Human Rights Module

Human Rights Module

On Crimes Against Humanity, Genocide, Other Crimes Against Human Rights, and War Crimes

THIRD EDITION

including revised extracts from

Paust, Bassiouni, Scharf, Sadat, Gurulé, Zagaris
International Criminal Law (4 ed. 2013)

CAROLINA ACADEMIC PRESS
Durham, North Carolina

ISBN 978-1-61163-498-3
LCCN 2013946722

Carolina Academic Press
700 Kent Street
Durham, NC 27701
Telephone (919) 489-7486
Fax (919) 493-5668
www.cap-press.com

Printed in the United States of America

Contents

Preface

The Human Rights Module has been prepared for those teaching human rights courses or seminars who wish to supplement whatever other materials they are using in order to assure adequate, up-to-date exploration of the nature and sources of human rights, human rights litigation in the U.S., and "core" international crimes most often associated with human rights infractions. "Core" crimes addressed here include attention to crimes against humanity, genocide, other crimes against human rights (such as torture, criminalized race discrimination, apartheid, hostage-taking, and disappearances), and war crimes. The Module should also prove useful as supplemental material for other international law courses or seminars where a focus on crimes against humanity, genocide, and other crimes against human rights, and/or war crimes is desired—perhaps a course or seminar on counter-terrorism addressing the law of war and human rights in particular. The Module is self-contained, providing needed cases and materials as well as a separate Documents Section in Part Two of the Module.

Some who use the Human Rights Module might prefer to concentrate on Chapters 1–3 and avoid inclusion of Chapter 4 on war crimes. Others might prefer to use the first four chapters and not Chapter 5 (which addresses civil sanctions) and some might prefer to use all five chapters in their course or seminar. Especially after the first AALS Workshop on Human Rights, held in 1999, it is our understanding that most law professors who teach human rights courses or seminars supplement assigned textbooks with other materials or find that present textbooks preclude adequate or more detailed and up-to-date attention to areas of special interest, such as those reflected in the special focus of the Module. The Module was prepared in part to meet such needs and to provide a self-contained set of cases, materials and documents that can be used in a few or several weeks.

We hope that you find the Module especially useful and we are eager to receive your comments and suggestions for improvement.

The Editors
2013

PART ONE

CASES AND MATERIALS

Chapter 1

Human Rights Law

Section 1
Nature and Sources
of International Law

Introduction

There are two basic types of international law: (1) international agreements, and (2) customary international law. International agreements are technically binding only upon the parties to such agreements (which in the past have included states, nations, peoples, tribes, international organizations, belligerents, and other entities) and their nationals (or possibly also those with a significant nexus with a party to an agreement, such as resident aliens). In general, it does not matter that the international agreement is termed a treaty, convention, covenant, protocol, or something else. It is an international agreement, subject to international law concerning such agreements. According to some, general principles of law are also a possible source of international law. *See* M. Cherif Bassiouni, *A Functional Approach to General Principles of International Law,* 11 MICH. J. INT'L L. 768 (1990). For others, general principles of law common to most domestic legal processes can at least evidence normative content and can shape international legal content. They can also fill gaps where international law is unclear. These are the same sources mentioned as being within the jurisdictional competence of the International Court of Justice (I.C.J.), as set forth in Article 38 of its Statute, appended to the United Nations Charter.[1]

International agreements may also reflect customary international law, in whole or in part, either at the time of formation or later. Unlike international agreements as such, customary international law is universally obligatory. Therefore, what was at one time an international agreement binding merely signatories and their nationals can later become customary law for the entire international community. The 1907 Hague Conven-

---

1. It should be noted that the International Court of Justice (or ICJ) does not have jurisdiction to prosecute individual violators of international law. Its competence generally involves advisory opinions at the request of certain U.N. entities and cases arising between states. See Statute of the I.C.J., art. 36.

tion No. IV Respecting the Laws and Customs of War on Land is a well-known example of this transformation. As recognized by the International Military Tribunal at Nuremberg in 1946, rights and duties reflected in the treaty had become customary international law at least by 1939 at the outset of World War II (some 32 years later) and, thus, binding on Germany (as a party) and some of Germany's allies that had not been parties and their nationals despite the persistent refusal of some states to ratify the treaty and a clause in the treaty making it applicable only during armed conflicts among signatories. In view of the name of the treaty, it is also likely that portions thereof were recognizably customary at the time of formation. *See, e.g.,* Anthony D'Amato, International Law: Process and Prospect 123–47 (1987); Clive Parry, The Sources and Evidences of International Law 62–67 (1965); Richard R. Baxter, *Multilateral Treaties as Evidence of Customary International Law,* 41 Brit. Y.B. Int'l L. 275 (1968).

What is "custom" or the customary law of nations? Article 38 of the Statute of the International Court of Justice recognizes that customary international law is evidenced by "a general practice accepted as law." See also Restatement of the Foreign Relations Law of the United States §102(2) and Comments b & c (3 ed. 1987)[hereinafter Restatement]. Therefore, customary law is comprised of two elements: (a) general patterns of practice or behavior (what people generally do), and (b) general acceptance as law (what people generally think) or general patterns of legal expectation or *opinio juris* (*i.e.,* expectations generally shared that something is legally required or appropriate). Both elements or patterns must exist or coincide. See North Sea Continental Shelf Cases (Federal Republic of Germany v. Denmark; Federal Republic of Germany v. Netherlands), 1969 I.C.J. 3, 44; *United States v. La Jeune Eugenie*, 26 F. Cas. 832 (C.C.D. Mass. 1821); *The Antelope*, 23 U.S. 66 (1825); and *Charge to Grand Jury*, 30 F. Cas. 1026 (C.C.D. Ga. 1859).

Fairly obviously, customary law can be dynamic—a law reflected in a dynamic process of behavior and expectation. What once was custom can change to non-custom if one or both of the elements are no longer extant, and what once was not customary law can grow into customary law recognizable, for example, by a judicial tribunal. *See, e.g., The Paquete Habana*, 175 U.S. 677 (1900); *Hilton v. Guyot*, 159 U.S. 113, 163 (1895); *The Scotia*, 81 U.S. (14 Wall.) 170, 187–88 (1871) ("Undoubtedly, no single nation can change the law of the sea. That law is of universal obligation, and no statute of one or two nations can create obligations for the world. Like all the laws of nations, it rests upon the common consent of civilized communities. It is of force, not because it was prescribed by any superior power, but because it has been generally accepted as a rule of conduct. Whatever may have been its origin, whether in the usages of navigation or in the ordinances of maritime states, or in both, it has become the law of the sea only by the concurrent sanction of those nations who may be said to constitute the commercial world.... They all became the law of the sea, not on account of their origin, but by reason of their acceptance as such.... Changes in nautical rules have taken place. How have they been accomplished, if not by the concurrent assent, express or understood, of maritime nations? ... This is not giving to the statutes of any nation extraterritorial effect. It is not treating them as general maritime laws, but it is recognition of the historical fact that by common consent of mankind, these rules have been acquiesced in as of general obligation. Of that fact we think we may take judicial notice. Foreign municipal laws must indeed be proved as facts, but it is not so with the law of nations."); *cf. Thirty Hogsheads of Sugar v. Boyle*, 13 U.S. (9 Cranch) 191, 198 (1815) (Marshall, C.J.); 1 Op. Att'y Gen. 30, 32 (1793).

Moreover, the traditional view is that custom rests upon the general patterns of legal expectation (*opinio juris*) of humankind, not merely that of their representatives (*i.e.,* nation-states). *See, e.g., The Scotia, supra; The Prize Cases*, 67 U.S. (2 Black) 635, 670 (1863) ("founded on the common consent as well as the common sense of the world"); *Ware v. Hylton*, 3 U.S. (3 Dall.) 199, 227 (1796) ("established by the general consent of mankind"); IV W. Blackstone, Commentaries on the Law of England 66 (1765).

The preamble to the 1907 Hague Convention No. IV Respecting the Laws and Customs of War on Land contained an early recognition that the "law of nations … [results] from the usages established among civilized peoples, from the laws of humanity, and from the dictates of the public conscience" (see the Documents Section). Similar phrases appear in the 1949 Geneva Conventions. *See, e.g.,* Article 158 of the 1949 Geneva Convention Relative to the Protection of Civilian Persons in Time of War [hereinafter Geneva Civilian Convention], in the Documents Section.

It should be noted that "usage" as such is merely long-term practice, not law (unless conjoined with relevant patterns of *opinio juris*).

A. *Obligatio Erga Omnes* and *Jus Cogens*

As materials below demonstrate, there are two other higher-level categories of international law. One category has been termed *obligatio erga omnes*, which are obligations owing not merely to certain states and their nationals, but to all of humankind. Another category, termed *jus cogens*, involves customary peremptory norms that preempt any other inconsistent international law. The prohibition of genocide is a well-recognized example of customary *jus cogens*—so are the customary prohibitions of torture or cruel, inhuman, or degrading treatment; forced disappearance of persons; and slavery and the slave trade. *See, e.g.,* Restatement, *supra*, § 702 (identifying as customary *jus cogens*: (a) genocide, (b) slavery or slave trade, (c) the murder or causing the disappearance of individuals, (d) torture or other cruel, inhuman, or degrading treatment or punishment, (e) prolonged arbitrary detention, (f) systematic racial discrimination, and (g) a consistent pattern of gross violations of internationally recognized human rights). See also *id.* Comments d, n and Reporters' Note 1. For this reason, an agreement to commit or tolerate genocide or the other prohibited conduct noted above would be trumped by a *jus cogens* prohibition, and such an agreement would be void *ab initio* as a matter of law. Consider also:

Human Rights Committee, General Comment on Issues Relating to Reservations Made Upon Ratification or Accession to the Covenant and Optional Protocols, U.N. Doc. CCPR/c/21/rev.1/add.6, General Comment No. 24, Para. 8 (Nov. 2, 1994).

[Editors' note: The Human Rights Committee has been established under the International Covenant on Civil and Political Rights (ICCPR). See Articles 28–46 of the ICCPR in the Documents Section. Portions of this General Comment also appear in Chapter Five. As reflected in Article 19(c) of the Vienna Convention on the Law of Treaties, attempted reservations (by any name) to an international agreement that are incompatible with the object and purpose of the agreement are void *ab initio* as a matter of law.]

8. Reservations that offend peremptory norms would not be compatible with the object and purpose of the Covenant [on Civil and Political Rights]. Although treaties that are mere exchanges of obligations between States allow them to reserve *inter se* applica-

tion of rules of general international law, it is otherwise in human rights treaties, which are for the benefit of persons within their jurisdiction. Accordingly, provisions in the Covenant that represent customary international law (and *a fortiori* when they have the character of peremptory norms) may not be the subject of reservations. Accordingly, a State may not reserve the right to engage in slavery, to torture, to subject persons to cruel, inhuman or degrading treatment or punishment, to arbitrarily deprive persons of their lives, to arbitrarily arrest and detain persons, to deny freedom of thought, conscience and religion, to presume a person guilty unless he proves his innocence, to execute pregnant women or children, to permit the advocacy of national, racial or religious hatred, to deny to persons of marriageable age the right to marry, or to deny to minorities the right to enjoy their own culture, profess their own religion, or use their own language. And while reservations to particular clauses of Article 14 may be acceptable, a general reservation to the right to a fair trial would not be.

Johann Bluntschli, Modern Law of Nations of Civilized States (1867)

… [T]reaties the contents of which violate the generally recognized human right … are invalid.

Note

1. The Inter-American Court of Human Rights has stated that judicial guarantees essential for the protection of nonderogable human rights under the American Convention on Human Rights are also nonderogable in time of public emergency. Judicial Guarantees in States of Emergency (Arts. 27(2), 25, and 8 of the American Convention on Human Rights), Advisory Opinion OC-9/97, Inter-Am. Ct. H.R., Ser. A, No. 9 (1987). Additionally, the Inter-American Court has recognized that the human right to be brought promptly before a judge must be subject to judicial control and that judicial protection must include the right to habeas corpus or *amparo* petitions and cannot be suspended during an emergency. See *Castillo Petruzzi*, Merits, Judgment, Inter-Am. Ct. Hum. Rts., Ser. C, No. 52 (30 May 1999), addressed in J. Becherer, 'International Decisions,' 95 Am. J. Int'l L. 171 *ff* (2001). Are such judicial guarantees effectively *jus cogens* norms as well?

B. Additional Consideration of Customary International Law

Jordan J. Paust, *Customary International Law: Its Nature, Sources and Status as Law of the United States* 12 Mich. J. Int'l L. 59, 63–74 (1990), revised in International Law as Law of the United States 4-7 (2 ed. 2003)

Of further significance is the fact that relevant patterns of legal expectation, perhaps contrary to Blackstone, need only be generally shared in the international community. Universality or unanimity are not required. Yet, for fuller exposition and understanding it is suggested that the researcher identify not merely how widespread a particular pattern of expectation is or has been, but also how intensely held or demanded a particular norm is or has been within the community. Awareness of the *degree* and *intensity* of general acceptance provides a more realistic approach to the identification and clarification of normative content and should aid those who must apply customary international law in making informed and rational choices. It would also be useful to know how long such patterns of expectation have existed, although a prior stability evident through time is no guarantee of continued acceptance in the future and time is not otherwise a determinative factor. It is possible, of course, to have a relatively recently widespread and intensely held expectation that something is legally appropriate or required and that such a pattern of *opinio juris* could form one of the components of a new rule of customary international law, one that will even be more stable in the future.

It is also significant that the behavioral element of custom (*i.e.*, general practice) is similarly free from the need for total conformity, and it rests not merely upon the practice of States as such but ultimately upon the practice of all participants in the international legal process. Thus, a particular nation-state might disagree whether a particular norm is customary and might even violate such a norm, but it would still be bound if the norm is supported by patterns of generally shared legal expectation and conforming behavior extant in the community. If the patterns of violation become too widespread, however, one of the primary bases of customary law can be lost. Similarly, if it is no longer generally expected that a norm is legally appropriate or required, the other base of customary law can be lost. When either base is no loner generally extant, there can be no conjoining of general patterns of legal expectation and behavior and, for such a social moment at least, a prior customary law will no longer be operative.

Since each nation-state, indeed each human being, is a participant in both the attitudinal and behavioral aspects of dynamic customary international law, each may initiate a change in such law or, with others, reaffirm its validity. Indeed, such a law at least, born of what people think and do is constantly reviewed and "re-enacted" in the social process, changed, or terminated. In the long-term, one wants to view such law with a movie camera; and yet at any given social moment (or at the time of a particular decision or activity), the existence of a customary international law will be dependent upon relevant patterns of expectation and behavior then extant.

These recognitions are also critical for the researcher's task. In one sense, they simplify that task since one need only identify patterns of what real people generally think and do. Yet, in another sense, researching customary law is significantly complicated by the fact that each person ultimately is a participant in the shaping of customary law and thus each viewpoint and every sort of human interaction could be relevant....

... [I]t is often impossible for one researcher to identify every relevant pattern of expectation and behavior. However, far less than perfect investigation has been accepted by courts and others, especially if documentation of such patterns is with reference to "judicial decisions, ... the works of jurists and commentators, and [documented] ... acts and usages of ... nations." Any evidence of customary norms and relevant patterns of expectation or behavior can be useful. In fact, in addition to judicial opinions and the works of textwriters, U.S. courts have considered treaties and other international agreements; domestic constitutions or legislation; executive orders, declarations or recognitions; draft conventions or codes; reports, resolutions or decisions of international organizations; and even the testimony or affidavits of textwriters.

Since any such evidence of expectation and behavior can be useful, it is also particularly misleading to ask whether a United Nations General Assembly resolution can be a source of customary law. A more realistic question, for example, might be whether a nearly unanimous resolution concerning the content or application of a norm of international law evidences a pattern of generally shared legal expectation or *opinio juris*.

The very act of voting on a resolution is in some sense also an instance of behavior, but the most relevant forms of behavior will probably involve other patterns of action and inaction outside the U.N. plaza. Importantly also, U.N. resolutions have been utilized by U.S. courts as aids in identifying the content of customary international law....

With respect to general practice, it is also important to note that "inaction" or compliance because of a choice to not violate a norm may often be more relevant than the nonconforming practice of a few violators of the norm, and yet such a practice may be difficult to measure.... Too often textwriters argue that the death of a norm, even a treaty norm, has occurred because of the actions of a few States. Instead, what should be investigated are the patterns of expectation more generally extant (including those even of such law violators), and the actions and inactions of all participants. It is also too simplistic to argue that law violations which, in a relatively unorganized community, have not been subject to effective sanctions have, therefore, necessarily led to the demise of a customary norm. It would be ludicrous to argue, for example, that when a law-violating elite of a State knows that its actions are prohibited by customary law, when others generally expect that such conduct is an remains illegal, and when violations are scarce, the customary norm is obviated by a failure effectively to ensure sanctions against such an elite. Even in a relatively organized community the lack of effective sanctions against several law violators (*e.g.*, those who commit murder) does not necessarily lead one to the conclusion that a norm (*e.g.*, the prohibition of murder) has thereby been obviated.

[Editors' note: An early international criminal law case after formation of the U.N. Charter recognized the authoritativeness of certain General Assembly resolutions. See *United States v. Altstoetter*, 3 Trials of War Criminals 983 (1948) ("The General Assembly is not an international legislature but it is the most authoritative organ in existence for the interpretation of world opinion.").

C. Constitutional Bases and Status

Jordan J. Paust, International Law as Law of the United States 7–14 (2 ed. 2003)

The Founders clearly expected that the customary law of nations was binding, was supreme law, created (among others) private and governmental rights and duties, and would be applicable in U.S. federal courts. For example, at the time of the formation of the Constitution John Jay had written: "Under the national government ... the laws of nations, will always be expounded in one sense ... [and there is] wisdom ... in committing such questions to the jurisdiction and judgment of courts appointed by and responsible only to one national government...." In 1792, the supremacy of the customary law of nations within the United States was affirmed in *Ross v. Rittenhouse*; and Attorney General Randolph declared: "[t]he law of nations, although not specially adopted ... is essentially a part of the law of the land."

In 1793, then Chief Justice Jay recognized that "the laws of the United States," the same phrase found in Article III, section 2, clause 1 and in Article VI, clause 2 of the Constitution, includes the customary "law of nations" and that such law was directly incorporable for the purpose of criminal sanctions. [*Henfield's Case*, 11 F. Cas. 1099, 1101 (C.C.D. Pa. 1793) (Jay, C.J.)] Also in 1793, the Chief Justice stated that prior to the Constitution:

> the United States had ... become amenable to the laws of nations; and it was their interest as well as their duty to provide, that those laws should be re-

spected and obeyed; in their national character and capacity, the United States were responsible to foreign nations for the conduct of each state, relative to the laws of nations, and the performance of treaties; and there the inexpediency of referring all such questions to State Courts, and particularly to the Courts of delinquent States, became apparent.... These were among the evils which it was proper for the nation ... to provide by a national judiciary.

That same year it was affirmed that the "law of nations is part of the law of the United States." Justice Wilson also declared that the Supreme Court has original jurisdiction in certain cases addressing such law, but that Congress can nevertheless provide a concurrent jurisdiction in lower federal courts. Chief Justice Jay had also charged a grand jury in Virginia that year in markedly familiar words: "The Constitution, the statutes of Congress, the law of nations, and treaties constitutionally made compose the laws of the United States." In that year also, Secretary of State Thomas Jefferson reassured the French Minister Genet that the law of nations is an "integral part" of the law of the land, and in his home state of Virginia it was declared in *Page v. Pendleton* : "the legislature ... admitted, that the law and usages of nations require ... the legislature could not retract their consent to observe the praecepts of the law, and conform to the usages, of nations...." In 1795, Justice Iredell addressed direct incorporation of customary international law and affirmed the fact of incorporation with or without a statutory base in a consistent and telling fashion: "[t]his is so palpable a violation of our own law ... of which the law of nations is a part, as it subsisted either before the act of Congress on the subject, or since...." With respect to the broad range of matters subject to incorporation, he added: "all ... trespasses committed against the general law of nations, are enquirable...." An early case had also expressly related the duty to incorporate customary international law to the Constitution: "courts ... [i]n this country ... are bound, by the Constitution of the United States, to determine according to treaties and the law of nations, wherever they apply."

Similar recognitions had occurred previously and would occur throughout our history. For example, in 1942 [in *Ex parte Quirin*] the Supreme Court summarized its practice in ascertaining and applying a portion of customary international law, the law of war:

From the very beginning of its history this Court has recognized and applied the law of war as including that part of the law of nations which prescribes, for the conduct of war, the status, rights and duties of enemy nations as well as of enemy individuals.

Although customary international law has been incorporated both directly and indirectly in civil and criminal cases from the beginning of the United States, the only express reference to the "law of nations" found in the Constitution is that aligned with a congressional power (*i.e.*, Article I, section 8, clause 10). It would be incorrect to assume, however, that incorporation of customary international law has no other adequate constitutional base. Indeed, as explained below, there are several relevant textual bases....

Historic Reach of the Law of Nations

By the time of the formation of the Constitution and within a generation or so thereafter, it was apparent that customary international law was relevant to various powers, rights and duties in civil, criminal, prize and admiralty, and other types of cases. As noted, customary international law pertained with respect to constitutional and jurisdictional questions and could reach governmental and private conduct. The significant reach of such law is also evident in the following survey of subjects addressed. Most generally, the Supreme Court noted that "all … trespasses committed against the general law of nations, are enquirable.…" More specifically, earliest subjects included piracy, acts of hostility or breaches of neutrality, assaults on foreign governmental personnel, terroristic publications, prizes of war and unlawful captures, the laws of war, slave trading, territorial infractions, "poisoners, assassins, and incendiaries by profession," violation of passports, violation of safe-conducts, extradition and "refuge" or asylum, human rights (itself of rich and of varied orientation), denials of justice to aliens, remedies, jurisdiction, nonimmunity, confiscation of property, war, reprisals, lawful intervention, oppression, tyrannicide, revolution, title to land by discovery and conquest, settlement of controversies between nations, and the law concerning treaties, including the primacy of the law of nations over treaties. Since that early period, the subjects addressed have grown.

Forms of Incorporation of International Law

There are various forms of incorporation of international law into U.S. domestic legal processes. For convenience, three primary forms of incorporation are identified: (1) direct incorporation, (2) indirect incorporation, and (3) incorporation by reference. Direct incorporation of international law involves use of an international agreement or customary international law directly as law forming the basis for a claim, right, duty, power, civil cause of action, criminal prosecution, or other type of sanction. In such cases, direct incorporation occurs whether or not there is a specific statutory basis for such uses of international law.

Another primary form of incorporation is indirect incorporation involving the use of international law as an interpretive aid. This form of incorporation can involve use of international law indirectly to clarify or supplement the meaning of, for example, the U.S. Constitution, a federal statute, a state constitution or statute, common law, a private contract, or some other legal provision. In this instance, international law is not used directly as the basis for a civil claim or criminal prosecution, but indirectly to inform the meaning of some other law or legal instrument. When international law is used to clarify duties or powers under the U.S. Constitution, it is the Constitution that provides the direct basis for the duty or power addressed and international law is used indirectly as an interpretive aid concerning the identification, limitation, or enhancement of a duty or competence. With respect to presidential powers, it is interesting to note that precisely because the President is bound under Article II, Section 3 of the Constitution faithfully to execute the "law," presidents have claimed the power to execute international agreements. For example, with respect to the war power, presidents have claimed the competence to execute resolutions of the U.N. Security Council (based ultimately on the U.N. Charter) that authorize the use of armed force.

Indirect incorporation happens to be the most frequent use of international law throughout United States history. Even treaties that had not been ratified yet by the U.S. have been used indirectly to clarify or provide content of federal law. Since most lawyers and judges in the U.S. have never taken a course in international law, it is not surprising that some judges may be more comfortable applying a domestic law as the direct basis for a civil claim, but utilizing international law as an aid to interpret such domestic law.

A form of indirect incorporation also occurs when a U.S. court uses customary international law as a background for interpretation of a treaty applicable in a case, which is preferable under the Vienna Convention on the Law of Treaties. An example of the use of U.N. General Assembly resolutions as evidence of customary international legal norms that can be used to identify and clarify rights and obligations under the U.N. Charter, all of which was incorporated through a U.S. statute for purposes of domestic litigation (a type of indirect incorporation through a U.S. statute), was the use of the Universal Declaration of Human Rights and the 1970 Declaration on Principles of International Law in the landmark human rights case *Filartiga v. Pena Irala*, 630 F.2d 876, 882 (2d Cir. 1980). In *Filartiga*, the Court of Appeals for the Second Circuit recognized:

> [A]lthough there is no universal agreement as to the precise extent of the "human rights and fundamental freedoms" guaranteed to all by the Charter, there is at present no dissent from the view that the guarantees include, as a bare minimum, the right to be free from torture. This prohibition has become part of customary international law, as evidenced and defined by the Universal Declaration of Human Rights ... which states, in the plainest of terms, "no one shall be subjected to torture." The General Assembly has declared that the Charter precepts embodied in this Universal Declaration "constitute basic principles of international law." G.A. Res. 2625 (XXV) (Oct. 24, 1970).

Interestingly, U.S. courts have used I.C.J. and P.C.I.J. decisions and advisory opinions to identify and clarify international law, especially customary international law, that was relevant to cases brought before the courts despite the fact that international judicial decisions and opinions are not directly binding in the U.S. The types of international norms addressed by U.S. courts have been varied, demonstrating a general relevance of international court decisions and opinions for interpretive purposes.

Another form of incorporation involves legislation that expressly refers to international law and incorporates such law in whole or in part "by reference." Some U.S. statutes contain language that compels one to identify relevant international norms that are incorporated through the language of the statute, whether the legislation addresses civil or criminal matters. Statutes that expressly refer to international law (*e.g.*, the "law of nations") or to phrases obviously based in or part of international law (*e.g.*, the "law of war") are examples. More generally, the power of Congress to "define and punish" violations of international law allows Congress to create legislation implementing international criminal law. This power is supplemented by the "necessary and proper" clause in Article I, Section 8, clause 18, which confirms congressional power to enact any laws necessary and proper to carry into execution a power such as the "define and punish" power as well as all other powers vested by the Constitution in the Government of the United States or any department or officer thereof. The treaty power is one such power.

When exercising such powers, Congress need not declare in the legislation that it is incorporating international law. Further, the legislation might specify the nature and elements of an offense with as much detail as is found in a treaty or customary law, provide greater detail, or simply incorporate international law by reference. Well-known criminal statutes that merely "incorporate by reference" include the federal statutes proscribing "piracy as defined by the law of nations"[2] and all violations of the "law of war" as offenses against the laws of the United States.[3] A newer statute also incorporates

---

2. 18 U.S.C. § 1651; United States v. Smith, 18 U.S. (5 Wheat.) 153, 158-62 (1820).

3. See 10 U.S.C. §§ 818, 821; *Ex parte* Quirin, 317 U.S. 1, 27-31 (1942); see also *In re* Yamashita, 327 U.S. 1, 7 (1946).

"grave breaches" of the 1949 Geneva Conventions by reference.[4] It is constitutionally permissible and not unusual in the U.S. for legislation to incorporate international crimes by reference, *i.e.*, without identifying each such crime, each (or any) element of an offense, or types of penalties that might obtain, nor does this practice appear to be impermissible or unusual at the international level or in other countries.

Federal statutes permitting civil sanctions against violators of international law and incorporating international law by reference also exist. Domestically, it is the statute that forms the direct basis for a civil suit against the perpetrator, while international normative content and even relevant sanctions or remedies are incorporated indirectly through the statutory basis. An example is the Alien Tort Claims Act (ATCA or ATS) noted above. As explained in another writing, the ATCA has been in existence in the U.S. since 1789 and had achieved early, precedential attention, but significantly increased use of the ATCA has occurred since the landmark decision in *Filartiga v. Pena-Irala* in 1980. The ATCA requires that a plaintiff be an alien, although a defendant can be a U.S. or foreign perpetrator of a private (individual, group or corporate) or public character. It provides that an alien can sue for what we term a "tort" or "wrong" "in violation of the law of nations or a treaty of the United States" and, as the statute states, the substantive law to be applied is international law. See Chapter Five.

Notes

1. Section 111 of the RESTATEMENT notes: "(1) International law and international agreements of the United States are law of the United States and supreme over the law of the several States. (2) Cases arising under international law or international agreements of the United States are within the Judicial Power of the United States and, subject to Constitutional and statutory limitations and requirements of justiciability, are within the jurisdiction of the federal courts. (3) Courts in the United States are bound to give effect to international law and to international agreements of the United States, except that a 'non-self-executing' agreement will not be given effect as law in the absence of necessary implementation."

Comment e of Section 111 notes:

"*Federal jurisdiction over cases "arising under" international law and agreements.* Cases arising under treaties to which the United States is a party, as well as cases arising under customary international law, or under international agreements of the United States other than treaties, are "Cases ... arising under ... the Laws of the United States, and Treaties made ... under their Authority," and therefore within the Judicial Power of the United States under Article III, Section 2 of the Constitution. Civil actions arising under international law or under a treaty or other international agreement of the United States are within the jurisdiction of the United States district courts. 28 U.S.C. § 1331.... For the purpose of Section 1331, all valid international agreements of the United States, whatever their designation and whatever the form by which they are concluded..., are "treaties of the United States." Customary international law, like other federal law, is part of the "laws ... of the United States.".....

2. When faced with a claim that the customary "law of nations forms a part of the laws of the United States only to the extent that Congress has acted to define it," the Second Circuit in *Filartiga* aptly noted: "This extravagant claim is amply refuted by the numerous decisions applying rules of international law uncodified in any act of Con-

---

4. See 18 U.S.C. § 2441 (2003) (set forth below).

gress.... A similar argument was offered to and rejected by the Supreme Court in *United States v. Smith*, ... 18 U.S. (5 Wheat.) 153, 158-60 ... [1820] and we reject it today." 630 F.2d at 886.

3. With respect to federal district court jurisdiction for civil and criminal sanctions, note:

28 U.S.C. § 1331

The district courts shall have original jurisdiction of all civil actions arising under the Constitution, laws, or treaties of the United States.

18 U.S.C. § 3231

The district courts of the United States shall have original jurisdiction, exclusive of the courts of the States, of all offenses against the laws of the United States.

Ex parte Quirin, 317 U.S. 1, 27–30 (1942)

[Editors' note: No federal statute existed to specifically implement the laws of war until the 1916 Articles of War addressed herein. Today, the same language in the 1916 statute addressed by the Court appears in 10 U.S.C. §§ 818, 821.]

From the very beginning of its history this Court has recognized and applied the law of war as including that part of the law of nations which prescribes, for the conduct of war, the status, rights and duties of enemy nations as well as of enemy individuals. By the Articles of War, and especially Article 15, Congress has explicitly provided, so far as it may constitutionally do so, that military tribunals shall have jurisdiction to try offenders or offenses against the law of war in appropriate cases. Congress, in addition to making rules for the government of our Armed Forces, has thus exercised its authority to define and punish offenses against the law of nations by sanctioning, within constitutional limitations, the jurisdiction of military commissions to try persons for offenses which, according to the rules and precepts of the law of nations, and more particularly the law of war, are cognizable by such tribunals. And the President, as Commander in Chief, by his Proclamation in time of war has invoked that law. By his Order creating the present Commission he has undertaken to exercise the authority conferred upon him by Congress, and also such authority as the Constitution itself gives the Commander in Chief, to direct the performance of those functions which may constitutionally be performed by the military arm of the nation in time of war.

An important incident to the conduct of war is the adoption of measures by the military command not only to repel and defeat the enemy, but to seize and subject to disciplinary measures those enemies who in their attempt to thwart or impede our military effort have violated the law of war. It is unnecessary for present purposes to determine to what extent the President as Commander in Chief has constitutional power to create military commissions without the support of Congressional legislation. For here Congress has authorized trial of offenses against the law of war before such commissions. We are concerned only with the question whether it is within the constitutional power of the national government to place petitioners upon trial before a military commission for the offenses with which they are charged. We must therefore first inquire whether any of the acts charged is an offense against the law of war cognizable before a military tribunal, and if so whether the Constitution prohibits the trial. We may assume that there are acts regarded in other countries, or by some writers on international law, as offenses against the law of war which would not be triable by military tribunal here, either because they are not recognized by our courts as violations of the law of war or because they are of that class of offenses constitutionally triable only by a jury. It was upon such grounds that the Court denied the right to proceed by military tribunal in *Ex parte Milligan, supra*. But as we shall show, these petitioners were charged with an offense against the law of war which the Constitution does not require to be tried by jury.

It is no objection that Congress in providing for the trial of such offenses has not itself undertaken to codify that branch of international law or to mark its precise boundaries, or to enumerate or define by statute all the acts which that law condemns. An Act of Congress punishing "the crime of piracy as defined by the law of nations" is an appropriate exercise of this constitutional authority, Art. I, sec. 8, cl. 10, "to define and punish" the offense since it has adopted by reference the sufficiently precise definition of international law. *United States v. Smith*, 5 Wheat. 153, 5 L.Ed. 57; see *The Marianna Flora*, 11 Wheat. 1, 40, 41, 6 L.Ed. 405; *United States v. The Malek Adhel*, 2 How. 210, 232, 11 L.Ed. 239; *The Ambrose Light*, D.C., 25 F. 408, 423, 428; 18 U.S.C. § 481, 18 U.S.C.A. § 481. Similarly by the reference in the 15th Article of War to "offenders or offenses that ... by the law of war may be triable by such military commissions", Congress has incorporated by reference, as within the jurisdiction of military commissions, all offenses which are defined as such by the law of war (compare *Dynes v. Hoover*, 20 How. 65, 82, 15 L.Ed. 838), and which may constitutionally be included within that jurisdiction. Congress had the choice of crystallizing in permanent form and in minute detail every offense against the law of war, or of adopting the system of common law applied by military tribunals so far as it should be recognized and deemed applicable by the courts. It chose the latter course.

Note

1. Today, 10 U.S.C. §§ 818, 821 perform the same incorporating role as the older Articles of War. § 818 states: "General courts-martial also have jurisdiction to try any person who by the law of war is subject to trial by a military tribunal and may adjudge any punishment permitted by the law of war...."

Does the incorporation of the laws of war as offenses against the laws of the United States also implicate federal district court jurisdiction under 18 U.S.C. § 3231, which states: "The district courts of the United States shall have original jurisdiction, exclusive of the courts of the States, of all offenses against the laws of the United States"? See Jordan J. Paust, *After My Lai: The Case for War Crime Jurisdiction Over Civilians in Federal District Courts*, 50 Tex. L. Rev. 6 (1971). If so, the United States can prosecute civilians who are not otherwise subject to the jurisdiction of U.S. military tribunals in the federal district courts?

Alternative legislation incorporating part of the laws of war as offenses against the laws of the United States is set forth below:

The War Crimes Act, 18 U.S.C. § 2441 (2006)

(a) Offense. Whoever, whether inside or outside the United States, commits a war crime, in any of the circumstances described in subsection (b), shall be fined under this title or imprisoned for life or any term of years, or both, and if death results to the victim, shall also be subject to the penalty of death.

(b) Circumstances. The circumstances referred to in subsection (a) are that the person committing such war crime or the victim of such war crime is a member of the

Armed Forces of the United States or a national of the United States (as defined in section 101 of the Immigration and Nationality Act [8 U.S.C. § 1101].

(c) Definition. As used in this section the term "war crime" means any conduct–

(1) defined as a grave breach in any of the international conventions signed at Geneva 12 August 1949, or any protocol to such convention to which the United States is a party;

(2) prohibited by Article 23, 25, 27, or 28 of the Annex to the Hague Convention IV, Respecting the Laws and Customs of War on Land, signed 18 October 1907;

(3) which constitutes a grave breach of common Article 3 (as defined in subsection (d)) when committed in the context of and in association with an armed conflict not of an international character; or

(4) of a person who, in relation to an armed conflict and contrary to the provisions of the Protocol on Prohibitions or Restrictions on the Use of Mines, Booby–Traps and Other Devices as amended at Geneva on 3 May 1996 (Protocol II as amended on 3 May 1996), when the United States is a party to such Protocol, willfully kills or causes serious injury to civilians.

(d) Common Article 3 Violations–

(1) Prohibited Conduct. In subsection (c)(3), the term "grave breach of common Article 3" means any conduct (such conduct constituting a grave breach of common Article 3 of the international conventions done at Geneva August 12, 1949), as follows:

(A) Torture.– The act of a person who commits, or conspires or attempts to commit, an act specifically intended to inflict severe physical or mental pain or suffering (other than pain or suffering incidental to lawful sanctions) upon another person within his custody of physical control for the purpose of obtaining information or a confession, punishment, intimidation, coercion, or any reason based on discrimination of any kind.

(B) Cruel of Inhuman Treatment.– The act of a person who commits, or conspires or attempts to commit, an act intended to inflict severe or serious physical or mental pain or suffering (other than pain or suffering incidental to lawful sanctions), including serious physical abuse, upon another within his custody or control.

(C) Performing Biological Experiments.– The act of a person who subjects, or conspires or attempts to subject, one or more persons within his custody or physical control to biological experiments without a legitimate medical or dental purpose and in so doing endangers the body or health of such person or persons.

(D) Murder.– The act of a person who intentionally kills, or conspires or attempts to kill, or kills whether intentionally or unintentionally in the course of committing any other offense under this subsection, one or more persons taking no active part in the hostilities, including those placed out of combat by sickness, wounds, detention, or any other cause.

(E) Mutilation or Maiming.– The act of a person who intentionally injures, or conspires or attempts to injure, or injures whether intentionally or unintentionally in the course of committing any other offense under this subsection, one or more persons taking no active part in the hostilities, including those placed out of combat by sickness, wounds, detention, or any other cause, by disfiguring the person or persons by any mutilation thereof or by permanently disabling any member, limb, or organ of his body, without any legitimate medical or dental purpose.

(F) Intentionally Causing Serious Bodily Injury.– The act of a person who intentionally causes, or conspires or attempts to cause, serious bodily injury to one or more persons, including lawful combatants, in violation of the law of war.

(G) Rape.– The act of a person who forcibly or with coercion or threat of force wrongfully invades, or conspires or attempts to invade, the body of a person by penetrating, however slightly, the anal or genital opening of the victim with any part of the body of the accused, or with any foreign object.

(H) Sexual Assault or Abuse.– The act of a person who forcibly or with coercion or threat of force engages, or conspires or attempt to engage, in sexual contact with one or more persons, or causes, or conspires or attempts to cause, one or more persons to engage in sexual conduct.

(I) Taking Hostages.– The act of a person who, having knowingly seized or detained one or more persons, threatens to kill, injure, or continue to detain such person or persons with the intent of compelling any nation, person other than the hostage, or group of persons to act or refrain from acting as an explicit or implicit condition for the safety or release of such person or persons.

(2) Definitions. In the case of an offense under subsection (a) by reason of subsection (c)(3)–

(A) the term "severe mental pain or suffering" shall be applied for purposes of paragraphs (1)(A) and (1)(B) in accordance with the meaning given the term in section 2340(2) of this title;

(B) the term "serious bodily injury: shall be applied for purposes of paragraph (1)(F) in accordance with the meaning given that term in section 113(b)(2) of this title;

(C) the term "sexual contact" shall be applied for purposes of subsection (1)(G) in accordance with the meaning given that term in section 2246(3) of this title;

(D) the term "serious physical pain and suffering" shall be applied for purposes of paragraph (1)(B) as meaning bodily injury that involves–

   (i) a substantial risk of death;

   (ii) extreme physical pain;

   (iii) a burn or physical disfigurement of a serious nature (other than cuts, abrasions, or bruises); or

   (iv) significant loss of impairment of the function of a bodily member, organ, or mental faculty; and

(E) the term "serious mental pain or suffering" shall be applied for purposes of subsection (1)(B) in accordance with the meaning given the term "severe mental pain or suffering" (as defined in section 2340(2) of this title), except that–

   (i) the term "serious" shall replace the term "severe" where it appears; and

(ii) as to conduct occurring after the date of the enactment of the Military Commissions Act of 2006, the term "serious and non-transitory mental harm (which need not be prolonged)" shall replace the term "prolonged mental harm" where it appears.

(3) Inapplicability of Certain Provisions With Respect to Collateral Damage or Incident of Lawful Attack. The intent specified for the conduct stated in subparagraphs (D), (E), and (F) or paragraph (1) precludes the applicability of those subparagraphs to an offense under subsection (a) by reasons of subsection (c)(3) with respect to–

(A) collateral damage; or

(B) death, damage, or injury incident to a lawful attack.

(4) Inapplicability of Taking Hostages to Prisoner Exchange. Paragraph (1)(1) does not apply to an offense under subsection (a) by reason of subsection (c)(3) in the case of a prisoner exchange during wartime.

(5) Definition of Grave Breaches. The definitions in this subsection are intended only to define the grave breaches of common Article 3 and not the full scope of United States obligations under that Article.

Note

1. When you have a chance to address the Convention Against Torture in this Chapter and the Chapter on the Laws of War you should become aware of the fact that some of the definitions and limitations contained in the War Crimes Act do not reflect international law.

Section 2
Individual Responsibility

An Introduction to General Types of Responsibility

Who can be held responsible for violations of international law? For example, can private individuals commit international crimes? Can public officials, including heads of state and diplomats, be prosecuted? Do leaders have a responsibility to assure compliance with international law by those under their effective control? Can one be prosecuted for complicity or other forms of connection to an international crime primarily committed by others? Are there limits to any such responsibility and related defenses? Does sovereign immunity pertain with respect to international crime? Do domestic laws or superior orders limit individual responsibility or provide excuses for international crime?

Resolution of 1781, 21 Journals of the Continental Congress 1136–37

On a report of a committee, consisting of Mr. [Edmund] Randolph, Mr. [James] Duane, Mr. [John] Witherspoon, appointed to prepare a recommendation to the states to enact laws for punishing infractions of the laws of nations:

The committee, to whom was referred the motion for a recommendation to the several legislatures to enact punishments against violators of the law of nations, report:

That the scheme of criminal justice in the several states does not sufficiently comprehend offenses against the law of nations:

That a prince, to whom it may be hereafter necessary to disavow any transgression of that law by a citizen of the United States, will receive such disavowal with reluctance and suspicion, if regular and adequate punishment shall not have been provided against the transgressor:

That as instances may occur, in which, for the avoidance of war, it may be expedient to repair out of the public treasury injuries committed by individuals, and the property of the innocent to be exposed to reprisal, the author of those injuries should compensate the damage out of his private fortune.

Resolved, That it be recommended to the legislatures of the several states to provide expeditious, exemplary and adequate punishment:

First. For the violation of safe conducts or passports, expressly granted under the authority of Congress to the subjects of a foreign power in time of war:

Secondly. For the commission of acts of hostility against such as are in amity, league or truce with the United States, or who are within the same, under a general implied safe conduct:

Thirdly. For the infractions of the immunities of ambassadors and other public ministers, authorised and received as such by the United States in Congress assembled, by animadverting on violence offered to their persons, houses, carriages and property, under the limitations allowed by the usages of nations; and on disturbance given to the free exercise of their religion: by annulling all writs and processes, at any time sued forth against an ambassador, or other public minister, or against their goods and chattels, or against their domestic servants, whereby his person may be arrested: and,

Fourthly. For infractions of treaties and conventions to which the United States are a party.

The preceding being only those offences against the law of nations which are most obvious, and public faith and safety requiring that punishment should be co-extensive with such crimes:

Resolved, That it be farther recommended to the several states to erect a tribunal in each State, or to vest one already existing with power to decide on offences against the law of nations, not contained in the foregoing enumeration, under convenient restrictions.

Resolved, That it be farther recommended to authorise suits to be instituted for damages by the party injured, and for compensation to the United States for damage sustained by them from an injury done to a foreign power by a citizen.

Opinion and Judgment of the International Military Tribunal at Nuremberg, (October 1, 1946)

[Editors' note: the I.M.T. at Nuremberg was an international criminal tribunal set up by four of the victors after World War II, the U.S., France, Great Britain, and the Soviet Union to prosecute certain German nationals accused of crimes against peace, crimes against humanity, and/or war crimes. See Charter of the International Military Tribunal at Nuremberg, extract in the Documents Section.]

It was submitted that international law is concerned with the actions of sovereign States, and provides no punishment for individuals; and further, that where the act in question is an act of State, those who carry it out are not personally responsible, but are protected by the doctrine of the sovereignty of the State. In the opinion of the Tribunal, both these submissions must be rejected. That international law imposes duties and liabilities upon individuals as well as upon States has long been recognized. In the recent case of *Ex parte Quirin* (1942, 317 U.S. 1), before the Supreme Court of the United States, persons were charged during the war with landing in the United States for purposes of spying and sabotage. The late Chief Justice Stone, speaking for the court, said: "From the very beginning of its history this court has applied the law of war as including that part of the law of nations which prescribes for the conduct of war, the status, rights, and duties of enemy nations as well as enemy individuals."

He went on to give a list of cases tried by the courts, where individual offenders were charged with offences against the laws of nations, and particularly the laws of war. Many other authorities could be cited, but enough has been said to show that individuals can be punished for violations of international law. Crimes against international law are committed by men, not by abstract entities, and only by punishing individuals who commit such crimes can the provisions of international law be enforced.

The provisions of Article 228 of the Treaty of Versailles already referred to illustrate and enforce this view of individual responsibility.

The principle of international law, which under certain circumstances, protects the representatives of a State, cannot be applied to acts which are condemned as criminal by international law. The authors of these acts cannot shelter themselves behind their official position in order to be freed from punishment in appropriate proceedings. Article 7 of the Charter expressly declares: "The official position of defendants, whether as heads of state, or responsible officials in government departments, shall not be considered as freeing them from responsibility, or mitigating punishment."

On the other hand the very essence of the Charter is that individuals have international duties which transcend the national obligations of obedience imposed by the individual State. He who violates the laws of war cannot obtain immunity while acting in pursuance of the authority of the State if the State in authorizing action moves outside its competence under international law.

Principles of the Nuremberg Charter and Judgment, Formulated by the International Law Commission, and adopted by G.A. Res. 177 (II)(a), 5 U.N. GAOR, Supp. No. 12, at 11–14, para. 99, U.N. Doc. A/1316 (1950)

I. Any person who commits an act which constitutes a crime under international law is responsible therefor and liable to punishment.

II. The fact that internal law does not impose a penalty for an act which constitutes a crime under international law does not relieve the person who committed the act from responsibility under international law.

III. The fact that a person who committed an act which constitutes a crime under international law acted as Head of State or responsible Government official does not relieve him from responsibility under international law....

VII. Complicity in the commission of a crime against peace, a war crime, or a crime against humanity as set forth in Principle VI is a crime under international law.

Report of the Secretary-General Pursuant to Paragraph 2 of Security Council Resolution 808 (1993) paras. 52–59, U.N. Doc. S/25704 (3 May 1993)

adopted by the U.N. Security Council in Res. 827 (25 May 1993), establishing the Statute for the International Tribunal for Prosecution of Persons Responsible for Serious Violations of International Humanitarian Law Committed in the Territory of the Former Yugoslavia.

Article 6

Personal jurisdiction

The International Tribunal shall have jurisdiction over natural persons pursuant to the provisions of the present Statute.

Individual criminal responsibility

53. An important element in relation to the competence *ratione personae* (personal jurisdiction) of the International Tribunal is the principle of individual criminal responsibility. As noted above, the Security Council has reaffirmed in a number of resolutions that persons committing serious violations of international humanitarian law in the former Yugoslavia are individually responsible for such violations.

54. The Secretary-General believes that all persons who participate in the planning, preparation or execution of serious violations of international humanitarian law in the former Yugoslavia contribute to the commission of the violation and are, therefore, individually responsible.

55. Virtually all of the written comments received by the Secretary-General have suggested that the statute of the International Tribunal should contain provisions with regard to the individual criminal responsibility of heads of State, government officials and persons acting in an official capacity. These suggestions draw upon the precedents following the Second World War. The Statute should, therefore, contain provisions which specify that a plea of head of State immunity or that an act was committed in the official capacity of the accused will not constitute a defence, nor will it mitigate punishment.

56. A person in a position of superior authority should, therefore, be held individually responsible for giving the unlawful order to commit a crime under the present statute. But he should also be held responsible for failure to prevent a crime or to deter the unlawful behaviour of his subordinates. This imputed responsibility or criminal negligence is engaged if the person in superior authority knew or had reason to know that his subordinates were about to commit or had committed crimes and yet failed to take the necessary and reasonable steps to prevent or repress the commission of such crimes or to punish those who had committed them.

57. Acting upon an order of a Government or a superior cannot relieve the perpetrator of the crime of his criminal responsibility and should not be a defence. Obedience to superior orders may, however, be considered a mitigating factor, should the International Tribunal determine that justice so requires. For example, the International Tribunal may consider the factor of superior orders in connection with other defences such as coercion or lack of moral choice.

58. The International Tribunal itself will have to decide on various personal defences which may relieve a person of individual criminal responsibility, such as minimum age or mental incapacity, drawing upon general principles of law recognized by all nations.

59. The corresponding article of the statute would read:

Article 7

Individual criminal responsibility

1. A person who planned, instigated, ordered, committed or otherwise aided and abetted in the planning, preparation or execution of a crime referred to in articles 2 to 5 of the present Statute, shall be individually responsible for the crime.

2. The official position of any accused person, whether as Head of State or Government or as a responsible Government official, shall not relieve such person of criminal responsibility nor mitigate punishment.

3. The fact that any of the acts referred to in articles 2 to 5 of the present Statute was committed by a subordinate does not relieve his superior of criminal responsibility if he knew or had reason to know that the subordinate was about to commit such acts or had done so and the superior failed to take the necessary and reasonable measures to prevent such acts or to punish the perpetrators thereof.

4. The fact that an accused person acted pursuant to an order of a Government or of a superior shall not relieve him of criminal responsibility, but may be considered in mitigation of punishment if the International Tribunal determines that justice so requires.

The Prosecutor v. Blagojevic & Jokic, IT-02-60-T (Trial Chamber, Judgement on Motions for Acquittal Pursuant to Rule 98 *bis*) (5 April 2004)

[footnote material appears in the text]

25. "Planning" means that one or more persons design the commission of a crime at both the preparatory and execution phases. *Prosecutor v. Akayesu*, ICTR-96-4-T (Judgment, 2 Sept. 1998), para. 480, reiterated in *Prosecutor v. Krstic*, IT-98-33-T (Judgment, 2 Aug. 2001), para. 601, in *Prosecutor v. Blaskic*, IT-95-14-T (Judgment, 3 Mar. 2000), para. 279, in *Prosecutor v. Kordic & Cerkez*, IT-95-14/2-T (Judgment, 26 Feb. 2001), para. 386.

26. "Instigating" means prompting another to commit an offence. *Blaskic*, para. 280, *Krstic*, para. 601, *Kordic*, para. 387, *Akayesu*, para. 482.

27. "Ordering" entails a person in a position of authority using that position to command another to commit an offence. *Krstic*, para. 601.

28. Planning, instigating and ordering require that the accused has criminal intent, either direct or indirect. Regarding planning: *Blaskic*, para. 278; *Kordic*, para. 386. Regarding instigating, see *Kvocka*, IT-98-30/1 (Trial Judgment, 15 Dec. 2000), para. 252. Regarding ordering, see *Blaskic*, para. 282.

29. "Committing" supposes that the accused carries out, physically or otherwise directly, the *actus reus* of the crime. *Prosecutor v. Tadic*, IT-95-1-A (Appeals Chamber, 15 July 1999), para. 189. This can be achieved individually or jointly with others. Co-perpetration and the theory of joint criminal enterprise are modes of joint commission that have been recognised in the Tribunal's jurisprudence. Regarding co-perpetration as a form of commission, see *Prosecutor v. Stakic*, IT-97-24-T (Judgment, 31 July 2003), para. 439.

Notes and Questions

1. Nearly all of the international criminal law treaties address crimes committed, for example, by "any person," *i.e.*, regardless of status. *See also* Jordan J. Paust, International Law as Law of the United States 8, 48–50, 201, 264–70, 289-91, 393, 407–09, *passim* (1996); Jordan J. Paust, *The Other Side of Right: Private Duties Under Human Rights Law*, 5 Harv. H.R.J. 51, 56–59 (1992); Sharon A. Williams, *The Role of the Individual in International Criminal Law: An Overview*, (Special Edition) Queen's L.J., International Law: Critical Choices for Canada 1985–2000, at 505 (1986); *Kadic v. Karadzic*, 70 F.3d 232, 239–43 (2d Cir. 1995) (private individuals can commit piracy, slave trade, war crimes, and genocide); *Adra v. Clift*, 195 F. Supp. 857, 864 (D. Md. 1961) (*quoting* 1 Hyde, International Law § 11A, at 33–34 (2 ed. 1945): "regardless of the character of the actors"). The Genocide Convention seems more particular in this regard. Article IV reads: "Persons committing genocide ... shall be punished whether they are constitutionally responsible rulers, public officials or private individuals." Article III of the Genocide Convention also states: "The following acts shall be punishable: (a) Genocide; (b) Conspiracy to commit genocide; (c) Direct and public incitement to commit genocide; (d) Attempt to commit genocide; (e) complicity in genocide." See also Article III of the International Convention on the Suppression and Punishment of the Crime of "Apartheid". These general developments are consistent with trends since the trial of Peter von Hagenbach in 1474 for crimes committed during his administration of territories on the upper Rhine. *Compare* Articles 25-27 of the Statute of the ICC, in the Documents Section. Under international law more generally, any person may be tried for the commission of an international crime. Consider especially the Opinion and Judgment of the I.M.T. at Nuremberg (Oct. 1, 1946) ("It was submitted that international law is concerned with the actions of sovereign States, and provides no punishment for individuals, and further, that where the act in question is an act of State, those who carry it out are not personally responsible, but are protected by the doctrine of the sovereignty of the State.... both submissions must be rejected. That international law imposes duties and liabilities upon individuals as well as upon States has long been recognized.... Crimes against international law are committed by men, not by abstract entities.... The Principle of international law, which under certain circumstances, protects the representatives of a State, cannot be applied to acts which are condemned as criminal by international law. The authors of these acts cannot shelter themselves behind their official position.... He who violates the laws of war cannot obtain immunity while acting in pursuance of the authority of the State if the State in authorizing action moves outside its competence under international law.").

2. In *United States v. von Leeb* (The High Command Case), U.S. Military Tribunal, 1948, XI Trials of War Criminals 462 (1950), the tribunal affirmed:

> "International law operates as a restriction and limitation on the sovereignty of nations. It may also limit the obligations which individuals owe to their states, and create for them international obligations which are binding upon them to an extent that they must be carried out even if to do so violates a positive law or directive of the state."

See also 9 Op. Att'y Gen. 356, 357 (1859) ("a law which operates on the interests and rights of other States or peoples must be made and executed according to the law of nations. A sovereign who tramples upon the public law of the world cannot excuse himself by pointing to a provision in his own municipal code."); *see also Johnson v. Eisentrager*, 339 U.S. 763, 765, 789 (1950) (no public official immunity exists for war crimes); *The*

Santissima Trinidad, 20 U.S. (7 Wheat.) 283, 350-55 (1822) ("If … he [a foreign sovereign] comes personally within our limits, although he generally enjoy a personal immunity, he may become liable to judicial process in the same way, and under the same circumstances, as public ships of the nation [that violate international law]"); *The Prosecutor v. Furundzija*, ICTY-95-17/1, at para. 140 (10 Dec. 1998); *The Prosecutor v. Milosevic*, ICTY-99-37-PT, at paras. 26-34 (Nov. 8, 2001) (the ICTY Chamber famously ruled that Milosevic had no immunity from alleged international crimes as a head of state and that Article 7 of the Statute of the ICTY, which rejects head of state immunity, "reflects a rule of customary international law"). In *The Prosecutor v. Tadic*, ICTY-94-1-AR72 (2 Oct. 1995), the Appeals Chamber of the International Criminal Tribunal for Former Yugoslavia recognized: "It would be a travesty of law and a betrayal of the universal need for justice, should the concept of State sovereignty be allowed to be raised successfully against human rights. Borders should not be considered as a shield against the reach of the law and as a protection for those who trample underfoot the most elementary rights of humanity." *Id*. para. 58.

3. If a relevant treaty, code, or documentation of custom does not mention individual responsibility, much less criminal sanctions, are criminal sanctions nevertheless appropriate under international law? *See, e.g.*, Opinion of the I.M.T. at Nuremberg (Oct. 1946); *Henfield's Case*, 11 F. Cas. 1099 (C.C.d. Pa. 1793).

4. U.S. Dep't of Army FM 27-10, The Law of Land Warfare at 183, paras. 510–511 (1956) recognizes the Nuremberg principles of nonimmunity for government officials and the lack of a defense based on domestic law "for an act which constitutes a crime under international law." With respect to criminal responsibility, the Field Manual adds:

Section II. Crimes Under International Law

498. Crimes Under International Law

Any person, whether a member of the armed forces or a civilian, who commits an act which constitutes a crime under international law is responsible therefor and liable to punishment. Such offenses in connection with war comprise:

a. Crimes against peace.

b. Crimes against humanity.

c. War crimes.

Although this manual recognizes the criminal responsibility of individuals for those offenses which may comprise any of the foregoing types of crimes, members of the armed forces will normally be concerned only with those offenses constituting "war crimes."

499. War Crimes

The term "war crime" is the technical expression for a violation of the law of war by any person or persons, military or civilian. Every violation of the law of war is a war crime.

500. Conspiracy, Incitement, Attempts and Complicity

Conspiracy, direct incitement, and attempts to commit, as well as complicity in the commission of, crimes against peace, crimes against humanity, and war crimes are punishable.

5. Do you agree with the *Blagojevic & Jokic* statements about planning, instigating, ordering, and committing? In *The Prosecutor v. Semanza*, ICTR-97-20-A (Appeals

Chamber, 20 May 2005), para. 257, it was recognized that although a person could not be found guilty of dereliction of duty because the person lacked sufficient authority over perpetrators of the crime of rape, the accused can be prosecuted for "instigating" rape by others. In *The Prosecutor v. Kordic & Cerkez*, IT-95-14/2 (Appeals Chamber Judgment, 17 Dec. 2004), para. 32, the Appeals Chamber declared that a person can be guilty of "instigating" by instigating another person to commit an act or omission with the awareness of the substantial likelihood that a crime will be committed in the execution of that instigation and that instigating with such awareness has to be regarded as "accepting" that crime. The Appeals Chamber also stated that "planning" can occur if the person plans an act or omission with the awareness of the substantial likelihood that a crime will be committed in the execution of that plan and that planning with such awareness has to be regarded as accepting that crime. *Id.* para. 31. With respect to "incitement," see also U.N. S.C. Res. 1296, S/RES/1296, para. 17 (19 April 2000) (the Security Council "reaffirms its condemnation of all incitements to violence against civilians in situations of armed conflict, further reaffirms the need to bring to justice individuals who incite or otherwise cause such violence....").

In *The Prosecutor v. Blaskic*, IT-95-14-T-A (Appeals Chamber Judgment, 29 July 2004), para. 40, declared that "ordering" can involve a lower *mens rea* standard than "direct intent" and include "awareness of a higher likelihood of risk and a volitional element" than plain reckless disregard, adding: "A person who orders an act or omission with the awareness of the substantial likelihood that a crime will be committed in the execution of that order, has the requisite *mens rea* for establishing liability under Article 7(1) [of the Statute of the ICTY] pursuant to ordering. Ordering with such awareness has to be regarded as accepting that crime." *Id.* para. 42.

6. In The *Prosecutor v. Kordic & Cerkez*, IT-95-14/2-A (Appeals Chamber Judgment, 17 Dec. 2004), para. 311, it was declared: "The *nullum crimen sine lege* [no crime without law] principle does not require that an accused knew that specific legal definition of each element of a crime he committed. It suffices that he was aware of the [relevant] factual circumstances."

7. The general standard for complicity or accomplice liability under customary international law is set forth in the following:

"Any person who aids and abets torture has liability as a complicitor or aider and abettor before the fact, during the fact, or after the fact. Liability exists whether or not the person knows that his or her conduct is criminal or that the conduct of the direct perpetrator of torture is criminal or even constitutes torture as such. Under customary international law, a complicitor or aider and abettor need only be aware that his or her conduct (which can include inaction) would or does assist a direct perpetrator or facilitates conduct that is criminal. In any case, ignorance of the law is no excuse. Especially relevant in this respect are the criminal memoranda and behavior of various German lawyers in the German Ministry of Justice, high level executive positions outside the Ministry, and the courts in the 1930s and 1940s that were addressed in informing detail in *United States v. Altstoetter* (The Justice Case). Clearly, several memo writers and others during the Bush Administration abetted the 'common, unifying' plan to use 'coercive interrogation' and their memos and conduct substantially facilitated its effectuation."

Jordan J. Paust, *The Absolute Prohibition of Torture and Necessary and Appropriate Sanctions*, 43 Val. U. L. Rev. 1535, 1544-45 (2009), available at http://ssrn.com/abstract=1331159. See Jordan J. Paust, M. Cherif Bassiouni, et al., International Criminal Law 69-74 (4 ed. 2013). *But see* Rome Statute of the International Criminal

Court, art. 25(3)(c), in the Documents Section. What new limitation of responsibility appears in the article?

8. A long line of cases documents the fact that companies and corporations can have duties and rights under international law. Regarding duties, *see, e.g.*, Jonathan A. Bush, *The Prehistory of Corporations and Conspiracy in International Criminal Law: What Nuremberg Really Said*, 109 Colum. L. Rev. 1094 (2009); Emeka Duruigbo, *Corporate Accountability and Liability for International Human Rights Abuses: Recent Changes and Recurring Challenges*, 6 Nw. U. J. Int'l Hum. Rts. 222 (2008); Günther Handl, *In Re South African Apartheid Litigation and Beyond: Corporate Liability for Aiding and Abetting under the Alien Tort Statute*, 53 German Yrbk. Int'l L. 425, 431-41 (2010)http://ssrn.com/abstract=1677638; Harold Hongju Koh, *Separating Myth From Reality About Corporate Responsibility Litigation*, 7 J. Int'l Econ. L. 263 (2004); Jordan J. Paust, *Nonstate Actor Participation in International Law and the Pretense of Exclusion*, 51 Va. J. Int'l L. 977, 986-89 (2011) (citing twenty U.S.Supreme Court cases on point as well as a large number of other U.S. and foreign cases); Jordan J. Paust, *Human Rights Responsibilities of Private Corporations*, 35 Vand. J. Transnat'l. L. 801, 803-10 (2002), and U.S. and foreigncases cited, available at http://ssrn.com/abstract=154812; Jordan J. Paust, *The Other Side of Right: Private Duties Under Human Rights Law*, 5 Harv. Hum. Rts. J. 51 (1992); Jordan J. Paust, *The History, Nature, and Reach of the Alien Tort Claims Act*, 16 Fla. J. Int'l L. 249, 252 n.7 (2004) (also demonstrating that the ATCA "had achieved early and informing precedential attention with respect to violations of international law by U.S. and foreign perpetrators here and abroad" and, therefore, that the ATCA has been partly extraterritorial in its reach. *Id.* at 250-52 & n.3), available at http://ssrn.com/abstract=1497122 [hereinafter Paust, *History*]; Robert C. Thompson, *et al.*, *Translating Unocal: The Expanding Web of Liability for Business Entities Implicated in International Crimes*, 40 Geo. Wash. Int'l L. Rev. 841 (2009); Baloco v. Drummond Co., Inc., 631 F.3d 1350, 1362-63 (11th Cir. 2011); Sinaltrainal v. Coca-Cola Co., 578 F.3d 1252, 1263 (11th Cir. 2009); Abdullahi v. Pfizer, Inc., 562 F.3d 163 (2d Cir. 2009); Romero v. Drummond Co., Inc., 552 F.3d 1303, 1315 (11th Cir. 2008); Khulumani v. Barclay Nat. Bank Ltd., 504 F.3d 254 (2d Cir. 2007); Sarei v. Rio Tinto, PLC, 487 F.3d 1193 (9th Cir. 2007); Aldana v. Del Monte Fresh Produce, N.A., Inc., 416 F.3d 1242 (11th Cir. 2005); Boim v. Quranic Literary Inst., 297 F.3d 542 (7th Cir. 2002); *id.*, 291 F.3d 1000 (7th Cir. 2002); Bigio v. Coca-Cola Co., 239 F.3d 440, 447 (2d Cir. 2000); Wiwa v. Royal Dutch Petroleum Co., 226 F.3d 88, 92 (2d Cir. 2000), *cert. denied*, 532 U.S. 941 (2001); Weisshaus v. Swiss Bankers Ass'n, 225 F.3d 191 (2d Cir. 2000); Jota v. Texaco, Inc., 157 F.3d 153 (2d Cir. 1998); Klinghoffer v. S.N.C. Achille Lauro, 937 F.2d at 49; Al-Quraishi v. Nakhla, 728 F. Supp.2d 702, 71-48 (D. Md. 2010); *In re* XE Services Alien Tort Litigation, 665 F. Supp.2d 569, 584-85, 588 (E.D. Va. 2009); Ntsebeza v. Daimler, 617 F. Supp.2d 228, 250, 254-55 (S.D.N.Y. 2009); Licea v. Curacao Drydock Co., Inc., 584 F. Supp. 2d 1355 (S.D. Fla. 2008); Roe v. Bridgestone Corp., 492 F. Supp.2d 988, 1008 (S.D. Ind. 2007); Almog v. Arab Bank, PLC, 471 F. Supp.2d 257, 271, 274-78, 289, 293 (E.D.N.Y. 2007) (also recognizing private actor conduct as crimes against humanity and genocide and private actor complicity with respect to each international crime); Burnett v. Al Baraka Inv. & Dev. Corp., 274 F. Supp.2d 86, 99-100 (D.D.C. 2003); Estate of Rodriquez v. Drummond Co., 256 F. Supp.2d 1250, 1258 (N.D. Ala. 2003); Presbyterian Church of Sudan v. Talisman Energy, Inc., 244 F. Supp.2d 289, 305-23, 327, 338 (S.D.N.Y. 2003); Bodner v. Banque Paribas, 114 F. Supp.2d 117, 128 (E.D.N.Y. 2000); *In re* Holocaust Victim Assets Litig., 105 F. Supp.2d 139, 141 (E.D.N.Y. 2000); Iwanowa v. Ford Motor Co., 67 F. Supp.2d 424, 443-45 n.26 (D.N.J. 1999); Burger-Fischer v. DeGussa Corp., 65 F. Supp.2d

248, 272-73 (D.N.J. 1999); Jama v. Immigration and Naturalization Service, 22 F. Supp.2d 353, 362-63 (D.N.J. 1998); Eastman Kodak Co. v. Kavlin, 978 F. Supp. 1078, 1090-95 (S.D. Fla. 1997); Doe v. Unocal Corp., 963 F. Supp. 880 (C.D. Cal. 1997); Bowoto v. Chevron Corp., WL 2349336, at *29 (N.D. Cal. 2007); Barton v. Tampa Elec. Co., 1997 WL 128158 (M.D. Fla. 1997) (company's "outrageous restriction on human rights"); United States v. Flick, 6 Trials of War Criminals Before the Nuremberg Military Tribunals Under Control Council Law No. 10, 1217 (1952) (recognizing that "[a]n organization which on a large scale is responsible for crimes can be nothing else than criminal," especially the SS); United States v. United States v. Krauch (I.G. Farben Case), 8 Trials of War Criminals Before the Nuremberg Military Tribunals Under Control Council Law No. 10, 1132-33 (addressing conduct of "private individuals, including juristic persons, ... in violation of international law"), 1140 ("proof establishes beyond a reasonable doubt that offenses" under international law "were committed by Farben.... The action of Farben ... cannot be differentiated from acts of plunder or pillage committed by" natural persons, and "[s]uch action on the part of Farben constituted a violation of the Hague Regulations") (1952); United States v. Krupp, 9 Trials of War Criminals Before the Nuremberg Military Tribunals Under Control Council Law No. 10, 1352-53 ("the confiscation of the Austin plant ... and its subsequent detention by the Krupp firm constitute a violation of Article 43 of the Hague Regulations."), 1370 ("we conclude that ... illegal acts of spoliation and plunder were committed by, and on behalf of, the Krupp firm"), 1372 ("the initiative ... was that of the Krupp firm") (1950); see also Charter of the International Military Tribunal at Nuremberg, art. 10 ("where a group or organization is declared criminal by the Tribunal, ... the criminal nature of the group or organization is considered proved"), Annex to the London Agreement (8 Aug. 1945), 82 U.N.T.S. 279; see also Dubai Petroleum Co. v. Kazi, 12 S.W.3d 71, 82 (Tex. 2000) (ICCPR "guarantees foreign citizens equal treatment ... [and] equal access to these courts" in suit against oil companies); Donahue v. Pemacel Tape Corp., 234 Ind. 398, 409-10, 127 N.E.2d 235, 240 (1955) ("one of the most basic rights of man" was at stake regarding former employee's covenant not to compete and corporation could not enforce it in violation of such rights); Crenshaw Bros. Produce Co. v. Harper, 142 Fla. 27, 47, 194 So. 353, 361 (Fla. 1940) ("The general rule of respondeat superior should not any longer contain an exception which is so callous to human rights."); Lobach v. Kansas City Southern Railway Co., 172 Mo. App. 278, 158 S.W. 397, 398 (Mo. App. 1913) (company's engineer's conduct, if proven, would be "wilful and wanton disregard of the most sacred of human rights"); Grubb v. Galveston, H. & S.A. Railway Co., 153 S.W. 694, 696 (Tex. Civ. App. 1913) ("it is absolutely essential to the preservation of life and human rights ... [that] corporations ... [are] liable for the wrongful acts and omissions of their servants"); State v. Southern Railway Co., 145 N.C. 495, 59 S.E. 570, 592 (N.C. 1907) (Brown, J., concurring) (addressing "a great and beneficent principle of human rights, applicable to individuals as well as to corporations"); Slack v. Marysville & Lexington R.R. Co., 13 B.Mon. 1, 68, WL 3378 (Ky. App. 1852) (Hise, J., dissenting) (stating that a corporation has no right to commit "wrong and injury upon the sacred and inalienable rights of man"); but see Kiobel v. Royal Dutch Petroleum Co., 621 F.3d 111 (2d Cir. 2010) (demonstrating use of remarkably ahistorical and troubling conclusions about a supposed lack of corporate and other non-natural-actor liability under international law while ignoring twenty U.S. Supreme Court cases on point and numerous others). With respect to rights under international law, see, e.g., Bonito Boats, Inc. v. Thunder Craft Boats, Inc., 489 U.S. 141, 155 (1989) (a "'fundamental human right, that of privacy, is threatened ... [by] industrial espionage"), quoting Kewanee Oil Co. v. Bicron Corp., 416 U.S. 470, 487 (1974); Sumitomo

Shoji America, Inc. v. Avagliano, 457 U.S. 176, 186-87 & n.16 (1982) (purpose of various FCN treaties is to give corporations rights); La Reunion Aerienne v. Socialist People's Libyan Arab Jamahiriya, 533 F.3d 837 (D.C. Cir. 2008) (unlawful bombing of a UTA flight); Banco Nacional de Cuba v. Chemical Bank New York Trust Co., 822 F.2d 230, 234-35, 237 (2d Cir. 1987) (counterclaims against Cuban national bank arising out of discrimination in violation of international law allowed and compensation will be governed by international law standards); Kalamazoo Spice Extraction Co. v. Provisional Military Government of Socialist Ethiopia, 729 F.2d 422 (6th Cir. 1984) (taking of property in violation of an FCN treaty and customary international legal standards); Banco Nacional de Cuba v. Farr, Whitlock & Co., 383 F.2d 166, 177 (2d Cir. 1967) (sugar expropriated by Cuba from a Cuban company violated international law), *cert. denied*, 390 U.S. 956 (1968); Faysound Ltd. v. Walter Fuller Aircraft Sales, Inc., 748 F. Supp. 1365, 1371-74 (E.D. Ark. 1990) (expropriation in violation of treaty-based and customary international law); American International Group, Inc. v. Islamic Republic of Iran, 493 F. Supp. 522, 524-25 (D.D.C. 1980) (Iran's nationalization of insurance industry violated FCN treaty and customary international law); *supra* notes 31, 37. *See also* Amerada Hess Shipping Corp. v. Argentine Republic, 830 F.2d 421 (2d Cir. 1987) (unlawful attack on corporate vessel), *rev'd on other gds.*, 488 U.S. 428 (1989); Standard Oil Co. of Indiana v. United States, 164 F. 376, 389 (7th Cir. 1908) (recognizing "the fundamental human right of being judged only after having been duly tried—a right just as essential to men in the associated relationship of the corporation, as to men in the relationship of co-partners, or to men individually"). See also First National City Bank v. Banco Para el Comercio Exterior de Cuba, 462 U.S. 611, 623, 632 (1983) (regarding a permissible set off, also noting that "the seizure of Citibank's assets ... [by Cuba] violated international law." *Id.* at 632.).

For a Japanese case, see Paust, Van Dyke, Malone, International Law and Litigation in the U.S. 118 (3 ed. 2009) (ruling that a Japanese store was liable for discrimination against foreign nationals). For an English case, see *Johnson v. Unisys, Ltd.*, [2001] UKHL/13, at [37] (22 Mar. 2001) (Lord Hoffmann) (explaining that responsibilities of private companies under domestic employment law are also "[s]ubject to observance of fundamental human rights"). In 1998, the Supreme Court of Canada also recognized that it is possible "for a non-state actor to perpetuate human rights violations on a scale amounting to persecution" within the reach of the Refugee Convention and, thus more generally, that private actors can engage in human rights violations. *Pushpanathan v. Canada*, 160 D.L.R. (4th) 193, 231 (S. Ct. Canada 1998) (also noting a related practice of Australia. The Court addressed whether private violations of human rights fell within the scope of Article 1 F (c) of the Convention Relating to the Status of Refugees, 189 U.N.T.S. 150, which deals with denial of refugee protections to persons "guilty of acts contrary to the purposes and principles of the United Nations."); *Hevra Kadisha, Jerusalem Burial Company v. Kestenbaum*, C.A. 294/93, 46(2) P.D. 464, 530 (S. Ct. Israel 1992) (Barak, J.) (human rights apply "also to the mutual relations between individuals themselves"); *In Matter of the Republic of the Philippines*, 46 BverfGE 342, 362 (2 BvM 1/76, Dec. 13, 1977) (direct duties of private individuals are created in human rights law), addressed in Memorandum for the United States as *Amicus Curiae, Filartiga v. Pena-Irala*, at 21 (1980), *reprinted in* 19 I.L.M. 585 (1980).

9. Concerning private duties under human rights law, *see, e.g.*, ICCPR, prmbl., art. 5(1); Universal Declaration of Human Rights, prmbl., arts. 1, 29-30; American Declaration of the Rights and Duties of Man; Note 8 above.

10. Private duties are also expressly recognized in the preamble to and Articles 27–29 of the African Charter on Human and Peoples' Rights. The preamble to the American

Declaration of the Rights and Duties of Man acknowledges that "the fulfillment of duty by each individual is a prerequisite to the rights of all. Rights and duties are interrelated....", and Articles XXIX through XXXVIII set forth several express duties of private actors. Indeed, the very title of the American Declaration is an express affirmation of private human rights duties. The American Convention on Human Rights also contains express recognition in Article 32(1) that "[e]very person has responsibilities to ... his community, and mankind," and Article 29(a) commands that the treaty not be interpreted to allow "any ... group, or person to suppress the enjoyment or exercise of the rights and freedoms recognized ... or to restrict them to a greater extent than is provided for" in the Convention, and thus an implied duty of groups and persons exists to not suppress or restrict human rights. Article 17 of the European Convention for the Protection of Human Rights and Fundamental Freedoms contains a "group or person" provision similar to that in the International Covenant and the American Convention.

11. With respect to individual duties under international law, consider also the following statement of Justice Wilson on circuit in *Henfield's Case*, 11 F. Cas. 1099, 1107 (C.C.D. Pa. 1793) (No. 6,360): "Under all the obligations due to the universal society of the human race, the citizens of a state still continue. To this universal society it is the duty that each nation should contribute to the welfare, the perfection and the happiness of the others. If so, the first degree of this duty is to do no injury. Among states as well as among men, justice is a sacred law.... On states as well as individuals the duties of humanity are strictly incumbent; what each is obliged to perform for others, from others it is entitled to receive." *Henfield's Case* involved direct incorporation of treaty law and customary international law termed the "law of nations" for criminal sanction purposes, that is, prosecution of an individual for alleged violations of international law without a federal criminal statute forming the basis for prosecution. *Henfield's Case* also recognized that private duties may pertain even when a treaty makes no express mention of individuals or individual duties. *Id.* at 1120 (Wilson, J.).

12. The European Court of Human Rights has stated that private "terrorist activities ... of individuals or groups ... are in clear disregard of human rights." See *Ireland v. United Kingdom*, Eur. Ct. H.R., Ser. A, No. 25, para. 149 (13 Dec. 1977). See also Human Rights and Terrorism, U.N. G.A. Res. 59/195 (20 Dec. 2004); U.N. G.A. Res. 49/60, Annex, art. 1(2)-(3) (9 Dec. 1994). Other U.S. cases and opinions recognizing responsibilities of non-state or private entities include: *Linder v. Portocarrero*, 963 F.2d 332, 336–37 (11th Cir. 1992) (the Contras can be civilly liable for torture and unlawful killing); *Klinghoffer v. S.N.C. Achille Lauro*, 937 F.2d 44, 49 (2d Cir. 1991) (the PLO and various organizations can be civilly liable for murder); *id.*, 739 F.Supp. 854, 858, 860 (S.D.N.Y. 1990); *Bolchos v. Darrel*, 3 F. Cas. 810 (D.S.C. 1795) (No. 1,607); Jama v. U.S. I.N.S., 22 F.Supp.2d 353, 362–63 (D.N.J. 1998); *Doe I v. Islamic Salvation Front*, 993 F. Supp. 3, 8 (D.D.C. 1998); *Mushiki-wabo v. Barayagwiza*, 1996 WL 164496 (S.D.N.Y. 1996); *Adra v. Clift*, 195 F. Supp. 857, 864 (D. Md. 1961) (private plaintiff and private defendant); 1 Op. Att'y Gen. 57, 58 (1795).

Section 3
General Human Rights

Human rights are at stake with respect to most international crimes. As noted in Chapter Four, human rights law also applies during any armed conflict as well as in times of relative peace. Consider what types of human rights are at stake with respect to abductions, assassinations, certain breaches of neutrality, war crimes, genocide, other crimes against humanity, slavery, impermissible terrorism, and piracy. In *United States v. Haun*, 26 F. Cas. 227 (C.C.S.D. Ala. 1860) (No. 15,329), Justice Campbell, sitting on circuit, ruled that congressional legislation to suppress the slave trade was supported by several treaties and was valid. He also quoted President Jefferson's Message to Congress in 1806 concerning private duties with respect to human rights, recognizing that Congress "'might interpose their authority constitutionally to withdraw the citizens of the United States from all further violations of human rights which have been so long continued on the unoffending inhabitants of Africa.'" *Id.* at 231.

In this section, we emphasize the prohibitions of torture and other cruel, inhuman, and degrading acts; race-based discrimination, including apartheid; hostage-taking; secret detention and the "disappearance" of persons.

A. The United Nations Charter

[read the preamble to and Articles 1, 55(c), 56, and 103 of the U.N. Charter]

More generally, all states have a duty under Articles 55(c) and 56 of the United Nations Charter to take joint and separate action to achieve "universal respect for, and observance of, human rights" and, thus, not to authorize their violation or to violate human rights law in any location or circumstance with respect to any person. See also U.N. G.A. Res. 59/195, Human Rights and Terrorism, preamble (2004); U.N. G.A. Res. 59/191, Protection of Human Rights and Fundamental Freedoms While Countering Terrorism, preamble and para. 1 (2004), both in the Documents Section; Declaration on Principles of International Law Concerning Friendly Relations and Co-Operation Among States in Accordance With the Charter of the United Nations, U.N. G.A. Res. 2625 (Oct. 24, 1970), 25 U.N. GAOR, Supp. No. 28, at 121, U.N. Doc. A/8028 (1971) ("Every State has the duty to promote through joint and separate action universal respect for and observance of human rights and fundamental freedoms in accordance with the Charter.").

One uses evidences of the content of customary human rights to identify those rights "guaranteed to all by the Charter." See *Filartiga v. Pena-Irala*, 630 F.2d 876, 882 (2d Cir. 1980), adding: "the guarantees include, at a bare minimum, the right to be free from torture. This prohibition has become part of customary international law as evidenced and defined by the Universal Declaration of Human Rights.... Charter precepts embodied in this Universal Declaration 'constitute basic principles of international law.' G.A. Res. 2625 (XXV) (Oct. 24, 1970)." *Id.* In addition to the prohibition of torture, Article 5 of the Universal Declaration prohibits "cruel, inhuman or degrading treatment or punishment." U.N. G.A. Res. 217A, art. 5, 3 U.N. GAOR, U.N. Doc. A/810, at 71 (1948). As a matter of customary international law, these prohibitions are absolute. The more general right to human dignity is mirrored in Article 1. *Id.* art. 1. Concerning the status of the Universal Declaration and its use as an authoritative interpretive aid, *see, e.g.,* McDougal, Lasswell, Chen, Human Rights and World Public Order 274, 302, 325-27 (1980); see also Paust, *Executive Plans and Authorizations to Violate International Law Concerning Treatment and Interrogation of Detainees*, 43 Columbia J. Transnat'l L. 811, 822 n.40 (2005) (Executive recognition of Article 5, among others, as customary international law) [hereinafter Paust, *Executive Plans*]. The same absolute prohibitions are found in the Resolution on Torture and other Cruel, Inhuman or Degrading Treatment or Punishment, G.A. Res. 59/182, U.N. Doc. A/RES/59/182 (2004), and the 1975 Declaration on the Protection of All Persons from Being Subjected to Torture and Other

Cruel, Inhuman or Degrading Treatment or Punishment, U.N. G.A. Res. 3452, 30 U.N. GAOR, Supp. No. 34, at 91, U.N. Doc. A/1034 (1976). Article 2 of the 1975 Declaration affirms that each form of prohibited conduct violates human rights under the U.N. Charter. The 1975 Declaration was also used in *Filartiga* to identify U.N. Charter-based and customary human rights prohibitions. 630 F.2d at 882-83. *See also Kadic v. Karadzic*, 70 F.3d 232, 240 (2d Cir. 1995), *cert. denied*, 518 U.S. 1005 (1996); *In re Estate of Marcos Human Rights Litig.*, 978 F.2d 493, 499 (9th Cir. 1992), *cert. denied*, 508 U.S. 972 (1993).

The 1988 Body of Principles for the Protection of All Persons Under Any Form of Detention or Imprisonment also affirms that "[a]ll persons under any form of detention … shall be treated in a humane manner and with respect for the inherent dignity of the human person." U.N. G.A. Res. 43/173, 43 U.N. GAOR, Supp. No. 49, at 297, U.N. Doc. A/43/49 (1988). *See also Kane v. Winn*, 319 F. Supp.2d 162, 197-99 (D. Mass. 2004) (use of the Body of Principles as evidence of customary law).

B. The International Covenant on Civil and Political Rights

[read Articles 1–27 and 50 of the International Covenant, in the Documents Section]

The International Covenant on Civil and Political Rights (ICCPR), 999 U.N.T.S. 171 (1966), contains articles relevant to detention of individuals (*e.g.*, art. 9), treatment of persons (*e.g.*, art. 7), minimum rights to due process (*e.g.*, art. 14), and other rights relevant to international law responsibilities and enforcement. Article 7 expressly prohibits torture and cruel, inhuman, or degrading treatment or punishment and Article 4(2) assures that such prohibitions are absolute and non-derogable even in time of national emergency. What other human rights identified in the ICCPR are also non-derogable under Article 4(2)? What is the test set forth that would allow derogations of derogable rights? Note that some rights contain their own set of limitations, such as the right of free speech set forth in Article 19.

Does the ICCPR apply anywhere that U.S. government personnel or agents detain individuals? Consider the following commentary: the ICCPR applies wherever a person is subject to the jurisdiction or effective control of a party to the treaty. *See, e.g.*, ICCPR, *supra* art. 2(1); Advisory Opinion, Legal Consequences of the Construction of a Wall in the Occupied Palestinian Territory, 2004 I.C.J. paras. 108-111 (The ICCPR "is applicable in respect of acts done by a State in the exercise of its jurisdiction outside its own territory"); Human Rights Committee, General Comment No. 31, at para. 10 (applies "to all persons subject to their jurisdiction. This means … anyone within the power or effective control of that State party, even if not situated within the territory of the State.… [The ICCPR applies] to all individuals … who may find themselves in the territory or subject to the jurisdiction of a State Party.… [It] also applies to those within the power or effective control of the forces of a State Party acting outside its territory, regardless of the circumstances in which such power or effective control was obtained), para. 11 ("the Covenant applies also in the situation of armed conflict to which the rules of international humanitarian law are applicable."), U.N. Doc. CCPR/C/21/Rev.1/Add.13 (2004); General Comment No. 24, at paras. 4, 12 ("all those under a State party's jurisdiction"), U.N. Doc. CCPR/C/21/Rev.1/Add.6 (1994); Coard, *et al.* v. United States, Case No. 10.951, Report No. 109/99, Annual Report of the Inter-Am. Comm. H.R. (Sept. 29, 1999); Alejandre, *et al.* v. Cuba, Case No. 11.589, Annual Report of the Inter-Am. Comm. H.R. (Sept. 29, 1999); Human Rights Comm., Concluding Observations on

Croatia, 28/12/92, U.N. Doc. CCPR/C/79/Add.15 (1992), § 9; Leila Zerrougui, *et al.*, Report, *Situation of Detainees at Guantanamo Bay*, Commission on Human Rights, 62nd sess., items 10 and 11 of the provisional agenda, U.N. Doc. E/CN.4/2006/120 (Feb. 15, 2006), at 8-9, para. 11; Paust, *Executive Plans*, *supra* at 822 n.40. More specifically, there is no territorial limitation set forth with respect to the absolute rights and duties contained in Article 7 of the ICCPR. The authoritative decisions and patterns of *opinio juris* noted above are part of subsequent practice and expectation relevant to proper interpretation of the treaty. *See* Vienna Convention on the Law of Treaties, art. 31(3)(b), 1155 U.N.T.S. 331 (1969) [hereinafter Vienna Convention]. Treaties must also be interpreted in light of their object and purpose (*see, e.g.*, *id.* art. 31(1)), which in this instance is to assure universal respect for and observance of the human rights set forth in the treaty. *See* ICCPR, *supra* preamble (recognizing "equal and inalienable rights of all," recognizing that "everyone … [should] enjoy" human rights, and "[c]onsidering the obligation of States under the Charter of the United Nations to promote universal respect for, and observance of, human rights"). The preamble to the treaty must also be used for interpretive purposes (*see, e.g.*, Vienna Convention, *supra* art. 31(2)), which in this instance reflects the object and purpose of the ICCPR to achieve universal respect for and observance of the human rights set forth in the treaty. More generally, human rights treaties are presumptively universal in reach in view of the general and preemptive duty of States under the United Nations Charter to achieve universal respect for and observance of human rights. *See, e.g.*, U.N. Charter, arts. 55(c), 56; ICCPR, *supra* preamble; Vienna Convention, *supra* art. 31(3)(c) ("any relevant rules of international law" (such as the preemptive human rights duties under the U.N. Charter) are to be taken into account when interpreting a treaty (such as the ICCPR). Further, the Supreme Court has recognized that treaties are to be interpreted in a broad manner in order to protect express and implied rights. *See, e.g.*, Paust, *Executive Plans*, *supra* at 832 n.76.

Read Article 50 of the ICCPR. In mandatory language, Article 50 expressly applies to all of "[t]he provisions" of the ICCPR and assures that orders, authorizations, conspiracies, complicitous conduct (including memos that abet violations), and other acts within the territory of a Party that are in violation of the treaty are proscribed "without any limitations or exceptions." Although the United States attempted set of reservations to the ICCPR, none was claimed with respect to Article 50 and the Executive Branch proclaimed: "In light of Article 50…, it is appropriate to clarify that, even though the Covenant will apply to state and local authorities, it will be implemented consistent with U.S. concepts of federalism…. A reservation is not necessary with respect to Article 50 since the intent is not to modify or limit U.S. undertakings under the Covenant…. the U.S. will implement its obligations under the Covenant by appropriate legislative, executive and judicial means, federal or state as appropriate…." Executive Explanation of Proposed Reservations, Understandings and Declarations, U.S. Senate Executive Report of the Bush Administration 102–23, 102d Cong., 2d Sess., *reprinted in* 31 I.L.M. 645, 656–57 (1992).

Concerning the invalidity of an attempted U.S. reservation to Article 7's reach to *all* forms of torture, cruel, inhuman, and degrading treatment, *see, e.g.*, *id.* at 823 n.42; Concluding Observations of the Human Rights Committee: United States of America, U.N. Doc. CCPR/C/79/Add.50, para. 14 (1995); Human Rights Committee, General Comment No. 24, para. 8, U.N. Doc. CCPR/C/21/Rev.1/Add.6 (1994). Article 7 is also expressly among the nonderogable articles in the treaty. See ICCPR, *supra* art. 4(2). Moreover, the rights and duties reflected in Article 7 are part of customary and *jus cogens* international law of a nonderogable and universal reach regardless of attempted treaty reservations or understandings. *See, e.g.*, Paust, *Executive Plans*, *supra* at 821-23;

Jordan J. Paust, *The Bush-Cheney Legacy: Serial Torture and Forced Disappearance in Violation of Global Human Rights Law*, 18 Barry L. Rev. 61-85 (2012), available at http://ssrn.com/asbtract=1989099.

When interpreting Article 7 of the ICCPR, the Human Rights Committee created by the Covenant declared: "Complaints about ill-treatment must be investigated.... Those found guilty must be held responsible, and the alleged victims must themselves have effective remedies at their disposal, including the right to obtain compensation." General Comment No. 7, para. 1, Report of the H.R. Comm., 37 U.N. GAOR, Supp. No. 40, Annex V, U.N. Doc. E/CN.4/Sub.2/Add.1/963 (1982). General Comment No. 20 (1992) replaced No. 7 and recognized that "it is not sufficient" merely to make violations "a crime" (para. 8), states should report "the provisions of their criminal law which penalize torture and cruel, inhuman and degrading treatment or punishment, specifying the penalties applicable to such acts, whether committed by public officials or other persons acting on behalf of the State, or by private persons. Those who violate article 7, whether by encouraging, ordering, tolerating or perpetrating prohibited acts, must be held responsible" (para. 13), states have a duty to afford protection against such acts "whether inflicted by people acting in their official capacity, outside their official capacity or in a private capacity" (para. 2), and "[a]mnesties are generally incompatible with" such duties and "States must not deprive individuals of the right to an effective remedy...." (para. 15), in International Human Rights Instruments, U.N. Doc. HRI/GEN/1 (4 Sept. 1992), at 29-32. Note that this General Comment is merely one of a number of instruments and decisions that have recognized private duties under human rights law and that the existence of private duties is often expressed or implied in human rights treaties. *See, e.g.*, ICCPR, art. 5(1); Jordan J. Paust, *The Reality of Private Rights, Duties, and Participation in the International Legal Process*, 25 Mich. J. Int'l L. 1229, 1241-45 (2004).

C. The American Declaration and O.A.S. Charter

[read the American Declaration of the Rights and Duties of Man, in the Documents Section]

Many of the same rights, duties and prohibitions apply to conduct within the Americas through the Charter of the Organization of American States and the American Declaration of the Rights and Duties of Man, O.A.S. Res. XXX (1948), arts. I ("Every human being has the right to life, liberty and the security of person."), XXV (" ... Every individual who has been deprived of his liberty ... has the right to humane treatment"), O.A.S. Off. Rec. OEA/Ser. L/V/I.4, Rev. (1965). As a party to the Charter of the Organization of American States, the U.S. is bound by the American Declaration, which is a legally authoritative indicia of human rights protected through Article 3(k) of the O.A.S. Charter [*see also id.* arts. 44, 111]. *See, e.g.*, Advisory Opinion OC-10/89, I-A, Inter-Am. Court H.R., Ser. A: Judgments and Opinions, No. 10, paras. 45, 47 (1989); Inter-Am. Comm. H.R., Report on the Situation of the Inhabitants of the Interior of Ecuador Affected by Development Activities, Chapter VIII (1996), OEA/Ser.L/V/II.96, doc. 10 rev. 1 (Apr. 24, 1977) ("The American Declaration ... continues to serve as a source of international obligation for all member states"); The "Baby Boy" Opinion, Case 2141, Inter-Am. Comm. H.R. 25, OEA/Ser.L/V/II.54, doc. 9 rev. 1 (1981), at para. 15 ("As a consequence of Article 3j, 16, 51e, 112 and 150 of [the Charter], the provisions of other instruments and resolutions of the OAS on human rights acquired binding force. Those instruments and resolutions of the OAS on human rights approved with the vote of the U.S. Government" include the American Declaration of the Rights and Duties of Man. That Declaration affirms several human rights, now protected through the O.A.S. Charter, including the right to "resort to the courts to ensure respect for ... [one's] legal rights" documented in Article XVIII); Roach Case, No. 9647, Inter-Am. Comm. H.R. 147, OEA/Ser.L/V/II.71, doc. 9 rev. 1 (1987), at para. 48; *see also* RICHARD B. LILLICH & HURST HANNUM, INTERNATIONAL HUMAN RIGHTS 802-04 (3 ed. 1995); DAVID WEISSBRODT, JOAN FITZPATRICK, FRANK NEWMAN, INTERNATIONAL HUMAN RIGHTS 598-600 (3 ed. 1996); McDOUGAL, LASSWELL, CHEN, *supra* at 198, 316.

Within the Americas, the United States is also bound to take no action inconsistent with the object and purpose of the American Convention on Human Rights, 1144 U.N.T.S. 123 (1969), which would necessarily include orders, authorizations, complicity, and more direct acts in violation of the human rights protected in the Convention. This obligation arises because the U.S. has singed the treaty while awaiting ratification. *See, e.g.,* Vienna Convention, *supra* art. 18. Article 5 of the American Convention requires:

(1) Every person has the right to have his physical, mental, and moral integrity respected.

(2) No one shall be subjected to torture or to cruel, inhuman, or degrading punishment or treatment. All persons deprived of their liberty shall be treated with respect for the inherent dignity of the human person....

D. Torture and Other Inhumane Acts

Convention Against Torture and Other Cruel, Inhuman or Degrading Treatment or Punishment, Dec. 10, 1984, 1465 U.N.T.S. 85

[Read the Torture Convention, in the Documents Section]

Questions

1. As of May, 2013, there are 153 signatories to the Convention. How is torture defined in Article 1 of the treaty? One textwriter and former President of the Appeals Chamber of the ICTY has noted that torture thus defined has the following elements: (1) an act that causes severe pain or suffering, whether physical or mental; (2) intentionally inflicted; (3) for a purpose listed or some other purpose; (4) inflicted by or at the instigation of or with the consent or acquiescence of a public official or other person acting in an official capacity; and (5) such pain or suffering does not arise "only from" nor is it "inherent in or incidental to lawful sanctions." *See* ANTONIO CASSESE, INTERNATIONAL CRIMINAL LAW, 119-20 (2003). Thus, the *actus reus* requires an "act" that causes severe pain or suffering, whether physical or mental. Under the Convention, torture does not involve every act that causes pain or suffering. The pain or suffering caused must be "severe." The CAT, however, does not elaborate on the key aspect of "severe." *See also* Notes 13-14 *infra*.

Thus also, there are two *mens rea* requirements. First, the act that causes severe pain and suffering must be "intentionally" inflicted on a person (not recklessly or negligently). The second aspect is not entirely clear. It is stated that the infliction of severe pain or suffering must be done for a purpose, such as for the purpose of: (1) obtaining from the victim or a third person information or a confession, (2) punishing the victim for an act he or a third person committed or is suspected of committing, (3) intimidating or coercing the victim or a third person; or (4) for any reason based on discrimination of any kind. However, the list of purposes is illustrative and not exhaustive, as noted by the phrase "for such purposes as". Moreover, paragraph 2 of Article 1 adds that the definition contained therein "is without prejudice to any international instrument ... which does or may contain provisions of wider application." Since most human rights instruments and the Geneva Conventions prohibit "torture" for any purpose and two of the major human rights instruments are addressed in the preamble as instruments that prohibit torture regardless of purpose, it is logical that the CAT did not attempt to restrict relevant purposes to those that are expressly listed in Article 1. *See also* Article 2(2); *The Prosecutor v. Delalic*, IT-96-21-T (Trial Chamber Judgment, 16 Nov. 1998), para. 470 ("there is no requirement that the conduct must be solely perpetrated for a prohibited purpose. Thus, ... the prohibited purpose must simply be part of the motivation behind the conduct and need not be the predominating or sole purpose."). Must the relevant purpose be more than a mere purpose to torture, *i.e.*, more than use of torture as an end in itself?

2. Are rape and other sexual offenses covered in Article 1? in Article 16? Note the recognitions of the ICTR and ICTY in Chapter Four that rape and other forms of sexual violence can constitute torture.

3. Can members of al Qaeda be prosecuted for violations of the Convention? Under this Convention, can there be some private perpetrators? See J. Paust, *The Other Side of Right: Private Duties Under Human Rights Law,* 5 Harv. H.R.J. 51, 61 (1992). See also para. 2 of Article 1. Other human rights treaties proscribe torture and cruel, inhuman or degrading treatment and punishment without mention of the status of perpetrators. *See, e.g.*, ICCPR, art. 7; *see also id.* art. 5(1) (implied duties of groups and persons). The CAT Committee has noted that the phrase "other persons acting in an official capacity" can include some non-state actors in Somalia with quasi-governmental authority. Elmi v. Australia, Comm. No. 120/1998, U.N. Doc. CAT/C/22/D/120/1998 (1999).

4. In the U.S., the Violence Against Women Act (VAWA), 42 U.S.C. § 13,981, which provides civil remedies for "a crime of violence motivated by gender," was enacted in part to protect human rights of women from private acts of violence. *See, e.g.*, Paust, *Human Rights Purposes of the Violence Against Women Act and International Law's Enhancement of Congressional Power*, 22 Hous. J. Int'l L. 209 (2000).

5. Do obligations of a Party to the treaty apply merely in the territory of the Party? See preamble and arts. 2(1), 4(1), 5(1) and (2), 16. See Committee Against Torture, *Consideration of Reports Submitted by States Parties Under Article 19 of the Convention: Conclusions and*

Recommendations of the Committee against Torture, United States of America, 36th sess., U.N. Doc. CAT/C/USA/CO/2 (18 May 2006), paras. ("The State party should recognize and ensure that the Convention applies at all times, whether in peace, war or armed conflict, in any territory under its jurisdiction"), 15 ("provisions of the Convention expressed as applicable to 'territory under the State party's jurisdiction' apply to, and are fully enjoyed by, all persons under the effective control of its authorities, of whichever type, wherever located in the world."), 17 (detention "in any secret detention facility under its de facto effective control ... constitutes, per se, a violation of the Convention"), 18 ("enforced disappearance in any territory under its jurisdiction ... constitutes, per se, a violation of the Convention"), 24 ("in all places of detention under its de facto effective control"), 26 ("eradicate all forms of torture and ill-treatment of detainees by its military or civilian personnel, in any territory under its jurisdiction") [hereinafter U.N. CAT Report].

6. With respect to Article 2, para. 1 ("territory under its jurisdiction"), *see also Loizidou v. Turkey,* 310 Eur. Ct. H.R., Ser. A (23 Mar. 1995) (portions of Cyprus were occupied territory under the jurisdiction of Turkey), examined in J. Kokott & B. Rudolf, International Decisions, 90 AM. J. INT'L L. 98, 98–100 (1996).

7. Under Article 2, para. 3, can a superior order be used in mitigation? Recall that customary international law concerning the reach of individual responsibility with respect to superior orders can be read into any treaty.

8. With respect to money damages, *compare* Article 14, para. 1, *with id.*, para. 2 and Article 16, paras. 1 and 2. See also U.N. CAT Report, *supra* at paras. 28 ("full redress, compensation and rehabilitation"), 32 ("redress, including appropriate compensation"). With respect to U.S. cases addressing civil liability for torture, cruel, inhuman, and/or degrading treatment, *see, e.g., Cabello v. Fernandez-Larios*, 402 F.3d 1148 (11th Cir. 2005) (Fernandos Larios, who served as a bodyguard to the general in command of a death squad during Pinochet's regime in Chile, was found liable for crimes against humanity, extrajudicial killing, torture, and cruelty with respect to massacres in 5 Chilean cities); *Kadic v. Karadzic*, 70 F.3d 232 (2d Cir. 1995); *Filartiga v. Pena-Irala*, 630 F.2d 876 (2d Cir. 1980); *Presbyterian Church of Sudan v. Talisman Energy, Inc.*, 244 F. Supp.2d 289, 305-06, 326 (S.D.N.Y. 2003); *Mehinovic v. Vuckovic,* 198 F. Supp.2d 1322, 1347-49 (N.D. Ga. 2002) ("Cruel, inhuman, or degrading treatment is a discrete and well-recognized violation of customary international law and is, therefore, a separate ground for liability," adding: "cruel, inhuman, or degrading treatment includes acts which inflict mental or physical suffering, anguish, humiliation, fear and debasement, which do not rise to the level of 'torture'" and that being "forced to observe the suffering of their friends and neighbors … [is] another form of inhumane and degrading treatment"); *Estate of Cabello v. Fernandez-Larios*, 157 F. Supp.2d 1345, 1360-61 (S.D. Fla. 2001); *Daliberti v. Republic of Iraq*, 97 F. Supp.2d 38, 45 (D.D.C. 2000); *Cicippio v. Islamic Republic of Iran*, 18 F. Supp.2d 62, 65-69 (D.D.C. 1998); *Xuncax v. Gramajo*, 886 F. Supp. 162, 187 (D. Mass. 1995); *Forti v. Suarez-Mason*, 672 F. Supp. 1531 (N.D. Cal. 1987) (torture and summary execution). See also Note 14 below concerning inhumane and degrading treatment.

9. Article 37 of the Convention on the Rights of the Child, 1577 U.N.T.S. 3 (1989), similarly requires that signatories "shall ensure that: (a) No child shall be subjected to torture or other cruel, inhuman or degrading treatment or punishment" and adds: "Neither capital punishment nor life imprisonment without possibility of release shall be imposed for offences committed by persons below 18 years of age."

This treaty also requires signatories to "take all appropriate measures … to protect children from the illicit use of narcotic drugs and psychotropic substances" (art. 33); "to protect the child from all forms of sexual exploitation and sexual abuse, … [including taking] all appropriate national, bilateral and multilateral measures to prevent: (a) The inducement or coercion of a child to engage in any unlawful sexual activity; (b) The exploitative use of children in prostitution or other unlawful sexual practices; (c) The exploitative use of children in pornographic performances and materials" (art. 34); and to "take all appropriate national, bilateral and multilateral measures to prevent the abduction, the sale of or traffic in children for any purpose or in any form" (art. 35). The treaty also requires that signatories "take all appropriate measures to promote physical and psychological recovery and social re-integration of a child victim of: any form of neglect, exploitation, or abuse; torture or any other form of cruel, inhuman or degrading treatment or punishment; or armed conflicts...." *Id.* art. 39.

10. Article 6 of the Convention on the Elimination of All Forms of Discrimination Against Women, 1249 U.N.T.S. 13 (1979), mandates that all signatories "shall take all appropriate measures, including legislation, to suppress all forms of traffic in women and exploitation of prostitution of women."

11. The U.S. statute proscribing torture is 18 U.S.C. §2340 *et seq.* Section 2340A(a), Torture, states: "Whoever outside the United States commits or attempts to commit torture shall be fined under this title or imprisoned not more than 20 years, or both, and if death results to any person from conduct prohibited by this subsection, shall be punished by death or imprisonment for any term or years or for life." The U.N. Committee Against Torture found the legislation lacking: "sections 2340 and 2340 A of the United States Code limit federal criminal jurisdiction over acts of torture to extraterritorial cases. The Committee also regrets that, despite the occurrence of cases of extraterritorial torture of detainees, no prosecutions have been initiated under the extraterritorial torture statute.... [The U.S.] should enact a federal crime of torture consistent with article 1 of the Convention ... to prevent and eliminate acts of torture ... in all its forms.... [The U.S.] should ensure that acts of psychological torture ... are not limited to 'prolonged mental harm' as set out in the State party's understandings lodged at the time of ratification of the Convention, but constitute a wider category of acts, which cause severe mental suffering, irrespective of their prolongation or its duration." U.N. CAT Report, *supra* at para. 13. The Committee also stated that the U.S. "should promptly, thoroughly, and impartially investigate any responsibility of senior military and civilian officials authorizing, acquiescing or consenting, in any way, to acts of torture committed by their subordinates." *Id.* para. 19.

12. During the wars in Afghanistan and Iraq, the Bush Administration attempted to interpret "torture" in a very narrow way that was not consistent with Article 1 of the Convention. *See, e.g.*, Jay S. Bybee, Memorandum for Alberto R. Gonzales, Counsel to the President, Re: Standards of Conduct for Interrogation under 18 U.S.C. §§ 2340-2340A (Aug. 1, 2002) (claiming that torture must involve death or organ failure and that mental suffering must be permanent), available at http://news.findlaw.com/wp/docs/doj/bybee80102mem.pdf;http://pegc.no-ip.info/archive/DOJ/20022602_bybee.pdf Jeffrey Smith, *Memo Offered Justification for Use of Torture*, Wash. Post, June 8, 2002, at A1; Paust, *Executive Plans, supra* at 834-36. A second Bybee memo argued that waterboarding and putting a person in a closed box was not torture). Is only "torture" prohibited under the CAT, arts. 1, 16, the ICCPR, art. 7; GC art. 3, and customary international law reflected therein? The Administration also claimed that a U.S. reservation to the treaty and an understanding limited the reach of the treaty. *See* Reservation No. 1, available at Cong. Rec. S17486-01 (daily ed., Oct. 27, 1990) ("the United States considers itself bound by the obligation under Article 16 to prevent 'cruel, inhuman or degrading treatment or punishment,' only insofar as the term 'cruel, inhuman or degrading treatment or punishment' means the cruel, unusual and inhumane treatment or punishment prohibited by the Fifth, Eighth, and/or Fourteenth Amendments to the Constitution of the United States."). Professor Paust has remarked: Clearly, the attempted reservation would be incompatible with the object and purpose of the Convention, since application of the reservation would preclude coverage of all forms of cruel, inhuman and degrading treatment as required under the Convention. As such, it is void

ab initio as a matter of law. *See* Vienna Convention on the Law of Treaties, *supra* art. 19(c). It was claimed recently by Alberto Gonzales that the putative reservation not only sought to limit the type of treatment proscribed (*i.e.*, that the phrase "cruel, inhuman, or degrading" set forth in a multilateral treaty "means" merely that which is recognized under U.S. constitutional amendments), but also sought to limit the treaty's reach overseas (*i.e.*, "means" treatment or punishment prohibited by the amendments and, if they don't apply overseas, such treatment or punishment overseas is o.k.). *See* Sonni Efron, *Torture Becomes a Matter of Definition: Bush Nominees Refuse to Say What's Prohibited*, N.Y. Times, Jan. 23, 2005, at A1. Such an attempted reservation would be doubly incompatible with the object and purpose of the oftlinetreaty and void as a matter of law. [*See also* Note 5 above] In any event, the customary prohibitions reflected in the treaty are universally applicable and have no such limitations. Paust, *Executive Plans*, *supra* at 823 n.43. See also Leila Zerrougui, *et al.*, Report, *Situation of Detainees at Guantanamo Bay*, Commission on Human Rights, 62nd sess., items 10 and 11 of the provisional agenda, U.N. Doc. E/CN.4/2006/120 (Feb. 15, 2006) [hereinafter U.N. Experts' Report], at 45 n.48, quoting Conclusions and Recommendations of the Committee against Torture: United States of America, 15/05/2000, U.N. Doc. A/55/44, paras. 179-180 (2000). See also The United States and Torture (Marjorie Chon ed. 2011); M. Cherif Bassiouni, The Institutionalization of Torture by the Bush Administration (2010); Christopher L. Blakesley, Terror and Anti-Terrorism: A Normative and Practical Assessment (2006); Marjorie Cohn, Cowboy Republic: Six Ways the Bush Gang Has Defied the Law (2007); Mark Danner, Abu Ghraib and the War on Terror (2004); John W. Dean, Worse Than Watergate: The Secret Presidency of George W. Bush (2004); Amos N. Guiora, Constitutional Limits on Coercive Interrogation (2008); Seymour M. Hersh, Chain of Command: The Road From 9/11 to Abu Ghraib (2004); Peter Jan Honigsberg, Our Nation Unhinged: TheHuman Consequences of the War on Terror (2009); Joseph Margulies, Guantánamo and the Abuse of Presidential Power (2006); Thomas Michael McDonnell, The United States, International Law, and the Struggle Against Terrorism 47-57, 60 (2009); Jordan J. Paust, Beyond the Law: The Bush Administration's Unlawful Responses in the "War" on Terror (2007); Philippe Sands, Torture Team: Rumsfeld's Memo and the Betrayal of American Values (2008); Michael P. Scharf & Paul R. Williams, Shaping Foreign Policy in Times of Crisis 129-30, 181-95 (2010); Diane Marie Amann, *Abu Ghraib*, 153 U. Pa. L. Rev. 2085, 2086, 2094 (2005); Karima Bennoune, *"To Respect and to Ensure": Reconciling International Human Rights Obligations in a Time of Terror*, 97 Proc., Am. Soc'y Int'l L. 23, 24 (2003); Jordan J. Paust, *The Bush-Cheney Legacy: Serial Torture and Forced Disappearance in Manifest Violation of Global Human Rights Law*, 18 Barry L. Rev. 61 (2012), available at http://ssrn.com/abstract=1989099 (concerning nine false claims of the Bush-Cheney Administration, "there has been notable rejection of their false claims that (1) relevant human rights law that is binding on the United States and its nationals does not apply outside United States territory; (2) human rights law does not apply during war or armed conflict; (3) alleged necessity can allow deviation from the absolute prohibitions of torture and cruel, inhuman, and degrading treatment under the laws of war and human rights law; (4) certain detained persons have no rights under applicable laws of war; (5) attempted U.S. reservations to two human rights treaties (which are facially and were known to be void *ab initio* as a matter of law) precluded their full reach regarding absolute and peremptory prohibitions of all forms of torture, cruel, inhuman, and other unlawful treatment; (6) certain interrogation tactics that had already been recognized as torture were not torture; (7) non-prisoners of war could be lawfully transferred from occupied territory to secret detention sites and to Guantanamo Bay for coercive interrogation or even lawful interrogation or detention; (8) the President and his entourage are not bound by the laws of war and, more generally, that they were above the law; and (9) through such manifestly unacceptable ploys members of the Administration could avoid criminal prosecution for authorizing or aiding and abetting international criminal conduct.").

13. With respect to authorizations within the Bush Administration, including the military, to strip persons naked and use of hooding as interrogation tactics, to use dogs to strike fear during interrogation and for terroristic purposes, to use water-boarding (which induces a significant fear of drowning), to use "fear up harsh: significantly increasing the fear level of a detainee," and to use other interrogation tactics not previously approved in U.S. military interrogation manuals, *see, e.g.*, Paust, *Executive Plans, supra* at 812, 824-51; Note 12 above.

In October 2006, former President Bush admitted that he had a "program" of secret detention and "tough" interrogation. *See, e.g.*, GEORGE W. BUSH, DECISION POINTS 170 (2010) (Bush admitted authorizing waterboarding, which is decidedly torture); JANE MAYER, THE DARK SIDE: THE INSIDE STORY OF HOW THE WAR ON TERROR TURNED INTO A WAR ON AMERICAN IDEALS 150 (noting an early 2002 meeting of Yoo, Gonzales, Addington, Flanigan, and Haynes discussing "what sorts of pain" to inflict), 185 (noting conflicts between Addington and Bellinger), 198-99 (noting that Addington, Gonzales, Haynes, Goldsmith, and others had flown to Guantanamo in September 2002 to discuss and observe use of patently unlawful SERE [Survival Evasion Resistance and Escape] tactics on detainees who were still held in secret detention or forced disappearance), 304, 307, 311-2 (noting the facilitating role of Gonzales) (2008); JOSE RODRIGUEZ, HARD MEASURES (2012) (admissions regarding waterboarding and other coercive tactics by former Deputy Director of Operations (Nov. 16—Dec. 2004) and Director, National Clandestine Service (Dec. 2004—Nov. 30, 2007), CIA); JOHN YOO, WAR BY OTHER MEANS ix, 35, 39-40, 43, 171-72, 187, 190-92, 200, 231 (2006); Jens David Ohlin, *The Torture Lawyers*, 51 HARV. INT'L L.J. 193 (2010); Jordan J. Paust, *The Absolute Prohibition of Torture and Necessary and Appropriate Sanctions*, 43 VALPARAISO U. L. REV. 1535, 1544-45, 1559-69 (2009) (also noting certain facilitating and abetting roles of Cheney, Addington, Gonzales, Rice, Rumsfeld, Tenet, Ashcroft, Yoo, Bybee, Haynes, Bradbury, Rizzo, Feith, Philbin, Flanigan, Goldsmith, and others), available at http://ssrn.com/abstract=1331159; Report, *Senate Armed Services Committee Inquiry Into the Treatment of Detainees in U.S. Custody*, Dec. 20, 2008; Majority Staff Report, House Committee on the Judiciary, *Reining in the Imperial Presidency: Lessons and Recommendations Relating to the Presidency of George W. Bush*, Jan. 13, 2009, at 110-46 (also noting: "in Secretary Powell's view, Mr. Bush was 'complicit' in those abuses." *Id.* at 136).

Would any of these tactics amount to cruel, inhuman, or degrading treatment, if not torture? See Paust, *The Absolute Prohibition, supra* at 1553-58 (water-boarding or a related inducement of suffocation, use of dogs to create intense fear, threatening to kill the detainee or family members, and the cold cell or a related inducement of hypothermia are each manifestly forms of torture. For example, there were 29 U.S. federal and state court cases, 7 U.S. Dep't of State Human Rights Country Reports, a decision of the European Court of Human Rights, and 2 decisions of the Inter-American Court of Human Rights that had recognized that water-boarding and related conduct is torture. *Id.* at 1553-54 n.69); U.N. CAT Report, *supra* at para. 24 (the U.S. "should rescind any interrogation technique, including methods involving sexual humiliation, 'water boarding,' 'short shackling' [*e.g.*, shackling a detainee to a hook in the floor], and using dogs to induce fear, that constitute torture, cruel, inhuman or degrading treatment or punishment, in all places of detention under its *de facto* effective control, in order to comply with its obligations under the Convention."); U.N. Experts' Report, *supra* Note 12, at 9-10, paras. 12-14, 21-22, paras. 41-45, 24-25, paras. 51-52, 37, para. 87; Council of Europe, Parliamentary Assembly, Res. 1433, *Lawfulness of Detentions by the United States in Guantanamo Bay*, paras. 7(i)-(vi), 8(i)-(iii), (vii) (2005), in the Documents Section; International Committee of the Red Cross, *ICRC Report on the Treatment of Fourteen "High Value Detainees" in CIA Custody* (Feb. 2007), quoted in Mark Danner, *Voices from the Black Sites*, 56 THE N.Y. REV. OF BKS. no. 6 (Apr. 9, 2009), available at http://www.nybooks.com/articles/22530. See also Evan Wallach, *Drop by Drop: Forgetting the History of Water Torture in U.S. Courts*, 45 COLUMBIA J. TRANSNAT'L L. 468 (2007) (also noting early uses of waterboarding and related inducement of suffocation during World War II and convictions); M. Cherif Bassiouni, *The Future of Human Rights in the Age of Globalization*, in PERSPECTIVES ON INTERNATIONAL LAW IN AN ERA OF CHANGE 22, 31 (2012).

14. What constitutes torture or cruel, inhuman or degrading treatment? See Convention, art. 1; recall Notes 8 and 13 above, and consider: In *Ireland v. United Kingdom*, 25 Eur. Ct. H.R. (ser. A) at 5 (1978), the European Court of Human Rights ruled that British interrogation tactics of wall-standing (forcing the detainees to remain for periods of some hours in a "stress position"), hooding, subjection to noise, deprivation of sleep, and deprivation of food and drink "constituted a practice of inhuman and degrading treatment" proscribed under human rights law.[5] In 1996, the European Court recognized that where a detainee "was stripped naked, with his arms tied behind his back and suspended by his arms ... [, s]uch treatment amounted to torture."[6] In another case, the European Court stated that treatment was "'degrading' because it was such as to arouse in its victims feelings of fear, anguish and inferiority capable of humiliating and debasing them."[7] The International Criminal Tribunal for Former Yugoslavia has also identified criteria for determining whether certain conduct constitutes criminally

---

5. *Id.* at 41, para. 96, 66, para. 167. The court noted that the "techniques were applied in combination, with premeditation and for hours at a stretch; they caused, if not bodily injury, at least intense physical and mental suffering to the persons subjected thereto and also led to acute psychiatric disturbances during interrogation," and, "accordingly," were forms of inhuman treatment. *Id.* at 66, para. 167. The Court concluded that the "techniques were also degrading, since they were such as to arouse in their victims feelings of fear, anguish and inferiority capable of humiliating and debasing them and possibly breaking their physical or moral resistance." *Id.*

6. *Aksoy v. Turkey*, 6 Eur. Ct. H.R. 2260, 23 EHRR 553, at paras. 60, 64 (18 Dec. 1996). The Court stated that "torture attaches only to deliberate inhuman treatment causing very serious and cruel suffering." *Id.* at paras. 63-64. The victim was detained for some two weeks and had claimed to have been subjected to beatings and had been stripped naked, hooded, and subjected to electric shocks. *Id.* at paras. 60, 64.

7. *T & V v. United Kingdom*, Judgment of 16 Dec. 1999, at para. 71, 30 EHRR 121 (2000).

sanctionable "torture"[8] or "cruel" or "inhuman" treatment.[9] Moreover, the Committee against Torture created under the Convention Against Torture and Other Cruel, Inhuman or Degrading Treatment or Punishment has condemned the use of the following interrogation tactics as either torture or cruel, inhuman or degrading treatment: (1) restraining in very painful conditions, (2) hooding under special conditions, (3) sounding of loud music for prolonged periods, (4) sleep deprivation for prolonged periods, (5) threats, including death threats, (6) violent shaking, and (7) using cold air to chill.[10] Earlier, a U.S. Army pamphlet addressing Geneva and other law of war proscriptions warned that an illegal means of interrogation of a detainee included "dunking his head into a barrel of water, or putting a plastic bag over his head to make him talk," adding: "No American soldier can commit these brutal acts, nor permit his fellow soldiers to do so."[11] Paust, *Executive Plans*, *supra* at 845-46.

15. For discussion of why the threat of administering truth serum constitute torture whereas the administration of such does not, see Linda M. Keller, *Is Truth Serum Torture?*, 20 Am. U. Int'l L. Rev. 521 (2005).

16. The authors of the U.N. Experts' Report, *supra* Note 12, maintain that force-feeding to deter Guantanamo detainees from carrying out long-term hunger strikes to protest their incarceration constitutes "torture" as defined by CAT. *Id*. paras. 54 & n.73, 70, 82. Do you agree; would you prefer more facts? Does force-feeding of detainees rise to the level of the infliction of "severe" pain or suffering? If so, was the in-

---

8. *See, e.g.*, *The Prosecutor v. Kunarac*, IT-96-23-T & IT-96-23/1-T (Trial Chamber, International Criminal Tribunal for Former Yugoslavia), para. 497 (22 Feb. 2001) (intentional "infliction, by act or omission, of severe pain or suffering, whether physical or mental"); *Id*. (Appeals Chamber, 12 June 2002), para. 149, adding "but there are no more specific requirements which allow an exhaustive classification or enumeration of acts which may constitute torture. Existing case law has not determined the absolute degree of pain required for an act to amount to torture"), para. 150 (rape can constitute torture); Johan D. van der Vyver, *Torture as a Crime Under International Law*, 67 Albany L. Rev. 427 (2003). In *The Prosecutor v. Naletilic & Martinovic*, IT-98-34-A (Appeals Chamber, 3 May 2006), paras. 299-300, the Appeals Chamber used the test stated in *Kunarac* and added: "while the suffering inflicted by some acts may be so obvious that the acts amount *per se* to torture, in general allegations of torture must be considered on a case-by-case basis so as to determine whether, in light of the acts committed and their context, severe physical or mental pain or suffering was inflicted. Similar case-by-case analysis is necessary regarding the crime of wilfully causing great suffering." Para. 299. In the case before the tribunal, "the Appeals Chamber agrees that telling prisoners falsely that they will be executed, in a "brutal context that makes the statement believable, can amount to wilfully causing great suffering. In addition, severe physical abuse in the course of interrogation ... also generally amounts to wilfully causing great suffering, particularly when combined with acts designed to cause psychological torment, such as falsely informing a prisoner that his father had been killed or firing guns at prisoners so as to create an atmosphere of terror." Para. 300.

9. With respect to "cruel" treatment, a trial chamber of the ICTY declared that "cruel treatment is treatment which causes serious mental or physical suffering and constitutes a serious attack on human dignity." *The Prosecutor v. Delalic*, IT-96-21-T (Trial Chamber, International Criminal Tribunal for Former Yugoslavia), para. 551 (Nov. 16, 1998). The same decision recognized that "inhuman treatment is an intentional act or omission, that is an act which, when judged objectively, is deliberate and not accidental, which causes serious mental or physical suffering or injury or constitutes a serious attack on human dignity." *Id*. at para. 543. Other ICTY cases confirm the *Delalic* recognitions. *See, e.g.*, Knut Dormann, Elements of War Crimes under the Rome Statute of the International Criminal Court 65 n.72 (re: inhuman), 398-99 ns. 7-8 (re: cruel) (2003). With respect to torture, see also *Zubeda v. Ashcroft*, 333 F.3d 463, 472 (3d Cir. 2003) ("[r]ape can constitute torture"); *Al-Saher v. I.N.S.*, 268 F.3d 1143, 1147 (9th Cir. 2001).

10. 0 Concluding Observations of the Committee against Torture: Israel, 18th Sess., U.N. Doc. A/52/44 (1997) at paras. 256-257.

11. 1 U.S. Dep't of Army Subject Schedule 27-1, *The Geneva Conventions of 1949 and Hague Convention No. IV of 1907*, at 7 (8 Oct. 1970).

fliction of severe pain or suffering committed for the purpose of obtaining information or a confession (short term or long term, *e.g.*, to keep detainees alive in order to obtain information later)? To punish the victim? To intimidate or coerce the victim? For an unlawful discriminatory purpose? Does force-feeding constitute "other acts of cruel, inhuman or degrading treatment or punishment" within the meaning of Article 16 of CAT?

17. The U.N. Committee Against Torture has also recognized that "secret detention … constitutes, *per se*, a violation of the Convention" and that "enforced disappearance … constitutes, *per se*, a violation of the Convention." U.N. CAT Report, *supra* at paras. 17-18. The Committee also declared that "detaining persons indefinitely without charge, constitutes *per se* a violation of the Convention." *Id.* para. 22. With respect to U.S. attempts to deny *habeas corpus* review of the propriety of detention, the Committee warned that the U.S. "should ensure that independent, prompt and thorough procedures to review the circumstances of detention and the status of detainees are available to all detainees as required by article 13 of the Convention." *Id.* para. 27. With respect to Guantanamo Bay, the Committee stated that the U.S. "should cease to detain any person at Guantanamo Bay and close this detention facility, permit access by the detainees to judicial process or release them as soon as possible, ensuring that they are not returned to any State where they could face a real risk of being tortured." *Id.* para. 22. With respect to a U.S. claim that its obligation under Article 3 does not extend to persons detained outside U.S. territory, the Committee declared that the U.S. "should apply the *non-refoulement* guarantee to all detainees in its custody, cease the rendition of suspects, in particular by its intelligence agencies, to Stateswhere they face a real risk of torture, in order to comply with its obligations under article 3 of the Convention. The State party should always ensure that suspects have the possibility to challenge decisions of *refoulement*." *Id.* para. 20. *See also* Leila Nadya Sadat, *Ghost Prisoners and Black Sites: Extraordinary Rendition Under International Law*, 57 Case W. Res. J. Int'l L. _ (2006); Diane Marie Amann, *The Committee Against Torture Urges an End to Guantanamo Detention*, ASIL Insight (June 8, 2006), available at http://www.asil.org/insights/2006/06/insights060608.html.

18. In *The Prosecutor v. Furundzija*, ICTY-95-17/1, at paras. 153-155 (10 Dec. 1998), it was recognized that the prohibition of torture "has evolved into a peremptory norm or *jus cogens*, that is, a norm that enjoys a higher rank in the international hierarchy than treaty law and even 'ordinary' customary rules. The most conspicuous consequence of this higher rank is that the principle at issue could not be derogated from by States.… [para. 154] an absolute value from which nobody must deviate. 155. The fact that torture is prohibited by a peremptory norm of international law has other effects at the inter-state and individual levels. At the inter-state level, it serves to internationally de-legitimise any legislative, administrative or judicial act authorizing torture. It would be senseless to argue, on the one hand, that on account of the *jus cogens* value of the prohibition against torture, treaties or customary rules providing for torture would be null and void *ab initio*, and then be unmindful of a State say, taking national measures authorising or condoning torture or absolving its perpetrators through an amnesty law. If such a situation were to arise, the national measures, violating the general principles and any relevant treaty provision, would produce the legal effects discussed above and in addition would not be accorded international legal recognition.…" *See also* remarks of U.N. Secretary-General Kofi Annan: "[t]orture is an atrocious violation of human dignity. It dehumanizes both the victimand the perpetrator. The pain and terror deliberately inflicted by one human being upon another leavepermanent scars.… Freedom from torture is a fundamental human right that must be protected under all circumstances. Growing awareness of inter-

national legal instruments and protection mechanisms gives hope that the wall of silence around this terrible practice is gradually being eroded." Freedom from Torture "Fundamental Right," Says Secretary-General, SG/SM/7855, OBV/223 (June 26, 2001), available at www.unis.unvienna.org/unis/pressrels/2001/sgsm7855.html.

19. In addition to Article 25 of the American Declaration (requiring "humane treatment") and Article 5 of the American Convention, other regional human rights instruments recognize the absolute prohibition of torture and cruel, inhuman, and degrading treatment. *See, e.g.*, African Charter of Human and Peoples' Rights, art. 5; Arab Charter on Human Rights, art. 8 (which also requires that "[t]he commission of, or participation in, such acts shall be regarded as crimes"); and the European Convention, art. 3.

20. Foreign prosecutions of individuals for torture include: (1) in June, 2005, a French trial in absentia of Ould Dah, a Mauritanian military officer, accused of torturing two other officers in 1991, led to a 10 year prison sentence ("universal jurisdiction" was used in connection with a 1994 law implementing the Torture Convention and Dah was detained in Montpellier, France while participating in a training course); (2) the Spanish conviction of Adolfo Scilingo of crimes against humanity, torture, and illegal detention in connection with the Argentinian "dirty war" between 1976 and 1983, admitting that he was on board two "death flights" during which detainees were mistreated and thrown to their deaths over the ocean (Third Section of the Criminal Division of the Audiencia Nacional (National Court) (19 April 2005); and (3) the Rotterdam District Court judgment of April 7, 2004, against one Sebastien Nzapali in *Prosecutor v. N*, who "in or around October 1996, in Matadi, jointly and in conjunction with others ... as head of the Garde Civile for the province of Bas-Zaire" in the Congo during the reign of Mobutu, engaged in "complicity in torture, repeatedly committed" within the meaning of the Dutch Torture Convention Implementation Act and Section 8 of the International Crimes Act. The case proceeded on the basis of universal jurisdiction and the crime of torture involved Nzapali's use of his bodyguards to against a harbor official who did not clear a car of a friend through customs. Nzapali had the victim beaten "'as a punching bag'" while defendant watched from a balcony. The court found that "the acts of the accused, whereby he abused his position, and seriously affected the physical and mental integrity of the victim, acting in violation of the universal respect for human rights and the fundamental freedoms, show a complete lack of respect for the dignity of a fellow human being." See Ward Ferdinandusse, Comment on *Prosecutor v. N.*, Case No. AO7178, 99 Am. J. Int'l L. 686 (2005). See also *Jones v. Saudi Arabia* (Ct. App., U.K. 2004) (allowing civil suit by four U.K. citizens against several Saudi officials for alleged torture and denying claims to immunity).

E. Race Discrimination

1. General Discrimination

International Convention on the Elimination of All Forms of Racial Discrimination, 660 U.N.T.S. 195

[Read Article 4 of the Race Discrimination Convention, in the Documents Section]

Question

1. When the United States ratified this convention in 1994 it attached a reservation to the effect that nothing in the Convention shall require the United States to authorize

legislation or other action incompatible with the U.S. Constitution, including those provisions relating to free speech. The reservation saves the United States from violating the treaty if it does not, in accordance with the Constitution, enact legislation to criminalize racist speech and organizations. Does the reservation guarantee a specific interpretation of the First Amendment of the U.S. Constitution? See J. Paust, International Law as Law of the United States 313 *ff*. (1996).

2. Apartheid

International Convention on the Suppression and Punishment of the Crime of "Apartheid," done in New York, Nov. 30, 1973, 1015 U.N.T.S. 243

[Read the Apartheid Convention, in the Documents Section]

Notes and Questions

1. In 1984, the U.N. General Assembly passed a resolution recalling that the Security Council had rejected "the so-called 'new constitution' [of the apartheid regime in South Africa] and declared it null and void," commended "the united resistance of the oppressed people of South Africa ... and recogniz[ed] the legitimacy of their struggle to eliminate apartheid and establish a society based on majority rule with equal participation by all the people of South Africa...," urged "all Governments and organizations ... to assist the oppressed people of South Africa in their legitimate struggle for national liberation;" and condemned "the South African racist regime for ... persisting with the further entrenchment of apartheid, a system declared a crime against humanity and a threat to international peace and security". G.A. Res. 39/2 (28 Sept. 1984) (vote: 133–0–2 abstentions).

2. Is mere membership a crime under Article III?

3. Is leader responsibility, as part of customary law, impliedly covered in Article IV (b), or is it limited to circumstances noted in Article III?

F. Hostage-Taking

International Convention Against the Taking of Hostages, 1316 U.N.T.S. 205 (1979)

[Read the Hostage-Taking Convention, in the Documents Section]

Questions

1. Is asylum or amnesty possible under Article 15 of the Convention if the accused has not been subject to initiation of prosecution under Article 8 (1)? See also preamble ("either be prosecuted or extradited").

2. Is hostage-taking covered if a U.S. perpetrator takes a foreign tourist hostage, within the meaning of Article 1 (1), in a convenience store in Texas? See also Article 13.

3. Can a member of al Qaeda who engages in hostage-taking of European victims in Iraq be prosecuted for a violation of the Convention?

Security Council Resolution Condemning Hostage-Taking, U.N. S.C. Res. 579 (1985)

The Security Council,

Deeply disturbed at the prevalence of incidents of hostage-taking and abduction, several of which are of protracted duration and have included loss of life,

Considering that the taking of hostages and abductions are offences of grave concern to the international community, having severe adverse consequences for the rights of the victims and for the promotion of friendly relations and co-operation among States,....

1. *Condemns unequivocally* all acts of hostage-taking and abduction;

2. *Calls for* the immediate safe release of all hostages and abducted persons wherever and by whomever they are being held;

3. *Affirms* the obligation of all States in whose territory hostages or abducted persons are held urgently to take all appropriate measures to secure their safe release and to prevent the commission of acts of hostage-taking and abduction in the future;

4. *Appeals* to all States that have not yet done so to consider the possibility of becoming parties to [various Conventions listed] ... ;

5. *Urges* the further development of international co-operation among States in devising and adopting effective measures which are in accordance with the rules of international law to facilitate the prevention, prosecution and punishment of all acts of hostage-taking and abduction as manifestations of international terrorism.

G. Disappearances

Section 702 (c) of the RESTATEMENT notes that "causing the disappearance of individuals" is a violation of the customary international law of human rights. U.S. cases have addressed civil remedies for such a violation, and one such case has offered a definitional orientation: It has "two essential elements: (1) abduction by state officials or their agents; followed by (2) official refusals to acknowledge the abduction or to disclose the detainee's fate." *Forti v. Suarez-Mason,* 694 F. Supp. 707, 711 (N.D. Cal. 1988); see also *id.* at 710. The court noted that the Organization of American States "has also denounced 'disappearance' as 'an affront to the conscience of the hemisphere and ... a crime against humanity'", *id.* at 710, citing O.A.S. Inter-Am. Comm. H.R. "General Assembly Resolution 666 (November 18, 1983)." Also see *The Prosecutor v. Kupreskic,* IT-‐95-16-T (ICTY Trial Chamber, Judgment, 14 Jan. 2000); *In re Estate of Marcos, Human Rights Litigation,* 25 F.3d 1467, 1475 (9th Cir. 1994); *Bowoto v. Chevron Corp.,* WL 2349336 at *29 (N.D. Cal. 2007); *Tachiona v. Mugabe,* 234 F. Supp.2d 401, 406 (S.D.N.Y. 2002); *Xuncax v. Gramajo,* 886 F. Supp. 162, 184-85 (D. Mass. 1995).

In 1992, the United Nations General Assembly also adopted the Declaration on the Protection of All Persons from Enforced Disappearance, U.N. G.A. Res. 47/133 (8 Dec. 1992), reprinted in 32 I.L.M. 904 (1993). In Article 1 of the Declaration, it was stated: "Any act of enforced disappearance is an offence to human dignity. It is condemned as a denial of the purposes of the Charter of the United Nations and as a grave and flagrant violation of the human rights and fundamental freedoms proclaimed in the Universal Declaration of Human Rights and reaffirmed in international instruments in this field." Article 4, paragraph 1, declares: "All acts of enforced disappearance shall be offences under criminal law punishable by appropriate penalties which shall take into account their extreme seriousness." Article 5 also declares that such acts render "perpetrators and the State or State authorities which organize, acquiesce in or tolerate such disappearances liable under civil law...." In 2006, the U.N. adopted the International Convention for the Protection of All Persons from Enforced Disappearance, read the Convention in the Documents Section. Article 7(1)(i) of the Rome Statute of the International Criminal Court lists enforced disappearance of persons as a crime against humanity and paragraph (2)(i) thereof contains a definition of enforced disappearance for purposes of ICC prosecution — see the Documents Section. See also Note 17 in Section 1 above.

Inter-American Convention on the Forced Disappearance of Persons, done in Belen, Brazil, June 9, 1994

[Read the Disappearance of Persons Convention, in the Documents Section]

Questions

1. Is amnesty possible in view of Articles I (a), (b), (c), III ("mitigating" circumstances), VI, IX (no "immunities" or "special dispensations")? Should amnesty ever pertain with respect to international crime? The preamble to the U.N. Convention on Enforced Disappearance expresses the determination "to prevent enforced disappearance and to combat impunity for the crime of enforced disappearance."

2. More generally, are criminal sanctions for human rights violations appropriate? Should greater attention be paid to the concept of crimes against human rights? See Paust, *Applicability of International Criminal Laws to Events in the Former Yugoslavia*, 9 Am. U.J. Int'l L. & Pol. 499, 518–21 (1994); *Aggression Against Authority: The Crime of Oppression, Politicide and Other Crimes Against Human Rights*, 18 Case W. Res. J. Int'l L. 283, 290–92 (1986), and references cited; Chapter Two.

3. Since the preamble to the Inter-American Convention reaffirms that systematic disappearance is a crime against humanity, could General Pinochet of Chile have been rightly prosecuted for such acts committed during his regime? *See also* Articles I (b), IX. Could he have been extradited to countries within the Americas? See Article V.

4. Is the prohibition derogable? See the preamble and Article X.

5. During the wars in Afghanistan and Iraq, the Bush Administration had detained numerous individuals there; at Guantanamo Bay, Cuba; and in many other places without disclosing the whereabouts of all persons detained or their names. As noted above, in 2006 former President Bush admitted that he had a "program" of secret detention. Are such forms of secret detention violations of the prohibition of forced disappearance? *See, e.g.,* Statute of the ICC, art. 7(2)(i); Inter-American Convention on the Forced Disappearance of Persons, art. II; Council of Europe Parliamentary Assembly, Res. 1433, *Lawfulness of Detentions by the United States in Guantanamo Bay*, paras. 7(vi), 8(vii)-(viii), in the Documents Section; Maureen R. Berman, Roger C. Clark, *State Terrorism: Disappearances*, 13 Rutgers L.J. 531 (1982); Jordan J. Paust, *Post-9/11 Overreaction and Fallacies Regarding War and Defense, Guantanamo, the Status of Persons, Treatment, Judicial Review of Detention, and Due Process in Military Commissions*, 70 Notre Dame L. Rev. 1335, 1352-56 (2004); Sadat, *Ghost Prisoners*, *supra*; Xuncax v. Gramajo, 886 F. Supp. 162, 184-85 (D. Mass. 1995); Forti v. Suarez-Mason, 694 F. Supp. 707, 710-12 (N.D. Cal. 1988); see also U.N. CAT Report, *supra* at paras.

17-18 (quoted above). Are they violations of the Geneva Conventions? *See* Geneva Civilian Convention, arts. 5, 25, 71, 106-07; IV COMMENTARY, GENEVA CONVENTION RELATIVE TO THE TREATMENT OF CIVILIAN PERSONS IN TIME OF WAR 56-58 (ICRC, J. Pictet ed. 1958).

6. If a member of al Qaeda engages in hostage-taking of some European nationals in Iraq and the location of the hostages is otherwise unknown, can the member of al Qaeda be prosecuted for forced disappearance of the hostages?

7. Article 8(2) of the European Convention for the Prevention of Torture and Inhuman or Degrading Treatment or Punishment requires signatories to provide the European Committee for the Prevention of Torture and Inhuman or Degrading Treatment or Punishment full information on all places where persons deprived of their liberty are held. Eur. T.S. No. 126 (1987), art. 8(2). The European Court of Human Rights has held that a state violates Article 2 of the European Convention for the Protection of Human Rights and Fundamental Freedoms if the authorities fail to take reasonable measures to prevent the disappearance of a person with respect to whom there is a particular risk of disappearance. *See Mahmut Kaya v. Turkey*, 28 EHRR 1 (28 Mar. 2000); *Gongadze v. Ukraine*, judgment of (8 Nov. 2005). Further, Articles 2 and 13 are violated by the failure of authorities to carry out an investigation of disappearances. *See Cyprus v. Turkey*, 35 EHRR 30 (10 May 2001); *Kurt v. Turkey*, 27 EHRR 373 (25 May 1998), adding that Article 5 requires the authorities to take effective measures to safeguard against a risk of disappearance and to conduct prompt and effective investigations.

8. Note that Article 1(2) of the U.N. Convention on Enforced Disappearance expressly states that "[n]o exceptional circumstances whatsoever, whether a state of war or a threat of war, internal political instability or any other public emergency, may be invoked as a justification." This recognition of the absolute nature of the prohibition of forced disappearance is mirrored in Article X of the Inter-American Convention. Necessarily, secret detention is a *per se* crime that is never justifiable.

9. Note that Article 13 of the U.N. Convention expressly precludes consideration of forced disappearance as a political offense for purposes of extradition. This is mirrored in Article V of the Inter-American Convention.

The Velásques Rodríguez Case, Inter-Am. Ct. Hum. Rts., Judgment (29 July 1988)

186. As a result of the disappearance, Manfredo Velasquez was the victim of an arbitrary detention, which deprive him of his physical liberty without legal cause and without a determination of the lawfulness of his detention by a judge or competent tribunal. Those acts directly violate the right to personal liberty recognized by Article 7 of the [American] Convention [on Human Rights] ... and are a violation imputable to Honduras of the duties to respect and ensure the right under Article 1(1).

187. The disappearance of Manfredo Velasquez violates the right to personal integrity recognized by Article 5 of the Convention.... First, the mere subjection of an individual to prolonged isolation and deprivation of communication is in itself cruel and inhuman treatment which harms the psychological and moral integrity of the person, and violates the right of every detainee under Article 5(1) and 5(2) to treatment respectful of his dignity. Second, although it has not been directly shown that Manfredo Velasquez was physically tortured, his kidnapping and imprisonment by governmental authorities, who have been shown to subject detainees to indignities, cruelty and tor-

ture, constitute a failure of Honduras to fulfill the duty imposed by Article 1(1) to ensure the right under Article 5(1) and 5(2) of the Convention. The guarantee of physical integrity and the right of detainees to treatment respectful of their human dignity require States Parties to take reasonable steps to prevent situations which are truly harmful to the rights protected.

188. The above reasoning is applicable to the right to life recognized by Article 4 of the Convention.... The context in which the disappearance of Manfredo Velasquez occurred and the lack of knowledge seven years later about his fate create a reasonable presumption that he was killed. Even if there is a minimal margin of doubt in this respect, it must be presumed that his fate was decided by authorities who systematically executed detainees without trial and concealed their bodies in order to avoid punishment. This, together with the failure to investigate, is a violation by Honduras of a legal duty under Article 1(1) of the Convention to ensure the rights recognized by Article 4(1). That duty is to ensure to every person subject to its jurisdiction the inviolability of the right to life and the right not to have one's life taken arbitrarily. These rights imply an obligation on the part of States Parties to take reasonable steps to prevent situations that could result in the violation of that right.

[Editors' note: Later, the Inter-American Court of Human Rights ordered money damages to be paid to his family, which was eventually paid some six years after the Court's order.]

Chapter 2

Crimes Against Humanity

Fictional Introductory Problem

For purposes of this problem, assume that you are a judge presiding over the trial of Andre Bagosora, who is being prosecuted in Burundi for committing crimes against humanity and genocide in neighboring Rwanda. The indictment and the Defendant's motion for dismissal are reproduced below. Based on the materials on crimes against humanity and genocide contained in this chapter and Chapter Three, you should assess the validity of each of the defendant's grounds for dismissal. What other issues might arise or legal policies appear to be at stake?

Burundi v. Bagosora, Indictment # 3-19-97, in the Trial Court of Burundi

1. The Defendant, Andre Bagosora, is a 35 year old Tutsi male of Rwandan citizenship. He is a private businessman who had close ties to the previously ruling governmental elite in Rwanda.

2. The population of the neighboring country of Rwanda is composed primarily of two groups, the majority Hutu and the minority Tutsi. In 1933, the colonial power (Belgium) conducted a census in order to issue identity cards, which labeled every Rwandan as either Hutu or Tutsi. Tribal classifications were determined on a patrilineal basis, taking sole account of the father's ethnicity. Thus, a person whose father was Tutsi was considered a Tutsi, regardless of the mother's ethnic background.

3. The Hutus and Tutsis had been fighting in Rwanda since Rwanda became an independent country in 1959. After the plane carrying the President of Rwanda (a Hutu) was shot down on April 6, 1994, the Hutus launched a genocidal campaign against the Tutsi, killing as many as one million Tutsi during a four month period. Tutsis were targeted because of their ethnic, political, and gender identifications. The genocide was halted when the Tutsis militarily defeated the Hutus and most of the Hutus fled to neighboring Zaire. In December of 1997, two million Hutu refugees returned peacefully to Rwanda.

4. In January of 1997, Radio Milles Collines, which since 1995 has been owned and operated by the defendant, began a campaign of hatred against the returning Hutu refugees. Cassette recordings exist of a speech by the defendant, in which he called on Tutsis "to capture the returning Hutu women, strip them naked, and rape them in order to create Tutsi children."

5. Subsequently, in 1998, thousands of Tutsi civilians undertook a campaign of mass rape against the female Hutu refugees. Amnesty International estimates that 10,000 female Hutu refugees were victims of sexual abuse at the hands of the Tutsis.

6. The defendant was taken into custody during a visit to Burundi. He is charged with committing crimes against humanity and genocide. The Burundi Court has universal jurisdiction over his crimes. There is no statute of limitations.

Motion to Dismiss the Indictment

The Defendant requests a dismissal of the indictment against him on the following grounds:

1. Burundi lacks jurisdiction under international law to prosecute the Defendant, who is a Rwandan citizen and is charged with crimes that occurred in Rwanda.

2. The acts alleged could not constitute crimes against humanity because they occurred during peacetime, not in the course of an armed conflict.

3. Since there has been so much intermarriage between Hutus and Tutsis through the years that ethnographers and historians question whether Hutus and Tutsis are technically distinct ethnic groups, violence against the Hutus cannot constitute a crime against humanity or the crime of genocide.

4. Because the defendant was a non-governmental actor, he cannot be convicted of crimes against humanity or genocide. Further, both types of crime must be committed in the context of a state policy to engage in widespread acts of extermination.

5. Since gender is not one of the protected groups under the Genocide Convention, alleged rapes cannot constitute the crime of genocide. Moreover, the defendant is alleged only to have urged radio listeners to commit rape, not to kill or otherwise destroy a group. Thus, his alleged act does not constitute the crime of genocide. Further, acts of rape are not covered as acts constituting crimes against humanity or genocide.

6. The charges against the Defendant contravene the free speech provisions of the Burundi Constitution (which is identical to the U.S. First Amendment), and the Burundi Constitution must control.

Section 1
Nuremberg and Earlier

One should recall that in the late 1700s and early 1800s there were references to "duties of humanity," "duty of humanity," "crimes against mankind," "crimes against the human family," "enemies of the whole human family," which seem related to concepts of laws of humanity, offenses against the laws of humanity, and crimes against humanity. During the 1915 massacres of Armenians by Turks, the governments of Great Britain, France and Russia had condemned the massacres as "crimes against humanity and civilization." See QUINCY WRIGHT, HISTORY OF THE UNITED NATIONS WAR CRIMES COMMISSION 35 (1948); *The Prosecutor v. Akayesu, infra*, paras. 565-566. Some low to mid-level Turkish persons were prosecuted in military commissions after World War I. See www.armeniangenocide.org/genocide.htm. A few years later, a former U.S. Secretary of State wrote that the slave trade had become a "crime against humanity." See Lansing,

Notes on World Sovereignty, 15 Am. J. Int'l L. 13, 25 (1921). Already in 1874 in the United States George Curtis had labeled slavery a "crime against humanity." See III Orations and Addresses of George William Curtis 208 (C. Norton ed. 1894). *See also* McMullen v. Hodge and Others, 5 Tex. 34, 71 (1849)Norris v. Newton, 18 F. Cas. 322, 324 (C.C.D. Indiana 1850) (No. 10,307) ("There can be no higher offense against the laws of humanity and justice … than to arrest a free man … with the view of making him a slave."); O'Loughlin v. People, 90 Colo. 368, 378, 10 P. 543 (1932) ("rape of a stepdaughter is …'a crime against humanity'"), quoting Wilkinson v. People, 86 Colo. 406, 411, 282 P. 257 (1929); State v. Robins, 221 Ind. 125, 46 N.E.2d 691 (1943); Toth v. State, 141 Neb. 448, 464, 3 N.W.2d 899 (1942) (re: incest and rape, also quoting *Wilkinson*); State v. Hogan, 63 Ohio St. 202, 214, 58 N.E. 572 (1900) ("piracy and the slave trade were offenses not only against humanity, but against civilization"); Rodriguiz v. State, 20 Tex. Ct. App. 542, 546 (Tex. Crim. App. 1886) (sexual intercourse with a female of severely diminished mental capacity was not covered by state criminal law but is one of the "heinous crimes against humanity"); Compton v. State, 13 Tex. Ct. App. 271, 274 (Tex. Crim. App. 1882) (incest with a stepdaughter is "a crime against humanity"); State v. Lilly, 47 W.Va. 496, 500, 35 S.E. 837 (1900) (dictum re: abortion: "[t]here is no crime more heinous against humanity"); 1 Op. Att'y Gen. 509, 513 (1821) ("crimes against mankind," citing H. Grotius, The Law of War and Peace, Book One, ch. 21, § 3). In 1855, the slave trade was also related to a "crime against mankind." United States v. Darnaud, 25 F. Cas. 754, 760 (C.C. Pa. 1855) (sodomy of a girl is a "crime against mankind"); see also United States v. Haun, 26 F. Cas. 227, (C.C.S.D. Ala. 1860) (Campbell, J., on circuit) (slave trade is a crime against "human rights" and against "humanity"); Henfield's Case, 11 F. Cas. 1099, 1107 (C.C.D. Pa. 1793) (No. 6,360) (Wilson, J., on circuit) (breaches of neutrality involve violations of the "duties of humanity").

Also recall that in the 1919 Report of the Commission on the Responsibility of the Authors of the War and on Enforcement of Penalties formulated by representatives from several States and presented to the Paris Peace Conference, criminal responsibility was identified in terms such as "offences against … the laws of humanity" and "violations," "breach[es] of," and "outrages against … the laws of humanity." The 1868 Declaration of St. Petersburg also referred to violations of the "laws of humanity" (see Chapter Four) and so did the preamble to the 1907 Hague Convention No. IV (in the "Martens clause"). Perhaps the trial of von Hagenbach in 1474 for violations of the "laws of God and man" is relevant, especially in view of the nature of the crimes charged. Of apparent rhetorical significance was the statement of Charles Darwin in 1881, who opposed limits on "experiments on living animals," and opined "that to retard the progress of physiology is to commit a crime against humanity." Quoted in Penn. Co. for Ins. v. Commissioner, 25 B.T.A. 1168, 1172 (U.S. Bd. Tax App. 1932).

The Prosecutor v. Akayesu, ICTR-96-4-T (2 Sept. 1998)

Before: Judge Laïty Kama, Presiding

Judge Lennart Aspegren

Judge Navanethem Pillay

565. Crimes against humanity are aimed at any civilian population and are prohibited regardless of whether they are committed in any armed conflict, international or internal in character. In fact, the concept of crimes against humanity had been recognised long before Nuremberg. On 28 May 1915, the Governments of France, Great Britain and Russia made a declaration regarding the massacres of the Armenian popula-

tion in Turkey, denouncing them as "crimes against humanity and civilisation for which all the members of the Turkish government will be held responsible together with its agents implicated in the massacres." The 1919 Report of the Commission on the Responsibility of the Authors of the War and on Enforcement of Penalties formulated by representatives from several States and presented to the Paris Peace Conference also referred to "offences against ... the laws of humanity."

566. These World War I notions derived, in part, from the Martens clause of the Hague Convention (IV) of 1907, which referred to "the usages established among civilised peoples, from the laws of humanity, and the dictates of the public conscience." In 1874, George Curtis called slavery a "crime against humanity." Other such phrases as "crimes against mankind" and "crimes against the human family" appear far earlier in human history (see 12 N.Y.L. Sch. J. Hum. Rts. 545 (1995) [extract printed in this chapter, *supra*]).

What is interesting with respect to historic recognitions of "laws of humanity" and "crimes against humanity" is that the reach of these precepts was potentially quite broad, perhaps as far-reaching as human rights. They involved several types of conduct and were not limited to state actors or war contexts. *See generally* J. Paust, *Threats to Accountability After Nuremberg, infra*. It should be noted that the phrase "any civilian population" addressed in *Musema* can include merely civilians as such and that in The Prosecutor v. Tadic, IT-94-1-T (Judgment), para. 634 (7 May 1997), it was recognized that the phrase makes it clear that crimes against humanity can be committed against civilians of the same nationality as the perpetrator or those who are stateless, as well as those of a different nationality.

Justice Robert Jackson in his report to the President of the United States in 1945 concerning crimes addressed at Nuremberg (another extract of which follows) recognized the relevance of the "Martens clause"when stating: "[t]hese principles have been assimilated as a part of International Law at least since 1907. The Fourth Hague Convention provided that the inhabitants and belligerents shall remain under the protection and the rule of 'the principles of the law of nations, as they result from the usages established among civilized peoples, from the laws of humanity and the dictates of public conscience.'"

Report of Justice Robert H. Jackson to the President of the United States, released June 7, 1945

The Legal Charges [Before the IMT, Nuremberg]

Against this background it may be useful to restate in more technical lawyer's terms the legal charges against the top Nazi leaders and those voluntary associations such as the S.S. and Gestapo which clustered about them and were ever the prime instrumentalities, first, in capturing the German state, and then, in directing the German state to its spoliations against the rest of the world.

(a) Atrocities and offenses against persons or property constituting violations of International Law, including the laws, rules, and customs of land and naval warfare. The rules of warfare are well established and generally accepted by the nations. They make offenses of such conduct as killing of the wounded, refusal of quarter, ill treatment of prisoners of war, firing on undefended localities, poisoning of wells and streams, pillage and wanton destruction, and ill treatment of inhabitants in occupied territory.

(b) Atrocities and offenses, including atrocities and persecutions on racial or religious grounds, committed since 1933. This is only to recognize the principles of criminal law as they are generally observed in civilized states. These principles have been assimilated as a part of International Law at least since 1907. The Fourth Hague Convention provided that inhabitants and belligerents shall remain under the protection and the rule of "the principles of the law of nations, as they result from the usages established among civilized peoples, from the laws of humanity and the dictates of the public conscience."

(c) Invasions of other countries and initiation of wars of aggression in violation of International Law or treaties.

International Military Tribunal at Nuremberg, Indictment Number 1

COUNT FOUR—CRIMES AGAINST HUMANITY

[Read the Charter of the I.M.T. at Nuremberg, Article 6 (c), in the Documents Section]

Statement of the Offense

All the defendants committed Crimes against Humanity during a period of years preceding 8th May, 1945 in Germany and in all those countries and territories occupied by the German armed forces since 1st September, 1939 and in Austria and Czechoslovakia and in Italy and on the High Seas.

All the defendants, acting in concert with others, formulated and executed a common plan or conspiracy to commit Crimes against Humanity as defined in Article 6(c) of the Charter. This plan involved, among other things, the murder and persecution of all who were or who were suspected of being hostile to the Nazi Party and all who were or who were suspected of being opposed to the common plan alleged in Count One.

The said Crimes against Humanity were committed by the defendants and by other persons for whose acts the defendants are responsible, (under Article 6 of the Charter) as such other persons, when committing the said War Crimes, performed their acts in execution of a common plan and conspiracy to commit the said War Crimes, in the formulation and execution of which plan and conspiracy all the defendants participated as leaders, organizers, instigators and accomplices.

These methods and crimes constituted violations of international conventions, of internal penal laws, of the general principles of criminal law as derived from the criminal law of all civilized nations and were involved in and part of a systematic course of conduct. The said acts were contrary to Article 6 of the Charter.

The prosecution will rely upon the facts pleaded under Count Three as also constituting Crimes against Humanity.

(A) MURDER, EXTERMINATION, ENSLAVEMENT, DEPORTATION AND OTHER INHUMANE ACTS COMMITTED AGAINST CIVILIAN POPULATIONS BEFORE AND DURING THE WAR

For the purposes set out above, the defendants adopted a policy of persecution, repression, and extermination of all civilians in Germany who were, or who were believed to, or who were believed likely to become, hostile to the Nazi Government and the common plan or conspiracy described in Count One. They imprisoned such persons without judicial process, holding them in "protective custody" and concentration camps, and subjected them to persecution, degradation, despoilment, enslavement, torture and murder.

Special courts were established to carry out the will of the conspirators; favored branches or agencies of the State and Party were permitted to operate outside the range even of nazified law and to crush all tendencies and elements which were considered "undesirable." The various concentration camps included Buchenwald, which was established in 1933 and Dachau, which was established in 1934. At these and other camps the civilians were put to slave labor, and murdered and ill-treated by diverse means, including those set out in Count Three above, and these acts and policies were continued and extended to the occupied countries after the 1st September, 1939, and until 8th May, 1945.

(B) Persecution on Political, Racial and Religious Grounds in Execution of and in Connection With the Common Plan Mentioned in Count One

As above stated, in execution of and in connection with the common plan mentioned in Count One, opponents of the German Government were exterminated and persecuted. These persecutions were directed against Jews. They were also directed against persons whose political belief or spiritual aspirations were deemed to be in conflict with the aims of the Nazis.

Jews were systematically persecuted since 1933; they were deprived of their liberty, thrown into concentration camps where they were murdered and ill-treated. Their property was confiscated. Hundreds of thousands of Jews were so treated before the 1st September 1939.

Since the 1st September, 1939, the persecution of the Jews was redoubled; millions of Jews from Germany and from the occupied Western Countries were sent to the Eastern Countries for extermination.

Particulars by way of example and without prejudice to the production of evidence of other cases are as follows:

The Nazis murdered amongst others Chancellor Dollfuss, the Social Democrat Breitscheid and the Communist Thaelmann. They imprisoned in concentration camps numerous political and religious personages, for example Chancellor Schuschnigg and Pastor Niemoller.

In November, 1938 by orders of the Chief of the Gestapo, anti-Jewish demonstrations all over Germany took place. Jewish property was destroyed, 30,000 Jews were arrested and sent to concentration camps and their property confiscated.

Under Paragraph VIII A, above, millions of the persons there mentioned as having been murdered and ill-treated were Jews.

Among other mass murders of Jews were the following:

At Kislovdosk all Jews were made to give up their property: 2,000 were shot in an anti-tank ditch at Mineraliye Vodi: 4,300 other Jews were shot in the same ditch.

60,000 Jews were shot on an island on the Dvina near Riga.

20,000 Jews were shot at Lutsk.

32,000 Jews were shot at Sarny.

60,000 Jews were shot at Kiev and Dniepropetrovsk.

Thousands of Jews were gassed weekly by means of gas-wagons which broke down from overwork.

As the Germans retreated before the Soviet Army they exterminated Jews rather than allow them to be liberated. Many concentration camps and ghettos were set up in which Jews were incarcerated and tortured, starved, subjected to merciless atrocities and finally exterminated.

About 70,000 Jews were exterminated in Yugoslavia....

Wherefore, this Indictment is lodged with the Tribunal in English, French and Russian, each text having equal authenticity, and the charges herein made against the above named defendants are hereby presented to the Tribunal.

ROBERT H. JACKSON

Acting on Behalf of the United States of America

FRANCOIS DE MENTHON

Acting on Behalf of the French Republic

HARTLEY SHAWCROSS

Acting on Behalf of the United Kingdom of Great Britain and Northern Ireland

R. A. RUDENKO

Acting on Behalf of the Union of Soviet Socialist Republics

Judgment of the International Military Tribunal at Nuremberg (1946)

(E) Persecution of the Jews

The persecution of the Jews at the hands of the Nazi Government has been proved in the greatest detail before the Tribunal. It is a record of consistent and systematic inhumanity on the greatest scale....

... Adolf Eichmann, who had been put in charge of this program by Hitler, has estimated that the policy pursued resulted in the killing of 6,000,000 Jews, of which 4,000,000 were killed in the extermination institutions....

Notes

1. Note that the Indictment identifies two types of crimes against humanity. At Nuremberg before the IMT, 16 were convicted of crimes against humanity.

2. Note also with respect to the Indictment that if the accused had a "common plan ... to commit Crimes against Humanity," obviously a "common plan" was not a necessary element of or subsumed within a crime against humanity. See also Sadat, *The Interpretation of the Nuremberg Principles*, *infra*; The Rome Statute of the ICC requires that the defendant's action be linked to a "State or organizational policy." *Id.* art. 7(2)(a). Therefore, is this an example of why the ICC only has limited jurisdiction over crimes against humanity. The language of the Rome Statute has generated difficulties at the ICC. See *Situation in the Republic of Kenya*, ICC (2010), *infra*; Leila Nadya Sadat, *Crimes Against Humanity in the Modern Age*, 106 AM. J. INT'L L. _ (2012). *See also* Paust, *The International Criminal Court Does Not Have Complete Jurisdiction Over Customary Crimes Against Humanity and War Crimes*, 43 THE JOHN MARSHALL L. REV. 681, 693-97 (2010).

3. Professor Cherif Bassiouni has written:

> The Tribunal did find that crimes against humanity actually were committed prior to the War; the judgment against defendant Neurath is illustrative of this fact. His offenses under counts three and four were categorized as "Criminal Activity in Czechoslovakia," some of which occurred before the War. However, since the offenses were committed in connection with crimes against peace, that is, the takeover of Czechoslovakia, they were considered proper subjects of prosecution under the Charter. Thus, it was not the "nature" of the act that was determinative

of its punishability but rather the "circumstances" under which it was committed, surely an artificial criterion.

The judgment of acquittal of defendant Streicher further illuminates the curious way in which crimes against humanity were defined. The reasoning supportive of the acquittal was that since the program of extermination of the Jews was initiated before the War, and hence already in progress, Streicher committed no crime connected with the War.

M.C. Bassiouni, *Crimes Against Humanity*, in 3 INTERNATIONAL CRIMINAL LAW 51, 68 (M.C. Bassiouni ed. 1987). See Article 7 of the ICC. Is it different? See also M. CHERIF BASSIOUNI, CRIMES AGAINST HUMANITY: HISTORICAL EVOLUTION AND CONTEMPORARY APPLICATION 14-19 (2011).

Control Council Law No. 10, art. II(1)(c) (1945)

Crimes against Humanity. Atrocities and offenses, including but not limited to murder, extermination, enslavement, deportation, imprisonment, torture, rape, or other inhumane acts committed against any civilian population, or persecutions on political, racial or religious grounds whether or not in violation of the domestic laws of the country where perpetrated.

Telford Taylor, Final Report to the Secretary of the Army on the Nuernberg War Crimes Trials Under Control Council Law No. 10, at 64–65, 69, 224–226 (1949)

Finally, there were the crimes which the average man would think of as most characteristic of the Nazis, and which we may describe as *degradation or extermination of national, political, racial, religious, or other groups*. These crimes cover the vast and terrible world of the Nuernberg laws, yellow arm bands, "Aryanization," concentration camps, medical experiments, extermination squads, and so on. These were the sort of deeds and practices which the provisions of the definition concerning "crimes against humanity" were intended to reach. Actually, when committed in the course of belligerent occupation (whether in the occupied country or elsewhere), these were also "war crimes." But the concept of "crimes against humanity" comprises atrocities which are part of a campaign of discrimination or persecution, and which are crimes against international law even when committed by nationals of one country against their fellow nationals or against those of other nations irrespective of belligerent status....

The fourth and largest category—"crimes against humanity," consisting of atrocities committed in the course or as a result of racial or religious persecutions—played a part in all 12 of the trials. Murderous "experiments," perpetrated in the name of medicine, had been inflicted on Jews, gypsies, and other unfortunate inmates of the concentration camps, as was developed in the "Medical," "Milch,"" and "Pohl" cases (Cases No. 1, 2, 4, respectively). The entire system of concentration-camp administration was explored in the "Pohl case." In the "Justice case" (Case No. 3) the Nazi judges and legal officials were accused of "judicial murder" by perverting the German legal system so as to deny to Poles, Czechs, and others the protection of law. Concentration-camp inmates were among the most miserable victims of the slave-labor program, as was disclosed in the "Krupp," "Farben," "Ministries," and "Pohl" cases. The notorious "final solution of the Jewish question," the objective of which was nothing less than the extermination of European Jewry, was the basis of the "Einsatz case" (Case No. 9), and an important facet of the "Ministries case" (Case No. 11). The complicity of the military leaders in the "solution" was dealt with in the "Hostage" and "High Command" cases (Cases No. 7 and 12). In the "RuSHA case" (Case No. 8), the defendants were the principal officials in the so-called resettlement program, under which thousands of farmers in eastern Europe and the Balkans were robbed of their land or the benefit for German "settlers," and Germanic-looking children of Polish, Czech, or other eastern European parentage were torn from their parents and taken to the Reich for "Germanization."

In two cases, an entire count of each indictment was devoted to the charge that the defendants had committed crimes against humanity during the early years of the Third Reich, and before the outbreak of war in 1939. In the "Flick case" the defendants were accused of complicity in the forced "Aryanization" of Jewish industrial and mining properties. In the "Ministries case" a number of the defendants were charged with responsibility for the discriminatory laws and abuses, and the misery and atrocities resulting therefrom, under which German Jewry suffered during those years. In each [such] case [under Control Council Law 10], the Tribunal dismissed the charge as outside its competence....

Crimes Against Humanity

None of the Nuremberg judgments squarely passed on the question whether mass atrocities committed by or with the approval of a government against a racial or religious group of its own inhabitants in peacetime constitute crimes under international law. Such a contention was made by the prosecution before the IMT, but the Tribunal disposed of this charge by holding that the language of the London Charter limited its jurisdiction to such crimes as were committed in the course of or in connection with aggressive war. Again in the "Flick Case" and in the "Ministries Case" the prosecution raised the same question; in each indictment an entire count was devoted to the charge of prewar atrocities, chiefly against Jews. Although the language of Law No. 10 defining "crimes against humanity" differed in certain particulars from the comparable definition in the London Charter, the "Flick" and "Ministries" tribunals followed the decision of the IMT and declined to take jurisdiction of the charge.

However, in two other Nuremberg cases where the question was raised only collaterally, the Nuremberg tribunals made significant and important observations on this question. Thus, in the "Einsatzgruppen Case" the Jewish exterminations of which the defendants were accused occurred during and after 1941, but it was charged that these murders constituted not only "war crimes" but also "crimes against humanity." Since no acts prior to 1939 were involved, the Tribunal had no occasion to pass upon the question of construction of Law No. 10 which confronted the "Flick" and "Ministries" tribunals. But in convicting the defendants of "crimes against humanity" the court expressly stated that "this law is not limited to offenses committed during war," and observed that—

> Crimes against humanity are acts committed in the course of wholesale and systematic violation of life and liberty. It is to be observed that insofar as international jurisdiction is concerned the concept of crimes against humanity does not apply to offenses for which the criminal code of any well-ordered State makes adequate provision. They can only come within the purview of this basic code of humanity because the State involved, owing to indifference, impotency or complicity, has been unable or has refused to halt the crimes and punish the criminals.

So, too, in the "Justice Case," where "crimes against humanity" committed after 1939 were also charged against the defendants, the Tribunal stated:

... it can no longer be said that violations of the laws and customs of war are the only offenses recognized by common international law. The force of circumstance, the grim fact of worldwide interdependence, and the moral pressure of public opinion have resulted in international recognition that certain crimes against humanity committed by Nazi authority against German nationals constituted violations not alone of statute but also of common international law.

The court proceeded to review a number of incidents extending over a century where nations or their chiefs of state had intervened or protested against religious or racial atrocities in Turkey, Rumania, and elsewhere, and quoted with approval Bluntschli's statement that "states are allowed to interfere in the name of international law if 'human rights' are violated to the detriment of any single race."

The practical importance of this question can hardly be overstated, and the convention recently concluded by the United Nations on the subject of "genocide" is a manifestation of the lively interest which it has awakened. Important as is the concept of "aggressive war," and beneficent as the Hague and Geneva Conventions may be, we can hardly expect much further judicial development and interpretation of "crimes against peace" or "war crimes" except in the unhappy event of another war. The concept of "crimes against humanity," however, if it becomes an established part of international penal law—as it seems to be doing—will be of the greatest practical importance in peacetime. Indeed, it may prove to be a most important safeguard against future wars, inasmuch as large-scale domestic atrocities caused by racial or religious issues always constitute a serious threat to peace.

United States v. Altstoetter, *et al.* ("The Justice Case")

III Trials of War Criminals Before the Nuremberg Military Tribunals Under Control Council Law No. 10, 1946–1949

C.C. Law 10 is not limited to the punishment of persons guilty of violating the laws and customs of war in the narrow sense....

As the prime illustration of a crime against humanity under C.C. Law 10, which by reason of its magnitude and its international repercussions has been recognized as a violation of common international law, we cite "genocide" which will shortly receive our full consideration. A resolution recently adopted by the General Assembly of the United Nations is in part as follows:

"The General Assembly therefore—

Affirms that genocide is a crime under international law which the civilized world condemns, and for the commission of which principals and accomplices— whether private individuals, public officials, or statesmen, and whether the crime is committed on religious, racial, political or any other grounds—are punishable; ...

The General Assembly is not an international legislature, but it is the most authoritative organ in existence for the interpretation of world opinion. Its recognition of genocide as an international crime is persuasive evidence of the fact. We approve and adopt its conclusions. Whether the crime against humanity is the product of statute or of common international law, or, as we believe, of both, we find no injustice to persons tried for such crimes. They are chargeable with knowledge that such acts were wrong and were punishable when committed....

The very essence of the prosecution's case is that the laws, the Hitlerian decrees and the Draconic, corrupt, and perverted Nazi judicial system themselves constituted the substance of war crimes and crimes against humanity and that participation in the enactment and enforcement of them amounts to complicity in crime. We have pointed out that governmental participation is a material element of the crime against humanity. Only when official organs of sovereignty participated in atrocities and persecutions did those crimes assume international proportions. It can scarcely be said that governmental participation, the proof of which is necessary for conviction, can also be a defense to the charge.

Notes and Questions

1. The 1950 Principles of the Nuremberg Charter and Judgment formulated by the International Law Commission of the United Nations (5 U.N. GAOR, Supp. No. 12, at 11–14, para. 99, U.N. Doc. A/1316, 1950) attached the following phrase to the paragraph on crimes against humanity: "when such acts are done or such persecutions are carried out in execution of or in connection with any act of aggression or any war crime." No such phrase appeared in Control Council Law No. 10. Further, the 1950 Principles did not retain the categories of "imprisonment, torture, rape" found in Control Council Law No. 10, but missing from Article 6(c) of the Nuremberg Charter. Were such words necessary?

Some eighteen years later, the U.N. General Assembly adopted the Convention on the Nonapplicability of Statutory Limitations to War Crimes and Crimes Against Humanity by resolution, article 1(b) of which states:

> "Crimes against humanity whether committed in time of war or in time of peace as they are defined in the Charter of the International Military Tribunal, Nuremberg, of August 8, 1945, and confirmed by resolutions 3(I) of February 13, 1946 and 95(I) of December 11, 1946, of the General Assembly of the United Nations...."

G.A. Res 2391 (XXIII), 23 U.N. GAOR, Supp. (No. 18) 40, U.N. Doc. A/7218 (1968)

Thus, it seems that the phrase added in the 1950 Principles was dropped. Additionally, the 1968 resolution contained the broad phrase "committed in time of war or in time of peace." The Nuremberg Charter (see the Documents Section) had utilized a similar phrase, "before or during the war," only in connection with the first category of crimes against humanity, while limiting issues of persecution as such by the phrase "in execution of or in connection with any crime within the jurisdiction of the Tribunal." What differences might attach? Which phrase or set of phrases is most authoritative, those in the 1945 Charter of the IMT (approved generally by the U.N. General Assembly in 1946), the 1950 I.L.C. Principles (approved by the U.N. General Assembly), Control Council Law No. 10, or the 1968 U.N. General Assembly resolution?

2. Article 5(c) of the Tokyo Charter for the I.M.T. for the Far East reads:

> *Crimes against Humanity*: Namely, murder, extermination, enslavement, deportation, and other inhumane acts committed before or during the war, or persecutions on political or racial grounds in execution of or in connection with any crime within the jurisdiction of the Tribunal, whether or not in violation of the domestic law of the country where perpetrated.

3. Does language in any of the abovementioned Charters, Laws, Principles or resolutions require that crimes against humanity be "widespread," "systematic," "serious,"

"cruel," or part of a "state policy," "common plan," or conspiracy? Need such crimes be committed by those acting on behalf of a state? See J. Paust, *Threats to Accountability After Nuremberg: Crimes Against Humanity, Leader Responsibility and National Fora*, 12 N.Y.L.S. J. H.R. 547 (1995); *see also* Article IV of the 1948 Genocide Convention (in Chapter Three); *but see* language quoted from the Einsatzgruppen Case, *supra*, and *Altstoetter*, *supra*; *The Prosecutor v. Akayesu*, ICTR-96-4-T, *infra*.

In The Prosecutor v. Krstic, IT-98-33-A (Appeals Chamber Judgment, 19 Apr. 2004), para. 223, it was declared that the existence of a plan or policy is not required for crimes against humanity or genocide, although such can be relevant concerning an intent to engage in widespread or systematic conduct. Twelve ICTY and four ICTR cases and the Special Court for Sierra Leon have recognized that a plan is not required.

4. Are there two basic types of crimes against humanity identified in those documents?

5. It has been stated that "[t]he Nuremberg Charter applied a customary international law of human rights in charging the Nazi war criminals, inter alia, with 'crimes against humanity'... The U.N. Charter codifies that customary law and renders applicable to all states at least such human rights law as was invoked at Nuremberg." L. HENKIN, R. PUGH, O. SCHACHTER, H. SMIT, INTERNATIONAL LAW 986 (2 ed. 1987). See also HERSCH LAUTERPACHT, INTERNATIONAL LAW AND HUMAN RIGHTS 35–38, 61–62 (1968); RICHARD B. LILLICH, INTERNATIONAL HUMAN RIGHTS 896–99 (2 ed. 1991); MYRES M. McDOUGAL, HAROLD D. LASSWELL, LUNG-CHU CHEN, HUMAN RIGHTS AND WORLD PUBLIC ORDER 354–56, 535–36, 542–46 (1980); FRANK NEWMAN & DAVID WEISSBRODT, INTERNATIONAL HUMAN RIGHTS 663–64, 715–17 (1990); TELFORD TAYLOR, NUREMBERG AND VIETNAM: AN AMERICAN TRAGEDY 79 (1970); M. Cherif Bassiouni, Crimes Against Humanity, in 3 INTERNATIONAL CRIMINAL LAW — ENFORCEMENT 51, 52 (M. Cherif Bassiouni ed. 1987); M. Cherif Bassiouni, *The Proscribing Function of International Criminal Law in the Processes of International Protection of Human Rights*, 9 YALE J. WORLD PUB. ORD. 193, 201 (1982).

6. Would the list of "crimes against humanity" recognized at Nuremberg, if committed during war, also constitute war crimes under then customary international law? See Chapter Four. What is the significance of the International Tribunal's recognition that "from the beginning of the war in 1939 war crimes were committed on a vast scale, which were also crimes against humanity...."? Are war crimes war crimes by any other name? See also *Eichmann, infra; but see* Egon Schwelb, *Crimes Against Humanity*, 23 BRIT. Y.B. INT'L L. 178, 206 (1946). Today, recall Geneva Civilian Convention, arts. 3, 13, 16, *passim* (in Chapter Four) with respect to the reach of Geneva law to one's own nationals. Also recall the laws of war applicable to a belligerency that were extant prior to 1939.

7. Can crimes against humanity be committed against combatants or, at least, former combatants? The Tokyo Charter did not limit either type of crimes against humanity to civilian victims and other customary documents only limited the first type to civilian victims. In The Prosecutor v. Krstic, *supra*, para. 223, the Appeals Chamber recognized that genocidal intent need not involve an intent to destroy civilians as such and that genocide can occur where a perpetrator seeks to target military personnel at least in part because they are members of a relevant group. Since genocide is a type of crime against humanity, the decision appears to be relevant here as well. In The Prosecutor v. Martic, IT-95-11-A (Appeals Chamber, Judgment) (9 Oct. 2008), the Appeals Chamber held that the term "civilian" means person who are not members of the armed forces. *Id.* para. 297.

Consider also the war crimes listed *supra* in Chapter Four. Is it significant that the 1919 list applied to "[a]ll persons ... guilty of offenses against the laws and customs of war or the laws of humanity"? *But see* M.C. Bassiouni, *Crimes Against Humanity*, in 3 INTERNATIONAL CRIMINAL LAW: ENFORCEMENT 5, 53–4 (M.C. Bassiouni ed. 1987). The 1919 Commission relied in part on the "Martens clause" to the 1907 Hague Convention No. IV which had referred to the "laws of humanity". See Note 3 below. During the conference, representatives from the U.S. and Japan had objected to use of the phrase "laws of humanity," arguing that it was vague and not a part of positive international law. See Annex to the Report, Memorandum of Reservations presented by the Representatives of the United States to the Report of the Commission. For a critical appraisal, see Lord Wright, *War Crimes Under International Law*, 62 L.Q. REV. 40, 48–9 (1946); *see also* J. Garner, *Punishment of Offenders Against the Laws and Customs of War*, 14 AM. J. INT'L L. 70 (1920). Clearly, however, it was a part of treaty law and had referred to general and overarching principles. Lord Wright was the Chairman of the United Nations War Crimes Commission established by the Declaration of St. James in 1942 which investigated war crimes during WW II. *See* QUINCY WRIGHT, HISTORY OF THE UNITED NATIONS WAR CRIMES COMMISSION(1948), wherein the prior position of the U.S. was also criticized.

According to Professor Bassiouni: at Versailles in 1919, it did not suit the foreign policy interests of the U.S. government to recognize such a principle. By 1945, however, the concept was revised in order to prosecute Nazi offenders who had committed horrible crimes against their fellow nationals—crimes not covered by the laws of war except in cases of belligerency. The failed attempt of a few years past was transformed by a new political will into a valid precedent and, in this case, the facts drove the law. *See* M. Cherif Bassiouni, *International Law and the Holocaust*, 9 CAL. WEST. INT'L L. J. 201, 274 (1979); *see also* J. F. WILLIS, PROLOGUE TO NUREMBERG: THE POLITICS AND DIPLOMACY OF PUNISHING WAR CRIMINALS OF THE FIRST WORLD WAR(1982); D. Mamas, *Prosecuting Crimes Against Humanity: The Lessons of World War I*, 13 FORDHAM J. INT'L L. 86 (1990).

8. In 1985, a U.S. Circuit Court has recognized that Israeli law enacted to punish war crimes and "crimes against humanity" committed in 1942 or 1943 reaches "crimes [that are] universally recognized and condemned by the community of nations" and that Israel "has jurisdiction to punish … war crimes and crimes against humanity" committed at such times under the universality principle. *Demjanjuk v. Petrovsky*, 776 F.2d 571, 582–83 (6th Cir. 1985), *cert. denied*, 475 U.S. 1016 (1986). Demjanjuk was subsequently tried and convicted in Israel. See L.A. Times, April 26, 1988, § 1, at 1, col. 3. However, he was later released upon proof of mistaken identity and returned to the U.S. in 1993 where lengthy deportation proceedings began.

9. In 2005, a three-judge panel of a Spanish court convicted Adolfo Scilingo, a former Argentinian naval officer, of crimes against humanity, torture, and illegal detention of persons during Argentina's "dirty war" between 1976 and 1983. The Scilingo Case, Judgement No. 16/2005, Audiencia Nacional (National Court) de Madrid (3d Sec., Crim. Div., 19 Apr. 2005). He was sentenced to 21 years in prison for each death of 31 persons and 5 years each for torture and illegal detention for a total of 640 years. During the proceedings, Scilingo admitted to being on board two "death flights" during which detainees were stripped naked, drugged, and thrown to their deaths over the ocean. He also testified about abuses committed at a torture center, the Buenos Aires Navy School of Mechanics. Human rights groups claim that over 30,000 persons were "disappeared" during the "dirty war".

10. Would non-state actor attacks by members of al Qaeda on the World Trade Center in New York on September 11, 2001 be prosecutable as crimes against humanity?

Would the attack at that date on the Pentagon? Although not required in the customary World War II instruments, were the 9/11 attacks "widespread" or "systematic"? See M. Cherif Bassiouni, *Legal Control of International Terrorism: A Policy-Oriented Assessment*, 43 HARV. INT'L L.J. 83, 101 (2002) ("the attacks upon the United States of September 11 constitute 'Crimes Against Humanity' as defined in Article 7 of the Statute of" the ICC); Antonio Cassese, *Terrorism is also Disrupting Some Crucial Legal Categories of International Law*, 12 EUR. J. INT'L L. 993, 994-95 (2011); Jordan J. Paust, *The International Criminal Court Does Not Have Complete Jurisdiction Over Customary Crimes Against Humanity and War Crimes*, 43 THE JOHN MARSHALL L. REV. 681, 691, 694 n.37 (2010) (citing many other authors); Leila Nadya Sadat, *Terrorism and the Rule of Law*, 3 WASH. U. GLOBAL STUD. L. REV. 135, 148-49 (2004); David J. Scheffer, *Staying the Course with the International Criminal Court*, 35 CORNELL INT'L L.J. 47, 49, 50 n.6 (2002); Susan Tiefenbrun, *A Semiotic Approach to a Legal Definition of Terrorism*, 9 ILSA J. INT'L & COMP. L. 357, 386 n.115 (2003) (quoting Professor Michael P. Scharf); *cf* William A. Schabas, *State Policy as an Element of International Crimes*, 98 J. CRIM. L. & CRIMINOLOGY 953 (2008) (arguing that, contrary to trends in decision in the ICTY and a majority viewpoint, "state policy" should be a requirement).

Canadian courts have also recognized private actor complicity or leader responsibility for crimes against humanity committed by the Sri Lanka insurgent group LLTE. *See, e.g.*, Sivakumar v. R, 1997 WL 1913825, 37 Imm. L.R. (2d) 191 (Fed. Ct. Can. 1997) (leader responsibility); Pushpanathan v. Canada, 2002 WL 31918433, 25 Imm. L.R. (3d) 242 (Imm. & Refugee Bd. (App. Div.) 2002) (private actor complicity).

Section 2
Eichmann Trial (Israel)

The Attorney General of the Government of Israel v. Adolf, the Son of Karl Adolf Eichmann, Criminal Case No. 40/61 (1961)

[Editors' note: These excerpts are taken from the opinion and judgment of the 3 judge District Court of Jerusalem, presided over by Mr. Justice Landau]

Our jurisdiction to try this case is based on the Nazis and Nazi Collaborators (Punishment) law, *a statutory law the provisions of which are unequivocal....*

... we have reached the conclusion that the law in question conforms to the best traditions of the law of nations.

The power of the State of Israel to enact the law in question or Israel's right to punish is based, with respect to the offences in question, from the point of view of international law, on a dual foundation: The universal character of the crimes in question and their specific character as being designated to exterminate the Jewish people. In what follows we shall deal with each of these two aspects separately....

The abhorrent crimes defined in this law are crimes not under Israel law alone. These crimes which afflicted the whole of mankind and shocked the conscience of nations are grave offenses against the law of nations itself ('*delicta juris gentium*'). Therefore, so far from international law negating or limiting the jurisdiction of countries with respect to such crimes, in the absence of an International Court the international law is in need of the judicial and legislative authorities of every country, to give effect to its penal injunctions and to bring criminals to trial. The authority and jurisdiction to try crimes under international law are universal....

The 'crime against the Jewish people' is defined on the pattern of the genocide crime defined in the "Convention for the prevention and punishment of genocide' which was adopted by the United Nations Assembly on 9.12.48. The 'crime against humanity' and the 'war crime' are defined on the pattern of crimes of identical designations defined in the Charter of the International Military Tribunal, (which is the Statute of the Nuremberg Court) annexed to the Four-Power Agreement of 8.8.45 on the subject of the trial of the principal war criminals (the London Agreement), and also in Law No. 10 of the Control Council of Germany of 20.12.45. The offence of 'membership of a hostile organization' is defined by the pronouncement in the judgment of the Nuremberg Tribunal, according to its Charter, to declare the organizations in question as 'criminal organizations', and is also patterned on the Council of Control Law No. 10. For purposes of comparison we shall set forth in what follows the parallel articles and clauses side by side....

In the light of the recurrent affirmation by the United Nations in the 1946 Assembly resolution and in the 1948 convention, and in the light of the advisory opinion of the International Court of Justice, there is no doubt that genocide has been recognized as a crime under international law in the full legal meaning of this term, and at that *ex tunc*; that is to say: the crimes of genocide which were committed against the Jewish people and other peoples were crimes under international law. It follows therefore, in the light of the acknowledged principles of international law, that the jurisdiction to try such crimes is universal.

Attorney General of Israel v. Eichmann, Israel, Supreme Court 1962, 36 INT'L L. REP. 277, 277–78, 287–89, 294–97, 304 (1968)

1. The appellant, Adolf Eichmann, was found guilty by the District Court of Jerusalem of offenses of the most extreme gravity against the Nazi and Nazi Collaborators (Punishment) Law, 1950 (hereinafter referred to as "the Law") and was sentenced to death. These offences may be divided into four groups:

(a) Crimes against the Jewish people, contrary to Section I (a)(1) of the Law;

(b) Crimes against humanity, contrary to Section I(a)(2);

(c) War crimes, contrary to Section I(a)(3);

(d) Membership of hostile organizations, contrary to Section 3.

2. The acts constituting these offences, which the Court attributed to the appellant, have been specified in paragraph 244 of the judgment of the District Court.

The acts comprised in Group (a) are:

(1) that during the period from August 1941 to May 1945, in Germany, in the Axis States and in the areas which were subject to the authority of Germany and the Axis States, he, together with others, caused the killing of millions of Jews for the purpose of carrying out the plan known as "the Final Solution of the Jewish Problem" with the intent to exterminate the Jewish people;

(2) that during that period and in the same places he, together with others, placed millions of Jews in living conditions which were calculated to bring about their physical destruction, for the purpose of carrying out the plan above mentioned with the intent to exterminate the Jewish people;

(3) that during that period and in the same places he, together with others, caused serious physical and mental harm to millions of Jews with the intent to exterminate the Jewish people;

(4) that during the years 1943 and 1944 he, together with others, "devised measures the purpose of which was to prevent births among Jews by his instructions forbidding child bearing and ordering the interruption of pregnancies of Jewish women in the Theresin Ghetto with the intent to exterminate the Jewish people".

The acts constituting the crimes in Group (b) are as follows:

(5) that during the period from August 1941 to May 1945 he, together with others, caused in the territories and areas mentioned in clause (1) the murder, extermination, enslavement, starvation and deportation of the civilian Jewish population;

(6) that during the period from December 1939 to March 1941 he, together with others, caused the deportation of Jews to Nisco, and the deportation of Jews from the areas in the East annexed to the Reich, and from the Reich area proper, to the German Occupied Territories in the East, and to France;

(7) that in carrying out the above-mentioned activities he persecuted Jews on national, racial, religious and political grounds;

(8) that during the period from March 1938 to May 1945 in the places mentioned above he, together with others, caused the spoliation of the property of millions of Jews by means of mass terror linked with the murder, extermination, starvation and deportation of these Jews;

(9) that during the years 1940–1942 he, together with others, caused the expulsion of hundreds of thousands of Poles from their places of residence;

(10) that during 1941 he, together with others, caused the expulsion of more than 14,000 Slovenes from their places of residence;

(11) that during the Second World War he, together with others, caused the expulsion of scores of thousands of gipsies from Germany and German-occupied areas and their transportation to the German-occupied areas in the East;

(12) that in 1942 he, together with others, caused the expulsion of 93 children of the Czech village of Lidice....

(1) Thus, the category of "crime against the Jewish People" is, as the District Court held in paragraph 26 of its judgment, "nothing but the gravest type of 'crime against humanity'". Although certain differences exist between them—for example, the first offence requires a specific criminal intent—these are not differences material to this case....

[*The Character of International Crimes*]

II. *The first proposition.* Our view that the crimes in question must today be regarded as crimes which were also in the past banned by the law of nations and entailed individual criminal responsibility, is based upon the following reasons:

(a) As is well known, the rules of the law of nations are not derived solely from international treaties and crystallized international custom. In the absence of a supreme legislative authority and international codes the process of its evolution resembles that of the common law; in other words, its rules are fashioned piecemeal by analogy with the rules embedded in treaties and custom, on the basis of the "general principles of law recognized by civilized nations" and having regard to vital international needs that compel an immediate solution. A principle which constitutes a common denominator of the legal systems current in many countries must clearly be regarded as a "general principle of law recognized by civilized nations"....

(c) In view of the characteristic traits that mark the international crimes discussed above and having regard to the organic development of the law of nations—a development that advances from case to case under the impact of the humane sentiments common to civilized nations and by virtue of the needs vital for the survival of mankind and for ensuring the stability of the world order—it definitely cannot be said that, when the Charter of the Nuremberg International Military Tribunal was signed and the categories of "War Crimes" and "Crimes against Humanity" were defined in it, this merely amounted to an act of legislation by the victorious countries. The truth, as the Tribunal itself said, is that the Charter, with all the principles embodied in it—including that of individual responsibility—must be seen as "the expression of international law existing at the time of its creation; and to that extent (the Charter) is itself a contribution to international law." (I.M.T. (1947), vol. I, p. 218.) See also the identical view expressed by Court No. III in the American Zone of Germany concerning two of the types of crimes mentioned in Control Council Law No. 10.

"All of the war crimes and many, if not all, of the crimes against humanity as charged in the indictment ... were ... (not) violative of pre-existing principles of international law. To the extent to which this is true, C.C. law may be deemed to be a codification, rather than original substantive legislation" (*U.S. v. Altstoetter,* T.W.C., vol. 3, p. 966).

It should be added that many of those who voiced criticism of the Charter and of the Judgment of the International Military Tribunal at Nuremberg directed it against the incorporation into the Charter of the "Crime against Peace" but not against the other two categories (see the articles by Finch in *American Journal of International Law*, 41 (1947), pp. 22, 23, and Doman in *Columbia Law Review*, 60 (1960), p. 413). In so far as other writers have criticized the incorporation of "Crimes against Humanity" as being contrary to international law *de lege lata*, they have done so on the ground that the punishment of the Nazi criminals for the commission of such crimes within Germany and against German citizens imported an excessive interference with the domestic competence of the State (see the article by Schick in the same volume of the *American Journal of International Law*, pp. 778–779). The reply to this argument is first that it is possible to trace a direct line to the inclusion of the crimes mentioned from the wording of the provision of Hague Convention No. IV of 1907, above cited, which refers to "the Laws of Humanity" and "the dictates of public conscience". It stands to reason, as Quincy Wright said (see his article, *ibid.*, p. 60), that this wording should apply "to atrocities against nationals as well as against aliens". In the graphic language of Friedmann (*Legal Theory*, 4th ed., p. 316), "it is hardly necessary to invoke natural law to condemn the mass slaughter of helpless human beings. Murder is generally taken to be a crime in positive international law.".... ..if any doubt existed as to this appraisal of the Nuremberg Principles as principles that have formed part of the customary law of nations "since time immemorial", two international documents justify it. We allude to the United Nations General Assembly Resolution of December 11, 1946, which "affirms the principles of international law recognized by the Charter of the Nuremberg Tribunal and the Judgment of the Tribunal", and also to the General Assembly Resolution of the same date, No. 96 (I), in which the General Assembly "affirms that Genocide is a crime under international law"....

What is more, in the wake of Resolution 96 (I) of December 11, 1946, the United Nations General Assembly unanimously adopted on December 9, 1948, the Convention for the Prevention and Punishment of the Crime of Genocide. Article I of this Convention provides:

> "The Contracting Parties confirm that genocide, whether committed in time of peace or in time of war, is a crime under international law."

As the District Court has shown, relying on the Advisory Opinion of the International Court of Justice dated May 28, 1951, the import of this provision is that the principles inherent in the Convention—as distinct from the contractual obligations embodied therein—"were already part of customary international law when the dreadful crimes were perpetrated, which led to the United Nations Resolution and the drafting of the Convention—the crimes of Genocide committed by the Nazis" (paragraph 21 of the judgment).

The outcome of the above analysis is that the crimes set out in the Law of 1950, which we have grouped under the inclusive caption "crimes against humanity", must be seen today as acts that have always been forbidden by customary international law— acts which are of a "universal" criminal character and entail individual criminal responsibility. That being so, the enactment of the Law was not from the point of view of international law a legislative act which conflicted with the principle *nulla poena* or the operation of which was retroactive, but rather one by which the Knesset gave effect to international law and its objectives....

We sum up our views on this subject as follows. Not only do all the crimes attributed to the appellant bear an international character, but their harmful and murderous effects were so embracing and widespread as to shake the international community to its very foundations. The State of Israel therefore was entitled, pursuant to the principle of universal jurisdiction and in the capacity of a guardian of international law and an agent for its enforcement, to try the appellant. That being the case, no importance attaches to the fact that the State of Israel did not exist when the offences were committed. Here therefore is an additional reason—and one based on a positive approach—for rejecting the second, "jurisdictional", submission of counsel for the appellant.

Notes and Questions

1. What was the smallest number of direct victims identified in *Eichmann* as an example of a crime against humanity (in Group (b))?

2. In 1984, a nearly unanimous resolution of the U.N. General Assembly condemned the illegal regime in South Africa "for defying relevant resolutions of the United Nations and persisting with the further entrenchment of apartheid, a system declared a crime against humanity and a threat to international peace and security." G.A. Res. 2, 39 U.N. GAOR, Supp. No. 51, at 14-5, § 3, U.N. Doc. A/39/51 (Sept. 28, 1984) (vote: 133–0–2).

A decade earlier, the U.N. General Assembly adopted the International Convention on the Suppression and Punishment of the Crime of Apartheid by resolution, Article 1 of which declares that "apartheid is a crime against humanity" and that relevant acts "are crimes violating the principles of international law, in particular the purposes and principles of the Charter of the United Nations." (see Chapter One).

3. The U.S. Army Field Manual 27-10, THE LAW OF LAND WARFARE (1956), para. 498, recognized that any person who commits a crime against humanity has committed "a crime under international law" and "is responsible therefor and liable to punishment."

Crimes against humanity as such are not defined therein. If such crimes are not also war crimes, how might they be prosecuted within or by the United States? Consider also the chapter on genocide, *infra*.

For a recommended addition to Title 18 of the United States Code, *see, e.g.*, 85 Proc., Am. Soc. Int'l L. 16 (1991); Paust, *Threats to Accountability After Nuremberg, supra*.

Section 3
Barbie, Touvier and Papon Trials (France)

Matter of Barbie, France, Court of Cassation (Criminal Chamber) Oct. 6, 1983 and Jan. 26, 1984, extract from: 78 Int'l L. Rep. 125 (1988)

Summary: *The facts:*—Klaus Barbie was head of the Gestapo in Lyons from November 1942 to August 1944, during the wartime German occupation of France. At the end of the war a warrant for his arrest was issued by the French authorities but, although arrested, he later disappeared. He was tried *in absentia* for war crimes and sentenced to death by the *Tribunal Permanent des Forces Armées de Lyon* in two judgments of 29 April 1952 and 25 November 1954.

It was eventually discovered that Barbie had taken refuge in Bolivia. The French Government sought in vain to obtain his extradition. In a judgment of 11 December 1974 the Supreme Court of Bolivia rejected the French extradition request on the ground that there was no extradition treaty between the two countries. Following the election of a new President in December 1982, the Bolivian authorities decided to expel Barbie on the ground that he had used a false identity to obtain Bolivian citizenship.

Meanwhile new proceedings relating to crimes against humanity had been instituted against him in February 1982 in Lyons. Barbie was accused of murder, torture and arbitrary arrests, detentions and imprisonment. In Lyons alone he was alleged to have been responsible for the murder of 4,342 persons, the deportation of 7,591 Jews and the arrest and deportation of 14,311 members of the French Resistance. An arrest warrant was issued by the Examining Magistrate of Lyons on 3 November 1982. On 3 February 1983 he was expelled by the Bolivian authorities and put on board an aircraft bound for French Guiana. On arrival he was apprehended by the airport police and immediately flown to France where he was transferred to the custody of the Examining Magistrate in Lyons.

[extract from decision of Oct. 6, 1983]

Furthermore, reference should be made to the combined provisions of the Preamble and Article 4 of the London Agreement of 8 August 1945, Article 6 of the Charter of the International Military Tribunal of Nuremberg which is annexed to that Agreement, as well as to the recommendations contained in the United Nations Resolution of 13 February 1946. Both the Agreement and the Resolution refer to the Moscow Declaration of 30 October 1943 and are themselves referred to in the [French] Law of 26 December 1964. It results from these provisions that "all necessary measures" are to be taken by the Member States of the United Nations to ensure that war crimes, crimes against peace and crimes against humanity are punished and that those persons suspected of being responsible for such crimes are sent back "to the countries in which their abominable deeds were done in order that they may be judged and punished according to the laws of those countries".

By reason of the nature of those crimes, these provisions are in accordance with the general principles of law recognized by the community of nations, referred to in Article 15(2) of the International Covenant on Civil and Political Rights and Article 7(2) of the European Convention for the Protection of Human Rights and Fundamental Freedoms. The provisions in question arise from international treaties which have been properly integrated into the municipal legal order and have an authority superior to that of laws by virtue of Article 55 of the Constitution of 4 October 1958.

The ground of cassation must therefore be rejected.

[extract from submission of the French Advocate General]

... the *Chambre d'accusation* of Lyons ... did not take account of certain essential factors, which I have endeavoured to specify, and therefore failed to draw the conclusions which ought to have resulted from its examination of the case.

The *Chambre d'accusation* remained aloof from the historic implications of the problem before it.

I also believe that the judgment under appeal, faced with the task of determining the scope of the crimes against humanity with which Klaus Barbie could be charged, adopted an approach which was too restrictive and even altered the definition of such crimes....

The concept of the protection of humanity, the "conscience" of humanity, is very old. I have read much on the subject but will not burden you with my reflections, which are not in place here.

When, in fact, does the first indication appear of the transposition into positive law of this protection of humanity? When do we find that it is translated into an indictment, proceedings or a trial? Curiously I have discovered that a rough outline of the exercise of jurisdiction which goes beyond the strict traditional framework already appeared in the fifteenth century. I hope that I will be excused a short excursion into history! It is rare ... On 9 May 1474 Pierre de Hagenbach, a bailiff of Charles the Foolish responsible for the administration of Alsace which had recently been annexed, was condemned to death and executed for acts which were not all specified or personalized and which included numerous acts of brutality which he had committed on that territory, in violation of the law of nations. His judges were not those who would have had territorial jurisdiction but rather the representatives of a number of free cities including Strasbourg, Colmar and Basle, meeting specially for that purpose. Please excuse this digression which, taking account of the geographical dimensions of the period, allows certain parallels to be drawn.

In fact the idea of the protection of humanity only really came to life in concrete form after the 1914–18 war in an abortive attempt at judgment of Guillaume II, to which I have already referred in previous submissions which I have had the honour to present to you in this case. But it was only the calculated, systematic atrocities of the last war which really caused the world community to react. That reaction came first in the form of the voices of several Heads of State including Churchill who, from 1942 onwards, raised his voice in solemn warning against the "inhuman acts" committed in occupied countries....

... [T]he Charter of the International Military Tribunal, which links procedure and prosecution and forms an integral part of the London Agreements which were formally incorporated into municipal law by the Law of 1964, constitutes the "first stone", which has remained the only source of positive law....

The Charter, in Article 6, contains two definitions with regard to war crimes and crimes against humanity....

Article 6(b) gives the following description of war crimes:

> Murder, ill-treatment or deportation to slave labour ... killing of hostages, plunder ... destruction ... devastation ...

Article 6(c) which deals with crimes against humanity covers specifically:

> Murder, extermination, enslavement, deportation and other inhumane acts ... or persecutions ...

The careful choice of each term used surely makes it clear that the intention of those who drafted this text was to make a distinction between brutality which is unfortunately inherent in many wars and a major, orchestrated attack on the very dignity of man.

My second remark constitutes a linchpin in my argument ...

Article 6(c) uses a series of terms defining a certain number of atrocities without making them subject to any particular condition and it is only after the conjunction "or" that political, racial or religious grounds are mentioned and tied, it is true, to the word "persecution".

This break in the sentence is of vital importance because it implies two distinct categories of crimes against humanity, acts which are inhuman in themselves and acts of clearly directed persecution.

One could give an infinite number of glosses but I prefer to rely on the text itself ... because despite the uneasy compromise which influenced its drafting, it is nevertheless the common denominator of the conscience of mankind. Was it not again taken as a reference point by the United Nations in 1968?

How, and according to what lines, was this text applied by the Nuremberg Tribunal?

A constant theme emerges from their deliberations. The exacerbation in the methods used, their systematic nature and the fact that the victims came from all horizons often led to the conclusion that crimes against humanity exceeded the classical notion of war crimes, of which they constituted an aggravated form.

Everyone has in mind the phrase of M. de Menthon which has so often been cited and which so aptly describes the escalating nature of the crime. The striking example which he gave has constantly overshadowed my study of the case. I refer to it again whilst underlining several other passages in his indictment:

> The most frightful aspect of these crimes is perhaps the deliberate moral degradation, the debasement of those detained to the point of making them lose, if that were possible, all character as human beings ...

> The terrible accumulation and confused tangle of crimes against humanity at once includes and surpasses the two more precise legal notions of crimes against peace and war crimes....

Surely these lines constitute a statement of the essential overlap of the different crimes, which the civil parties have criticized the judgment under appeal for failing to perceive.

Since Nuremberg the matter has been clouded over. The courts of several countries have examined, prosecuted and convicted the perpetrators of such acts without finding it necessary to trace the delicate dividing line which this Court is called upon to establish today.

This Chamber has in fact already been required to pronounce on crimes against humanity ... albeit initially in an incidental manner.

In a judgment of 6 February 1975 (*Glaeser v. Touvier*) ... this Chamber allowed the application for designation as a civil party in a case of prosecution for crimes against humanity and stated that such crimes are crimes under ordinary law committed in certain circumstances and for certain reasons "specified in the text which defines them"....

That case concerned the authorization of a private prosecution and in particular the designation of the competent court which was held to be neither the *Tribunal Permanent des Forces Armées* (war crimes) nor the *Cour de Sûreté de l'État* (giving secrets to the enemy) but rather the *Cour d'assises*.

Subsequently in a judgment of this Chamber of 30 June 1976, a first response was given to the problem of the non-application of statutory limitation to the prosecution of crimes against humanity. It should be stressed that the acts at issue in that case had been committed "against persons or groups of persons by reason of their membership of the Resistance or the Jewish community" which, in the view of the eminent Rapporteur Le Gunehec, were capable "of being designated as crimes against humanity"....

Crimes against humanity are not to be confused with genocide which is merely one abominable aspect of such crimes. The only relevant membership, of a victim of action which has reached such a level of horror that it is no more than a mechanism of negation, is his membership of the human race....

But remaining on the plane of ideas, I ask the question whether the notion of a State system or State ideology of which so much has been spoken is not rather too restrictive.

Are there not forces and organizations whose powers might be greater and whose actions might be more extensive than those of certain countries represented institutionally at the United Nations? Care is required because other methods of total abuse of the human condition could equal in horror, albeit from other aspects, those of which we have just spoken. Certain forms of international terrorism are surely in the process of giving us just such an example.

Your judgment, gentlemen, is awaited well beyond the frontiers of France. To my knowledge it is the first occasion when a supreme court anywhere in the world has been called upon to give a precise definition of crimes against humanity....

[extract from decision of the Cour de Cassation, Dec. 20, 1985]

The following acts constitute crimes against humanity within the meaning of Article 6(c) of the Charter of the Nuremberg International Military Tribunal annexed to the London Agreement of 8 August 1945, which are not subject to statutory limitation of the right of prosecution, even if they are crimes which can also be classified as war crimes within the meaning of Article 6(b) of the Charter: inhumane acts and persecution committed in a systematic manner in the name of a State practicing a policy of ideological supremacy, not only against persons by reason of their membership of a racial or religious community, but also against the opponents of that policy, whatever the form of their opposition.

The indictment which is the subject of the judgment under appeal lists various counts of crimes against humanity, arising from a series of acts which are indisputably quite separate from those for which Klaus Barbie was convicted *in absentia* by judgments handed down in 1952 and 1954. These acts, as detailed by the judges of the lower court, consisted in the arrest and illegal imprisonment of numerous persons, followed by brutality and physical torture or deportation to concentration camps normally resulting in the death of the victims. These acts were allegedly committed in 1943 and 1944 by or on the orders of Klaus Barbie, in his capacity as SS Lieutenant and head of the Gestapo of Lyons, which was responsible for the suppression of crimes and political offences. One of the five sections of the Gestapo in Lyons specialized in the fight against communism and sabotage whilst another was responsible for the fight against Jews. The judgment under appeal lists about thirty cases of persons arrested and subsequently tortured to death or deported or, more frequently, persons who died in the course of deportation. That judgment also lists four complete operations carried out on the instructions of the accused and with his participation:

—a raid carried out on 9 August 1944 on the workshops of the SNCF [French Railways] at Oullins, followed by the assassination of one railman and the unlawful imprisonment of ten others;

—a raid on 9 February 1943 at the Lyons headquarters of the Union Generale des Israelites de France, in the course of which eighty-six persons were arrested and brutalized or tortured, before eighty-five of them were deported to the camp of Auschwitz from which only one returned;

—a raid on 6 April 1944 on a reception centre for Jewish children at Izieu, whose forty-four inmates and seven members of staff were also deported to Auschwitz and immediately exterminated in the gas chambers, with the exception of a teacher who was the only person to return from that deportation and the director and two adolescent inmates of the centre, who were transferred to a camp in Lithuania and shot;

—the deportation by the last rail convoy to leave Lyons for Germany on 11 August 1944, of more than six hundred persons who had been held in the three prisons in that city, having been arrested in their capacity, real or presumed, as Jews or resistance fighters and who had been subjected to violence and torture. Following a journey of more than eight days without any supplies, those persons were brought to various concentration camps in Struthof, Dachau, Ravensbruck and Auschwitz. The precise number of persons deported and those who died and those who survived is unknown.

The *Chambre d'accusation*, having analysed Article 6 of the Charter of the Nuremberg International Military Tribunal, stated that

> Only the persecution of persons who are non-combatants, committed in furtherance of a deliberate State policy and for racial, religious or political motives, is of such a nature as to constitute a crime against humanity whose prosecution is not subject to statutory limitation. On the other hand a war crime, even if it may be committed by the same means, is characterized, in contrast to a crime against humanity, by the fact that it appears to assist the conduct of the war.

By application of these principles, the *Chambre d'accusation* ordered that an indictment should be drawn up against Klaus Barbie and he should be sent for trial by the *Cour d'assises* for crimes against humanity, but only for those acts established by the examining magistrate which constituted "persecution against innocent Jews", carried out for racial and religious motives with a view to their extermination, that is to say in furtherance of the "final solution" sought by the leaders of the Nazi regime. In this regard, the judgment under appeal is final since no appeal has been lodged against its provisions seising the trial court.

In addition the judgment under appeal, in considering the appeal of the civil parties, confirmed the order of the examining magistrate by which he held that

> ... the prosecution is barred by statutory limitation to the extent that it relates to the unlawful imprisonment without judgment, torture, deportation and

death of combatants who were members of the Resistance, or persons whom Barbie supposed to be members of the Resistance, even if they were Jewish. Even if such acts were heinous and were committed in violation of human dignity and the laws of war, they could only constitute war crimes, whose prosecution was barred by statutory limitation.

It is evident that the combatants in the Resistance were particularly effective in their struggle against the German armed forces, in particular in creating insecurity over the whole of the territory and in neutralizing or destroying entire units. Furthermore the combatants constitute dangerous adversaries requiring elimination and this was the view of all Germans, whether Nazis or not and regardless of any ideology. The security police known as SIPOSD, of which the Gestapo in Lyons directed by Klaus Barbie was a part, fought the combatants by the heinous means which are well known.

The combatants in the Resistance were motivated firstly by the desire to chase out the invader of their country and give freedom to their children. Their political ideology, by comparison with their patriotism, was merely a secondary impetus for their action, inseparable from their patriotism. On the other hand, when the Nazis took into account the political philosophies of their adversaries, they classified them without distinction as "Judeo-Bolsheviks and Communists" in order to render their fight against these "combatants of darkness" more effective.

Finally the judgment under appeal adds that the deportation of persons with regard to whom there was information allowing Barbie to think that they were members of the Resistance was to be considered as a war crime whose prosecution was barred by statutory limitation and not as a crime against humanity, in the absence of the element of intention necessary for the latter crime. With regard to Professor Gompel, a Jewish member of the Resistance, the judgment under appeal states that

> Proof has not been furnished that he was arrested and tortured to death because he was Jewish and the accused was rightly given the benefit of the doubt on this point.

[This Court considers] however that the judgment under appeal states that the "heinous" crimes committed systematically or collectively against persons who were members or could have been members of the Resistance were presented, by those in whose name they were perpetrated, as justified politically by the national socialist ideology. Neither the driving force which motivated the victims, nor their possible membership of the Resistance, excludes the possibility that the accused acted with the element of intent necessary for the commission of crimes against humanity. In pronouncing as it did and excluding from the category of crimes against humanity all the acts imputed to the accused committed against members or possible members of the Resistance, the *Chambre d'accusation* misconstrued the meaning and the scope of the provisions listed in these grounds of appeal.

I.L.R.'s

NOTE. — The *Chambre d'accusation* of the Court of Appeal of Paris, to which the case was remitted by the Court of Cassation, subsequently considered which additional charges should be added to the indictments against Barbie, in the light of the definition of crimes against humanity given by the Court of Cassation. The *Chambre d'accusation* first ordered an additional investigation of the facts (*Barbie*, judgment of 5 March 1986, *Gaz. Pal.* 1986, 1, p. 412).

After examining the results of this investigation the *Chambre d'accusation* held that three additional sets of charges should be added to the indictments as crimes against humanity: the torture and death in prison of Professor Gompel, a Jew who was also a member of the Resistance, in January/February 1944; the arrest and deportation of actual or possible Resistance members in 1943 and 1944; and the deportation and, in many cases, subsequent death of those actual or possible Resistance members taken out of France by the last train to leave Lyons for Germany before the liberation of that city, on 11 August 1944. The *Chambre d'accusation* ordered that *Barbie* should be committed for trial for these additional crimes against humanity and remitted his case to the *Cour d'Assises du Rhône* (*Barbie*, judgment of 9 July 1986, *Gaz. Pal.* 1986, 2, p. 599).

In a later decision the Court of Cassation, explicitly referring to the definition of crimes against humanity given in its judgment of 20 December 1985, quashed a judgment of the *Chambre d'accusation* of the Court of Appeal of Lyons of 25 April 1986. The Court of Cassation held that the torture and deportation of a woman who had belonged to the Resistance, as well as the torture, deportation and murder of her husband and son, by reason of their links with her, could all constitute crimes against humanity. Neither the motives of the victims nor the fact that they might have been detained as hostages were relevant. The case was remitted to the *Chambre d'accusation* of the Court of Appeal of Paris which ordered that further charges should be added to the indictments against Barbie in respect of the crimes committed against all three members of the family in question (*Bogatto, widow of Lesevre*, judgment of 25 November 1986, summarized in *La Semaine Juridique* 1987, IV, p. 42).

The trial of Barbie before the *Cour d'Assises du Rhône* (Judge Cerdini, President) began on 11 May 1987. On 4 July 1987 the Court found him guilty on all 340 counts of the seventeen crimes against humanity with which he was charged. The Court found that there were no extenuating circumstances and he was sentenced to life imprisonment (*Le Monde*, 5–6 July 1987). [Barbie died in prison on Sept. 25, 1991]

Notes and Questions

1. Do you agree with the Court's 1985 opinion? Did the Court merely state that certain acts committed "in a systematic manner in the name of a State practicing a policy of ideological supremacy" can constitute crimes against humanity? Was such a statement merely illustrative of the facts or did the Court state that such crimes must be both "systematic" and "in the name of the State" and that the State must be "practicing a policy of ideological supremacy"? Did the Court expressly approve the statement of the *Chambre d'accusation* concerning the need for a "deliberate State policy"? At the end of the 1985 opinion, what intent was thought to be required–merely an intent to target "politically"? Would even such a requirement be consistent with the customary instruments noted above? Can persecutions other than political persecutions be covered? Are non-state actors immune from prosecution for "crimes against humanity"? Consider also Article IV of the Genocide Convention.

2. Are you convinced by the Advocate General's or the Court's attempt to distinguish "crimes against humanity" from "war crimes," *e.g.*, on the basis of noncombatant status of the victims and/or that war crimes are "characterized ... by the fact that [they appear] to assist the conduct of the war"?

Can crimes against humanity be committed against combatants? Or, at least, former combatants who are captured and are not "civilians"? What types? Can such crimes "assist the conduct" of war in some manner?

3. Are there any international crimes, or any addressed thus far, that can *only* be committed by state officials or "under color of" state authority? Did the Nuremberg Charter, the Tokyo Charter, the Nuremberg Principles, or Control Council Law No. 10 make any reference to a requirement of state official status or actions under state authority?

4. Does anything in the customary World War II instruments support the notion that crimes against humanity require an ideologic or philosophic element?

5. The Court recognized that a series of acts supported "various counts of crimes against humanity." What number of direct victims supported various counts? Consider especially the 1986 decision identified in the I.L.R. note. What appears to be the minimum number of direct victims with respect to several such crimes? Also recall *Eichmann*, and see *Touvier, infra* re: such numbers.

6. The Advocate General rightly recognized that genocide is a type of crime against humanity. Can genocide be committed by non-state actors? Without an ideological motivation or pretext? See Chapter Three.

7. Note that private suits for money damages with respect to crimes against humanity are recognized in the French cases.

Matter of Touvier

[Editors' note: Paul Touvier was the Regional Chief of the Second Division of the Milice (a special paramilitary force formed by the Vichy Government to combat the Resistance and others) at Lyon. In 1989, he was finally arrested. Charges had already been filed and others were added after his arrest—mostly by civil parties. All cases were transferred to Paris and consolidated in 1990.]

Leila Sadat Wexler, *The Interpretation of the Nuremberg Principles by the French Court of Cassation: From Touvier to Barbie and Back Again*, 32 COLUM. J. TRANSNAT'L. L. 289, 347–56, 358–62, 366–67, 379–80 (1994)*

The charges were as follows:

(1) Touvier organized the bombing of the Synagogue at Quai Tilsitt in Lyon on December 10, 1943;

(2) Touvier organized and/or participated in a raid by the Milice of Mrs. Vogel's family, and others, which occurred on June 13, 1944;

(3) Touvier participated in the assassination of Victor and Hélène Basch on January 10, 1944;

(4) Touvier, among others in the Gestapo and the Milice, arrested a resister, Jean de Filippis, on January 16, 1944, who was later tortured (in Touvier's presence) and deported;

(5) Touvier arrested and tortured André Laroche on March 29, 1944;

(6) Touvier participated in a raid at the Pré de Foire de Montmelian on April 24, 1944;

* Copyright © 1994 by The Columbia Journal of Transnational Law Association, Inc. This article is reprinted from an article published in *The Columbia Journal of Transnational Law*, Volume 32, Issue 2, with the kind permission of The Columbia Journal of Transnational Law Association, Inc. Translations are her own.

(7) Touvier arrested and later assassinated Albert Nathan on August 17, 1944;

(8) Touvier participated in the Milice's arrest and torture of Émile Medina on May 19, 1944;

(9) Touvier participated in the arrest and torture of Robert Nant on May 27, 1944;

(10) Touvier participated in the massacre [of seven Jews] at Rillieux la-Pape on June 29, 1944;

(11) Touvier was responsible for the arrest and deportation of Eliette Meyer and Claude Bloch, as well as the assassination of Lucien Meyer, on June 29, 1944.

Judge Getti [*juge d'instruction*] carefully examined the above charges and concluded that Touvier could be prosecuted with respect to five: the attack on the Synagogue at Quai Tilsitt (1); the assassination of Mr. & Mrs. Basch (3); the arrest, torture and deportation of Jean de Filippis (4); the massacre at Rillieux (10); and the arrest and deportation of Eliette Meyer and Claude Bloch, and the assassination of Lucien Meyer (11). With respect to the others, the evidence was inconclusive.

The case was sent to the Indicting Chamber of the Paris Court of Appeals for review. In a 215-page decision that provoked an uproar in France, the Indicting Chamber reversed the *juge d'instruction* and concluded that there was no cause to prosecute Touvier on any of the charges. The appellate court reasoned that either the evidence was insufficient to support the charge in question, or that, even if Touvier's participation in the criminal activity was clear, he could not, as a matter of law, be guilty....

Turning to the third decision in the *Barbie* case, the court found that to be guilty of a crime against humanity, one must intend to take part in carrying out a common plan by systematically committing inhumane acts and illegal persecutions in the name of a state practicing a hegemonic political ideology. To determine whether this was so, the court analyzed the historical record of the Vichy government: its policies toward the Jews and its relationship with the Germans then occupying France. To oversimplify somewhat, although the court agreed that there were certain antisemitic tendencies in the Milice and in the Vichy government, it found that Vichy France simply could not be considered a hegemonic state. Therefore, Touvier could not, as a matter of law, have committed a crime against humanity in carrying out the orders of such a state.... Finally, the court dismissed the idea that Touvier could be guilty due to his work with the Gestapo, finding that Touvier was not carrying out any German plan at Rillieux — it was entirely "*une affaire entre Français*" (a French affair).

It was more the court's revisionist approach to the historical record than its acquittal of Paul Touvier that outraged the public. Seventy-three percent of French men and women reported that they were "shocked" by the decision. A document entitled "*Nous accusons*" (after Zola's *J'accuse*) was signed and published by 188 famous personalities, accusing the three judges of a miscarriage of justice. And, the French National Assembly denounced the verdict. The historical record showed that the Milice specifically excluded Jews from their number and repeatedly targeted them for abuse. Moreover, as the civil parties pointed out in their appeal, the appellate court's own words led one to the conclusion that the Vichy state practiced an ideology of exclusion, hate, and collaboration with the Germans. Finally, Touvier himself admitted that the Milice carried out this assassination under German orders as retaliation for the execution of Philippe Henriot by the Resistance.

An Indictment is Rendered in the Touvier *case*

The decision of the Paris Court of Appeals was brought to the Criminal Chamber, and all waited to see what the High Court would do....

Because none of the parties appealed the six charges that both the *juge d'instruction* and the Court of Appeals dismissed, those charges were not before the Court of Cassation. Thus, only the five incidents for which the *juge d'instruction* had recommended indictment were at issue. As for the four charges that the Court of Appeals had reversed due to insufficient evidence, the Court of Cassation affirmed without much discussion, summarily rejecting the appellants' contention that the Court of Appeals had infected its evaluation of the evidence by systematically discrediting all the witnesses except Touvier. Turning to the massacre at Rillieux, the Court reviewed without editorial comment the "historical" analysis of the Court of Appeals. It then reversed on very narrow grounds: because the criminal acts committed at Rillieux had been accomplished at the instigation of the Gestapo, and because, under Article 6 of the IMT Charter, only those acting "in the interests of the European Axis countries" could be tried under Article 6(c), the Court of Appeals had contradicted itself by finding that Touvier could not have committed a crime against humanity, while conceding that he acted at the instigation of the Gestapo. Thus, the case would be sent to yet another court of appeals for a review of the massacre at Rillieux....

The court of *renvoi* was the Court of Appeals of Versailles, which held on June 2, 1993, that Touvier could be tried for his participation in the massacre at Rillieux, concluding that:

> Touvier actively participated in the criminal acts charged by the prosecution. In this respect, the testimony [to that effect] of the former milicians or former Resistance members is corroborated by own declarations, whether made before or after the start of the judicial investigation.

The court then found that act was a crime against humanity. It was a crime listed in Article 6(c), committed against persons by reason of their membership in a religious group, with the intent of furthering the plan of a state practicing a hegemonic political ideology. Moreover, [Touvier's] French nationality could not protect him; he knowingly and voluntarily associated himself with the Nazis' policy of extermination and persecution that was inspired by political, racial or religious motivations.

Touvier's attorneys pleaded one last defense: duress. They claimed that the pressure of the Gestapo on Touvier was so great that it was a *fait justificatif*, exculpating him from criminal liability. The court summarily rejected this claim, pointing out that Touvier had joined the Milice of his own free will, knowing that its motto included a promise to struggle "against the Jewish leper and for French purity." ...

A Critique of the French Case Law

The jurisprudence of the Court of Cassation in the *Touvier* case leaves one strangely dissatisfied. Touvier was made to stand trial—but only because he was implicated in the murder of the seven men at Rillieux as an accomplice of the Gestapo. Had he carried out the executions, even had they been in the hundreds or thousands, either on his own initiative, or on orders from his superiors at the Milice, the indictment would have failed.

As postulated in the introduction, this uneasiness about the result is due to three problems in the case law. First, the Court misinterprets the spirit of the law it is applying. Second, the Court compounds this with several errors of statutory construction and thereby misinterprets the letter of the law it is applying. Finally, the greatest failure of the jurisprudence was to establish a legal regime to cover the prosecution of crimes against humanity in French law that would not only have applied in this case, but to future cases. Each of these critiques will be set forth in turn.

The Court's Approach to the Case

I will not belabor this point, but feel compelled to point out that at least certain decisions in the *Touvier* case lead one to question the courts' judgment if not impartiality.

Article 6(c) and the Nuremberg Charter, to which the law of 1964 refers, were based on the desire of the Allies to try and to punish the perpetrators of crimes committed during the war. Moreover, the United Nations Resolution of February 13, 1946, to which the law also referred, evinced a desire to try not only the "major" war criminals, but also minor offenders. The former were tried at Nuremberg, the latter in the countries in which their crimes were committed. Paul Touvier was tried and convicted once; the question then simply became, could his case be reopened applying a different, international law, using the 1964 law as a basis?

It is true that in constructing their jurisprudence on crimes against humanity, the French courts had little with which to work. The 1964 law was laconic in its pronouncements ("*un fragment de vide circonscrit*"), leaving the courts with little guidance as to its application. Yet, the message of the French legislature was unmistakable: crimes against humanity should be prosecuted regardless of when and where they were committed. Notwithstanding, it took the courts over ten years and the intervention of the executive branch to agree (in the *Barbie* case) that the legislature meant what it said. Moreover, one might surmise that it was only Barbie's German nationality that made this possible. The most egregious error, by far, however, was the introduction of the requirements of "hegemonic state" and "execution of a common plan" to the long list of elements of the crime against humanity. Neither was justified as a matter of statutory interpretation, as explained below, and both appear to be blatant attempts to exonerate, in advance, the Vichy government from wrong. (Others have suggested that the worry was about possible liability concerning certain "events" in Algeria.) Moreover, these elements shift the focus from Touvier's own individual moral culpability (or lack thereof), which was, after all, one of Nuremberg's greatest legacies, to that of his government. Thus, the introduction of these elements by the Court of Cassation, and its failure to censure the Paris Court of Appeals' misapplication of their meaning, leaves the 1964 law with very few teeth.

Problems of Statutory Construction

The French jurisprudence has also led to the evolution of a definition of crimes against humanity that contradicts the text of Article 6(c). I will address these errors of interpretation in chronological fashion, following the order in which they arose.

> 1. 1975: "crimes against humanity are ordinary crimes (*crimes de droit commun*) committed under certain circumstances and for certain motives specified in the text that defines them"

Distinguishing crimes against humanity both from war crimes and from "ordinary" crimes of murder, rape, etc., has been problematic since the IMT Judgment, which failed to address this issue. The position adopted by the Court of Cassation in the 1975 decisions clearly accepts that crimes against humanity are distinct from war crimes; yet it denies them a special status in French law by assimilating them to "ordinary crimes." Although the Court appeared to depart from this standard in its December 20, 1985 decision in the *Barbie* case, it apparently returned to it in subsequent decisions in the *Touvier* case....

2. 1985: "systematically committing inhumane acts and persecutions in the name of a State practicing a hegemonic political ideology"

When articulated by the Court of Cassation in the *Barbie* case, it was unclear what the judges were driving at with this language, which cannot, of course, be found anywhere in Article 6(c) or elsewhere in the IMT Charter or judgment. In the context of the questions presented for decision in the particular case, one could argue that the Court added this simply to show that members of the Resistance as well as Jews were among the members of the "civilian population" protected by Article 6(c). Moreover, in rejecting the notion that it was the victim's intent or activities in an occupied territory that qualified the perpetrator's activities as a crime against humanity or not, the Court is only to be praised. Unfortunately, however, the language of this decision later came to stand for several propositions: first, that the perpetrator must have as his mental intent both an intent to hurt the victim and an intent to attack the group to which the victim belongs (as evidenced by the attack on the victim); second, that only if the perpetrator (i) carried out his crimes on behalf of a State and (ii) that State was one practicing a hegemonic political ideology, could the perpetrator's act or acts be characterized as crimes against humanity. Both propositions are foreign to Article 6(c) and are arguably erroneous.

First, although Article 6(c), in speaking in terms of "humanity" and a civilian "population," implied that one was necessarily speaking of collective victims, the persecution-type crimes (which are based on the victim's membership in a particular group) are separate from the "murder-type" crimes. Thus the text of Article 6(c) would imply that the special intent required by the Court of Cassation is not applicable with respect to this second type of crime. Indeed, if a government (ignoring for now the possibility of private action) wished to engage in random purges as a means to terrorize its population into submission, who would not argue that this constitutes a crime against humanity? With this language the Court of Cassation appears to be equating the crime against humanity to genocide, which proves too much — genocide is merely one form of crime against humanity.

Second, the Court requires state action. So does the majority of the scholarship in this area, but it is worth noting at least two contra-indications. First, the Genocide Convention does not require "state action" but rather states that "persons committing genocide ... shall be punished, whether they are constitutionally responsible rulers, public officials or private individuals." This was certainly a possible interpretation of Article 6(c). Second, the Court does not really define what it means by state or government — is it referring to an international or municipal definition? Moreover, what if no "State" or recognized government exists due to a civil war in the country, such as may be true in the former Yugoslavia?

Finally, the Court adds to its requirement that the crimes be perpetrated on behalf of a State, the requirement that the State be one "practicing a hegemonic political ideology." This phrase is one of the Court's own making, although it echoes language used to this effect in the writings [European Scholars] and others [to] ... describ[e] Nazi Germany. The first objection one can make to this is, of course, that it is not in Article 6(c) and therefore should not be embroidered thereon by the French courts. Second, the term is impossibly vague.

"Hegemony" may mean the "predominance of one element of a system over others." However, although an ideology is clearly encompassed within the meaning of "hegemony," that ideology need not be either uniform or totalitarian. Thus, to the extent the

Court used this phraseology to refer to Nazi Germany, the word may have been accurate; but it is certainly not accurate to say that a state which does not live up to the level of totalitarianism exhibited by Nazi Germany cannot be a hegemonic state. Indeed, the term may simply describe the internal political order of a nation. Thus, as there is a continuum of State behavior that may correctly be characterized as "hegemonic," the term "hegemony" can provide no precise litmus test for a court of law.

3. 1988: "in carrying out a common plan"

In its final word in the *Barbie* case, the Court of Cassation added this requirement to the others: that the defendant must intend to further a "common plan" of a state practicing a hegemonic political ideology. This appears to be an erroneous reading of the third paragraph of Article 6, which included the "common plan or conspiracy" language to add an additional crime to the list of crimes with which the defendants could be charged at Nuremberg. That is, the conspiracy charges were separate from the charges based on the substantive provisions of Articles 6(a), 6(b), and 6(c). This addition may result from the unfamiliarity of continental legal systems with the law of conspiracy, but is nonetheless an unfortunate gloss on Article 6(c).

4. 1992: crimes against humanity are restricted to those working "in the interests of the European Axis countries"

This language, which the Court of Cassation presumably added to its 1992 decision in order to find that Touvier could stand trial for his participation in the massacre at Rillieux, also appears to be based on a mistaken reading of the IMT Charter. The language appears in the first paragraph of Article 6, as follows:

The Tribunal established ... hereof for the trial and punishment of the major war criminals of the European Axis countries shall have the power to try and punish persons who, acting in the interests of the European Axis countries ... committed any of the following crimes.

Like so many other aspects of Article 6 (which is entitled "jurisdiction and general principles") this language appears to be jurisdictional, not a substantive limit on the definition of crimes against humanity in Article 6(c). Thus it was rather disingenuous for the Court to rely on this language as the basis for holding as it did....

Conclusion

"sur une base fragile, on n'édifie rien de solide."

Perhaps reacting to the disarray of the case law, in 1992 the French legislature adopted a new "crimes against humanity" law, codifying the jurisprudence in part, rejecting the jurisprudence in part, and innovating in part.... Although certain aspects of the new law could not be considered an improvement over the jurisprudence to date, its adoption reiterates the commitment of the French legislature to the pursuit and prosecution of perpetrators of crimes against humanity.

The failure of the Court of Cassation to take up the challenge posed by the 1964 law leaves little hope that its approach to the new law will be any more coherent, or more consistent with the spirit of Nuremberg. Like the IMT judgment itself, the French jurisprudence leaves one wishing for more. It also leaves one depressed about the effectiveness of municipal courts as the primary enforcers of international law. Yet, there may be a silver lining....

New French Criminal Code

Title I

Of Crimes against Humanity

Chapter I

Genocide

Art. 211-1. Constitutes genocide the fact, in carrying out a common plan tending to the destruction in whole or in part of a national, ethnic, racial or religious group, or of a group determined by any arbitrary criteria, to commit or cause to be committed, against any members of this group, one of the following acts:

— intentional harm to life;

— causing serious bodily or mental harm;

— inflicting on the group conditions of life of such a nature as to bring about its destruction in whole or in part;

— imposing measures intended to prevent births;

— forcibly transferring children.

Genocide is punishable by life imprisonment....

Chapter II

Other Crimes against Humanity

Art. 212-1. Deportation, enslavement, or the practice of massive and systematic summary executions, the abduction of persons followed by their disappearance, torture or other inhumane acts, inspired by political, philosophical, racial or religious motives and organized in carrying out a common plan against a civil population group are punishable by life imprisonment....

Art. 212-2. When committed in wartime in carrying out a common plan against those fighting the ideological system in the name of which the crimes against humanity are being perpetrated, the acts listed in Article 212-1 are punishable by life imprisonment.

Art. 212-3. Participation in a group formed or a conspiracy (*entente*) established in order to prepare, characterized by one or more acts (*faits matériels*), one of the crimes defined in Articles 211-1, 212-1 and 212-2 is punishable by life imprisonment.

Notes and Questions

1. Do you agree with Professor Sadat or the French legislature or courts? Does the legislature agree with the courts?

2. The legislation ominously deletes "persecution" as such and requires all acts to be "against a civilian population group." Such is quite different than the recognition of two general types of crimes against humanity in the customary World War II instruments. See Paust, *Threats to Accountability After Nuremberg, supra.*

3. Why do you suspect the French legislation is so different?

4. In 2012, France enacted legislation aimed at implementing the complementarity principle of the Rome Statute for the ICC. The French law punishes public, direct incitement to commit genocide; defines the conditions necessary for superior responsibil-

ity for crimes against humanity; and extends the definition of crimes against humanity to conform to Article 7 of the Rome Statute. See *Loi 2010-930 du 9 août 2010, portent adaptation du droit pénal à l'institution de la cour pénale internationale* [Law 2010-930 of August 9, 2010 Law to Adapt France's Criminal Code to the International Criminal Court], Journal Officiel de la République Française [J.O.] [Official Gazette of France], Aug. 10, 2010, p. 14678.

5. Compare the French definition of genocide with the customary definition contained in Article II of the Genocide Convention, in Chapter Three. Since the French legislation is far more restrictive, how will France be able to comply with its obligations under the Genocide Convention? If treaties are superior to the laws by virtue of Article 55 of the French Constitution, should the definition of genocide contained in the 1948 Genocide Convention prevail over the inconsistent legislation?

6. Following the *Touvier* affair, an additional French defendant was prosecuted under the 1964 Law, when Maurice Papon, Secretary-General for the Gironde *Prefecture* was tried in 1997 for his role in the deportation of almost 1600 Jews from the Bordeaux area in France. Unlike Paul Touvier, Papon maintained his innocence, arguing that although his signature did indeed appear on the deportation orders he signed, he was unaware of the ultimate fate awaiting those deported. Following a highly public and controversial trial, the French Court of Assizes found Papon guilty on charges of arrest and detention, but innocent on the charges of murder. Papon was sentenced on April 2, 1998 to 10 years in prison for "complicity in crimes against humanity." In a bizarre twist to an already unusual case, Papon fled to Switzerland when the verdict was announced, thereby forfeiting his right to an appeal. He thereupon successfully appealed to the European Court of Human Rights, in Strasbourg, which ruled on July 25, 2002, that he was entitled to appeal his conviction even though he had fled. *Affaire Papon v. France*, Case No. 54210/00 (ECHR July 25, 2002). A committee of the French Court of Cassation subsequently held that Papon should have an appeal, but on points of law only arising from the original trial, not on questions of fact. John Lichfield, *Nazi War Criminal Papon wins Right to Appeal*, The Independent, Feb. 27, 2004. In the interim, Papon successfully petitioned to be released from prison on medical grounds, provoking an additional controversy from relatives of his victims and Jewish groups in France. His medical release was unsuccessfully appealed by the government, and he remains free while he pursues his other legal remedies. Pierre-Antoine Souchard, *War criminal Papon Spared Jail Return by Appeal Court*, The Independent, Feb. 14, 2003. For analysis of the indictment and trial in the *Papon* case, see Leila Nadya Sadat, *The Legal Legacy of Maurice Papon*, in Memory and Justice on Trial: The Papon Affair (Richard J. Golsan, ed., Routledge, 2000).

Section 4
Mugesera Case (Canada)

Mugesera v. Canada 2005 SCC 40 (S. Ct. Canada 2005), 2 S.C.R. 100

[Editors' note: Mugesera was a permanent resident in Canada who was alleged to have incited murder, genocide, and hate speech and to have committed a crime against humanity in Rwanda before entry into Canada. the Supreme Court ruled that his deportation order was valid and should be reinstated.]

The Elements of a Crime Against Humanity

118. At the time relevant to this appeal, crimes against humanity were defined in and proscribed by ss. 7(3.76) and 7(3.77) of the *Criminal Code* [reproduced in *Finta, supra*]

Sections 7(3.76) and 7(3.77) of the *Criminal Code* have since been repealed. Crimes against humanity are now defined in and proscribed by ss. 4 and 6 of the *Crimes Against Humanity and War Crimes Act*, S.C. 2000, c. 24. Those sections define crimes against humanity in a manner which differs slightly from the definition in the sections of the *Criminal Code* relevant to this appeal. However, the differences are not material to the discussion that follows.

119. As we shall see, based on the provisions of the *Criminal Code* and the principles of international law, a criminal act rises to the level of a crime against humanity when four elements are made out:

1. An enumerated proscribed act was committed (this involves showing that the accused committed the criminal act and had the requisite guilty state of mind for the underlying act);

2. The act was committed as part of a widespread or systematic attack;

3. The attack was directed against any civilian population or any identifiable group of persons; and

4. The person committing the proscribed act knew of the attack and knew or took the risk that his or her act comprised a part of that attack.

120. Despite relying on essentially the same authorities, the lower courts and the tribunal in this appeal were inconsistent in their identification and application of the elements of a crime against humanity under s. 7(3.76) of the *Criminal Code*. We will now briefly review their views on these questions.

121. For the IAD [Immigration & Refugee Board, Appeals Division], Mr. Duquette, relying on this Court's decision in *R. v. Finta*, [1994] 1 S.C.R. 701, found that a crime against humanity must be committed against a civilian population or an identifiable group, must be cruel and must shock the conscience of all right-thinking people (para. 335). He also held that the individual who commits the crime must be aware of the circumstances which render the act inhumane and must be motivated by discriminatory intent (paras. 337-38). To these requirements, he added, relying on *Sivakumar*, that crimes against humanity must occur on a widespread and systematic basis (para. 339).

122. Applying these principles to the facts, Mr. Duquette concluded that counselling murder, even where no murder is subsequently committed, is sufficient to constitute a crime against humanity, particularly where murders have been happening on a widespread and systematic basis (para. 344). In his opinion, Mr. Mugesera had acted with discriminatory intent, and was an educated man who was aware of his country's history, the current political situation and the fact that civilians were being massacred (para. 338). He was therefore aware of the circumstances which rendered his speech a crime against humanity.

123. Nadon J., reviewing the IAD's decision, did not elaborate on the elements of a crime against humanity. He limited his consideration of the issue to finding that Mr. Duquette had erred in law because Mr. Mugesera's counselling of murder and incitement to hatred, absent proof that actual murders had ensued, was not sufficiently "cruel

and terrible" to constitute a crime against humanity (paras. 55-56). Nadon J. relied on this Court's decision in *Finta*, at p. 814, to support the proposition that the alleged acts must show an added degree of inhumanity.

124. Decary J.A., for the FCA [Federal Court of Appeals], who apparently also drew on *Finta* and *Sivakumar*, reached an entirely different outcome, both on the law and on its application to the facts. He found that a crime against humanity must occur in the context of a widespread or systematic attack directed against a civilian population with discriminatory intent (para. 57). Having set aside the IAD's findings of fact, he concluded that there was no evidence that the speech had taken place in the context of a widespread or systematic attack, since the massacres which had occurred to that point were not part of a common plan and since there was no evidence that Mr. Mugesera's speech was part of an overall strategy of attack (para. 58).

125. The decisions below leave no doubt as to the existence of a great deal of confusion about the elements of a crime against humanity. Though this Court has commented on the issue in the past, most notably in *Finta*, it is apparent that further clarification is needed.

126. Since *Finta* was rendered in 1994, a vast body of international jurisprudence has emerged from the International Criminal Tribunal for the Former Yugoslavia (ICTY) and the ICTR. These tribunals have generated a unique body of authority which cogently reviews the sources, evolution and application of customary international law. Though the decisions of the ICTY and the ICTR are not binding upon this Court, the expertise of these tribunals and the authority in respect of customary international law with which they are vested suggest that their findings should not be disregarded lightly by Canadian courts applying domestic legislative provisions, such as ss. 7(3.76) and 7(3.77) of the *Criminal Code*, which expressly incorporate customary international law. Therefore, to the extent that *Finta* is in need of clarification and does not accord with the jurisprudence of the ICTY and the ICTR, it warrants reconsideration....

170. In sum, we have seen that the criminal act requirement for crimes against humanity in ss. 7(3.76) and 7(3.77) is made up of three essential elements: (1) a proscribed act is carried out; (2) the act occurs as part of a widespread or systematic attack; and (3) the attack is directed against any civilian population. The first element means that all the elements of an enumerated act "both physical and moral" must be made out. The second and third elements require that the act take place in a particular context: a widespread or systematic attack directed against any civilian population. Each of these elements has been made out in Mr. Mugesera's case.

171. However, as noted above, making out the criminal act of a crime against humanity will not necessarily imply that there are reasonable grounds to believe that Mr. Mugesera has committed a crime against humanity. Mr. Mugesera must also have had a guilty mind. As a result, we must now go on to consider the mental element of s. 7(3.76) of the *Criminal Code*.

(b) *The Guilty Mind for Crimes Against Humanity*

172. We have seen that an individual accused of crimes against humanity must possess the required guilty state of mind in respect of the underlying proscribed act. We have also underlined that, contrary to what was said in *Finta*, discriminatory intent need not be made out in respect of all crimes against humanity, but only in respect of those which take the form of persecution. This leaves a final question: in addition to the mental element required for the underlying act, what is the mental element required to make out a crime against humanity under s. 7(3.76) of the *Criminal Code*?

173. The question of whether a superadded mental element exists for crimes against humanity was a point of significant contention in *Finta*. Cory J., for the majority, found that the accused must have an awareness of the facts or circumstances which would bring the act within the definition of a crime against humanity (p. 819). La Forest J. penned dissenting reasons suggesting that establishing the mental element for the underlying act was sufficient in itself and thus no additional element of moral blameworthiness was required (p. 754). At the time, there was little international jurisprudence on the question. It is now well settled that in addition to the *mens rea* for the underlying act, the accused must have knowledge of the attack and must know that his or her acts comprise part of it *or* take the risk that his or her acts will comprise part of it: *see, e.g., Tadic*, Appeals Chamber, at para. 248; *Ruggiu*, at para. 20; *Kunarac*, Trial Chamber, at para. 434; *Blaskic*, at para. 251.

174. It is important to stress that the person committing the act need only be cognizant of the link between his or her act and the attack. The person need not intend that the act be directed against the targeted population, and motive is irrelevant once knowledge of the attack has been established together with knowledge that the act forms a part of the attack or with recklessness in this regard: *Kunarac*, Appeals Chamber, at para. 103. Even if the person's motive is purely personal, the act may be a crime against humanity if the relevant knowledge is made out.

175. Knowledge may be factually implied from the circumstances: *Tadic*, Trial Chamber, at para. 657. In assessing whether an accused possessed the requisite knowledge, the court may consider the accused's position in a military or other government hierarchy, public knowledge about the existence of the attack, the scale of the violence and the general historical and political environment in which the acts occurred: *see, e.g., Blaskic*, at para. 259. The accused need not know the details of the attack: *Kunarac*, Appeals Chamber, at para. 102.

176. In *Finta*, the majority of this Court found that subjective knowledge on the part of the accused of the circumstances rendering his or her actions a crime against humanity was required (p. 819). This remains true in the sense that the accused must have knowledge of the attack and must know that his or her acts are part of the attack, or at least take the risk that they are part of the attack.

177. Returning to the case at bar, the findings of the IAD leave no doubt that Mr. Mugesera possessed the culpable mental state required by s. 7(3.76) of the *Criminal Code*. Mr. Duquette found that Mr. Mugesera was a well-educated man who was aware of his country's history and of past massacres of Tutsi (para. 338). He was aware of the ethnic tensions in his country and knew that civilians were being killed merely by reason of ethnicity or political affiliation (para. 338). Moreover, Mr. Duquette found that the speech itself left no doubt that Mr. Mugesera knew of the violent and dangerous state of affairs in Rwanda in the early 1990s (para. 338). These findings of fact clearly show that Mr. Mugesera was aware of the attack occurring against Tutsi and moderate Hutu. Furthermore, a man of his education, status and prominence on the local political scene would necessarily have known that a speech vilifying and encouraging acts of violence against the target group would have the effect of furthering the attack.

178. In the face of certain unspeakable tragedies, the community of nations must provide a unified response. Crimes against humanity fall within this category. The interpretation and application of Canadian provisions regarding crimes against humanity must

therefore accord with international law. Our nation's deeply held commitment to individual human dignity, freedom and fundamental rights requires nothing less.

179. Based on Mr. Duquette's findings of fact, each element of the offence in s. 7(3.76) of the *Criminal Code* has been made out. We are therefore of the opinion that reasonable grounds exist to believe that Mr. Mugesera committed a crime against humanity and is therefore inadmissible to Canada by virtue of ss. 27(1)(*g*) and 19(1)(*j*) of the *Immigration Act*.

Note

1. In a prior case, Judge La Forest made the following observation concerning *mens rea*:

In my view, these instructions introduced elements of knowledge of both the *legal* and *moral* status of the conduct, in a way that is not required by either domestic or international law.

It is well established in our domestic criminal law jurisprudence that knowledge of illegality is not required for an accused. Section 19 of the Criminal Code echoes a requirement found in earlier codes (including the one in effect at the time the actions in this case were alleged to have been committed): ignorance of the law by one who commits an offence is not an excuse for committing the offence. At common law the principle is well established....

Nor should it be forgotten that awareness that the act is morally wrong is also immaterial....

The underlying rationale behind the *mens rea* requirement is that there is a lack of sense of personal blame if the person did not in some way even intend to do the action or omission. In finding a war crime or crime against humanity, the trial judge must, of course, look for the normal intent or recklessness requirement in relation to the act or omission that is impugned. However, there is rarely any requirement that the accused knew the legal status or description of his behaviour. This is not part of the rules of our criminal law and, in my view, is not required under international law.

To summarize, then, the correct approach, in my view, is that the accused have intended the *factual* quality of the offence, *e.g.*, that he was shooting a civilian, or that he knew that the conditions in the train were such that harm could occur to occupants. It is not possible to give an exhaustive treatment of which circumstances must have an equivalent knowledge component. Whether there is an equivalent mental element for circumstances will depend on the *particular* war crime or crime against humanity involved. However, in almost if not every case, I think that our domestic definition of the underlying offence will capture the requisite *mens rea* for the war crime or crime against humanity as well. Thus, the accused need not have known that his act, if it constitutes manslaughter or forcible confinement, amounted to an "inhumane act" either in the legal or moral sense....

R. v. Imre Finta, [1994] 28 C.R. (4th) 265 (S. Ct. Canada) (La Forest, dissenting).

Section 5
Newer International Prosecutions

A. The International Criminal Tribunals for the Former Yugoslavia and Rwanda and the Special Court for Sierra Leone

The Security Council established the International Criminal Tribunal for the Former Yugoslavia in 1993 with jurisdiction over "serious violations of international humanitarian law" committed in the territory of the Former Yugoslavia. ICTY Statute, art. 1. One year later, the Council established the International Criminal Tribunal for Rwanda, which likewise had within its purview "serious violations of international humanitarian law" committed in Rwandan territory or by Rwandan citizens in "neighboring States" in 1994. ICTR Statute, art. 1. Both Statutes included the crime against humanity in their texts, the first international elaboration of the crime since the 1950 Nuremberg Principles. However, confusingly, the definitions of the crime in the Rwanda Statute (article 3) and Yugoslavia Statute (article 5) are different. The differences between the two Statutes, as well as their arguable departure from customary international law, gave rise to certain controversies about the scope and meaning of the crime, difficulties that persist even today after the Tribunals' operation and the adoption of the Rome Statute for the International Criminal Court (ICC), discussed *infra* in Section 5(B). The following excerpt details some of the controversies.

J. Paust, *Threats to Accountability After Nuremberg: Crimes Against Humanity, Leader Responsibility and National Fora*, 12 N.Y.L.S. J. H.R. 547 (1995)

Despite the broad historic reach of the concept of crimes against humanity and well-documented definitions in the World War II era, there have been certain recent definitions that might needlessly restrict coverage and accountability. One such definition appears in Article 5 of the Statute of the International Criminal Tribunal for the Former Yugoslavia. Unlike all of the definitions in the international instruments arising from the World War II era, Article 5 of the Statute fuses the two types together as one, listing "persecutions on political, racial and religious grounds" as merely one form of inhumane acts and requiring that all categories of crimes against humanity be "directed against any civilian population." Article 5 of the Statute also changes the Nuremberg phrase "committed against" (which, in the 1950 ILC Principles, reads "done against") to "directed against," a phrase that may require a slightly higher threshold of *mens rea* (or may involve a shift from an *actus reus* element to a new additional *mens rea* element); and it adds three relevant methods or acts ("imprisonment," "torture" and "rape"), although each is most likely covered by the Nuremberg phrase "other inhumane acts" and each appeared in Control Council Law No. 10. This definitional orientation was adopted despite the fact that the U.N. Secretary-General's Report adopting such a focus had noted that such crimes were recognized in the Nuremberg Charter and Control Council Law No. 10 and that the law "which has beyond doubt become part of international customary law ... is embodied in" the Nuremberg Charter and the Genocide Convention.

Presumably customary definitions contained in those instruments will guide the Tribunal, since they are recognizably those accepted under customary international law and such law was stated to be the law that the Tribunal is required to apply in order to avoid problems connected with "the principle *nullum crimen sine lege*" or *sine jus*.... Certainly customary international law was meant to be the guiding force, a necessary background, the only delimiting criterion, and what the Tribunal is required to apply.

If so, it should not be possible for an accused to escape accountability for criminal persecutions on the ground that they were not "directed against" a "civilian population" as such or in any other way. First, neither the persecution-types of crimes against humanity, nor genocide under customary international law have such a limiting phrase. Second, as the U.N. War Crimes Commission reported in 1948, even when such a phrase is applicable (*i.e.*, to the first type), the words "appear to indicate ... [acts] against civilians" as opposed to a population as such, the Commission also speculating "that single or isolated acts against individuals may be considered to fall outside" the phrase. Thus, it is the commission of an act against (*i.e.*, "committed against" or "done against") civilians that is covered and not merely the intentional targeting of civilians as such (*i.e.*, "directed against"). Even the slightly higher *mens rea* threshold is met, however, when civilians are targeted. With respect to single acts, it is arguable that commission of one act injuring one victim fits the definition if there is an intent thereby to act against or to target other civilians (*e.g.*, as in the case of a terroristic murder or inhumane act against an instrumental target with the object of producing intense fear or anxiety in a primary target involving other civilians). The same double or terroristic-type targeting may also exist with respect to certain persecutions. Moreover, merely because the word persecutions is in the plural does not answer the question whether one persecution is sufficient because the definitions also refer to crimes in the plural (*i.e.*, crimes against humanity, and thus "persecutions" constitute "crimes").

It should be noted that the Report of the U.N. Secretary-General stated that crimes against humanity are "inhumane" and "very serious," but such labels do not appear in Article 5 of the Statute of the International Tribunal, nor are they general elements of the offense or limiting criteria for all types of crimes against humanity. Thus, the Tribunal need not entertain defense claims that some acts were not really "inhumane" or "very serious".

Similarly, the Report noted that some such crimes were part of a "widespread" or "systematic" attack, but these words were not considered to be required elements of the crime that prosecutors must prove and they do not appear in Article 5 of the Statute. Clearly also, the words "serious," "widespread," and "systematic" appear in none of the Charters or formulations noted above, nor do they exist in the definition of genocide contained in the Genocide Convention which, as noted, is a special form of *crimen contra omnes*. Such phrases sometimes appear in judicial opinions or works of textwriters in connection with particular cases or as occasional rhetorical flourish. They are at times descriptive of actual events or partly poetic, but such expressions should not be confused with required elements of the general crime under customary international law. To stress the point, it should not be a defense that an individual's acts were not "systematic" or "widespread".* These are not defenses to genocide, slavery, or more general

---

* In *Attorney General of Israel v. Eichmann*, as few as ninety-three people sufficed in one circumstance. Moreover, in *Matter of Barbie*, sometimes as few as one, three, seven, eleven, thirty, or forty-four victims comprised the number of persons covered. In a later decision of the French Supreme Court in 1986, the Court held that acts against a woman, her husband and son "could all constitute crimes against humanity." In the *Touvier* case, the defendant was convicted of being an accomplice to crimes against humanity involving merely the death of seven persons. In *The Prosecutor v. Akayesu*, ICTR-96-4-T (2 Sept. 1998), paras. 57, 59-63, the number of direct victims were as few as 3,

human rights violations, nor do they appear as elements or defenses in the customary international instruments.

Most unfortunately, however, the newer Rwandan Statute has adopted a restrictive approach that will not serve accountability. Article 3 of the Rwandan Statute also fuses the two basic types and addresses merely those acts that are "part of a widespread or systematic attack against any civilian population...." Why this far more limited form of crimes against humanity was utilized is not explained. In any event, it should not be repeated in a more permanent code or statute. Thus, I disagree with certain statements in the 1994 Report of the International Law Commission. While arguing for a similar fusion of the two types recognized at Nuremberg and a severely restrictive definition, the I.L.C. Report stated:

> It is the understanding of the Commission that the definition of crimes against humanity encompasses inhumane acts of a very serious character involving widespread or systematic violations aimed at the civilian population in whole or part. The hallmarks of such crimes lie in their large-scale and systematic nature. The particular forms of unlawful act (murder, enslavement, deportation, torture, rape, imprisonment etc.) are less crucial to the definition that (sic) the factors of scale and deliberate policy, as well as in their being targeted against the civilian population in whole or in part. This idea is sought to be reflected in the phrase "directed against any civilian population" in article 5 of the Yugoslav Tribunal Statute ... The term "directed against any civilian population" should be taken to refer to acts committed as part of a widespread and systematic attack against a civilian population on national, political, ethnic, racial or religious grounds. The particular acts referred to in the definition are acts deliberately committed as part of such an attack.

If adopted, such a codification would fail humanity. Political persecution, religious persecution, and racial persecution should not be less significant than nearly all other international crimes, and the I.L.C. should not create new thresholds of accountability that are not only missing from customary law reflected in the Charter of the IMT at Nuremberg, but are also not found in connection with the vast majority of international crimes.

Some may argue that it is not practical to convince state elites that they should retain a Nuremberg-oriented prohibition of political or religious persecution, but such a parading of the word "practical," in Orwellian garb, would merely serve political and religious oppression. Surely such a word has lost any redeeming value for the victims of politicide. For them, the word "practical" smacks of an elite or self-oriented view that is partly unreal, socially dangerous and simply outrageous!

Another potentially restrictive definition of crimes against humanity appears in the Canadian Criminal Code. It fuses the two types recognized at Nuremberg into one, requiring that the act or omission be "committed against any civilian population or any identifiable group of persons." Clearly, such a requirement does not comply with cus-

---

5, 8, 8, and 8 in various instances, and the Tribunal noted that even under the restrictive Statute of the ICTR (requiring "widespread or systematic attack") the defendant need not directly perpetrate widespread criminal acts if the defendant acted "during" or "as part of" a relevant pattern of crimes against humanity. Relevant acts included murder, torture, rape, and "other inhumane acts." Clearly the number of direct victims need not be large or the crime "widespread." *See also* LYAL S. SUNGA, INDIVIDUAL RESPONSIBILITY IN INTERNATIONAL LAW FOR SERIOUS HUMAN RIGHTS VIOLATIONS 136 (1992) (an attack on one person can suffice); other materials in this chapter.

tomary definitions, since not all types must be committed against a civilian population or group of persons. It appears then that accountability after Nuremberg and uniform application of international criminal law is endangered by imperfect national legislation.

The problem is exacerbated by loose rhetoric found in national judicial opinions. While addressing the Canadian law in 1994, Justice Cory of the Supreme Court of Canada seemed particularly fond of adding phrases or descriptions that should not mistakenly be considered as elements of the general crime. Among the phrases used by Justice Cory that are clearly absent from the customary international instruments and that do not reflect elements or limitations under international law are the following: "so grave that they shock the conscience of all right thinking people," "cruel and terrible actions which are the essential elements," "grievous," "stigma ... must ... [be] overwhelming ... [and have] particularly heavy public opprobrium," "high degree of moral outrage," "untold misery," "immense suffering," "calculated malevolence," "barbarous cruelty," "requisite added dimension of cruelty and barbarism," and the "element of inhumanity must be demonstrated."

Notes and Questions

1. In *The Prosecutor v. Dusko Tadic,* at para. 141, the Appellate Chamber of the ICTY recognized that it is "a settled rule of customary international law that crimes against humanity do not require a connection to international armed conflicts. Indeed, ... customary international law may not require a connection between crimes against humanity and any conflict at all."

2. Did the Statute of the ICTY also define crimes against humanity too narrowly in other ways? See Article 5, in the Documents Section.

3. The Trial Chamber in *Nikolic,* IT-94-2-R61 (20 Oct. 1995), para. 26, defined these crimes even more narrowly by requiring: (1) that each type be directed against a civilian population (a limiting element in the Statute); (2) that each be organized and systematic and not the work of isolated individuals; and (3) that the crimes, considered as a whole, must be of a certain scale and gravity. Why do you suspect that certain persons make up limiting elements that are not reflected in the customary instruments and are not called for even in a far too limiting statute? Will these limitations, supposedly made in the name of humanity, actually serve humanity? Who will they tend to serve?

4. Note that, unlike the historic World War II documents, Article 5 of the Statute of the ICTY had required a linkage between crimes against humanity and an "armed conflict, whether of an international or internal character." Neither Article 3 of the Statute of the ICTR nor Article 7 of the Statute of the ICC require such a linkage, and as the tribunal in *Tadic* correctly notes, *supra*, it is not required by customary international law.

Problems concerning crimes against humanity arose perhaps because there has been no general codification in a multilateral convention since the Charters for the I.M.T.s at Nuremberg and for the Far East, although specific subsets are codified in the Genocide Convention and the Apartheid Convention, which are species of crimes against humanity that clearly can occur during times of peace (see Chapters One and Three). *See* M. Cherif Bassiouni, *"Crimes Against Humanity": The Need for a Specialized Convention,* 31 Colum. J. Trans. L. 457 (1994).

If you were to draft a new Convention on Crimes Against Humanity, what elements and definitions would you include? Earlier, for Professor Bassiouni and others, among the problems to be resolved in the 1990s were: (a) whether there should be a linkage to armed conflict, (b) whether there is a need for a policy of persecution or a policy of systematic harm to a segment of the civilian population, and (c) whether more specific acts which constitute the crime can be enumerated. For Professor Paust and others:˙(a) today, at least, there is no need for a linkage with an armed conflict;˙ and (b) there is no need for any such policy, nor should the customary documents be rewritten in order to establish higher thresholds for accountability at the expense of humanity. For Professor Bassiouni, textual phrases such as "other inhumane acts" are too vague and can therefore violate "principles of legality." *See* M. Cherif Bassiouni, Crimes Against Humanity in International Criminal Law 320 *ff.* (1992). For others, they are no more vague than similar human rights provisions, similar provisions in the Hague and Geneva law and the Torture Convention (see Chapter One) and related constitutional provisions applied in various legal systems. Should a Convention on Crimes Against Humanity cover merely what is mirrored in Article 7 of the Rome Statute or should it cover what appears in several of the customary international legal instruments created after World War II? See also Paust, *The International Criminal Court Does Not Have Complete Jurisdiction Over Customary Crimes Against Humanity and War Crimes, supra* at 684-700.

5. Recently, a group of nearly 250 distinguished experts drafted a Proposed International Convention on the Prevention and Punishment of Crimes Against Humanity. See Leila Nadya Sadat, *Preface*, in Forging A Convention for Crimes Against Humanity xxvi (Leila Nadya Sadat ed., 2011), stating:

> "The *Proposed Convention* builds upon and complements the ICC Statute by retaining the Rome Statute definition of crimes against humanity but has added robust interstate cooperation, extradition, and mutual legal assistance provisions.... the creative work of the Initiative was to meld these and our own ideas into a single, coherent international convention that establishes the principle of State Responsibility as well as individual criminal responsibility (including the possibility of responsibility for the criminal acts of legal persons) for the commission of crimes against humanity. The Proposed Convention innovates in many respects by attempting to bring prevention into the instrument in a much more explicit way than predecessor instruments, by including the possibility of responsibility for the criminal acts of legal persons, by excluding defenses of immunities and statutory limitations, by prohibiting reservations, and by establishing a unique institutional mechanism for supervision of the Convention."

6. Should crimes against humanity include gender-specific targeting as a category (even though some such targeting, as part of a mixed targeting otherwise covered by customary definitions, is prosecutable)? *See generally* Rhonda Copelon, *Surfacing Gender: Re-Engraving Crimes Against Women in Humanitarian Law*, 5 Hast. Women's L. J. 243, 248, 259, 261–63 (1994) (adding: "The expansion of the concept of crimes against humanity explicitly to include gender is … part of the broader movement to end the historical invisibility of gender violence as a humanitarian and human rights violation."); J. Paust, *Women and International Criminal Law Instruments and Processes*, in 2 Women and International Human Rights Law 349 (Kelly D. Askin & Dorean M.

---

* See early uses of the concept documented above (*e.g.,* including contexts of slavery or the slave trade); Art. II (1)(c) of Control Council Law No. 10; the Genocide Convention; the Apartheid Convention; Art. 1(b) of the Convention on the Nonapplicability of Statutory Limitations to War Crimes and Crimes Against Humanity; Art. 3 of the Statute of the ICTR; *see also* Art. 5(c) of the Charter of the IMT for the Far East (first type of crime against humanity); *Attorney General of Israel v. Eichmann, supra*; *The Prosecutor v. Dusko Tadic, supra*, in Note 1 above; Paust, *Threats to Accountability, supra*.

Koenig eds. 2000); Adrien Katherine Wing & Sylke Merchan, *Rape, Ethnicity, and Culture: Spirit Injury From Bosnia to Black America*, 25 COLUM. H.R.L. REV. 1, 43–44 (1993).

Article 7(1)(h) of the Statute of the ICC includes gender-based persecution among conduct constituting a crime against humanity. See also Brook S. Moshan, *Women, War, and Words: The Gender Component in the Permanent International Criminal Court's Definition of Crimes Against Humanity*, 22 FORDHAM INT'L L.J. 154, 176 (1998).

7. Concerning the fact that Article 7 of the Rome Statute of the ICC does not cover all customary crimes against humanity, see also Jordan J. Paust, *The International Criminal Court Does Not Have Complete Jurisdiction Over Customary Crimes Against Humanity and War Crimes*, 43 JOHN MARSHALL L. REV. 681 (2010), available at http://ssrn.com/abstract=1598440.

The Prosecutor v. Rutaganda, ICTR-96-3-T (6 Dec. 1999)

Before: Judge Laïty Kama, Presiding

Judge Lennart Aspegren

Judge Navanethem Pillay

Crimes against Humanity pursuant to Article 3 of the Statute of the Tribunal

65. Article 3 of the Statute confers on the Tribunal the jurisdiction to prosecute persons for various inhumane acts which constitute crimes against humanity. The Chamber concurs with the reasoning in the *Akayesu Judgement* that offences falling within the ambit of crimes against humanity may be broadly broken down into four essential elements, namely:

> (a) the *actus reus* must be inhumane in nature and character, causing great suffering, or serious injury to body or to mental or physical health

> (b) the *actus reus* must be committed as part of a widespread or systematic attack

> (c) the *actus reus* must be committed against members of the civilian population

> (d) the *actus reus* must be committed on one or more discriminatory grounds, namely, national, political, ethnic, racial or religious grounds.

The *Actus Reus* Must be Committed as Part of a Widespread or Systematic Attack

66. The Chamber is of the opinion that the *actus reus* cannot be a random inhumane act, but rather an act committed as part of an attack. With regard to the nature of this attack, the Chamber notes that Article 3 of the English version of the Statute reads "[…] as part of a widespread or systematic attack […]" whilst the French version of the Statute reads "[…] *dans le cadre d'une attaque généralisée et systématique* […]". The French version requires that the attack be both of a widespread *and* systematic nature, whilst the English version requires that the attack be of a widespread *or* systematic nature and need not be both.

The Chamber notes that customary international law requires that the attack be either of a widespread *or* systematic nature and need not be both. The English version of the Statute conforms more closely with customary international law and the Chamber therefore accepts the elements as set forth in Article 3 of the English version of the Statute and follows the interpretation in other ICTR judgements namely: that the "attack" under Article 3 of the Statute, must be either of a widespread or systematic nature and need not be both.

67. The Chamber notes that "widespread", as an element of crimes against humanity, was defined in the *Akayesu Judgement*, as massive, frequent, large scale action, carried out collectively with considerable seriousness and directed against a multiplicity of victims, whilst "systematic" was defined as thoroughly organised action, following a regular pattern on the basis of a common policy and involving substantial public or private resources. The Chamber concurs with these definitions and finds that it is not essential for this policy to be adopted formally as a policy of a State. There must, however, be some kind of preconceived plan or policy.

68. The Chamber notes that "attack", as an element of crimes against humanity, was defined in the *Akayesu Judgement*, as an unlawful act of the kind enumerated in Article 3(a) to (i) of the Statute, such as murder, extermination, enslavement, etc. An attack may also be non-violent in nature, like imposing a system of apartheid, which is declared a crime against humanity in Article 1 of the Apartheid Convention of 1973, or exerting pressure on the population to act in a particular manner may also come under the purview of an attack, if orchestrated on a massive scale or in a systematic manner. The Chamber concurs with this definition.

69. The Chamber considers that the perpetrator must have:

> "[…]actual or constructive knowledge of the broader context of the attack, meaning that the accused must know that his act(s) is part of a widespread or systematic attack on a civilian population and pursuant to some kind of policy or plan."

The *Actus Reus* Must be Directed against the Civilian Population

70. The Chamber notes that the *actus reus* must be directed against the civilian population, if it is to constitute a crime against humanity. In the *Akayesu Judgement*, the civilian population was defined as people who were not taking any active part in the hostilities. The fact that there are certain individuals among the civilian population who are not civilians does not deprive the population of its civilian character. The Chamber concurs with this definition.

The Enumerated Acts

76. The Chamber notes that in respect of crimes against humanity, the Accused is indicted for murder and extermination. The Chamber, in interpreting Article 3 of the Statute, will focus its discussion on these offences only.

Murder

77. Pursuant to Article 3(a) of the Statute, murder constitutes a crime against humanity. The Chamber notes that Article 3(a) of the English version of the Statute refers to "Murder", whilst the French version of the Statute refers to "*Assassinat*". Customary International Law dictates that it is the offence of "Murder" that constitutes a crime against humanity and not "*Assassinat*".

78. The *Akayesu Judgement* defined Murder as the unlawful, intentional killing of a human being. The requisite elements of murder are:

(a) The victim is dead;

(b) The death resulted from an unlawful act or omission of the accused or a subordinate;

(c) At the time of the killing the accused or a subordinate had the intention to kill or inflict grievous bodily harm on the deceased having known that such bodily harm is likely to cause the victim's death, and is reckless as to whether or not death ensues;

(d) The victim was discriminated against on any one of the enumerated discriminatory grounds;

(e) The victim was a member of the civilian population; and

(f) The act or omission was part of a widespread or systematic attack on the civilian population.

79. The Chamber concurs with this definition of murder and is of the opinion that the act or omission that constitutes murder must be discriminatory in nature and directed against a member of the civilian population.

Extermination

80. Pursuant to Article 3(c) of the Statute, extermination constitutes a crime against humanity. By its very nature, extermination is a crime which is directed against a group of individuals. Extermination differs from murder in that it requires an element of mass destruction which is not a pre-requisite for murder.

81. The *Akayesu Judgement*, defined the essential elements of extermination as follows:

(a) the accused or his subordinate participated in the killing of certain named or described persons;

(b) the act or omission was unlawful and intentional;

(c) the unlawful act or omission must be part of a widespread or systematic attack;

(d) the attack must be against the civilian population; and

(e) the attack must be on discriminatory grounds, namely: national, political, ethnic, racial, or religious grounds.

82. The Chamber concurs with this definition of extermination and is of the opinion that the act or omission that constitutes extermination must be discriminatory in nature and directed against members of the civilian population. Further, this act or omission includes, but is not limited to the direct act of killing. It can be any act or omission, or cumulative acts or omissions, that cause the death of the targeted group of individuals.

The Prosecutor v. Musema, ICTR-96-13-T (27 Jan. 2000)

Before: Judge Lennart Aspegren, Presiding

Judge Laïty Kama

Judge Navanethem Pillay

Rape

220. Rape may constitute a crime against humanity, pursuant to Article 3(g) of the Statute. In the *Akayesu* Judgement, rape as a crime against humanity was defined as:

"[…] a physical invasion of a sexual nature, committed on a person under circumstances which are coercive. Sexual violence, which includes rape, is considered to be any act of a sexual nature which is committed on a person under circumstances which are coercive. This act [under the Statute of the ICTR] must be committed:

(a) as part of a widespread or systematic attack;

(b) on a civilian population;

(c) on certain catalogued discriminatory grounds, namely: national, ethnic, political, racial, or religious grounds."

221. The Chamber notes that, while rape has been defined in certain national jurisdictions as non-consensual intercourse, variations on the acts of rape may include acts which involve the insertions of objects and/or the use of bodily orifices not considered to be intrinsically sexual.

222. The Chamber also observes that in defining rape, as a crime against humanity, the Trial Chamber in the *Akayesu* Judgement acknowledged:

> "that rape is a form of aggression and that the central elements of the crime of rape cannot be captured in a mechanical description of objects and body parts. The Convention against Torture and Other Cruel, Inhuman and Degrading Treatment or Punishment does not catalogue specific acts in its definition of torture, focusing rather on the conceptual framework of state sanctioned violence. This approach is more useful in international law. Like torture, rape is used for such purposes as intimidation, degradation, humiliation, discrimination, punishment, control or destruction of a person. Like torture, rape is a violation of personal dignity, and rape in fact constitutes torture when inflicted by or at the instigation of or with the consent or acquiescence of a public official or other person acting in an official capacity."

223. The Chamber notes that the definition of rape and sexual violence articulated in the *Akayesu* Judgement was adopted by the Trial Chamber II of the ICTY in its *Delalic* Judgement.

224. The Chamber has considered the alternative definition of rape set forth by Trial Chamber I of the ICTY in its *Furundzija* Judgement, which relies on a detailed description of objects and body parts. In this judgement the Trial Chamber looked to national legislation and noted:

"The Trial Chamber would emphasise at the outset, that a trend can be discerned in the national legislation of a number of States of broadening the definition of rape so that it now embraces acts that were previously classified as comparatively less serious offences, that is sexual or indecent assault. This trend shows that at the national level States tend to take a stricter attitude towards serious forms of sexual assault; the stigma of rape now attaches to a growing category of sexual offences, provided of course they meet certain requirements, chiefly that of forced physical penetration."

225. The *Furundzija* Judgement further noted that "most legal systems in the common and civil law worlds consider rape to be the forcible sexual penetration of the human body by the penis or the forcible insertion of any other object into either the vagina or the anus". Nevertheless, after due consideration of the practice of forced oral penetration, which is treated as rape in some States and sexual assault in other States, the Trial Chamber in that case determined as follows:

"183. The Trial Chamber holds that the forced penetration of the mouth by the male sexual organ constitutes a most humiliating and degrading attack upon human dignity. The essence of the whole corpus of international humanitarian law as well as human rights law lies in the protection of the human dignity of every person, whatever his or her gender. The general principle of respect for human dignity is the basic underpinning and indeed the very *raison d'être* of international humanitarian law and human rights law, indeed in modern times it has become of such paramount importance as to permeate the whole body of international law. This principle is intended to shield human beings from outrages upon their personal dignity, whether such outrages are carried out by unlawfully attacking the body or by humiliating and debasing the honour, the self-respect or the mental well-being of a person. It is consonant with this principle that such an extremely serious sexual outrage as forced oral penetration should be classified as rape."

226. The Chamber concurs with the conceptual approach set forth in the *Akayesu* Judgement for the definition of rape, which recognizes that the essence of rape is not the particular details of the body parts and objects involved, but rather the aggression that is expressed in a sexual manner under conditions of coercion.

227. The Chamber considers that the distinction between rape and other forms of sexual violence drawn by the *Akayesu* Judgement, that is "a physical invasion of a sexual nature" as contrasted with "any act of a sexual nature" which is committed on a person under circumstances which are coercive is clear and establishes a framework for judicial consideration of individual incidents of sexual violence and a determination, on a case by case basis, of whether such incidents constitute rape. The definition of rape, as set forth in the *Akayesu* Judgement, clearly encompasses all the conduct described in the definition of rape set forth in *Furundzija*.

228. The Chamber notes that in the *Furundzija* Judgement, the Trial Chamber considered forced penetration of the mouth as a humiliating and degrading attack on human dignity and largely for this reason included such conduct in its definition of rape even though State jurisdictions are divided as to whether such conduct constitutes rape. The Chamber further notes, as the *Furundzija* Judgement acknowledges, that there is a trend in national legislation to broaden the definition of rape. In light of the dynamic ongoing evolution of the understanding of rape and the incorporation of this understanding into principles of international law, the Chamber considers that a conceptual definition is preferable to a mechanical definition of rape. The conceptual definition will better accommodate evolving norms of criminal justice.

229. For these reasons, the Chamber adopts the definition of rape and sexual violence set forth in the *Akayesu* Judgement.

Questions

1. Are the factors identified in *Rutaganda* concerning "widespread" and "systematic" too limiting? Is "frequent" merely relevant to what is "systematic"? Is "with ... seriousness" really necessary to either? Also recall that in *Akayesu* the number of direct victims were as few as three, five, and eight persons. In The Prosecutor v. Kordic & Cerkez, IT-95-14/2-T (Trial Chamber Judgment, 26 Feb. 2001), para. 179, it was recognized that "widespread" conduct can involve the "cumulative effect of a series of inhumane acts or the singular effect of an inhumane act of extraordinary magnitude." In The Prosecutor v. Naletilic & Martinovic, IT-98-34-T (Trial Chamber Judgment, 31 Mar. 2003), para. 236, it was stated that "systematic" conduct "requires an organized nature of the acts and the improbability of their random occurrence."

Note that *Rutaganda*, in para. 67, did not accept a claim that a state policy must be involved. This is noticeably different than the limit found in French cases in Section 3. Nonetheless, can crimes against humanity be committed in the absence of some "policy"? See other materials in this chapter and Chapter Three.

Rutaganda cited *Akayesu* concerning a supposed requirement of "widespread" or "systematic" conduct. See ICTR-96-3-T, para. 63 and note 10. *Akayesu* cited nothing for this proposition but the French cases. See ICTR-96-4-T, paras. 567-574 and notes 139-141, arguing that the French cases somehow changed customary international law for the international community. *Id.* at para. 567 ("underwent a gradual evolution in the *Eichmann, Barbie, Touvier* and *Papon* cases.").

2. Regarding "murder," is "intentional killing" the same as an intent to inflict grievous harm knowing that such is "likely" to kill? In the U.S. generally, what factors tend to differentiate "murder 1" from "murder 2"?

3. If "constructive knowledge" of an "attack" on civilian persons suffices, why "must" one "know"? In *The Prosecutor v. Blaskic*, IT-95-14-A (Appeals Chamber Judgment, 29 July 2004), ruled that "knowledge on the part of the accused that there is an attack on the civilian population, as well as knowledge that his act is part thereof" is required. *Id.* para. 126. "The *Blaskic* Appeals Chamber affirmed a number of findings by the Trial Chamber with respect to certain underlying offences as persecutions under Article 5 [of the ICTY Statute]. Although some of these findings reiterate and reaffirm the jurisprudence of the ICTY, the Appeals Chamber succinctly summarized these ... and confirmed the customary nature of these crimes as persecutions.... Thus, the Appeals Chamber concluded that the following offences may constitute persecutions: killing (murder) and causing serious injury; deportation, forcible transfer and forcible displacement; inhumane treatment of civilians; and attacks on cities, towns and villages ... [as well as] destruction and plunder of property." Daryl A. Mundis & Fergal Gaynor, *Current Developments at the Ad Hoc International Criminal Tribunals*, 3 J. INT'L CRIM. JUSTICE 268, 274-75 (2005).

Consider also *The Prosecutor v. Naletilic & Martinovic*, IT-98-34-A (Appeals Chamber Judgment, 3 May 2006), paras. 129-130: "in the case of *Kvocka et al*, [the Appeals Chamber stated] 'the discriminatory intent of crimes cannot be inferred directly from the general discriminatory nature of an attack characterised as a crime against humanity. However, the discriminatory intent may be inferred from the context of the attack, provided it is substantiated by the surrounding circumstances of the crime.' [IT-98-30/1-A, 28 Feb. 2005, para. 366] According to the *Krnojelac* Appeal Judgment, such circumstances include the operation of a prison, in particular the systematic nature of crimes committed against a particular group within the prison, and the general attitude of the alleged perpetrator as seen through his behaviour. [IT-97-25-A, 2 Aug. 2001, para. 184]

[para.] 130. The Appeals Chamber has had occasion to apply this approach in a number of cases. According to the Appeals Chamber in the case of *Kordic and Cerkez*, in the situation in which all the guards belong to one ethnic group and all the prisoners to another, it could reasonably be inferred that the latter group was being discriminated against. [IT-95-14/2-A, 17 Dec. 2004, para. 950] In the *Kvocka et al.* Appeal Judgment, the Appeals Chamber stated that since almost all the detainees in the camp belonged to the non-Serb group, it could reasonably be concluded that the reason for their detention was membership of that group and that the detention was therefore of a discriminatory character." [IT-98-30/1-A, 28 Feb. 2005, para. 366]

With respect to knowledge that ones crimes against humanity are related to an attack on civilians, the Appeals Chamber reiterated a statement in *The Prosecutor v. Tadic*, IT-94-1-A (Appeals Chamber Judgment, 15 July 1999), para. 271, that "'it must be proved that the crimes were *related* to the attack on a civilian population (occurring during an armed conflict) and that the accused *knew* that his crimes were so related.'" *Naletilic &*

Martinovic, para. 118. The opinion analogized such a requirement to that contained in Article 2 of the Statute of the ICTY with respect to war crimes and stated that "the Prosecution has to show 'that the accused *knew* that his crimes' had a nexus to an international armed conflict, or at least that he had knowledge of the factual circumstances later bringing the Judges to the conclusion that the armed conflict was an international one.... The perpetrator only needs to be aware of the factual circumstances on which the judge finally determines the existence of the armed conflict and the international (or internal) character thereof. It is a general principle of criminal law that the correct legal classification of a conduct of the perpetrator is not required. The principle of individual guilt, however, demands sufficient awareness of *factual* circumstances establishing the armed conflict and its (international or internal) character." *Id*. paras. 118-119.

The Appeals Chamber in *Naletilic & Martinovic* also recognized that "persecutions may be undertaken by individuals at all levels of a hierarchy; there is no requirement that the individual be a senior figure." *Id*. para. 580.

With respect to alleged cumulative convictions for war crimes of unlawful transfer of persons and plunder of public and private property as well as "conduct underlying these offences [that] also formed part of the basis of the charge of persecutions as a crime against humanity," "the offences ... cannot be said to be consumed within persecutions since the unlawful transfer and plunder were charged as a grave breach of the Geneva Conventions and as a violations of the laws or customs of war while persecutions was charged as a crime against humanity," and "crimes against humanity under Article 5 of the Statute and grave breaches under Article 2 of the Statute contain different elements.... [T]he *Celibici* Appeal Judgment states that the test for permissible cumulative convictions for the same underlying conduct is whether 'each applicable provision contains a materially distinct legal element not present in the other, bearing in mind that an element is materially distinct from another if it requires proof of a fact not required by the other' and [in *Kordic & Cerkez*, para. 1037] '[w]hile Article 5 requires proof that the act occurred as part of a widespread or systematic attack against a civilian population, Article 2 requires proof of a nexus between the acts of the accused and the existence of an international armed conflict as well as the protected persons status of the victims under the Geneva Conventions.'" *Id*. paras. 561-562, citing The Prosecutor v. Celibici, IT-96-21-A (Appeals Chamber Judgment, 20 Feb. 2001), para. 421.

4. In *The Prosecutor v. Stakic*, IT-97-24-T (Trial Chamber Judgment, 31 July 2003), it was recognized that when a person is accused of having been an indirect perpetrator of an attack conviction can rest on the general discriminatory intent of the accused in relation to an attack committed by direct perpetrators even if the direct perpetrators had no such discriminatory intent if the direct perpetrators were used as an innocent instrument or tool of the indirect perpetrator. *Id*. paras. 737-744.

5. Concerning the difference between murder and extermination, is the word "mass" too limiting? Can a small number of direct victims be "exterminated"? In *The Prosecutor v. Stakic, supra*, a physician, Milomir Stakic, was convicted of extermination, stating that the perpetrator must intend to kill on a massive scale or intend to create conditions of life that lead to the death of a large number of persons or "the annihilation of a mass of people." *Id*. para. 641. Gross negligence or recklessness is not sufficient regarding the *mens rea* required for extermination as a crime against humanity. *Id*. para. 642.

6. Concerning "inhumane" treatment, is the *Rutaganda* approach, requiring "great" suffering or "serious" injury, too limiting? In *The Prosecutor v. Kordic & Cerkez*, IT-95-14/2-A (Appeals Chamber Judgment, 17 Dec. 2004), para. 117, the Appeals Chamber of

the ICTY stated that "inhumane" acts as crimes against humanity fulfill the following conditions: (1) the victim must have suffered serious bodily or mental harm, (2) the degree of severity must be assessed on a case-by-case basis with due regard for the individual circumstances, (3) the suffering must be the result of an act or omission of the accused or his subordinate, and (4) when the offence was committed, the accused or his subordinate must have been motivated by the intent to inflict serious bodily or mental harm upon the victim.

7. With respect to the factual quality of "inhumane," the accused "need not have known that his or her act … amounted to an 'inhumane act' either in the legal or moral sense." Guenael Mettraux, *Crimes Against Humanity in the Jurisprudence of the ICTs for the Former Yugoslavia and for Rwanda*, 43 HARV. INT'L L.J. 237, 297 n.323 (2002).

8. In *The Prosecutor v. Muhimana*, ICTR-95-1B-T (Trial Chamber Judgment, 28 Apr. 2005), para. 546, it was recognized that "coercion is an element that may obviate the relevance of consent as an evidentiary factor in the crime of rape" and "circumstances prevailing in most cases charged under international criminal law, as either genocide, crimes against humanity, or war crimes, will be almost universally coercive, thus vitiating consent." See also Daryl A. Mundis & Fergal Gaynor, *Current Developments at the Ad Hoc International Criminal Tribunals*, 3 J. INT'L CRIM. JUSTICE 1134, 1136-37 (2005).

9. An issue concerning rape as a crime against humanity was presented in *The Prosecutor v. Cesic*, IT-95-10/1-S (Trial Chamber Sentencing Judgment, 11 Mar. 2004). "The question arises whether another person could be [an] object or instrument [used for penetrating a person]. In general terms, a person is not considered an object. But you could use another person as an object or an instrument if you depersonalise him, if you take from him what makes him a person; that is, his own free will. Under the circumstances … [where] both detainees [were] instructed to penetrate in the body of the other detainee … [they] were deprived of their own free will." *Id.*, Transcript (8 Oct. 2003), para. 85. Under the circumstances, Cesic "actively participated in the violence inflicted upon the victims before the assault and initiated the assault by ordering it." *Id.*, Sentencing Judgment, para. 36; see also Daryl A. Mundis & Fergal Gaynor, *Current Developments at the Ad Hoc International Criminal Tribunals*, 2 J. INT'L CRIM JUSTICE 879, 884 (2004).

10. Concerning "hate speech" as an element of persecution, *The Prosecutor v. Nahimana, et al.*, ICTR-99-52-T (Trial Chamber Judgment and Sentence, 3 Dec. 2003), stated that "hate speech is a discriminatory form of aggression that destroys the dignity of those in the group under attack" and found that newspaper articles in question "created the conditions for extermination and genocide in Rwanda." *Id.* paras. 1072-1074. The Trial Chamber also stated that persecution is "broader than direct and public incitement, including advocacy of ethnic hatred in other forms." *Id.* para. 1078.

B. The Rome Statute for the International Criminal Court and its Application

In 1998 the Rome Statute for the International Criminal Court was adopted. Crimes against humanity are defined in Article 7 of the ICC Statute, and are one of the three crimes currently falling within the ICC's jurisdiction. Article 7 of the Statute has been criticized by some commentators as being overly restrictive, and, indeed, was the object of long negotiations between delegates, as the following extract suggests:

Leila Nadya Sadat, The International Criminal Court and the Transformation of International Law: Justice for the New Millennium 146-52 (Transnational 2002)[*]

The Statute adopted by the Diplomatic Conference is a montage of historically-based texts, massaged during difficult political negotiations, that improved the existing law in some respects, but left it either unchanged or more restrictive in other cases. One particularly thorny problem left unresolved by the Statute, for example, is its failure to distinguish jurisdictional from material elements of offenses. By jurisdictional elements, I mean elements that must be established in order for the Court to have jurisdiction over the crime. By material elements, I mean the traditional elements of the underlying crime that render an individual criminally liable, *i.e.*, the *actus reus* and *mens rea* or the *élément materiel* and the *élément moral*. The confusion was no doubt a direct result of the unconscious manner by which theories of universal jurisdiction were converted from international law norms addressing the distribution of competences between States to a norm of international law addressing the negotiation of competence between the international legal order and national legal systems....

Defining crimes against humanity presented one of the most difficult challenges at Rome, for no accepted definition existed, either as a matter of treaty or customary international law.

The disparity in definitions underscores the two major problems in defining the scope of crimes against humanity: first, distinguishing the crime from war crimes and from crimes under domestic law; second, determining which acts are punishable under international law as a matter of individual criminal responsibility, as opposed to State responsibility for violations of human rights. The Rome Statute attempts to address both problems through an extensive *chapeau*. The text is quite restrictive in overall character, although two positive outcomes should be noted. First, the Rome Statute does not require any nexus to an "armed conflict." Although some delegations in Rome repeatedly urged retention of the words "armed conflict," which was a bracketed option in the Zutphen Intersessional Draft and the April Draft Statute, that proposal was properly defeated as contrary to the weight of judicial decisions, national legislation, and other authority.

Second, absent from the *chapeau* is any requirement that the crimes be committed as part of an attack based on political, philosophical, racial, ethnic, religious, or other grounds. Instead, the Statute maintains the historic difference between "murder-type" crimes and "persecution-type" crimes that originated with article 6(c) of the IMT Charter. In this way the Statute tracks the ICTY approach (which was confirmed by the Appeals Chamber in the *Tadic* case) and appears consistent with the weight of authority on this point. The Statute, however, reinserts the linkage later by requiring that the crime of persecution be committed in connection either with another crime against humanity or any other crime within the jurisdiction of the Court.

Article 7 contains four separate preconditions that must be satisfied before jurisdiction attaches in a particular case in which crimes against humanity are charged. Some appear to be purely jurisdictional, meaning that once they have been proved as regards a particular situation, they need not be reestablished *ab initio* with respect to each defendant. Others, however, are material elements of the offense, meaning that they must be

---

committed with intent or knowledge on the part of the defendant, and proven with particularity in each case. The text is essentially a codification of compromises between those who thought the Statute was too innovative in character and too broad in its reach, and those who thought it did not go far enough......

Notes and Questions

1. With respect to crimes against humanity prosecutable before the ICC, Article 7(1) begins with the phrase "[f]or purposes of this Statute...." Does Article 7 reach all crimes against humanity identified in customary instruments such as the Charters of the I.M.T.s and Control Council Law No. 10? *See also* Bangladesh International Crimes (Tribunals) Act, art. 3(2)(a), in the Documents Section.

2. Does Article 7(1) of the Statute of the ICC fuse the two general types of crimes against humanity into one and reach crimes of persecution only when committed as part of an attack against a civilian population? Does Article 7(1)(h) further limit the reach of customary crimes of persecution of "persons" by use of the phrase "against any identifiable group or collectivity," thus limiting the reach to exclude ICC jurisdiction over persecutions of persons as such, as well as persecution of persons who may not be part of a group or collectivity? *See, e.g.*, Paust, *Content and Contours of Genocide, Crimes Against Humanity, and War Crimes*, in International Law in the Post-Cold War World: Essays in Memory of Li Haopei (Wang Tieya & Sienho Yee eds. 2000). Professor Paust adds: "Article 7(2)(a) ... provides an even more limiting and an illogical definition of 'attack' as 'a course of conduct involving the multiple commission of acts.' Clearly, an 'attack' can otherwise involve a single act. The limitations [of ICC jurisdiction over customary crimes] are compounded by an additional requirement in Article 7(2)(a) that a covered attack be engaged in 'pursuant to or in furtherance of a State or organizational policy.' Thus needlessly excluded are customary crimes against humanity perpetrated by: (a) governmental actors whose crimes are not 'pursuant to or in furtherance of' a State or organizational policy, (b) private unorganized actors, and (c) private actors who do not act pursuant to or in furtherance of a State or 'organizational' policy." *Id*. See also 93 Proc., Am. Soc. Int'l L. 73 (1999); Paust, *The International Criminal Court Does Not Have Complete Jurisdiction Over Customary Crimes Against Humanity and War Crimes*, 43 John Marshall L. Rev. 681 (2010).

3. Article 7(1) defines the target of crimes against humanity as "any civilian population." Thus under the ICC Statute, non-civilians (*e.g.*, members of the military) are excluded from the class of victims. Any of the prohibited acts enumerated in Article 7(1)(a)-(c), (f)-(i) and (k), if perpetrated against captured combatants, would amount to a war crime or grave breach of the 1949 Geneva Conventions. Does the term "civilian population" include belligerents *hors de combat* who have laid down their weapons, either because they are wounded or because they have been captured? *See* Antonio Cassese, International Criminal Law 93 (2003). As noted in Chapter Four, combatant status hinges upon membership in the armed forces of a party to an armed conflict and not whether the person is fighting or captured. *See, e.g.*, The Prosecutor v. Kordic & Cerkez, IT-95-14/2-A (Appeals Chamber, 17 Dec. 2004), quoted in Chapter Four.

4. Article 7 both narrows and broadens the customary international law understanding of crimes against humanity. Article 7(2)(a) defines "attack directed against a civilian population" to mean a course of conduct "involving the multiple commission of acts referred to in paragraph 1 against any civilian population, pursuant to or in furtherance

of a State or organizational policy to commit such attack." The requirement that an "attack directed against a civilian population" be in furtherance of a State or organizational policy to constitute crimes against humanity significantly narrows the reach of the statute. One commentator who is highly critical of the restrictive definition, posits:

> [I]n the case of murder, or rape, or forced pregnancy, why should it be required that the general practice constitute a policy pursued by a State or an organization? Would it not be sufficient for the practice to be accepted, or tolerated, or acquiesced in by the State or the organization, for those offences to constitute crimes against humanity? Clearly, this requirement goes beyond what is required under international customary law and unduly restricts the notion under discussion.

Cassese, *supra* at 93.

At the same time, in dealing with persecution-type crimes, Article 7 greatly expands the category of discriminatory grounds. While under customary international law these grounds may be political, racial, ethnic, or religious, Article 7(1)(h) adds "cultural," "gender," and "other grounds that are universally recognized as impermissible under international law."

5. Saddam Hussein has been charged with crimes against humanity for the murder of 148 Shiites from the town of Dujail, north of Baghdad. The victims were killed in response to a failed assassination attempt against Saddam. Would the allegations arising from the Dujail, Iraq killings support conviction of Saddam Hussein for crimes against humanity under the definition set forth in Article 5 of the Statute of the ICTY, Article 3 of the Statute of the ICTR, Article 7 of the Statute of the ICC, or Article 13 of the Iraqi High Criminal Court Law?

6. In an historic decision on December 11, 2001, the Special Panel of the Dili District Court in East Timor (consisting of three judges from Brazil, Burundi, and East Timor) convicted ten men of crimes against humanity charges in the Los Palos case. The case was the first involving crimes against humanity to reach trial, and is one of the ten priority cases of the Serious Crimes Unit. The ten accused received sentences of between 4 years' and the maximum 33 years 4 months' imprisonment. The Special Panel found that there was a widespread and systematic campaign of violence directed at the civilian population during 1999 at the direction of the Indonesian armed forces, and that contrary to many of the claims of the accused, they were aware that their acts (including murder, torture, and forced deportation) were part of that campaign. *See generally* Suzannah Linton, *New Approaches to International Justice in Cambodia and East Timor*, 84 IRRC 93 (March 2002). The Serious Crimes Panel of the District Court of Dili, which heard the case, was applying UNTAET (the United Nations Transitional Administration for East Timor) Regulation 2000/15, which incorporates many provisions from the 1998 Statute for the ICC, including Article 7 (which is section 5 of UNTAET Regulation 2000/15), defining crimes against humanity, with just three differences, each of which are relatively minor. See Kai Ambos & Steffen Wirth, *The Current Law of Crimes Against Humanity*, 13 Crim. L. F. 1 (2002).

7. One of the problems that arises in crimes against humanity cases decided in international courts and tribunals is not only the legal definition of the *chapeaux* elements, but the definition of the predicate crimes (*e.g.*, murder, torture, deportation) as well. Judges and lawyers from different legal systems have a tendency to assume the crimes will be defined internationally as they are in the domestic legal system from whence they come, which is not always true of course. For example, questions have arisen in the

Tribunals as to the definition of murder, and particularly whether premeditation is an element the crime, as well as with regard to the definition of extermination and deportation. *See, e.g., The Prosecutor v. Kordic*, IT-95-14/2-T (Trial Chamber Judgement, 26 Feb. 2001); *The Prosecutor v. Blaskic*, IT-95-14-T (Trial Chamber Judgement, 3 Mar. 2000). Obviously, none of the decisions of the ICTY, ICTR, East Timor Special Panels will bind the ICC. However, they may prove instructive to the ICC. The adoption of the Elements of Crimes for the interpretation of the ICC Statute (see the Documents Section) by the Assembly of States Parties somewhat ameliorates the ambiguity of these terms in international law, but the ICC will no doubt wrestle with the difficult task of international criminal harmonization.

Decision Pursuant to Article 15 of the Rome Statute on the Authorization of an Investigation into the Situation in the Republic of Kenya, No. ICC-01/09 (31 Mar. 2010)

[Editors' Note: On November 26, 2009, the Prosecutor of the ICC requested authorization to open an investigation into the post-election violence that took place in six out of the eight regions of Kenya, resulting in a reported 1,133 to 1,200 killings of civilians, 900 acts of sexual violence, internal displacement of 350,000, and 3,561 acts causing serious injury.]

II. Whether the Requisite Criteria Have Been Met

A. Whether there is a reasonable basis to believe that crimes against humanity within the jurisdiction of the Court have been committed

70. In the Prosecutor's Request, it is alleged that there is a reasonable basis to believe that the crimes against humanity of murder, rape and other forms of sexual violence, deportation or forcible transfer of population and other inhumane acts were committed and that therefore the Court's material jurisdiction is established. The Prosecutor further submits that these crimes fall under the temporal jurisdiction of the Court since they occurred after the entry into force of the Statute for the Republic of Kenya. Finally, he contends that, since the alleged crimes were committed on Kenyan territory, they fall within the Court's territorial jurisdiction.

71. The Chamber recalls that, to fall under the jurisdiction of the Court, a crime must fulfill the jurisdictional parameters *ratione materiae*, *ratione temporis* and—in the alternative–*ratione personae* or *ratione loci*. In the following sections, the Chamber will address each of these requirements in turn.

1. Jurisdiction *ratione materiae....*

a) Contextual elements of crimes against humanity

(i) The law and its interpretation....

79. The Chamber observes that the following requirements can be distinguished: ...

(aa) An attack directed against any civilian population

80. The meaning of the term "attack," although not addressed in the Statute, is clarified by the Elements of Crimes, which state that, for the purposes of article 7(1) of the Statute, an attack is not restricted to a "military attack." Instead, the term refers to "a campaign or operation carried out against the civilian population."

82. The Chamber need not be satisfied that the entire civilian population of the geographical area in question was being targeted. However, the civilian population must be the primary object of the attack in question and cannot merely be an incidental victim.

The term "civilian population" refers to persons who are civilians, as opposed to members of armed forces and other legitimate combatants.

(bb) State or organizational policy

83. Further, article 7(2)(a) of the Statute imposes the additional requirement that the attack against any civilian population be committed "pursuant to or in furtherance of a State or organizational policy to commit such attack." The Elements of Crimes offer further clarification in paragraph 3, in fine, of the Introduction to Crimes against humanity, where it is stated that:

[it] is understood that "policy to commit such an attack" requires that the State or organization actively promote or encourage such an attack against a civilian population;

and in footnote 6 of the same Introduction to Crimes against Humanity, where it is stated that

[a] policy which has a civilian population as the object of the attack would be implemented by State or organizational action. Such a policy may, in exceptional circumstances, be implemented by a deliberate failure to take action, which is consciously aimed at encouraging such attack. The existence of such a policy cannot be inferred solely from the absence of governmental or organizational action.

84. The Chamber notes that the Statute does not provide definitions of the terms "policy" or "State or organizational". However, both this Chamber and Pre-Trial Chamber I have addressed the policy requirement in previous decisions. In the case against Katanga and Ngudjolo Chui, Pre-Trial Chamber I found that this requirement:

[…] ensures that the attack, even if carried out over a large geographical area or directed against a large number of victims, must still be thoroughly organised and follow a regular pattern. It must also be conducted in furtherance of a common policy involving public or private resources. Such a policy may be made either by groups of persons who govern a specific territory or by any organisation with the capability to commit a widespread or systematic attack against a civilian population. The policy need not be explicitly defined by the organisational group. Indeed, an attack which is planned, directed or organized—as opposed to spontaneous or isolated acts of violence—will satisfy this criterion.

85. In the "Decision Pursuant to Article 61(7)(a) and (b) of the Rome Statute on the Charges of the Prosecutor Against Jean-Pierre Bemba Gombo," this Chamber also addressed the issue, stating that:

[t]he requirement of 'a State or organisational policy' implies that the attack follows a regular pattern. Such a policy may be made by groups of persons who govern a specific territory or by any organization with the capability to commit a widespread or systematic attack against a civilian population. The policy need not be formalised. Indeed, an attack which is planned, directed or organised—as opposed to spontaneous or isolated acts of violence—will satisfy this criterion.

86. Regarding the meaning of the term "policy," the Chamber will apply, in accordance with article 21(2) of the Statute, the definitions given in the abovementioned precedents. The Chamber also takes note of the jurisprudence of the ad hoc tribunals, and the work of the International Law Commission (the "ILC").

87. In particular, the Chamber takes note of the judgment in the case against Tihomir Blaskic, in which the ICTY Trial Chamber held that the plan to commit an attack:

[…] need not necessarily be declared expressly or even stated clearly and precisely. It may be surmised from the occurrence of a series of events, inter alia:

1. the general historical circumstances and the overall political background against which the criminal acts are set;

2. the establishment and implementation of autonomous political structures at any level of authority in a given territory;

3. the general content of a political programme, as it appears in the writings and speeches of its authors;

4. media propaganda;

5. the establishment and implementation of autonomous military structures;

6. the mobilisation of armed forces;

7. temporally and geographically repeated and co-ordinated military offensives;

8. links between the military hierarchy and the political structure and its political programme;

9. alterations to the "ethnic" composition of populations;

10. discriminatory measures, whether administrative or other (banking restrictions, laissez-passer, …);

11. the scale of the acts of violence perpetrated—in particular, murders and other

12. physical acts of violence, rape, arbitrary imprisonment, deportations and expulsions or the destruction of non-military property, in particular, sacral sites.

89. With regard to the definition of the terms "State or organizational", the Chamber firstly notes that while, in the present case, the term "State" is self-explanatory, it is worth mentioning that in the case of a State policy to commit an attack, this policy "does not necessarily need to have been conceived 'at the highest level of the State machinery.'" Hence, a policy adopted by regional or even local organs of the State could satisfy the requirement of a State policy.

90. With regard to the term "organizational," the Chamber notes that the Statute is unclear as to the criteria pursuant to which a group may qualify as "organization" for the purposes of article 7(2) (a) of the Statute. Whereas some have argued that only State-like organizations may qualify, the Chamber opines that the formal nature of a group and the level of its organization should not be the defining criterion. Instead, as others have convincingly put forward, a distinction should be drawn on whether a group has the capability to perform acts which infringe on basic human values:

the associative element, and its inherently aggravating effect, could eventually be satisfied by 'purely private criminal organizations, thus not finding sufficient reasons for distinguishing the gravity of patterns of conduct directed by 'territorial' entities or by private groups, given the latter's acquired capacity to infringe basic human values.

92. The Chamber finds that had the drafters of the Statute intended to exclude non-State actors from the term "organization," they would not have included this term in article 7(2)(a) of the Statute. The Chamber thus determines that organizations not linked to a State may, for the purposes of the Statute, elaborate and carry out a policy to commit an attack against a civilian population.

93. In the view of the Chamber, the determination of whether a given group qualifies as an organization under the Statute must be made on a case-by-case basis. In making this determination, the Chamber may take into account a number of considerations, inter alia: (i) whether the group is under a responsible command, or has an established hierarchy; (ii) whether the group possesses, in fact, the means to carry out a widespread or systematic attack against a civilian population; (iii) whether the group exercises control over part of the territory of a State; (iv) whether the group has criminal activities against the civilian population as a primary purpose; (v) whether the group articulates, explicitly or implicitly, an intention to attack a civilian population; (vi) whether the group is part of a larger group, which fulfills some or all of the abovementioned criteria. It is important to clarify that, while these considerations may assist the Chamber in its determination, they do not constitute a rigid legal definition, and do not need to be exhaustively fulfilled.

(cc) Widespread or systematic nature of the attack

110. The supporting material further indicates that, depending on the respective location and the phase of the violence, the attacks were directed against members of specifically identified communities. These communities were targeted on behalf of their ethnicity which was, in turn, associated with the support of one of the two major political parties, PNU and ODM.

111. Accordingly, during the initial phase of the violence. Rift Valley was the scene of attacks specifically targeting the non-Kalenjin community and in particular people of Kikuyu, Kisii, and Luhya ethnicity, perceived as affiliated with the PNU.…

112. During the phase of retaliatory violence, the attacks were directed mainly against the non-Kikuyu communities.…

(bb) State or organizational policy

117. Upon examination of the available information, the Chamber observes that some of the violent events which occurred during the period under examination spontaneously arose after the announcement of the election results. Additionally, there were accounts of opportunistic crime which accompanied the general situation of lawlessness. However, the Chamber is of the view that the violence was not a mere accumulation of spontaneous or isolated acts. Rather, a number of the attacks were planned, directed or organized by various groups including local leaders, businessmen and politicians associated with the two leading political parties, as well as by members of the police force.

118. With regard to the initial attacks, the Chamber notes various accounts of meetings of local leaders, businessmen and politicians. Most of these meetings were convened in Rift Valley, with the alleged aims to discuss the eviction of the Kikuyu community, to coordinate violence and to organize funding.

119. The supporting material includes additional accounts of meetings between businessmen or politicians and groups of young people. It is alleged that during these meetings, the youth were given instructions, supplied with weapons and distributed money. Moreover, it is reported that training and oathing in camps or at private residences took place in preparation for the attacks. In some instances, such meetings were directly followed by violent attacks against specific communities.

120. The supporting material further indicates that prior to the elections, some politicians employed inflammatory rhetoric to articulate their aim to evict the Kikuyus. Such statements were publicly disseminated through leaflets or the media. In addition, there are references to warnings given to people in anticipation of the violence.

121. The Chamber also considers that the organized nature of some of the attacks may further be inferred from the strategy and method employed in the attack. In this regard, it is reported that the attacks were well coordinated and organized....

122. The supporting material also highlights phenomena such as the large supply of petrol and the use of sophisticated weaponry. Such phenomena are consistent with allegations that businessmen or politicians financed the violence or directly supplied vehicles, petrol or weapons which were to be used in the attacks.

123. With regard to the entity behind the initial attacks, the supporting material contains references pointing to the involvement of Kalenjin leaders, businessmen and ODM politicians, including cabinet ministers. Finally, several ODM politicians reportedly announced in public their determination to evict the Kikuyu community.

124. Some of the retaliatory attacks showed similar features pointing to forms of organization and planning. In this regard, the Chamber notes a number of references to meetings organized by politicians, local businessmen and local leaders where attacks against communities associated with the ODM were reportedly discussed....

125. There are accounts of politicians employing hate speech against non-Kikuyu communities as well as ethnic propaganda disseminated by religious leaders and local language media. In addition, it is reported that prior to the violence, verbal warnings and leaflets were circulated among the non-Kikuyus.

126.... It is further alleged that PNU politicians financed the violence or supplied weapons, vehicles and petrol....

127. Groups associated with the planning of the retaliatory attacks included Kikuyu leaders, businessmen and PNU politicians who reportedly planned the attacks against perceived rival communities during their meetings. Furthermore, with regard to the violence which occurred in Naivasha between 27 and 30 January 2008, the Waki Commission claimed it had evidence that "government and political leaders in Nairobi, including key office holders at the highest level of government may have directly participated in the preparation of the attacks." Finally, the supporting material contains a number of contentions to the effect that, especially in Rift Valley and in the slums of Nairobi, Kikuyu leaders enlisted Kikuyu gangs, and in particular the Mungiki gang, to unleash violence on perceived rival communities.

128. With regard to the attacks emanating from the police, it is reported that the killings of the suspected Mungiki members occurred pursuant to a government campaign aimed at the suppression of this gang while the killings of suspected SLDF members and Mt Elgon residents reportedly occurred in the context of a government joint military-police operation.

(cc) Widespread nature of the attack

179. Accordingly, since the requirement of jurisdiction *ratione loci* is fulfilled, the Chamber is under no obligation to examine jurisdiction *ratione personae* under article 12(2)(b) of the Statute....

Dissenting Opinion of Judge Hans-Peter Kaul

I. Introduction and Main Conclusions

1. The majority concluded, upon examination of the Prosecutor's "Request for authorization of an investigation pursuant to Article 15" (the "Prosecutor's Request") and the facts contained in the supporting material, including the victims' representations, that there is a reasonable basis pursuant to article 15(4) of the Rome Statute (the

"Statute") to proceed with an investigation of alleged crimes against humanity on the territory of the Republic of Kenya from 1 June 2005 until 26 November 2009.

2. I regret that I am unable to accept the decision of the majority and the analysis that underpins it.

3. Basing my analysis on the supporting material, including the victims' representations, I am of the considered view that Pre-Trial Chamber II (the "Chamber") should not authorize the commencement of the Prosecutor's *proprio motu* investigation in the situation of the Republic of Kenya....

6.... The question is not whether or not those crimes have happened. The issue is whether the ICC is the right forum before which to investigate and prosecute those crimes....

8. As a Judge of the International Criminal Court (the "Court" or the "ICC"), I would like to ask all in the Republic of Kenya who yearn for justice and who support the intervention of the Court in this country for understanding the following: there are, in law and in the existing systems of criminal justice in this world, essentially two different categories of crimes which are crucial in the present case. There are, on the one side, international crimes of concern to the international community as a whole, in particular genocide, crimes against humanity and war crimes pursuant to articles 6, 7, and 8 of the Statute. There are, on the other side, common crimes, albeit of a serious nature, prosecuted by national criminal justice systems, such as that of the Republic of Kenya.

9. There is, in my view, a demarcation line between crimes against humanity pursuant to article 7 of the Statute, and crimes under national law. There is, for example, such a demarcation line between murder as a crime against humanity pursuant to article 7(1)(a) of the Statute and murder under the national law of the Republic of Kenya. It is my considered view that the existing demarcation line between those crimes must not be marginalized or downgraded, even in an incremental way. I also opine that the distinction between those crimes must not be blurred.

10. Furthermore, it is my considered view that this would not be in the interest of criminal justice in general and international criminal justice in particular.... As a Judge of the ICC, I feel, however, duty-bound to point at least to the following: such an approach might infringe on State sovereignty and the action of national courts for crimes which should not be within the ambit of the Statute. It would broaden the scope of possible ICC intervention almost indefinitely. This might turn the ICC, which is fully dependent on State cooperation, in a hopelessly overstretched, inefficient international court, with related risks for its standing and credibility. Taken into consideration the limited financial and material means of the institution, it might be unable to tackle all the situations which could fall under its jurisdiction with the consequence that the selection of the situations under actual investigation might be quite arbitrary to the dismay of the numerous victims in the situations disregarded by the Court who would be deprived of any access to justice without any convincing justification.

32. I now turn to the Statute of the ICC which seems to follow another route by establishing that a "State or organizational policy" is a legal requirement radiating on the entire chapeau of article 7 of the Statute as it is linked with the element of "attack" and not the component "systematic." This fact compels me to conduct a careful analysis before drawing an analogy with or relying on the jurisprudence of other tribunals. Article 10 of the Statute reinforces the assumption that the drafters of the Statute may have deliberately deviated from customary rules as evinced in the jurisprudence of other courts and tribunals in providing that "[n]othing in this Statute shall be interpreted as limiting

or prejudicing in any way existing or developing rules of international law for purposes other than in the Statute."

3. Interpretation of Article 7(2)(a) of the Statute According to Article 31 of the Vienna Convention.

34.... I apply the principles comprised in article 31 of the Vienna Convention on the Law of Treaties (the "VCLT")....

36. An "attack directed against any civilian population" *per definitionem legis* is a course of conduct involving the multiple commission of acts against such population "pursuant to or in furtherance of a State or organizational policy to commit such attack". The Statute suggests that the attack is not any attack that has been directed against any civilian population. Rather, it is qualified by the added features that it is "widespread" or "systematic" and that it was conducted "pursuant to or in furtherance of a State or organizational policy." As the latter qualification represents a point of disagreement with the majority's decision, I shall develop my understanding on this aspect of article 7 of the Statute only.

37. The Statute clarifies that, on the one hand, either a State may adopt such a policy or, on the other hand, that an "organizational policy" may be found to exist. I observe that the Statute does not provide any guidance regarding the notion "organizational policy." Based on the English text of the Statute one might arrive to the conclusion that in this case the policy need only be "organizational," seemingly referring to the nature of such policy as being (only) of an organized, planned or systematic manner, leaving aside the question of attribution to a specific authorship. However, I note that the English text of the Statute is phrased more broadly than other authentic versions of the Statute, leaving some doubt as to its exact meaning. The original of the Statute in Arabic, Chinese, English, French, Russian and Spanish are equally authentic. A look at the French, Spanish and Arabic text reveals the following.

38. [After reviewing the other authentic texts,] I conclude that while the English text would accept the meaning of a policy to be of a systematic nature but does not necessarily need to be authored by an entity like that of an "organization", the other authentic texts of the Statute clearly refer to the requirement that a policy be adopted by an 'organization'. In case where two or more versions possess equal authority and one appears to have a wider bearing than the other, I shall adopt the interpretation which offers the more limited interpretation and which accords with the intention of the drafters as enshrined in the other texts. I therefore believe that the Statute has opted for the meaning whereby "organizational" shall be construed as meaning to pertain to an organization....

51. I read the provision such that the juxtaposition of the notions "State" and 'organization' in article 7(2)(a) of the Statute are an indication that even though the constitutive elements of statehood need not be established those 'organizations' should partake of some characteristics of a State. Those characteristics eventually turn the private 'organization' into an entity which may act like a State or has quasi-State abilities. These characteristics could involve the following: (a) a collectivity of persons; (b) which was established and acts for a common purpose; (c) over a prolonged period of time; (d) which is under responsible command or adopted a certain degree of hierarchical structure, including, as a minimum, some kind of policy level; (e) with the capacity to impose the policy on its members and to sanction them; and (f) which has the capacity and means available to attack any civilian population on a large scale.

52. In contrast, I believe that non-state actors which do not reach the level described above are not able to carry out a policy of this nature, such as groups of organized

crime, a mob, groups of (armed) civilians or criminal gangs.... For it is not the cruelty or mass victimization that turns a crime into a *delictum iuris gentium* but the constitutive contextual elements in which the act is embedded.

53. In this respect, the general argument that any kind of non-state actors may be qualified as an 'organization' within the meaning of article 7(2)(a) of the Statute on the grounds that it "has the capability to perform acts which infringe on basic human values" without any further specification seems unconvincing to me. In fact this approach may expand the concept of crimes against humanity to any infringement of human rights. I am convinced that a distinction must be upheld between human rights violations on the one side and international crimes on the other side, the latter forming the nucleus of the most heinous violations of human rights representing the most serious crimes of concern to the international community as a whole.

b) Contextual Interpretation....

c) Object and Purpose

56. The restricted interpretation of this contextual requirement is also warranted by a teleological interpretation of article 7(2)(a) of the Statute, i.e., in light of its object and purpose.... What is the object and purpose of crimes against humanity? What is in fact the underlying rationale or raison d'être of crimes against humanity? What makes it different from other common crimes which fall solely under the jurisdiction of States? ...

V. General Conclusions

148. On a general note, I observe that the information available does not lead to the conclusion of 'one' "attack" during the time frame under examination but a series of numerous incidents, as suggested by the Prosecutor. Numerous violent acts were launched at different times by different groups and against different groups throughout the country. The violence was at the occasion of the as rigged perceived presidential elections in December 2007. The reasons for the violence appear to go beyond allegations of manipulated elections. Information in the supporting material and the victims' representations suggests that the cause of the violence may be found in long-lasting and unresolved issues, such as land distribution, poverty, unemployment, rental issues, inter-ethnic tensions, xenophobia, disenfranchisement, perceived discrimination, desire for ethnically homogenous neighbourhoods, organized crime, retaliation and anger over the support of the opposing political party. The origin of such issues may sometimes date back to colonial times. Albeit the motives of the perpetrators are not decisive and may vary, it nevertheless sheds light on the question of the existence of a possible policy....

150. While I accept that some of the violence appears to have been organized and planned in advance, I fail to see the existence of an 'organization' behind the violent acts which may have established a policy to attack the civilian population within the meaning of article 7(2)(a) of the Statute. I find indications in the supporting material that some local leaders, some local businessmen, some local politicians, some religious leaders, some journalists at local vernacular radio stations, some chiefs of communities and some civic and parliamentary aspirants were involved in the preparation of the violence. But I do not see an 'organization' meeting the prerequisites of structure, membership, duration and means to attack the civilian population. To the contrary, the overall assessment of the information in the supporting material, including the victims' representations leads me to conclude that several centres of violence in several provinces existed which each do not rise to the level of crimes against humanity.

151. In the event that those centres of violence was to be considered as 'one' attack, the unifying element would be the policy implemented by an 'organization' at the national level. As I don't have information available indicating that such policy was adopted at the national level, I fail to see how those crimes and centres of violence could be assessed in light of article 7(1) of the Statute.

152. A different aspect involves the conduct of law enforcement agencies and the military. The reactions of the police during the "post-election violence" range from being mere passive observers, assisting civilians, being overwhelmed with the situation to actively engaging in the violence. In many areas of Kenya, the police had to be assisted by the military to re-gain control. Another distinct aspect of police involvement concerns its participation in addressing organized crime and combating movements which do not necessarily relate to the events surrounding the "post-election violence." In sum, I have not found any information in the supporting material, including the victims' representations, suggesting that a State policy existed pursuant to which the civilian population was attacked.

153. In total, the overall picture is characterized by chaos, anarchy, a collapse of State authority in most parts of the country and almost total failure of law enforcement agencies.

In light of all of the above, I feel unable to authorize the commencement of an investigation in the situation in the Republic of Kenya.

Notes and Questions

1. Which opinion is the more persuasive, the majority or the dissent? For a discussion of each side's persuasiveness and precedential value, *see* Leila Nadya Sadat, *Crimes Against Humanity in the Modern Age*, 106 Am. J. Int'l L. _ (2012). *See also* Charles C. Jalloh, *Situation in the Republic of Kenya*, 105 Am. J. Int'l L. 540 (2011); Claus Kress, *On the Outer Limits of Crimes Against Humanity: The Concept of Organization within the Policy Requirement: Some Reflections on the March 2010 ICC* Kenya *Decision*, 23 Leiden J. Int'l L. 855 (2010); Darryl Robinson, *Essence of Crimes Against Humanity Raised by Challenges at ICC*, EJIL Talk, Sept. 27, 2011, http://www.ejiltalk.org/essence-of-crimes-against-humanity-raised-by-challenges-at-icc/#more-3782; William A. Schabas, *Prosecuting Dr. Strangelove, Goldfinger, and the Joker at the International Criminal Court: Closing the Loopholes*, 23 Leiden J. Int'l L. 847 (2010).

2. The Pre-Trial Chamber in the Kenya case adopted the factors articulated in *Prosecutor v. Blaskic*, No. IT-9Fli5-14-T (Trial Chamber Judgement, 3 March 2000), as relevant and probative in deciding whether there was a "policy" to commit an attack against the Kenyan civilian population. Consider the list of factors in paragraph 87 of the opinion. Which of these factors are most probative as to whether there was a policy to commit an attack against a civilian population?

In earlier ICTY and ICTR cases, the policy element was considered to be a requisite element of crimes against humanity. *See, e.g., Prosecutor v. Tadic,* Case No. IT-94-1-T (Trial Chamber Judgement, 7 May 1997), para. 653; *Prosecutor v. Akayesu,* Case No. ICTR-96-4-T (Trial Chamber Judgment, 2 Sept. 1998), para. 653; *Prosecutor v. Rutaganda,* Case No. ICTR-96-3-T (Trial Chamber Judgement, 6 Dec. 1999), para. 69; *Prosecutor v. Musema*, Case No. ICTR-96-13-T (Trial Chamber Judgement, 27 Jan. 2000), para. 204; *Prosecutor v. Kayishema and Ruzindana*, Case No. ICTR-95-1-T (Trial Chamber Judgement, 21 May 1999), paras. 123-25, 581. However, the policy requirement was abandoned by the *Kunarac* Appeal Judgement, which held that the attack need not be supported by any form of "policy" or "plan." *See Prosecutor v. Kunarac*, et al., Case No.

IT-96-23 & IT-96-23/1-A (Appeal Chamber Judgement, 12 June 2002), para. 98. This conclusion was affirmed in *Prosecutor v. Vasiljevic*, Case No. IT-98-32-T (Trial Chamber Judgement, 29 Nov. 2002), para. 36; *Prosecutor v. Naletilic and Martinovic*, Case No. IT-98-34-T (Trial Chamber Judgement, 31 March 2003), para. 234; *Prosecutor v Semanza*, Case No. ICTR-97-20-T (Trial Chamber Judgement, 15 May 2003), para. 329.

3. In the case of a "State" policy to commit an attack, the policy "does not necessarily need to have been conceived 'at the highest level of the State machinery.'" *Prosecutor v. Blaskic*, Case No. IT-95-14-T (Trial Chamber Judgement, 3 March 2000), para. 205. A policy adopted by regional or local governmental agencies could satisfy the requirement of a State policy. Must the "organizational policy" be established, endorsed or condoned at the highest policy-level of the "organization"?

4. The Pre-Trial Chamber in the Kenya case maintained that a distinction should be drawn on whether a group has the capability to perform acts which "infringe on basic human values." Para. 90. Is this standard too vague? Does the Chamber's definition of "organizational" risk expanding the concept of crimes against humanity to any infringement of human rights?

Judge Kaul's dissent stated that the juxtaposition of the notions of "State" and "organization" in Article 7(2)(a) of the ICC statute require that the "organization" possess some characteristics of a State. Para. 51. For Judge Kaul, this means that criminal organizations and syndicates would not qualify as "organizations" under Article 7(2)(a). However, what about more sophisticated criminal enterprises such as violent drug cartels or terrorist organizations? Do these groups possess State-like characteristics? Should their members be prosecuted for crimes against humanity? Review the opinion of the French Advocate General in the *Barbie* case, *supra* Section 3. Would he agree with Judge Kaul? The preamble of the ICC statute accentuates the gravity of the crimes subject to the jurisdiction of the ICC. The preamble states:

Mindful that during this century millions of children, women and men have been victims of unimaginable atrocities that deeply shock the conscience of humanity,

Recognizing that such grave crimes threaten the peace, security and well-being of the world,

Affirming that the most serious crimes of concern to the international community as a whole must not go unpunished and that their effective prosecution must be ensured by taking measures at the national level and by enhancing international cooperation, ...

Determined to these ends and for the sake of present and future generations, to establish an independent permanent International Criminal Court in relationship with the United Nations system, with jurisdiction over the most serious crimes of concern to the international community as a whole.

Would the prosecution of members of organized crime for crimes against humanity be consistent with the fundamental principles set forth in the preamble to the ICC statute? Concerning claims that organized criminal activities can be covered, see, for example, Sonia Merzon, *Extraterritorial Reach of the Trafficking Victims Protection Act*, 39 Geo. Wash. Int'l L. Rev. 887, 913 (2007), *citing* Tom Obokata, *Trafficking of Human Beings as a Crime Against Humanity: Some Implications for the International Legal System*, 54 Int'l & Comp. L.Q. 445 (2005); Paust, *The International Criminal Court Does Not Have Complete Jurisdiction Over Customary Crimes Against Humanity and War Crimes*, *supra* at 694; Jennifer M. Smith, *An International Hit Job: Prosecuting Organized*

Crime Acts as Crimes Against Humanity, 97 Geo. L.J. 1111, 1122-24, 1126-28 & nn.148-149, 1129-30, 1139-52 (2009) (adding: national courts and the ICTY have "recognized that private actors could commit crimes against humanity" and "state policy" is not required; and since the Appeals Chamber decision in *The Prosecutor v. Kunarac* "explicitly held that a policy or plan is not even an element of crimes against humanity under customary international law, ... other ICTY and ICTR judgments have consistently reaffirmed that a plan or policy is not a requisite legal element.... [listing 12 ICTY cases and 4 ICTR cases] For example, the ICTR Appeals Chamber in *Semanza v. Prosecutor* reaffirmed that the existence of a plan or policy is not" required "and rejected the defendant's contention that crimes against humanity require 'the existence of a political objective' and 'the implication of high level political and/or military authorities in the definition and establishment of [a] methodical plan'"); Bruce Zagaris, *U.S. International Cooperation Against Transnational Organized Crime*, 44 Wayne L. Rev. 1401, 1462 (1998) ("genocide and crimes against humanity by transnational organized crime groups").

5. Consider the following hypothetical:

The dictatorial President of country Z, Ur R. Ong, has been publicly accused of a crime against humanity involving a successful bomb attack on the elite of his political opposition during their annual meeting, at which all three hundred or so of the conferees were killed. Ong claims that he, with the aid of a few of his most loyal colonels, planned this on his own in self-defense and in order to save the civilian population from political extremists who were plotting a terrorist campaign. When asked about the Nuremberg Charter, On said that it only applied during war, that it has been replaced by the Rome Statute of the ICC, and that the killing of the terrorists occurred during peace, was the internal affair of country Z, and was certainly not a crime against humanity under customary international law? Is Ong correct?

6. For further discussion of crimes against humanity in the Rome Statute, *see, e.g.*, Kelly Dawn Askin, *Crimes within the Jurisdiction of the International Criminal Court*, 10 Crim. L. F. 33 (1999); Kai Ambos & Steffen Wirth, *The Current Law of Crimes Against Humanity*, 13 Crim. L. F. 1 (2002). *See also generally* M. Cherif Bassiouni, Crimes Against Humanity in International Criminal Law (2d ed. 1999); David Luban, *A Theory of Crimes Against Humanity*, 29 Yale J. Int'l L. 85 (2004).

Chapter 3

Genocide

Section 1
The Convention

Convention on the Prevention and Punishment of the Crime of Genocide, 78 U.N.T.S. 277*

[Read the Genocide Convention, in the Documents Section]

Article II of the Genocide Convention, which defines genocide, arguably has certain flaws. One problem is that the protected "group" is limited to "national, ethnical, racial or religious" and does not directly include social, cultural, or political groups as such.[2] The latter two were part of the original draft definition of Article II, but were opposed by the U.S.S.R. and thus not included in the approved text. Nevertheless, the negotiating history of the Convention reveals that the drafters intended the definition to be flexible and progressive to meet evolving exigencies.[3] This was needed because the definition was essentially reactive to the Nazi practices between 1932–1945, but was never intended to be limited to events during the Holocaust. In a 1992 authoritative interpretation, the Final Report of the Commission of Experts Established Pursuant to Security Council Resolution 780 (1992) to Investigate Violations of International Humanitarian

---

* This Convention was adopted by the U.N. General Assembly on December 9, 1948 (G.A. Res. 2670), 3 GAOR, Part 1, U.N. Doc. A/810, p. 174); entered into force on January 12, 1951. There are 142 state parties as of May 2013.

2. Note, however, that these might be factors relevant to the determination of other groupings (like ethnic, national or religious). Cultural groups are not directly included within the customary definition of genocide, but cultural characteristics might similarly relate to conclusions whether other groups exist.

3. *See* United Nations Report on the Study of the Question of the Prevention and Punishment of the Crime of Genocide, E/CN.4/Sub. 2/416, 4 July 1978, pp. 13–24, particularly paras. 46–91; *reprinted in* 1 International Criminal Law 389–97 (M. Cherif Bassiouni ed. 1986). *See also* Revised and Updated Report on the Question of the Prevention and Punishment of the Crime of Genocide Prepared by Mr. B. Whitaker, Review of Further Developments in Fields with which the Sub-Commission has been concerned, U.N. ESCOR, Human Rights Sub-Commission on the Prevention of Discrimination and Protection of Minorities, 38th Sess., U.N. Doc. E/CN.4/Sub. 2/1985, 16, 2 July 1985. For a distinction between intent and motive, *see, e.g.,* Wayne R. LaFave & Austin W. Scott, Jr., Criminal Law 216 (2d ed. 1986). For an approach to "specific intent," *see, e.g., Michalic v. Cleveland Taubers*, 346 U.S. 325 (1960); *Holland v. United States*, 348 U.S. 121 (1954).

Law in the Former Yugoslavia, the Commission took the position that the definition of the crime of genocide is not static.[4] Further, the definition encompasses not merely a "group" in its entirety, but also a "part" thereof, like the intellectual elite or women who are targeted because they are members of a relevant group.[5] Moreover, a given group can be defined on the basis of its localized or regional existence, as opposed to an all-inclusive concept encompassing all members wherever they may be.

According to Professor Bassiouni:

> A second flaw in the Convention is the element of intent which requires "specific intent." While this type of intent is more readily identifiable in leaders or decision-makers, it is not always easily demonstrated with respect to the different layers or levels of executors of the policy. Thus, proving specific intent of lower level executors can be difficult. Yet it would be unfair, for example, to convict a prison guard who kills a prisoner of the crime of genocide without the specific intent to carry out the policy of genocide. That crime would also be a "war crime" if committed during an armed conflict. [see Chapter Four] When the accused are other than decision-makers, the mental element should include at least knowledge by the executor that he is carrying out a genocidal policy. The major difference between "genocide" and "crimes against humanity" is that the former requires a specific intent to "destroy, in whole or in part" a given "group," while the latter does not.[6]

According to others, there is no such flaw in the Convention. There is merely the need to prove a specific intent to commit one of the acts defined in Articles II and III. Further, there is no unfairness in prosecuting any person, of any rank, who in fact has the "intent to destroy, in whole or in part," within the meaning of Article II, or who has been reasonably accused of conspiracy, incitement, attempt, or complicity within the meaning of Article III. It is not necessary that there be a "policy" of genocide or some further specific intent unspecified in the customary definition of genocide contained in Article II.

Questions

1. Under the Convention, is there a duty to prosecute those reasonably accused of genocide? See Articles I ("undertake to prevent and to punish"), IV ("Persons committing … shall be punished"), and V; 1993 Report of the Secretary-General, at para. 45 ("shall be tried and punished"). Given the fact that the crime of genocide is a violation of customary international law over which there is universal jurisdiction, is there also a universal duty to initiate prosecution or extradite?

---

4. . U.N. SCOR, U.N. DOC. S/1994/674, 27 May 1994, para. 96. *See also* M. Cherif Bassiouni, *The Commission of Experts Established Pursuant to Security Council Resolution 780: Investigating Violations of International Humanitarian Law in the Former Yugoslavia,* 5 CRIM. L.F. 279 (1994); M. Cherif Bassiouni, *Current Developments: The United Nations Commission of Experts Established Pursuant to Security Council Resolution 780 (1992),* 88 AM. J. INT'L L. 784 (1994).

5. Annex to the Final Report *(supra)*, U.N. SCOR, Annex IV, "The Policy of Ethnic Cleansing" and Annex "Prijedor", U.N. DOC. S/1994/674/Add. 2 (Vol. I) (Dec. 28, 1994), and Annex IX, "Rape and Sexual Assault", U.N. DOC. S/1994/674/Add. 2 (Vol. V) (May 31, 1995). *See also* M. Cherif Bassiouni & Marcia McCormick, *Sexual Violence: An Invisible Weapon of War in the Former Yugoslavia* (Occasional Paper No. 1 International Human Rights Law Institute, DePaul University College of Law 1996); Lawrence J. LeBlanc, *The Intent to Destroy Groups in the Genocide Convention: The Proposed U.S. Understanding,* 78 AM. J. INT'L L. 369 (1984); materials that follow in this chapter.

6. *See, e.g.,* M. CHERIF BASSIOUNI, CRIMES AGAINST HUMANITY IN INTERNATIONAL CRIMINAL LAW (1992).

2. Under the Convention, is there a duty to prevent genocide? See Articles I, VIII. Professor Schabas has written: "The Outcome Document, adopted at the United Nations summit in September 2005, affirms that 'each individual state has the responsibility to protect its populations from genocide, war crimes, ethnic cleansing and crimes against humanity.'... It is uncontroversial to maintain that the duty to prevent genocide is one of customary international law.... Perhaps the Outcome Document will help to lay to rest a controversy ... whether or not the 'ethnic cleansing' that has been an ugly feature of the civil war in Darfur [Sudan] constitutes the crime of genocide." William A. Schabas, *Genocide, Crimes Against Humanity, and Darfur: The Commission of Inquiry's Findings on Genocide*, 27 Cardozo L. Rev. 1703 (2006). In response partly to U.S. claims that conduct in Darfur amounts to genocide, the U.N. Security Council created a Commission of Inquiry in 2004 to address the issue. The 2005 Report of the Commission concluded that "genocidal intent" appeared to be lacking with respect to a Sudanese "policy of attacking, killing and forcibly displacing members of some tribes," which did not prove "a specific intent to annihilate, in whole or in part" but rather "that those who planned and organized attacks on villages pursued the intent to drive the victims from their homes, primarily for purposes of counter-insurgency warfare." See U.N. Secretary-General, Report of the International Commission of Inquiry on Violations of International Law and Humanitarian Law and Human Rights Law in Darfur, para. 518, U.N. Doc. S/2005/60 (31 Jan. 2005); Schabas, *supra* at 1705-06, adding that the Commission nonetheless "characterized the behaviour of the pro-government Janjaweed paramilitaries as 'crimes against humanity'" and that the Security Council has referred "'the situation in Darfur since 1 July 2002' to the International Criminal Court."

In one example investigated, the Darfur Commission Report concluded that instead of genocidal intentions, the intention was to murder all those men they considered as rebels, as well as [to] forcibly expel the whole population so as to vacate the villages and prevent rebels from hiding among or getting support from the local population" and in some instances "populations surviving attacks on villages are not killed outright in an effort to eradicate the group; rather, they are forced to abandon their homes and live together in areas selected by the Government." Report, *supra* at paras. 514-515.

3. What constitutes genocide within the meaning of Article II?

4. What is the specific intent required? With respect to specific acts covered in Article II (a)–e), are there additional *mens rea* requirements concerning the specific acts or methods? In *Prosecutor v. Niyitegeka*, ICTR-96-14-A (Appeals Chamber Judgement, 9 July 2004), the Appeals Chamber held that the term "as such" in the definition of genocide does not prohibit a conviction for genocide where the perpetrator was also driven by other motivations. The Court stated that term "as such" means that the proscribed acts were committed against the victims *because of* their membership in the protected group, but not *solely* because of such membership.

5. In order to commit genocide, as opposed to an attempt to commit genocide under Article III (d), must the perpetrator destroy a relevant group "in whole or in part" or must the perpetrator merely intend to do so while committing one or more of the listed acts?

Must there be an intent to destroy the group in whole or in part or merely its identity? In *The Prosecutor v. Milosevic*, IT-02-54-T (Decision on Motion for Judgment of Acquittal, 16 June 2004), the Trial Chamber declared that "[i]t is the material destruction of the group which must be intended and not the destruction of its identity." *Id.* para. 124. Is the "intent to destroy" requirement limited to the intent to "physically" or "biologically" destroy members of the protected group? In *Prosecutor v. Krajisnik*, IT-00-

39-T (Trial Chamber Judgement, 27 Sept. 2006), the Trial Chamber indicated that the "intent to destroy" can encompass more than physical or biological destruction:

> It is not accurate to speak of "the group" as being amenable to physical or biological destruction. Its members are, of course, physical or biological beings, but the bonds among its members, as well as such aspects of the group as its members' culture and beliefs, are neither physical nor biological. Hence the Genocide Convention's "intent to destroy" the group cannot sensibly be regarded as reducible to an intent to destroy the group physically or biologically, as has occasionally been said.

6. Could al Qaeda attacks on the World Trade Center and the Pentagon in the U.S. on September 11, 2001 constitute acts of genocide under Article II? Near the end of this chapter, consider whether those involved in conspiracy or complicity to commit such attacks could be prosecuted under the U.S. genocide legislation (especially 18 U.S.C. §§ 1091, 1093(8)).

7. If U.S. military personnel targeted armed Iraqi military personnel during the Iraq war because they were Iraqi soldiers, would such targetings involve the killings of a national group with the intent to destroy that group "in part"? Is it relevant that such conduct is permissible under the laws of war? *Cf* The Prosecutor v. Krstic, IT-98-33-A (Appeals Chamber Judgment, 19 Apr. 2004), para. 226, genocide can be committed against military personnel if they are killed because they are part of a relevant group with the intent to destroy in whole or in part members of that group.

8. If Serbian military units intentionally killed Muslim persons in Bosnia-Herzegovina in order to "ethnically cleanse" areas of Muslims by causing those left alive to flee, were the killings genocide? Does it depend on one's definition of "ethnically cleanse"? Consider Antonio Cassese, International Criminal Law 98-100 (2003) ("It would seem that Article IV does not cover the conduct currently termed in nontechnical language 'ethnic cleansing,' that is the forcible expulsion of civilians belonging to a particular group from an area, a village, or a town.").

9. What do you think is meant by the phrase "ethnic cleansing"? Like the former President of the Appeals Chamber of the ICTY, Antonio Cassese, Judge Lauterpacht has stated that this phrase encompasses "the forced migration of civilians." See Application of the Convention on the Prevention and Punishment of the Crime of Genocide (Bosnia and Herzegovina v. Yugoslavia (Serbia and Montenegro)), 1993 I.C.J. 325, 431 (separated op., Judge Elihu Lauterpacht). Is this all that the phrase might encompass? See also John Quigley, *State Responsibility for Ethnic Cleansing*, 32 U.C. Davis L. Rev. 341 (1999) ("It is an umbrella term that covers a variety of delictual acts aimed at driving members of an ethnic group from their home area"); Final Report of the Commission of Experts Established Pursuant to Security Council Resolution 780 (1992), U.N. SCOR, Annex 1, at 33, U.N. Doc. E/CN.4/1995/176 (1995) ("a purposeful policy designed by one ethnic or religious group to remove by violent and terror-inspiring means the civilian populations of another ethnic or religious group from certain geographic areas").

A. Prosecutions Before the International Criminal Tribunal for Rwanda, The Prosecutor v. Jean-Paul Akayesu, ICTR-96-4-T (2 Sept. 1998)

Before: Judge Laïty Kama, Presiding

Judge Lennart Aspegren

Judge Navanethem Pillay

12. Before rendering its findings on the acts with which Akayesu is charged and the applicable law, the Chamber is of the opinion that it would be appropriate, for a better understanding of the events alleged in the Indictment, to briefly summarise the history of Rwanda. To this end, it recalled the most important events in the country's history, from the pre-colonial period up to 1994, reviewing the colonial period and the "Revolution" of 1959 by Gregoire Kayibanda. The Chamber most particularly highlighted the military and political conflict between the Rwandan Armed Forces (RAF) and the Rwandan Patriotic Front(RPF) and its armed wing, from 1990. This conflict led to the signing of the Arusha Peace Accords and the deployment of a United Nations peacekeeping force, UNAMIR.

13. The Chamber then considered whether the events that took place in Rwanda in 1994 occurred solely within the context of the conflict between the RAF and the RPF, as some maintain, or whether the massacres that occurred between April and July 1994 constituted genocide. To that end, and even if the Chamber later goes back on its definition of genocide, it should be noted that genocide means, as defined in the Convention for the Prevention and Punishment of the Crime of Genocide, as the act of committing certain crimes, including the killing of members of the group or causing serious physical or mental harm to members of the group with the intent to destroy, in whole or in part, a national, ethnical, racial or religious group, as such.

14. Even though the number of victims is yet to be known with accuracy, no one can reasonably refute the fact that widespread killings took place during this period throughout the country. Dr. Zachariah, who appeared as an expert witness before this Tribunal, described the piles of bodies he saw everywhere, on the roads, on the footpaths and in rivers and, particularly, the manner in which all these people had been killed. He saw many wounded people who, according to him, were mostly Tutsi and who, apparently, had sustained wounds inflicted with machetes to the face, the neck, the ankle and also to the Achilles' tendon to prevent them from fleeing. Similarly, the testimony of Major-General Dallaire, former Commander of UNAMIR, before the Chamber indicated that, from 6 April 1994, the date of the crash that claimed the life of President Habyarimana, members of FAR and the Presidential Guard were going into houses in Kigali that had been previously identified in order to kill. Another witness, the British cameraman, Simon Cox, took photographs of bodies in various localities in Rwanda, and mentioned identity cards strewn on the ground, all of which were marked "Tutsi".

15. Consequently, in view of these widespread killings the victims of which were mainly Tutsi, the Trial Chamber is of the opinion that the first requirement for there to be genocide has been met, to wit, killing and causing serious bodily harm to members of a group. The second requirement is that these killings and serious bodily harm be committed with the intent to destroy, in whole or in part, a particular group targeted as such.

16. In the opinion of the Chamber, many facts show that the intention of the perpetrators of these killings was to cause the complete disappearance of the Tutsi people. In this connection, Alison DesForges, a specialist historian on Rwanda, who appeared as an expert witness, stated as follows: "on the basis of the statements made by certain political leaders, on the basis of songs and slogans popular among the interahamwe, I believe that these people had the intention of completely wiping out the Tutsi from Rwanda so that—as they said on certain occasions—their children, later on, should not know what a Tutsi looked like, unless they referred to history books". This testimony given by Dr. DesForges was confirmed by two prosecution witnesses, who testified separately be-

fore the Tribunal that one Silas Kubwimana said during a public meeting chaired by the Accused himself that all the Tutsi had to be killed so that someday Hutu children would not know what a Tutsi looked like. Dr. Zachariah also testified that the Achilles' tendons of many wounded persons were cut to prevent them from fleeing. In the opinion of the Chamber, this demonstrates the resolve of the perpetrators of these massacres not to spare any Tutsi. Their plan called for doing whatever was possible to prevent any Tutsi from escaping and, thus, to destroy the whole group. Dr. Alison DesForges stated that numerous Tutsi corpses were systematically thrown into the River Nyabarongo, a tributary of the Nile, as seen, incidentally, in several photographs shown in court throughout the trial. She explained that the intent in that gesture was "to send the Tutsi back to their origin", to make them "return to Abyssinia", in accordance with the notion that the Tutsi are a "foreign" group in Rwanda, believed to have come from the Nilotic regions.

17. Other testimonies heard, especially that of Major-General Dallaire, also show that there was an intention to wipe out the Tutsi group in its entirety, since even newborn babies were not spared. Many testimonies given before the Chamber concur on the fact that it was the Tutsi as members of an ethnic group who were targeted in the massacres. General Dallaire, Doctor Zachariah and, particularly, the Accused himself, unanimously stated so before the Chamber.

18. Numerous witnesses testified before the Chamber that the systematic checking of identity cards, on which the ethnic group was mentioned, made it possible to separate the Hutu from the Tutsi, with the latter being immediately arrested and often killed, sometimes on the spot, at the roadblocks which were erected in Kigali soon after the crash of the plane of President Habyarimana, and thereafter everywhere in the country.

19. Based on the evidence submitted to the Chamber, it is clear that the massacres which occurred in Rwanda in 1994 had a specific objective, namely the extermination of the Tutsi, who were targeted especially because of their Tutsi origin and not because they were RPF fighters. In any case, the Tutsi children and pregnant women would, naturally, not have been among the fighters. The Chamber concludes that, alongside the conflict between the RAF and the RPF, genocide was committed in Rwanda in 1994 against the Tutsi as a group. The execution of this genocide was probably facilitated by the conflict, in the sense that the conflict with the RPF forces served as a pretext for the propaganda inciting genocide against the Tutsi, by branding RPF fighters and Tutsi civilians together through the notion widely disseminated, particularly by Radio Television Libre des Mille Collines (RTLM), to the effect that every Tutsi was allegedly an accomplice of the RPF soldiers or "Inkotanyi". However, the fact that the genocide occurred while the RAF were in conflict with the RPF, obviously, cannot serve as a mitigating circumstance for the genocide.

20. Consequently, the Chamber concludes from all the foregoing that it was, indeed, genocide that was committed in Rwanda in 1994, against the Tutsi as a group. The Chamber is of the opinion that the genocide appears to have been meticulously organized. In fact, Dr. Alison Desforges testifying before the Chamber on 24 May 1997, talked of "centrally organized and supervised massacres". Some evidence supports this view that the genocide had been planned. First, the existence of lists of Tutsi to be eliminated is corroborated by many testimonies. In this respect, Dr. Zachariah mentioned the case of patients and nurses killed in a hospital because a soldier had a list including their names.

21. The Chamber holds that the genocide was organized and planned not only by members of the RAF, but also by the political forces who were behind the "Hutu-

power", that it was executed essentially by civilians including the armed militia and even ordinary citizens, and above all, that the majority of the Tutsi victims were non-combatants, including thousands of women and children.…

37. Having made its factual findings, the Chamber analysed the legal definitions proposed by the Prosecutor for each of the facts. It thus considered the applicable law for each of the three crimes under its jurisdiction, which is all the more important since this is the very first Judgement on the legal definitions of genocide on the one hand, and of serious violations of Additional Protocol II of the Geneva Conventions, on the other. Moreover, the Chamber also had to define certain crimes which constitute offences under its jurisdiction, in particular, rape, because to date, there is no commonly accepted definition of this term in international law.

38. In the opinion of the Chamber, rape is a form of aggression the central elements of which cannot be captured in a mechanical description of objects and body parts. The Chamber also notes the cultural sensitivities involved in public discussion of intimate matters and recalls the painful reluctance and inability of witnesses to disclose graphic anatomical details of the sexual violence they endured. The Chamber defines rape as a physical invasion of a sexual nature, committed on a person under circumstances which are coercive. Sexual violence, including rape, is not limited to physical invasion of the human body and may include acts which do not involve penetration or even physical contact. The Chamber notes in this context that coercive circumstances need not be evidenced by a show of physical force. Threats, intimidation, extortion and other forms of duress which prey on fear or desperation may constitute coercion.

39. The Chamber reviewed Article 6 (1) of its Statute, on the individual criminal responsibility of the accused for the three crimes constituting *ratione materiae* of the Chamber. Article 6(1) enunciates the basic principles of individual criminal liability which are probably common to most national criminal jurisdictions. Article 6(3), by contrast, constitutes something of an exception to the principles articulated in Article 6(1), an exception which derives from military law, particularly the principle of the liability of a commander for the acts of his subordinates or "command responsibility". Article 6(3) does not necessarily require the superior to have had knowledge of such to render him criminally liable. The only requirement is that he had reason to know that his subordinates were about to commit or had committed and failed to take the necessary or reasonable measures to prevent such acts or punish the perpetrators thereof.

40. The Chamber then expressed its opinion that with respect to the crimes under its jurisdiction, it should adhere to the concept of notional plurality of offences (cumulative charges) which would render multiple convictions permissible for the same act. As a result, a particular act may constitute both genocide and a crime against humanity.

41. On the crime of genocide, the Chamber recalls that the definition given by Article 2 of the Statute is echoed exactly by the Convention for the Prevention and Repression of the Crime of Genocide. The Chamber notes that Rwanda acceded, by legislative decree, to the Convention on Genocide on 12 February 1975. Thus, punishment of the crime of genocide did exist in Rwanda in 1994, at the time of the acts alleged in the Indictment, and the perpetrator was liable to be brought before the competent courts of Rwanda to answer for this crime.

42. Contrary to popular belief, the crime of genocide does not imply the actual extermination of a group in its entirety, but is understood as such once any one of the acts mentioned in Article 2 of the Statute is committed with the specific intent to destroy "in whole or in part" a national, ethnical, racial or religious group. Genocide is distinct

from other crimes inasmuch as it embodies a special intent or *dolus specialis*. Special intent of a crime is the specific intention, required as a constitutive element of the crime, which requires that the perpetrator clearly seek to produce the act charged. The special intent in the crime of genocide lies in "the intent to destroy, in whole or in part, a national, ethnical, racial or religious group, as such".

43. Specifically, for any of the acts charged under Article 2(2) of the Statute to be a constitutive element of genocide, the act must have been committed against one or several individuals, because such individual or individuals were members of a specific group, and specifically because they belonged to this group. Thus, the victim is chosen not because of his individual identity, but rather on account of his being a member of a national, ethnical, racial or religious group. The victim of the act is therefore a member of a group, targeted as such; hence, the victim of the crime of genocide is the group itself and not the individual alone.

44. On the issue of determining the offender's specific intent, the Chamber considers that intent is a mental factor which is difficult, even impossible, to determine. This is the reason why, in the absence of a confession from the Accused, his intent can be inferred from a certain number of presumptions of fact. The Chamber considers that it is possible to deduce the genocidal intent inherent in a particular act charged from the general context of the perpetration of other culpable acts systematically directed against that same group, whether these acts were committed by the same offender or by others. Other factors, such as the scale of atrocities committed, their general nature, in a region or a country, or furthermore, the fact of deliberately and systematically targeting victims on account of their membership of a particular group, while excluding the members of other groups, can enable the Chamber to infer the genocidal intent of a particular act.

45. Apart from the crime of genocide, Jean-Paul Akayesu is charged with complicity in genocide and direct and public incitement to commit genocide.

46. In the opinion of the Chamber, an Accused is an accomplice in genocide if he knowingly aided and abetted or provoked a person or persons to commit genocide, knowing that this person or persons were committing genocide, even if the Accused himself lacked the specific intent of destroying in whole or in part, the national, ethnical, racial or religious group, as such.

47. Regarding the crime of direct and public incitement to commit genocide, the Chamber defines it mainly on the basis of Article 91 of the Rwandan Penal Code, as directly provoking another to commit genocide, either through speeches, shouting or threats uttered in public places or at public gatherings, or through the sale or dissemination, offer for sale or display of written material or printed matter in public places or at public gatherings or through the public display of placards or posters, or by any other means of audiovisual communication. The moral element of this crime lies in the intent to directly encourage or provoke another to commit genocide. It presupposes the desire of the guilty to create, by his actions, within the person or persons whom he is addressing, the state of mind which is appropriate to the commission of a crime. In other words, the person who is inciting to commit genocide must have the specific intent of genocide: that of destroying in whole or in part, a national, ethnical, racial or religious group, as such. The Chamber believes that incitement is a formal offence, for which the mere method used is culpable. In other words, the offence is considered to have been completed once the incitement has taken place and that it is direct and public, whether or not it was successful....

51. With regard to count one on genocide, the Chamber having regard, particularly, to the acts described in paragraphs 12(A) and 12(B) of the Indictment, that is, rape and

sexual violence, the Chamber wishes to underscore the fact that in its opinion, they constitute genocide in the same way as any other act as long as they were committed with the specific intent to destroy, in whole or in part, a particular group, targeted as such. Indeed, rape and sexual violence certainly constitute infliction of serious bodily and mental harm on the victims. See above, the findings of the Trial Chamber on the Chapter relating to the law applicable to the crime of genocide, in particular, the definition of the constituent elements of genocide, and are even, according to the Chamber, one of the worst ways of inflicting harm on the victim as he or she suffers both bodily and mental harm. In light of all the evidence before it, the Chamber is satisfied that the acts of rape and sexual violence described above, were committed solely against Tutsi women, many of whom were subjected to the worst public humiliation, mutilated, and raped several times, often in public, in the Bureau Communal premises or in other public places, and often by more than one assailant. These rapes resulted in physical and psychological destruction of Tutsi women, their families and their communities. Sexual violence was an integral part of the process of destruction, specifically targeting Tutsi women and specifically contributing to their destruction and to the destruction of the Tutsi group as a whole.

52. The rape of Tutsi women was systematic and was perpetrated against all Tutsi women and solely against them. A Tutsi woman, married to a Hutu, testified before the Chamber that she was not raped because her ethnic background was unknown. As part of the propaganda campaign geared to mobilizing the Hutu against the Tutsi, the Tutsi women were presented as sexual objects. Indeed, the Chamber was told, for an example, that before being raped and killed, Alexia, who was the wife of the Professor, Ntereye, and her two nieces, were forced by the Interahamwe to undress and ordered to run and do exercises "in order to display the thighs of Tutsi women". The Interahamwe who raped Alexia said, as he threw her on the ground and got on top of her, "let us now see what the vagina of a Tutsi woman tastes like". As stated above, Akayesu himself, speaking to the Interahamwe who were committing the rapes, said to them: "don't ever ask again what a Tutsi woman tastes like".

53. On the basis of the substantial testimonies brought before it, the Chamber finds that in most cases, the rapes of Tutsi women in Taba, were accompanied with the intent to kill those women. Many rapes were perpetrated near mass graves where the women were taken to be killed. A victim testified that Tutsi women caught could be taken away by peasants and men with the promise that they would be collected later to be executed. Following an act of gang rape, a witness heard Akayesu say, "tomorrow they will be killed" and they were actually killed. In this respect, it appears clearly to the Chamber that the acts of rape and sexual violence, as other acts of serious bodily and mental harm committed against the Tutsi, reflected the determination to make Tutsi women suffer and to mutilate them even before killing them, the intent being to destroy the Tutsi group while inflicting acute suffering on its members in the process.

54. The Chamber has already established that genocide was committed against the Tutsi group in Rwanda in 1994, throughout the period covering the events alleged in the Indictment. Owing to the very high number of atrocities committed against the Tutsi, their widespread nature not only in the commune of Taba, but also throughout Rwanda, and to the fact that the victims were systematically and deliberately selected because they belonged to the Tutsi group, with persons belonging to other groups being excluded, the Chamber is also able to infer, beyond reasonable doubt, the genocidal intent of the accused in the commission of the above-mentioned crimes; to the extent that the actions and words of Akayesu during the period of the facts alleged in the

Indictment, the Chamber is convinced beyond reasonable doubt, on the basis of evidence adduced before it during the hearing, that he repeatedly made statements more or less explicitly calling for the commission of genocide. Yet, according to the Chamber, he who incites another to commit genocide must have the specific intent to commit genocide: that of destroying in whole or in part, a national, ethnical, racial, or religious group, as such.

55. In conclusion, regarding Count One on genocide, the Chamber is satisfied beyond reasonable doubt that these various acts were committed by Akayesu with the specific intent to destroy the Tutsi group, as such. Consequently, the Chamber is of the opinion that the acts alleged in paragraphs 12, 12A, 12B, 16, 18, 19, 20, 22 and 23 of the Indictment, constitute the crimes of killing members of the Tutsi group and causing serious bodily and mental harm to members of the Tutsi group. Furthermore, the Chamber is satisfied beyond reasonable doubt that in committing the various acts alleged, Akayesu had the specific intent of destroying the Tutsi group as such.

56. Regarding Count Two, on the crime of complicity in genocide, the Chamber indicated *supra* that, in its opinion, the crime of genocide and that of complicity in genocide were two distinct crimes, and that the same person could certainly not be both the principal perpetrator of, and accomplice to, the same offence. Given that genocide and complicity in genocide are mutually exclusive by definition, the accused cannot obviously be found guilty of both these crimes for the same act. However, since the Prosecutor has charged the accused with both genocide and complicity in genocide for each of the alleged acts, the Chamber deems it necessary, in the instant case, to rule on Counts 1 and 2 simultaneously, so as to determine, as far as each proven fact is concerned, whether it constituted genocide or complicity in genocide....

Notes and Questions

1. The *Akayesu* Judgment also recognized that "[t]he Genocide Convention is undeniably ... customary international law...." *Id.* at para. 495. The Chamber also recognized that bodily or mental harm "does not necessarily mean ... permanent and irremediable" harm (*id.* at para. 502); that an "ethnic group is generally defined as a group whose members share a common language or culture" (*id.* at para. 513); that, according to the *travaux préparatoires* concerning the Convention, groups covered include "any group which is stable and permanent like the said four groups ... and [if] membership is by birth" (*id.* at para. 516); and that with respect to *mens rea* there should be a "clear intent to destroy, in whole or in part," and the "offender is culpable because he knew or should have known that the act committed would destroy, in whole or in part, a group" (*id.* at para. 520).

2. In *The Prosecutor v. Karemera, Ngirumpatse, and Nzirorera*, ICTR-98-44-AR73(C) (Appeals Chamber, 16 June 2006), the Appeals Chamber ruled that Trial Chambers of the ICTR must henceforth take judicial notice of the following: (1) the existence of Twa, Tutsi and Hutu as protected groups falling under the Genocide Convention; (2) between 6 April and 17 July 1994 there were throughout Rwanda widespread or systematic attacks against a civilian population based on Tutsi ethnic identification, during the attacks some Rwandan citizens killed or caused serious bodily injury or mental harm to persons perceived to be Tutsi, as a result there were a large number of deaths of persons of Tutsi ethnic identify; and (3) between 6 April and 17 July 1994 there was genocide in Rwanda against the Tutsi ethnic group.

3. In *Akayesu*, the Trial Chamber held that "the crime of genocide and that of complicity in genocide were two distinct crimes" with different mental elements. *Id.* at para. 56. The Trial Chamber stated:

> In the opinion of the Chamber, an Accused is an accomplice in genocide if he knowingly aided and abetted or provoked a person or persons to commit genocide, knowing that this person or persons were committing genocide, even if the Accused himself lacked the specific intent of destroying in whole or in part, the national, ethnical, racial or religious group, as such.

Id. at para. 46.

Therefore, according to the Trial Chamber in *Akayesu*, "complicity," "accomplice," and "aided and abetted" reflect basically the same type of responsibility and in order to convict a person of complicity in genocide the prosecutor is not required to prove that the accused acted with genocidal intent. The prosecutor is only required to prove that the accused knowingly assisted persons to commit genocide, knowing that such persons were committing genocide.

The *Akayesu* Trial Chamber's view of complicity in genocide has been rejected by other Trial Chambers and affirmed by others. Apparently, one question exists whether "complicity in genocide" (which is the phrase found in Article III (e) of the Genocide Convention and in some parts of the Statutes of the ICTY and ICTR) should be treated differently than complicity to commit other international crimes, since genocide as such requires a special criminal intent. Does complicity in genocide also require a special *mens rea*? In *Prosecutor v. Karemera, et al.,* ICTR-98-44-T (Trial Chamber Judgement, 18 May 2006), the Trial Chamber held that "complicity is one of the forms of criminal responsibility that is applicable to the crime of genocide, and not a crime itself." *Id.* at para. 7. The Trial Chamber in *Karemera* further stated:

> Whereas the genocide is the crime, joint criminal enterprise and complicity in genocide are two modes of liability, two methods by which the crime of genocide can be committed and individuals held responsible for this crime.... Complicity can only be pleaded as a form of liability for the crime of genocide.

Id. at para. 8. Therefore, according to Karemera, *in order to convict an accused of genocide under a theory of complicity, the prosecution must prove genocidal intent.* But see Prosecutor v. Semanza, *ICTR-97-20-T, at 394 (Trial Judgement, 15 May 2003), at para. 394 (finding no material distinction between aiding and abetting and complicity in genocide).*

The *Karemera* Trial Chamber's construction of complicity in genocide seems at odds with the Statute of the ICTY. Article 4(3) provides:

The following acts shall be punishable:

(a) genocide;

(b) conspiracy to commit genocide;

(c) direct and public incitement to commit genocide;

(d) attempt to commit genocide;

(e) complicity in genocide.

Article 4(3) lists different genocide-related crimes, including complicity in genocide. Article 7(1) sets forth a list of different forms of liability, different ways in which the crimes within the jurisdiction of the ICTY can be committed, including the acts of genocide proscribed in Article 4(3). Article 7(1) provides:

> A person who planned, instigated, ordered, committed or otherwise aided and abetted in planning, preparation or execution of a crime referred to in articles 2 to 5 of the present Statute, shall be individually responsible for the crime.

Complicity as such is not mentioned in the different methods of criminal responsibility set forth in Article 7(1), although the Statute authorizes individual criminal liability for aiding and abetting. As noted in *Akayesu* and *Semanza*, are they basically the same forms of responsibility? The Statute of the ICTR is similarly structured. *See* Statute of the ICTR, arts. 2(3) and 6(1).

Which position do you prefer? Should complicity in genocide be construed as a separate crime or merely a method by which genocide can be committed? For articles discussing the inconsistent application of complicity in genocide by the ICTY and ICTR, *see* Grant Dawson & Rachel Boynton, *Reconciling Complicity in Genocide and Aiding and Abetting Genocide in the Jurisprudence of the United Nations Ad Hoc Tribunals*, 21 HARV. HUM. RTS. J. 241 (2008); Daniel M. Greenfield, *The Crime of Complicity in Genocide: How the International Criminal Tribunals for Rwanda and Yugoslavia Got It Wrong, and Why It Matters,* 98 J. CRIM. L. & CRIMINOLOGY 921 (2008). Professor Elies van Sliedregt of the University of Amsterdam has written that under the case law of the ICTY and ICTR "the content and meaning of complicity in genocide remains unclear and contested" and the fact that the Statutes of the tribunals both contain separate parts with respect to complicity in genocide and aiding and abetting "has given rise to contradictory rulings." Elies van Sliedregt, *Complicity to Commit Genocide*, in THE UN GENOCIDE CONVENTION: A COMMENTARY 162, 163, 169 (Paola Gaeta ed. 2009), adding: "it is by now accepted that the reason for this coexistence [of the two phrases] in the Statutes is bad drafting." *Id.* at 167 (citing *Krstic*, *Semanza*, and G. METTRAUX, INTERNATIONAL CRIMES AND THE AD HOC TRIBUNALS 257 (2006). He also notes: "At the ICTY, it is by now a well-established rule that the *mens rea* for aiding and abetting is knowledge of the intent of the principal and the awareness that one's acts or conduct will assist the principal in the commission of the crimes. The aider and abettor need not share the principal's *mens rea*.... Eventually, the ICTR Appeals Chamber in *Ntakirutimana* brought the ICTR law in harmony with ICTY case law.... [But] the *ad hoc* Tribunal's case law remains unclear as to what the appropriate mental standard for complicity in genocide is." *Id.* at 170-71.

4. In *Prosecutor of Kalimanzira*, ICTR-05-88-A (Appeals Chamber Judgement, 20 Oct. 2010), the Appeals Chamber distinguished the crime of direct and public incitement to commit genocide (which is punishable under Article 2(3)(c)) from instigating genocide (punishable under Article 6(1)). The most important difference is that the acts constituting incitement must be "direct" and unequivocally "public." The Appeals Chamber observed that "all convictions before the Tribunal for direct and public incitement to commit genocide involve speeches made to large, fully public assemblies, messages disseminated by the media, and communications made through public address system over a broad public area." *Id.* at para. 156. The Chamber held that public incitement to genocide pertained to mass communications, and that private incitement such as private conversations, meetings or messages, was specifically excluded. *Id.* at para. 158.

5. In the Rome Statute of the ICC, the offense of direct and public incitement to commit genocide has been eliminated as a separate offense. "Direct and public incitement" is recast under Article 25(3)(e) as a mode of individual criminal responsibility. Should "direct and public incitement" to commit genocide be treated as a separate crime, as it is under Articles 2(3)(c) and 4(3)(c), respectively, of the ICTR and ICTY statutes, or merely as a form of individual criminal liability, the position embraced by

Article 25(3)(e) of the Statute of the ICC? *See* Chile Eboe-Osuji, *"Complicity in Geno-cide" versus "Aiding and Abetting Genocide": Construing the Difference in the ICTR and ICTY Statutes*, 3 J. Int'l Crim. Just. 56, 60 n. 15 (2005) (arguing that "direct and public incitement" should be a separate crime).

The Prosecutor v. Rutaganda, ICTR-96-3-T (6 Dec. 1999)

Before: Judge Laïty Kama, Presiding

        Judge Lennart Aspegren

        Judge Navanethem Pillay

48. The Chamber accepts that the crime of genocide involves, firstly, that one of the acts listed under Article 2(2) of the Statute be committed; secondly, that such an act be committed against a national, ethnical, racial or religious group, specifically targeted as such; and, thirdly, that the "act be committed with the intent to destroy, in whole or in part, the targeted group".

The Acts Enumerated under Article 2(2)(a) to (e) of the Statute

49. Article 2(2)(a) of the Statute, like the corresponding provisions of the Genocide Convention, refers to "*meurtre*" in the French version and to "killing" in the English version. In the opinion of the Chamber, the term "killing" includes both intentional and unintentional homicides, whereas the word "*meurtre*" covers homicide committed with the intent to cause death. Given the presumption of innocence, and pursuant to the general principles of criminal law, the Chamber holds that the version more favourable to the Accused should be adopted, and finds that Article 2(2)(a) of the Statute must be interpreted in accordance with the definition of murder in the Criminal Code of Rwanda, which provides, under Article 311, that "Homicide committed with intent to cause death shall be treated as murder".

50. For the purposes of interpreting Article 2(2)(b) of the Statute, the Chamber understands the words "serious bodily or mental harm" to include acts of bodily or mental torture, inhumane or degrading treatment, rape, sexual violence, and persecution. The Chamber is of the opinion that "serious harm" need not entail permanent or irremediable harm.

51. In the opinion of the Chamber, the words "deliberately inflicting on the group conditions of life calculated to bring about its physical destruction in whole or in part", as indicated in Article 2(2)(c) of the Statute, are to be construed "as methods of destruction by which the perpetrator does not necessarily intend to immediately kill the members of the group", but which are, ultimately, aimed at their physical destruction. The Chamber holds that the means … include subjecting a group of people to a subsistence diet, systematic expulsion from their homes and deprivation of essential medical supplies below a minimum vital standard.

52. For the purposes of interpreting Article 2(2)(d) of the Statute, the Chamber holds that the words "measures intended to prevent births within the group" should be construed as including sexual mutilation, enforced sterilization, forced birth control, forced separation of males and females, and prohibition of marriages. The Chamber notes that measures intended to prevent births within the group may be not only physical, but also mental.

53. The Chamber is of the opinion that the provisions of Article 2(2)(e) of the Statute, on the forcible transfer of children from one group to another, are aimed at

sanctioning not only any direct act of forcible physical transfer, but also any acts of threats or trauma which would lead to the forcible transfer of children from one group to another group.

Potential Groups of Victims of the Crime of Genocide

55. The Chamber notes that the concepts of national, ethnical, racial and religious groups have been researched extensively and that, at present, there are no generally and internationally accepted precise definitions thereof. Each of these concepts must be assessed in the light of a particular political, social and cultural context. Moreover, the Chamber notes that for the purposes of applying the Genocide Convention, membership of a group is, in essence, a subjective rather than an objective concept. The victim is perceived by the perpetrator of genocide as belonging to a group slated for destruction. In some instances, the victim may perceive himself/herself as belonging to the said group.

56. Nevertheless, the Chamber is of the view that a subjective definition alone is not enough to determine victim groups, as provided for in the Genocide Convention. It appears, from a reading of the *travaux préparatoires* of the Genocide Convention, that certain groups, such as political and economic groups, have been excluded from the protected groups, because they are considered to be "mobile groups" which one joins through individual, political commitment. That would seem to suggest *a contrario* that the Convention was presumably intended to cover relatively stable and permanent groups.

57. Therefore, the Chamber holds that in assessing whether a particular group may be considered as protected from the crime of genocide, it will proceed on a case-by-case basis, taking into account both the relevant evidence proffered and the political and cultural context as indicated *supra....*

60. The *dolus specialis* is a key element of an intentional offence, which offence is characterized by a psychological nexus between the physical result and the mental state of the perpetrator. With regard to the issue of determining the offender's specific intent, the Chamber applies the following reasoning, as held in the *Akayesu Judgement*:

> " [...] intent is a mental factor which is difficult, even impossible, to determine. This is the reason why, in the absence of a confession from the accused, his intent can be inferred from a certain number of presumptions of fact. The Chamber is of the view that the genocidal intent inherent in a particular act charged can be inferred from the general context of the perpetration of other culpable acts systematically directed against that same group, whether these acts were committed by the same offender or by others. Other factors, such as the scale of atrocities committed, their general nature, in a region or a country, or furthermore, the fact of deliberately and systematically targeting victims on account of their membership of a particular group, while excluding the members of other groups, can enable the Chamber to infer the genocidal intent of a particular act."

61. Similarly, in the *Kayishema and Ruzindana Judgement*, Trial Chamber II held that:

> "[...] The Chamber finds that the intent can be inferred either from words or deeds and may be determined by a pattern of purposeful action. In particular, the Chamber considers evidence such as [...] the methodical way of planning, the systematic manner of killing. [...]"

62. Therefore, the Chamber is of the view that, in practice, intent can be, on a case-by-case basis, inferred from the material evidence submitted to the Chamber, including the evidence which demonstrates a consistent pattern of conduct by the Accused.

The Prosecutor v. Musema, ICTR-96-13-T (27 Jan. 2000)

Before: Judge Lennart Aspegren, Presiding

      Judge Laïty Kama

      Judge Navanethem Pillay

      Conspiracy to Commit Genocide

195.... [T]he Chamber raised the question as to whether an accused could be convicted of both genocide and conspiracy to commit genocide.

196. Under Civil Law systems, if the conspiracy is successful and the substantive offence is consummated, the accused will only be convicted of the substantive offence and not of the conspiracy. Further, once the substantive crime has been accomplished and the criminal conduct of the accused is established, there is no reason to punish the accused for his mere *résolution criminelle* (criminal intent), or even for the preparatory acts committed in furtherance of the substantive offence. Therefore an accused can only be convicted of conspiracy if the substantive offence has not been realized or if the Accused was part of a conspiracy which has been perpetrated by his co-conspirators, without his direct participation.

197. Under Common Law, an accused can, in principle, be convicted of both conspiracy and a substantive offence, in particular, where the objective of the conspiracy extends beyond the offences actually committed. However, this position has incurred much criticism. Thus, for example, according to Don Stuart:

> "The true issue is not whether evidence has been used twice to achieve convictions but rather whether the fundamental nature of the conspiracy offence is best seen [...] as purely preventive, incomplete offence, auxiliary offence to the principal offence and having no true independent rationale to exist on its own alongside the full offence. On this view it inexorably follows that once the completed offence has been committed there is no justification for also punishing the incomplete offence."

198. In the instant case, the Chamber has adopted the definition of conspiracy most favourable to Musema, whereby an accused cannot be convicted of both genocide and conspiracy to commit genocide on the basis of the same acts. Such a definition is in keeping with the intention of the Genocide Convention. Indeed, the "*Travaux Préparatoires*" show that the crime of conspiracy was included to punish acts which, in and of themselves, did not constitute genocide. The converse implication of this is that no purpose would be served in convicting an accused, who has already been found guilty of genocide, for conspiracy to commit genocide, on the basis of the same acts.

Notes and Questions

1. Can conspiracy to commit genocide amount to more than an "incomplete offence," involving a greater threat or evil than acts of genocide because of the conspiratorial agreement to commit genocide? Does the evil of acts of genocide relate more to the intent of the perpetrator (*i.e.*, to target persons because they are thought to be members of a certain group(s)) than the acts of killing, etc., that are also elements of the offense and numbers of direct victims? If so, is the evil intent that is connected with acts of genocide magnified when there is a conspiracy as opposed to lone, ad hoc acts of genocide by one perpetrator?

Professor Jens David Ohlin has noted that "conspiracy is an inchoate offence, and a completed genocide need not occur for a conviction to obtain." He adds: "The Trial Chamber's view [in *Musema*] was rejected by other trial chambers in several cases which allowed convictions for both genocide and conspiracy to commit genocide," citing *The Prosecutor v. Nahimana*, ICTR-99-52-T (3 Dec. 2003), at para. 1043; *The Prosecutor v. Niyitegeka*, ICTR-96-14-T (16 May 2003), at para. 502. Jens David Ohlin, *Incitement and Conspiracy to Commit Genocide* in The Genocide Convention: A Commentary 218, 220 (Paola Gaeta ed., 2009).

2. In *The Prosecutor v. Niyitegeka*, ICTR-96-14-T (May 15, 2003), *aff'd* (Appeals Chamber July 9, 2004), the Trial Chamber used circumstantial evidence of intent to find a broadcaster guilty of conspiracy to commit genocide and direct and public incitement of genocide. The Trial Chamber stated that conspiracy to commit genocide is "defined as an agreement between two or more persons to commit the crime of genocide. *Id.* para. 423. *The Prosecutor v. Nahimana, Barayagwiza, and Ngeze*, ICTR-99-52-T (Dec. 3, 2003), found defendants guilty of conspiracy to commit genocide and direct and public incitement to commit genocide on the basis of circumstantial evidence, citing the Trial Chamber in *Niyitegeka*. In *The Prosecutor v. Semanza*, ICTR-97-20-T (May 15, 2003), the Trial Chamber found the defendant guilty of complicity to commit genocide and crimes against humanity.

3. In *Prosecutor v. Nahimana, et al.*, ICTR-99-52-A (Appeals Chamber Judgement, 28 Nov. 2007), the Appeals Chamber held that a concerted agreement may be inferred from the alleged conspirators' conduct, in particular their "concerted or coordinated action," but that the existence of a concerted agreement "must be the only reasonable inference based on the totality of the evidence" for the *actus reus* to be satisfied. The Appeals Chamber, by a 4-1 majority, set aside the convictions of Nahimana, Barayagwizq and Ngeze for conspiracy to commit genocide, finding that the existence of a conspiracy was not the only reasonable inference from the appellants' concerted activities. What is the legal authority for requiring that the existence of a conspiratorial agreement "must be the only reasonable inference" to be drawn for the appellants' concerted action? Does this standard impose an unreasonable burden on the prosecution seeking to convict for conspiracy to commit genocide?

4. Concerning rape or sexual violence as a means of committing genocide, as an *actus reus*, also see Karen Engle, *Feminism and Its (Dis)contents: Criminalizing Wartime Rape in Bosnia and Herzegovina*, 99 Am. J. Int'l L. 778 (2005); Johan D. van der Vyver, *Prosecution and Punishment of the Crime of Genocide*, 23 Fordham Int'l L.J. 286, 300-01, 310-12 (1999), also offering an expanded conceptualization of *dolus directus* versus *indirectus* and *eventualis*. *Id.* at 307-08. Also recall the extract from *Musema* in Chapter Two.

5. The ICTY and ICTR have used two approaches to define the notion of a national, ethnic, racial, or religious group: objective and subjective. In accordance with the objective approach, "the group should be regarded as a social fact, a reality regarded as stable and permanent. Individuals are members of the group automatically and irreversibly by way of being born within the group." Agnieszka Szpak, *National, Ethnic, Racial, and Religious Groups Protected Against Genocide in the Jurisprudence of the Ad Hoc International Criminal Tribunals*, 23 Eur. J. Int'l L. 155, 173 (2012). "The subjective approach presupposes in turn that the group exists as much as its members perceive themselves as belonging to that group (self-identification) or are as such perceived by the perpetrators of the genocide (identification by others)." *Id.* Which is the better approach, the objective or subjective? Should a hybrid objective/subjective approach be used to identify whether the victims were members of a protected group?

6. Concerning the "extension" of groups listed in Article II of the Convention in *Akayesu* and *Rutaganda* and claims that genocide under customary international law includes a broader reach with respect to targeted groups, *see, e.g.*, van der Vyver, *supra* at 304-06, 318 ("jurisprudence of international tribunals exceeds the bounds ... by extending the protection afforded to target groups to include all institutional groups (those whose membership are not exclusively determined by voluntary entry into and exit from the group), such as gay and lesbian communities."), 355 ("provided only that one is ... born into the social group"); Schabas, *supra* at 1713 (The Darfur Commission Report "went too far in suggesting that the interpretive expansion of the four groups enumerated in the Genocide Convention 'has become part and parcel of international customary law.'"). The Trial Chamber in *Akayesu* declared that the prohibited targetings reach "'stable' groups, constituting in a permanent fashion and membership ... which is determined by birth, with the exclusion of the more 'mobile' groups which one joins through individual voluntary commitment, such as political and economic groups." ICTR-96-4-T, para. 510 (2 Sept. 1998). Recall para. 56 in *Rutaganda*, *supra*.

Should the crime of genocide punish killings committed with the "intent to destroy in whole or part" "stable" groups, but exempt from coverage killings committed with the same intent directed against "mobile" groups? What is the justification for this distinction? How do you determine whether someone is a member of a "stable" or "mobile" group? Is gender a "stable" group? Should genocide be extended to include gender killings committed with genocidal intent?

7. The 2005 Darfur Commission of Inquiry Report recognized that "various tribes that have been the object of attacks and killings ... do not appear to make up ethnic groups distinct from the ethnic group to which persons or militias that attack them belong. They speak the same language (Arabic) and embrace the same religion (Muslim)" and "objectively the two sets of persons at issue do not make up two distinct protected groups," but there has grown "a self-perception of two distinct groups," one "African" and the other "Arab" and what is important in this context is that the perpetrator and victim "see each other and themselves as constituting distinct groups." See Report, *supra* at paras. 508-509, 511. The Report adds: "What matters from a legal point of view is the fact that the interpretive expansion of one of the elements of the notion of genocide (the concept of protected group) by the two International Criminal Tribunals is in line with the object and scope of the rules on genocide (to protect from deliberate annihilation essentially stable and permanent human groups), ... which are no longer identified only by their objective connotations but also on the basis of the subjective perceptions of members of groups." *Id.* para. 501.

What is critical under the Convention, that targetings actually be made against the types of human groups listed in Article II or that there be a genocidal intent to destroy such a human group in whole or in part? Could a mistaken genocidal targeting constitute genocide or merely an attempt? Note that the Darfur Commission Report accepts both an expansion of groups to include "stable and permanent human groups" and a subjective approach to genocidal targetings based primarily on intent as opposed to objective features of context. Professor Schabas is critical of both of these approaches, but notes acceptance of the "subjective approach" in other ICTR cases. Schabas, *supra* at 1712-14, citing *The Prosecutor v. Semanza*, ICTR-97-20-T (Judgement and Sentence, May 15, 2003), para. 317; *The Prosecutor v. Kajelijeli*, ICTR-98-44A-T (Judgment and Sentence, Dec. 1, 2003), para. 811. Which approaches do you prefer?

8. Concerning claims that the reach of customary prohibitions of genocide include targetings of political groups as such, *see, e.g.,* U.N. G.A. Res. 96(I) (1946); Matthew Lippman, *The Convention on the Prevention and Punishment of the Crime of Genocide: Fifty Years Later*, 15 ARIZ. J. INT'L & COMP. L. 415, 464 (1998); Beth Van Schaack, *The Crime of Political Genocide: Repairing the Genocide Convention's Blind Spot*, 106 YALE L.J. 2259 (1997); van der Vyver, *supra* at 355; materials in Section 3. Recall from Chapter Two that political "persecution" can constitute a crime against humanity.

9. In *The Prosecutor v. Rwamakuba*, ICTR-98-44-AR72.4 (Appeals Chamber, Decision on Interlocutory Appeal Regarding Application of Joint Criminal Enterprise to the Crime of Genocide, 22 Oct. 2004), the Appeals Chamber found that customary international law prior to 1992 criminalized the intentional participation in a common plan to commit genocide and recognized application of the doctrine of joint criminal enterprise to the crime of genocide, noting that the doctrine of "joint criminal enterprise does not create a separate crime of participating through the means identified in that doctrine ... [and] is only concerned with the mode of liability of committing crimes within the jurisdiction of the Tribunal." *Id.* paras. 14, 30-31. The drafting history of the Convention, the Chamber declared, makes "clear that the Contracting Parties sought to ensure that all persons involved in a campaign to commit genocide, at whatever stage, were subject to criminal responsibility ... [although i]t is not clear whether the drafters viewed criminal responsibility through intentional participation in a common plan as a form of commission of genocide, complicity in genocide, or conspiracy to commit genocide." *Id.* paras. 26-28.

10. In April, 2001, four Rwandan nationals (Messrs. Ntezimana and Higaniro, and two nuns, Mukangango, and Mukabutera) appeared before Belgium's Cour d'Assises. They were accused of genocide and crimes against humanity with respect to several homicides in the Butare region of Rwanda. It was the first prosecution under a 1993 Belgian law allowing prosecution for war crimes, human rights violations, and related crimes. The two nuns were found guilty in 2001. In June, 2005, two Rwandans (Nzabonimana and Ndashyikirwa) were found guilty of war crimes and murder in connection with genocidal massacres. The Belgian law was amended in 2003, limiting jurisdiction to cases involving Belgian citizens and residents.

11. Regarding domestic prosecutions, see also Wolfgang Kaleck, *From Pinochet to Rumsfeld: Universal Jurisdiction in Europe 1998-2008*, 30 MICH. J. INT'L L. 927, 932-33 (four convicted in Belgium), 935 (Belgian conviction of Rwandan Major), 938 (French cases), 939 (Swiss conviction and some cases transferred to the ICTR), 944 (case in the Netherlands), 946-47 (in Denmark, case against former official dropped because of insufficient evidence), 948 (investigations in Norway), 957 (investigations in Spain) (2009); Máximo Langer, *The Diplomacy of Universal Jurisdiction: The Political Branches*

and the Transnational Prosecution of International Crimes, 105 A_M. J. I_NT'_L_ L. 1, 8-9, 13-14 (current proceedings in Germany), 22-23 (pending cases in France), 28, 32 (convictions in Belgium), 42 (trials in Belgium, Canada, the Netherlands, and Switzerland) (2011); BBC, Rwandan Genocide Conviction, May 23, 2009 (conviction in Canada), available at http://www.bbc.co.uk/worldservice/africa/2009/05/090523_rwanda_canada.shtml; Edmund Kagire, *Another Genocide Fugitive Arrested in Belgium*, N.Y. T_IMES_, Apr. 21, 2011; Matti Huuhtanen, *Ex-Pastor Jailed for Life in Finland Genocide Conviction*, T_HE_ S_TAR_, June 11, 2010; Jordan J. Paust, *Genocide in Rwanda, State Responsibility to Prosecute or Extradite, and Nonimmunity for Heads of State and Other Public Officials*, 34 H_OUS_. J. I_NT'_L L. 57, 58-62 (2011) (also addressing prosecutions in Rwanda).http://www.thestar.com/printarticle/822213

B. Prosecutions Before the International Criminal Tribunal for Former Yugoslavia

Crimes against humanity, including genocide, were committed on a vast scale in Rwanda in 1994 and have led to prosecutions within Rwanda and in an International Criminal Tribunal for Rwanda (ICTR) that was created by the United Nations Security Council in November 1994. By August 2011, there had been eighty-two cases before the ICTR that resulted in fifty-seven convictions or cases pending appeal, one case awaiting trial, ten cases in progress, eight acquittals, two detainees released, two detainees deceased before judgment, and two cases transferred to national jurisdiction in France.

Prosecutions of genocide before the Trial Chambers of the ICTY demonstrated a problem concerning proof beyond a reasonable doubt of genocidal intent to destroy a group in whole or in part when circumstantial evidence of such an intent is utilized.

In *The Prosecutor v. Jelisic*, IT-95-10-T (Trial Chamber, Dec. 14, 1999 and Appeals Chamber, Judgment, July 5, 2001), Goran Jelisic, a low ranking policeman who tortured and killed detainees in concentration camps in 1992 in Brcko, was convicted of 31 counts of war crimes and crimes against humanity but acquitted of genocide. The Trial Chamber ruled that there was insufficient evidence to establish beyond a reasonable doubt that he had the requisite intent to destroy a group of Muslims in whole or in part, although he chose victims because they belonged to such a group. The Trial Chamber stressed that the prosecution had not proven that his conduct was engaged in as part of a larger plan to destroy such a group and that the number of direct victims was not a substantial number of the overall group, which presumably would aid in the use of circumstantial evidence to prove genocidal intent.

In *The Prosecutor v. Sikirica*, IT-95-8-T (Trial Chamber, Judgment on Defence Motions to Acquit, Sept. 3, 2001), the same problem of proof was evident. Dusko Sikirica was the commander of a concentration camp at Prijedor where hundreds of Bosnian Muslims and Croats were tortured and killed. The Trial Chamber ruled that the prosecution had not proven genocidal intent beyond a reasonable doubt when the existence of large numbers of victims might have been the result of random killings as opposed to genocidal killings, especially when they were not simply exterminated soon after capture, the victims did not seem to have any special significance to their community except that most were young men who could be used for military service, and the Bosnian

Serb leaders in the area had transferred women, children and elderly Muslims and Croats out of the area instead of killing them.

In *The Prosecutor v. Krstic*, IT-98-33-T (Trial Chamber, Aug. 2, 2001), the Trial Chamber found General Radislav Krstic guilty of genocide during his Bosnian Serb Drina Corps capture of Srebrenica in 1995 where thousands were massacred. General Krstic was also a member of the Bosnian Serb Army's Main Staff. The Trial Chamber also found him guilty of persecution, cruel and inhumane treatment, terrorizing a civilian population, forcible transfer of persons, and destruction of property as crimes against humanity, as well as murder as a war crime. *See, e.g.,* Mark Drumbl, *ICTY Authenticates Genocide at Srebrenica and Convicts for Aiding and Abetting,* 5 MELBOURNE J. INT'L L. 434, 435 n.5 (2004). The prosecution proved that genocide had occurred in the area of Srebrenica, since the widespread and systematic killings could not have occurred without a genocidal plan even though women and children had been transferred out of the area. Moreover, the Trial Chamber used a "joint criminal enterprise" aspect of criminal responsibility that had been established in *The Prosecutor v. Tadic,* IT-94-1-A and IT-94-1-A*bis* (Jan. 26, 2000), whereby guilt can be established when one knowingly participates in acts to advance the goal of a joint criminal enterprise (which "embraces actions perpetrated by a collectivity of persons in furtherance of a common criminal design." *Tadic* at paras. 193, 220). However, his conviction was reduced by the Appeals Chamber from genocide and complicity in genocide (under Article 4(3)(e) of the Statute of the ICTY) to aiding and abetting genocide under Article 7(1) of the Statute. The Appeals Chamber found that evidence supported the conclusion that General Krstic was aware of the intent to commit genocide by troops under his command, but that this alone did not prove that he had a genocidal intent. IT-98-33-A, at paras. 129, 134, 140 (Appeals Chamber, judgment, Apr. 19, 2004). Nonetheless, at a later time he became clearly involved as an aider and abettor of genocide committed by others and he participated in a criminal enterprise in that fashion, *i.e.,* he knowingly aided others who had genocidal intent as they engaged in acts of genocide.

Confusion exists with respect to the statement of the Appeals Chamber in *Krstic* that "[i]t is well established that where a conviction of genocide relies on the intent to destroy a protected group 'in part,' the part must be a substantial part of that group," since there is no such requirement in the Genocide Convention or in the Statute of the ICTY. Was this a statement as to elements of the crime or merely a statement concerning use of circumstantial evidence as proof of genocidal intent? Adding to the confusion, the Appeals Chamber set forth circumstantially-based elements of a supposed "substantial" part requirement, including the number of persons targeted, the prominence of the targeted part (especially men of military age) within the overall group, the area of targetings, the likely impact of the targetings on the survival of the group (*e.g.,* killing of Muslim men of military age could have "severe procreative implications for the Srebrenica Muslim community, potentially consigning the community to extinction." Moreover, the killing of more than 7,000 men of military age was, "assuredly, a physical destruction [in part], and given the scope of the killings, the Trial Chamber could legitimately draw the inference that their extermination was motivated by genocidal intent." *Id.* para. 27. *See also* Trial Chamber, Judgment, para. 91: "the elimination of virtually all the men [from Srebrenica] has made it almost impossible for the Bosnian Muslim women ... to successfully re-establish their lives"), and the fact that Muslim women and children were removed because their "transfer completed the removal of all Bosnian Muslims from Srebrenica, thereby eliminating even the residual possibility that the Muslim community in the area could reconstitute itself." The Appeals Chamber "found a causal connection between the murder of 7,000 men and the intent to destroy the Srebrenica Bosnian Muslims; it then found a further causal link between the intended destruction of the Srebrenica Bosnian Muslims as a targeted group and the intended destruction of the protected group, namely Bosnian Muslims as a whole." Drumbl, *supra* at 440.

The Appeals Chamber also ruled that the existence of a plan or policy to commit genocide is not required, although if it exists such a plan or policy can aid in recognition of genocidal intent of a perpetrator or aid in demonstrating that an attack on a civilian population was widespread or systematic. *Id.* para. 223.

In *The Prosecutor v. Blagojevic & Jokic*, IT-02-60-T (Trial Chamber, Judgment, Jan. 17, 2005), the Trial Chamber found Colonel Vidoje Blagojevic, a commander of an infantry brigade within the Bosnian Serb Drina Coprs, guilty of complicity in genocide by aiding and abetting genocide within the meaning of Articles 4(3)(e) and 7(1) of the Statute of the ICTY. Aiding and abetting genocide occurs when the person (1) carried out an act which consisted of practical assistance, encouragement or moral support to the principal that had a "substantial effect" on the commission of the crime, (2) had knowledge that his or her own acts assisted in the commission of the specific crime by the principle offender, and (3) knew that the crime was committed with specific intent. *Id.* para. 782.

Importantly, "forcible transfer of a population" can constitute an act or method of genocide—in particular, the term "destroy" "can encompass the forcible transfer of a population." *Id.* para. 665. *Compare* Article II(e) of the Convention. The Trial Chamber added: "the physical or biological destruction of a group is not necessarily the death of the group members. While killing large numbers of a group may be the most direct means of destroying a group, other acts or series of acts, can also lead to the destruction of the group. A group is comprised of its individuals, but also of its history, traditions, the relationship between its members, the relationship with other groups, the relationship with the land. The Trial Chamber finds that the physical or biological destruction of the group is the likely outcome of a forcible transfer of the population when this transfer is conducted in such a way that the group can no longer constitute itself—particularly when it involves the separation of its members.... [this] reasoning and conclusion are not an argument for the recognition of cultural genocide, but rather an attempt to clarify the meaning of physical or biological destruction." *Id.* para. 666. "The forcible transfer of the women, children and elderly is a manifestation of the specific intent to rid the Srebrenica enclave of its Bosnian Muslim population. The manner in which the transfer was carried out—through force and coercion, by not registering those who were transferred, by burning the houses of some of the people, sending the clear message that they had nothing to return to, and significantly, through its targeting of literally the entire Bosnian Muslim population of Srebrenica, including the elderly and children—clearly indicates that it was a means to eradicate the Bosnian Muslim population from the territory where they had lived." *Id.* para. 675. "Bosnian Serb forces not only knew that the combination of the killings of the men with the forcible transfer of the women, children and elderly, would inevitably result in the physical disappearance of the Bosnian Muslim population of Srebrenica, but clearly intended through these acts to physically destroy this group." *Id.* para. 677.

In *The Prosecutor v. Brdanin*, IT-99-36-T(Trial Chamber, Judgment, Sept. 1, 2004), the Bosnian Serb entity's regional Vice President and later President in the region of Krajina was charged with genocidal deaths of Bosnian Muslims and Croats. Although the Trial Chamber did not accept the charges of genocide (with a high *mens rea* requirement) based on a joint criminal enterprise (with a lower standard of reasonable foreseeability of the criminal acts of others), the Appeals Chamber reversed this decision because, although Brdanin intended that Bosnian Muslims and Croats would be forcibly transferred out of the region, he was also responsible for resultant genocide that was a foreseeable outcome of the criminal enterprise of forced removal. On remand, the Trial Chamber (9 Sept. 2004) found him not guilty of genocide because circumstantial evidence of genocidal intent must provide an inference that could be the only reasonable inference under the circumstances. In context, the forced removal of persons did not support an intent to destroy the group in whole or in part and, supposedly, the acts or methods of genocide listed in the Convention "prohibit only the physical or biological destruction of a human group."

In *The Prosecutor v. Plavsic*, IT-00-39&40/1-S (Sentencing Judgment, Feb. 27, 2003), former President of the Bosnian Serb group Biljana Plavsic plead guilty to one count of persecutions on political, racial, and religious grounds, a crime against humanity, in exchange for dismissal of a charge of genocide.

Notes and Questions

1. Was the Trial Chamber in *Brdanin* correct that only acts involving "physical or biological destruction" are covered in Article II(a)–(e) of the Convention? Is "bodily ... harm" "destruction"?, Is "mental harm"? Are "conditions of life"? Is "forcibly transferring children"? Moreover, is the intent to destroy through these and other acts or methods of primary significance?

2. Professor Schabas has written that ICTY cases have recognized "that an individual, acting alone, may commit genocide." Schabas, *supra* at 1710, citing *Jelisic*, Trial Chamber Judgment at para. 100; Appeals Chamber Judgment, at para. 48. However, he prefers that a "state plan or policy" be "an essential ingredient of the crime." *Id.* at 1711. Do you agree? Again, is the primary evil involved a genocidal intent by the perpetrator or numbers or a state plan (which does not appear in the Convention as a limitation)?

3. The ICTR and ICTY have consistently held that the existence of a state policy is not an element of genocide. *See Prosecutor v. Popovic, et al.*, IT-05-88-T (Trial Chamber Judgement, 10 June 2010) (citing cases); *Prosecutor v. Simba*, ICTR-01-76-A (Appeals Chamber Judgement, 18 March 2010). *See also Prosecutor v. Nchamihigo*, (ICTR-2001-63-A (Appeals Chamber Judgement, 18 March 2010) (a high-level plan is not required for genocide).

Section 2
Application in Bangladesh

Paust & Blaustein, *War Crimes Jurisdiction and Due Process: The Bangladesh Experience*, 11 Vand. J. Trans. L. 1 (1978)

Genocide

Since Pakistan had ratified the Genocide Convention prior to the period during which the conduct in violation of the Convention is alleged to have occurred, it clearly applied to the accused. Furthermore, since article 1 of the Genocide Convention states that "genocide, whether committed in time of peace or in time of war, is a crime under international law," it clearly applies during both peace and war times....

Article 6 requires that persons charged with genocide be tried "by a competent tribunal of the State in the territory of which the act was committed, or by such international penal tribunal as may have jurisdiction." It seems reasonable to interpret this provision as granting jurisdictional competence to the new government with authority over the same territory in which the acts were committed.[7] Furthermore, there is no stated restriction as to when such a state should have come into legal existence, and Bangladesh is "the State in the territory of which the act was committed."

The United Nations General Assembly has declared that the crime of genocide as defined in the 1948 Genocide Convention also constitutes a crime against humanity, "even if such acts do not constitute a violation of the domestic law of the country in which they were committed."[8] Thus, Bangladesh has jurisdiction over such acts when they are committed in connection with either crimes against peace or war crimes, even though there is no implementing legislation in Pakistan or in Bangladesh. Two days after the surrender of Pakistani troops to India and Bangladesh the General Assembly additionally affirmed "that refusal by States to co-operate in the arrest, extradition, trial and punishment of persons guilty of war crimes and crimes against humanity is contrary to the purposes and principles of the Charter of the United Nations and to generally recognized norms of international law."[9]

It is also relevant that the early code of Bluntschli on the law of war contained the following declaration:

Inter-necine wars and wars of annihilation against nations or races susceptible of existence and culture constitute a violation of the law of war.

1. The war of extermination against the idolatrous inhabitants of Palestine, which the ancient Jews regarded as a holy duty, is today condemned as an act of barbarity, and can no longer be praised as an example worthy of imitation.[10]

There is ample evidence of a customary, inherited expectation that genocide was actually prohibited as a violation of the customary international law of war.[11]

---

7. *See generally* Genocide Convention, *supra,* preamble; *id.* art. 1. Nothing in article 6 states that persons charged with genocide *must* be tried in such a state and no other.

8. G.A. Res. 2391, at 3 (formally adopting the Convention on the Non-Applicability of Statutory Limitations to War Crimes and Crimes Against Humanity (in force Nov. 11, 1970). *See also* G.A. Res. 2583, 24 U.N. GAOR (1834th plen. mtg.), U.N. Doc. A/RES/2583 (1970); Miller, *The Convention on the Non-Applicability of Statutory Limitations to War Crimes and Crimes Against Humanity,* 65 Am. J. Int'l L. 476 (1971).

9. G.A. Res. 2840, at 2. Those purposes and principles would include the obligation to take action to assure "universal respect for, and observance of," international human rights and fundamental freedoms (including human rights in times of armed conflict). *See* U.N. Charter, preamble; *id.* arts. 1(2)-(3), 55(c), 56.

10. Bluntschli, at 15. The current example of such fanatically barbarous misdeeds can come under the heading of a terroristic *Jihad* or holy war.

11. See G.A. Res. 96, *supra*; Lemkin, *Genocide as a Crime Under International Law,* 41 Am. J. Int'l L. 145 (1947); Schwelb, *Crimes Against Humanity,* 23 Brit. Y.B. Int'l L. 178 (1946). *Cf.* Kunz, *The Genocide Convention,* 43 Am. J. Int'l L. 738 (1948) (considering the effect of the Convention on prior law). For authoritative comment on the customary nature of the crime of genocide, see *Attorney General of Israel v. Eichmann,* 36 Int'l L. Rep. 18, §§ 17–20. ("According to an Advisory Opinion of the International Court of Justice of May 28, 1951, given at the request of the United Nations General Assembly on the question of the reservations to the convention, the principles inherent in the convention are acknowledged by the civilized nations as binding on the country even without conventional obligation").

Notes

1. Concerning the fact that jurisdiction over genocide under customary international law is not territorially limited, also see *Case Concerning Application of the Convention on the Prevention and Prosecution of the Crime of Genocide* (Bosnia and Herzegovina v. Yugoslavia), 1996 I.C.J. 595, 616; *Attorney General of Israel v. Eichmann*, 36 Int'l L. Rpt. 18, 39 (Dist. Ct. Jerusalem 1961) ("The reference of Article 6 to territorial jurisdiction, apart from the jurisdiction of the non-existent international tribunal, is not exhaustive. Every sovereign State may exercise its existing powers within the limits of customary international law...."); van der Vyver, *supra* at 287, 319-20.

Section 3
Genocide and Politicide

Paust, *Aggression Against Authority: The Crime of Oppression, Politicide and Other Crimes Against Human Rights*, 18 Case W. Res. J. Int'l L. 283, 292–94, 304–05 (1986)

Genocide and Political Oppression

Acts of genocide directed against "a national, ethnical, racial or religious group, as such,"[1] may be motivated by, or result in, the political oppression of members of such groups and impermissibly interfere with the process of authority and self-determination. To that extent, the customary prohibition of genocide, with concomitant universal enforcement jurisdiction, can be useful in opposing aggression against authority and political oppression. Additionally, it does not matter that such attacks happen to coincide with attacks on "political" groups.[2] Attacks on the groups specified in the treaty and which are motivated by, or result in, political oppression of such persons can be

---

1. I share the viewpoint that the prohibition of genocide now at least is customary. *See* Case Concerning The Barcelona Traction, Light and Power Co., Ltd., (Belgium v. Spain), 1970 I.C.J. 3, paras. 33–34 (Judgment of February 5); G.A. Res. 96, 1 U.N. GAOR at 189, U.N. Doc. A/64/Add. 1 (1946) *reprinted in* [1946–1947] U.N. Y.B. 255 (unanimously affirming that genocide already "is a crime under international law"); Genocide Convention, *supra*, at preamble ("genocide *is* a crime under international law"), art. 1 ("The Contracting parties confirm that genocide ... *is* a crime under international law") (emphasis added); M. McDougal, H. Lasswell & L. Chen, Human Rights and World Public Order 215, 355–56 (1980); Edwards, *Contributions of the Genocide Convention to the Development of International Law*, 8 Ohio N.U.L. Rev. 300, 305–06, 308-09 (1981); Paust & Blaustein, *supra* at 22–23, ns. 76–77; Comment, *The United States and the 1948 Genocide Convention*, 16 Harv. Int'l L.J. 683 (1975). *But see* Starkman, *Genocide and International Law: Is There a Cause of Action?*, 8 A.S.I.L.S. Int'l L.J. 1, 13–21 (1984). The new Restatement also adopts this view. Restatement of the Foreign Relations Law of the United States §702(a) and Reporters' Note 1 thereto, §702(a) and Comment d and Reporters' Note 3 thereto (3 ed. 1987).

2. *See* M. C. Bassiouni, International Criminal Law—A Draft International Criminal Code 72 (1980); P. Drost, II The Crime of State: Genocide 62 (1959); L. Sohn & T. Buergenthal, International Protection of Human Rights 929 (1973). Although the United States favored inclusion of an express category of "political" group within article 2 of the Genocide Convention, and such was included in the 1946 General Assembly resolution on Genocide, such a category was dropped later in order to gain a quicker and more widespread ratification. Comment, *Genocide: A Commentary on the Convention*, 58 Yale L.J. 1142, 1145 (1949). Early in 1986, the U.S. Senate voted 92 to 1 in favor of a resolution directing the President to seek renewed negotiations concerning inclusion of political groups within those specified in the Genocide Convention. *See* Washington Weekly Report, vol. 12, No. 7, at 3 (UNA-USA Feb. 21, 1986).

criminally sanctioned. Moreover, today it can be recognized that whether or not attacks on "political" groups as such involve acts of genocide, such attacks are necessarily violative of the precept of self-determination and fundamental human rights. As such, they constitute aggression against authority, a violation of the U.N. Charter, the crime of oppression, and what the International Law Commission has recognized as a crime against self-determination. To the extent that violations of relevant human rights are criminally sanctioned, any gap in coverage by the Genocide Convention will prove to be of little import.

Nevertheless, it may be important to emphasize these recognitions in a new international instrument, if only to further sanctify criminal proscription and to provide additional guidance concerning the contours of present prohibitions. For that purpose, a draft Convention on the Prevention and Punishment of the Crime of Politicide is offered in the annex to this article. Politicide, as a useful rallying term, can encompass more odious forms of aggression against authority, the crime against self-determination, the crime of political oppression, and so forth, while providing a logically related focus in supplementation of the Genocide Convention.

Hurst Hannum, *International Law and Cambodian Genocide: The Sounds of Silence*, 11 HUMAN RIGHTS Q. 82 (1989)[*]

This article examines the feasibility of bringing an application to the International Court of Justice, under the terms of Article IX of the Genocide Convention or Article 36 of the Statute of the Court. It concludes that such an application would be legally feasible and politically desirable and that the failure of any state thus far to institute proceedings before the Court is an indefensible abdication of international responsibility.

The first part of this article considers in some detail the factual evidence of genocide in Cambodia, countering the view expressed by some that, however deplorable they might have been, the Khmer Rouge killings were not technically "genocide." The second part outlines the elements of a successful application under the Genocide Convention, including questions of the Court's jurisdiction, the existence of a dispute between an applicant state and Democratic Kampuchea and whether the killings of Cambodians themselves by the Khmer Rouge leadership constitute genocide against a "national" group within the meaning of the convention. The third part considers the application under the Court's compulsory jurisdiction, charging Democratic Kampuchea with violations of customary international law and crimes against humanity, *i.e.*, mass arbitrary killings and widespread systematic torture....

Killings

Three distinct categories of deliberate killings occurred in Democratic Kampuchea: waves of massacres; individual executions following imprisonment and interrogation; and arbitrary and summary executions. To an extent, similar patterns can be seen in all three methods of state-sponsored murder, and all were directed to the same goal: the relentless purge from the Cambodian nation of elements deemed tainted and corrupted.

The first groups to be identified, isolated, and executed were the officer corps and the defeated army, the higher ranking civil servants of the previous two regimes, and, in some instances, their entire families. In 1976, corresponding to what the Khmer Rouge identified as an intensification of the class struggle, the more highly educated

---

professional classes were targeted. Later, to advance the progress of the new social order, the Khmer Rouge leadership decided to purge the Cambodian nation of those they described as having lingering attitudes of "privateness" or "propertyism"—attitudes that should have disappeared with the abolition of markets and private property and the dissolution of the capitalist classes. This was the theoretical foundation for waves of massacres directed against Khmer Rouge cadres and elements of the Cambodian peasantry.

The most thoroughly documented regional purge occurred in the Eastern Zone in 1978, in which an estimated minimum of 100,000 people were executed in a six-month period. While some of those executed in the Eastern Zone belonged to a recognizable political group judged disloyal by Democratic Kampuchea's central leadership, far larger numbers of people were killed because they were deemed to be tainted merely by having lived under the jurisdiction of the presumedly disloyal political faction. The overwhelming number of those massacred were simple peasants or urban evacuees without any particular political affiliation, who were not members of any "political group" in the common sense meaning of those words.

In addition to those destroyed in the expanding massacres directed against successive segments of the populace, scores of thousands were individually executed, usually following interrogation and torture, in a nationwide system of prison-execution centers. The apex of this nationwide prison-execution system was S.21, the central prison-execution facility in Phnom Penh. S.21, now known as "Tuol Sleng," was an extermination facility operating under the direct control of Democratic Kampuchea's highest leadership. Only seven prisoners, whose skills were useful to the prison authorities and the leadership, are known to have survived; twenty thousand died. One of the last acts of the Democratic Kampuchea prison officials before fleeing in January 1979 was to slit the throats of the prisoners then chained to their interrogation cots; when Tuol Sleng was discovered, pools of blood were still coagulating beneath their bodies.

Execution schedules recorded each day's work, and the highest daily figure was 582 people executed on 27 May 1978. The composition of a particular day's execution schedule usually reflected the mix of prisoners at that time, but particular days were occasionally reserved to kill certain types of prisoners. For example, 1 July 1977 was devoted to executing the imprisoned wives and children of those killed previously; 22 July 1977 was devoted to "smashing" people from the Ministry of Public Works. Because the victims' names are identified by occupation and place of arrest, the daily arrest and execution schedules make it possible to reconstruct the patterns of killings by Democratic Kampuchea, as waves of victims washed through the prison to their deaths....

Finally, refugee and survivor accounts contain innumerable references to killings by lower-level Khmer Rouge cadres, often intended as punishments for minor infractions or "bad" attitudes, which served to ensure Khmer Rouge control through indiscriminate terror. As a Khmer Rouge slogan noted, *tuk meun chamnenh, dak meun khat*: "there is no profit in keeping them; there is no loss in removing them." These arbitrary and summary executions also are "killings" within the meaning of Article II(a) of the Genocide Convention and contributed to the partial destruction of the Cambodian national group itself....

... There is no statute of limitations on crimes against humanity, including genocide. So long as those persons responsible for planning, directing or committing acts of genocide have not been punished, "whether they are constitutionally responsible rulers, public officials, or private individuals," Democratic Kampuchea is in violation of its obligations under Article IV....

The meaning of the phrase "national group"

The fundamental rule of treaty interpretation is set forth in Article 31 of the Vienna Convention of the Law of Treaties:

> A treaty shall be interpreted in good faith in accordance with the ordinary meaning to be given to the terms of the treaty in their context and in the light of its object and purpose....

The first clause of Article II of the Genocide Convention identifies "a national, ethnical, racial or religious group" as within its scope. Applying the principles set forth immediately above, it is clear that a national group such as the Khmer people of Kampuchea, falls within the ambit of Article II of the Genocide Convention, whether or not such a group constitutes a majority or a minority within a particular state.

That the Khmer people decimated by the government of Democratic Kampuchea constitutes a "national group" within any generally accepted definition of that term cannot be doubted. The Khmers have a distinct language and a political and social history that spans centuries, and they are ethnically distinct from neighboring peoples. Whether or not they also constitute an ethnical or racial group within the meaning of Article II does not detract from their status as a national group as well. Indeed, under the injunction by the Court in the *Anglo-Iranian Oil Co.* case, the word "national" must be given a different meaning than the other adjectives utilized in the text, or it would be merely superfluous.

The term "national minority" was widely understood by the drafters of the Convention, as demonstrated in greater detail below, and the absence of the term "minority" from the Convention must be presumed to be intentional. Any interpretation which seeks to equate "national group" with "national minority" is inconsistent with the plain language chosen by the drafters and cannot be sustained....

If the Khmer national group falls within the ambit of Article II even when it constitutes a majority in a given state, the question then becomes whether the group allegedly committing or tolerating genocide must be nationally, ethnically, racially, or religiously distinct from its intended victims. A search of the text of the treaty reveals no such requirement; indeed, there is no reference whatsoever to the nature of the "persons" liable for punishment under Articles IV, V, and VI, nor is there any limitation on the "state" responsible for implementing the treaty. As stated in the 1985 United Nations *Study on Genocide*, "[i]t is noteworthy that the definition [of genocide] does not exclude cases where the victims are part of the violator's own group." ...

A careful survey of the preparatory work of the Genocide Convention—including the meetings of the Ad Hoc Committee on Genocide established by the Economic and Social Council in 1948, and the debates in the Economic and Social Council, Sixth Committee of the General Assembly, and the General Assembly itself—reveals no specific vote or consensual decision with respect to the term "national". There are, however, general references to the terms "national" and "ethnical" and to the phrase "as such," as well as discussions of cultural genocide and general consideration of those persons who should be protected under the Convention....

The concept of cultural genocide was ultimately excluded from the Convention by a vote of the Sixth Committee. While there were undoubtedly many different reasons for the votes of various delegations, the identification of "cultural genocide" with "minority" rights by some delegations supports the interpretation put forward herein that the concept of "national" and other groups is not limited to minorities....

The debate over a Swedish amendment to add the term "ethnical" to the list of protected groups supports a broad interpretation of the word "national." As noted by the Soviet representative, "An ethnical group was a sub-group of a national group; it was a smaller collectivity than the nation, but one whose existence could nevertheless be of benefit to humanity." Some believed that there was no difference between an "ethnical" and a "national" group or between "ethnical" and "racial" group. Nevertheless, "ethnical" was added to the list of protected groups by narrow margin.

Despite a request early in the debate on Article II for a definition of the term "national group," the full committee did not judge further definition to be required. In the context of the present application, however, nothing in the *travaux préparatoires* is contrary to or incompatible with the proposition that the Khmer people of Kampuchea constitute a national group within the meaning of Article II....

The contention that groups such as the Buddhist monkhood or Cham were primarily political groups and that their destruction therefore is not covered by the Genocide Convention cannot be sustained. Even if political motives coincided with the hatred of religion, "foreigners," and ideological deviance, the targeted destruction of religious and ethnical groups by the government of Democratic Kampuchea is precisely the kind of "odious scourge" the Genocide Convention is intended to prohibit.

With respect to the Khmer national group, there was obviously no intention on the part of the Democratic Kampuchean authorities to destroy the Khmer group "in whole," as this would have implied their own demise. Nevertheless, there was a clear intent to destroy the national group "in part," which becomes apparent when one analyses the scope and scale of the destruction visited upon the Khmer people by the Khmer Rouge government. The wholesale massacres of families, villages, and other subgroups of the Khmer people provide persuasive evidence that the aim of the Democratic Kampuchean government was not merely the elimination of political opponents or reform of the socioeconomic structure of the country, but rather the wholesale remaking of the Khmer people according to a deliberately imposed vision. If the Genocide Convention means anything, it means that a state cannot destroy those parts of its own people that do not conform sufficiently to the government's own view of social, racial, or ideological purity....

In the only official analysis under UN auspices of the massive human rights violations in Democratic Kampuchea, the Chairman of the UN Sub-Commission on Prevention of Discrimination and Protection of Minorities concluded that the destruction of Kampuchean society by the government of Democratic Kampuchea amounted to "nothing less than auto-genocide." While "auto-genocide" as a term has no legal status, the terrible reality it describes is what the Genocide Convention defines as the destruction "in part" of a "national group"....

It is difficult to imagine a more persuasive "series of facts linked together" than the evidence of murder and partial destruction of religious and ethnical groups and the Cambodian national group itself than is presently available with respect to the period of Khmer Rouge rule in Democratic Kampuchea from 1975 to 1979. The single conclusion required by this evidence is that Democratic Kampuchea has violated its obligations under the Genocide Convention not to commit or tolerate genocide.

Questions

1. Do you agree with Professor Hannum? What types of persons were targets and why were they targeted?

2. Is "auto-genocide" covered by Article II? Whether or not it is, would it constitute a crime against humanity?

3. What was the probable intent of perpetrators? Who was targeted and why? Were Cambodians or Khmer people targeted because they were Cambodians or Khmer people as such? What does Article II of the Genocide Convention require?

4. If Spanish nationals were targeted by the Pinochet regime in Chile because they were Spanish, would such targetings constitute genocide? What if they were targeted because they were "liberal"?

5. Should the Genocide Convention be amended to include gender-based targeting as such? See J. Paust, *Women and International Criminal Law Instruments and Processes*, in 2 Women and International Human Rights Law 349 (Kelly D. Askin & Dorean M. Koenig eds. 2000); Berta Esperanza Hernandez-Truyol, *Women's Rights as Human Rights — Rules, Realities and the Role of Culture: A Formula for Reform*, 21 Brook. J. Int'l L. 605, 649–50 (1996).

6. Consider also the following hypotheticals involving mixed motives. If a group of women is targeted because the women are Muslim and because they are women, is the targeting genocidal in purpose? If the same mixed motives exist but the women killed or seriously bodily injured are not in fact Muslim, is the targeting genocidal? Besides the specific intent, what do you need to know? Must there be an impact on the relevant group (*i.e.*, the group covered in Article II of the Convention)? If a genocidal intent exists, can some impacts be indirect as where an instrumental target (*e.g.*, a group of women) is not part of a covered group, but the covered group is the primary target of the perpetrators and the primary group suffers certain effects? Consider Article II and prohibited acts (b) and (d). What about acts (a), (c), or (e)?

In The Prosecutor v. Niyitegeka, ICTR-96-14-A (Appeals Chamber Judgment, 9 July 2004), the Appeals Chamber ruled that the phrase "as such" (reflected in Article II of the Convention) does not require that the intent of the perpetrator be merely or "solely" to target a relevant group and that the perpetrator can have other motivations but still be responsible for genocide. *Id*. para. 53. The Appeals Chamber upheld the conviction of Niyitegeka (who had been a Minister of Information in Rwanda in 1994) for genocide, conspiracy to commit genocide, direct and public incitement to commit genocide, murder, extermination, and other inhumane acts as crimes against humanity.

Section 4
U.S. Implementation

Senate Committee on Foreign Relations, International Convention on the Prevention and Punishment of the Crime of Genocide, S. Exec. Rept. No. 92-6, 92d Cong., 1st Sess. 1–18 (4 May 1971)

The Committee on Foreign Relations, to which was referred the International Convention on the Prevention and Punishment of the Crime of Genocide (Ex. O, 81st Cong., first sess.), having considered the same, reports favorably thereon with three understandings and one declaration and recommends that the Senate advise and consent to ratification thereof....

Since the treaty, in article I, specifically refers to "time of war," the possible effect of the Genocide Convention on U.S. military forces abroad, especially when in combat, was carefully considered. This is particularly relevant since the word "genocide" has been loosely applied to the incidents at My Lai. However, as will be seen in the discussion of article II below where genocide is defined, whatever occurred at My Lai—and the committee does not prejudge the matter—it was not genocide, as defined in the treaty. Combat actions do not fall within the meaning of the Genocide Convention. They are subject to other international and national laws....

Acts Constituting Genocide ...

The testimony and discussion of article II turned on the alleged vagueness of certain of its terms—"in whole or in part," "group", "as such," and "mental harm." While the committee had no particular problem with the meaning of these words, in order to allay any misconceptions, it recommends to the Senate two understandings to this article:

"(1) That the U.S. Government understands and construes the words 'intent to destroy, in whole or in part, a national, ethnical, racial, or religious group, as such' appearing in article II to mean the intent to destroy a national, ethnical, racial, or religious group by the acts specified in article II in such a manner as to affect a substantial part of the group concerned.

"(2) That the U.S. Government understands and construes the words 'mental harm' appearing in article II(b) to mean permanent impairment of mental faculties."

The first of these understandings serves to emphasize the importance which the committee attaches to the word "intent." Basic to any charge of genocide must be the *intent* to destroy an entire group because of the fact that it is a certain national, ethnical, racial, or religious group, in such a manner as to affect a substantial part of the group. There have been allegations that school busing, birth control clinics, lynchings, police actions with respect to the Black Panthers, and the incidents at My Lai constitute genocide. The committee wants to make clear that under the terms of article II none of these and similar acts is genocide unless the *intent* to destroy the group as a group is proven. Harassment of minority groups and racial and religious intolerance generally, no matter how much to be deplored, are not outlawed per se by the Genocide Convention. Far from outlawing discrimination, article II is so written as to make it, in fact, difficult to prove the "intent" element necessary to sustain a charge of genocide against anyone....

The second of the understandings was suggested by the executive branch in 1949 and while the executive branch no longer considers this understanding to be necessary, the committee thinks it will be helpful to eliminate any doubt as to what is meant by "mental harm.".…

Punishable Acts …

The principal question about the meaning of article III concerned the relationship of the words "direct and public incitement to commit genocide" to the freedom of speech guarantees of the first amendment.

The 1969 case of *Brandenburg v. Ohio* was cited by several witnesses as the most recent reaffirmation of the line drawn by the Supreme Court between protected speech and prohibited direct and immediate incitement to action. In that case, the Court said: " … the constitutional guarantees of free speech and free press do not permit a State to forbid or proscribe advocacy of the use of force or of law violation except where such advocacy is directed to inciting or producing imminent lawless action and is likely to incite or produce such action." (395 U.S. 444.) This is a 1969 per curiam decision of the Supreme Court and there is no reason to expect any reversal of this doctrine, with which the language of the Genocide Convention is consistent.…

Punishment of Persons …

While most of the testimony on [article IV] attempted to establish that governments, as well as individuals, could be held responsible for commission of genocidal acts, the committee believes that this argument is somewhat strained. The article clearly refers to "persons." The government's responsibility is to punish such persons, whether they are constitutionally responsible rulers, public officials, or private individuals.…

Implementing Legislation …

[Article V] makes clear that the convention is construed not [to] be self-executing and that implementing legislation is required to give effect to its provisions. Indeed, the committee regards Senate approval of the convention as the first in a two-step procedure. The Department of State is already on record as proposing to recommend to the President that the instrument of ratification of the convention not be deposited until the implementing legislation has been enacted. This statement by the Department has been incorporated into a declaration to be included in the resolution of ratification as follows:

"4. That the United States Government declares that it will not deposit its instrument of ratification until after the implementing legislation referred to in article V has been enacted." …

Trial of Persons Charged With Genocide …

[Article VI] provoked considerable discussion, not because of its language but because of the means suggested for its implementation. Executive branch and other testimony brought out that the negotiating history of the convention makes it clear that the courts of the country in which the accused has citizenship can likewise have jurisdiction over the crime. This theory of concurrent jurisdiction—jurisdiction based on the site of the alleged offense and jurisdiction based on the nationality of the offender— was thoroughly explored during the hearings. It was pointed out that a number of nations, particularly colonial powers, have consistently asserted the right to try their own nationals for crimes committed outside their territory. Even the United States in certain limited areas—counterfeiting, theft of Government property, treason, antitrust violations—has exercised jurisdiction over its citizens for acts committed abroad. This concept of concurrent jurisdiction no doubt will be closely examined during consideration of the implementing legislation. However, the U.S. Government should make it clear to the other contracting parties that it intends to construe article VI so as to permit it to try its own nationals for punishable genocide acts whether committed at home or abroad. For this reason, the committee recommends to the Senate the following understanding:

"(3) That the U.S. Government understands and construes article VI of the convention in accordance with the agreed language of the report of the Legal Committee of the United Nations General Assembly that nothing in article VI shall affect the right of any State to bring to trial before its own tribunals any of its nationals for acts committed outside the State...."

Role of the United Nations

In the discussion of [article VIII], the question was raised whether it would broaden or enlarge the powers of the United Nations. Genocide, as the term is accepted by the committee, namely, mass murder on a broad scale, would pose a threat to world peace and it would clearly be within the powers of the United Nations to discuss it. The article itself moreover refers to "action under the Charter of the United Nations" which limits its scope to that document, including the article 2(7) proscription against intervention "in matters which are essentially within the domestic jurisdiction of any state...."

As a practical matter, whether we are a party to the Genocide Convention or not, the United Nations can discuss alleged genocide in the United States or anywhere else any time it so chooses. The committee moreover is quite certain that for propaganda and other purposes spurious charges of this nature will continue to be made in the United Nations, whether we do or do not ratify the Genocide Convention, if only because our position in the world makes us a visible target of discontent. Indeed, we lend more color to such charges by not being a party to the Genocide Convention. This being the case, the question whether article VIII gives the United Nations greater scope to discuss genocide seems relatively immaterial. It is important, moreover, in this connection to bear in mind that such enforcement powers as the United Nations has are lodged in the Security Council, subject to the veto power, which the United States now has demonstrated it will not hesitate to exercise.

Settlement of Disputes ...

The jurisdiction of the Court [under article IX] will extend to disputes relating to the interpretation, application, or fulfillment of the convention, including those relating to the responsibility of a state for genocide. It must be noted that such cases will fall under article 36(1) of the Court's statute which provides:

"1. The jurisdiction of the Court comprises all cases which the parties refer to it and all matters specially provided for in the Charter of the United Nations or *in treaties and conventions in force*." [emphasis added.]

Cases arising under the Genocide Convention will not be covered by the Connally amendment under which the United States reserves to itself the right to determine which cases it considers to be within its domestic jurisdiction and therefore outside the jurisdiction of the Court. The Connally amendment applies only to article 36(2)—the so-called compulsory jurisdiction clause....

THE CONVENTION AND THE CONSTITUTION

Discussion of the Genocide Convention during the hearings renewed the debate over whether a treaty can authorize what the Constitution prohibits. The Supreme Court, in its own words, "has regularly and uniformly recognized the supremacy of the Constitution over a treaty" (*Reid v. Covert*). It is therefore fallacious to claim that the Genocide Convention will supersede or set aside the Constitution of the United States. It will not and cannot do so.

A related argument was raised by some witnesses to the effect that the Congress would have no power to enact legislation making genocide a crime if the convention were not approved. The power of Congress to do so rests on article I, section 8, clause 10, of the Constitution: "The Congress shall have the Power … To Define and Punish Piracies and Felonies committed on the high Seas, and Offences against the Law of Nations…. ," as well as on the necessary and proper clause. The fact that the Congress enacts a statute pursuant to a treaty, as would be the case in the Genocide Convention, does not alter its competence to enact such legislation in any event….

Questions

1. Do you agree the "whatever occurred at My Lai" was not genocide? What would the prosecutor have to prove?

2. Can genocide occur in time of armed conflict?

3. Does Article II of the Convention require that the intent of the perpetrator to destroy in whole or in part be an intent "in such a manner as to affect a substantial part of the group concerned"? Does Article II require that the acts of the perpetrator "affect a substantial part of the group concerned"?

4. Must there be an "intent to destroy the group as a group"?

1986 Lugar/Helms/Hatch Provisos as Approved by the Foreign Relations Committee

Resolved (two-thirds of the Senators present concurring therein), That the Senate advise and consent to the ratification of the International Convention on the Prevention and Punishment of the Crime of Genocide, adopted unanimously by the General Assembly of the United Nations in Paris on December 9, 1948 (Executive O, Eighty-first Congress, first session), Provided that—

I. The Senate's advice and consent is subject to the following reservations:

(1) That with reference to Article IX of the Convention, before any dispute to which the United States is a party may be submitted to the jurisdiction of the International Court of Justice under this article, the specific consent of the United States is required in each case.

(2) That nothing in the Convention requires or authorizes legislation or other action by the United States of America prohibited by the Constitution of the United States as interpreted by the United States.

II. The Senate's advice and consent is subject to the following understandings, which shall apply to the obligations of the United States under this Convention:

(1) That the term "intent to destroy, in whole or in part, a national, ethnical, racial, or religious group as such" appearing in Article II means the specific intent to destroy, in whole or in substantial part, a national, ethnical, racial, of religious group as such by the acts specified in Article II.

(2) That the term "mental harm" in Article II(b) means permanent impairment of mental faculties through drugs, torture, or similar techniques.

(3) That the pledge to grant extradition in accordance with a state's laws and treaties in force found in Article VII extends only to acts which are criminal under the laws of both the requesting and the requested state and nothing in Article VI affects the rights of any state to bring to trial before its own tribunals any of its nationals for acts committed outside a state.

(4) That acts in the course of armed conflicts committed without the specific intent required by Article II are not sufficient to constitute genocide as defined by this Convention.

(5) That with regard to the reference to an international penal tribunal in Article VI of the Convention, the United States declares that it reserves the right to effect its participation in any such tribunal by a treaty entered into specifically for that purpose with the advice and consent of the Senate.

III. The Senate's advice and consent is subject to the following declaration:

That the President will not deposit the instrument of ratification until after the implementing legislation referred to in Article V has been enacted.

Extract: Vol. XII-7 UNA/USA Washington Weekly Report 1-3 (21 Feb. 1986)

SENATE LENDS CONSENT TO GENOCIDE CONVENTION

By a vote of 83 ayes to 11 noes, the Senate has given its advice and consent to the ratification of the Genocide Convention....

Senate Leadership Seeks to Bridge Gap

Sen. Richard Lugar (R-IN), Chairman of the Committee on Foreign Relations, opened debate on the treaty by acknowledging the thirty-six year stalemate between those who have believed that ratification has strong symbolic value and those who have sought a definition of precise obligations under the treaty and its impact on U.S. sovereignty. He explained that the eight provisos seek to delineate those obligations. To reaffirm our commitment to human rights and rule of law, to prevent the United States from being unfairly criticized and to recall the Holocaust—these are the reasons why I believe the Senate should approve the Genocide Convention," said Lugar. Added Sen. Claiborne Pell (D-RI), ranking minority member of the Committee on Foreign Relations, "By making genocide a crime under international law, the convention is a powerful instrument for the protection of life and the advancement of human rights throughout this planet."

Sen. Jesse Helms (R-NC), the principal advocate of treaty obligation clarifications in the Foreign Relations Committee, argued that, "From the very beginning my chief object with regard to the Genocide Convention has been to see that the independent sovereignty of the United States is protected from interference by an international regime of law." Helms termed inclusion of the eight provisions the 'sovereignty package' since it is designed to protect this nation's sovereignty from the intrusion of the United Nations into the domestic matters of the United States, and the people of this country. Sen. Orrin Hatch (R-UT), another proponent of the reservations package, commented that, "While it is time to resolve these issues, we must not compromise our constitutional form of government in the process. Participation in world affairs need not and should not result in any diminution of liberty in the United States." Although Hatch eventually voted in favor of Senate consent, Helms announced early in the debate that he would be unable to vote for the treaty with the attached reservations. "I think that the United States should be moving away from entangling alliances, not moving toward more in an uncertain future," he said.

Reservations Package Clarifies U.S. Obligations

As consented to by the Senate, the United States expresses eight reservations to the convention. The two most contentious provisions require the specific consent of the United States for any appearance before the International Court of Justice on a legal question involving genocide and assert the sovereignty of the U.S. Constitution. In the second case, no provision of the convention could authorize or permit legislation, executive conduct or legal action contrary to the U.S. Constitution as interpreted by the United States. Other reservations include a statement that armed conflict, by itself, does not constitute genocide; a prohibition on the extradition of American citizens for crimes not in violation of U.S. law; a stricter definition of the mental state necessary to commit genocide; clarification of mental harm through the use of drugs and torture; the requirement for a specific treaty for U.S. involvement in any international genocide penal tribunal; and a declaration preventing the President from depositing the instrument of ratification until Congress passes implementing legislation. This last reservation prevents the treaty's provisions from becoming self-executing. Implementing legislation would make the convention part of the U.S. legal code; Congress is expected to act on it shortly.

Attachment of the reservations package to the treaty caused considerable controversy during Foreign Relations Committee deliberations in May 1985. Most of the Democratic members of the Committee argued that several of the reservations weakened the treaty and made it meaningless. Committee Chairman Lugar, however, insisted that the eight conditions be attached to the convention to overcome conservative concerns that the treaty would supersede the authority of the U.S. Constitution and threaten the rights of U.S. citizens. Lugar reinforced his commitment to including the conditions by threatening to suspend Committee markup of the treaty if the package was not accepted. At that time, the panel voted 9 ayes to 8 noes to include the most contentious reservations in the treaty. Restating his position on the Senate floor, Lugar noted that, "These provisos delineate and qualify the U.S. obligations under the convention; they in no way detract from the symbolic value that will inhere from ratification." Sen. Christopher Dodd (D-CT), an opponent of the reservations package who tried to weaken the World Court reservation in Committee, noted on the Senate floor that, "If it comes to the question of voting on the treaty with the present conditions or putting off this issue once again, I will vote for ratification."

Symms Rebuffed on "Killer Amendment"

By a vote of 31 ayes to 62 noes, Sen. Steven Symms (R-ID) was defeated in his attempt to amend the treaty to include political groups among those listed for protection in the convention. Amendment of the convention in any form would have effectively nullified it; the President would find it necessary to gain the assent of the ninety-six other signatories to such an amendment before he could ratify it on behalf of the

United States. Lugar argued that the Symms amendment " … is effectively a killer amendment. It is the same as a vote against the treaty." The Senate later voted 93 ayes to 1 no on a resolution directing the President to seek renewed negotiations on the treaty with a view to including political genocide in the convention.…

U.S. Legislation

Genocide, 18 U.S.C. §§ 1091–1093 (as amended 2007)

§ 1091. Genocide

(a) **Basic offense.**—Whoever, whether in time of peace or in time of war, in a circumstance described in subsection (d) and with the specific intent to destroy, in whole or in substantial part, a national, ethnic, racial, or religious group as such—

> (1) kills members of that group;

> (2) causes serious bodily injury to members of that group;

> (3) causes the permanent impairment of the mental faculties of members of the group through drugs, torture, or similar techniques;

> (4) subjects the group to conditions of life that are intended to cause the physical destruction of the group in whole or in part;

> (5) imposes measures intended to prevent births within the group; or

> (6) transfers by force children of the group to another group; or attempts to do so, shall be punished as provided in subsection (b).

(b) **Punishment for basic offense.**—The punishment for an offense under subsection (a) is—

> (1) in the case of an offense under subsection (a)(1) where death results, by death or imprisonment for life and a fine of not more than $1,000,000, or both; and

> (2) a fine of not more than $1,000,000 or imprisonment for not more than twenty years, or both, in any other case.

(c) **Incitement offense.**—Whoever in a circumstance described in subsection (d) directly and publicly incites another to violate subsection (a) shall be fined not more than $500,000 or imprisoned not more than five years, or both.

(d) **Required circumstance for offenses.**—The circumstance referred to in subsections (a) and (c) is that—

> (1) the offense is committed in whole or in part within the United States;

> (2) the alleged offender is a national of the United States (as that term is defined in section 101 of the Immigration and Nationality act (8 U.S.C. 1101));

> (3) the alleged offender is an alien lawfully admitted for permanent residence in the United States (as that term is defined in section 101 of the Immigration and Nationality Act (8 U.S.C. 1101));

> (4) the alleged offender is a stateless person whose habitual residence is in the United States; or

> (5) after the conduct required for the offense occurs, the alleged offender is brought into, or found in, the United States, even if that conduct occurred outside the United States.

(e) **Nonapplicability of certain limitations.** — Notwithstanding section 3282 of this title, in the case of an offense under subsection (a)(1), an indictment may be found, or information instituted, at any time without limitation.

[§ 3282 provides a 5 year statutory limitation regarding "offenses not capital"]

§ 1092. Exclusive remedies

Nothing in this chapter shall be construed as precluding the application of State or local laws to the conduct proscribed by this chapter, nor shall anything in this chapter be construed as creating any substantive or procedural right enforceable by law by any party in any proceeding.

§ 1093. Definitions

As used in this chapter—

(1) the term "children" means the plural and means individuals who have not attained the age of eighteen years;

(2) the term "ethnic group" means a set of individuals whose identity as such is distinctive in terms of common cultural traditions or heritage;

(3) the term "incites" means urges another to engage imminently in conduct in circumstances under which there is a substantial likelihood of imminently causing such conduct;

(4) the term "members" means the plural;

(5) the term "national group" means a set of individuals whose identity as such is distinctive in terms of nationality or national origins;

(6) the term "racial group" means a set of individuals whose identity as such is distinctive in terms of physical characteristics or biological descent;

(7) the term "religious group" means a set of individuals whose identity as such is distinctive in terms of common religious creed, beliefs, doctrines, practices, or rituals; and

(8) the term "substantial part" means a part of a group of such numerical significance that the destruction or loss of that part would cause the destruction of the group as a viable entity within the nation of which such group is a part.

U.N. Human Rights Commission, Res. 1987/25, Status of the Convention on the Prevention and Punishment of the Crime of Genocide

The Commission on Human Rights,

Recalling General Assembly resolutions 40/142 of 13 December 1985 and 41/147 of 4 December 1986,

Also recalling its resolution 1986/18 of 10 March 1986,

Further recalling General Assembly resolution 260 A (III) of 9 December 1948, in which the Assembly approved the Convention on the Prevention and Punishment of the Crime of Genocide and proposed it for signature and ratification or accession,

Reaffirming its conviction that genocide is a crime which violates the norms of international law and runs counter to the spirit and aims of the United Nations,

Expressing its conviction that strict observance by all States of the provisions of the Convention is necessary for the prevention and punishment of the crime of genocide,

1. *Strongly condemns once again* the crime of genocide;

2. *Affirms* the necessity of international co-operation in order to liberate mankind from this odious crime....

Notes and Questions

1. Is Genocide now (whether or not it had been in 1948) a violation of customary international law? See text *supra*; RESTATEMENT OF THE FOREIGN RELATIONS LAW OF THE UNITED STATES §404 and Reporters' Note 1, §702, Comments d and n and Reporters' Note 3 (3 ed. 1987); the 1993 Report of the Secretary-General, at paras. 35, 45; Paust, *Congress and Genocide: They're Not Going to Get Away With It*, 11 MICH. J. INT'L L. 90, 90–92 (1989). The latter article contains a survey of numerous textwriters on the status of the prohibition of genocide as customary international law (*id.* at 90–91 and n.1) and as *jus cogens* (*id.* at 92–93 & n.3). Newer affirmations include: Johan D. van der Vyver, *Prosecution and Punishment, supra* at 287, 319-20.

2. Does Article II of the Convention define that which is prohibited under customary international law, with a possible exception regarding extended groups ? See Paust, *id.* at 93–4; RESTATEMENT, §702, Comment d; Statute of the ICTY, art. 4; Statute of the ICTR, art. 2; Statute of the ICC, art. 6; questions in Section 1. If so, has the U.S. attempt to redefine "genocide" come too late? Note that in 2004 a concurrent resolution of the U.S. House and Senate used the customary definition of genocide when declaring "the actions in Darfur, Sudan, are genocide." H.R. Concurrent Res. 467, 108th Cong.; S. Concurrent Res. 133 (2004). Consider also:

Paust, Congress and Genocide

First, the attempted "understanding" [regarding "substantial" part] is fundamentally incompatible with the object and purpose of the treaty and will thereby be legally unacceptable. Second, the attempt to redefine genocide in such a radical manner has been obviated by the development of a customary international law independent of a long, abnegative effort of the Senate to allow the United States to participate in the treaty process.

Part of the radical effort to gut the Convention of any functional criminal effect hinged upon a blatant attempt to unilaterally rewrite article II of the Convention. In particular, the treaty phrase "with intent to destroy, in whole or in part," appears in the Senate's 1986 "understanding" as [with] the specific intent to destroy, in whole or in *substantial* part...." The phrase "specific intent" actually is appropriate under the circumstances, but the threshold element of the crime of genocide would be shifted by the last portion of such language from the treaty's lower threshold of intent to destroy a relevant group "in part" to the Senate's nearly impossible threshold of intent to destroy a relevant group "in substantial part."

One can imagine the type of defenses that the Senate's "understanding" might permit. For example, is a nuclear incineration of all of the Jews in and around the state of Israel to be excused under such an "understanding" merely because a "substantial part" of the Jews of the world were not targeted? If Hitler himself had been prosecuted under the Senate's present version, a defense to what the world knows as acts of genocide might have been: "Yes, I attempted to exterminate Jews as such and thousands, even millions, of Jews, but I never had the specific intent to destroy a 'substantial' part of such a group, nor could I or my followers have done so—we never had control of even half the Jews of the world." Or take the putative defense of a member of the KKK in the United States: "Sure, I intended to exterminate as many blacks as I could get my sights on, but I never had more than 2,000 in my gun sights and never had the intent to destroy a 'substantial' part of such group, nor could I physically do so." Even nationwide conspirators in the KKK, each responsible for the known acts of co-conspirators, might defend: "We never intended to kill more than six million blacks and thus never intended to kill a 'substantial' part of the blacks in the U.S., much less in the world." It is evident, therefore, that U.S. prosecutors (under the Senate's present "understanding") would have a nearly impossible burden in proving an intent to destroy a relevant group "in substantial part." When half the persons within a large group were not even targeted by an accused, how could a prosecuting attorney prove that there was an intent to destroy a "substantial part" of such a group? Even if the phrase "substantial part" could theoretically include just more than one third, one fourth or ten percent, why would we want such threshold quotas set against what the world still knows as acts of genocide? The significant evil involved (and the fundamental difference between murder and genocide) hinges not upon percentages of group extermination but upon the singling out of victims of a certain group because they are members of such a group—the targeting of members of a group as such. That evil is not merely against a particular group or its members. In the long run it involves an attack upon our common dignity, an attack upon us all.

The Senate also attempted to rewrite section b of article II of the treaty. The treaty prohibition of an intent to cause "serious ... mental harm to members" of a relevant group would be changed by the present Senate "understanding" to an intent to cause "*permanent* impairment of mental faculties through drugs, torture or similar techniques." Thus, it would be possible for alleged terrorists or Nazi war criminals to defend their actions with proof of the fact that intense fear or anxiety produced in the primary victims was not intended to be "permanent" but temporary. Indeed, how would prosecutors meet the even more difficult burden of proving beyond a reasonable doubt that an intent existed not merely to cause "serious" but "permanent" mental harm? It might also be alleged by an accused that specific terroristic tactics utilized did not equate with "torture or similar techniques" because the primary victims were never captured or under the control of the accused. Here again, U.S. prosecutors would be at a serious disadvantage and the object and purpose of the Convention would be needlessly thwarted.

Even more incredible was a 1987 bill in the House of Representatives designed supposedly "to implement" the Genocide Convention. A definitions portion of H.R. 807 would have redefined "substantial part" to mean "a part of a group of such numerical significance that the destruction or loss of that part would cause the destruction of the group as a viable entity...." How would a U.S. prosecutor prove such an element? If ninety-five percent of a group of thirty-five million men, women and children was brutally and systematically exterminated at the hands of some nationwide conspirators, would a defense be that the remaining five percent, now even more unified in its group identification and determination, was never targeted and still constitutes a viable entity? Under such a definition, must "the group as a viable entity" be exterminated or an intent to do so be proven beyond a reasonable doubt before genocide recognizably exists? Hitler's defense under such a definitional scheme would have been even stronger, and so would that of any future exterminators of racial, religious, national, or ethnic groups as long as they intend to leave some "viable" portion of the group or as long as it cannot be proven that they did not. Frankly, I've never heard of a more ludicrous, if not egregious, effort at drafting an "Implementation Act." There can be no doubt that adoption of the putative definition of "substantial part" in H.R. 807 would be fundamentally incompatible with the object and purpose of the Genocide Convention and leave the United States effort at meaningful adherence to the treaty and customary international law a laughable disgrace....

From the above, it is evident that the Senate's 1986 "understanding" should be changed. The present understanding would clash so seriously with the ordinary meaning of the terms of the treaty as well as its object and purpose that it could not survive a good faith, legally appropriate interpretation of the treaty. As an attempted "reservation," the Senate's "understanding" would be legally unacceptable since it is incompatible with the object and purpose of the Convention. Further, such an "understanding" cannot be legally operative in the case of a contrary *jus cogens*, which is the case here.

Questions

1. On October 14, 1988, S.1851 (which followed H.R. 807) was passed by the U.S. Senate. The House also passed its version of S.1851 on October 19th. President Reagan signed the legislation on November 4, 1988, and deposited the U.S. instrument of ratification of the Convention with the U.N. on November 25, 1988. Is the treaty thus "last in time" for the United States as opposed to U.S. legislation? Did the 2007 amendment to the legislation make it last in time? What differences exist? What statutory provisions would not prevail under the "last in time" rule, especially if some of the "understandings" concerning the treaty are void because they are incompatible with the object and purpose of the treaty? If the legislation is trumped entirely under the last-in-time rule, can prosecutors use the treaty directly for prosecution of genocide or, alternatively, use customary international law as the basis for prosecution? See also Johan D. van der Vyver, *Prosecution and Punishment, supra* at 353.

2. Under the legislation, can the U.S. prosecute members of al Qaeda for genocide in connection with the attacks on the World Trade Center and the Pentagon on September 11, 2001? Within the meaning of Section 1091(d), was "the offense" committed by bin Laden (the leader of al Qaeda) "committed within the United States"? Would Section 1093(8) fit? Do Sections 1091 and 1098(3) require the actual destruction of the group as a viable entity or an intent to destroy "a part of a group of such numerical significance that the destruction or loss of that part would cause the destruction of the group as a viable entity"?

3. Could the U.S. have prosecuted the former Iraqi dictator Saddam Hussein under the U.S. legislation for his widespread attacks on Iraqi Kurds in Northern Iraq after numerous Kurds engaged in armed violence against his regime? Would such attacks fit within Article II of the Genocide Convention?

4. If the United States does not have adequate legislation to prosecute all acts of genocide, is the U.S. in violation of Articles I, IV and V of the Convention? Also see Lee A. Steven, *Genocide and the Duty to Extradite or Prosecute: Why the United States is in Breach of Its International Obligations*, 39 Va. J. Int'l L. 425 (1999); *see also* van der Vyver, *supra* at 352. What legislation would you recommend now to adequately implement U.S. obligations under the Genocide Convention? Under customary international law? Would your legislation incorporate the Convention by reference?

5. Presently, can the U.S. prosecute some acts of genocide that are not covered by the 1988 legislation? as violations of customary international law? With respect to war crimes, recall 18 U.S.C. § 2441 and 10 U.S.C. §§ 818, 821; hostage-taking, 18 U.S.C. § 1203; U.S. national victims of murder or serious bodily harm, 18 U.S.C. §§ 2331–2332.

6. Section 1092 of the U.S. statute expressly does not preempt state jurisdiction. Can states within the United States exercise universal jurisdiction over acts of genocide committed outside their territory? There have been state prosecutions of war crimes, piracy, and other infractions of the law of nations. Assume that you have been requested by a state legislator to draft a criminal statute to cover genocide under the Convention and/ or customary international law. Draft the statute.

7. Note that Section 1092 merely states that it does not create a "substantive or procedural right". It does not preclude use of direct incorporation of customary international law or use of other federal statutory bases for incorporation such as the Alien Tort Claims Act, 28 U.S.C. § 1350, and the Torture Victim Protection Act—both of which execute relevant treaty law. *See, e.g.,* J. PAUST, INTERNATIONAL LAW AS LAW OF THE UNITED STATES 10, 14-15, 63-66, 284, 311, 373-74 (2 ed. 2003). Congressional intent to override the treaty, not even mentioned, would have to be clear and unequivocal. *See, e.g., id.* at 99, 107–08, *passim.* Even then, there would be exceptions to the last in time rule protecting rights under treaties and customary law. *See id.* at 86–100, *passim.*

8. When humans come, the extermination of species has been a common consequence for at least ten thousand years. Intended, negligent, unintended, it has still been a result. Should the intentional extermination of a life species be regulated by international law? What of new but threatening species we encounter in the future? Are we really prepared for space exploration? More generally, see M. Scharf & L. Roberts, *The Interstellar Relations of the Federation: International Law and "Star Trek: The Next Generation,"* 25 TOLEDO L. REV. 577 (1995).

Are the following relevant or earth-bound? Convention on International Trade in Endangered Species of Wild Fauna and Flora, 27 U.S.T. 1087, T.I.A.S. No. 8249, in 12 I.L.M. 1085 (1973); Convention on Biological Diversity (With Annexes), done at Rio de Janeiro, 5 June 1992, in 31 I.L.M. 818 (1992).

Chapter 4

War Crimes

Introductory Note

War crimes are offenses against the laws of war, more recently termed the laws of armed conflict or humanitarian law which apply during wars or armed conflicts. Although war has never been merely state-to-state, whether a state is at war and it is international in character depends upon the status of opponents (*e.g.*, whether they are states, nations, peoples, belligerents, or insurgents). In general, theorists prefer to separate laws concerning (1) the regulation of methods and means of combat, weaponry, and area controls (*e.g.*, those concerning occupied territory), such as those stressed in the 1907 Hague Convention No. IV, from those laws of armed conflict concerning (2) the protection of human beings, most notably the newer 1949 Geneva Conventions and Protocols thereto (extracts of which are in the Documents Section). However, no neat, ever-determinative lines are possible, since the laws of armed conflict ultimately relate to protections of persons or property and the policies of human dignity and of lessening unnecessary death, injury and suffering. For example, the 1863 Lieber Code (which was created to reflect certain customary laws of war at the time) emphasized both strands of the law of war. See the Documents Section. Within the 1907 Hague Convention, one also finds norms relating to the protection of persons; and within Geneva law, one finds norms relevant to selection of targets (especially in Protocol I), approaches to combat, and occupied territory. More important is an understanding of what provisions are applicable, in what contexts, to whom, with what sorts of rights and protections, and with what probable consequences.

The history of the law of war and its rich content is much more extensive than our chapter allows.[1] In more modern times, one of the first codifications of what was perceived to be the customary law of war was the 1863 Lieber Code, Instructions for the Government of Armies of the United States in the Field, General Orders No. 100 (April

---

1. For background, consider M. Cherif Bassiouni, Crimes Against Humanity in International Law 192–234 (1992); Antonio Cassese, The New Humanitarian Law of Armed Conflict (1979); M. Keen, The Law of War in the Late Middle Ages (1965); Myres S. McDougal & Florentino P. Feliciano, Law and Minimum World Public Order: The Legal Regulation of International Coercion (1961); Howard S. Levie, *The Laws of War and Neutrality,* in John N. Moore, Frederick S. Tipson, Robert F. Turner (eds.), National Security Law 307–13 (1990); Jean S. Pictet, I Commentary, Geneva Convention for the Amelioration of the Condition of the Wounded and Sick in Armed Forces in the Field 9-16 (1952); J. Paust, *My Lai and Vietnam: Norms, Myths and Leader Responsibility,* 57 Mil. L. Rev. 99, 108–18, *passim* (1972).

24, 1863). This document, used during the U.S. Civil War and later by the Germans during the Franco-Prussian War, became an historic base for further codifications such as those portions of the 1899 and 1907 Hague Conventions concerning war on land. The 1907 Hague Convention No. IV was recognizably customary international law applicable during World War II. Already, in 1864, the first Geneva Convention had been codified—with ten articles for protection of the wounded and sick. Geneva law was supplemented with new conventions in 1906 and 1929–with extended coverage for wounded and sick at sea and prisoners of war. In 1949, the four Geneva Conventions took form: GWS (Wounded & Sick), GWS at Sea, GPW (Prisoners of War), and GC (Civilians)—the latter providing the first Geneva Convention directed to protections of civilians as such. The 1949 Conventions were supplemented in 1977 with the adoption of two Protocols. Numerous other treaties adopted in the twentieth century have further supplemented normative guarantees, rights, and prohibitions found in the law of the Hague and Geneva law, including the more general law of human rights and several international criminal treaties such as the 1948 Genocide Convention (see Chapter Three) and customary legal trends, such as those concerning Crimes Against Humanity (see Chapter Two). As recognized by the Swiss scholar and professor at Heidelberg, Johann Bluntschli, in 1866: "Human rights remain in force during war." Quoted in J. Paust, International Law as Law of the United States 206 (2 ed. 2003).

Introductory Problem

For purposes of this problem, assume that you are a district judge presiding over the trial of General Fawaz Hussein, the (fictional) cousin of Iraqi President Saddam Hussein. Assume that General Hussein was captured by U.S. forces during the War in Iraq that began in 2003, and is being tried today in a federal district court. The indictment, containing the allegations against General Hussein, is reproduced below. General Hussein has moved for dismissal of any or all of the charges on the grounds that the facts alleged do not constitute a basis for criminal liability under the laws of war. Based on the materials on war crimes contained in this chapter, you should assess whether each of the charges alleges facts which, if proved, would constitute grounds for criminal liability under the laws of war. In addition, you should address the following defense claims: (a) "lack of knowledge," (b) "obedience to orders," (c) "military necessity," (d) lack of protected status under the Geneva law for Kuwaiti "terrorist" detainees. Consider also other challenges the General might argue.

Indictment of Fawaz Hussein

Background.

1. The defendant, General Fawaz Hussein, was the commander of the Iraqi National Tank and Artillery Battalion. As such, the defendant had 1,000 troops under his command. The defendant answered directly to Saddam Hussein, the President of Iraq and the Commander-in-Chief of the Iraqi army as well as the Iraqi Minister of Defense, Donsni Beersfeld.

2. The crimes charged herein are violations of the laws of war as reflected and codified in the following instruments, among others: (1) the 1949 Geneva Conventions (to which the U.S. and Iraq are parties); (2) Protocols I and II (1977) Additional to the

Geneva Conventions (which apply as customary international law); and (3) the opinions and judgments of the trials of Nazi war criminals in the *Dreierwalde* case, the *Von Leeb* case, and the *List* case, among others.

3. Even if the defendant had no actual knowledge of the actions of his troops described below, his personal criminal liability may be grounded on the principle of command responsibility. Nor may he escape liability relying on the defense that he was following Saddam Hussein's orders, since such orders were patently unlawful. Nor may he escape liability relying on the necessity defense, since the acts described below went beyond what was absolutely necessary for the conduct of military operations.

Count 1.

4. The defendant violated Protocol I of the Geneva Conventions and the customary law of war when, in 1990, he ordered his troops to surround Kuwait City, to cut off all power and water into the city, to bomb it into submission with artillery fire, and to confiscate the city's foodstuffs and medical stores to feed and care for the members of the Iraqi army. The fact that there was a small enemy military garrison in Kuwait City does not absolve defendant of liability.

Count 2.

5. The defendant violated the Geneva Convention Relative to the Protection of Civilian Persons in Time of War when, after the takeover of Kuwait City, troops under his command entered the Kuwait City Hospital and, when they discovered that the hospital personnel were hiding uninjured armed Kuwaiti soldiers there, they destroyed the facility, raped several nurses, and shot several doctors. In addition, the surviving hospital personnel were taken into custody as hostages in order to ensure the cooperation of the subjugated Kuwaiti population during the Iraqi occupation. In a televised broadcast, Saddam Hussein warned that, in accordance with a classified presidential directive and a court order, two of the captured Kuwaiti hospital "terrorist" personnel would be killed for every Iraqi killed by Kuwaiti resistance fighters. Altogether, 50 of the captured hospital personnel were executed by Fawaz Hussein's troops pursuant to this directive.

Count 3.

6. The defendant violated the Geneva Convention Relative to the Treatment of Prisoners of War and the customary law of war when troops under his command seized hundreds of Kuwaiti soldiers and civilians, and placed them in detention near Iraqi command bunkers and military bases as "human shields" so as to ensure that the bunkers and bases would not be subject to attack. Under two written directives from Iraqi Minister of Defense Beersfeld, captured Kuwaiti soldiers and civilians were authorized to be stripped naked and hooded during interrogation, use of dogs were authorized as part of "fear up harsh" interrogation, and the tactic of "water boarding" was authorized (whereby a detainee is made to experience an intense, terroristic fear of drowning). General Hussein ordered his troops to use the interrogation tactics on several detainees.

Count 4.

7. The defendant violated the Geneva Convention Relative to the Protection of Civilian Persons when the troops under his command destroyed Kuwait's seven oil processing plants and set at least 500 Kuwaiti oil wells on fire.

> Wherefor, the Special Prosecutor submits that this court should find the defendant, Fawaz Hussein, guilty of the aforementioned violations of the laws of war and impose such sentence as the Tribunal may deem just and proper.

Sources of International Humanitarian Law

International humanitarian law is not a completely cohesive body of law, but an amalgam of separate legal principles and proscriptions[2] applicable to international and non-international armed conflicts. Hans-Peter Gasser defines international humanitarian law in the following manner:

> previously known as the *law of war* [international humanitarian law] is a special branch of law governing situations of armed conflict—in a word, war. International humanitarian law seeks to mitigate the effects of war, first in that it limits the choice of means and methods of conducting military operations, and secondly in that it obliges the belligerents to spare persons who do not or no longer participate in hostile actions.[3]

These and other proscriptions are also included under the label of international criminal law.[4] Because international criminal law and international humanitarian law have not been completely codified, each proscription generally arises from a different source of law, *i.e.*, international agreements or treaties and customary law, although the two can constantly influence each other and what used to be merely treaty-based law can later reflect customary law (see Chapter One). Thus, it is useful to distinguish the particular source of conventional or customary international law.[5] Yet, distinctions between conventional and customary sources are not necessarily clear-cut, especially when some instruments are meant to reflect custom at the time of their formation (*e.g.*, the 1863 Lieber Code, *infra*) and, as soon as ink is dry on a new instrument, custom can

---

2. Hans-Peter Gasser, *International Humanitarian Law, Introduction* to Hans Haug, Humanity for All 1, 3 (1993). Gasser also lists the sources of international humanitarian law as the 1949 Geneva Conventions, Protocols I and II, and the rules of international customary law which are *jus cogens*. *Id.* at 18; *see also* Theodor Meron, Human Rights and Humanitarian Norms as Customary Law (1989); M. Cherif Bassiouni, *The Commission of Experts Established pursuant to Security Council Resolution 780: Investigating Violations of International Humanitarian law in the Former Yugoslavia*, 5 Crim. L.F. 279, 321–24 (1994).

3. Gasser, *supra* note 1, at 3.

4. *See* M. Cherif Bassiouni, International Crimes: Digest/Index of International Instruments 1815–1985, at 143–314 (1986); Yves Sandoz, *Penal Aspects of International Humanitarian Law*, in 1 International Criminal Law 201 (M. Cherif Bassiouni ed., 1986) [hereinafter Bassiouni, ICL].

5. For the law of armed conflict applicable to different types of conflicts, *see, e.g.*, G. Abi-Saab, Droit Humanitaire et Conflits Internes (1986); A. Andries, Eléments de Droit Pénal National et International (1992); Michael Bothe, *et al.*, New Rules for Victims of Armed Conflicts (1982); E. David, Principles de Droit des Conflits Armés (1994); The Laws of Armed Conflicts: A Collection of Conventions, Resolutions and Other Documents (Dietrich Schindler & Jiri Toman eds., 1981); The Law of War: A Documentary History (Leon Friedman ed., 1972); Howard S. Levie, The Code of International Armed Conflict (1986); F. Thomas, Debestraffing van Oorlogsmisdaden (1993); Michel Veuthey, Guérilla et Droit Humanitaire (1983); G. Abi-Saab, *War of National Liberation in the Geneva Conventions and Protocols*, 1979 Recueil des Cours D'Academie de Droit Intern'l 411; A. Cassese, *War of National Liberation and Humanitarian Law*, in Mélanges Pictet 319 (1984); F. Ouguergouz, *Guerres de libération nationale en droit humanitaire: quelques classifications*, in Mise en Oeuvre du Droit International Humanitaire 345 (F. Kalshoven & Y. Sandoz eds., 1988); J. Paust & A. Blaustein, *War Crimes Jurisdiction and Due Process: The Bangladesh Experience*, 11 Vand. J. Trans. L. 1 (1978); D. Plattern, *Law répression des violations du droit international humanitaire applicable aux conflits armés non internationaux*, Revue Internationale de Croix-Rouge Sept.-Oct. 1990, at 447; Sandoz, *supra* note 3; Michel Veuthey, *Non-International Armed Conflict and Guerilla Warfare*, in 1 Bassiouni, ICL, *supra* note 3, at 243.

have its influence with respect to the interpretation of printed words. It is widely recognized that the 1949 Geneva Conventions, including common Article 3 and the grave breach provisions, and Articles 11, 48-54, 75, and 85 of Protocol I, in addition to other provisions therein, embody customary international law. Recall the 1993 Report of the Secretary-General, at para. 35 ("beyond doubt" customary international law includes "the Geneva Conventions of 12 August 1949"). As recognized at Nuremberg, the laws and customs of war include the 1907 Hague Convention and customary law as it has evolved since then. War crimes, as they emerge from customary laws of war, are criminally punishable.[6] These few distinctions illustrate the separate nature of the applicable sources of law and the overlap of some of their proscriptive norms. Genocide and Crimes Against Humanity are considered part of international humanitarian law even though they apply in time of peace as well as in time of war.

Section 1
Applicability

When do the laws of war apply?

U.S. Army Field Manual 27-10, The Law of Land Warfare (1956)

8. Situations to Which Law of War Is Applicable

a. Types of Hostilities. War may be defined as a legal condition of armed hostility between States. While it is usually accompanied by the commission of acts of violence, a state of war may exist prior to or subsequent to the use of force. The outbreak of war is usually accompanied by a declaration of war.

Instances of armed conflict without a declaration of war may include, but are not necessarily limited to the exercise of armed force pursuant to a recommendation, decision or call by the United Nations, in the exercise of the inherent right of individual or collective self-defense against armed attack, or in the performance of enforcement measures through a regional arrangement, or otherwise, in conformity with appropriate provisions of the United Nations Charter.

b. Customary Law. The customary law of war applies to all cases of declared war or any other armed conflict which may arise between the United States and other nations, even if the state of war is not recognized by one of them. The customary law is also applicable to all cases of occupation of foreign territory by the exercise of armed force, even if the occupation meets with no armed resistance.

c. Treaties. Treaties governing land warfare are applicable to various forms of war and armed conflict as provided by their terms. The Hague Conventions apply to "war". Common Article 2 of the Geneva Conventions of 1949 states:

---

6. *See generally* J. PICTET, IV COMMENTARY at 583 ("Geneva Conventions form part of what are generally called the laws and customs of war, violations of which are commonly called 'war crimes.'"); FM 27-10, paras. 499 ("Every violation of the law of war is a war crime"), 506b; HOWARD S. LEVIE, TERRORISM IN WAR: THE LAW OF WAR CRIMES (1993). As noted in other chapters, this is so even though some treaties, like the 1907 Hague Convention, do not expressly refer to criminal sanctions.

In addition to the provisions which shall be implemented in peacetime, the present Convention shall apply to all cases of declared war or of any other armed conflict which may arise between two or more of the High Contracting Parties, even if the state of war is not recognized by one of them.

The Convention shall also apply to all cases of partial or total occupation of the territory of a High Contracting Party, even if the said occupation meets with no armed resistance.

Although one of the Powers in conflict may not be a party to the present Convention, the Powers who are parties thereto shall remain bound by it in their mutual relations. They shall furthermore be bound by the Convention in relation to the said Power, if the latter accepts and applies the provisions thereof. (*GWS, GWS Sea, GPW, GC, art. 2*)

d. Special Case of Civil Wars. See paragraph 11.

9. Applicability of Law of Land Warfare in Absence of a Declaration of War

As the customary law of war applies to cases of international armed conflict and to the forcible occupation of enemy territory generally as well as to declared war in its strict sense, a declaration of war is not an essential condition of the application of this body of law. Similarly, treaties relating to "war" may become operative notwithstanding the absence of a formal declaration war.

10. When Law of Land Warfare Ceases to Be Applicable

The law of land warfare generally ceases to be applicable upon:

a. The termination of a war by agreement, normally in the form of a treaty of peace; or

b. The termination of a war by unilateral declaration of one of the parties, provided the other party does not continue hostilities or otherwise decline to recognize the act of its enemy; or

c. The complete subjugation of an enemy State and its allies, if prior to a or b; or

d. The termination of a declared war or armed conflict by simple cessation of hostilities.

However, certain designated provisions of the Geneva Conventions of 1949 (see GC, art. 6) continue to be operative, notwithstanding the termination of any antecedent hostilities, during the continuance of military occupation. Insofar as the unwritten law of war and the Hague Regulations extend certain fundamental safeguards to the persons and property of the populations of occupied territory, their protection continues until the termination of any occupation having its origin in the military supremacy of the occupant, notwithstanding the fact the Geneva Convention relative to the Protection of Civilian Persons may have ceased to be applicable.

11. Civil War

a. Customary Law. The customary law of war becomes applicable to civil war upon recognition of the rebels as belligerents.

b. Geneva Conventions of 1949.

[common Article 3]

In the case of armed conflict not of an international character occurring in the territory of one of the High Contracting Parties, each party to the conflict shall be bound to apply, as a minimum, the following provisions:

(1) Persons taking no active part in the hostilities, including members of armed forces who have laid down their arms and those placed *hors de combat* by sickness, wounds, detention, or any other cause, shall in all circumstances be treated humanely,

without any adverse distinction founded on race, colour, religion or faith, sex, birth or wealth, or any other similar criteria.

To this end, the following acts are and shall remain prohibited at any time and in any place whatsoever with respect to the above-mentioned persons:

(a) violence to life and person, in particular murder of all kinds, mutilation, cruel treatment and torture;

(b) taking of hostages;

(c) outrages upon personal dignity, in particular, humiliating and degrading treatment;

(d) the passing of sentences and the carrying out of executions without previous judgment pronounced by a regularly constituted court, affording all the judicial guarantees which are recognized as indispensable by civilized peoples.

(2) The wounded and sick shall be collected and cared for.

An impartial humanitarian body, such as the International Committee of the Red Cross, may offer its services to the Parties to the conflict.

The Parties to the conflict should further endeavor to bring into force, by means of special agreements, all or part of the other provisions of the present Convention.

The application of the preceding provisions shall not affect the legal status of the Parties to the conflict. (GWS, GPW, GWS Sea, GC, art. 3)

J. Pictet (ed.), IV Commentary, Geneva Convention Relative to the Protection of Civilian Persons in Time of War (1958)

[re: common Article 2]

PARAGRAPH 1—ARMED CONFLICTS INVOLVING THE APPLICATION OF THE CONVENTION

By its general character, this paragraph deprives belligerents, in advance, of the pretexts they might in theory put forward for evading their obligations. There is no need for a formal declaration of war, or for recognition of the existence of a state of war, as preliminaries to the application of the Convention. The occurrence of *de facto* hostilities is sufficient.

It remains to ascertain what is meant by "armed conflict". The substitution of this much more general expression for the word "war" was deliberate. It is possible to argue almost endlessly about the legal definition of "war". A State which uses arms to commit a hostile act against another State can always maintain that it is not making war, but merely engaging in a police action, or acting in legitimate self-defence. The expression "armed conflict" makes such arguments less easy. Any difference arising between two States and leading to the intervention of members of the armed forces is an armed conflict within the meaning of Article 2, even if one of the parties denies the existence of a state of war. It makes no difference how long the conflict lasts, or how much slaughter takes place. The respect due to the human person as such is not measured by the number of victims....

1. *Introductory sentence — Field of application of the Article* [common Article 3]

A. *Cases of armed conflict* — What is meant by "armed conflict not of an international character"?

That was the burning question which arose again and again at the Diplomatic Conference. The expression was so general, so vague, that many of the delegations feared that it might be taken to cover any act committed by force of arms — any form of anarchy, rebellion, or even plain banditry. For example, if a handful of individuals were to rise in rebellion against the State and attack a police station, would that suffice to bring into being an armed conflict within the meaning of the Article? In order to reply to questions of this sort, it was suggested that the term "conflict" should be defined or — and this would come to the same thing — that a list should be given of a certain number of conditions on which the application of the Convention would depend. The idea was finally abandoned — wisely, we think. Nevertheless, these different conditions, although in no way obligatory, constitute convenient criteria, and we therefore think it well to give a list drawn from the various amendments discussed: they are as follows:

> (1) That the Party in revolt against the *de jure* Government possesses an organized military force, an authority responsible for its acts, acting within a determinate territory and having the means of respecting and ensuring respect for the Convention.

> (2) That the legal Government is obliged to have recourse to the regular military forces against insurgents organized as military and in possession of a part of the national territory.

> (3) (a) That the *de jure* Government has recognized the insurgents as belligerents; or

> (b) That it has claimed for itself the rights of a belligerent; or

> (c) That it has accorded the insurgents recognition as belligerents for the purposes only of the present Convention; or

> (d) That the dispute has been admitted to the agenda of the Security Council or the General Assembly of the United Nations as being a threat to international peace, a breach of the peace, or an act of aggression.

> (4)(a) That the insurgents have an organization purporting to have the characteristics of a State.

> (b) That the insurgent civil authority exercises *de facto* authority over persons within a determinate portion of the national territory.

> (c) That the armed forces act under the direction of an organized authority and are prepared to observe the ordinary laws of war.

> (d) That the insurgent civil authority agrees to be bound by the provisions of the Convention.

The above criteria are useful as a means of distinguishing a genuine armed conflict from a mere act of banditry or an unorganized and short-lived insurrection.

Does this mean that Article 3 is not applicable in cases where armed strife breaks out in a country, but does not fulfill any of the above conditions (which are not obligatory and are only mentioned as an indication)? We do not subscribe to this view. We think, on the contrary, that the scope of application of the article must be as wide as possible. There can be no drawbacks in this, since the Article in its reduced form, contrary to what might be thought, does not in any way limit the right of a State to put down rebellion, nor does it increase in the slightest the authority of the rebel party. It merely demands respect for certain rules, which were already recognized as essential in all civilized countries, and embodied in the municipal law of the States in question, long before the Convention was signed ...

The obligation resting on the Party to the conflict which represents established authority is not open to question. The mere fact of the legality of a Government involved in an internal conflict suffices to bind that Government as a Contracting Party to the

Convention. On the other hand, what justification is there for the obligation on the adverse Party in revolt against the established authority? At the Diplomatic Conference doubt was expressed as to whether insurgents could be legally bound by a Convention which they had not themselves signed. But if the responsible authority at their head exercises effective sovereignty, it is bound by the very fact that it claims to represent the country, or part of the country. The "authority" in question can only free itself from its obligations under the Convention by following the procedure for denunciation laid down in Article 158. But the denunciation would not be valid, and could not in point of fact be effected, unless the denouncing authority was recognized internationally as a competent Government. It should, moreover, be noted that under Article 158 denunciation does not take effect immediately....

PARAGRAPH 4.—LACK OF EFFECTS ON THE LEGAL STATUS OF THE PARTIES TO THE CONFLICT

This clause is essential. Without it neither Article 3, nor any other Article in its place, would ever have been adopted. It meets the fear—always the same one—that the application of the Convention, even to a very limited extent, in cases of civil war may interfere with the *de jure* Government's lawful suppression of the revolt, or that it may confer belligerent status, and consequently increased authority and power, upon the adverse Party....

Consequently, the fact of applying Article 3 does not in itself constitute any recognition by the *de jure* Government that the adverse Party has authority of any kind; it does not limit in any way the Government's right to suppress a rebellion by all the means—including arms—provided by its own laws; nor does it in any way affect that Government's right to prosecute, try and sentence its adversaries for their crimes, according to its own laws.

In the same way, the fact of the adverse party applying the Article does not give it any right to special protection or any immunity, whatever it may be and whatever title it may give itself or claim.

Article 3 resembles the rest of the Convention in that it is only concerned with the individual and the physical treatment to which he is entitled as a human being without regard to his other qualities. It does not affect the legal or political treatment which he may receive as a result of his behaviour.

Paust & Blaustein, *War Crimes Jurisdiction and Due Process: The Bangladesh Experience,* 11 VAND. J. TRANS. L. 1, 11–15 (1978)

Customary Law of War

The customary international law of war applied to the armed conflict between Pakistan and the forces of the subsequent state of Bangladesh from the period of belligerency. That period began prior to the formal recognition of Bangladesh by India on December 6, 1971, prior to general armed intervention into the conflict by Indian troops in early December 1971, and after the Bangladesh Proclamation of Independence on April 10, 1971. The forces of the subsequent state of Bangladesh had (1) an armed force with a responsible command structure, (2) the semblance of a government, (3) control of significant amounts of territory in East Pakistan, (4) recognition by others as a belligerent force, ... (5) generally followed the laws of war [and (6) engaged in sustained or protracted hostilities].

The customary law of war includes the principles of the 1907 Hague Convention, No. IV, and numerous additional prescriptions on the conduct of hostilities, the treatment of captives, and the basic protections of the populations involved in armed conflict.

The 1949 Geneva Conventions

Bangladesh considered itself bound by the Geneva Conventions by virtue of the previous ratification by Pakistan which was at all times bound by the Conventions. The remaining questions were: (1) when did certain provisions of those Conventions apply, and (2) who was entitled to what sort of protection?

It is submitted that sometime after the March 25, 1971, actions in Dacca and the April 10th Bangladesh Proclamation of Independence, common article 3 of the 1949 Geneva Conventions applied specifically in the context of emerging independence and generally to the outbreak of armed hostilities within East Pakistan. There is no definitive view on when this jurisdictional event occurs, but several useful criteria for policy-conscious and rational decision-making have been elaborated by the textwriters. More certain is that once the conflict has reached the level of an actual belligerency (as opposed to an insurgency or some lesser form of armed violence), article 2 of the Geneva Conventions, and thus the bulk of Convention provisions, apply to the conflict. Thus, as the conflict intensifies and the insurgent group gains recognition as a belligerent, the application of the Geneva precepts is expanded. The advent of an armed conflict between troops of Pakistan and India, including the exchange of fire across their borders, undoubtedly made the conflict an international armed conflict governed by article 2 of the Conventions.

A determination must be made of who was entitled to what sort of protection at each stage of the conflict, given the expanded applicability of Geneva law. This poses no major difficulty, for under common article 3 of the Conventions the people of East Pakistan were all entitled to protection outlined in the article if they were not directly engaged in combat. When the conflict became an article 2 conflict the people of East Pakistan, in a state of belligerency, were at least entitled to the protection outlined in Part II of the 1949 Geneva Convention Relative to the Protection of Civilian Persons, and a growing body of authority supports the argument that the provisions of common article 3 should have continued to apply as well. When the state of Bangladesh became a reality, the relevant conduct had already occurred, so questions of shifting nationality were not technically relevant. Where the Geneva law seeks to govern the relations of distinct national groups (states or belligerents) under common article 2 and, presumably, more homogeneous entities under common article 3, a policy consideration is raised in contradistinction to the formal language of article 4 of the Geneva Civilian Convention, which would technically preclude the protections of Part III (but expressly not Part II) of that Convention to "nationals" of the offending party. In the context of a belligerency (to which common article 2 applies as well as Part II) where there are substantial differences in group make-up and one of the groups is striving for self-determination, it is both unrealistic and unresponsive to overall community policy and Geneva goal values to continue to treat the populace of such a belligerent as "nationals" of the other belligerent within the meaning of article 4—especially when common interpretation of the word "nation" or "nationals" is not equated with "state" but can refer also to a group of people. Formalistic thinking would otherwise require that the same persons who are entitled to the protection of the customary law of war do not also receive the full protection of Geneva law, which was enacted to increase protection for civilians in times of armed conflict.

In this case, however, the problem may be mooted by the fact that the alleged misconduct would not only be prohibited by common article 3 of the Geneva Conventions (at such a level of conflict), but also by the language of articles 13 and 16 of the Geneva Civilian Convention which prohibits attacks upon, ill-treatment of, or a failure to affirmatively protect all those who are (1) exposed to grave danger in any manner, (2) wounded, (3) sick, (4) infirm, (5) expectant mothers, (6) children under the age of fifteen who were orphans or had been separated from their families as a result of war, or (7) members of a hospital staff protected under article 20 of that Convention.

Protocol Additional to the Geneva Conventions of 12 August 1949, and relating to the protection of victims of international armed conflicts (Protocol I) 8 June 1977

[Read the preamble and Articles 1, 3 and 4 of Protocol I]

Protocol Additional to the Geneva Conventions of 12 August 1949, and relating to the protection of victims of non-international armed conflicts (Protocol II) 8 June 1977

[Read the preamble and Articles 1-3 of Protocol II]

Notes and Questions

1. Today, it is widely recognized that although common Article 3 of the 1949 Geneva Conventions was designed to apply to an insurgency (the lowest level of armed conflict under the laws of war), the rights, duties and prohibitions reflected in common Article 3 are now part of customary international law applicable "in all circumstances" during any armed conflict. *See, e.g.*, 4 COMMENTARY, *supra* at 14 ("This minimum requirement in the case of a non-international armed conflict, is *a fortiori* applicable in international conflicts."), 58; ICRC, INTERNATIONAL HUMANITARIAN LAW AND THE CHALLENGES OF CONTEMPORARY ARMED CONFLICT 9 (2003); JEAN-MARIE HENCKAERTS & LOUIS DOSWALD-BECK, 1 CUSTOMARY INTERNATIONAL HUMANITARIAN LAW: RULES 299, 306-19 (ICRC 2005) (the prohibitions reflected in common Article 3 are "fundamental guarantees" that apply as "customary international law applicable in both international and non-international armed conflicts"); U.S. Dep't of Army, TJAG School, OPERATIONAL LAW HANDBOOK 8-9 (2003); Derek Jinks, *Protective Parity and the Law of War*, 79 NOTRE DAME L. REV. 1493, 1508-11 (2004); Paust, *Judicial Power to Determine the Status and Rights of Persons Detained Without Trial*, 44 HARV. INT'L L.J. 503, 512 n.27 (2003) [hereinafter Paust, *Judicial Power*]; Paust, *Executive Plans andAuthorizations to Violate International Law Concerning Treatment and Interrogation of Detainees*, 43 COLUMBIA J. TRANSNAT'L L. 811, 816 & nn.17, 19 (2005) [hereinafter Paust, *Executive Plans*], available at http://ssrn.com/abstract=903349http://www.columbia.edu/cu/jtl/Vol_43_3_files/Paust.pdf; Case Concerning Military and Paramilitary Activities in and Against Nicaragua (Nicaragua v. United States), 1986 I.C.J. 4, at 113-14, paras. 218 ("There is no doubt that, in the event of international armed conflicts, these rules also constitute a minimum yardstick, in addition to the more elaborate rules which are also to apply to international conflicts; and they are rules which ... reflect ...'elementary considerations of humanity'"), 255 (is included in "general principles of humanitarian law ... in the context of armed conflicts, whether international in character or not"); The Prosecutor

v. Delalic, IT-96-21-A, Judgment (Appeals Chamber, International Criminal Tribunal for Former Yugoslavia, 20 Feb. 2001), at paras. 143, 150, *reprinted in* 40 I.L.M. 630 (2001); The Prosecutor v. Tadic, Appeals Chamber, *supra* at para. 102 ("The International Court of Justice has confirmed that these rules reflect 'elementary considerations of humanity' applicable under customary international law to any armed conflict, whether it is of an internal or international character. (Nicaragua Case, at para. 218). Therefore, at least with respect to the minimum rules in common Article 3, the character of the conflict is irrelevant."); The Prosecutor v. Tadic, Trial Chamber, *supra* at paras. 65, 67, 74; The Prosecutor v. Naletilic and Martinovic, IT-98-34, Judgment (Trial Chamber, ICTY, Mar. 31, 2003), para. 228 (common Article 3 "applies regardless of the internal or international character of the conflict");

The Prosecutor v. Mucic, *et al.* (Appeals Chamber, ICTY, Feb. 20, 2001), paras. 140-50; Abella v. Argentina, Case 11,137, Inter-Am. C.H.R., paras. 155-56, OEA/ser.L/V.97, doc. 38 (1997); Hamdan v. Rumsfeld, 344 F. Supp.2d 152, 162-63 (D.D.C. 2004); *see also* 2004 UK Ministry of Defence, The Manual of the Law of Armed Conflict 5 n.13 (2004) (recognizing that among "important judgments" the I.C.J. "referred to the rules in Common Art. 3 as constituting 'a minimum yardstick' in international armed conflicts"). It is also widely recognized that the same customary and absolute rights and duties are mirrored in Article 75 of Protocol I to the Geneva Conventions, which is applicable during any international armed conflict.

2. What, within the meaning of Article 3(2) of Protocol II, is an "internal or external affair *of*" a particular state (emphasis added)? When an affair is also "of" the international community, does such a phrase not apply? In general, application of human rights law is of concern to the international community and is not simplistically the prerogative of the state in whose territory and/or at whose hands violations occur. The same pertains with respect to application of common Article 3 of the Geneva Conventions to an internal insurgency. See also common Article l; J. Pictet, III Commentary Relative to the Treatment of Prisoners of War 18, 35, 38, 43 (1960); IV Commentary, *supra* at 15, 37–38, 41, 44; *but see id.* at 16.

3. The first major war to which the 1949 Geneva Conventions applied was the Korean Conflict during which some nineteen countries participated under a U.N. flag.

4. Did the customary laws of war apply to the social violence that occurred in Libya in early 2011 (*e.g.*, were the criteria for an "insurgency" met when Libyan rebels fought Libyan governmental forces under Muammar Qaddafi)? Did Protocol II's provisions apply if Libya was a party to the Protocol? See Article 1 (1) and (2). Did Protocol I? How would you interpret the phrase "armed conflict" in Article 1 (4) of Protocol I? Must such a conflict satisfy the criteria that must be met for the existence of an insurgency? a belligerency? Clearly, once the United States and NATO forces engaged in the armed conflict in Libya (under U.N. S.C. Res. 1973 (March 17, 2011)) an armed conflict of an international character had occurred.

5. Did the laws of armed conflict apply to the fighting between the Contras and the Government of Nicaragua in the 1980s? Had the Contras met the criteria for an "insurgency"? What facts would you like to know? Did they apply to U.S. involvement? See Nicaragua v. United States, [1986] I.C.J. paras. 218–220; Separate Opinion of Judge Ago, *id.* at para. 11; Separate Opinion of Judge Schwebel, *id.* at para. 257. See also discussion below in Note 9.

6. As noted, all of the customary laws of war apply to a belligerency, such as during the U.S. Civil War. In 1949, when the Geneva Conventions first applied certain laws of

war to what is strictly an internal insurgency under common Article 3, it was a radical change of the laws of war. Richard R. Baxter, *Modernizing the Law of War*, 78 Mil. L. Rev. 165, 168-73 (1978).

What is the difference between an "insurgency" and a "belligerency" (or "true civil war"), to which all of the customary laws of war apply? Recall FM 27-10, para. 11 a; Paust & Blaustein, *supra*. See also J. Pictet, III Commentary, *supra* at 38 ("For instance, if one Party to a conflict is recognized by third parties as being a belligerent, that Party would then have to respect the Hague rules."); The Prize Cases, 67 U.S. (2 Black) 635, 666 ("When the party in rebellion occupy and hold in a hostile manner a certain portion of territory; have declared their independence; have cast off their allegiance; have organized armies; have committed hostilities against their former sovereign, the world acknowledges them as belligerents"), 669 ("Foreign nations acknowledge it as a war by a declaration of neutrality ... recognizing hostilities as existing....") (1862); The Santissima Trinidad, 20 U.S. (7 Wheat.) 283, 337 (1822) ("The government of the United States has recognized the existence of a civil war between Spain and her colonies.... Each party is, therefore, deemed by us a belligerent nation"); U.S. Dep't of Army, Pamphlet 27-161-2, 2 International Law 27 (1962) ("If the rebellious side conducts its war by guerrilla tactics it seldom achieves the status of a belligerent because it does not hold territory and it has no semblence of a government."). Note that the belligerent or insurgent remains bound by the treaty obligations of the state of their nationality as well as by any applicable customary laws of war and human rights law. See also Chacon v. Eighty-Nine Bales of Cochineal, 5 F. Cas. 390, 394 (No. 2,568) (C.C.D. Va. 1821) (Marshall, C.J.), aff'd in The Santissima Trinidad, *supra* ("Whether Buenos Ayres be a state or not, if she is in a condition to make war, and to claim the character and rights of a belligerent, she is bound to respect the laws of war").

One important difference is that during an insurgency the insurgent fighters do not have combatant status and combatant immunity for what would be lawful acts of war. See ICRC, The Relevance of IHL in the Context of Terrorism (2011) (there is no combatant or pow status for fighters during an insurgency). Therefore, they can be prosecuted under relevant domestic law for murder, assault and battery, and so forth, even with respect to conduct that would provide combatant immunity for combatants during a belligerency or other international armed conflict for acts that are lawful under the laws of war (such as the killing of an enemy combatant who has not surrendered or been captured) and that are not otherwise violative of other international laws (*e.g.*, those proscribing aircraft sabotage, aircraft hijacking, forced disappearance, genocide, or other crimes against humanity). An insurgent who kills an enemy fighter can be prosecuted for murder under relevant domestic law, but the murder is not a war crime. If an insurgent intentionally kills civilians who are not directly participating in hostilities, such killings are violations of the customary laws of war that apply today during an insurgency and, therefore, the insurgent can be prosecuted for the war crime of killing such civilians.

The normal test for "combatant" status during an international armed conflict is membership in the armed forces of a party to the conflict. *See, e.g.*, Paust, *War and Enemy Status After 9/11: Attacks on the Laws of War*, 28 Yale J. Int'l L.325, 329-34 (2003) [hereinafter Paust, *Status*]; see also The Prosecutor v. Kordic & Cerkez, IT-95-14/2-A (Appeals Chamber, 17 Dec. 2004), para. 51, "members of the armed forces resting in their homes in the area of the conflict, as well as members of the [Territorial Defence forces] residing in their homes, remain combatants whether or not they are in combat, or for the time being armed." Also note: Article 1 of the Annex to the 1907 Hague Convention expressly states that belligerent status during war will "apply ... to armies" and it expressly sets forth additional criteria that are to be met merely by "militia" or "volunteer corps." The customary 1863 Lieber Code also affirmed: "So soon as a man is armed by a sovereign government and takes the soldier's oath of fidelity, he is a belligerent; his killing, wounding, or other warlike acts are not individual crimes or offenses." Therefore, the Lieber Code reflected both the membership test for what we term "combatant" status and the fact that the combatant has what we term "combatant immunity" for lawful acts of war.

During either an insurgency or an international armed conflict, a fighter who does not meet the test for "combatant" status is an "unprivileged" fighter. Such a person can be prosecuted under domestic law for acts of violence engaged in by such person, but the mere act of unprivileged fighting of enemy fighters is not a war crime. The unprivileged fighter lacks combatant immunity for what would otherwise be lawful acts of war by a combatant during an international armed conflict, however such a person has protections once detained, like any civilian who is not directly participating in hostilities. *Cf* IV Commentary, *supra* at 53 (noting while addressing considerations during formation of Article 5: "[t]hose who take part in the struggle while not belonging to the armed forces are acting deliberately outside the laws of warfare," but will nonetheless benefit from the requirement of humane treatment in Article 5). "Outside," that is, with respect to combatant status and combatant immunity, but nonetheless persons who are protected at least under customary law reflected in common Article 3 once detained.

Language in *Ex parte* Quirin, 317 U.S. 1 (1942), can create confusion. In that case, German "enemy belligerents," "who though combatants," were prosecuted for the war crime of engaging in combat activity out of uniform (prior to creation of the 1949 Geneva Conventions). See 317 U.S. at 35-37, 44; Hays Parks, Special Forces' Wear of Non-Standard Uniforms, 4 Chi. J. Int'l L. 493, 547 n.31 (2003); Paust, Status, supra at 331-32. Yet, the Court stated that it was appropriate "to charge all the petitioners with the offense of unlawful belligerency." 317 U.S. at 23 (emphasis added). The Court also stated that participation in combat "without uniform" subjects the individual "to the punishment prescribed by the law of war for unlawful belligerents." 317 U.S. at 37. Even a combatant who is entitled to prisoner of war status could be charged with the war crime of fighting while out of uniform, which was the major war crime addressed. See also IV Commentary, supra at 53 ("irregular combatants" are "[t]hose who take part in the struggle while not belonging to the armed forces [and] are acting deliberately outside the laws of warfare." Yet, the acts are not labeled as war crimes). Any person (e.g., a combatant or an unprivileged belligerent) can be prosecuted for their conduct that constitutes a war crime.

Perhaps unwittingly, the Bush Administration turned the meaning of "combatant" on its head and has preferred to classify detainees at Guantanamo as "enemy combatants." *See, e.g.*, Hamdi v. Rumsfeld, 542 U.S. 507, 510 (2004); Padilla v. Hanft, 423 F.3d 386, 388-93 (4th Cir. 2005); *In re* Guantanamo Detainee Cases, 355 F. Supp.2d 443, 445-50 (D.D.C. 2005). It has also used an overly broad definition of enemy combatant that has no support elsewhere. As noted in *In re Guantanamo Detainee Cases*, "[o]n July 7, 2004, nine days after the issuance of the *Rasul* decision, Deputy Secretary of Defense Paul Wolfowitz issued an Order creating a military tribunal called the Combatant Status Review Tribunal (hereinafter "CSRT") to review the status of each detainee at Guantanamo Bay as an 'enemy combatant.' [The document can be found at http:// www.defenselink.mil/news/Jul2004/d20040707review.pdf.] That definition is as follows:

[T]he term 'enemy combatant' shall mean an individual who was part of *or supporting* Taliban *or al Qaeda forces, or associated forces* that are engaged in hostilities against the United States or its coalition partners. This includes any person who has committed a belligerent act *or has directly supported hostilities* in aid of enemy armed forces."

355 F. Supp.2d at 450 (emphasis added).

Contrary to international law, the Bush Administration also made efforts to prosecute unprivileged fighters for merely fighting in an armed conflict as a war crime. As noted, this "unprecedented effort to characterize all direct participation in hostilities [by civilians] as a war crime … has largely been a failure—yielding only one guilty plea based on a direct attack on a U.S. soldier—after nearly a decade of efforts to prosecute Guantanamo detainees in military tribunals." David J.R. Frakt, *Direct Participation in Hostilities as a War Crime: America's Failed Efforts to Change the Law of War*, 46 Valp. U. L. Rev. 729, 762 (2012).

7. What was the status of the U.S. Civil War and what laws of war applied? See the 1863 Lieber Code, which applied the customary laws of war codified therein in the context of the U.S. Civil War (some portions are extracted in the Documents Section); Paust, *My Lai and Vietnam: Norms, Myths and Leader Responsibility*, 57 Mil. L. Rev. 99, 115–16, 130–31 (1972).

8. Note that some treaties and customary norms apply in all social contexts, *e.g.*, in times of relative peace or times of armed conflict. The customary prohibition of genocide and human rights law (which contains its own set of derogation provisions with respect to derogable rights) are examples. That customary and treaty-based human rights laws apply during war, recall Bluntschli (quoted *supra*) and *see, e.g.*, Louise Doswald-Beck, Human Rights in Times of Conflict and Terrorism (2011); Paust, *Executive Plans, supra* at 820-23, and the many references cited; Protocol Additional to the Geneva Conventions of 12 August 1949, and Relating to the Protection of Victims of International Armed Conflicts, art. 72 ("other applicable rules of international law relating to protection of fundamental human rights during international armed conflict"), 1125 U.N.T.S. 3 (June 8, 1977); Protocol Additional to the Geneva Conventions of 12 August 1949, and Relating to the Protection of Victims of Non-International Armed Conflicts, prmbl. ("Recalling … that international instruments relating to human rights offer a basic protection to the human person"), 1125 U.N.T.S. 609 (June 8, 1977); In the case Armed Activities on the Territory of the Congo (Dem. Rep. Congo v. Uganda), 2005 I.C.J. paras. 216-20, 345(3); Advisory Opinion, Legal Consequences of the Construction of a Wall in the Occupied Palestinian Territory, 2004 I.C.J. paras. 104-106; Advisory Opinion, Legality of the Threat or Use of Nuclear Weapons, 1996 I.C.J. 95, 226, 239-40, para. 25 ("The protection of the International Covenant on Civil and Political Rights does not cease in times of war, except by operation of Article 4" regarding derogable rights) (July 8); Human Rights Comm., General Comment No. 31, U.N. Doc. CCPR/C/21/Rev.1/Add.13 (May 26, 2004), para. 11 ("the Covenant applies also in situations of armed conflict to which the rules of international humanitarian law are applicable. While … more specific rules of international humanitarian law may be specially relevant for the purposes of the interpretation of Covenant rights, both spheres of law are complementary, not mutually exclusive"); Human Rights Comm., General Comment No. 29, paras. 3, 9, 11 & n.6 , U.N. Doc. CCPR/C/21/Rev.1/Add.11 (2001); U.N. Committee Against Torture, *Consideration of Reports Submitted by States Parties Under Article 19 of the Convention: Conclusions and Recommendations of the Committee against Torture, United States of America*, 36th sess., U.N. Doc. CAT/C/USA/CO/2 (18 May 2006), paras. 14 (the U.S. "should recognize and ensure that the Convention applies at all times, whether in peace, war or armed conflict, in any territory under its jurisdiction.…"), 15 ("provisions of the Convention … apply to, and are fully enjoyed by, all

persons under the effective control of its authorities, of whichever type, wherever located in the world"), 19 (there exists an "absolute prohibition of torture ... without any possible derogation"), 24 (the U.S. "should rescind any interrogation technique—including methods involving sexual humiliation, 'water boarding,' 'short shackling,' and using dogs to induce fear, that constitute torture or cruel, inhuman or degrading treatment or punishment, in all places of detention under its *de facto* effective control, in order to comply with the Convention."); Human Rights Comm., *Concluding Observations of the Human Rights Committee, United States of America*, 87th Sess., July 10-28, 2006, paras. 10, 16, U.N. Doc. CCPR/C/USA/CO/3/Rev. 1 (18 Dec. 2006); Leila Zerrougui, *et al.*, Report, *Situation of Detainees at Guantánamo Bay*, U.N. Comm. on Human Rights, 62nd sess., U.N. Doc. E/CN.4/2006/120 (15 Feb. 2006), at paras. 15-16 (adding: "The application of international humanitarian law and of international human rights law are not mutually exclusive, but are complementary."), 83; U.N. S.C. Res. 1378, para. 9 (2006) ("violations of international humanitarian and human rights law in situations of armed conflict"); U.N. S.C. Res. 1265, para. 4, U.N. Doc. S/RES/1265 (Sept. 17, 1999); U.N. S.C. Res. 1100, prmbl., U.N. Doc. S/RES/1194 (1998) ("violations of human rights and of international humanitarian law"); U.N. G.A. Res. 63/166, prmbl. (2008), U.N. Doc. A/RES/63/166 (19 Feb. 2009) ("freedom from torture and other cruel, inhuman or degrading treatment or punishment is a non-derogable right that must be protected under all circumstances, including in times of international or internal armed conflict or disturbance"); U.N. G.A. Res. 59/191, Protection of Human Rights and Fundamental Freedoms While Countering Terrorism, para. 1 (2004), in the Documents Section; Council of Europe Parliamentary Assembly Resolution 1433, Lawfulness of Detentions by the United States at Guantanamo Bay (26 April 2005), in the Documents Section.

What types of rights, duties, and prohibitions are contained in common Article 3 of the Geneva Conventions? What types of nonderogable human rights are contained in Article 7 of the International Covenant on Civil and Political Rights (ICCPR)? The rights reflected in Article 7 are customary rights of universal application and are also peremptory rights *jus cogens* (*i.e.*, they prevail in all contexts and preempt any inconsistent international agreements or limitations therein). Note that common Article 3 also incorporates customary rights to due process by reference. Today, it is widely recognized that Article 14 of the ICCPR reflects minimum customary human rights to due process. Recall *Hamdan v. Rumsfeld*, 548 U.S. 557 (2006). Thus, they are incorporated by reference through common Article 3. Concerning other relevant customary and treaty-based human rights, see Chapter One.

9. Is the following definition of "armed conflict" too broad? In *The Prosecutor v. Dusko Tadic,* the Appeals Chamber of the ICTY stated in para. 70:

> "We find that an armed conflict exists whenever there is resort to armed force between states or protracted armed violence between governmental authorities and organized armed groups or between such groups within a state."

Does the definition cover armed conflict between organized armed groups across state lines? Under Geneva law, what sort of conflict might the latter be? Does the phrase "armed force" require that traditional criteria for an insurgency be used? Does the phrase "organized armed groups" include U.N. or NATO peacemakers using armed force as part of their mission? Recall FM 27-10, *supra* para. 8 a. Does the definition cover armed conflict by organized armed groups on the high seas or in outer space? Are these international armed conflicts under Geneva law? Would this definition cover armed violence between members of al Qaeda and the regime in Iraq? What is the meaning of "protracted" armed violence? What traditional criteria for an insurgency or application of Geneva Protocol II, art. 1(1) are missing?

See also id. (Trial Chamber, Judgment, May 17, 1997), para. 562 ("terrorist activities ... are not subject to international humanitarian law"); The Prosecutor v. Boskoski & Tareulovski, IT-04-82-T (Trial Chamber, Judgment, Jul. 10, 2008), paras. 175, 177-78 ("the Trial Chamber in *Tadic* interpreted this test ... as consisting of two criteria, namely (i) the intensity of the conflict, and (ii) the organization of the parties to the conflict" and "care is needed not to lose sight of the requirement for protracted armed violence..., when assessing the intensity of the conflict. The criteria are closely related"), 185 (regarding "protracted" violence, what matters is whether the acts are perpetrated in isolation or as part of a protracted campaign that entails the engagement of both parties in hostilities," and quoting The Prosecutor v. Kordic: "'[t]he requirement of protracted fighting is significant'"), 199-203 (identifying various other factors); The Prosecutor v. Musema, ICTR-96-13-T (Trial Chamber, Judgment, Jan. 27, 2000), para. 248 ("The expression 'armed conflicts' introduces a material criterion: the existence of open hostilities between armed forces which are organized to a greater or lesser degree"); Rome Statute of the International Criminal Court, art. 8(2)(d) ("isolated and sporadic acts of violence" are not "armed conflict"), 2187 U.N.T.S. 90. Has al Qaeda ever engaged in a "protracted campaign that entails engagement of ... [other] parties in hostilities," "open hostilities," or use "armed forces" in "protracted fighting"? It should be noted that Professor Cassese, as Judge in the Appeals Chamber of the ICTY, wrote the opinion noted above in *Tadic*, and he later recognized that members of al Qaeda are mere civilians engaged in criminal activities. Antonio Cassese, International Law 410 (2 ed. 2005).

In *The Prosecutor v. Rutaganda*, ICTR-96-3-T, at paras. 91-92 (6 Dec. 1999), the Trial Chamber of the ICTR stated:

91. It can thence be seen that the definition of an armed conflict *per se* is termed in the abstract, and whether or not a situation can be described as an "armed conflict", meeting the criteria of Common Article 3, is to be decided upon on a case-by-case basis. Hence, in dealing with this issue, the *Akayesu Judgement* suggested an "evaluation test", whereby it is necessary to evaluate the intensity and the organization of the parties to the conflict to make a finding on the existence of an armed conflict. This approach also finds favour with the Trial Chamber in this instance.

92. In addition to armed conflicts of a non-international character, satisfying the requirements of Common Article 3, under Article 4 of the Statute, the Tribunal has the power to prosecute persons responsible for serious violations of the 1977 Additional Protocol II, a legal instrument whose overall purpose is to afford protection to persons affected by non-international armed conflicts. As aforesaid, this instrument develops and supplements the rules contained in Common Article 3, without modifying its existing conditions of applicability. Additional Protocol II reaffirms Common Article 3, which, although it objectively characterized internal armed conflicts, lacked clarity and enabled the States to have a wide area of discretion in its application. Thus the impetus behind the Conference of Government Experts and the Diplomatic Conference in this regard was to improve the protection afforded to victims in non-international armed conflicts and to develop objective criteria which would not be dependent on the subjective judgements of the parties. The result is, on the one hand, that conflicts covered by Additional Protocol II have a higher intensity threshold than Common Article 3, and on the other, that Additional Proto-

col II is immediately applicable once the defined material conditions have been fulfilled. If an internal armed conflict meets the material conditions of Additional Protocol II, it then also automatically satisfies the threshold requirements of the broader Common Article 3.

10. Can a state be at "war" against a non-state actor such as al Qaeda? Or at "war" with a mere tactic of "terrorism"? The Bush Administration so claimed, but most textwriters disagree. *See, e.g.*, Bruce Ackerman, *This Is Not a War*, 113 YALE L.J. 1871 (2004); Michael Byers, *Terrorism, the Use of Force, and International Law After 11 September*, 51 INT'L & COMP. L.Q. 401 (2002); David Cole, *Enemy Aliens*, 54 STAN. L. REV. 953, 958 (2002); Christopher Greenwood, *War, Terrorism, and International Law*, 56 CURRENT L. PROBS. 505, 529 (2004); Joan Fitzpatrick, *Jurisdiction of Military Commissions and the Ambiguous War on Terrorism*, 96 AM. J. INT'L L. 345, 347-48 (2002); Wayne McCormack, *Emergency Powers and Terrorism*, 185 MIL. L. REV. 69, 70 & n.6 (2005); Mary Ellen O'Connell, symposium, "Terrorism on Trial," *The Legal Case Against the Global War on Terror*, 37 CASE W. RES. J. INT'L L. 349, 349-57 (2005); Paust, *Status, supra* at 326-28; Kenneth Roth, *The Law of War in the War on Terror*, FOREIGN AFF. 2 (Jan.-Feb. 2004); Leila N. Sadat, *Terrorism and the Rule of Law*, 3 WASH. U. GLOBAL STUD. L. REV. 135, 140 (2004); Marco Sassoli, *Use and Abuse of the Laws of War in the "War on Terrorism,"* 22 LAW & INEQ. 195 (2004); Warren Richey, *Tribunals on Trial*, THE CHRISTIAN SCIENCE MONITOR, Dec. 14, 2001, at 1 (*quoting* Professor Leila Sadat: not a war); *see also* Leila Zerrougui, *et al.*, Report, Situation of Detainees at Guantanamo Bay, Commission on Human Rights, 62nd sess., items 10 and 11 of the provisional agenda, U.N. Doc. E/CN.4/2006/120 (Feb. 15, 2006), at 36, para. 83 ("The war on terror, as such, does not constitute an armed conflict for the purposes of the applicability of international humanitarian law."); *cf* Norman C. Bay, *Executive Power and the War on Terror*, 83 DENV. L. REV. 335, 337 n.6 (2005); *but see* John C. Yoo & James C. Ho, *The Status of Terrorists*, 44 VA. J. INT'L L. 207 (2003); Curtis A. Bradley & Jack L. Goldsmith, *Congressional Authorization and the War on Terrorism*, 118 HARV. L. REV. 2047, 2068 (2005) ("[D]espite its novel features, the post-September 11 war on terrorism possesses more characteristics of a traditional war than some commentators have acknowledged.... The United States's continuing combat operations and related use of significant military resources against al Qaeda in Afghanistan and other countries also make a war characterization at least plausible."). In *Pan American World Airways, Inc. v. Aetna Casualty & Surety Co.*, 505 F.2d 989, 1013-15 (2d Cir. 1974), the Second Circuit declared that the U.S. could not have been at war with the Palestinian Front for the Liberation of Palestine, despite alleged terrorist attacks.

If not, can members of al Qaeda rightly be prosecuted for "war crimes" with respect to the 9/11 attacks on the U.S. World Trade Center and the Pentagon in 2001? What sort of other international crimes might apply to such events?

11. In any event, the United States has been involved in international armed conflicts in Afghanistan (since October 2001) and Iraq (since 2003), to which all of the customary laws of war apply as well as relevant treaty based laws of war. *See, e.g.*, Paust, *Executive Plans, supra* at 813-20. During such armed conflicts, the Bush Administration claimed a right to deny rights and protections under Geneva law when "military necessity" allegedly prevailed. Is this claim acceptable under the Geneva Conventions? Consider the following: Common Article 1 of the Geneva Conventions expressly requires that all of the signatories respect and ensure respect for the Conventions "in all circumstances." It is widely recognized that common Article 1, among other provisions, thereby assures that Geneva law is nonderogable, and that alleged necessity poses no exception

unless a particular article allows derogations on the basis of necessity. Article 1 also provides that the duty to respect and to ensure respect for Geneva law is not based on reciprocal compliance by an enemy but rests upon a customary *obligatio erga omnes* (an obligation owing by and to all humankind) as well as an express treaty-based obligation assumed by each signatory that is owing to every other signatory whether or not they are involved in a particular armed conflict. Further, Article 1 ensures that reprisals in response to enemy violations are not permissible. Each recognition above assures that, indeed, as expressly mandated in Article 1 the rights and duties set forth in the Geneva Conventions must be observed "in all circumstances." *Id*. at 814-16.

See also U.N. S.C. Res. 1674, para. 6, U.N. Doc. S/RES/1674 (28 Apr. 2006) (the Security Council demanded that all parties to an armed conflict "comply strictly with the obligations applicable to them under international law, in particular those contained in the Hague Conventions of 1899 and 1907 and in the Geneva Conventions of 1949 and their Additional Protocols of 1977").

12. Under the Geneva Conventions, any person (thus, including a civilian, prisoner of war, unprivileged belligerent, terrorist, state or non-state actor) has rights under the Geneva Civilian Convention, including the customary law reflected in common Article 3 and Article 75 of Protocol I. *See, e.g.*, Paust, *Executive Plans*, *supra* at 817-18; IV COMMENTARY, *supra* at 51 ("Every person in enemy hands must have some status under international law: he is either a prisoner of war and, as such, covered by the Third Convention, a civilian covered by the Fourth Convention, or ... a member of the medical personnel.... There is no intermediate status; nobody in enemy hands can be outside the law."), 595 ("applying the same system to all accused whatever their status"), 595; J. PICTET, III COMMENTARY, *supra* at 51 n.1, 76, 423; FM 27-10, *supra* at 31, para. 73 (persons who are not prisoners of war are covered under the Geneva Civilian Convention, where applicable: "he is not entitled to be treated as a prisoner of war. He is, however, a 'protected person' within the meaning of Article 4, GC...."); 2004 UK MANUAL, *supra* at 145, 148, 150, 216, 225; UK War Office, THE LAW OF WAR ON LAND pt. 3, at 96 (1958); The Prosecutor v. Delalic, IT-96-21-T (Trial Chamber, ICTY, Nov. 16, 1998), at para. 271 ("there is no gap between the Third and the Fourth Geneva Contentions"); MICHAEL BOTHE, *ET AL*., NEW RULES FOR VICTIMS OF ARMED CONFLICTS: COMMENTARY ON THE TWO 1977 PROTOCOLS ADDITIONAL TO THE GENEVA CONVENTIONS OF 1949, at 261-63 (1982); HENCKAERTS & DOSWALD-BECK, *supra* at 389; HILLARE MCCOUBREY, INTERNATIONAL HUMANITARIAN LAW: MODERN DEVELOPMENTS IN THE LIMITATION OF WARFARE 137 (2 ed. 1998); Knut Dormann, *The Legal Situation of "Unlawful/Unprivileged Combatants,"* 85 INT'L REV. RED CROSS 849 (2003); Jinks, *supra* at 1504, 1510-11; Derek Jinks, *The Declining Significance of POW Status*, 45 HARV. INT'L L.J. 367, 374 (2004) ("irrespective of whether war detainees are assigned POW status, humanitarian law accords protections that mirror, in most important respects, the rights accorded POWs."); Legal Adviser, U.S. Dep't of State, William H. Taft IV, *The Law of Armed Conflict After 9/11: Some Salient Features*, 28 YALE J. INT'L L. 319, 321-22 (2003) (non-pows "are not 'outside the law'... [and] they do not forfeit their right to humane treatment" under the 1949 Geneva Civilian Convention and "customary law" reflected "in Article 75 of Additional Protocol I to the Geneva Conventions," "safeguards to which all persons in the hands of an enemy are entitled"); Johannes van Aggelen, *A Response to John C. Yoo, "The Status of Soldiers and Terrorists Under the Geneva Convention,"* 3 CHINESE J. INT'L L. 1, 5, 8-9 (2004); *see also* Hamdan v. Rumsfeld, 548 U.S. 557, 629-31 & n.63 (2006) (no gaps in coverage exist under the laws of war with respect to detainees of any status and, at a minimum, common Article 3 of the 1949 Geneva Conventions is applicable during an

armed conflict); Hamdan v. Rumsfeld, 344 F. Supp.2d at 161 (if a detainee is not a pw, rights and protections exist under common Article 3); U.S. Dep't of Army, Subject Schedule 27-1, THE GENEVA CONVENTIONS OF 1949 AND HAGUE CONVENTION NO. IV OF 1907, at 7-8 ("these rules are embodied in one general principle: treat all prisoners of war, civilians, or other detained personnel *humanely*.... To repeat, we must insure that all persons are treated humanely. These persons may not be subjected to murder, torture, corporal punishment, mutilation, or any form of physical or mental coercion.") (Oct. 8, 1970) (emphasis in original); Council of Europe, Parliamentary Assembly Resolution 1433 (2005) ("At no time have detentions at Guantanamo Bay been within a 'legal black hole'"), in the Documents Section.

13. During the armed conflicts involving the U.S. in Afghanistan and Iraq, the Bush Administration attempted to deny Geneva protections to members of al Qaeda because al Qaeda "cannot be considered a state party to" them. Does this make sense? Do the Conventions provide protections for captured personnel from Halliburton or other corporations operating in Iraq? Do the rights and duties reflected in common Article 3 apply to any detainee? Is it likely that any member of al Qaeda captured during such conflicts is a national of a state that has ratified the treaties, since every state but Taiwan is a signatory? Additionally, are the rights and duties reflected in the Geneva Conventions that are customary international law (especially common Article 3) of universal applicability? *See* Hamdan v. Rumsfeld, 344 F. Supp.2d 152, 161 (D.D.C. 2004) (the Conventions "are triggered by the place of the conflict, and not by what particular faction a fighter is associated with"); Paust, *Executive Plans*, *supra* at 829-31; William H. Taft, IV, Memorandum to Counsel to the President, Comments on Your Paper on the Geneva Convention (Feb. 2, 2002), at 2, available at http://www.nytimes.com/packages/html/politics/20040608_DOC.pdf.

In *Hamdan v. Rumsfeld*, 415 F.3d 33, 41 (D.C. Cir.), a panel of the D.C. Circuit Court of Appeals embraced the Bush Administration's view: "Another problem for Hamdan is that the 1949 Convention does not apply to al Qaeda and its members.... Under Common Article 2, the provisions of the Convention apply to 'all cases of declared war or any other armed conflict which may arise between two or more of the High Contracting Parties, even if the state of war is not recognized by one of them.' Needless to say, al Qaeda is not a state and it was not a 'High Contracting Party.'" If the Conventions actually did not apply to members of al Qaeda in Afghanistan, how can they rightly be detained under GC Article 5 or prosecuted for violations?

14. Are certain nationals of a neutral country denied protections under Part III of the Geneva Civilian Convention (although, if not prisoners of war, they would be protected by customary law reflected in common Article 3 and Article 75 of Protocol I, if not also under certain portions of Part II of the Convention)? If the U.S. detains such persons outside U.S. territory, does the narrow exclusion in GC Article 4 with respect to those found "in the territory" of the U.S. apply? Regarding occupied territory, see also IV COMMENTARY, *supra* at 48 ("in occupied territory they are protected persons and the Convention is applicable to them"); U.S. Dep't of Army, Pam. 27-161-2, II INTERNATIONAL LAW 132 (1962) ("If they are in occupied territory, they remain entitled to protection."); 2004 UK MANUAL, *supra* at 274 ("Neutral nationals in occupied territory are entitled to treatment as protected persons under Geneva Convention IV whether or not there are normal diplomatic relations between the neutral states concerned and the occupying power.").

Professor Paust has stated: "In any event, limitations in Article 4 are obviated once the general rights, duties and protections in the Convention become customary international law of universal application. In a related manner, the International Military Tribunal at Nuremberg ruled that the fact that (1) Germany refused to ratify the 1907 Hague Convention, and (2) the treaty contained a general participation clause in Article 2 that limited the treaty's reach to armed conflicts between contracting parties became irrelevant once the rules mirrored in the treaty became customary international law." Paust, *Executive Plans, supra* at 819 n.28.

15. Note that with respect to the 1949 Geneva Civilian Convention, one can organize inquiry in terms of the following questions (some of which we have begun to address):

(a) when do certain provisions of the Convention apply?

Through Article 2: to an armed conflict of an international character, including a belligerency (see also FM 27-10, para. 8a re: other "international" conflicts).

Through Article 3: to an armed conflict not of an international character (*e.g.,* an insurgency).

(b) who is protected in Article 2 or Article 3 conflicts?

(1) in the case of an Article 2 conflict:

—those protected in common Article 3 (because what is reflected in the article now provides a minimum set of customary protections even during an international armed conflict, by treaty interpretation and/or customary international law); and

—those identified in Article 4, which refers to certain persons and excludes certain others (*e.g.,* co-nationals and certain nationals of a neutral state while "in the territory" of a detaining state) from Part III protections (*i.e.,* protections that are contained in Articles 27–141), but which does not exclude even such persons from the protections contained in Part II (*i.e.,* in Articles 13–26, some of which have been referred to above). This can involve technical differences because of the scheme set forth in Articles 4 and 13 of the Geneva Civilian Convention.

(2) in the case of an Article 3 conflict: those persons protected within common Article 3 (who include those persons of any status who are no longer taking an active part in hostilities).

(c) what sort of protections apply?

(1) in the case of an Article 2 conflict:

—the customary minimum protections reflected in common Article 3 and in Article 75 of Protocol I;

—for some persons, the protections found in Part II; and

—for some persons, also the protections found in Part III.

(2) in the case of an Article 3 conflict: the protections found in common Article 3.

(d) what sort of sanctions are expressed, although others can also pertain?

(1) in the case of an Article 2 conflict: those found in Part IV, Section I (*i.e.,* Articles 142–149), including the "grave breach" provisions (with "grave breaches" set forth in Article 146).

(2) in the case of an Article 3 conflict: (see below).

What human rights protections apply to detainees of any status. See, for example, Articles 6, 7, 9, 14, 26 of the International Covenant on Civil and Political Rights.

16. Under GPW art. 4, who is entitled to prisoner of war status? During the international armed conflict in Afghanistan that began in October, 2001, the Bush Administra-

tion denied pw status to members of the armed forces of the Taliban (which had been at least a *de facto* regime and a belligerent involved in a civil war with the Northern Alliance prior to U.S. entry and which was recognized as the *de jure* regime of Afghanistan by at least three other states). The Bush Administration alleged (incorrectly) that the Taliban in general did not carry arms openly during battle or wear distinctive insignia within the meaning of GPW art. 4(A)(2), although all fighters carry their arms in the open during battles and members of the Taliban generally wore distinctive turbans. What should be the test for Taliban pow status? For U.S. military pow status? Consider the following commentary: "The test for combatant or individual belligerent status under the laws of war is straightforward. It is membership in the armed forces of a party to an armed conflict of an international character. Thus, privileged or lawful belligerents include members of the armed forces of a state, nation, or belligerent during an armed conflict. As noted in U.S. military texts, '[a]nyone engaging in hostilities in an armed conflict on behalf of a party to the conflict' is a 'combatant'[7] and '[c]ombatants ... include all members of the regularly organized armed forces of a party to the conflict.'[8] Article 1 of the Annex to the 1907 Hague Convention expressly states that belligerent status will 'apply ... to armies' and expressly sets forth additional criteria to be met merely by 'militia.' The customary 1863 Lieber Code also affirmed: 'So soon as a man is armed by a sovereign government and takes the soldier's oath of fidelity, he is a belligerent; his killing, wounding, or other warlike acts are not individual crimes or offenses.'

"The 1949 Convention's list of six separate categories involved a clear change of certain prior interpretations of coverage under the 1929 Convention. Under express terms of the treaty, only one category out of six contains criteria limiting prisoner of war status to those belonging to a group that carries arms openly, wears a fixed distinctive sign recognizable at a distance, and conducts operations generally in accordance with the law of war. Under GPW Article 4(A)(2), these limiting criteria expressly apply only to certain 'militias or volunteer corps' or 'organized resistance movements.' They expressly do not apply to '[m]embers of the armed forces of a Party to the conflict, as well as members of militias or volunteer corps forming part of such armed forces' covered under 4(A)(1) or to '[m]embers of regular armed forces who profess allegiance to a government or an authority not recognized by the Detaining Power' covered under 4(A)(3).

"With respect to the armed forces of a party to the armed conflict in Afghanistan (such as those of the Taliban and the United States), the determinative criterion for prisoner of war status is membership. Thus, members of the armed forces of each party qualify as prisoners of war under GPW Article 4(A)(1), if not 4(A)(3), and the authoritative ICRC has expressly recognized combatant and pw status for all members of the armed forces of the Taliban. Moreover, pw status does not inhibit the ability to detain enemy pws for the duration of an armed conflict, whether or not particular pws can also be prosecuted for war crimes or other violations of international law. Indeed, prisoners of war subject to prosecution do not thereby lose their status as a prisoner of war. There is no need to change the laws of war in that regard.

"A new extension of the four criteria expressly applicable only to one of six categories addressed in GPW Article 4(A), *i.e.* those covered in 4(A)(2), to the 'armed forces' of a party to an armed conflict (who are presently covered by Article 4(A)(1)) would result in

---

7. U.S. Army Judge Advocate General's School, Operational Law Handbook 12 (2002), available at http://www.jagcnet.army.mil.
8. The U.S. Navy, Annotated Supplement to the Commander's Handbook of Naval Operations 296 (Naval War College, Int'l L. Studies vol. 73, 1999).

a nonsensical, policy-thwarting denial of pw status to all members of the armed forces of a party to an armed conflict whenever several members do not wear a fixed distinctive sign recognizable at a distance or several members violate the laws of war. Such an approach is illogical and contrary to normal approaches to treaty interpretation; would seriously threaten pw status, combat immunity, and protections for soldiers of various countries including U.S. military; and would be inconsistent with general state practice (which is also relevant for treaty interpretation). In Afghanistan and more generally and in conformity with widespread state practice, several types of U.S. soldiers (*e.g.*, special forces) and various regular soldiers at different times have used camouflage and have otherwise attempted to blend in with local flora or geography in an effort to avoid being recognizable at a distance, since they prefer not to be clearly recognizable at all. Indeed, various U.S. soldiers in Afghanistan have not only not met the criterion of wearing distinctive emblems or signs recognizable at a distance, but have also been spotted wearing Afghan civilian clothing and sporting beards to 'blend in.' Thus, under the nonsensical approach, all U.S. soldiers could be denied prisoner of war status during the conflict in Afghanistan and an upgraded war with Iraq." Paust, *Status, supra* at 332-34.

One district court adopted a contrary view. In *United States v. Lindh,* 212 F. Supp.2d 541, 557 n.35 (E.D. Va. 2002), the district court declared: "Lindh asserts that the Taliban is a 'regular armed force,' under the GPW, and because he is a member, he need not meet the four conditions of the Hague Regulations because only Article 4(2)(A), which addresses irregular armed forces, explicitly mentions the four criteria. This argument is unpersuasive; it ignores long-established practice under the GPW and, if accepted, leads to an absurd result. First, the four criteria have long been understood under customary international law to be the defining characteristics of any lawful armed force.... Thus, all armed forces or militias, regular and irregular, must meet the four criteria if their members are to receive combatant immunity. Were this not so, the anomalous result that would follow is that members of an armed force that meet none of the criteria could still claim lawful combatant immunity merely on the basis that the organization calls itself a 'regular armed force.' It would indeed be absurd for members of a so-called 'regular armed force' to enjoy lawful combatant immunity even though the force had no established command structure and its members wore no recognizable symbol or insignia, concealed their weapons, and did not abide by the customary laws of war. Simply put, the label 'regular armed force' cannot be used to mask unlawful combatant status."

What approach is preferable? What is the reason for requiring members of certain militias and other volunteer corps to wear a "fixed distinctive sign recognizable at a distance" as a precondition to being classified as a prisoner of war under GPW, art. 4(A)(2), but not 4(A)(1) or (3)? What is the reason for requiring them to carry arms openly during an attack? Doesn't every group carry arms openly during an attack? Should soldiers be denied pw status because they wear camouflage during missions?

The Geneva Protocols

Note also that the 1977 Protocols supplement this list, with Protocol I applying to Article 2 conflicts and Protocol II applying to Article 3 conflicts. Apparently every state has ratified the 1949 Geneva Conventions except Taiwan, but not all (yet most) states have ratified both Protocols. The United States has yet to ratify either Protocol, but considers most of the provisions to reflect customary law or to be relevant to interpretation of the general conventions. This point is addressed only partly in the *Tadic* decision of the Appeals Chamber of the ICT for Former Yugoslavia (below). Professor Scharf has also recognized: "[A] very strong case can be made that Protocol I has ripened into customary international law ... and, in any event, the United States already imposes the rules contained in Protocol I on U.S. military personnel operating abroad.... .155 [214 in 2012] States have ratified Protocol I, making it one of the most widely ratified treaties. With the addition of the United Kingdom this year, its parties include seventeen of the nineteen members of NATO and three of the Permanent Members of the Security Council. The Protocol has been frequently invoked in various conflicts by governments, U.N. investigative bodies, and the International Committee of the Red Cross. Moreover, U.S. soldiers are subject to arrest and prosecution/extradition for breaches of the Protocol when they are present in the territory of any State Party.... [T]he Reagan Administration declared that many of the other provisions of the Protocol (including most, if not all, of the substantive provisions that are referenced in the ICC's Statute) represent customary international law.[9] Reflecting this position, the U.S. Air Force and Navy commanders' handbooks employ the Protocol's language. When U.S. Troops are deployed to the U.N. for a peace-keeping mission they are subject to Protocol I. And, as a matter of policy on the conduct of hostilities during coalition actions (*e.g.*, in the Persian Gulf and Balkans), the United States has implemented the rules of the Protocol because of the need to coordinate rules of engagement with its coalition partners and because, as a Defense Department Report on the Persian Gulf Conflict explained, several provisions of Protocol I are 'generally regarded as codification of the customary practice of nations, and therefore binding on all.'" Michael P. Scharf, *The ICC's Jurisdiction over the Nationals of Non-Party States: A Critique of the U.S. Position*, 64 Law & Contemp. Probs. 67 (2001).

The applications of common Article 3 and Protocol II are not coextensive, although they are complementary. Application of either to insurgents does not depend on the insurgents being formal parties to the Geneva Conventions.[10] Application of Protocol II in its entirety, however, depends on whether the state involved is a signatory to the Protocol, since (unlike common Article 3) it is not fully customary law. Thus, common Article 3, especially as custom and as the minimum standard in Article 2 conflicts as well, applies to a broader range of conflicts than does Protocol II. Although both apply to "conflict[s] not of an international character," unlike Protocol II, common Article 3 does not provide definitional criteria with respect to identification of such conflicts.

To meet the jurisdictional requirements of Protocol II, there must be a showing that: (1) Protocol I does not apply and an armed conflict is taking place between the armed forces of a party to Protocol II and dissident armed forces; (2) the dissident armed forces are under responsible command; (3) the dissident forces exercise control over a portion of the territory, enabling them to carry out sustained and concerted military operations; and (4) the dissident forces are capable of implementing Protocol II.[11]

---

9. Message from the President of the United States transmitting Protocol II Additional to the Geneva Conventions, *reprinted in* 26 I.L.M. 561 (1987).

10. *See, e.g.,* J. Pictet, IV Commentary, *supra* at 37 (as reproduced above). For an example of the application of common Article 3 and Protocol II to one aspect of a conflict while applying the grave breaches provisions of the 1949 Geneva Conventions and Protocol I to other aspects, *see* Military and Paramilitary Activities in and against Nicaragua (Nicaragua v. U.S.), [1986] I.C.J. 14, para. 219. Does this make sense? Is it preferable? See also Note 5 above.

11. Protocol II, art. 1. For a discussion of the background concerning adoption of common Article 3 and Protocol II, *see, e.g.,* International Committee of the Red Cross, Commentary on the Additional Protocols of 8 June 1977 to the Geneva Conventions of 12 August 1949 1343–56 (Yves Sandoz, *et al.* eds., 1987); *see also* Bothe, *supra*; Sylvie Junod, *Additional Protocol II;*

Other Aspects of Internal Versus International Armed Conflicts

Under the customary law of war, an otherwise internal armed conflict will be considered international, for example, when the non-state party to the conflict is recognized as a belligerent or when a foreign state participates in the armed conflict. In these cases, the entire body of the international law of armed conflicts applies.[12] Effects of foreign government involvement have led to two general considerations:

A. Under what is perhaps a more traditional approach:

(1) if a foreign state assists an established government, the conflict is classified as internal and the rules of international conflict do not apply because the insurgents have no belligerent or higher status in international law, unless the conflict is governed by Protocol I, Article 1 (4), there is other outside intervention, or the conflict is international in character for some other reason (*e.g.,* because of U.N. Security Council action under Chapter VII);

(2) if a foreign state assists insurgents against an established government, the conflict can be classified as international and the rules of international armed conflict apply at least between the foreign state and the established government because both are subjects of international law and the conflict is also "between" Contracting Parties within the meaning of common Article 2.

Such an approach seems to stress criteria from another area of law, *i.e.,* issues relating to the permissibility of intervention, and, at times, the technical status of parties to the conflict. Under this approach, the relationship between an established government and insurgents is governed at least by the rules applicable to conflicts of a non-international character, and may include additional humanitarian norms in at least the following cases:

(1) the established government recognizes the insurgents as belligerents (an obsolete practice);

(2) outside recognition of the insurgents as belligerents occurs [then all of the customary laws of war apply];

(3) the established government and the insurgents enter into special agreements pursuant to common Article 3 of the Geneva Conventions, bringing into force some or all of the Geneva Conventions and Protocol I;

(4) Article 1 (4) of Protocol I applies; or

(5) the insurgents are classified as an organized resistance movement belonging to an intervening state.[13]

Under each of these scenarios, international humanitarian law will apply to all parties, including third party intervenors. Third party states rarely, if ever, recognize an in-

---

History and Scope, 33 Am. U. L. Rev. 29 (1983); Charles Lysaght, *The Scope of Protocol II and Its Relationship to Common Article 3 of the Geneva Conventions of 1949 and Other Human Rights Instruments*, 33 Am. U. L. Rev. 9 (1983).

12. See the many citations in Note 3 following the extract of the *Tadic* case below.

13. *See also* Dietrich Schindler II, *International Humanitarian Law and Internal Armed Conflicts*, 1982 Int'l Rev. Red Cross 230, 255–64.

surgent as a belligerent.[14] One notable example was the recognition of the Confederate States by England as a belligerent during the U.S. Civil War.

B. Another approach focuses more on the general process of armed violence in which parties participate and various internationalizing elements (in addition to the technical status of and relationships between some of the parties). The phrase "armed conflict not of an international character" found in common Article 3 is interpreted with more emphasis on various elements that may be relevant to the character of a general conflict and lead one to a conclusion that it is not "not of an international character" but "international".[15] Both approaches may hinge on orientations to treaty interpretation, but this latter approach may best serve to advance humanitarian purposes (*i.e.*, the general object and purpose of Geneva law) by tending more often to stress various internationalizing elements. For example, would the fact that Soviet military advisers were directly involved in combat missions of a recognized government's armed forces against what otherwise were mere insurgents sufficiently internationalize the conflict to move it beyond the language of common Article 3? If so, would it fit neatly within the language of common Article 2, especially the word "between" used in relation to another set of words—"Contracting Parties"? From a policy-oriented approach, which interpretive orientation would tend best to serve humanitarian law, especially since all of the customary laws of war apply to a "belligerency" and to other international armed conflicts? Might Article 1 (4) of Protocol I apply in some such situations? Is it policy-serving to have common Article 3 no longer technically applicable (*e.g.*, once the insurgency becomes a "belligerency" to which all of the customary laws of war apply), but common Article 2 to be technically not applicable (*e.g.*, because a "belligerent" is not a "Party" to the Geneva Conventions), but a belligerent can be a "Power" within the meaning of common Article 2? When Geneva Civilian Convention provisions become part of the customary laws of war, should the words "Parties" or "Power" become as irrelevant as the "general participation" clause of Article I of the 1907 Hague Convention, as recognized in the Opinion and Judgement of the IMT at Nuremberg, so that customary GC provisions apply whether or not a belligerent is a "Party" to the Convention? Why is it in the interest of U.S. soldiers to be considered combatants in an "international" armed conflict whenever they are deployed abroad to engage in fighting?

Another example demonstrates related differences. During the Vietnam War, Soviet military advisers were aiding North Vietnamese forces; U.S. and other nation-state forces were engaged in the general armed conflict, sometimes fighting what the U.S. considered to be Viet Cong insurgents in South Vietnam; and South Vietnamese forces fought Viet Cong and North Vietnamese forces. Several countries recognized either the North or South Vietnamese forces as military forces of a state. Was the Vietnam War an Article 2 conflict? Should one be more technical in focus and stress the status of participants—perhaps concluding that any clash between U.S. forces and Viet Cong forces was not part of the general international conflict but merely an armed conflict "not of an international character" (or that the U.S. was merely aiding a recognized government attempt to put down insurgents)? Alternatively, should one focus on the purposes of Geneva law and overall context, concluding that various participants were actually in-

---

14. *See* Evan Luard, *Civil Conflicts in Modern International Relations,* in The International Regulation of Civil Wars 21 (Evan Luard ed., 1972).

15. At times, Pictet uses the word "international" in contradistinction to common Article 3 conflicts. *See, e.g.,* IV Commentary at 14.

volved in an international armed conflict? *See generally* vols. 1–4, THE VIETNAM WAR AND INTERNATIONAL LAW (R. Falk ed. 1968–1976).

Section 2
Types of War Crimes

A. General

U.S. Dep't of Army Field Manual 27-10, The Law of Land Warfare (1956)

498. Crimes Under International Law

Any person, whether a member of the armed forces or a civilian, who commits an act which constitutes a crime under international law is responsible therefor and liable to punishment.

499. War Crimes

The term "war crime" is the technical expression for a violation of the law of war by any person or persons, military or civilian. Every violation of the law of war is a war crime....

502. Grave Breaches of the Geneva Conventions of 1949 as War Crimes

The Geneva Conventions of 1949 define the following acts as "grave breaches," if committed against persons or property protected by the Conventions:

a. *GWS and GWS Sea.*

Grave breaches to which the preceding Article relates shall be those involving any of the following acts, if committed against persons or property protected by the Convention: wilful killing, torture or inhuman treatment, including biological experiments, wilfully causing great suffering or serious injury to body or health, and extensive destruction and appropriation of property, not justified by military necessity and carried out unlawfully and wantonly. (GWS, art. 50; GWS Sea, art. 51.)

b. *GPW.*

Grave breaches to which the preceding Article relates shall be those involving any of the following acts, if committed against persons or property protected by the Convention: wilful killing, torture or inhuman treatment, including biological experiments, wilfully causing great suffering or serious injury to body or health, compelling a prisoner of war to serve in the forces of the hostile power or wilfully depriving a prisoner of war of the rights of fair and regular trial prescribed in this Convention. (GPW, art. 130.)

c. *GC.*

Grave breaches to which the preceding Article relates shall be those involving any of the following acts, if committed against persons or property protected by the present Convention: wilful killing, torture or inhuman treatment, including biological experiments, wilfully causing great suffering or serious injury to body or health, unlawful deportation or transfer or unlawful confinement of a protected person, compelling a protected person to serve in the forces of a hostile Power or wilfully depriving a protected person of the rights of fair and regular trial prescribed in the present Convention, taking of hostages and extensive destruction and appropriation of property, not justified by military necessity and carried out unlawfully and wantonly. (GC, art. 147.)

504. Other Types of War Crimes

In addition to the "grave breaches" of the Geneva Conventions of 1949, the following acts are representative of violations of the law of war ("war crimes"):

a. Making use of poisoned or otherwise forbidden arms or ammunition.

b. Treacherous request for quarter.

c. Maltreatment of dead bodies.

d. Firing on localities which are undefended and without military significance.

e. Abuse of or firing on the flag of truce.

f. Misuse of the Red Cross emblem.

g. Use of civilian clothing by troops to conceal their military character during battle.

h. Improper use of privileged buildings for military purposes.

i. Poisoning of wells or streams.

j. Pillage or purposeless destruction.

k. Compelling prisoners of war to perform prohibited labor.

l. Killing without trial spies or other persons who have committed hostile acts.

m. Compelling civilians to perform prohibited labor.

n. Violation of surrender terms.

Notes and Questions

1. For other lists, see the 1919 List in the Documents Section; *compare* Article 8 of the Statute of the ICC.

2. In the Principles of the Nuremberg Charter and Judgment, formulated by the U.N. International Law Commission in 1950, the following summary appears:

War Crimes:

Violations of the laws or customs of war which include, but are not limited to, murder, ill-treatment of prisoners of war or of persons on the seas, killing of hostages, plunder of public or private property, wanton destruction of cities, towns, or villages, or devastation not justified by military necessity.

See also Charter of the IMT at Nuremberg, art. 6 (b); Charter of the IMT for the Far East, art. 5 (b) ("Namely, violations of the laws and customs of war"); Control Council Law No. 10, art. II (1)(b) — each in the Documents Section. Concerning the fact that violations of the Geneva Conventions other than grave breaches are war crimes that must be punished, see Note 2 following the *Tadic* opinion, *infra*.

3. Most war crimes are committed by military personnel, but recall the recognition in FM 27-10, para. 498 that *any* person, including civilians (official or private), can be a perpetrator. At the IMT at Nuremberg, editor-in-chief Julius Streicher of *Der Stürmer* was convicted of crimes against humanity "in connection with war crimes" because of his "incitement to murder and extermination at the time when Jews in the East were

being killed under the most horrible conditions." 22 Trials of the Major War Crimi-nals Before the International Military Tribunal 549 (1949). Several of the Ger-man industrialists were also found guilty of "plunder of property." See also The Prosecu-tor v. Tadic, Decision on the Defense Motion on Jurisdiction (Trial Chamber, International Criminal Tribunal for Former Yugoslavia, 10 Aug. 1995), para. 61 ("Viola-tions of the laws or customs of war are commonly referred to as 'war crimes.' They can be defined as crimes committed by any person …'whether committed by combatants or civilians, including the nationals of neutral states'"); 11 Op. Att'y Gen. 297, 299-300 (1865); 4 Commentary, Geneva Convention Relative to the Protection of Civil-ian Persons in Time of War 13 ("any man or any woman"), 79 ,209-10, 591-94 602 ("all") (ICRC, Jean S. Pictet ed. 1958); U.K. Ministry of Defence, The Manual of the Law of Armed Conflict 428 ("civilians," "any person") (2004); Jordan J. Paust, After My Lai: The Case for War Crime Jurisdiction Over Civilians in Federal District Courts, 50 Tex. L. Rev. 6, 12-17 (1971); Weisshaus v. Swiss Bankers Ass'n, 225 F.3d 191 (2d Cir. 2000); Kadic v. Karadzic, 70 F.3d 232, 239-40, 242-43 (2d Cir. 1995), cert. denied, 518 U.S. 1005 (1996); Presbyterian Church of Sudan v. Talisman Energy, Inc., 374 F. Supp.2d 331 (S.D.N.Y. 2005); Id., 244 F. Supp.2d 289, 305, 308-19, 320-25 (S.D.N.Y. 2003); In re Agent Orange Product Liability Litig., 373 F. Supp.2d 7, 58-59 (E.D.N.Y. 2005); Estate of Ro-driquez v. Drummond Co., Inc., 256 F. Supp.2d 1250 (N.D. Ala. 2003); Doe v. Islamic Salvation Front, 993 F. Supp. 3, 7-8 (D.D.C. 1998); Ex parte Mudd, manuscript opinion (1868); The War Crimes Act, 18 U.S.C. § 2441(a) ("Whoever"); see also Linder v. Porto-carrero, 963 F.2d 332, 336-37 (11th Cir. 1992) (crimes of the Contras). Concerning pri-vate duties, see also Jordan J. Paust, The Reality of Private Rights, Duties, and Participation in the International Legal Process, 25 Mich. J. Int'l L. 1229 (2004).

4. In The Prosecutor v. Alfred Musema, ICTR-96-13-T (Trial Chamber, 27 Jan. 2000), addressing breaches of Common Article 3 of the Geneva Conventions and of Protocol II, the ICTR recognized that "civilians can be held responsible for violations of interna-tional humanitarian law committed in an armed conflict," and that "it is well-established that the post-World War II Trials unequivocally support the imposition of individual criminal liability for war crimes on civilians where they have a link or connection with a Party to the conflict." Id. at paras. 268, 274. Is it necessary that civilian perpetrators of any type of war crime have a "link" with a Party? Musema stated in para. 285(a): "nor would it be required that the acts [of humiliating or degrading treatment] be committed under state authority." Common Article 3 of the Geneva Conventions states that "each Party to the conflict shall be bound to apply, as a minimum, the following provisions…."

The Trial Chamber in Musema set forth a requirement "that there is a link or nexus between the offence committed and the armed conflict for Article 4 of the Statute [of the ICTR] to apply," that the crimes alleged "must be closely related to the hostilities or committed in conjunction with the armed conflict." Id. at paras. 259-260. Using this ap-proach, the Trial Chamber in The Prosecutor v. Rutaganda, ICTR-96-3-T (6 Dec. 1999), acquitted Rutaganda regarding three counts of violations of common Article 3. The Ap-peals Chamber in Rutaganda reversed and entered findings of guilt on two of the three counts, but accepted a so-called nexus requirement. ICTR-96-3-A (26 May 2003).
Must all war crimes be committed "in conjunction with … armed conflict"? Consider war crimes committed by civilians during an occupation. The Trial Chamber in Musema added: "In the Rutaganda Judgment it was held that the term nexus should not be defined in abstracto. Rather, the evidence adduced in support of the charges against the accused must satisfy the Chamber that such a nexus exists. Thus, the burden rests on the Prosecutor to prove beyond a reasonable doubt, that, on the basis of the facts, such a

nexus exists between the crime committed and the armed conflict." *Id.* at para. 262, *citing Rutaganda* Judgment, paras. 102-103 (which merely cited *Akayesu* Judgment, paras. 70, 643). Is there any other precedent for such a "nexus" requirement? Does it only apply regarding the reach of Article 4 of the Statute of the ICTR? The *Rutaganda* Judgment added that it was determined in the *Akayesu* Judgment and by the Appeals Chamber of the ICTY in *Tadic* that "the requirements of Common Article 3 and Additional Protocol II apply in the whole territory where the conflict is occurring and are not limited to the 'war front' or to the 'narrow geographical context of the actual theater of combat operations.'" At para. 101, *citing Akayesu* Judgment at paras. 635-636; *Tadic* (2 Oct. 1995), at para. 69. Where it applies, should the burden regarding proof of a "nexus" be "beyond a reasonable doubt"?

The Trial Chamber in *Musema* also noted that its jurisdiction under Article 4 of the Statute of the ICTR was limited to "serious violations" of Common Article 3 of the Geneva Conventions and of Protocol II; that the "Trial Chamber in the *Akayesu* Judgment understood, in line with the Appeals Chamber Decision in *Tadic* that the phrase 'serious violation' means 'a breach of a rule protecting important values which must involve grave consequences for the victim'"; that the list of violations in Article 4 of the Statute was taken from Common Article 3 and Protocol II; and that such violations are "serious" and are also violative of customary international law. *Id.* at paras. 286-288.

5. Do the "grave breach" provisions of the Geneva Conventions apply to situations regulated by common Article 3 of the Conventions? *Compare* M. Cherif Bassiouni, The Law of the International Criminal Tribunal for the Former Yugoslavia 441–632 (1996); O. Gross, *The Grave Breaches System and the Armed Conflict in the Former Yugoslavia*, 16 Mich. J. Int'l L. 783, 825 & n.178 (1995); T. Meron, *War Crimes in Yugoslavia and Developments in International Law*, 88 Am. J. Int'l L. 78, 80–81 (1994); M. Scharf, *Swapping Amnesty for Peace: Was there a Duty to Prosecute International Crimes in Haiti?*, 31 Tex. Int'l L. J. 1, 20(1996); *with* J. Paust, *Applicability of International Criminal Laws to Events in the Former Yugoslavia*, 9 Am. U. J. Int'l L. & Pol. 499, 510–12 & ns.39–42 (1994); Paust & Blaustein, *supra* at 2, 14–15, 28 n.101; J. Pictet, IV Commentary at 591 (citing common Article 3 in connection with discussion of the general section on criminal sanctions). *See also* T. Meron, *The Continuing Role of Custom in the Formation of International Humanitarian Law,* 90 Am. J. Int'l L. 238, 243 (1996) ("the appeals chamber should have devoted more attention to discussing the possibility that ... the core offenses listed in the grave breaches provisions may have an independent existence as a customary norm applicable also to violations of at least common Article 3.")[hereinafter Meron, *Continuing*]; *International Criminalization of Internal Atrocities,* 89 Am. J. Int'l L. 554 (1995).

The Prosecutor v. Dusko Tadic, Decision on the Defence Motion for Interlocutory Appeal on Jurisdiction, ICTY Appeals Chamber, IT-94-1-AR72 (2 Oct. 1995)

Cassese, J.

79. Article 2 of the Statute of the International Tribunal provides:

"The International Tribunal shall have the power to prosecute persons committing or ordering to be committed grave breaches of the Geneva Conventions of 12 August 1949...."

By its explicit terms, and as confirmed in the Report of the Secretary-General, this Article of the Statute is based on the Geneva Conventions of 1949 and, more specifically, the provisions of those Conventions relating to "grave breaches" of the Conventions. Each of the four Geneva Conventions of 1949 contains a "grave breaches" provision, specifying particular breaches of the Convention for which the High Contracting Parties have a duty to prosecute those responsible. In other words, for these specific acts, the Conventions create universal mandatory criminal jurisdiction among contracting States. Although the language of the Conventions might appear to be ambiguous and the question is open to some debate*(see, e.g.,* [*Amicus Curiae*] Submission of the Government of the United States of America Concerning Certain Arguments Made by Counsel for the Accused in the Case of *The Prosecutor of the Tribunal v. Dusko Tadic,* 17 July 1995, (Case No. IT-94-1-T), at 35–6 (hereinafter, U.S. *Amicus Curiae Brief)),* it is widely contended that the grave breaches provisions establish universal mandatory jurisdiction only with respect to those breaches of the Conventions committed in international armed conflicts [no citations were provided]. Appellant argues that, as the grave breaches enforcement system only applies to international armed conflicts, reference in Article 2 of the Statute to the grave breaches provisions of the Geneva Conventions limits the International Tribunal's jurisdiction under that Article to acts committed in the context of an international armed conflict.

The Trial Chamber has held that Article 2 [of the Statute of the Tribunal]:

"[H]as been so drafted as to be self-contained rather than referential, save for the identification of the victims of enumerated acts; that identification and that alone involves going to the Conventions themselves for the definition of 'persons or property protected....

[T]he requirement of international conflict does not appear on the face of Article 2. Certainly, nothing in the words of the Article expressly require its existence; once one of the specified acts is allegedly committed upon a protected person the power of the International Tribunal to prosecute arises if the spatial and temporal requirements of Article 1 are met....

[T]here is no ground for treating Article 2 as in effect importing into the Statute the whole of the terms of the Conventions, including the reference in common Article 2 of the Geneva Convention [sic] to international conflicts. As stated, Article 2 of the Statute is on its face, self-contained, save in relation to the definition of protected persons and things." (Decision at Trial, at paras. 49–51.)

80. With all due respect, the Trial Chamber's reasoning is based on a misconception of the grave breaches provisions and the extent of their incorporation into the Statute of the International Tribunal. The grave breaches system of the Geneva Conventions establishes a twofold system: there is on the one hand an enumeration of offences that are regarded so serious as to constitute "grave breaches", closely bound up with this enumeration a mandatory enforcement mechanism is set up, based on the concept of a duty and a right of all Contracting States to search for and try or extradite persons allegedly responsible for "grave breaches". The international armed conflict element generally attributed to the grave breaches provisions of the Geneva Conventions is merely a function of the system of universal mandatory jurisdiction that those provisions create. The international armed conflict requirement was a necessary limitation on the grave breaches system in light of the intrusion on State sovereignty that such mandatory universal jurisdiction represents. State parties to the 1949 Geneva Conventions did not want to give other States jurisdiction over serious violations of international humanitarian law committed in their internal armed conflicts—at least not the mandatory universal jurisdiction involved in the grave breaches system.

81. The Trial Chamber is right in implying that the enforcement mechanism has of course not been imported into the Statute of the International Tribunal, for the obvious reason that the International Tribunal itself constitutes a mechanism for the prosecution and punishment of the perpetrators of "grave breaches". However, the Trial Chamber has misinterpreted the reference to the Geneva Conventions contained in the sentence of Article 2: "persons or property protected under the provisions of the relevant Geneva Conventions". (Statute of the Tribunal, art. 2.) For the reasons set out above, this reference is clearly intended to indicate that the offences listed under Article 2 can only be prosecuted when perpetrated against persons or property regarded as "protected" by the Geneva Conventions under the strict conditions set out by the Conventions themselves. This reference in Article 2 to the notion of "protected persons or property" must perforce cover the persons mentioned in Articles 13, 24, 25 and 26 (protected persons) and 19 and 33 to 35 (protected objects) of Geneva Convention I; in Articles 13, 36, 37 (protected persons) and 29, 24, 25 and 27 (protected objects) of Convention II; in Article 4 of Convention III on prisoners of war; and in Articles 4 and 20 (protected persons) and Articles 18, 19, 21, 22, 33, 53, 57 etc. (protected property) of Convention IV on civilians. Clearly, these provisions of the Geneva Conventions apply to persons or objects protected only to the extent that they are caught up in an international armed conflict. By contrast, those provisions do not include persons or property coming within the purview of common Article 3 of the four Geneva Conventions....

83. We find that our interpretation of Article 2 is the only one warranted by the text of the Statute and the relevant provisions of the Geneva Conventions, as well as by a logical construction of their interplay as dictated by Article 2. However, we are aware that this conclusion may appear not to be consonant with recent trends of both State practice and the whole doctrine of human rights—which, as pointed out below (see paras. 97–127), tend to blur in many respects the traditional dichotomy between international wars and civil strife. In this connection the Chamber notes with satisfaction the statement in the *amicus curiae* brief submitted by the Government of the United States, where it is contended that:

> "the 'grave breaches' provisions of Article 2 of the International Tribunal Statute apply to armed conflicts of a non-international character as well as those of an international character." (U.S. Amicus Curiae Brief, at 35.)

This statement, unsupported by any authority, does not seem to be warranted as to the interpretation of Article 2 of the Statute. Nevertheless, seen from another viewpoint, there is no gainsaying its significance: that statement articulates the legal views of one of the permanent members of the Security Council on a delicate legal issue; on this score it provides the first indication of a possible change in *opinio juris* of States. Were other States and international bodies to come to share this view, a change in customary law concerning the scope of the "grave breaches" system might gradually materialize. Other elements pointing in the same direction can be found in the provision of the German Military Manual mentioned below (para. 131), whereby grave breaches of international humanitarian law include some violations of common Article 3. In addition, attention can be drawn to the Agreement of 1 October 1992 entered into by the conflicting parties in Bosnia-Herzegovina. Articles 3 and 4 of this Agreement implicitly provide for the prosecution and punishment of those responsible for grave breaches of the Geneva Conventions and Additional Protocol I. As the Agreement was clearly concluded within a framework of an internal armed conflict (see above, para. 73), it may be taken as an important indication of the present trend to extend the grave breaches provisions to such category of conflicts. One can also mention a recent judgement by a Danish court.

On 25 November 1994 the Third Chamber of the Eastern Division of the Danish High Court delivered a judgement on a person accused of crimes committed together with a number of Croatian military police on 5 August 1993 in the Croatian prison camp of Dretelj in Bosnia (The Prosecution v. Refik Saric, unpublished (Den. H. Ct. 1994)). The Court explicitly acted on the basis of the "grave breaches" provisions of the Geneva Conventions, more specifically Articles 129 and 130 of Convention III and Articles 146 and 147 of Convention IV (The Prosecution v. Refik Saric, Transcript, at 1 (25 Nov. 1994)), without however raising the preliminary question of whether the alleged offences had occurred within the framework of an international rather than an internal armed conflict (in the event the Court convicted the accused on the basis of those provisions and the relevant penal provisions of the Danish Penal Code. (see *id.* at 7–8)) This judgement indicates that some national courts are also taking the view that the "grave breaches" system may operate regardless of whether the armed conflict is international or internal.

84. Notwithstanding the foregoing, the Appeals Chamber must conclude that, in the present state of development of the law, Article 2 of the Statute only applies to offences committed within the context of international armed conflicts.

Li, J. (concurring in part)

7. Professor Meron states the customary international law of war crimes very correctly and clearly in the following terms:

"Whether the conflicts in Yugoslavia are characterized as internal or international is critically important. The fourth Hague Convention of 1907, which codified the principal laws of war and served as the normative core for the post-World War II war crimes prosecutions, applies to international wars only. The other principal prong of the penal laws of war, the grave breaches provisions of the Geneva Conventions and Protocol I, is also directed to international wars. Violations of common Article 3 of the Geneva Conventions, which concerns internal wars, do not constitute grave breaches giving rise to universal criminal jurisdiction. Were any part of the conflict deemed internal rather than international, the perpetrators of even the worst atrocities might try to challenge prosecutions for war crimes or grave breaches, but not for genocide or crimes against humanity." (Meron, *War Crimes in Yugoslavia and the Development of International Law,* 88 AJIL 78, 80 (1994).)

8. The Final Report of 27 May 1994 of the Commission of Experts established pursuant to Security Council resolution 780 (1992) takes the same view as Professor Meron:

> "If a conflict is classified as international, then the grave breaches of the Geneva Conventions, including Additional Protocol I, apply as well as violations of the laws and customs of war. The treaty and customary law applicable to international armed conflict is well-established. The treaty law designed for internal armed conflict is in common [A]rticle 3 of the Geneva Conventions, Additional Protocol II of 1977, and [A]rticle 19 of the 1954 Hague Convention for the Protection of Cultural Property in the Event of Armed Conflict. These legal sources do not use the terms 'grave breaches' or 'war crimes'. Further, the content of customary law applicable to internal armed conflict is debatable. As a result, in general, unless the parties to an internal armed conflict agree otherwise, the only offences committed in internal armed conflict for which universal jurisdiction exists are 'crimes against humanity' and genocide, which apply irrespective of the conflicts' classification." (S/1994/674, p. 13, para. 42.)

9. And the ICRC, an authority on international humanitarian law, in the Preliminary Remarks on the Setting-up of an International Tribunal for the Prosecution of Persons Responsible for Serious Violations of International Humanitarian Law Committed in the Territory of the Former Yugoslavia, "underline[s] the fact that, according to humanitarian law as it stands today, the notion of war crimes is limited to situations of international armed conflict". (DDM/JUR/442 b, 25 March 1993, para. 4.)

10. Now, I may turn to the difference of my opinion from that of the Decision. The Decision asserts that there has been development of customary international law to such an extent that all the various violations of the laws or customs of war as enumerated in lit. (a)-(e) of Article 3 of the Statute of this Tribunal are liable to be prosecuted and punished even if they are committed in internal armed conflict. I cannot agree with this assertion....

12. As regards the interpretative statements of the French, U.S. and U.K. delegates on Article 3 of the Statute in the Security Council when voting on the resolution adopting the Statute, I agree. But these interpretative statements only give grounds for interpreting Article 3 of the Statute as granting the Tribunal the power to prosecute the various violations specified in the two Additional Protocols of 1977 and common Article 3 of the Geneva Conventions of 1949, which interpretation I endorse; they, however, do not maintain that the violations of the laws or customs of war which are enumerated in lit. (a)-(e) and committed in an internal armed conflict should be prosecuted according to Article 3 of the Statute....

Sidhwa, J. (concurring)

117. Article 3 of the Statute lists five offences under paras. (a) to (e), with the condition that "such violations shall include, but not be limited to" the same. The list is therefore illustrative and not limited to the five offences stated. It is clear, therefore, that the 1907 Hague Regulations, the 1949 Geneva Conventions with Additional Protocols I and II, the 1945 Charter of the International Military Tribunal 1945, apart from other conventions, constitute laws of war and that war crimes embodied therein, if they constitute serious violations of international humanitarian law, become offences liable to punishment under Article 3 of the Statute. Likewise, the 1907 Hague Regulations, the 1949 Geneva Conventions with Additional Protocols I and II and the instances given in the decision of the Nurnberg Tribunal, on the authoritative pronouncement of the Secretary-General as contained in para. 44 of his report, constitute, apart from others, the customs of war. There is an overlapping between Articles 2 and 3 of the Statute qua the "grave breaches". Since Article 2 of the Statute specifically deals with the "grave breaches", Article 3 thereof must be taken to cover all other serious violations of the 1949 Geneva Conventions and the Additional Protocols apart from the "grave breaches". Thus, Article 3 of the Statute covers *inter alia* war crimes embodied in the 1949 Geneva Conventions and the two Protocols, excluding the "grave breaches" but including all others, such as Common Article 3 thereof, if they constitute serious violations of international humanitarian law. Article 3 of the Statute would, therefore, cover both international and internal armed conflicts....

Abi-Saab, J. (concurring in part)

One of the merits of the Decision is that by its finding that "grave breaches" are subsumed in the "serious violations of the laws or customs of war" it resituated the Statute firmly within the modern trend recognizing the essential identity of the legal regime of violations of the two strands of the *jus in bello*. But the Decision had to qualify this finding in a manner that would still preserve for Article 2 of the Statute an autonomous field of application in relation to Article 3, pursuant to the "*effet utile*" principle of interpretation.

While I agree with the way the Decision portrays the relationship between "grave breaches" and "serious violations of the laws or customs of war" as that of species to genus, and I can see some merit in applying them separately "grave breaches" being more concretely formulated by reference to the detailed provisions of the Geneva Conventions—I find the "division of labour" between the two Articles of the Statute in the Decision rather artificial. Instead of reaching, as the Decision does, for the acts expressly mentioned in Article 2 via Article 3 when they are committed in the course of an internal armed conflict, I consider, on the basis of the material presented in the Decision itself, that a strong case can be made for the application of Article 2, even when the incriminated act takes place in an internal conflict.

Admittedly the traditional view, as far as the interpretation of the Geneva Conventions is concerned, has been that the "grave breaches" regime does not apply to internal armed conflicts. But the minority view that it does is not devoid of merit if we go by the texts alone and their possible teleological interpretation.

Regardless, however, of the outcome of this initial debate, if we consider the recent developments which are aptly presented in the Decision, we can draw two conclusions from them. The first is that a growing practice and *opinio juris* both of States and international organizations, has established the principle of personal criminal responsibility for the acts figuring in the grave breaches articles as well as for the other serious violations of the *jus in bello*, even when they are committed in the course of an internal armed conflict. The second conclusion is that in much of this accumulating practice and *opinio juris*, the former acts are expressly designated as "grave breaches" (see Decision para. 83).

This is not a mere question of semantics, but of proper legal classification of this accumulated normative substance, with a view to introducing a modicum of order among the categories of crimes falling within the substantive jurisdiction of the Tribunal.

The legal significance of this substance can be understood in at least two ways other than the one followed by the Decision, in order to bring the acts committed in internal conflicts within the reach of the grave breaches regime in the Geneva Conventions, and consequently of Article 2 of the Statute.

As a matter of treaty interpretation—and assuming that the traditional reading of "grave breaches" has been correct—it can be said that this new normative substance has led to a new interpretation of the Conventions as a result of the "subsequent practice" and *opinio juris* of the States parties: a teleological interpretation of the Conventions in the light of their object and purpose to the effect of including internal conflicts within the regime of "grave breaches". The other possible rendering of the significance of the new normative substance is to consider it as establishing a new customary rule ancillary to the Conventions, whereby the regime of "grave breaches" is extended to internal conflicts. But the first seems to me as the better approach. And under either, Article 2 of the Statute applies—the same as Articles 3, 4 and 5—in both international and internal conflicts.

This construction of Article 2 is supported by the fact that it coincides with the understanding of the parties to the conflict themselves of the legal situation. Thus in their Agreement of 1 October 1992—concerning the implementation of their earlier Agreement of 22 May 1992 which they specifically concluded within the framework of common Article 3 of the Geneva Conventions—they excluded from the obligation to release prisoners those "accused of or sentenced for, grave breaches ..." (Article 3) . They thus recognized the applicability of the regime of grave breaches in their on-going conflict, which they had already classified as internal....

Notes and Questions

1. Judge Cassese states that "'persons ... protected under the provisions of the relevant Geneva Conventions'" [see GC art. 147] or "by the Geneva Conventions" do not include persons protected under common Article 3. See *id.* Opinion of Cassese, at para. 81. Does this make sense, especially since common Article 3 applies in all armed conflicts as a minimum standard? Further, he did not mention (but arguably did not exclude) Articles 13 and 16 of Convention IV (Geneva Civilian Convention). *See also id.*, para. 76. *Cf.* J. Paust, *Applicability of International Criminal Laws to Events in the Former Yugoslavia, supra* at 512–13, and references cited; *Legal Aspects of the My Lai Incident: A Response to Professor Rubin*, 50 ORE. L. REV. 138, 143–49 (1971), reprinted in 3 THE VIETNAM WAR AND INTERNATIONAL LAW 359 (R. Falk ed., ASIL 1972); Paust & Blaustein, *supra* (each demonstrating application of Geneva law even to one's own nationals in certain cases).

How should treaties be interpreted? Customary criteria are reflected in Article 31(1) of the Vienna Convention on the Law of Treaties, 1155 U.N.T.S. 331, (a treaty must be interpreted "in accordance with the ordinary meaning to be given to the terms of the treaty in their context and in light of its object and purpose") and Article 31(3)(b) (and in accordance with "any subsequent practice in the application of the treaty"). Which interpretation best complies?

2. Was the language quoted from Professor Meron's article by Judge Li (in his para. 7) correct? Does it ultimately matter whether a violation of common Article 3, which is a violation of the laws of war and a war crime, is a "grave" breach of the Conventions? FM 27-10, para. 506 b recognizes that "[t]he principles quoted in [, for example, Article 146 of the Geneva Civilian Convention, and addressing grave breaches as well as "all acts contrary to the provisions of the present Convention other than grave breaches"] are declaratory of the obligations of belligerents under customary international law to take measures for the punishment of war crimes committed by all persons, including members of a belligerent's own armed forces." Recall that paragraph 499 states that "Every violation of the law of war is a war crime" and that paragraph 507 recognizes "Universality of Jurisdiction" over war crimes. See also J. PICTET, I COMMENTARY, *supra* at 367–68 ("the 1929 Convention called for the punishment of *all* acts contrary to the provisions of the Convention ... *all* breaches of the present Convention should be repressed ... [national legislation] must include a general clause ... providing for the punishment of other breaches of the Convention."); IV COMMENTARY, *supra* at 583 ("The Geneva Conventions form part of what are generally called the laws and customs of war, violations of which are ...'war crimes'"), 587, 590–94 ("must also suppress all other acts contrary to the provisions of this Convention ... all breaches should be suppressed ... [and states] should institute judicial or disciplinary punishment for breaches of the Convention."), 597, 602 ("other breaches ... will be punished").

In light of the above, do you find the statements at the end of paragraph 80 of Judge Cassese's opinion persuasive? Do States have jurisdiction in any event? Do common Articles 1 and 3 of the Geneva Conventions provide another counter to "sovereignty" over internal armed conflicts? Does universal jurisdiction and responsibility over numerous sorts of international criminal activity that can occur completely within a State also constitute a counter to such "sovereignty" interests?

Also in light of the above, do you agree with Judges Sidhwa and Abi-Saab that violations of common article 3 of the Geneva Conventions and Protocol II, as part of the laws of war, constitute war crimes? Judge Cassese would also agree. See Cassese opinion, *supra* at paras. 87–127 (adding in para. 89 that Article 3 of the Statute covers, among other war crimes, "violations of common Article 3 and other customary rules on internal conflicts...."); *see also* Meron, *Continuing, supra* at 239, 243; Paust & Blaustein, *supra*. Is a "breach" of common Article 3 a breach of Geneva law?

3. Professor Meron was quoted for the proposition that the customary Hague Convention No. IV of 1907 applies only to "international wars". Do you suspect that a recognized belligerency or true civil war is an "international" war? Recall Paust & Blaustein, *supra*(H.C. IV of 1907, all other customary laws of war, and common Article 2 of the Geneva Conventions apply to a recognized belligerency); U.S. FM 27-10, para. 11 a, *supra*; see also U.S. Dep't of Army Pam. 27-161-2, INTERNATIONAL LAW 27 (1962) ("If a civil war has reached such proportions that the rebellious side is accorded the status of a belligerent the legal effect ... is the same as that of an international war."); 1863 Lieber Code, arts. 149–154; DIG. OPS. OF JAG, ARMY 244 (U.S. 1866) (considered as exemplifying customary international law); BLUNTSCHLI ON THE LAW OF WAR AND NEUTRALITY — A TRANSLATION FROM HIS CODE OF INTERNATIONAL LAW 3–4 (F. Lieber translation) (U.S. Army T.J.A.G. School, ICL library); H. HALLECK, ELEMENTS OF INTERNATIONAL LAW AND LAWS OF WAR 151–53 (1866); I. HYDE, INTERNATIONAL LAW 198 (2 ed. 1947); J. PICTET, III COMMENTARY, *supra* at 38 (quoted above concerning application of the customary laws of war to a belligerency); 2 OPPENHEIM'S INTERNATIONAL LAW 370–72 & n.1 (7 ed. H. Lauterpacht 1948); NATALINO RONZITTI, INTERNATIONAL LAW AND THE USE OF FORCE BY NATIONAL LIBERATION MOVEMENTS (1988); Tom Farer, *The Humanitarian Laws of War in Civil Strife: Toward a Definition of "International Armed Conflict,"* 7 REV. BELGE DE DROIT INT'L 20 (1971); Hans-Peter Gasser, *Der Internationale Strafgerichtshoffür das frühere Jugoslavewien und das "Kriegsrecht und die Kriegagebräuche": Eline Glosse zu Artikel 3 des Statuts,* 2 HUMANITÄREN VÖLKERRECHT INFORMATIONSSCHRIFTEN 60 (1993); Martin Hess, *Die Anwendbarkeit des Humanitären Völkerrechts, insbesondere in gemischten Konflikten,* in 39 SCHWEIZER STUDIEN ZUM INTERNATIONALEN RECHT 150 (1985); Theodor Meron, *War Crimes in Yugoslavia and the Development of International Law,* 88 AM. J. INT'L L. 78 (1994); John E. Parkerson, Jr., *United States Compliance with Humanitarian Law Respecting Civilians During Operation Just Cause,* 133 MIL. L. REV. 31, 35–39 (1991); J. Paust, *Applicability, supra* at 506–10; Yves Sandoz, *Reflexion sur la Mise en Oeuvre du Droit International Humanitaire et sur le Rôle du Comité International de la Croix-Rouge en Ex-Yougoslavie,* 4 REVUE SUISSE DE DROIT INTERNATIONAL ET DE DROIT EUROPÉEN 461 (1993); *see also* Meron, *Continuing, supra* at 242–43 ("I agree that, as a matter of law, some important Hague rules already apply to noninternational armed conflicts....").

The Appeals Chamber in *The Prosecutor v. Dusko Tadic,* at para. 127 (Cassese Op.), had recognized that customary norms applicable to "internal strife" "cover such areas as protection of civilians from hostilities, in particular from indiscriminate attacks, protection of civilian objects, in particular cultural property, protection of all those who do not (or no longer) take active part in hostilities, as well as prohibition of means of warfare proscribed in international armed conflicts and [the] ban of certain methods of conducting hostilities." In *The Prosecutor v. Hadzihasanovic & Kubura,* IT-01-47-AR73.3 (Appeals Chamber, Decision on Joint Defence Interlocutory Appeal of Trial Chamber

Decision on Rule 98bis Motions for Acquittal,11 Mar. 2005), the Appeals Chamber found that the war crimes of (1) "wanton destruction of cities, towns or villages not justified by military necessity"; (2) "plunder of public or private property"; and (3) "destruction or wilful damage done to institutions dedicated to religion" apply in internal armed conflicts as well as in international armed conflicts as offenses under customary international law. *Id.* paras. 26-30, 37-38, 44-48.

See also Geneva Protocol II, arts. 4, 13-14, 17; Statute of the ICC, art. 8(2)(e)(i)-(iv), regarding norms other than common Article 3 applicable during an insurgency.

4. It should be noted that Article 38 1(b) of the Statute of the I.C.J. does not include the limiting word "States" with respect to the formation of customary international law through general practice accepted as law.

5. Given the controversial decision in *Tadic* that "grave breaches" of the Geneva Conventions can only occur during an international armed conflict (which is not controversial within the ICTY), the ICTY has had to deal with the issue whether an accused should know that he or she is participating in such an armed conflict when "grave breaches" are charged. In *The Prosecutor v. Naletilic & Martinovic*, IT-98-34-A (Appeals Chamber, 3 May 2006), paras. 113-122, the Appeals Chamber decided that an Appeals Chamber decision in The Prosecutor v. Kordic & Cerkez, IT-95-14/2-A (Appeals Chamber Judgment, 17 Dec. 2004), para. 311, that the accused need not "make a correct legal evaluation as to the international character of the armed conflict," the accused must be "aware of the factual circumstances, *e.g.*, that a foreign state was involved in the armed conflict" [in that case, participation by Croatian troops] (*Kordic & Cerkez* at para. 311) "was correct, and follows logically from the principles established in *Tadic*." *Naletilic & Martinovic* at para. 113. "The principle of individual guilt requires that an accused can only be convicted for a crime if his *mens rea* comprises the *actus reus* of the crime ... that he knew of the facts that were necessary to make his conduct a crime ... [and] he must have had knowledge of the facts that made his or her conduct criminal." *Id.* para. 114. "The Appeals Chamber concludes that the existence and international character of an armed conflict are both jurisdictional prerequisites (as established in *Tadic*) and substantive elements of crimes pursuant to Article 2 of the Statute.... Thus, the Prosecution's obligation to prove intent also encompasses the accused's knowledge of the facts pertinent to the internationality of an armed conflict.... [T]here has to be a nexus between the act of the accused and the international armed conflict. It is illogical to say that there is such a nexus unless it is proved that the accused has been aware of the factual circumstances concerning the nature of the hostilities.... [T]he Prosecution has to show 'that the accused *knew* that his crimes' had a nexus to an international armed conflict, or at least that he had knowledge of the factual circumstances later bringing the Judges to the conclusion that the armed conflict was an international one.... It is a general principle of criminal law that the correct legal classification of a conduct by the perpetrator is not required. The principle of individual guilt, however, demands sufficient awareness of *factual* circumstances establishing the armed conflict and its (international or internal) character." *Id.* paras. 116-119.

6. The ICTR provided more detail concerning some of the violations of Common Article 3 of the Geneva Conventions, as limited by Article 4 (e) of the Statute of the ICTR (to "serious violations") in *The Prosecutor v. Musema*, ICTR-96-13-T (27 Jan. 2000):

285.... Required elements of Article 4 (e) of the Statute of the Tribunal

a) *Humiliating and degrading treatment*: Subjecting victims to treatment designed to subvert their self-regard. Like outrages upon personal dignity, these offences may be regarded as a lesser forms of torture; moreover ones in which the motives required for torture would not be required, nor would it be required that the acts be committed under state authority.

b) *Rape*: The specific elements of rape are stated in Section 3.3. on Crime against Humanity in the Applicable Law. [see Chapter Two, Section 5]

c) *Indecent assault*: The accused caused the infliction of pain or injury by an act which was of a sexual nature and inflicted by means of coercion, force, threat or intimidation and was non-consensual.

The violation must be serious

286. Article 4 of the Statute states that "The International Tribunal for Rwanda shall have the power to prosecute persons committing or ordering to be committed serious violations of Common Article 3 and of the Additional Protocol II". The Trial Chamber in the *Akayesu* Judgement understood, in line with the Appeals Chamber Decision in *Tadic* that the phrase "serious violation" means "a breach of a rule protecting important values which must involve grave consequences for the victim".

287. The list of serious violations provided in Article 4 of the Statute is taken from Common Article 3 of the Geneva Conventions and of Additional Protocol II, which outline "Fundamental Guarantees"as a humanitarian minimum of protection for war victims. The list in Article 4 of the Statute thus comprises serious violations of the fundamental humanitarian guarantees which, as has been stated above, are recognised as customary international law.

288. In the opinion of the Chamber, violations of these fundamental humanitarian guarantees, by their very nature, are therefore to be considered as serious.

7. In view of the above, do you think that stripping persons naked and hooding them as an interrogation tactic is "humiliating" and/or "degrading"? Is it "cruel" or "inhuman" treatment? Would the use of snarling dogs to instill intense fear or even terrorism constitute cruel, inhuman, degrading, or humiliating treatment? Would waterboarding (used to instill an intense and terrifying fear of drowning)? Would an interrogation tactic of "the cold cell" (where a naked detainee is kept in a cell cooled to 50 degrees and periodically doused with cold water), "fear up harsh: significantly increasing the fear level in a detainee," or "yelling to create fear" constitute cruel, inhuman, degrading, or humiliating treatment? These interrogation tactics were authorized by members of the Bush Administration for use against persons detained during the wars in Afghanistan and Iraq. *See, e.g.*, Paust, *The Absolute Prohibition of Torture and Necessary and Appropriate Sanctions*, 43 Valp. U. L. Rev. 1535, 1553-58 (2009), available at http://ssrn.com/asbtract=1331159; Paust, *Executive Plans*, *supra* at 812, 824-51, adding: in *Ireland v. United Kingdom* [25 Eur. Ct. H.R. (ser. A) at 5 (1971)], the European Court of Human Rights ruled that British interrogation tactics of wall-standing (forcing the detainees to remain for periods of some hours in a "stress position"), hoo, subjection to noise, deprivation of sleep, and deprivation of food and drink "constituted a practice of inhuman and degrading treatment" proscribed under human rights law.[16] In 1996, the European Court

---

16. *Id.* at 41, para. 96, 66, para. 167. The court noted that the "techniques were applied in combination, with premeditation and for hours at a stretch; they caused, if not bodily injury, at least intense physical and mental suffering to the persons subjected thereto and also led to acute psychiatric disturbances during interrogation," and, "accordingly," were forms of inhuman treatment. *Id.* at 66, para. 167. The Court concluded that the "techniques were also degrading, since they were such as to arouse in their victims feelings of fear, anguish and inferiority capable of humiliating and debasing them and possibly breaking their physical or moral resistance."

recognized that where a detainee "was stripped naked, with his arms tied behind his back and suspended by his arms ... [, s]uch treatment amounted to torture."[17] In another case, the European Court stated that treatment was "'degrading' because it was such as to arouse in its victims feelings of fear, anguish and inferiority capable of humiliating and debasing them."[18] The International Criminal Tribunal for Former Yugoslavia has also identified criteria for determining whether certain conduct constitutes criminally sanctionable "torture"[19] or "cruel" or "inhuman" treatment.[20] Moreover, the Committee against Torture created under the Convention Against Torture and Other Cruel, Inhuman or Degrading Treatment or Punishment has condemned the use of the following interrogation tactics as either torture or cruel, inhuman or degrading treatment: (1) restraining in very painful conditions, (2) hooding under special conditions, (3) sounding of loud music for prolonged periods, (4) sleep deprivation for prolonged periods, (5) threats, including death threats, (6) violent shaking, and (7) using cold air to chill [Concluding Observations of the Committee against Torture: Israel, 18th Sess., U.N. Doc. A/52/44 (1997) at paras. 256-257.]. Earlier, a U.S. Army pamphlet addressing Geneva and other law of war proscriptions warned that an illegal means of interrogation of a detainee included "dunking his head into a barrel of water, or putting a plastic bag over his head to make him talk," adding: "No American soldier can commit these brutal acts, nor permit his fellow soldiers to do so."

8. The Army has charged the former head of the interrogation center at Abu Ghraib prison with criminal charges in connection with the abuses at the prison. Ten lower-ranking soldiers who served at the prison outside Baghdad have been convicted for abusing prisoners, including an Army dog handler who was sentenced to incarceration

---

17. Aksoy v. Turkey, 6 Eur. Ct. H.R. 2260, 23 EHRR 553, at paras. 60, 64 (18 Dec. 1996). The Court stated that "torture attaches only to deliberate inhuman treatment causing very serious and cruel suffering." *Id.* at paras. 63-64. The victim was detained for some two weeks and had claimed to have been subjected to beatings and had been stripped naked, hooded, and subjected to electric shocks. *Id.* at paras. 60, 64.

18. T & V v. United Kingdom, Judgment of 16 Dec. 1999, at para. 71, 30 EHRR 121 (2000).

19. *See, e.g.*, The Prosecutor v. Kunarac, IT-96-23-T & IT-96-23/1-T (Trial Chamber, International Criminal Tribunal for Former Yugoslavia), para. 497 (22 Feb. 2001) (intentional "infliction, by act or omission, of severe pain or suffering, whether physical or mental"); *Id.* (Appeals Chamber, 12 June 2002), para. 149 (adding "but there are no more specific requirements which allow an exhaustive classification or enumeration of acts which may constitute torture. Existing case law has not determined the absolute degree of pain required for an act to amount to torture"), para. 150 (rape can constitute torture); The Prosecutor v. Naletilic & Martinovic, IT-98-34-A (Appeals Chamber, 3 May 2006), paras. 299-300; The Prosecutor v. Furundzija, IT-95-17/1 (Trial Chamber, Judgment), paras. 159-64 (10 Dec. 1998) (sexual violence can constitute torture); The Prosecutor v. Kvocka, IT-98-30/ 1 (Trial Chamber, Judgment), para. 149 (2 Nov. 2001) (same); William A. Schabas, *The Crime of Torture and the International Criminal Tribunals*, 37 Case W. Res. J. Int'l L. 349, 362-63 (2006) (addressing decisions of the ICTR and ICTY regarding rape and sexual violence as torture); Johan D. van der Vyver, *Torture as a Crime Under International Law*, 67 Albany L. Rev. 427 (2003).

20. With respect to "cruel" treatment, a trial chamber of the ICTY declared that "cruel treatment is treatment which causes serious mental or physical suffering and constitutes a serious attack on human dignity." The Prosecutor v. Delalic, IT-96-21-T (Trial Chamber, International Criminal Tribunal for Former Yugoslavia), para. 551 (Nov. 16, 1998). The same decision recognized that "inhuman treatment is an intentional act or omission, that is an act which, when judged objectively, is deliberate and not accidental, which causes serious mental or physical suffering or injury or constitutes a serious attack on human dignity." *Id.* at para. 543. Other ICTY cases confirm the *Delalic* recognitions. *See, e.g.*, Knut Dormann, Elements of War Crimes under the Rome Statute of the International Criminal Court 65 n.72 (re: inhuman), 398-99 ns. 7-8 (re: cruel) (2003).... With respect to torture, see also Zubeda v. Ashcroft, 333 F.3d 463, 472 (3d Cir. 2003) ("[r]ape can constitute torture"); Al-Saher v. I.N.S., 268 F.3d 1143, 1147 (9th Cir. 2001).

for six months for using his snarling canine to torment Iraqi prisoners. Former Cpl. Charles Graner Jr. received the longest sentence—10 years in prison. Army Reservist Lynndie England, photographed giving a thumbs-up in front of naked prisoners, is serving a three year prison term.

9. Is terrorism unknown to the laws of war? *See, e.g.*, the 1919 List of War Crimes, GC art. 33; United States v. von Leeb, extract *infra*.

B. Conduct of Hostilities and Other Protections

U.S. Dep't of Army FM 27-10, The Law of Land Warfare (1956)

[para. 3] a. Prohibitory Effect. The law of war places limits on the exercise of belligerent's power ... and requires that all belligerents refrain from employing any kind or degree of violence which is not actually necessary for military purposes and that they conduct hostilities with regard for the principles of humanity and chivalry.

The prohibitory effect of the law of war is not minimized by "military necessity" which has been defined as that principle which justifies those measures not forbidden by international law which are indispensable for securing the complete submission of the enemy as soon as possible. Military necessity has been generally rejected as a defense for acts forbidden by the customary and conventional laws of war inasmuch as the latter have been developed and framed with consideration for the concept of military necessity.

b. Binding on States and Individuals. The law of war is binding not only upon States as such but also upon individuals and, in particular, the members of their armed forces....

25.... [I]t is a generally recognized rule of international law that civilians must not be made the object of attack directed exclusively against them.... [*compare* Article 51(3) of Protocol I]

28. Refusal of Quarter

It is especially forbidden ... to declare that no quarter will be given.

29. Injury Forbidden After Surrender

It is especially forbidden ... to kill or wound an enemy who, having laid down his arms, or having no longer means of defense, has surrendered at discretion.

30. Persons Descending by Parachute

The law of war does not prohibit firing upon paratroopers or other persons who are or appear to be bound upon hostile missions while such persons are descending by parachute. Persons other than those mentioned in the preceding sentence who are descending by parachute from disabled aircraft may not be fired upon.

31. Assassination and Outlawry

[The Hague Convention] provides:

It is especially forbidden ... to kill or wound treacherously individuals belonging to the hostile nation or army.

This article is construed as prohibiting assassination, proscription, or outlawry of an enemy, or putting a price upon an enemy's head, as well as offering a reward for an enemy "dead or alive". It does not, however, preclude attacks on individual soldiers or officers of the enemy whether in the zone of hostilities, occupied territory or elsewhere....

39. Bombardment of Undefended Places Forbidden

The attack or bombardment, by whatever means, of towns, villages, dwellings, or buildings which are undefended is prohibited. (HR, art. 25.) ...

41. Unnecessary Killing and Devastation

Particularly in the circumstances referred to in the preceding paragraph, loss of life and damage to property must not be out of proportion to the military advantage to be gained. Once a fort or defended locality has surrendered, only such further damage is permitted as is demanded by the exigencies of war, such as the removal of fortifications, demolition of military buildings, and destruction of stores.

42. Aerial Bombardment

There is no prohibition of general application against bombardment from the air of combatant troops, defended places, or other legitimate military objectives.....

47. Pillage Forbidden

The pillage of a town or place, even when taken by assault, is prohibited. (HR, art. 28.) ...

56. Devastation

The measure of permissible devastation is found in the strict necessities of war. Devastation as an end in itself or as a separate measure of war is not sanctioned by the law of war. There must be some reasonably close connection between the destruction of property and the overcoming of the enemy's army. Thus the rule requiring respect for private property is not violated through damage resulting from operations, movements, or combat activity of the army; that is, real estate may be used for marches, camp sites, construction of field fortifications, etc. Buildings may be destroyed for sanitary purposes or used for shelter for troops, the wounded and sick and vehicles and for reconnaissance, cover, and defense. Fences, wood, crops, buildings, etc., may be demolished, cut down, and removed to clear a field of fire, to clear the ground for landing fields, or to furnish building materials or fuel if imperatively needed for the army.....

57. Protection of Artistic and Scientific Institutions and Historic Monuments

The United States and certain of the American Republics are parties to the so-called [1935] Roerich Pact, which accords a neutralized and protected status to historic monuments, museums, scientific, artistic, educational, and cultural institutions in the event of war between such States.

[See also Convention (and Regulations and Protocol) for the Protection of Cultural Property in the Event of Armed Conflict, done at the Hague, May 14, 1954, 249 U.N.T.S. 240.]

58. Destruction and Seizure of Property

It is especially forbidden ... to destroy or seize the enemy's property, unless such destruction or seizure be imperatively demanded by the necessities of war.

59. Booty of War

a. Public Property. All enemy public movable property captured or found on a battlefield becomes the property of the capturing State.

The Declaration of St. Petersburg, (1868) (extract)

... Considering that the progress of civilization should have the effect of alleviating as much as possible the calamities of war;

That the only legitimate object which States should endeavor to accomplish during War is to weaken the military forces of the enemy;

That for this purpose it is sufficient to disable the greatest number of men;

That this object would be exceeded by the employment of arms which uselessly aggravate the sufferings of disabled men, or renders their death inevitable;

That the employment of such arms would therefore be contrary to the laws of humanity;

The Contracting Parties engage mutually to renounce ... the employment by their military or naval troops of any projectile of a weight below 400 grammes [some 14 ounces], which is either explosive or charged with fulminating or inflammable substances....

Hague Declaration No. IV, July 29, 1899, para. 3

The Contracting Parties agree to abstain from the use of bullets which expand or flatten easily in the human body, such as bullets with a hard envelope which does not entirely cover the core, or is pierced with incisions.

Geneva Protocol of 1925, (Protocol prohibiting the use in War of Asphyxiating, Poisonous or other Gases, and of Bacteriological Methods of Warfare), done in Geneva 17 June 1925, L.N.T.S. 1929 No. 2138, 26 U.S.T. 571, T.I.A.S. No. 8061

... Whereas the use in war of asphyxiating, poisonous or other gases, and all analogous liquids, materials or devices, has been justly condemned by the general opinion of the civilized world; ...

To the end that this prohibition shall be universally accepted as a part of International Law, binding alike the conscience and the practice of nations;

Declare:

That the High Contracting Parties, so far as they are not already Parties to Treaties prohibiting such use, accept this prohibition, agree to extend this prohibition to the use of bacteriological methods of warfare and agree to be bound as between themselves according to the terms of this declaration....

Hague Convention (No. IV) Respecting the Laws and Customs of War (1907)

[read the extracts of HC IV in the Documents Section]

Notes and Questions

1. Concerning the prohibition of assassination, note that selective targeting that is lawful under the laws of war or the law of self-defense is not "assassination."

2. There are many developments concerning the regulation of weaponry. Consider, for example, Convention on the Prohibition of the Development, Production and Stockpiling of Bacteriological (Biological) and Toxin Weapons and on Their Destruction, done in London, Moscow and Washington, April 10, 1972, 26 U.S.T. 583, T.I.A.S.

No. 8062; Convention on the Prohibition of Military or Any Other Hostile Use of Environmental Modification Techniques, 1970, 1108 U.N.T.S. 88 (1977); Convention on Prohibitions or Restrictions on the Use of Certain Conventional Weapons Which May be Deemed to Be Excessively Injurious or to Have Indiscriminate Effects, and Protocols I-III, U.N. Doc. A/CONF. 95/15 (1980), in 19 I.L.M. 1523 (1980); Declaration on the Prohibition of Chemical Weapons, Paris, Jan. 11, 1989, in 28 I.L.M. 1020 (1989); Convention on the Prohibition of the Development, Production, Stockpiling and Use of Chemical Weapons and on their Destruction, Jan. 13, 1993, in 32 I.L.M. 800 (1993); Convention on the Prohibition of the Use, Stockpiling, Production and Transfer of Anti-Personnel Mines and their Destruction, in 36 I.L.M. 1507 (1997); Hans-Peter Gasser, *For Better Protection of the Natural Environment in Armed Conflict: A Proposal for Action*, 89 Am. J. Int'l L. 637 (1995); Janet Lord, *Legal Restraints in the Use of Landmines: Humanitarian and Environmental Crisis*, 25 Cal. W.L.J. 311 (1995); Rex J. Zedalis, *The Chemical Weapons Convention Implementation Act: United States Control over Exports*, 90 Am. J. Int'l L. 138 (1996); Special Issue on Disarmament, 28 McGill L. J. 453 (1983). Does the U.S. have the right unilaterally to destroy an Iranian chemical weapons facility? If it is targeted during an armed conflict with Iran?

3. Concerning conventional weaponry, it should be noted that some weapons are prohibited *per se* and, therefore, may never be used, while other weapons are regulated by general principles of necessity and proportionality and more specific customary or treaty-based norms. As noted below, the use of poison for any purpose is absolutely forbidden. Also, the absolute prohibitions of weapons covered by the 1868 St. Petersburg Declaration and the 1899 Hague Declaration No. IV are customary prohibitions, and the Hague Declaration's language appears in the Rome Statute of the ICC, art. 8(2)(ix). Language in the first part of the Geneva Protocol of 1925 appears in the Rome Statute, art. 8(2)(b)(xviii). *See generally* J. Paust, *Does Your Police Force Use Illegal Weapons? A Configurative Approach to Decision Integrating International and Domestic Law*, 18 Harv. Int'l L. J. 19, 29–37 (1977); U.S. FM 27-10, at paras. 34–38; Note 1 *supra*.

4. The French text of Article 23 (e) of the Annex to Hague Convention No. IV does not contain the word "calculated" and it is the authoritative text. The French text retained the wording from the 1899 Hague Convention No. II, July 29, 1899, Annex, Art. 23 (e): "of a nature to cause superfluous injury" ("*propres a causer des maux superflus*"). Under customary law, the words "unnecessary" and "superfluous" are now interchangeable in this regard. *See, e.g.,* Paust, *Does Your Police Force Use Illegal Weapons?, supra* at 30 n.43. *See also* Article 8 (2)(b)(xx) of the Statute of the ICC ("of a nature to cause"). However, there is a limitation in the ICC article which is not a customary limitation (*i.e.*, "provided that such … are the subject of a comprehensive prohibition and are included in an annex to this Statute" created by an amendment).

5. What is the nature of the prohibition of "poison" and "asphyxiating, poisonous or other gases"? Consider the following: Customary international law reflected in Article 23(a) of the 1907 Hague Convention expressly affirms the *per se* prohibition of poison—that is, it may never be used under any circumstances and, thus, regardless of attempts at justification or claims of military necessity. See also Captain Paul A. Robblee, *The Legitimacy of Modern Conventional Weaponry*, 71 Mil. L. Rev. 95, 101-02, 104-05, 110 (1976). It does not matter how poison is employed (*e.g.*, by pellet, liquid or gas, dropped by hand or modern aircraft) and it does not matter against whom the poison is employed (*e.g.*, solely against enemy combatants, against a mixture of enemy combatants and noncombatants, or in areas inhabited merely by noncombatants), since by the plain meaning of Article 23(a) it is prohibited "to employ" poison in any manner. Fur-

ther, the treaty does not merely prohibit "poisoned weapons," but also prohibits the employment of "poison," *i.e.*, one is prohibited "[t]o employ poison" of any sort in any manner. With respect to poisonous effects of herbicides, in 1945 the Judge Advocate General of the U.S. Army recognized the dynamic reach of the customary prohibition of poison to gases and "crop-destroying chemicals which can be sprayed by airplane." See Major General Myron C. Cramer, Memorandum for the Secretary of War, Subject: Destruction of Crops by Chemicals, SPJGW 1945/164 (Mar. 1945), reprinted in 10 I.L.M. 1304 (1971).

Long ago, the authoritative 1863 Lieber Code recognized that customary laws of war prohibited "the use of poison in any way," even in the face of claims of "military necessity" (Article 16) and that "[t]he use of poison in any manner, be it to poison wells, or food, or arms, is wholly excluded from modern warfare. He that uses it puts himself out of the pale of the law and usages of war" (Article 70). The "[p]oisoning of wells" also appears in a list of customary war crimes recognized by the Commission on the Responsibility of the Authors of the War and on Enforcement of Penalties that was presented to the Preliminary Peace Conference in Paris following World War I. See List of War Crimes, No. 32 (1919). The U.S. Army Field Manual utilized during the Vietnam War (and still today) also recognized that it is a war crime to employ poison. FM 27-10, *supra* at 18, para. 37, 180, para. 504(i). More generally, it was known by the Founders that "poisoners ... by profession" were international criminals. *See, e.g.*, 1 Op. Att'y Gen. 509, 515 (1821), quoting E. DE VATTEL, THE LAW OF NATIONS (1758).

The United Kingdom also recognized prior to the Vietnam War that "using asphyxiating, poisonous or other gases, and all analogous liquids, materials or devices" is a war crime. 1958 UK MANUAL, *supra* at 175, para. 626(r). Importantly, the "[u]se of deleterious and asphyxiating gases" also appears on the 1919 List of War Crimes, No. 26. Thus, prior to adoption of the 1925 Geneva Protocol, use of "deleterious and asphyxiating gases" as well as poison in any form had already been recognized as per se violations of the customary laws of war. An important issue, therefore, is whether use of particular herbicides or other chemicals in spray form or gas was "deleterious" or "asphyxiating" even if use of others would not have reached these customary legal triggers. Further, the customary prohibitions shed light on the meaning of certain phrases in the 1925 Geneva Protocol. When the drafters of the 1925 Protocol affirmed that "use in war of asphyxiating, poisonous or other gases, and of all analogous liquids, materials or devices, has been justly condemned by the general opinion of the civilized world," the drafters recognized and affirmed what we would term today a pattern of general *opinio juris* that recognizably condemned their use. Similarly, when the drafters recognized that "such use has been declared in Treaties to which the majority of Powers of the world are Parties," the drafters were affirming that a general *opinio juris* was extant and reflected also in treaties.

Importantly also, in 1945 the Cramer Memorandum addressed "certain crop-destroying chemicals which can be sprayed by airplane" recognized that "a customary rule of international law has developed by which poisonous gases and those causing unnecessary suffering are prohibited," these include "poisonous and deleterious gases," and customary law requires that "chemicals do not produce poisonous effects upon enemy personnel, either from direct contact, or indirectly from ingestion of plants and vegetables which have been exposed thereto," adding that "[w]hether ... agents ... are toxic ... is a question of fact which should definitely be ascertained." See Cramer, Memorandum, *supra*, reprinted in 10 I.L.M. 1304, 1305-06 (1971). *See also* DOD General Counsel J. Fred Buzhardt, letter to Senator J.W. Fulbright (Apr. 5, 1971) ("chemical herbicides, harmless to man," would not be proscribed per se, but "as poison…, their use against crops intended solely for the consumption by the enemy's forces would clearly have been prohibited by Article 23(a) of the Hague Regulations … [which], in effect, declares that any use of a lethal substance against human beings is, per se, a use which is calculated to cause unnecessary suffering."), reprinted in 10 I.L.M. 1300, 1302 (1971) (stating that his opinion was also "that of the Judge Advocate Generals of the Army, Navy and Air Force"). "The weight of opinion [in 1970] appears … to favor the view that customary international law proscribes the use in war of lethal chemical and biological weapons," but a question remained whether it outlawed *per se* any "use of tear gas and herbicides" as opposed to their particular use or effects that violated relevant international law. Richard R. Baxter & Thomas Buergenthal, *Legal Aspects of the Geneva Protocol of 1925*, 64 Am. J. Int'l L. 853, 853-54 (1970). Their study also noted that the U.S. was concerned whether all "irritant chemicals (tear gas) and anti-plant chemicals" fell per se "within the prohibition of the use in war of "'other gases.'" See *id*. at 855, 857 & n.18 (re: U.S. statement to the U.N. General Assembly regarding riot control agents), 859, 861. There were suggestions that the phrase "other gases" that were prohibited per se should only apply "to chemical agents similar to those of asphyxiating or poisonous gases." *Id*. at 856-57.

Was the use of certain herbicides during the Vietnam War a violation of the laws of war? *Cf In re* Agent Orange Litigation, 373 F. Supp.2d 7 (E.D.N.Y. 2005), *aff'd*, 517 F.3d 104 (2d Cir. 2008). Would they be today?

6. What is the nature of "military necessity"? Does this principle allow use of force that is merely beneficial in carrying out a necessary military operation or force that is proportionate to a military advantage? See Paust, *Weapons Regulation, Military Necessity and Legal Standards: Are Contemporary Department of Defense Practices Inconsistent with Legal Norms?*, 4 Den. J. Int'l L. & Pol. 229 (1974), adding:

> it must be emphasized that it has never been an accepted international legal standard in modern times that armed forces can employ any form or intensity of violence which is consistent with or helpful in the attainment of a legitimate military objective. Such an approach is far too broad. It amounts to a military "benefit" test as opposed to a military "necessity" test, and the military benefit or "*Kriegsraison*" theory was expressly repudiated at Nuremberg.

See also *United States v. List, infra*; M. McDougal & F. Feliciano, Law and Minimum World Public Order 520 (1961); M. Greenspan, The Modern Law of Land Warfare 297 (1959); U.S. Department of Army Pam. No. 27-161-2, International Law 9–10 (1962).

7. For an analysis of the law of air warfare or aerial bombardment *compare* H. DeSaussure, *The Laws of Air Warfare: Are There Any?*, in The Int'l Lawyer (1971); Law and Responsibility in Warfare: The Vietnam Experience 119–149 (P. Trooboff ed., ASIL 1975); *with* J. Paust, *My Lai and Vietnam, supra* at 140 n.156 and 146–153. See also J. M. Spaight, Air Power and War Rights (3 ed. 1947); M. Greenspan, The Modern Law of Land Warfare 351–353 (1959); M. McDougal & F. Feliciano, Law and Minimum World Public Order 79–80 (1961); II Oppenheim's International Law 516–533 (7 ed. 1952).

Do the 1949 Geneva Conventions apply? *See, e.g.,* common Article 3; Geneva Civilian Convention, Articles 4 ("in the hands of"), 13, 16; Protocol I, Articles 51, 75(1) ("in the power of"), 75(2); IV Commentary at 47 ("'in the hands of' is used in an extremely general sense. It is not merely a question of being in enemy hands directly, as a prisoner is. The mere fact of being in the territory of a Party to the conflict or in occupied territory implies that one is in the power or 'hands' of the Occupying Power").

When U.S. Navy Seals killed Osama bin Laden in his compound in norther Pakistan on May 2, 2011, assuming that he had not surrendered, was bin Laden "in the hands of" or "in the power of" the Seals team? Consider Hague Convention No. IV, Annex, art. 23 (b) ("it is especially forbidden ... [t]o kill or wound treacherously individuals belonging to the hostile nation or army"),(c) ("it is especially forbidden ... [t]o kill or wound an enemy who, having laid down his arms, or having no longer means of defence, has surrendered"); Rome Statute of the ICC, art. 8(2)(b)(vi) (same re: a "combatant" who "has surrendered"), (xi) (Killing or wounding treacherously individuals belonging to the hostile nation or army"); Jordan J. Paust, *Permissible Self-Defense Targeting and the Death of bin Laden*, 39 Denv. J. Int'l L. & Pol'y 569, 578-83 (2011).

8. Recall paragraph 25 of FM 27-10. Geneva Protocol I, arts. 48 and 51 require that parties to an international armed conflict "distinguish between the civilian population and combatants and between civilian objects and military objectives and accordingly shall direct their operations only against military objectives" (art. 48, which articulates the principle of distinction) and that "[t]he civilian population as such, as well as individual civilians, shall not be the object of attack" (art. 51(2)). However, "[c]ivilians shall enjoy the protection afforded ... unless and for such time as they take a direct part in hostilities" (art. 51(3)). When a civilian takes a direct part in hostilities such a person is a DPH and is targetable. This set of customary rules is well-known, but it is not always agreed exactly what forms of civilian participation in hostilities are "direct" and subject a civilian to permissible attack. Consider the following extract from Paust, *Self-Defense Targetings of Non-State Actors and Permissibility of U.S. Use of Drones in Pakistan*, 19 J. Transnat'l L. & Pol'y 237 (2010), available at http://ssrn.com/abstract=1520717 :

An extremely restrictive view of direct and active participation might involve the claim that civilians who are members of a non-state organization engaged in armed attacks can only be targeted during the time that they actually carry out the attacks. *See also* ... Inter-American Commission on Human Rights Report on Terrorism and Human Rights, OEA/Ser.L/v/II.116, Doc. 5, rev. 1 corr. (Oct. 22, 2002), at para. 69, which noted that "[i]t is possible ... [that the fighter "who engaged in hostilities"] cannot ... revert back to civilian status or otherwise alternate between combatant and civilian status"). The more realistic and policy-serving view is that such persons who directly participate in a process of armed attacks over time *are* directly and actively taking a part in hostilities. It is not a question of formal status, but of direct and active participation over time....

Importantly, the International Committee of the Red Cross has recognized that such non-state fighters can be recognized as "members" of "organized armed groups ... [that consist] of individuals whose continuous function is to take a direct part in hostilities ('continuous combat function' [CCF])" or "members of an organized armed group with a continuous combat function" and that they are targetable. *See* ICRC, Guidance on the Notion of Direct Participation in Hostilities under International Humanitarian Law 16, 27, 36, 70-73 (2009). The ICRC adds that "members of organized armed groups ... cease to be civilians ... and lose protection against direct attack." *Id.* at 17. The ICRC would distinguish such member-fighters or "fighting forces" "from civilians who directly participate in hostilities on a merely spontaneous, sporadic, or unorganized basis." *Id.* at 34. The latter are targetable when they directly participate in hostilities. Moreover, direct participation in hostilities by civilians includes their "[m]easures preparatory to the execution of a specific act ... as well as the deployment to and the return from a location of its execution." *Id.* at 17, 65-68. *See also* Yoram Dinstein, The Conduct of Hostilities Under the Law of International Armed Conflict 27-29 (2004) (preferring that civilians who are directly participating lose civilian status); Nils Melzer, Targeted Killing in International Law 56, 310, 314, 317 (general practice is "to directly attack insurgents" or organized armed groups "even when they are not engaged in a particular military operation," the practice is not internationally condemned, and "members of organized armed groups ... are not regarded as civilians, but as approximately equivalent to State armed forces" for targeting purposes), 319-20, 327-28 (those with "functional 'combatancy'" are targetable), 345 (direct participation is "reached where a civilian supplies ammunition to an operational firing position, arms an airplane with bombs for a concrete attack, or transports combatants to an operational combat area") (2008); *Public Committee Against Torture v. Government of Israel*, HCJ 769/02 (S.Ct. Israel Dec. 14, 2006), para. 39 ("a civilian who has joined a terrorist organization ... and in the framework of his role in that organization he commits a chain of hostilities, with short periods of rest between them, loses his immunity from attack").

A major problem with the ICRC's preference concerning "sporadic" fighters is that military forces engaged in targetings might not be able to tell whether a fighter is a member of an organized group or only joins in sporadically. *See also* Melzer, *supra* at 319 (it may be "problematic in operational reality").

Do you suspect that one who directly finances hostilities is a DPH? *See* ICRC Guidance, *supra* at 51-52, 54 (economic or financial activities engaged in by civilians may be "war-sustaining activities," but not direct participation in hostilities); Melzer, *supra* at 341, 345; *Public Committee Against Torture v. Israel, supra* at para. 35 ("a person who sells food or medicine to an unlawful combatant is not taking a direct part, rather an indirect part in hostilities. The same is the case regarding a person who aids the unlawful combatants by general strategic analysis, and grants them logistical general support, including monetary aid"). *But see* Amos N. Guiora, *Proportionality "Re-Configured,"* in 31 ABA Nat. Sec. L. Rpt. 9, 13 (Feb. 2009) (arguing for a change in law to allow targeting of those who are merely "passive supporters" of hostilities). http://ssrn.com/abstract=1364608.Professor David Luban notes why such an expansive form of targeting is unacceptable. *See* David Luban, *Was the Gaza Campaign Legal?, id.* at 15-16. Note that the 1863 Lieber Code contained two articles that recognized a need to make a distinction—Article 22 ("the distinction between the private individual ... and the hostile country itself, with its men in arms" and "the unarmed citizen is to be spared in person") and Article 23 ("Private citizens ... the inoffensive individual").

Do you agree with the ICRC approach, that persons who are not "combatants," but who are members of an organized armed group and have a continuous combat function (CCF) are targetable?

In 2009, the U.S. used a drone to kill a top Taliban leader inside Pakistan who was directly participating in armed hostilities. The targeting also resulted in the deaths of his wife, his wife's parents, his uncle, a Taliban lieutenant, and seven bodyguards. Was the targeting permissible? Was it in compliance with the principle of proportionality? Would you want to know additional facts? Why?

9. During the 1991 Gulf War, the U.S. used "smart" weaponry to specifically target what it stated was a sophisticated communications and intelligence center located in a bunker near civilian buildings and also misused by civilians as an air raid shelter. The Iraqis claimed that it was an example of unnecessary killing of civilians. Several bodies

were seen being lifted out of the targeted bunker, most without clothing (which may be suspicious). Do you suspect that such a targeting was a war crime? Explain. See also Article 51 of Geneva Protocol I (in the Documents Section).

10. During the 1991 Gulf War, if Iraq, which had occupied Kuwait, targeted Kuwaiti oil wells when leaving occupied Kuwait, what international norms do you suspect would have been violated? See Articles 53 and 147 of the 1949 Geneva Civilian Convention; Geneva Protocol I, arts. 52, 55; H.C. No. IV, Annex, arts. 23(g), 46, 55. What human rights might also be implicated with respect to massive environmental pollution? Would the targeting of oil storage tanks of use to the enemy military be impermissible?

11. During the 1999 NATO air strikes in Kosovo, would the targeting of a major bridge in Belgrade, Yugoslavia that was used by the Yugoslavian military have been a proper military target? When it was known that thousands of civilians were on the bridge in the evening during a candlelight procession to protect the bridge?

12. It is expected that there will be an increased use of drones and other robotics during armed conflicts and measures of self-defense within or outside the context of war. Already there have been uses of "remotely piloted" land-based, naval, and air and space robotics. For example, remotely controlled robots are used during war and domestic law enforcement to find and dismantle explosives and some can sniff for chemical or bacteriological/biological weaponry. Some fully autonomous vehicles, mines, and other mechanisms are not "piloted," but are addressed. One publication notes that "[a]utonomous systems are also part of the projected ground forces" and that there will be "a reconfigurable skirmishing vehicle," a "'stealth tank,'" "unmanned supply lorries and mine-clearing vehicles," "a small, tracked robot vehicle that can undertake missions normally done by a single soldier;" and "aerial robots dropping ground robots and using a few special forces to guide them." *Autonomous Vehicles: Robot Wars*, Engineer, June 6, 2011, at 20. Concerning various types of military robotics, see Patrick Lin, George Bekey & Keith Abney, *Autonomous Military Robotics: Risk, Ethics, and Design* 1, 5-6, 11-19 (Dec. 20, 2008), available at http://www.ethics.calpoly.edu/ONR_report.pdf. Consider this revised extract from Paust, *Remotely Piloted Warfare as a Challenge to the* Jus ad Bellum, in Oxford Handbook on the Use of Force in International Law (Marc Weller ed. 2013):

Drones can come in various sizes, and in the future some will predictably be the size of a dragonfly. Some drones and other robotics are also likely to use increasingly sophisticated computerized forms of intelligence gathering and analysis for decision making with respect to identification and engagement of targets during war and self-defense, perhaps even with a completely autonomous decisional, learning, and operational capability. Are there identifiable challenges posed by the foreseeable development and increasing availability and use of drones and other robotics? Will their increased use require changes in that laws of war, especially with respect to the need to adhere to basic legal principles that limit violence and its effects?

Presently, it is not generally expected that use of drones for targeting during war will require a change in the laws of war. However, there are at least two predictable developments in drone technology that raise concerns whether drones will be sufficiently controlled and permit compliance with general principles of necessity, distinction, and proportionality. First, there is concern that some drones will become completely autonomous and will be used to hunt and quickly eliminate human beings and objects within the matrix of programed targets. Presently, drones used for targeting during war and self-defense are operated by human beings, and there are often others who can participate in decisions concerning target identification and whether to engage a particular target. Drones often have the capability to fly over an area for hours, allowing nuanced human choice with respect to all features of context, including those concerning identification of the target; the importance of the target; whether equally effective alternative methods of targeting or capture exist; the presence, proximity, and number of civilians who are not targetable; whether some civilians are voluntary or coerced human shields; the precision in targeting that can obtain; and foreseeable consequences with respect to civilian death, injury, or suffering.

Some foresee a growing use of on-board computers to locate targets, provide valuable contextual input, and coordinate with other drones and aircraft, but assume that human beings will still make needed choices concerning proper application of the principles of distinction and proportionality and whether a target should even be engaged under the circumstances. Others foresee a problematic future use of drones that are completely autonomous and, if they do not kill and destroy needlessly because of computer glitches, they might kill and destroy without adequate consideration of all relevant features of context despite possible increased sophistication in their programing. In fact, some systems can be placed in an autonomous mode by a human decision maker and then hunt for human or material targets in a defensive or offensive manner. Depending on their capabilities, smart autonomous hunting drones and other hunting robots might be blind with respect to the need to comply with customary principles of distinction and proportionality.

Second, it has been reported that research "is headed away from single drones and towards a co-ordinated team or swarm of vehicles with a specified mission and location..., a swarm of robots," and that "inevitably there will be more autonomy; the robots will be required to make more decisions." It is also foreseeable that with respect to swarms, a human can provide the initial order to a swarm, but "drones in the armed swarm would work out between them which element would enact an attack order." Quite possibly, use of a swarm might pose greater danger with respect to computer glitches and the need for nuanced decision making with respect to identification and engagement of particular targets. Nonetheless, the swarm can prove to be valuable with respect to some forms of lawful uses of offensive and defensive force. Basic legal norms do not need to be changed, but efforts should be made to assure the existence of adequate computerized and human controls and the development of rules of engagement (ROE) to restrain their actual use. Wanton and reckless disregard of consequences can lead to criminal and civil sanctions, but these can occur with respect to misuse of any weapons system.

Also see generally, Eyal Benvenisti, *The Legal Battle to Define the Law on Transnational Asymmetric Warfare*, 20 DUKE J. COMP. & INT'L L. 339 (2010); Laurie R. Blank, *After Top Gun: How Drone Strikes Impact the Law of War*, 33 U. PA. J. INT'L L. 675 (2012); Aaron M. Drake, *Current U.S. Air Force Drone Operations and Their Conduct in Compliance with International Humanitarian Law — An Overview*, 39 DENV. J. INT'L L. & POL'Y 629 (2011); Chris Jenks, *Law From Above: Unmanned Aerial Systems, Use of Force, and the Law of Armed Conflict*, 85 N.D. L. REV. 649 (2009); Michael W. Lewis, *Drones and the Boundaries of the Battlefield*, 47 TEX. INT'L L.J. 293 (2012); Michael A. Newton, *Flying into the Future: Drone Warfare and the Changing Face of Humanitarian Law*, 39 DENV. J. INT'L L. & POL'Y 601 (2011); Mary Ellen O'Connell, *The Resort to Drones Under International Law*, 39 DENV. J. INT'L L. & POL'Y 585 (2011); Michael N. Schmitt, *Drone Attacks Under the* Jus ad Bellum *and* Jus in Bello: *Clearing the "Fog of Law,"* 13 Y.B. INT'L HUMANITARIAN L. 311 (2010); Markus Wagner, *Taking Humans Out of the Loop: Implications for International Humanitarian Law*, 21 J. L., INFO. & SCI. _(2011).

13. With respect to the taking of hostages, reprisals, violence against hostages, and the shooting of prisoners—all in connection with the general principles of necessity and proportionality—and all prior to the 1949 Geneva Conventions [which prohibit hostage-taking and reprisals], the 1977 Geneva Protocols, the 1979 Hostages Convention and other legal developments, consider the following:

THE DREIERWALDE CASE TRIAL OF KARL AMBERGER (FORMERLY OBERFELDWEBEL), CASE NO. 7, BRITISH MILITARY COURT, WUPPERTAL, 11th—14th March, 1946 from U.N. War Crimes Commission, Law Reports of Trials of War Criminals, 81, 86–87 (1947)

Shooting of unarmed prisoners of war. Plea that they were thought to be trying to escape. Hague Convention No. IV of 1907.

The accused was in charge of a party conducting five allied prisoners of war ostensibly to a Railway Station. On the way, the party, including the accused, began firing on them; all were killed except one, who escaped though wounded. The case for the Prosecution was that since the prisoners of war had made no attempt to escape, the shooting was in violation of the laws and usages of war. The Defence claimed that Amberger had genuinely believed that the prisoners were trying to escape. The Commission found him guilty and sentenced him to death by hanging.

The conventional rule of International Law which protects prisoners of war, whether or not they have surrendered, is now contained in the International Convention relative to the treatment of Prisoners of War, signed at Geneva on 27th July, 1929, and Article 2 states that:

"Prisoners of War are in the power of the hostile Government, but not of the individual or formation which captured them.

"They shall at all times be humanely treated and protected, particularly against acts of violence, from insults and from public curiosity.

"Measures of reprisal against them are forbidden."

This provision develops the principle already contained in Art. 4 of the 1907 Hague Regulations respecting the laws and customs of war on land.

There is no doubt that the allied airmen, who did not surrender to the German armed forces but were captured by German civilians, came under the protection of Art. 2 of the 1929 Convention. It is also safe to say that the killing of prisoners of war constituted a war crime under customary International Law even before the promulgation and ratification of the Conventions of 1907 and 1929....

Concerning the Legality of the Shooting of Prisoners While Attempting to Escape

The Judge Advocate in his summing up made the following statement:

"Gentlemen, war is a cruel thing, and there are certain rules which apply to war. One is that it is the duty of an officer or a man if he is captured to try and escape. The corollary to that is that the Power which holds him is entitled to prevent him from escaping, and in doing so no great niceties are called for by the Power that has him in his control: by that I mean it is quite right if it is reasonable in the circumstances, for a guard to open fire on an escaping prisoner, though he should pay great heed merely to wound him, but if he should be killed though that is very unfortunate it does not make a war crime.... If the accused, Karl Amberger, did see that his prisoners were trying to escape or had reasonable grounds for thinking that they were attempting to escape then that would not be a breach of the rules and customs of war, and therefore you would not be able to say a war crime had been committed."

It follows from this statement that a person who came under the protection of the Hague and Geneva Conventions and the provisions of customary International Law protecting prisoners of war would subsequently lose that protection on the rise of any set of circumstances which caused his captors reasonably to believe that he was attempting to escape. It should be noted that these circumstances need not, apparently, arise due to the acts or omissions of the captive. While it is not enough for the captor to have a merely subjective fear that an attempt to escape is being made, on the other hand the events which give rise to the requisite reasonable apprehension could on the face of the Judge Advocate's statement, be due to other agencies than the volition of the prisoner.

Chapter 3—"Penal Sanctions with regard to Prisoners of War"—of the 1929 Convention makes no mention of the shooting at, or killing of, prisoners attempting to escape.

Under Article 50, escaped prisoners who are recaptured before being able to rejoin their own armed forces or to leave the territory occupied by the armed forces which captured them shall be liable only to disciplinary punishment (*i.e.*, they shall not be liable to judicial proceedings). Under Article 54, imprisonment is the most severe disciplinary punishment which may be inflicted on a prisoner of war. These provisions, however, leave open the question of the procedure which can legally be followed while the prisoner is still in flight.

There is surprisingly little authority on this point. The 6th (Revised) Edition of Volume II of Oppenheim-Lauterpacht's *International Law* contains the following passage: "The conviction became general that captivity should only be the means of preventing prisoners from returning to their corps and taking up arms again" (p. 293). An escaping prisoner, it could be argued, was already potentially in arms again and this circumstance justified his being treated as already once again a member of the opposing forces. At all events, firing upon prisoners who reasonably appear to be attempting an escape seems to be accepted State practice.

United States v. von Leeb, *et al.*, 10 Trials of War Criminals 3, 11 Trials of War Criminals 528–29, 562–63 (1948) (The High Command Case)

Hostages and Reprisals

In the Southeast Case [Hostage Case], United States vs. Wilhelm List, *et al.*, (Case No. 7), the Tribunal had occasion to consider at considerable length the law relating to hostages and reprisals. It was therein held that under certain very restrictive conditions and subject to certain rather extensive safeguards, hostages may be taken, and after a judicial finding of strict compliance with all preconditions and as a last desperate remedy hostages may even be sentenced to death. It was held further that similar drastic safeguards, restrictions, and judicial preconditions apply to so-called "reprisal prisoners." If so inhumane a measure as the killing of innocent persons for offenses of others, even when drastically safeguarded and limited, is ever permissible under any theory of international law, killing without full compliance with all requirements would be murder. If killing is not permissible under any circumstances, then a killing with full compliance with all the mentioned prerequisites still would be murder.

In the case here presented, we find it unnecessary to approve or disapprove the conclusions of law announced in said judgment as to the permissibility of such killings. In the instance of so-called hostage taking and killing, and the so-called reprisal killings with which we have to deal in this case, the safeguards and preconditions required to be observed by the Southeast judgment were not even attempted to be met or even suggested as necessary. Killings without full compliance with such preconditions are merely terror murders. If the law is in fact that hostage and reprisal killings are never permissible at all, then also the so-called hostage and reprisal killings in this case are merely terror murders.

The responsibility of defendants for any such acts will be considered in our determination of the cases against the individual defendants....

[food and other property]

Pillage of public and private property—The prosecution relies upon two orders to sustain this charge. The first of these orders is from the 12th Panzer Division on 11 November 1941, directing an operation against certain villages "used by the partisans as a base of operations" with instructions to seize the cattle, horses, and chickens and most of the food, but further directing a small amount of food be left for the population at the direction of the commander of the operations. We cannot say this order was illegal.

Likewise an order of XXXIX Corps issued on 7 December 1941, regarding a forced retreat, called for the destruction of food and fodder that could not be taken along in the retreat. The destruction of these foodstuffs would tend to hamper the advancing enemy and we cannot find it was not justified under the exigency of the situation.

We do not find any criminality under this phase of the case.

[siege warfare]

Criminal conduct pertaining to the siege of Leningrad—Leningrad was encircled and besieged. Its defenders and the civilian population were in great straits and it was feared the population would undertake to flee through the German lines. Orders were issued to use artillery to "prevent any such attempt at the greatest possible distance from our own lines by opening fire as early as possible, so that the infantry, if possible, is spared shooting on civilians." We find this was known and approved by von Leeb. Was it an unlawful order?

"A belligerent commander may lawfully lay siege to a place controlled by the enemy and endeavor by a process of isolation to cause its surrender. The propriety of attempting to reduce it by starvation is not questioned. Hence, the cutting off of every source of sustenance from without is deemed legitimate. It is said that if the commander of a besieged place expels the noncombatants, in order to lessen the number of those who consume his stock of provisions, it is lawful, though an extreme measure, to drive them back so as to hasten the surrender" [quoting HYDE, III INTERNATIONAL LAW 1802–03 (2 ed. 1945)—see also Article 18 of the 1863 Lieber Code, in the Documents Section.]

We might wish the law were otherwise but we must administer it as we find it. Consequently, we hold no criminality attached on this charge.

United States v. List, *et al.*, 11 Trials of War Criminals 757, 1248–49, 1250, 1252–54, 1270–71 (1948) (The Southeast [Hostages] Case)

The major issues involved in the present case gravitate around the claimed right of the German armed forces to take hostages from the innocent civilian population to guarantee the peaceful conduct of the whole of the civilian population and its claimed right to execute hostages, members of the civil population, and captured members of the resistance forces in reprisal for armed attacks by resistance forces, acts of sabotage and injuries committed by unknown persons....

The question of hostages is closely integrated with that of reprisals. A reprisal is a response to an enemy's violation of the laws of war which would otherwise be a violation on one's own side. It is a fundamental rule that a reprisal may not exceed the degree of the criminal act it is designed to correct. Where an excess is knowingly indulged, it in turn is criminal and may be punished. Where innocent individuals are seized and punished for a violation of the laws of war which has already occurred, no question of hostages is involved. It is nothing more than the infliction of a reprisal. Throughout the evidence in the present case, we find the term hostage applied where a reprisal only was involved....

An examination of the available evidence on the subject convinces us that hostages may be taken in order to guarantee the peaceful conduct of the populations of occupied territories and, when certain conditions exist and the necessary preliminaries have been taken, they may, as a last resort, be shot. The taking of hostages is based fundamentally on a theory of collective responsibility. The effect of an occupation is to confer upon the invading force the right of control for the period of the occupation within the limitations and prohibitions of international law. The inhabitants owe a duty to carry on their ordinary peaceful pursuits and to refrain from all injurious acts toward the troops or in respect to their military operations. The occupant may properly insist upon compliance with regulations necessary to the security of the occupying forces and for the maintenance of law and order. In the accomplishment of this objective, the occupant may only, as a last resort, take and execute hostages.

Hostages may not be taken or executed as a matter of military expediency. The occupant is required to use every available method to secure order and tranquility before resort may be had to the taking and execution of hostages. Regulations of all kinds must be imposed to secure peace and tranquility before the shooting of hostages may be indulged. These regulations may include one or more of the following measures: (1) the registration of the inhabitants, (2) the possession of passes or identification certificates, (3) the establishment of restricted areas, (4) limitations of movement, (5) the adoption of curfew regulations, (6) the prohibition of assembly, (7) the detention of suspected persons, (8) restrictions on communication, (9) the imposition of restrictions on food supplies, (10) the evacuation of troublesome areas, (11) the levying of monetary contributions, (12) compulsory labor to repair damage from sabotage, (13) the destruction of property in proximity to the place of the crime, and any other regulation not prohibited by international law that would in all likelihood contribute to the desired result.

If attacks upon troops and military installations occur regardless of the foregoing precautionary measures and the perpetrators cannot be apprehended, hostages may be taken from the population to deter similar acts in the future provided it can be shown that the population generally is a party to the offense, either actively or passively....

It is essential to a lawful taking of hostages under customary law that proclamation be made, giving the names and addresses of hostages taken, notifying the population that upon the recurrence of stated acts of war treason the hostages will be shot. The number of hostages shot must not exceed in severity the offenses the shooting is designed to deter. Unless the foregoing requirements are met, the shooting of hostages is in contravention of international law and is a war crime in itself. Whether such fundamental requirements have been met is a question determinable by court martial proceedings. A military commander may not arbitrarily determine such facts. An order of a military commander for the killing of hostages must be based upon the finding of a competent court martial that necessary conditions exist and all preliminary steps have been taken which are essential to the issuance of a valid order. The taking of lives of innocent persons arrested as hostages is a very serious step....

That international agreement is badly needed in this field is self-evident.

International law is prohibitive law and no conventional prohibitions have been invoked to outlaw this barbarous practice. The extent to which the practice has been employed by the Germans exceeds the most elementary notions of humanity and justice. They invoke the plea of military necessity, a term which they confuse with convenience and strategical interests. Where legality and expediency have coincided, no fault can be found insofar as international law is concerned. But where legality of action is absent, the shooting of innocent members of the population as a measure of reprisal is not only criminal but it has the effect of destroying the basic relationship between the occupant and the population. Such a condition can progressively degenerate into a reign of terror. Unlawful reprisals may bring on counter reprisals and create an endless cycle productive of chaos and crime. To prevent a distortion of the right into a barbarous method of repression, international law provides a protective mantle against the abuse of the right.... Excessive reprisals are in themselves criminal and guilt attaches to the persons responsible for their commission.

It is a fundamental rule of justice that the lives of persons may not be arbitrarily taken. A fair trial before a judicial body affords the surest protection against arbitrary, vindictive, or whimsical application of the right to shoot human beings in reprisal. It is a rule of international law, based on these fundamental concepts of justice and the rights of individuals, that the lives of persons may not be taken in reprisal in the absence of a judicial finding that the necessary conditions exist and the essential steps have been taken to give validity to such action....

Military necessity has been invoked by the defendants as justifying the killing of innocent members of the population and the destruction of villages and towns in the occupied territory. Military necessity permits a belligerent, subject to the laws of war, to apply any amount and kind of force to compel the complete submission of the enemy with the least possible expenditure of time, life, and money. In general, it sanctions measures by an occupant necessary to protect the safety of his forces and to facilitate the success of his operations. It permits the destruction of life of armed enemies and other persons whose destruction is incidentally unavoidable by the armed conflicts of the war; it allows the capturing of armed enemies and others of peculiar danger, but it does not permit the killing of innocent inhabitants for purposes of revenge or the satisfaction of a lust to kill. The destruction of property to be lawful must be imperatively demanded by the necessities of war. Destruction as an end in itself is a violation of international law. There must be some reasonable connection between the destruction of property and the overcoming of the enemy forces. It is lawful to destroy railways, lines of communication, or any other property that might be utilized by the enemy. Private homes and churches even may be destroyed if necessary for military operations. It does not admit the wanton devastation of a district or the willful infliction of suffering upon its inhabitants for the sake of suffering alone....

... Unless civilization is to give way to barbarism in the conduct of war, crime must be punished. If international law as it applies to a given case is hopelessly inadequate such inadequacy should be pointed out. If customary international law has become outmoded, it should be so stated. If conventional international law sets forth an unjust rule, its enforcement will secure its correction. If all war criminals are not brought to the bar of justice under present procedures, such procedures should be made more inclusive and more effective. If the laws of war are to have any beneficent effective, they must be enforced.

The evidence in this case recites a record of killing and destruction seldom exceeded in modern history. Thousands of innocent inhabitants lost their lives by means of a firing squad, hangman's noose, people who had the same inherent desire to live as do these defendants....

An order, directory or mandatory, which fixes a ratio for the killing of hostages or reprisal prisoners, or requires the killing of hostages or reprisal prisoners for every act committed against the occupation forces is unlawful. International law places no such unrestrained and unlimited power in the hands of the commanding general of occupied territory. The reprisals taken under the authority of this order were clearly excessive. The shooting of 100 innocent persons for each German soldier killed at Topola, for instance, cannot be justified on any theory by the record. There is no evidence that the population of Topola were in any manner responsible for the act. In fact, the record shows that the responsible persons were an armed and officered band of partisans. There is nothing to infer that the population of Topola supported or shielded the guilty persons. Neither does the record show that the population had previously conducted themselves in such a manner as to have been subjected to previous reprisal actions. An order to shoot 100 persons for each German soldier killed under such circumstances is not only excessive but wholly unwarranted. We conclude that the reprisal measure taken for the ambushing and killing of 22 German soldiers at Topola were excessive and therefore criminal. It is urged that only 449 persons were actually shot in reprisal for the Topola incident. The evidence does not conclusively establish the shooting of more than 449 persons although it indicates the killing of a much greater number. But the killing of 20 reprisal prisoners for each German soldier killed was not warranted under the circumstances shown. Whether the number of innocent persons killed was 2,200 or 449, the killing was wholly unjustified and unlawful.

The reprisal measures taken for the Topola incident were unlawful for another reason. The reprisal prisoners killed were not taken from the community where the attack on the German soldiers occurred. The record shows that 805 Jews and gypsies were taken from the collection camp at Sabac and the rest from the Jewish transit camp at Belgrade to be shot in reprisal for the Topola incident. There is no evidence of any connection whatever, geographical, racial, or otherwise between the persons shot and the attack at Topola. Nor does the record disclose that judicial proceedings were held. The order for the killing in reprisal appears to have been arbitrarily issued and under the circumstances shown is nothing less than plain murder....

The defendant List also asserts that he had no knowledge of many of the unlawful killings of innocent inhabitants which took place because he was absent from his headquarters where the reports came in and that he gained no knowledge of the acts. A commanding general of occupied territory is charged with the duty of maintaining peace and order, punishing crime, and protecting lives and property within the area of his command. His responsibility is coextensive with his area of command. He is charged with notice of occurrences taking place within that territory. He may require adequate reports of all occurrences that come within the scope of his power and, if such reports are incomplete or otherwise inadequate, he is obliged to require supplementary reports to apprize him of all the pertinent facts. If he fails to require and obtain complete information, the dereliction of duty rests upon him and he is in no position to plead his own dereliction as a defense. Absence from headquarters cannot and does not relieve one from responsibility for acts committed in accordance with a policy he instituted or in which he acquiesced. He may not, of course, be charged with acts committed on the order of someone else which is outside the basic orders which he has issued. If time permits he is required to rescind such illegal orders, otherwise he is required to take steps to prevent a recurrence of their issue.

Want of knowledge of the contents of reports made to him is not a defense. Reports to commanding generals are made for their special benefit. Any failure to acquaint themselves with the contents of such reports, or a failure to require additional reports where inadequacy appears on their face, constitutes a dereliction of duty which he cannot use in his own behalf....

Notes and Questions

1. Today, does "military necessity" permit the killing of captured "noncombatants" without trial? Consider extracts from the Geneva Civilian and Prisoners of War Conventions (in the Documents Section), including common Article 3; and FM 27-10, paragraph 85:

> Killing of Prisoners
>
> A commander may not put his prisoners to death because their presence retards his movements or diminishes his power of resistance by necessitating a large guard, or by reason of their consuming supplies, or because it appears certain that they will regain their liberty through the impending success of their forces. It is likewise unlawful for a commander to kill his prisoners on grounds of self-preservation, even in the case of airborne or commando operations, although the circumstances of the operation may make necessary rigorous supervision of and restraint upon the movement of prisoners of war.

This is not a unilateral policy, and even in the absence of specific provisions in the 1949 Geneva Conventions requiring compliance "in all circumstances" and without a military necessity exception unless expressly stated, there exists an exemplification of customary international law which should not be unfamiliar to a war crimes prosecutor. In *United States v. List* the court stated:

> Military necessity or expediency do not justify a violation of positive rules. International law is prohibitive law. Articles 46, 47, and 50 of the Hague Regulations of 1907 make no exceptions to its enforcement. The rights of the innocent population therein set forth must be respected even if military necessity or expediency decree otherwise. [11 T.W.C. at 1255]

Furthermore, in actual combat situations it is not necessary to kill prisoners of war or other detainees. Effective alternatives are always available.

2. Assume that you are a military lawyer and your commander wants a decision as to the legality of the following extract from DOD GEN-25/ DA Pam 360-521, Handbook for U.S. Forces in Vietnam (1966) before he issues orders in conformity thereto:

[at p. 97, Section VII. Search and Destroy Operations. 29. General]

a. The primary objectives of search and destroy operations are to find, fix and destroy the enemy; to destroy or seize his equipment, foodstuffs, medical supplies and base areas; and, whenever possible, destroy his political and military infrastructure....

Check also: Hague Convention No. IV (1907), Annex, Article 23 (g); 1949 Geneva Civilian Convention, Articles 13, 16, 23, 53, 57; Protocol I, Article 54.

3. Concerning destruction of food and use of starvation as a weapon today, see Notes and Questions at the end of this chapter. With respect to siege warfare and firing artillery rounds at civilians today, consider Articles 3, 4 ("in the hands of"), 13, 16-17 of the Geneva Civilian Convention. Does GC Article 4 apply to civilians fleeing a besieged area? Consider also Protocol I, arts. 48, 51. Does Article 75(1) of Protocol I apply to such persons? Does Article 75(2)?

4. Early recognitions of violations of the laws of war included:

a. Thomas Jefferson's letter to Virginia Governor Patrick Henry in March 27, 1779 stating that captured enemy troops should be humanely treated and that it "is for the benefit of mankind to mitigate the horrors of war as much as possible." He also wrote to Major General Benedict Arnold, commander of the British force at Portsmouth, that he expected the General to "concur with us in endeavoring as far as possible to alleviate the inevitable miseries of war by treating captives as humanity and natural honor requires."

b. Henry Wheaton's treatise in 1836:

"No use of force is lawful, except so far as it is necessary. A belligerent has, therefore, no right to take away the lives of those subjects of the enemy whom he can subdue by any other means. Those who are actually in arms, and continue to resist, may be lawfully killed: but the inhabitants of the enemy's country who are not in arms, or who, being in arms, submit and surrender themselves, may not be slain, because their destruction is not necessary for obtaining the just ends of war.

"The custom of civilized nations, founded on this principle, has therefore exempted the persons of the sovereign and his family, the members of the civil government, women and children, cultivators of the earth, artisans, labourers, merchants, men of science and letters, and generally all other public or private individuals engaged in the ordinary civil pursuits of life, from the direct effect of military operations, unless actually taken in arms, or guilty of some misconduct in violation of the usages of war by which they forfeit their immunity."

HENRY WHEATON, ELEMENTS OF INTERNATIONAL LAW 250 § 2, 251-52 § 4 (1st ed. 1836).

Wheaton's recognition of the reach of the principle of necessity can be compared with the 1868 Declaration of St. Petersburg's affirmation "[t]hat the only legitimate object which States should endeavor to accomplish during War is to weaken the military forces of the enemy."

c. General Winfield Scott's General Orders No. 20, Head Quarters of the Army, Tampico, 19 Feb. 1847, which prohibited: "2. Assassination; murder; malicious stabbing or maiming; rape; malicious assault and battery; robbery; theft; the wanton destruction of churches, cemeteries or other religious edifices and fixtures, and the destruction, except by order of a superior officer, of public or private property...."

How were these earlier recognitions mirrored or expanded in the 1863 Lieber Code created by Professor Francis Lieber, Major General Halleck and others during the U.S. Civil War in an effort to reflect customary laws of war?

Instructions for the Government of Armies of the United States in the Field, General Orders No. 100 (1863) (the Lieber Code)

[Read the extracts from the Lieber Code in the Documents Section]

Geneva Convention Relative to the Protection of Civilian Persons in Time of War of August 12, 1949, 75 U.N.T.S. 287

[Read the extracts from the Geneva Civilian Convention]

Geneva Convention Relative to the Treatment of Prisoners of War, 12 August 1949, 75 U.N.T.S. 135

[Read Articles 12-14, 18-20, 22-23 of the Geneva Prisoner of War Convention]

Notes and Questions

1. With respect to Geneva Civilian Convention coverage of a state's own nationals from harm perpetrated by state forces or others of the same nationality, *see, e.g.*, GC arts. 1, 3, 4, 13-24; Protocol I, art. 75; J. Paust, *Applicability of International Criminal Laws to Events in the Former Yugoslavia*, 9 Am. U. J. Int'l L. & Pol. 499, 510, 512–13 (1994), and references cited.

2. Concerning the Israeli practice of administrative detention of Palestinians (without trial) in the West Bank and Gaza and applicable Hague and Geneva law (including GC arts. 5, 27), *see, e.g., Report of the ICJ Mission of Inquiry Into the Israeli Military Court System in the Occupied West Bank and Gaza*, 14 Hast. Int'l & Comp. L. Rev. 1, 52–61 (1990). What is the test or burden of proof regarding detention of persons who are security threats "in the territory of a Party to the conflict," "in occupied territory"? See also Jelena Pejic, *The European Court of Human Rights' Al-Jedda judgment: the oversight of international humanitarian law*, 93 Int'l Rev. of the Red Cross 1, 9 (no. 883Sept. 2011) (with respect to "'measures of control' that may be taken by a state with respect to civilians whose activity is deemed to pose a serious threat to its security[, i]t is uncontroversial that direct civilian participation in hostilities falls into that category [and] other civilian behaviour may also meet the threshold of posing a serious security threat to the detaining power," adding: "[e]xamples of activities ... are the financing of combat operations, general recruitment for combat, etc." *Id*. at n.38).

Did the U.S. meet this test with respect to detention of persons without trial in Afghanistan, Iraq, and Guantanamo Bay, Cuba and elsewhere during the wars in Afghanistan and Iraq? Are security detainees entitled to a review of the propriety of their detention? See GC arts. 42-43, 78; GPW, art. 5; Paust, *Judicial Power, supra* at 510-14. With respect to human rights at stake, including the right to take proceedings to an independent court of law concerning the propriety of detention, *see, e.g.,* International Covenant on Civil and Political Rights, art. 9; Paust, *Judicial Power, supra* at 503-10 (documenting evidence that the right to judicial review is a customary and nonderogable human right); Hamdi v. Rumsfeld, 542 U.S. 507 (2004); Rasul v. Bush, 542 U.S. 466 (2004); *In re* Guantanamo Detainee Cases, 355 F. Supp.2d 443 (D.D.C. 2005) (especially concerning U.S. military Combatant Status Review Tribunal (CSRT) procedures at Guantanamo); Hamdan v. Rumsfeld, 415 F.3d 33, 33, 41 (D.C. Cir.); Boumediene v. Bush, 553 U.S. 723 (2008) (constitutional habeas applies to aliens located at Guantanamo Bay, Cuba).

3. Read GC, arts. 49, 147. Is it ever lawful to transfer a non-prisoner of war out of occupied territory? Consider the following remarks:

The Bush Administration's claim [concerning the transfer of persons out of occupied territory is] set forth in a previously secret March 19, 2004 draft DOJ memo prepared by Jack L. Goldsmith [which] recognizes that everyone lawfully in Iraq is a protected person under the Geneva Conventions but argues that "protected persons," such as Iraqi nationals, can be transferred "from Iraq to another country to facilitate interrogation, for a brief but not indefinite period," and that persons who are not lawfully in Iraq can be denied protections and transferred.[1] Yet, the denial of protections under common Article 3 with respect to any detainee under any circumstances is a violation of Geneva law and, therefore, a war crime; and the transfer from occupied territory of any "protected person" under the Geneva Civilian Convention who is not a prisoner of war, such as those protected under common Article 3, is a war crime in violation of Article 49 of the Geneva Civilian Convention as well as a "grave breach" of the Convention under Article 147 [see also Article 85(4)(a) of Protocol I]. The Charter of the International Military Tribunal at Nuremberg [Article 6(b)] also lists "deportation ... for any other purpose of civilian population of or in occupied territory" as a war crime. [The Charter's use of "of or in" does not distinguish between persons who are nationals or aliens in occupied territory or who are lawfully or unlawfully under domestic law "in" occupied territory.] It also lists "deportation ... committed against any civilian population" as a crime against humanity. [*Id.* art. 6(c)] Additionally, transfer of any "person to another State where there are substantial grounds for believing that he would be in danger of being subjected to torture" is prohibited by the Convention Against Torture and Other Cruel, Inhuman or Degrading Treatment or Punishment. Paust, *Executive Plans, supra* at 850-51. More generally, under human rights law a person must not be rendered to another country where there is a "real risk" of human rights deprivations.

---

1. *See, e.g.,* Jack Goldsmith, Memorandum to William H. Taft, IV, *et al.,* re Draft Memorandum for Alberto R. Gonzales, Counsel to the President, Re: Permissibility of Relocating Certain "Protected Persons" from Occupied Iraq 2-5, 14 (Mar. 19, 2004), available at KAREN J. GREENBERG & JOSHUA L. DRATEL, EDS., THE TORTURE PAPERS: THE ROAD TO ABU GHRAIB 366 (2005). The Goldsmith memo offered a specious claim that to "remove" or "relocate" is not to "transfer" or "deport". See Goldsmith, *supra* at 2-5. However, treaties are to be interpreted with respect to their object and purpose as well as the ordinary meaning of their terms, which clearly encompasses transfer of any sort, for any purpose, and for however long. *See also* 2004 UK MANUAL, *supra* at 293 ("forbidden to *transfer* forcibly ... not *moved* outside occupied territory") (emphasis added). An earlier military pamphlet recognized that the prohibition involves "forced individual or mass *relocation.*" U.S. Dep't of Army Pam. No. 20-151, *Lectures of the Geneva Conventions of 1949,* at 19 (28 Apr. 1958) (emphasis added). The only exceptions are specifically addressed in the Geneva Civilian Convention. See GC, art. 49, paragraph 2 (certain types of "evacuation"); IV }plain COMMENTARY, *supra* at 279 ("The prohibition is absolute and allows of no exceptions, apart from those stipulated in paragraph 2.").

4. When does the Geneva Civilian Convention, or portions thereof, cease to apply? See Article 6. In general, the customary laws of war apply until "peace" occurs. See FM 27-10, para. 10 a; *cf. id.* para. 10 d.

5. What sort of protections pertain for prisoners of war? *See, e.g.*, GPW, arts. 7, 13-17, *passim.*

6. Rape is expressly prohibited in Article 27 of the Geneva Civilian Convention, a prohibition based in customary international law. See also the 1919 List of War Crimes; the 1863 Lieber Code, arts. 44, 47. Is rape also impliedly prohibited in common Article 3, in Article 16? Can rape constitute "torture," "violence to ... person," "cruel treatment," "outrages upon personal dignity," "humiliating and degrading treatment," exposure to "grave danger," "acts of violence or threats thereof," "inhuman treatment," "great suffering," "serious injury to body or health"? *See also The Prosecutor v. Musema*, ICTR-96-13-T, paras 220-229 (27 Jan. 2000), extract in Chapter Two, Section 5; and footnote 19 at the end of Section 2 A of this Chapter. Can rape constitute a "grave breach" of the Geneva Conventions? What are the elements of the war crime of "rape" or "sexual violence"? In the Elements of Crimes regarding the ICC?

For further affirmation of rape as a war crime, *see, e.g.*, U.S. Dep't of Army, Subject Schedule 27-1, *The Geneva Conventions of 1949 and Hague Convention No. IV of 1907*, at 8 (8 Oct. 1970) ("rape, or any other form of sexual assault"); William A. Schabas, *The Crime of Torture and the International Criminal Tribunals*, 37 Case W. Res. J. Int'l L. 349, 362-63 (2006); Theodor Meron, *Rape as a Crime under International Humanitarian Law*, 87 Am. J. Int'l L. 424 (1993); Madeline Morris, *By Force of Arms: Rape, War and Military Culture*, 45 Duke L.J. 651 (1996); Fionnuala Daibhnaid Ni Aolain, *The Entrenchment of Systematic Abuse—Mass Rape in the Former Yugoslavia*, 8 Harv. H.R.J. 285 (1995); Paust, correspondence, 88 Am. J. Int'l L. 88 (1994); Paust, *Applicability, supra* at 516–17 n.61 (prohibitions under Geneva law (including grave breach provisions), customary law, and other precepts); Cherif Bassiouni & Marcia McCormick, *Sexual Violence: An Invisible Weapon of War in the Former Yugoslavia* (DePaul Occas. Paper No. 1, 1996) (same); symposium, 5 Hast. Women's L.J. no. 2 (1994) (especially the contributions of Professors Koenig and Copelon); Adrien Katherine Wing & Sylke Merchan, *Rape, Ethnicity, and Culture: Spirit Injury From Bosnia to Black America*, 25 Colum. H.R.L. Rev. 1, 9–12, 20–25 (1993). The Indictments of Karadzic and Mladic and of Tadic expressly referred to rape and "sexual assault" as genocide, other crimes against humanity, and/or grave breaches of Geneva law. See also Article 8 (2)(a)(ii)-(iii), (b)(xxii) of the Statute of the ICC.

7. In 2006, the U.N. Security Council affirmed "that deliberately targeting civilians and other protected persons as such in situations of armed conflict is a flagrant violation of international humanitarian law"; reaffirmed "its condemnation in the strongest terms of all acts of violence or abuses committed against civilians in situations of armed conflict in violation of applicable international obligations with respect in particular to (i) torture and other prohibited treatment, (ii) gender-based and sexual violence, (iii) violence against children, (iv) the recruitment and use of child soldiers, (v) trafficking in humans, (vi) forced displacement, and (vii) the intentional denial of humanitarian assistance"; and condemned "in the strongest terms all sexual and other forms of violence committed against civilians in armed conflict, in particular women and children." U.N. S.C. Res. 1674, paras. 3, 5, 19 (28 Apr. 2006). In 2011, the Security Council authorized the use of armed force in Libya in order to protect civilians and civilian populated areas from attacks by the government of Libya. U.N. S.C. Res. 1973 (2011). In March 2011, the U.S., NATO, and other countries participated in an international armed con-

flict that lasted some seven months and led to regime change in Libya. By July 2011, thirty-two countries (including the U.S.) had recognized the Libyan National Transitional Council (NTC) as "the legitimate governing authority in Libya.

8. Outside the law of armed conflict, there are few gender-specific international criminal provisions. See J. Paust, *Women and International Criminal Law Instruments and Processes*, in 2 WOMEN AND INTERNATIONAL HUMAN RIGHTS LAW 349 (Kelly D. Askin & Dorean M. Koenig eds. 2000); Convention on the Elimination of All Forms of Discrimination Against Women, art. 6, 1249 U.N.T.S. 13. Should there be others? See Chapters Two and Three.

9. Note that the Optional Protocol to the Convention on the Rights of the Child prohibits the recruitment and use of children under 18 years of age in armed conflict. However, parties to the Rights of the Child Convention must assure that children under 15 not take a direct part in hostilities. *Id.* art. 38(2). Geneva Protocol I, art. 77 uses a 15 years old test. The first successful prosecution of an accused in a Trial Chamber of the ICC occurred in March 14, 2012, with the conviction of Thomas Lubanga Dyilo (head of the military wing of the Union of Congolese Patriots), as co-perpetrator, of the war crimes of conscripting and enlisting children under the age of 15 and using them to participate actively in hostilities during an internal armed conflict in the Democratic Republic of the Congo in 2002 and 2003. In July, 2012, he received a sentence of 14 years in prison.

10. Note that Article 29 of the Geneva Civilian Convention refers to state and individual responsibility. Such responsibility can be both criminal and civil in nature. Pictet's IV COMMENTARY, *supra* at 209–211 recognizes such dual and "distinct" responsibilities as well as the possibility of both criminal and civil sanctions, Pictet adding: "The principle of State responsibility further demands that a State whose agent has been guilty of an act in violation of the Convention, should be required to make reparation. This already followed from Article 3 of the Fourth Hague Convention of 1907 respecting the Laws and Customs of War on Land, which states that 'a belligerent Party which violates the provisions of the said Regulations [The Hague Regulations] shall, if the case demands, be liable to pay compensation. It shall be responsible for all acts committed by persons forming part of its armed forces.'" *Id.* at 210. Pictet also refers to Article 148 of the Geneva Civilian Convention, which provides that "No ... Party shall be allowed to absolve itself or any other ... Party of any liability incurred by itself or by another ... Party in respect of [grave] breaches...." See Pictet, *supra* at 211, 602–03, adding that the State "remains liable to pay compensation" even if it has prosecuted the individual perpetrators. Concerning money damages for war crimes, see Article 75 of the Statute of the ICC; RESTATEMENT§ 404, Comment b; *Sosa v. Alvarez-Machain*, 124 S.Ct. 2739, 2783 (2004) (Breyer, J., concurring in part and concurring in judgment); *The Paquete Habana*, 189 U.S. 453, 464 *ff* (1903); *id.*, 175 U.S. 677, 700, 711, 714 (1900); *Weisshaus v. Swiss Bankers Ass'n*, 225 F.3d 191 (2d Cir. 2000); *Kadic v. Karadzic*, 70 F.3d 232, 242–43 (2d Cir. 1995); *Linder v. Portocarrero*, 963 F.2d 332, 336-37 (11th Cir. 1992); *Estate of Rodriguez v. Drummond Co.*, 206 F. Supp.2d 1250, 1259-61 (N.D. Ala. 2003); *Presbyterian Church of Sudan v. Talisman Energy, Inc.*, 244 F. Supp.2d 289, 310-11, 320-25 (S.D.N.Y. 2003); *Mehinovic v. Vuckovic*, 198 F. Supp.2d 1322, 1350-52 (N.D. Ga. 2002); *Iwanowa v. Ford Motor Co.*, 57 F. Supp.2d 41 (D.N.J. 1999); *Doe v. Islamic Salvation Front*, 993 F. Supp. 3, 5, 8 (D.D.C. 1998); *Linder v. Portocarrero*, 963 F.2d 332, 336–37 (11th Cir. 1992); J. PAUST, INTERNATIONAL LAW AS LAW OF THE UNITED STATES 226-27, 291, 293, 313 (2 ed. 2003); Paust, *Suing Karadzic*, 10 LEIDEN J. INT'L L. 91 (1997); *Suing Saddam: Private Remedies for War Crimes and Hostage-Taking*, 31 VA. J. INT'L L. 351, 360–70, 378 (1991),

and references cited; Research in International Law, *The Law of Responsibility of States for Damage Done in Their Territory to the Person or Property of Foreigners* (Harvard Law School), Comment, 23 Am. J. Int'l L., Supp. 167 (1929); U.S. Dep't of Army Pam. 27--161-1, International Law 84–86 (1964).

11. Today, is it a violation of international law to use starvation as a weapon for military purposes? Against noncombatants, against combatants? Should food be considered neutral property (*e.g.*, property not subject to intentional destruction and that should pass freely through enemy lines), such as medicine and medical supplies?

See panel, *The Right to Food*, 69 Proceedings, Am. Soc. Int'l L. 50–51 (1975); J. Paust, *The Human Rights to Food, Medicine and Medical Supplies, and Freedom from Arbitrary and Inhumane Detention and Controls in Sri Lanka*, 31 Vand. J. Trans. L. 617 (1998); E. Rosenblad, *Starvation as a Method of Warfare—Conditions for Regulation by Convention*, 7 Int'l Lawyer 252 (1973); Mudge, *Starvation as a Means of Warfare*, 4 Int'l Lawyer 228 (1970); U.N. G.A. Res. 3102 (XXVIII) (12 Dec. 1973). FM 27-10, at 18, para. 37, affirms that use of poison is unlawful, but it states that efforts "to destroy, through chemical or bacterial agents harmless to man, crops intended solely for consumption by the armed forces (if that fact can be determined)" would be permissible. Nonetheless, the Manual makes clear (1) that the chemicals or bacterial agents used must not be "poison," (2) that they must be "harmless to man," (3) that the crops must be "solely for consumption" by the enemy military, and (4) that it must be "determined" that the crops are *solely* for military consumption. Clearly, crops that cannot be identified as those to be used solely for consumption by the enemy military must not be targeted. Thus, crops that could be used by enemy military as well as noncombatants cannot be targeted under any circumstances. This prohibition is especially important where combatants and civilians are intermingled. Also, if one cannot "determine" that they would be used solely by enemy military, a wanton or reckless targeting would not be compatible with the law of war prohibition. See also Sir Henry S. Maine, International Law: A Series of Lectures Delivered Before the University of Cambridge, 1887, Lecture VII ("The poisoning of water or food is a mode of warfare absolutely forbidden."), reprinted in the Avalon Project at Yale Law School; the 1863 Lieber Code, *supra* art. 70 (poisoning of "wells, or food," is proscribed).

FM 27-10 also recognized that "[p]oisoning of wells or streams" is a war crime. *Id.* at 180, para. 504(i). The Manual attempted to reflect customary law on this point recognized in a number of British texts prohibiting "[t]he contamination of sources of water." See U.S. Dep't of Army, Pam. 27-161-2, *supra* at 41. For example, the 1958 British Manual on The Law of War on Land recognized that "poisoning of wells, streams, and other sources of water supply" were examples of war crimes. 1958 UK Manual, *supra* at 175, para. 626(i). This same customary prohibition is reflected in U.S. Dep't of Army, *The Law of Land Warfare: A Self-Instructional Text* 36 (28 Apr. 1972), and in U.S. Dep't of Army Subject Schedule No. 27-1, *The Geneva Conventions of 1949 and Hague Convention No. IV of 1907*, at 10 (3 Oct. 1970), which also notes that an order to place a dead body in a well is clearly illegal because such conduct "poisons the water and the poisoning of wells and streams is a war crime" (*id.*) and which also identifies as a war crime the killing of "a farmer's water buffalo," *id.* at 5. It was also reflected in U.S. Dep't of Army Subject Schedule 27-1, *The Hague and Geneva Conventions* 24 (20 April 1967) and in MACV Directive 20-4, Inspections and Investigations of War Crimes, para. 3(c) (Headquarters, United States Military Assistance Command, Vietnam, 18 May 1968). That a "poisoning of springs and water courses" is a customary war crime was also recognized in 3 Commentary, Geneva Convention Relative to the Treatment of

PRISONERS OF WAR 421 (ICRC, Jean S. Pictet ed. 1960). The customary 1863 Lieber Code was also on point far earlier: "use of poison in any manner, be it to poison wells, or food ... is wholly excluded from modern warfare." Lieber Code, *supra*, art. 70.

Article 54 of Protocol I to the 1949 Geneva Conventions sets forth a newer customary standard. Read Article 54 in the Documents Section. *Compare* Article 8 (2)(b)(xxv) of the Statute of the ICC. Concerning the use of food as a weapon and the Statute of the ICC, see Paust, *Content and Contours of Genocide, Crimes Against Humanity, and War Crimes*, in INTERNATIONAL LAW IN THE POST-COLD WAR WORLD: ESSAYS IN MEMORY OF LI HAOPEI (Wang Tieya & Sienho Yee eds. 2000)*, adding:

A policy of denial and neglect involving starvation can also constitute other violations of humanitarian law when used wantonly or in reckless disregard of consequences. The indiscriminate use of food as a weapon is covered under Articles 51 (4) ("[i]ndiscriminate attacks") and 54 (1) ("[s]tarvation of civilians as a method of warfare") and, especially, 54 (2) of Protocol I, as well as under Article 14 (1) of Protocol II. A policy of denial and neglect involving starvation can also result in violations, for example, of Articles 3, 16, 23, 24, and 147 of the Geneva Civilian Convention. Such a policy should also be prosecutable, for example, under Article 8 (2) (a) (ii), (iv), (b) (x), (xi), (xiii), (xvi), (xxi), (c) (i)-(ii), and (e) (v), (ix), (xi), and (xii) of the Rome Statute even if starvation is not intentional. In my opinion, food, like medicine and medical supplies, should always be treated as neutral property during an armed conflict. Starvation, even of enemy combatants, seems necessarily inhumane and to involve unnecessary and lingering death and suffering.

Moreover, Article 8 (2) (b) (xxv), addressing starvation, is too limited for a different reason. Not all means of starvation are addressed, but only starvation perpetuated "by depriving them of objects indispensable to their survival." The latter phrase should at least be interpreted logically and in view of a plain meaning to include starvation by depriving persons of food and any other "object" that in context is indispensable to the survival of civilians. Article 54 (1) and (2) of Protocol I to the Geneva Conventions lists starvation of civilians and the deprivation of objects indispensable to their survival as separate crimes. In any event, "starvation of civilians," by any means, is already proscribed under customary international law.

12. The 1977 Protocol I to the 1949 Geneva Conventions adds important limitations on the actions of combatants, especially targetings involving "indiscriminate" attacks during relevant armed conflicts. Read Articles 51 and 75 of Protocol I, in the Documents Section. *Compare* Article 8 (2)(b) of the Statute of the ICC. How would each apply to Yugoslavian military targetings in Kosovo before NATO's intervention in 1999? How would they apply to NATO's use of air power in Kosovo before NATO ground troops arrived?

A press release from the Office of the Prosecutor, Carla Del Ponte, dated 13 June 2000 stated that the Prosecutor of the ICTY decided not to pursue a criminal investigation of "any aspect of NATO's 1999 air campaign" and that "[a]lthough some mistakes were made by NATO, the Prosecutor is satisfied that there was no deliberate targeting of civilians or unlawful military targets by NATO." The Prosecutor relied on a 26 page Final Report to the Prosecutor by the Committee Established to Review the NATO Bombing Campaign Against the Federal Republic of Yugoslavia, available at www.icty.org/x/file/Press/nato061300.pdf. The Report stated that with respect to crimi-

---

* Reproduced with permission of Routledge, Ltd.

nal responsibility for air targetings "[t]he *mens rea* for the offence is intention or reck-lessness, not simple negligence," adding: "In determining whether or not the *mens rea* requirement has been met, it should be borne in mind that commanders deciding on an attack have duties: a) to do everything practicable to verify that the objectives to be at-tacked are military objectives, b) to take all practicable precautions in the choice of methods and means of warfare with a view to avoiding or, in any event to minimizing incidental civilian casualties or civilian property damage, and c) to refrain from launch-ing attacks which may be expected to cause disproportionate civilian casualties or civil-ian property damage." *Id.* para. 28. Is the "expected to cause" standard like a criminal negligence standard, since it entails a lower threshold than wanton, reckless disregard? See also Geneva Protocol I, arts. 35(3), 51(5).

Note that ICC jurisdiction over war crimes involving air or artillery targeting is more limited than the reach of customary international law. *See, e.g.,* Paust, *Content and Con-tours,** *supra,* noting:

… Within Article 8 (2) (b) (iv), concerning attacks, for example, causing "incidental loss of life or injury to civilians or damage to civilian objects," one finds the only provi-sion containing the delimiting phrase "in the knowledge that such attack will cause." This is an improper standard or threshold with respect to all forms of relevant criminal liability and, thus, is another indication of the quite limited jurisdiction of the Court. The phrase "in the knowledge or in wanton disregard that such attack may cause" would have reached other serious war crimes, but was not chosen. Instead, the limiting phrase within Article 8 (2) (b) (iv) assures that an entire area of criminal responsibility attach-ing to wanton or reckless disregard of consequences will not be addressed by the ICC unless it falls within other sections of Article 8 (2), which is possible depending on the language used in other sections and various features of context. Sometimes the *mens rea* standard concerning customary war crimes is reflected in the words "wilful," "wilfully," or "deliberate," as used in Article 147 of the 1949 Geneva Civilian Convention or used a few times with respect to certain customary war crimes found in the 1919 List of War Crimes prepared by the Responsibilities Commission, but sometimes the standard in-cludes "wanton" or "wantonly," as in Article 147 of the Geneva Civilian Convention and certain crimes in the 1919 List. Both instruments are evidence of the fact that the two standards are different, that their drafters knew how to set higher or lower thresholds of criminal responsibility, and that they chose to set higher thresholds only in certain in-stances. Indeed, the same points pertain with respect to Article 8 of the Rome Statute.

More generally with respect to wanton or reckless disregard, it is informative that Ar-ticle 44 of the customary 1863 Lieber Code proscribed "[a]ll wanton violence" and Arti-cle 16 addressed "wanton devastation." "Wanton devastation and destruction" was also the standard used in crimes numbers 18 and 20 in the 1919 List prepared by the Re-sponsibilities Commission. With respect to World War II prosecutions, the Report of Robert H. Jackson to the President of the United States identified "wanton destruction" as among the "[a]trocities and offenses against persons or property" to be addressed at Nuremberg. Similarly, *United States v. List, et al.* noted that "military necessity … does not admit the wanton devastation of a district…." The crime of "wanton destruction of cities, towns or villages" was also expressly recognized in Article 6 (b) of the Charter of the International Military Tribunal at Nuremberg. Thereafter, the Principles of the Nuremberg Charter and Judgment formulated by the International Law Commission and adopted by the U.N. General Assembly affirmed that "[v]iolations of the laws or

---

* Also reproduced with permission of Routledge, Ltd.

customs of war … include, but are not limited to, … wanton destruction of cities, towns, or villages.…" The same crime was also recognized in Article 3(d) of the Bangladesh International Crimes (Tribunals) Act of 1973. More recently, the Indictment of Radovan Karadzic and Ratko Mladic issued by the International Criminal Tribunal for the Former Yugoslavia addresses crimes involving "wantonly appropriated and looted" property and "wanton and unlawful destruction of" property. The Statute of the International Criminal Tribunal for the Former Yugoslavia has also identified crimes involving "extensive destruction and appropriation of property … carried out unlawfully and wantonly" and "wanton destruction of cities, towns or villages.…" Interestingly, Article 8 (2) (b) (xiii) and (e) (xii) of the Rome Statute assures that the new ICC will be able to address "Destroying or seizing the enemy's property" without limiting words such as "intentionally" or "wantonly." In order to constitute a "grave breach" within the meaning of the Rome Statute, however, Article 8 (2) (a) (iv) requires "Extensive destruction or appropriation of property … [that is] carried out unlawfully and wantonly."

Article 51 (5) of Protocol I to the Geneva Conventions also provides a standard with perhaps a lower threshold when using the phrase "an attack which may be *expected* to cause incidental loss" (emphasis added). Similarly, the phrase "intended, or may be *expected*, to cause" found in Article 35 (3) of Protocol I (emphasis added) includes a standard of responsibility far less than "in the knowledge that such … will cause." The "or may be expected" language also appears in the preamble to the Convention on Prohibitions or Restrictions on the Use of Certain Conventional Weapons Which May be Deemed to be Excessively Injurious or to Have Indiscriminate Effects.…

A related problem concerning ICC coverage of customary crime involves the oft-repeated phrase "intentionally directing attacks" found in Article 8 (2) (b) (i)-(iii), (ix), (xxiv) and (e) (i)-(iv). For reasons noted above with respect to criminal responsibility for wanton or reckless disregard, the language used in the Rome Statute clearly does not reach all customary criminal responsibility.

13. The principles reflected in Article 51 of Protocol I are derived from custom.

14. Note that Article 51(2) prohibits "[a]cts or threats of violence the primary purpose of which is to spread terror.…" Must terror actually be produced? In The Prosecutor v. Galic, IT-98-29-T (Trial Chamber Judgment and Sentence, 5 Dec. 2003), Major General Stanislav Galic was convicted with respect to his role as commander of the Bosnian Serb Army's SRK Corps during the "Siege of Sarajevo." The Trial Chamber ruled that a terror outcome is not necessary with respect to a violation of Article 51(2) and stated that three elements of the offense must exist as follows: (1) acts of violence directed against the civilian population or individual civilians not taking direct part in hostilities causing death or serious injury to body or health within the civilian population, (2) the offender wilfully made the civilian population or individual civilians not taking direct part in hostilities the object of those acts of violence, and (3) the offence was committed with the primary purpose of spreading terror among the civilian population. *Id.* paras.133-134. Moreover, military necessity is not an excuse with respect to the crime of targeting of civilians. *Id.* para. 44. Also, indiscriminate attacks "may qualify as direct attacks against civilians" (*Id.* para. 57.) and "certain apparently disproportionate attacks may give rise to the inference that civilians were actually the object of attack (*Id.* para. 60), but the Prosecution must prove that the accused wilfully made the civilian population or relevant individual civilians the object of an attack for the crime of targeting civilians to be proven. *Id.* paras. 55-56. This is in contrast to the crime of indiscriminate attacks under Article 51(4)-(5), which requires that the Prosecution prove that an "attack was launched wilfully and in knowledge of circumstances giving rise to the expectation of excessive civilian casualties." *Id.* para. 59.

15. Are electrical power works and grids sometimes a lawful military target? During the 1991 Gulf War, it was claimed that the U.S. targeted Iraqi power plants with the result that some water systems in the city of Baghdad did not function. Was such a war crime? What else would you like to know? See also Protocol I, arts. 54, 56.

During the 1999 NATO air strikes in Kosovo, a television transmission tower was targeted. If intentionally targeted, would such a targeting be a war crime? Consider Protocol I, arts. 51-52, 54, 56. Also consider *United States v. Ohlendorf*, IV TRIALS OF WAR CRIMES BEFORE THE NUERNBERG MILITARY TRIBUNALS 466, 467 (1948): during the total warfare in WWII, "communications are to be destroyed, railroads wrecked, ammunition plants demolished, factories razed, all for the purpose of impeding the military. In these operations it inevitably happens that nonmilitary persons are killed." The Final Report to the Prosecutor stated that the NATO bombing of the Serbian TV and Radio Station in Belgrade was "part of a planned attack aimed at disrupting and degrading the C3 (Command, Control and Communications) network" and concluded that "[i]nsofar as the attack was actually aimed at disrupting the communications network, it was legally acceptable." *Id.* paras. 72, 75. Some 10 to 17 persons were estimated to have been killed during the attack. The Report addressed Article 52 of Protocol I and used a two-prong test: "was the station a legitimate military objective and; if it was, were the civilian casualties disproportionate to the military advantage gained by the attack." *Id.* para. 75. Does this "military advantage" test adequately reflect the "military necessity" test?

16. Consider the following hypothetical:

During an international armed conflict, General Mala has told you that he wants to target several "military objectives" whose destruction he claims will be strategically valuable. Would you agree to the destruction of the following:

– a new enemy soccer stadium during the evening when no one would be around, because it symbolizes national pride and its destruction would send an important demoralizing message;

– a military housing complex where enemy officers and their families reside;

– a civilian airliner headed to the enemy capital with its top general and aides among the 200+ passengers on board;

– a truck convoy carrying needed food to enemy military and a few civilians in the enemy capital;

– three civil nuclear reactors that power the electric grid in the enemy capital;

– a factory in the countryside that produces military weapons while the civilian workforce is on their day shift;

– the well-guarded home of the enemy President while he and his family are sleeping.

17. The Final Report to the Prosecutor contained terse consideration of admitted use of "depleted uranium projectiles" by NATO aircraft. The Report admitted that the principle of proportionality is applicable, but seemed to argue merely that use of such projectiles is not *per se* illegal and that its prior analysis concerning effects of NATO bombings on the environment are somehow determinative. What the Report did not address is whether use of such weaponry is violative of customary prohibitions of "poison or poisoned weapons," employment of "arms, projectiles or material of a nature to cause unnecessary suffering" (*e.g.*, a lingering death, injury or suffering after a person is taken out of combat, as in the case of neutron warheads—see Paust, remarks, 72 PROC., ASIL

39, 43-45 (1978)), or employment of radioactive weapons in circumstances where they may be expected to cause incidental loss to civilian life or injury that would be excessive.

18. Is espionage an international crime? During time of war? Article 30 of the 1907 Hague Convention, Annex, states: "A spy taken in the act shall not be punished without previous trial." See *United States ex rel. Wessels v. McDonald*, 265 F. 754, 762 (E.D.N.Y. 1920) ("A spy may not be tried under the international law when he returns to his own lines, even if subsequently captured, and the reason is that, under the international law, spying is not a crime, and the offense which is against the laws of war consists of being found during the war in the capacity of a spy. *Martin v. Mott*, 12 Wheat. 19...." See also Art. 31 of the 1907 Hague Convention; FM 27-10, The Law of Land Warfare 33, para. 77 (1956) ("no offense against international law. Spies are punished, not as violators of the laws of war...." but as crimes against that state).

Chapter 5

Civil Sanctions

A. The Right of Access and to a Remedy

[read Article 14(1) of the International Covenant, in the Documents Section]

General Comment No. 13, Report of the Human Rights Committee 39 U.N. GAOR, Supp. (No. 40), at 143, U.N. Doc. A/39/40 (Twenty-first session 1984), *reprinted at* International Human Rights Instruments, U.N. Doc. HRI/GEN/1 (4 September 1992), at 13.

1.... All of [Article 14's] provisions are aimed at ensuring the proper administration of justice and to this end uphold a series of individual rights to equality before the courts and tribunals and the right to a fair and public hearing by a competent, independent and impartial tribunal established by law....

2.... article 14 applies not only to procedures for the determination of criminal charges against individuals but also to procedures to determine their rights and obligations in a suit at law....

3.... ensure that equality before the courts, including equal access to courts, fair and public hearings and competence, impartiality and independence of the judiciary are established by law and guaranteed in practice....

4. The provisions of article 14 apply to all courts and tribunals within the scope of that article whether ordinary or specialized....

General Comment No. 15, 41 U.N. GAOR, Supp. No. 40, Annex VI, at 117, U.N. Doc. A/41/40 (Twenty-third session 1986), *reprinted at* International Human Rights Instruments, U.N. Doc. HRI/GEN/1 (4 September 1992), at 17–19.

The position of aliens under the Covenant

1.... each State party must ensure the rights in the Covenant to "all individuals within its territory and subject to its jurisdiction" (art. 2, para. 1). In general, the rights set forth in the Covenant apply to everyone, irrespective of reciprocity, and irrespective of his or her nationality or statelessness.

2. Thus, the general rule is that each one of the rights of the Covenant must be guaranteed without discrimination between citizens and aliens....

7.... Aliens shall be equal before the courts and tribunals, and shall be entitled to a fair and public hearing by a competent, independent and impartial tribunal established by law in the determination of any ... rights or obligations in a suit at law.... Aliens are entitled to equal protection of the law. There shall be no discrimination between aliens and citizens in the application of these rights....

General Comment No. 24, U.N. Doc. CCPR/c/21/rev.1/add/6 (Nov. 2, 1994)

11. The Covenant consists not just of the specified rights, but of important supportive guarantees. These guarantees provide the necessary framework for securing the rights in the Covenant and are thus essential to its object and purpose. Some operate at the national level and some at the international level. Reservations designed to remove these guarantees are thus not acceptable. Thus, a State could not make a reservation to Article 2, paragraph 3, of the Covenant, indicating that it intends to provide no remedies for human rights violations. Guarantees such as these are an integral part of the structure of the Covenant and underpin its efficacy. The Covenant also envisages, for the better attainment of its stated objectives, a monitoring role for the Committee. Reservations that purport to evade that essential element in the design of the Covenant, which is also directed to securing the enjoyment of the rights, are also incompatible with its object and purpose. A State may not reserve the right not to present a report and have it considered by the Committee. The Committee's role under the Covenant, whether under Article 40 or under the Optional Protocols, necessarily entails interpreting the provisions of the Covenant and the development of a jurisprudence. Accordingly, a reservation that rejects the Committee's competence to interpret the requirements of any provisions of the Covenant would also be contrary to the object and purpose of that treaty.

12. The intention of the Covenant is that the rights contained therein should be ensured to all those under a State party's jurisdiction. To this end certain attendant requirements are likely to be necessary. Domestic laws may need to be altered properly to reflect the requirements of the Covenant; and mechanisms at the domestic level will be needed to allow the Covenant rights to be enforceable at the local level. Reservations often reveal a tendency of States not to want to change a particular law. And sometimes that tendency is elevated to a general policy. Of particular concern are widely formulated reservations which essentially render ineffective all Covenant rights which would require any change in national law to ensure compliance with Covenant obligations. No real international rights or obligations have thus been accepted. And when there is an absence of provisions to ensure that Covenant rights may be sued on in domestic courts, and, further, a failure to allow individual complaints to be brought to the Committee under the first Optional Protocol, all the essential elements of the Covenant guarantees have been removed....

17.... [T]he Committee believes that ... [Vienna Convention Article 20] provisions on the role of State objections in relation to reservations are inappropriate to address the problem of reservations to human rights treaties. Such treaties, and the Covenant specifically, are not a web of inter-State exchanges of mutual obligations. They concern the endowment of individuals with rights. The principle of inter-State reciprocity has no place, save perhaps in the limited context of reservations to declarations on the

Committee's competence under Article 41.... The absence of protest by States cannot imply that a reservation is either compatible or incompatible with the object and purpose of the Covenant....

18. It necessarily falls to the Committee to determine whether a specific reservation is compatible with the object and purpose of the Covenant. This is in part because ... it is an inappropriate task for States parties in relation to human rights treaties, and in part because it is a task that the Committee cannot avoid in the performance of its functions.... Because of the special character of a human rights treaty, the compatibility of a reservation with the object and purpose of the Covenant must be established objectively, by reference to legal principles, and the Committee is particularly well placed to perform this task. The normal consequence of an unacceptable reservation is not that the Covenant will not be in effect at all for a reserving party. Rather, such a reservation will generally be severable, in the sense that the Covenant will be operative for the reserving party without benefit of the reservation.

Notes and Questions

1. When ratifying the 1966 International Covenant on Civil and Political Rights, the United States added the following "Declaration": " ... the United States declares that the provisions of Articles 1 through 27 of the Covenant are not self-executing." The Declaration does not apply to Article 50. In its explanation of the suggested declaration of partial non-self-execution, the Executive explained: "For reasons of prudence, we recommend including a declaration that the substantive provisions of the Covenant are not self-executing. The intent is to clarify that the Covenant will not create a private cause of action in U.S. courts ... existing U.S. law generally complies with the Covenant; hence, implementing legislation is not contemplated." See Report on the International Covenant on Civil and Political Rights, Explanation of Proposed Reservations, Understandings and Declarations, at 19, 102d Cong., 2d Sess., Mar. 24, 1992, *reprinted in* 31 I.L.M. 645 (1992). If operative, would the Declaration be treated as a putative reservation that is void *ab initio* as a matter of law because it is inconsistent with the object and purpose of the treaty? See ICCPR, prmbl., arts. 2, 9, 14, 50 JORDAN J. PAUST, INTERNATIONAL LAW AS LAW OF THE UNITED STATES 363-65 (2 ed. 2003).

2. Concerning the customary right of access to courts and to an effective remedy, *see, e.g.*, JORDAN J. PAUST, INTERNATIONAL LAW AS LAW OF THE UNITED STATES 224–38, 284–322 ns.468–623 (2 ed. 2003); Beth Stephens, *Translating* Filartiga: *A Comparative and International Law Analysis of Domestic Remedies for International Human Rights Violations*, 27 YALE J. INT'L L. 1, 20–21, 46–48 (2002); Jon M. Van Dyke, *The Fundamental Human Right to Prosecution and Compensation*, 29 DENV. J. INT'L L. & POL'Y 77 (2001); H.R. Comm., General Comment No. 7 (1982), para. 1 (victims of ill-treatment under ICCPR Article 7 "must themselves have effective remedies at their disposal, including the right to obtain compensation"); H.R. Comm., General Comment No. 20 (1992), paras. 2, 13, 15 (victims have a "right to an effective remedy, including compensation" whether violators of Article 7 were "public officials or other persons acting on behalf of the State ... or private persons" "acting in their official capacity, outside their official capacity or in a private capacity"); Torture and Other Cruel, Inhuman or Degrading Treatment or Punishment, U.N. G.A. Res. 62/148, para. 13 (18 Dec. 2007). For recognition of such rights under the 1966 Covenant, also see *Dubai Petroleum Co., et al. v. Kazi*, 12 S.W.3d 71, 82 (Tex. 2000) ("Article 14(1) requires all signatory countries to confer the right of equality before the courts to citizens of all other signatories.... The

Covenant not only guarantees foreign citizens equal treatment in the signatorie's courts, but also guarantees them equal access to these courts"), also citing General Comment No. 13 (1984).

3. With respect to the more extensive elaboration of human rights to due process in criminal proceedings, *see, e.g.*, *Hamdan v. Rumsfeld*, 548 U.S. 557 (2006) (in this chapter); International Covenant on Civil and Political Rights, arts. 9–10, 14; Rome Statute of the ICC, arts. 21(3), 63–69; Jordan J. Paust, *Antiterrorism Military Commissions: Courting Illegality*, 23 Mich. J. Int'l L. 1, 10–18 (2001); *Antiterrorism Military Commissions: The Ad Hoc DOD Rules of Procedure*, 23 Mich. J. Int'l L. 677 (2002).

B. U.S. Federal Statutes

Alien Tort Claims Act (ATCA or ATS), 28 U.S.C. § 1350

The district courts shall have original jurisdiction of any civil action by an alien for a tort only, committed in violation of the law of nations or a treaty of the United States.

Torture Victim Protection Act (TVPA), Public Law 102-256, 106 Stat. 73 (1992)

To carry out obligations of the United States under the United Nations Charter and other international agreements pertaining to the protection of human rights by establishing a civil action for recovery of damages from an individual who engages in torture or extrajudicial killing.

Be it enacted by the Senate and House of Representatives of the United States of America in Congress assembled,

Sec. 2. Establishment of Civil Action.

(a) Liability. An individual who, under actual or apparent authority, or color of law, of any foreign nation—

> (1) subjects an individual to torture shall, in a civil action, be liable for damages to that individual; or

> (2) subjects an individual to extrajudicial killing shall, in a civil action, be liable for damages to the individual's legal representative, or to any person who may be a claimant in an action for wrongful death.

(b) Exhaustion of Remedies. A court shall decline to hear a claim under this section if the claimant has not exhausted adequate an available remedies in the place in which the conduct giving rise to the claim occurred.

(c) Statute of Limitations. No action shall be maintained under this section unless it is commenced within 10 years after the cause of action arose.

Sec. 3. Definitions.

(a) Extrajudicial Killing. For the purpose of this Act, the term "extrajudicial killing" means a deliberated killing not authorized by a previous judgment pronounced by a regularly constituted court affording all the judicial guarantees which are recognized as indispensable by civilized peoples. Such term, however, does not include any such killing that, under international law, is lawfully carried out under the authority of a foreign nation.

(b) Torture. For the purposes of this Act—

(1) the term "torture" means any act, directed against an individual in the offender's custody or physical control, by which severe pain or suffering (other than pain or suffering arising only from or inherent in, or incidental to, lawful sanctions), whether physical or mental, is intentionally inflicted on that individual for such purposes as obtaining from that individual or a third person information or a confession, punishing that individual for an act that individual or a third person has committed or is suspected of having committed, intimidating or coercing that individual or a third person, or for any reason based on discrimination of any kind; and

(2) mental pain or suffering refers to prolonged mental harm caused by or resulting from—

(A) the intentional infliction or threatened infliction of severe physical pain or suffering;

(B) the administration or application, or threatened administration or application, of mind altering substances or other procedures calculated to disrupt profoundly the senses or the personality;

(C) the threat of imminent death; or

(D) the threat that another individual will imminently be subjected to death, severe physical pain or suffering, or the administration or application of mind altering substances or other procedures calculated to disrupt profoundly the senses or personality.

The Antiterrorism Act (ATA), 18 U.S.C. §§ 2331-2337

§ 2331. Definitions

As used in this chapter [18 USCS §§ 2331 *et seq.*]—

(1) the term "international terrorism" means activities that—

(A) involve violent acts or acts dangerous to human life that are a violation of the criminal laws of the United States or of any State, or that would be a criminal violation if committed within the jurisdiction of the United States or of any State;

(B) appear to be intended—

(i) to intimidate or coerce a civilian population;

(ii) to influence the policy of a government by intimidation or coercion; or

(iii) to affect the conduct of a government by assassination or kidnapping;

and

(C) occur primarily outside the territorial jurisdiction of the United States, or transcend national boundaries in terms of the means by which they are accomplished, the persons they appear intended to intimidate or coerce, or the locale in which their perpetrators operate or seek asylum;

(2) the term "national of the United States" has the meaning given such term in section 101(a)(22) of the Immigration and Nationality Act [8 USCS § 1101(a)(22)];

(3) the term "person" means any individual or entity capable of holding a legal or beneficial interest in property; and

(4) the term "act of war" means any act occurring in the course of—

(A) declared war;

(B) armed conflict, whether or not war has been declared, between two or more nations; or

(C) armed conflict between military forces of any origin....

§ 2333. Civil remedies

(a) Action and jurisdiction. Any national of the United States injured in his or her person, property, or business by reason of an act of international terrorism, or his or her estate, survivors, or heirs, may sue therefor in any appropriate district court of the United States and shall recover threefold the damages he or she sustains and the cost of the suit, including attorney's fees....

§ 2334. Jurisdiction and venue....

(d) Convenience of the forum. The district courts shall not dismiss ... unless—

(1) the action may be maintained in a foreign court that has jurisdiction over the subject matter and over all the defendants;

(2) that foreign court is significantly more convenient and appropriate; and

(3) that foreign court offers a remedy which is substantially the same as the one available in the courts of the United States....

§ 2335. Limitations of actions

(a) In general. Subject to subsection (b), a suit for recovery of damages under section 2333 of this title shall not be maintained unless commenced within 4 years after the date the cause of action accrued.

(b) Calculation of period. The time of the absence of the defendant from the United States or from any jurisdiction in which the same or a similar action arising from the same facts may be maintained by the plaintiff, or of any concealment of the defendant's whereabouts, shall not be included in the 4–year period set forth in subsection (a).

§ 2336. Other limitations.

(a) Acts of war. No action shall be maintained under section 2333 of this title for injury or loss by reason of an act of war....

§ 2337. Suits against Government officials

No action shall be maintained under section 2333 of this title against—

(1) the United States, an agency of the United States, or an officer or employee of the United States or any agency thereof acting within his or her official capacity or under color of legal authority; or

(2) a foreign state, an agency of a foreign state, or an officer or employee of a foreign state or an agency thereof acting within his or her official capacity or under color of legal authority.

Notes and Questions

1. What customary international law is reflected in the Torture Victim Protection Act (TVPA) and the Antiterrorism Act? Under each form of legislation, who can sue whom for what? Are private perpetrators outside the reach of the TVPA? Are public perpetrators immune under the TVPA? Are they immune under §2337 of the Antiterrorism Act? Are foreign states or foreign state entities suable under the TVPA? How are such lawsuits different from lawsuits under the Alien Tort Claims Act (ATCA), 28 U.S.C. §1350? *See generally*, Joan Fitzpatrick, *The Future of the Alien Tort Claims Act of 1789: Lessons from* In re Marcos Human Rights Litigation, 67 St. John's L. Rev. 491 (1993); Jordan J. Paust, *Suing Karadzic*, 10 Leiden J. Int'l L. 91 (1997). Does the word "individual" in the TVPA reach corporations? *See, e.g., Estate of Rodriquez v. Drummond Co.*, 256 F. Supp.2d 1250, 1268 (N.D. Ala. 2003).

In 2008, Congress amended the Foreign Sovereign Immunities Act (FSIA) to provide a cause of action against foreign states for torture, extrajudicial killing, aircraft sabotage, hostage taking, and the provision of material support or resources for any such conduct if the state has been designated as a "state sponsor of terrorism" and the claimant is a U.S. national or other person listed in 28 U.S.C. §1605A(c). The new legislation states that the definitions of torture and extrajudicial killing are those found in the TVPA.

Under §2333 of the Antiterrorism Act, can Holocaust survivors who subsequently became U.S. nationals sue an alleged Nazi perpetrator of "terrorism" within the meaning of §2331, as "[a]ny national" within the meaning of the statute, or must the plaintiffs be nationals at the time of the wrongful conduct?

2. Does the TVPA, which reaches an individual acting, for example, under "actual authority" of a foreign nation, override judicially-created or "common law" doctrines of immunity? Does every federal statute trump mere common law? See also references in the preceding note.

3. Is "nation" the same as "state" under international law? within the meaning of the TVPA?

4. Can a U.S. national ever be a proper defendant under the TVPA?

5. Why would an alien sue under the TVPA if suit is possible under the ATCA? Consider this question also after the Supreme Court's 2004 decision in *Sosa v. Alvarez–Machain, infra*. A Seventh Circuit panel ruled that the TVPA "preempts" the ATCA and, thus, requires exhaustion of remedies pursuant to the TVPA. See *Enahoro v. Abubakar*, 408 F.3d 877 (7th Cir. 2005). Does this seem correct? *But see Sarei v. Rio Tinto PLC*, 221 F. Supp.2d 1116, 1132–39, 1162 (C.D. Cal. 2002) ("the ATCA does not require the exhaustion of national remedies").

6. Precedential use of the ATCA prior to Filartiga included attention to claims against private violators of international law, U.S. and foreign. *See, e.g., Adra v. Clift*, 195 F. Supp. 857, 865 (D. Md. 1961); *Moxon v. The Fanny*, 17 F. Cas. 942, 943 (D.C.D. Pa. 1793) (No. 9,895) (federal courts are "particularly by law vested with authority where an alien sues for a tort only in violation of the laws of nations, & c."); *M'Grath v. Candalero*, 16 F. Cas. 128 (D.C.D. S.C. 1794) (No. 6,810) ("tort" remedy, ATCA addressed by analogy: "If an alien sue here for a tort under the law of nations or a treaty ... the suit will be sustained"); *Bolchos v. Darrel*, 3 F. Cas. 810 (D.S.C.1795) (No. 1,607); 26 Op. Att'y Gen. 250 (1907); 1 Op. Att'y Gen. 57, 58–59 (1795) ("there can be no doubt that the company or individuals who have been injured by these acts of hostility have a remedy by civil suit in the courts of the United States; jurisdiction being

expressly given to these courts in all cases where an alien sues for a tort only, in viola-tion of the law of nations, or a treaty of the United States."); see also symposium, 4 Hous. J. Int'l L. no. 1 (1981). As it does today, the ATCA applied to conduct and/or injuries or other harm here or abroad.

Under the ATCA, must a plaintiff be an alien at the time of filing? Can plaintiffs be U.S. citizens who, at the time their causes of action arose, were aliens?

7. The language of the ATCA expressly applies to a violation of any treaty of the U.S. and prior to *Sosa* in 2004 the ATCA provides a cause of action (see cases infra). In fact, the ATCA is congressional legislation that executes, implements or incorporates by refer-ence treaties of the United States. The ATCA performs the very role that implementing legislation plays with respect to a partly or wholly non-self-executing treaty and it also provides a cause of action and a remedy. Thus, treaties that are not self-executing are exe-cuted or implemented by the ATCA. *See, e.g., Estate of Cabello v. Fernandez–Larios*, 157 F. Supp.2d 1345, 1359–60 (S.D. Fla. 2001); *Ralk v. Lincoln County*, 81 F. Supp.2d 1372, 1380 (S.D. Ga. 2000) ("because the ICCPR is not self-executing, Ralk can advance no private right of action under the" treaty, but "could bring a claim under the Alien Tort Claims Act for violations of the ICCPR"); Paust, *supra*, at 207, 282 n.571, 371–72. An opinion miss-ing this point is *Iwanowa v. Ford Motor Co.*, 67 F. Supp.2d at 439 n.16 (stating in false dic-tum that two law of war treaties do not "confer rights enforceable by private parties" [*but see Weisshaus v. Swiss Bankers Ass'n (In re Holocaust Victim Assets Litigation)*, 225 F.3d 191 (2d Cir. 2000); *Kadic*, 70 F.3d at 242–43; *In re World War II Era Japanese Forced Labor Lit-igation*, 114 F. Supp.2d 939 (N.D. Cal. 2000) (private claims under HC IV settled by peace treaty); Paust, *Suing Saddam: Private Remedies for War Crimes and Hostage–Taking*, 31 Va. J. Int'l L. 351, 360–69 (1991); Paust, *Judicial Power To Determine the Status and Rights of Persons Detained Without Trial*, 44 Harv. Int'l L.J. 503 (2003)] and are entirely non-self-executing–then falsely concluding, in terse, unreasoned and unsupported dictum beyond what plaintiff had argued or briefed (see id. at 439), that "[s]ince neither … provide a pri-vate action, they cannot provide a basis for suit under the ATCA." Of course, human rights treaties are clearly distinguishable in any event since they provide rights enforce-able by private parties, access to domestic courts, and the right to an effective remedy).

Must treaties confer private rights expressly? The treaty addressed in 26 Op. Att'y Gen. 250 (1907) did not mention any right of action or "private action," individuals, or private rights, but the Attorney General found that a violation of the treaty by a U.S. company (also recognized as a treaty violation by an International Water Boundary Commission) was actionable in view of the fact that the ATCA provides a right of ac-tion. See Convention between the United States of America and the United States of Mexico touching the international boundary line where it follows the bed of the Rio Grande and the Rio Colorado, Nov. 12, 1884, 24 Stat. 1011. Article III of the treaty stated in pertinent part: "No artificial change in the navigable course of the river … or by dredging to deepen … shall be permitted to affect or alter the dividing line…." Id. art. III. This was also the approach at the time of formation of the ATCA. *See, e.g., Bol-chos v. Darrel*, 3 F. Cas. at 811 (Article 14 of the U.S.-France Treaty of Amity and Com-merce, 17 July 1778, 8 Stat. 12, T.S. 83, required forfeiture of property interest of Dar-rel's principal, treaty did not mention any "right of action" or "private action," but claimant Bolchos had an actionable claim under the ATCA to restitution of property wrongfully seized by Darrel); *M'Grath v. Candalero*, 16 F. Cas. at 128 (1778 U.S.-French Treaty of Amity and Commerce, supra, did not mention any "right of action" or "private action," but was used to support a U.S. plaintiff's "tort" remedy, and the ATCA was addressed by analogy and per dictum; cf arts. 17, 22 of the treaty, recognizing that some individuals shall be "bound to make Satisfaction for all Matter of Damage, and the Interest thereof, by reparation, under the Pain and obligation of their Person and Goods," "full Satisfaction shall be made"); 1 Op. Att'y Gen. 57 (1795) (apparently U.S.-British Treaty of Peace, 3 Sept. 1783, 8 Stat. 80, T.S. 104, was "a" treaty violated, and the ATCA provided a right of action even though the Treaty of Peace did not mention a relevant "right of action"; cf Treaty of Amity, Commerce and Navigation, 19 Nov. 1794, arts. 19, 21, 8 Stat. 116, not mentioning any "right of action" or "private action," but re: injuries by Men of War or Privateers, individuals "shall be bound in their persons and Estates to make satisfaction and reparation for all Damages, and the interest thereof, of whatever nature the said Damages may be." Injuries addressed in the Opinion occurred September 28, 1794, before ratification of the Treaty of Amity. The Opinion also emphasizes a warning to U.S. citizens by the President issued April 22, 1793–when only the Treaty of Peace was operative). More generally, the ATCA expressly incorporates all treaties of the United States by reference and it is the ATCA that provides the direct basis for a lawsuit, not the treaties as such.

8. Is the ten-year limitation in the TVPA tolled when a defendant is outside the territory of the United States? *See also Hilao v. Estate of Marcos*, 103 F.3d 767, 773 (9th Cir.1996) (the Senate Report on the TVPA states that the ten-year statute of limitation is subject to equitable tolling, including for periods in which the defendant is absent from the jurisdiction or immune from lawsuits and for periods in which the plaintiff is imprisoned or incapacitated.); *Barrueto, et al. v. Larios*, 205 F. Supp.2d 1325 (S.D. Fla. 2002); *Estate of Cabello, et al. v. Fernandez–Larios*, 157 F. Supp.2d 1345 (S.D. Fla. 2001).

9. There are no statutes of limitation under international law, and there are none expressed by Congress with respect to the ATCA. *See also Vietnam Ass'n for Victims of Agent Orange/Dioxin v. Dow Chemical Co. (In re Agent Orange Prod. Liab. Litig.)*, 373 F. Supp.2d 7, 63 (E.D.N.Y. 2005). When courts "legislate" by "borrowing" limitations in other federal statutes, the matter can become complex.

Addressing claims under the ATCA, the district court in *Forti v. Suarez–Mason*, 672 F. Supp. 1531 (N.D. Cal.1987) noted that there is no statute of limitation under international law regarding such claims, but addressed causes of action with "closest analogies" in state and ordinary federal law and statutes of limitation relating to such. The district court did so arguing that "[w]hile international law provides the substantive standard..., the cause of action itself is created by the federal statute," *i.e.*, the ATCA. *Id.* at 1547 n.10. Nonetheless, the court recognized that "because the claim itself is a federal claim, federal equitable tolling doctrines apply" and that such occurs: "(1) where defendant's wrongful conduct prevented plaintiff from timely asserting his claim, or (2) where extraordinary circumstances outside plaintiff's control make it impossible for plaintiff to timely assert his claim." *Id.* at 1549. Plaintiffs had claimed that international law's lack of a statute of limitation, which is itself part of the law of the U.S., is the most analogous federal law. *Id.* at 147 n.10. Which approach is preferable in view of the legal policies at stake with respect to serious violations of international law over which there is universal jurisdiction? Is it relevant that human rights law guarantees a right to an effective remedy in domestic tribunals? *See, e.g.*, Universal Declaration of Human Rights, art. 8; International Covenant on Civil and Political Rights, arts. 2, 14; PAUST, *supra* at 198–203. Is it relevant that Congress used a statute of limitations in the TVPA but did not amend the ATCA? *See also Kadic v. Karadzic*, 70 F.3d at 241 (Congress chose not to diminish the reach of the ATCA). Is it relevant that a purpose of the ATCA was to avoid a "denial of justice" to aliens under international law?

10. Are acts of terrorism proscribed under international law regardless of motive, the status of the perpetrator, and the method used? *See, e.g.*, the 1991, 1994, 2004, and 2006 U.N. General Assembly resolutions in the Documents Section). Are acts of terrorism contrary to human rights law? *See, e.g.*, the 2004 U.N. G.A. resolutions. Are some acts of terrorism crimes against humanity? *See, e.g.*, Charters of the International Military Tribunals at Nuremberg and for the Far East; Control Council Law No. 10.

What would be an objective and descriptive definition of terrorism? Should it include elements of (1) intent (as opposed to mere negligence), (2) to produce terror, (3) a terror outcome, and (4) by methods of violence or weapons (broadly defined to include chemical, biological, or bacteriological agents) or a threat thereof? *See* the 1994 General Assembly resolution, para. 3. Should "terrorism" involve a political, religious, or ideologic motive? Under § 2331 of the Antiterrorism Act, must all acts of "terrorism" involve acts of violence, political motives, or terror outcomes? Is the definitional orientation adequate or too broad? What would you recommend?

11. Are terroristic tactics used against civilians in time of war violations of the laws of war? *See, e.g.*, Geneva Civilian Convention (GC), art. 33; Geneva Protocol I, art. 51(2); 1919 List of War Crimes, in the Documents Section.

12. Under § 2336 (a) of the Antiterrorism Act, are only lawful acts of war impliedly covered? Recall that Supreme Court cases recognize that judges must try to interpret legislation consistently with international law if at all possible. Further, war crimes are nonimmune.

13. Under § 2337, with respect to states and agencies thereof, are they not immune when acting outside official capacity or color of legal authority? Was use of the phrase "his or her" sloppy (*e.g.*, should it have read: "its, his or her"?) or intentionally restrictive? Should § 2337 be interpreted consistently with U.S. treaty law on nonimmunity with respect to persons "acting in an official capacity," such as Article 2(3)(a) of the ICCPR? See also H.R. Comm., General Comment No. 20 (quoted above); Articles 1 and 14 of the Convention Against Torture; Article 25(1) of the American Convention on Human Rights; Article 13 of the European Convention for the Protection of Human Rights and Fundamental Freedoms. Concerning suits against foreign states and foreign state entities for certain terrorist acts, see also the Foreign Sovereign Immunities Act, 28 U.S.C. § 1605 (a) (7), in the Documents Section.

14. Consider § 2332 again when addressing jurisdiction to prescribe under international law (in Chapter 3). What basis(es) exist for prescription regarding murder and serious bodily injury to U.S. nationals? Is there universal jurisdiction with respect to human rights violations?

15. Cases utilizing § 2333 include: *Boim v. Quranic Literary Institute and Holy Land Foundation for Relief and Development*, 291 F.3d 1000 (7th Cir. 2002); *Sokolow v. Palestinian Liberation Organization*, 2008 WL 4449480 (S.D.N.Y. 2008); *Saperstein v. Palestinian Authority*, 2008 WL 4467535 (S.D. Fla. 2008); *Biton v. Palestinian Interim Self-Government Authority*, 252 F.R.D. 1 (D.D.C. 2008); *Almog v. Arab Bank*, 471 F. Supp.2d 257 (E.D.N.Y. 2007); *Weiss v. Arab Bank, PLC*, 2007 WL 4565060 (E.D.N.Y. 2007) (also noting that one cannot be at "war" with Hamas, PIJ and AAMB re: § 2336); *Estate of Ungar ex rel. Strachman v. Palestinian Authority*, 304 F. Supp.2d 232 (D.R.I. 2004), aff'd, 402 F.3d 272 (1st Cir. 2005); *Smith v. Islamic Emirate of Afghanistan, et al.*, 262 F. Supp.2d 217 (S.D.N.Y. 2003) (suit arising out of 9/11 attacks by al Qaeda, *et al.*); *Estate of Ungar v.*

Palestinian Authority, 304 F. Supp.2d 232 (D.R.I. 2004) and 153 F. Supp.2d 76, 85 (D.R.I. 2001) (complicity in killing of U.S. national in Israel); *Boim v. Quranic Literary Institute*, 127 F. Supp.2d 1002 (N.D. Ill. 2001) (claim of parents of U.S. national in Israel against an entity that allegedly funded terrorism), *aff'd*, 291 F.3d 1000 (7th Cir. 2002).

16. Recall the War Crimes Act of 2003, 18 U.S.C. §2441, in Chapter One. Are "grave breach" violations of the Geneva Conventions thereby tortious per se? Note the language used by Justice Breyer while concurring in *Sosa, infra* ("universal criminal jurisdiction necessarily contemplates a significant degree of civil tort recovery as well"). If so, can U.S. nationals sue under 28 U.S.C. §1331, using the tortious per se approach (without some other statute providing subject matter jurisdiction)? Aliens can sue for such infractions of the laws of war under the Alien Tort Claims Act (ATCA). What other statutes incorporate such customary international law for U.S. plaintiffs (and with respect to what sort of violations)? *See also* Jordan J. Paust, *Suing Saddam: Private Remedies for War Crimes and Hostage–Taking*, 31 VA. J. INT'L L. 351 (1991).

17, Recall 28 U.S.C. §1331, in Chapter One.

C. Cases

Filartiga v. Pena–Irala, 630 F.2d 876 (2d Cir.1980)

Kaufman, J.

Upon ratification of the Constitution, the thirteen former colonies were fused into a single nation, one which, in its relations with foreign states, is bound both to observe and construe the accepted norms of international law, formerly known as the law of nations. Under the Articles of Confederation, the several states had interpreted and applied this body of doctrine as a part of their common law, but with the founding of the "more perfect Union" of 1789, the law of nations became preeminently a federal concern.

Implementing the constitutional mandate for national control over foreign relations, the First Congress established original district court jurisdiction over "all causes where an alien sues for a tort only (committed) in violation of the law of nations." Judiciary Act of 1789, ch. 20, §9(b), 1 Stat. 73, 77 (1789), codified at 28 U.S.C. §1350 [the ATCA]. Construing this rarely-invoked provision, we hold that deliberate torture perpetrated under color of official authority violates universally accepted norms of the international law of human rights, regardless of the nationality of the parties. Thus, whenever an alleged torturer is found and served with process by an alien within our borders, §1350 provides federal jurisdiction. Accordingly, we reverse the judgment of the district court dismissing the complaint for want of federal jurisdiction.

I

The appellants, plaintiffs below, are citizens of the Republic of Paraguay. Dr. Joel Filartiga, a physician, describes himself as a longstanding opponent of the government of President Alfredo Stroessner, which has held power in Paraguay since 1954. His daughter, Dolly Filartiga, arrived in the United States in 1978 under a visitor's visa, and has since applied for permanent political asylum. The Filartigas brought this action in the Eastern District of New York against Americo Norberto Pena–Irala (Pena), also a citizen of Paraguay, for wrongfully causing the death of Dr. Filartiga's seventeen-year old son, Joelito. Because the district court dismissed the action for want of subject matter jurisdiction, we must accept as true the allegations contained in the Filartigas' complaint and affidavits for purposes of this appeal.

The appellants contend that on March 29, 1976, Joelito Filartiga was kidnapped and tortured to death by Pena, who was then Inspector General of Police in Asuncion, Paraguay. Later that day, the police brought Dolly Filartiga to Pena's home where she was confronted with the body of her brother, which evidenced marks of severe torture. As she fled, horrified, from the house, Pena followed after her shouting, "Here you have what you have been looking for for so long and what you deserve. Now shut up." The Filartigas claim that Joelito was tortured and killed in retaliation for his father's political activities and beliefs.

Shortly thereafter, Dr. Filartiga commenced a criminal action in the Paraguayan courts against Pena and the police for the murder of his son. As a result, Dr. Filartiga's attorney was arrested and brought to police headquarters where, shackled to a wall, Pena threatened him with death. This attorney, it is alleged, has since been disbarred without just cause.

During the course of the Paraguayan criminal proceeding, which is apparently still pending after four years, another man, Hugo Duarte, confessed to the murder. Duarte, who was a member of the Pena household, claimed that he had discovered his wife and Joelito in flagrante delicto, and that the crime was one of passion. The Filartigas have submitted a photograph of Joelito's corpse showing injuries they believe refute this claim. Dolly Filartiga, moreover, has stated that she will offer evidence of three independent autopsies demonstrating that her brother's death "was the result of professional methods of torture." Despite his confession, Duarte, we are told, has never been convicted or sentenced in connection with the crime.

In July of 1978, Pena sold his house in Paraguay and entered the United States under a visitor's visa. He was accompanied by Juana Bautista Fernandez Villalba, who had lived with him in Paraguay. The couple remained in the United States beyond the term of their visas, and were living in Brooklyn, New York, when Dolly Filartiga, who was then living in Washington, D. C., learned of their presence. Acting on information provided by Dolly the Immigration and Naturalization Service arrested Pena and his companion, both of whom were subsequently ordered deported on April 5, 1979 following a hearing. They had then resided in the United States for more than nine months.

Almost immediately, Dolly caused Pena to be served with a summons and civil complaint at the Brooklyn Navy Yard, where he was being held pending deportation. The complaint alleged that Pena had wrongfully caused Joelito's death by torture and sought compensatory and punitive damages of $10,000,000. The Filartigas also sought to enjoin Pena's deportation to ensure his availability for testimony at trial. The cause of action is stated as arising under "wrongful death statutes; the U. N. Charter; the Universal Declaration on Human Rights; the U. N. Declaration Against Torture; the American Declaration of the Rights and Duties of Man; and other pertinent declarations, documents and practices constituting the customary international law of human rights and the law of nations," as well as 28 U.S.C. § 1350, Article II, sec. 2 and the Supremacy Clause of the U.S. Constitution. Jurisdiction is claimed under the general federal question provision, 28 U.S.C. § 1331 and, principally on this appeal, under the Alien Tort Statute, 28 U.S.C. § 1350.

Judge Nickerson stayed the order of deportation, and Pena immediately moved to dismiss the complaint on the grounds that subject matter jurisdiction was absent and for forum non conveniens. On the jurisdictional issue, there has been no suggestion that Pena claims diplomatic immunity from suit. The Filartigas submitted the affidavits of a number of distinguished international legal scholars, who stated unanimously that the law of nations prohibits absolutely the use of torture as alleged in the complaint.[Profs. Falk, Franck, Lillich, and McDougal] Pena, in support of his motion to dismiss on the ground of forum non conveniens, submitted the affidavit of his Paraguayan counsel, Jose Emilio Gorostiaga, who averred that Paraguayan law provides a full and adequate civil remedy for the wrong alleged. Dr. Filartiga has not commenced such an action, however, believing that further resort to the courts of his own country would be futile.

Judge Nickerson heard argument on the motion to dismiss on May 14, 1979, and on May 15 dismissed the complaint on jurisdictional grounds. The district judge recognized the strength of appellants' argument that official torture violates an emerging norm of customary international law. Nonetheless, he felt constrained by dicta contained in two recent opinions of this Court, Dreyfus v. von Finck, 534 F.2d 24 (2d Cir.), *cert. denied*, 429 U.S. 835 ... (1976); IIT v. Vencap, Ltd., 519 F.2d 1001 (2d Cir.1975), to construe narrowly "the law of nations," as employed in § 1350, as excluding that law which governs a state's treatment of its own citizens.

The district court continued the stay of deportation for forty-eight hours while appellants applied for further stays. These applications were denied by a panel of this Court on May 22, 1979, and by the Supreme Court two days later. Shortly thereafter, Pena and his companion returned to Paraguay.

II

Appellants rest their principal argument in support of federal jurisdiction upon the Alien Tort Statute, 28 U.S.C. § 1350, which provides: "The district courts shall have original jurisdiction of any civil action by an alien for a tort only, committed in violation of the law of nations or a treaty of the United States." Since appellants do not contend that their action arises directly under a treaty of the United States,[1] a threshold question on the jurisdictional issue is whether the conduct alleged violates the law of nations. In light of the universal condemnation of torture in numerous international agreements, and the renunciation of torture as an instrument of official policy by virtually all of the nations of the world (in principle if not in practice), we find that an act of torture committed by a state official against one held in detention violates established norms of the international law of human rights, and hence the law of nations.

The Supreme Court has enumerated the appropriate sources of international law. The law of nations "may be ascertained by consulting the works of jurists, writing professedly on public law; or by the general usage and practice of nations; or by judicial decisions recognizing and enforcing that law." United States v. Smith, 18 U.S. (5 Wheat.) 153, 160–61 ... (1820); Lopes v. Reederei Richard Schroder, 225 F. Supp. 292, 295 (E.D. Pa.1963). In *Smith*, a statute proscribing "the crime of piracy (on the high seas) as defined by the law of nations," 3 Stat. 510(a) (1819), was held sufficiently determinate in meaning to afford the basis for a death sentence. The *Smith* Court discovered among the works of Lord Bacon, Grotius, Bochard and other commentators a genuine consensus that rendered the crime "sufficiently and constitutionally defined." *Smith, supra*, 18 U.S. (5 Wheat.) at 162....

The Paquete Habana, 175 U.S. 677 ... (1900), reaffirmed that:

---

1. [Court's note 7] Appellants "associate themselves with" the argument of some of the *amici curiae* that their claim arises directly under a treaty of the United States, Brief for Appellants at 23 n.*, but nonetheless primarily rely upon treaties and other international instruments as evidence of an emerging norm of customary international law, rather then independent sources of law.

where there is no treaty, and no controlling executive or legislative act or judicial decision, resort must be had to the customs and usages of civilized nations; and, as evidence of these, to the works of jurists and commentators, who by years of labor, research and experience, have made themselves peculiarly well acquainted with the subjects of which they treat. Such works are resorted to by judicial tribunals, not for the speculations of their authors concerning what the law ought to be, but for trustworthy evidence of what the law really is.

Id. at 700.... Modern international sources confirm the propriety of this approach.

Habana is particularly instructive for present purposes, for it held that the traditional prohibition against seizure of an enemy's coastal fishing vessels during wartime, a standard that began as one of comity only, had ripened over the preceding century into "a settled rule of international law" by "the general assent of civilized nations." *Id.* at 694 ...; *accord, id.* at 686.... Thus it is clear that courts must interpret international law not as it was in 1789, but as it has evolved and exists among the nations of the world today. See Ware v. Hylton, 3 U.S. (3 Dall.) 199 ... (1796) (distinguishing between "ancient" and "modern" law of nations).

The requirement that a rule command the "general assent of civilized nations" to become binding upon them all is a stringent one. Were this not so, the courts of one nation might feel free to impose idiosyncratic legal rules upon others, in the name of applying international law. Thus, in Banco Nacional de Cuba v. Sabbatino, 376 U.S. 398 ... (1964), the Court declined to pass on the validity of the Cuban government's expropriation of a foreign-owned corporation's assets, noting the sharply conflicting views on the issue propounded by the capital-exporting, capital-importing, socialist and capitalist nations. *Id.* at 428–30....

The case at bar presents us with a situation diametrically opposed to the conflicted state of law that confronted the *Sabbatino* Court. Indeed, to paraphrase that Court's statement, *id.* at 428..., there are few, if any, issues in international law today on which opinion seems to be so united as the limitations on a state's power to torture persons held in its custody.

The United Nations Charter ... makes it clear that in this modern age a state's treatment of its own citizens is a matter of international concern. It provides:

> With a view to the creation of conditions of stability and well-being which are necessary for peaceful and friendly relations among nations ... the United Nations shall promote ... universal respect for, and observance of, human rights and fundamental freedoms for all without distinctions as to race, sex, language or religion.

Id. Art. 55. And further:

> All members pledge themselves to take joint and separate action in cooperation with the Organization for the achievement of the purposes set forth in Article 55.

Id. Art. 56.

While this broad mandate has been held not to be wholly self-executing, Hitai v. Immigration and Naturalization Service, 343 F.2d 466, 468 (2d Cir.1965), this observation alone does not end our inquiry. For although there is no universal agreement as to the precise extent of the "human rights and fundamental freedoms" guaranteed to all by the Charter, there is at present no dissent from the view that the guaranties include, at a bare minimum, the right to be free from torture. This prohibition has become part of customary international law, as evidenced and defined by the Universal Declaration of Human Rights, General Assembly Resolution 217 (III)(A) (Dec. 10, 1948) which states, in the plainest of terms, "no one shall be subjected to torture." The General Assembly has declared that the Charter precepts embodied in this Universal Declaration "constitute basic principles of international law." G.A. Res. 2625 (XXV) (Oct. 24, 1970).

Particularly relevant is the Declaration on the Protection of All Persons from Being Subjected to Torture, General Assembly Resolution 3452, 30 U.N. GAOR Supp. (No. 34) 91, U.N.Doc. A/1034 (1975).... The Declaration expressly prohibits any state from permitting the dastardly and totally inhuman act of torture. Torture, in turn, is defined as "any act by which severe pain and suffering, whether physical or mental, is intentionally inflicted by or at the instigation of a public official on a person for such purposes as ... intimidating him or other persons." The Declaration goes on to provide that "[w]here it is proved that an act of torture or other cruel, inhuman or degrading treatment or punishment has been committed by or at the instigation of a public official, the victim shall be afforded redress and compensation, in accordance with national law." This Declaration, like the Declaration of Human Rights before it, was adopted without dissent by the General Assembly. Nayar, "*Human Rights: The United Nations and United States Foreign Policy,*" 19 Harv. Int'l L.J. 813, 816 n.18 (1978).

These U.N. declarations are significant because they specify with great precision the obligations of member nations under the Charter. Since their adoption, "[m]embers can no longer contend that they do not know what human rights they promised in the Charter to promote." Sohn, "*A Short History of United Nations Documents on Human Rights,*" in The United Nations and Human Rights, 18th Report of the Commission (Commission to Study the Organization of Peace ed. 1968). Moreover, a U.N. Declaration is, according to one authoritative definition, "a formal and solemn instrument, suitable for rare occasions when principles of great and lasting importance are being enunciated." 34 U.N. ESCOR, Supp. (No. 8) 15, U.N. Doc. E/cn.4/1/610 (1962) (memorandum of Office of Legal Affairs, U.N. Secretariat). Accordingly, it has been observed that the Universal Declaration of Human Rights "no longer fits into the dichotomy of 'binding treaty' against 'non-binding pronouncement,' but is rather an authoritative statement of the international community." E. Schwelb, Human Rights and the International Community 70 (1964). Thus, a Declaration creates an expectation of adherence, and "insofar as the expectation is gradually justified by State practice, a declaration may by custom become recognized as laying down rules binding upon the States." 34 U.N. ESCOR, *supra*. Indeed, several commentators have concluded that the Universal Declaration has become, in toto, a part of binding, customary international law. Nayar, *supra*, at 816–17; Waldlock, "*Human Rights in Contemporary International Law and the Significance of the European Convention,*" Int'l & Comp. L.Q., Supp. Publ. No. 11 at 15 (1965).

Turning to the act of torture, we have little difficulty discerning its universal renunciation in the modern usage and practice of nations. *Smith, supra,* 18 U.S. (5 Wheat.) at 160–61.... The international consensus surrounding torture has found expression in numerous international treaties and accords. *E.g.,* American Convention on Human Rights, Art. 5, OAS Treaty Series No. 36 at 1, OAS Off. Rec. OEA/Ser 4 v/II 23, Doc. 21, rev. 2 (English ed., 1975) ("No one shall be subjected to torture or to cruel, inhuman or degrading punishment or treatment"); International Covenant on Civil and Political Rights, U.N. General Assembly Res. 2200 (XXI)A, U.N. Doc. A/6316 (Dec. 16, 1966) (identical language); European Convention for the Protection of Human Rights and

Fundamental Freedoms, Art. 3, Council of Europe, European Treaty Series No. 5 (1968), 213 U.N.T.S. 211 (semble). The substance of these international agreements is reflected in modern municipal, *i.e.*, national law as well. Although torture was once a routine concomitant of criminal interrogations in many nations, during the modern and hopefully more enlightened era it has been universally renounced. According to one survey, torture is prohibited, expressly or implicitly, by the constitutions of over fifty-five nations, including both the United States and Paraguay. Our State Department reports a general recognition of this principle:

> There now exists an international consensus that recognizes basic human rights and obligations owed by all governments to their citizens.... There is no doubt that these rights are often violated; but virtually all governments acknowledge their validity.

Department of State, Country Reports on Human Rights for 1979, published as Joint Comm. Print, House Comm. on Foreign Affairs, and Senate Comm. on Foreign Relations, 96th Cong. 2d Sess. (Feb. 4, 1980), Introduction at 1. We have been directed to no assertion by any contemporary state of a right to torture its own or another nation's citizens. Indeed, United States diplomatic contacts confirm the universal abhorrence with which torture is viewed:

> In exchanges between United States embassies and all foreign states with which the United States maintains relations, it has been the Department of State's general experience that no government has asserted a right to torture its own nationals. Where reports of torture elicit some credence, a state usually responds by denial or, less frequently, by asserting that the conduct was unauthorized or constituted rough treatment short of torture.[2]

Memorandum of the United States as *Amicus Curiae* at 16 n.34.

Having examined the sources from which customary international law is derived the usage of nations, judicial opinions and the works of jurists we conclude that official torture is now prohibited by the law of nations. The prohibition is clear and unambiguous, and admits of no distinction between treatment of aliens and citizens. Accordingly, we must conclude that the dictum in *Dreyfus v. von Finck*, *supra*, 534 F.2d at 31, to the effect that "violations of international law do not occur when the aggrieved parties are nationals of the acting state," is clearly out of tune with the current usage and practice of international law. The treaties and accords cited above, as well as the express foreign policy of our own government, all make it clear that international law confers fundamental rights upon all people vis-a-vis their own governments. While the ultimate scope of those rights will be a subject for continuing refinement and elaboration, we hold that the right to be free from torture is now among them. We therefore turn to the question whether the other requirements for jurisdiction are met.

---

2. [Court's note 15] The fact that the prohibition of torture is often honored in the breach does not diminish its binding effect as a norm of international law. As one commentator has put it, "The best evidence for the existence of international law is that every actual State recognizes that it does exist and that it is itself under an obligation to observe it. States often violate international law, just as individuals often violate municipal law; but no more than individuals do States defend their violations by claiming that they are above the law." J. Brierly, The Outlook for International Law 4–5 (Oxford 1944).

III

Appellee submits that even if the tort alleged is a violation of modern international law, federal jurisdiction may not be exercised consistent with the dictates of Article III of the Constitution. The claim is without merit. Common law courts of general jurisdiction regularly adjudicate transitory tort claims between individuals over whom they exercise personal jurisdiction, wherever the tort occurred. Moreover, as part of an articulated scheme of federal control over external affairs, Congress provided, in the first Judiciary Act, §9(b), 1 Stat. 73, 77 (1789), for federal jurisdiction over suits by aliens where principles of international law are in issue. The constitutional basis for the Alien Tort Statute is the law of nations, which has always been part of the federal common law. . . .

During the eighteenth century, it was taken for granted on both sides of the Atlantic that the law of nations forms a part of the common law. 1 BLACKSTONE, COMMENTARIES 263–64 (1st Ed. 1765–69); 4 *id.* at 67. Under the Articles of Confederation, the Pennsylvania Court of Oyer and Terminer at Philadelphia, per McKean, Chief Justice, applied the law of nations to the criminal prosecution of the Chevalier de Longchamps for his assault upon the person of the French Consul–General to the United States, noting that "[t]his law, in its full extent, is a part of the law of this state ..." Respublica v. DeLongchamps, 1 U.S. (1 Dall.) 111, 119 (1784). Thus, a leading commentator has written:

> It is an ancient and a salutary feature of the Anglo–American legal tradition that the Law of Nations is a part of the law of the land to be ascertained and administered, like any other, in the appropriate case. This doctrine was originally conceived and formulated in England in response to the demands of an expanding commerce and under the influence of theories widely accepted in the late sixteenth, the seventeenth and the eighteenth centuries. It was brought to America in the colonial years as part of the legal heritage from England. It was well understood by men of legal learning in America in the eighteenth century when the United Colonies broke away from England to unite effectively, a little later, in the United States of America.

Dickinson, *The Law of Nations as Part of the National Law of the United States*, 101 U. PA. L. REV. 26, 27 (1952).

Indeed, Dickinson goes on to demonstrate, *id.* at 34–41, that one of the principal defects of the Confederation that our Constitution was intended to remedy was the central government's inability to "cause infractions of treaties or of the law of nations, to be punished." 1 FARRAND, RECORDS OF THE FEDERAL CONVENTION 19 (Rev. ed. 1937) (Notes of James Madison). And, in Jefferson's words, the very purpose of the proposed Union was "to make us one nation as to foreign concerns, and keep us distinct in domestic ones." Dickinson, *supra*, at 36 n. 28.

As ratified, the judiciary article contained no express reference to cases arising under the law of nations. Indeed, the only express reference to that body of law is contained in Article I, sec. 8, cl. 10, which grants to the Congress the power to "define and punish ... offenses against the law of nations." Appellees seize upon this circumstance and advance the proposition that the law of nations forms a part of the laws of the United States only to the extent that Congress has acted to define it. This extravagant claim is amply refuted by the numerous decisions applying rules of international law uncodified in any act of Congress. *E.g.,* Ware v. Hylton, 3 U.S. (3 Dall.) 199 ... (1796); *The Paquete Habana, supra,* 175 U.S. 677 ...; *Sabbatino, supra,* 376 U.S. 398 ... (1964). A similar argument was offered to and rejected by the Supreme Court in United States v. Smith, *supra,* 18 U.S. (5 Wheat.) 153, 158–60 ... and we reject it today. As John Jay wrote in THE FEDERALIST No. 3, at 22 (1 Bourne ed. 1901), "Under the national government, treaties and articles of treaties, as well as the laws of nations, will always be expounded in one sense and executed in the same manner, whereas adjudications on the same points and questions in the thirteen states will not always accord or be consistent." Federal jurisdiction over cases involving international law is clear.

Thus, it was hardly a radical initiative for Chief Justice Marshall to state in The Nereide, 13 U.S. (9 Cranch) 388, 422 ... (1815), that in the absence of a congressional enactment,[3] United States courts are "bound by the law of nations, which is a part of the law of the land." These words were echoed in The Paquete Habana, *supra*, 175 U.S. at 700 ... : "international law is part of our law, and must be ascertained and administered by the courts of justice of appropriate jurisdiction, as often as questions of right depending upon it are duly presented for their determination."

The Filartigas urge that 28 U.S.C. § 1350 be treated as an exercise of Congress's power to define offenses against the law of nations. While such a reading is possible, see Lincoln Mills v. Textile Workers, 353 U.S. 448 ... (1957) (jurisdictional statute authorizes judicial explication of federal common law), we believe it is sufficient here to construe the Alien Tort Statute, not as granting new rights to aliens, but simply as opening the federal courts for adjudication of the rights already recognized by international law. The statute nonetheless does inform our analysis of Article III, for we recognize that questions of jurisdiction "must be considered part of an organic growth part of an evolutionary process," and that the history of the judiciary article gives meaning to its pithy phrases. Romero v. International Terminal Operating Co., 358 U.S. 354, 360 ... (1959). The Framers' overarching concern that control over international affairs be vested in the new national government to safeguard the standing of the United States among the nations of the world therefore reinforces the result we reach today....

Pena also argues that "if the conduct complained of is alleged to be the act of the Paraguayan government, the suit is barred by the Act of State doctrine." This argument was not advanced below, and is therefore not before us on this appeal. We note in passing, however, that we doubt whether action by a state official in violation of the Constitution and laws of the Republic of Paraguay, and wholly unratified by that nation's government, could properly be characterized as an act of state. See Banco Nacionale de Cuba v. Sabbatino, *supra*, 376 U.S. 398 ... ; Underhill v. Hernandez, 168 U.S. 250 ... (1897). Paraguay's renunciation of torture as a legitimate instrument of state policy, however, does not strip the tort of its character as an international law violation, if it in fact occurred under color of government authority. See Declaration on the Protection of All Persons from Being Subjected to Torture, *supra* note 11; *cf.* Ex parte Young, 209 U.S. 123 ... (1908) (state official subject to suit for constitutional violations despite immunity of state)....

... In the modern age, humanitarian and practical considerations have combined to lead the nations of the world to recognize that respect for fundamental human rights is in their individual and collective interest. Among the rights universally proclaimed by all nations, as we have noted, is the right to be free of physical torture. Indeed, for pur-

---

3. [Court's note 20] The plainest evidence that international law has an existence in the federal courts independent of acts of Congress is the long-standing rule of construction first enunciated by Chief Justice Marshall: "an act of congress ought never to be construed to violate the law of nations, if any other possible construction remains...." *The Charming Betsy*, 6 U.S. (2 Cranch), 64, 67 ... (1804)....

poses of civil liability, the torturer has become like the pirate and slave trader before him *hostis humani generis*, an enemy of all mankind. Our holding today, giving effect to a jurisdictional provision enacted by our First Congress, is a small but important step in the fulfillment of the ageless dream to free all people from brutal violence.

Filartiga v. Pena–Irala, 577 F. Supp. 860 (E.D.N.Y. 1984)

Nickerson, J.

The Court of Appeals decided only that Section 1350 gave jurisdiction. We must now face the issue left open by the Court of Appeals, namely, the nature of the "action" over which the section affords jurisdiction. Does the "tort" to which the statute refers mean a wrong "in violation of the law of nations" or merely a wrong actionable under the law of the appropriate sovereign state?....

The word "tort" has historically meant simply "wrong" or "the opposite of right," so-called, according to Lord Coke, because it is "wrested" or "crooked," being contrary to that which is "right" and "straight". Sir Edward Coke on Littleton 158b; see also W. Prosser, Law of Torts 2 (1971). There was nothing about the contemporary usage of the word in 1789, when Section 1350 was adopted, to suggest that it should be read to encompass wrongs defined as such by a national state but not by international law. Even before the adoption of the Constitution piracy was defined as a crime by the law of nations. United States v. Smith, 18 U.S. (5 Wheat.) 153, 157 ... (1820). As late as 1819 Congress passed legislation, now 18 U.S.C. § 1651, providing for punishment of "the crime of piracy, as defined by the law of nations." 3 Stat. 510 (1819). Congress would hardly have supposed when it enacted Section 1350 that a "crime," but not the comparable "tort," was definable by the law of nations. Nor is there any legislative history of the section to suggest such a limitation.

Accordingly, there is no basis for adopting a narrow interpretation of Section 1350 inviting frustration of the purposes of international law by individual states that enact immunities for government personnel or other such exemptions or limitations. The court concludes that it should determine the substantive principles to be applied by looking to international law....

The international law described by the Court of Appeals does not ordain detailed remedies but sets forth norms. But plainly international "law" does not consist of mere benevolent yearnings never to be given effect. Indeed, the Declaration on the Protection of All Persons from Being Subjected to Torture, General Assembly Resolution 3452, 30 U.N. GAOR Supp. (No.34) 91, U.N. Doc. A/1034 (1975), adopted without dissent by the General Assembly, recites that where an act of torture has been committed by or at the instigation of a public official, the victim shall be afforded redress and compensation "in accordance with national law," art. 11, and that "each state" shall ensure that all acts of torture are offenses under its criminal law, art. 7.

The international law prohibiting torture established the standard and referred to the national states the task of enforcing it. By enacting Section 1350 Congress entrusted that task to the federal courts and gave them power to choose and develop federal remedies to effectuate the purposes of the international law incorporated into United States common law.

In order to take the international condemnation of torture seriously this court must adopt a remedy appropriate to the ends and reflective of the nature of the condemnation. Torture is viewed with universal abhorrence.... If the courts of the United States are to adhere to the consensus of the community of humankind, any remedy they fashion must recognize that this case concerns an act so monstrous as to make its perpetrator an outlaw around the globe....

Plaintiffs claim punitive damages, and the Magistrate recommended they be denied on the ground that they are not recoverable under the Paraguayan Civil Code....

Yet because, as the record establishes, Paraguay will not undertake to prosecute Pena for his acts, the objective of the international law making torture punishable as a crime can only be vindicated by imposing punitive damages....

Moreover, there is some precedent for the award of punitive damages in tort even against a national government. In *I'm Alone* (Canada v. United States), U.N. REP. INT. ARB. AWARDS, vol. 3, at 1609, the American and Canadian claims Commissioners recommended, in addition to compensatory damages, payment of $25,000 by the United States to Canada for intentionally sinking a Canadian ship. In de Letelier v. Republic of Chile, 502 F. Supp. 259, 266, 267 (D.D.C.1980), the court awarded $2,000,000 in punitive damages against the Republic of Chile and various of its employees to the survivors and personal representatives of the former Chilean Ambassador to the United States and a passenger in his car, both killed by the explosion of a bomb. While the court imposed the damages under domestic laws, it mentioned that the "tortious actions" proven were "in violation of international law." *Id*. at 266.

Where the defendant is an individual, the same diplomatic considerations that prompt reluctance to impose punitive damages are not present. The Supreme Court in dicta has recognized that punishment is an appropriate objective under the law of nations, saying in The Marianna Flora, 24 U.S. (11 Wheat.) 1, 41 ... (1826), that "an attack from revenge and malignity, from gross abuse of power, and a settled purpose of mischief ... may be punished by all the penalties which the law of nations can properly administer." ...

This court concludes that it is essential and proper to grant the remedy of punitive damages in order to give effect to the manifest objectives of the international prohibition against torture.

In concluding that the plaintiffs were entitled only to damages recoverable under Paraguayan law, the Magistrate recommended they be awarded $150,000 each as compensation for emotional pain and suffering, loss of companionship and disruption of family life. He also suggested that Dolly Filartiga receive $25,000 for her future medical expenses for treatment of her psychiatric impairment and that Dr. Filartiga receive $50,000 for past expenses related to funeral and medical expenses and to lost income. The Magistrate recommended against an award of punitive damages and of $10,364 in expenses incurred in connection with this action. Plaintiffs object only to these last recommendations....

The record in this case shows that torture and death are bound to recur unless deterred. This court concludes that an award of punitive damages of no less than $5,000,000 to each plaintiff is appropriate to reflect adherence to the world community's proscription of torture and to attempt to deter its practice.

Judgment may be entered for plaintiff Dolly M. E. Filartiga in the amount of $5,175,000 and for plaintiff Joel Filartiga in the amount of $5,210,364, a total judgment of $10,385,364. So ordered.

Notes and Questions

1. In *Filartiga*, both the Second Circuit and the district court paid some attention to Paraguayan law. In view of the fact that the substantive legal standards incorporated by

reference under the ATCA are those under international law, should a court look to foreign domestic law? Near the time of formation of the ATCA, violations of international law were also the focus of attention. *See, e.g., Bolchos v. Darrel*, 3 F. Cas. 810 (D.S.C. 1795); 1 Op. Att'y Gen. 57 (1795); *see also Moxon v. The Fanny*, 17 F. Cas. 942, 943 (D.C.D. Pa. 1793) (No. 9,895); *M'Grath v. Candalero,* 16 F. Cas. 128 (D.C.D.S.C. 1794) (No. 6,810). What dangers might occur if courts looked to foreign law and the foreign state allowed torture, cruel treatment, disappearances of individuals?

2. How was the United Nations Charter utilized in *Filartiga*? How was the Universal Declaration of Human Rights?

When identifying and clarifying actionable human rights, one need only identify rights that are "sufficiently determinable." *See, e.g.,* Alvarez–Machain v. United States, *et al.,* 331 F.3d 604, 612 (9th Cir. 2003) ("sufficient consensus," " 'sufficiently ... defined,' " *quoting* United States v. Smith, 18 U.S. (5 Wheat.) 153, 162 (1820)); *id.,* 266 F.3d 1045 (9th Cir. 2001) (norm need not be specific in human rights instruments); Hilao v. Estate of Marcos (*In re* Estate of Ferdinand Marcos Human Rights Litig.), 25 F.3d at 1475 (" 'definable' "); Tel–Oren v. Libyan Arab Republic, 726 F.2d at 781 (Edwards, J.) ("definable"); Filartiga v. Pena–Irala, 630 F.2d at 880–82 (above); Xuncax v. Gramajo, 886 F. Supp. at 185 ("adequately defined"), 187 ("not necessary that every aspect ... be fully defined"); Forti v. Suarez–Mason, 672 F. Supp. at 1540–42 (below: "definable," "sufficient consensus to evince"); *id.,* 694 F. Supp. at 710–11 (below: "sufficient to establish"); *see also* Kadic v. Karadzic, 70 F.3d at 238 (courts ascertain the evolving content of the law of nations); *cf id.* at 239 ("well-established" norms). *See also* Sosa v. Alvarez–Machain, 542 U.S. 692 (2004) ("courts should require any claim based on the present day law of nations to rest on a norm of international character accepted by the civilized world and defined with a specificity comparable to the features of the 18th-century paradigms" recognized by the Court, which included piracy, acts of hostility or breaches of neutrality, infringements of rights of ambassadors, violations of safe conduct, and war crimes [and how were these defined?], also addressing *United States v. Smith* as a case "illustrating the specificity with which the law of nations defined piracy" and *In re Estate of Marcos*, and stating that the issue is "whether a norm is sufficiently definite to support a cause of action."

Further, as noted in *Filartiga*, 630 F.2d at 881, courts must use international law as it has evolved. *See, e.g.,* Kadic v. Karadzic, 70 F.3d at 238, 241; Amerada Hess Shipping Corp. v. Argentine Republic, 830 F.2d at 425; Tel–Oren v. Libyan Arab Republic, 726 F.2d at 777 (Edwards, J.); Estate of Rodriquez v. Drummond Co., Inc., 256 F. Supp.2d at 1263; Presbyterian Church of Sudan v. Talisman Energy, Inc., 374 F. Supp.2d 331 (S.D.N.Y. 2005), *id.,* 244 F. Supp.2d at 304; Maria v. McElroy, 68 F. Supp. 2d 206, 233 (E.D.N.Y. 1999); Iwanowa v. Ford Motor Co., 67 F. Supp.2d at 445; Jama v. U.S. I.N.S., 22 F. Supp.2d at 362; Doe v. Islamic Salvation Front, 993 F. Supp. at 8; Xuncax v. Gramajo, 886 F. Supp. at 179 n.18; Forti v. Suarez–Mason, 672 F. Supp. at 1539; Paust, *supra*, at 206, 281–82 n.562; H.R. Rep. No. 102–367, at 3–4 (1991), *reprinted in* 4 U.S.C.C.A.N. 86 (1992) ("norms ... may ripen in the future into rules of customary international law").

3. The U.S. and all states in the Americas are bound by the American Declaration of the Rights and Duties of Man, which is now a legally authoritative indicia of human rights protected through Article 3(k) of the O.A.S. Charter, done April 30, 1948, 119 U.N.T.S. 3, 2 U.S.T. 2394, T.I.A.S. No. 2631, amended by the Protocol of Buenos Aires, done 27 Feb. 1967, 21 U.S.T. 607, T.I.A.S. No. 6847 [*see also id.* arts. 44, 111]. *See, e.g.,* Advisory Opinion OC–10/89, Inter–Am. Court H.R., Ser. A, No. 10, para. 45 (1989); Inter–American Comm. on Human Rights, Report on the Situation of the Inhabitants

of the Interior of Ecuador Affected by Development Activities, Chapter VII (1996), O.A.S. Doc. OEA/Ser.L/V/II.96, doc. 10, rev. 1 (April 24, 1997) ("The American Declaration ... continues to serve as a source of international obligation for all member states...."); *see also* American Convention on Human Rights, preamble and art. 29 (d). The U.S. has signed but has not yet ratified the American Convention. In view of Article 18(a) of the Vienna Convention on the Law of Treaties, what is the U.S. obligation with respect to rights protected by the American Convention?

4. Another case not mentioned in *Filartiga* concerning punitive or aggravated damages is *The Apollon*, 22 U.S. (9 Wheat.) 362, 374, 377 (1824) (foreign private plaintiff has standing and can sue the U.S. for a violation of the law of nations by unlawfully seizing a foreign ship in foreign territorial waters and can obtain damages, travel expenses concerning the suit, attorney fees, and "vindictive" or "aggravated" damages).

5. Several of the post-*Filartiga* cases (*infra*) recognized jurisdictional competence in U.S. courts even though there was no nexus with the forum. Under customary international law, all states have jurisdictional competence to provide civil or criminal proceedings with respect to violations of customary international law, if not other violations by treaty. See *Talbot v. Janson*, 3 U.S. (3 Dall.) 133 (1795); *Demjanjuk v. Petrovsky*, 776 F.2d 571 (6th Cir. 1985); Restatement § 404. Also under international law, litigation or prosecution of such claims can occur once the defendant is on U.S. territory. In domestic U.S. law, court's would recognize the existence of "personal jurisdiction" at that point. Personal jurisdiction is possible, for example, if an individual is served process, or arrested, while the person is temporarily within the U.S.

Would universal jurisdiction be a basis for U.S. application of the ATCA in *Filartiga*? Note that the customary international law that provides universal jurisdictional competence is part of the law of the United States. Is such a jurisdictional competence relevant to general federal judicial jurisdiction (under the U.S. Const., Art. III) and federal question jurisdiction (under 28 U.S.C. § 1331)? Recall Section 2 B 1 of this chapter. Several of the cases in this section address additional jurisdictional issues under domestic law (*e.g.*, federal question jurisdiction and subject matter jurisdiction).

6. Concerning universal jurisdiction over customary human rights violations, *see, e.g.*, Beth Stephens, *Translating* Filartiga: *A Comparative and International Law Analysis of Domestic Remedies for International Human Rights Violations*, 27 Yale J. Int'l L. 1, 35, 42, 49–50 (2002); Jordan J. Paust, *Suing Karadzic*, 10 Leiden J. Int'l L. 91, 95–96 (1997); Paust, *Suing Saddam: Private Remedies for War Crimes and Hostage–Taking*, 31 Va. J. Int'l L. 351, 371–74 (1991); and cases that follow.

7. Are leaders liable for more than direct participation in, complicity in, or giving orders to violate international law? What if a leader merely tolerates torture, cruel treatment, or other war crimes or human rights violations by those under the leader's effective control? Consider the extract from *Kadic v. Karadzic*, *infra*, and the international legal precept of leader or command responsibility or dereliction of duty mirrored partly in several cases that follow.

Concerning leader or command responsibility under the knew or should have known test, *see, e.g.*, Jordan J. Paust, M. Cherif Bassiouni, et al., International Criminal Law 91-122 (4 ed. 2013); Ilias Bantekas, *The Contemporary Law of Superior Responsibility*, 93 Am. J. Int'l L. 573 (1999); William Hays Parks, *Command Responsibility for War Crimes*, 62 Mil. L. Rev. 1 (1973); Jordan J. Paust, *My Lai and Vietnam: Norms, Myths and Leader Responsibility*, 57 Mil. L. Rev. 99, 175–85 (1972). The general test includes responsibility for negligence or dereliction of duty if a leader, under the circumstances,

(1) should have known that persons under his or her authority or control had committed, were committing or were about to commit relevant infractions; (2) the leader had an opportunity to act; and (3) the leader took no reasonable corrective action. Article 28(1)(a) of the Rome Statute for the ICC generally reflects this customary test with respect to military leaders, but paragraph (b) sets forth a far more limiting test for civilian leaders prosecutable before the ICC. It changes "should have known" to "or consciously disregarded information which clearly indicated," and thus does not reflect a long and rich history of leader responsibility under the "knew or should have known" test that has been applied to nonmilitary officials, leaders, and persons with actual control.

Forti v. Suarez–Mason, 672 F. Supp. 1531 (N.D. Cal. 1987)

Jensen, J.

This is a civil action brought against a former Argentine general by two Argentine citizens currently residing in the United States. Plaintiffs Forti and Benchoam sue on their own behalf and on behalf of family members, seeking damages from defendant Suarez–Mason for actions which include, *inter alia*, torture, murder, and prolonged arbitrary detention, allegedly committed by military and police personnel under defendant's authority and control. As will be discussed more fully below, plaintiffs predicate federal jurisdiction on 28 U.S.C. §§ 1350 (the "Alien Tort Statute") and 1331. They claim jurisdiction for their various state-law claims under the doctrine of pendent and ancillary jurisdiction....

Plaintiffs' action arises out of events alleged to have occurred in the mid-to late 1970s during Argentina's so-called "dirty war" against suspected subversives. In 1975 the activities of terrorists representing the extremes of both ends of the political spectrum induced the constitutional government of President Peron to declare a "state of siege" under Article 23 of the Argentine Constitution. President Peron also decreed that the Argentine Armed Forces should assume responsibility for suppressing terrorism. The country was accordingly divided into defense zones, each assigned to an army corps. In each zone the military was authorized to detain suspects and hold them in prison or in military installations pursuant to the terms of the "state of siege." Zone One—which included most of the Province of Buenos Aires and encompassed the national capital—was assigned to the First Army Corps. From January 1976 until January 1979 defendant Suarez–Mason was Commander of the First Army Corps.

On March 24, 1976 the commanding officers of the Armed Forces seized the government from President Peron. The ruling military junta continued the "state of siege" and caused the enactment of legislation providing that civilians accused of crimes of subversion would be judged by military law. *See, e.g.*, Law 21.264. In the period from 1976 to 1979, tens of thousands of persons were detained without charges by the military, and it is estimated that more than 12,000 were "disappeared," never to be seen again. *See generally* Nunca Mas: The Report of the Argentine National Commission on the Disappeared (1986).

In January 1984 the constitutionally elected government of President Raul Alfonsin assumed power. The Alfonsin government commenced investigations of alleged human rights abuses by the military, and the criminal prosecution of certain former military authorities followed. The government vested the Supreme Council of the Armed Forces with jurisdiction over the prosecution of military commanders. Summoned by the Supreme Council in March 1984, defendant failed to appear and in fact fled the country. In January of 1987 Suarez–Mason was arrested in Foster City, California pursuant to a provisional arrest warrant at the request of the Republic of Argentina. While defendant was in custody awaiting an extradition hearing he was served with the Complaint herein....

B. Allegations of the Complaint

The Complaint alleges claims for damages based on acts allegedly committed by personnel within the defense zone under General Suarez–Mason's command. According to the Complaint, police and military officials seized plaintiff Alfredo Forti, along with his mother and four brothers, from an airplane at Buenos Aires' Ezeiza International Airport on February 18, 1977. Compl. paras. 3, 10. The entire family was held at the "Pozo de Quilmes" detention center, located in a suburb of Buenos Aires in Buenos Aires Province.... No charges were ever filed against the Fortis. After six days the five sons were released, dropped blindfolded on a street in the capital. The mother, Nelida Azucena Sosa de Forti, was not released, and remains "disappeared" to this day, despite efforts on behalf of the Forti family by the Interamerican Commission on Human Rights and several members of the United States Congress....

When seizing the six members of the Forti family at Ezeiza Airport, the authorities also allegedly seized all of the family's belongings, which included several thousand dollars in cash. To date, only some personal effects have been returned....

An Argentine court which adjudicated criminal liability of the nine former junta members has attributed direct responsibility for the February 18, 1977 seizure of the Forti family to the First Army Corps....

As to plaintiff Debora Benchoam, the Complaint alleges that Benchoam and her brother were abducted from their Buenos Aires bedroom before dawn on July 25, 1977 by military authorities in plain clothes.... At the time Benchoam was sixteen years old and her brother, seventeen.

Benchoam was blindfolded and taken first to an unidentified house and later to a police station in Buenos Aires, where she was held incommunicado for a month.... For the first week of detention Benchoam was kept blindfolded with her hands handcuffed behind her back, and was provided neither food nor clothing. A guard attempted to rape her....

On August 28, 1977, allegedly at the direction of defendant Suarez–Mason, Benchoam was transferred to Devoto Prison in Buenos Aires. Here she was imprisoned, without charge, for more than four years.... In 1979 or 1980 plaintiff obtained a writ of habeas corpus, but the writ was reversed on appeal. Finally, as a result of international and domestic appeals, plaintiff was granted the "right of option" and allowed to leave the country. She was released from prison on November 5, 1981 and came to the United States as a refugee....

The military personnel also abducted plaintiff's seventeen-year-old brother on July 25, 1977.... The brother's body was returned to the Benchoam family the following day. He had died of internal bleeding from bullet wounds, and his face was "severely disfigured" from blows....

Additionally, plaintiff's abductors allegedly stole jewelry, cash, and clothing valued at $20,000, none of which has ever been returned....

Although the individual acts are alleged to have been committed by military and police officials, plaintiffs allege that these actors were all agents, employees, or representatives of defendant acting pursuant to a "policy, pattern and practice" of the First Army Corps under defendant's command. Plaintiffs assert that defendant "held the highest position of authority" in Buenos Aires Province; that defendant was responsible for maintaining the prisons and detention centers there, as well as the conduct of Army officers and agents; and that he "authorized, approved, directed and ratified" the acts complained of....

Plaintiff Forti filed a criminal complaint against defendant and others in November 1983, shortly after the election of President Alfonsin. That complaint has not yet been adjudicated as against Suarez–Mason.... Plaintiff Benchoam has apparently not filed criminal charges against defendant. Although both plaintiffs retain their Argentine citizenship, both reside currently in Virginia.... Plaintiffs predicate federal jurisdiction principally on the "Alien Tort Statute," 28 U.S.C. § 1350, and alternatively on federal question jurisdiction, 28 U.S.C. § 1331. Additionally, they assert jurisdiction for their common-law tort claims under principles of pendent and ancillary jurisdiction....

Based on these above allegations, plaintiffs seek compensatory and punitive damages for violations of customary international law and laws of the United States, Argentina, and California. They press eleven causes of action. Both allege claims for torture; prolonged arbitrary detention without trial; cruel, inhuman and degrading treatment; false imprisonment; assault and battery; intentional infliction of emotional distress; and conversion. Additionally Forti claims damages for "causing the disappearance of individuals," and Benchoam asserts claims for "murder and summary execution," wrongful death, and a survival action.

In response to these allegations, defendant moves to dismiss the entire Complaint under Federal Rule of Civil Procedure 12(b), subsections (1) and (6). He argues that the Court lacks subject matter jurisdiction under 28 U.S.C. § 1350 to adjudicate tort claims arising out of "politically motivated acts of violence in other countries" and, alternatively, that not all of the torts alleged constitute violations of the law of nations. Defendant also argues that adjudication of plaintiffs' claims is barred by the act of state doctrine, which prohibits United States courts from adjudicating the legality of the actions of a foreign government official acting in his official capacity. Further, he contends that plaintiffs' claims are time-barred under the applicable Argentine statute of limitations; that plaintiffs have failed to join indispensable parties, and that plaintiff Benchoam lacks capacity to sue for her brother's death....

Subject Matter Jurisdiction

As a threshold matter, defendant argues that the Court lacks subject matter jurisdiction under 28 U.S.C. § 1350, the "Alien Tort Statute." Defendant urges the Court to follow the interpretation of § 1350 as a purely jurisdictional statute which requires that plaintiffs invoking it establish the existence of an independent, private right of action in international law. Defendant argues that the law of nations provides no tort cause of action for the acts of "politically motivated terrorism" challenged by plaintiffs' Complaint. Alternatively, defendant argues that even if § 1350 provides a cause of action for violations of the law of nations, not all of the torts alleged by plaintiffs qualify as violations of the law of nations. For the reasons set out below, the Court rejects defendant's construction of § 1350 and finds that plaintiffs allege sufficient facts to establish subject matter jurisdiction under both the Alien Tort Statute and 28 U.S.C. § 1331. However, the Court agrees with defendant that not all of the alleged claims constitute "international torts" cognizable under 28 U.S.C. § 1350. Accordingly, the Court dismisses with prejudice the claims for "causing disappearance" and "cruel, inhuman, or degrading treatment." Further, the Court orders plaintiffs to amend the Complaint to state more definitely the facts constituting their claim for official torture.

A. The Alien Tort Statute

The Alien Tort Statute provides that federal district courts shall have "original jurisdiction of any civil action by an alien for a tort only, committed in violation of the law of nations or a treaty of the United States." 28 U.S.C. § 1350 (1982). The district courts' jurisdiction is concurrent with that of state courts. See Act of Sept. 24, 1789 (First Judiciary Act), ch. 20, § 9, 1 Stat. 73, 77. As the cases and commentaries recognize, the history of the Alien Tort Statute is obscure. *See, e.g.,* IIT v. Vencap, Ltd., 519 F.2d 1001, 1015 (2d Cir.1975) (§ 1350 a "kind of legal Lohengrin"). Nonetheless, the proper interpretation of the statute has been discussed at some length in the principal decisions upon which the parties rely: the unanimous decision in Filartiga v. Pena–Irala, 630 F.2d 876 (2d Cir.1980) and the three concurring opinions in Tel–Oren v. Libyan Arab Republic, ... 726 F.2d 774 (D.C.Cir.1984), *cert. denied,* 470 U.S. 1003 ... (1985).

Defendant urges the Court to adopt the reasoning of Judges Bork and Robb in *Tel-Oren, supra,* where the court affirmed the dismissal of a § 1350 tort action against various defendants based on a terrorist attack in Israel by members of the Palestine Liberation Organization. While the three judges concurred in the result, they were unable to agree on the rationale. Judge Bork found that § 1350 constitutes no more than a grant of jurisdiction; that plaintiffs seeking to invoke it must establish a private right of action under either a treaty or the law of nations; and that in the latter category the statute can support jurisdiction at most over only three international crimes recognized in 1789 — violation of safe-conducts, infringement of ambassadorial rights, and piracy. *Tel-Oren, supra,* 726 F.2d at 798–823 (Bork, J., concurring). Judge Robb, on the other hand, found that the dispute involved international political violence and so was "nonjusticiable" within the meaning of the political question doctrine. *Id.* at 823–27 (Robb, Jr., concurring).

The Court is persuaded, however, that the interpretation of § 1350 forwarded by the Second Circuit in *Filartiga, supra,* and largely adopted by Judge Edwards in *Tel-Oren,* is better reasoned and more consistent with principles of international law. There appears to be a growing consensus that § 1350 provides a cause of action for certain "international common law torts." *See, e.g., Filartiga, supra; Tel-Oren, supra* (Edwards, J., concurring); Guinto v. Marcos, 654 F. Supp. 276, 279–80 (S.D.Cal.1986); Von Dardel v. USSR, 623 F. Supp. 246, 256–59 (D.D.C.1985) (finding violation under any of the three *Tel-Oren* approaches); Siderman v. Republic of Argentina, No. CV 82–1772–RMT(MCx) (C.D. Cal. September 28, 1984), *vacated on other grounds.* (C.D. Cal March 7, 1985) (Lexis, Genfed library, Dist. file). It is unnecessary that plaintiffs establish the existence of an independent, express right of action, since the law of nations clearly does not create or define civil actions, and to require such an explicit grant under international law would effectively nullify that portion of the statute which confers jurisdiction over tort suits involving the law of nations. See Tel–Oren, 726 F.2d at 778 (Edwards, J., concurring). Rather, a plaintiff seeking to predicate jurisdiction on the Alien Tort Statute need only plead a "tort ... in violation of the law of nations."

The contours of this requirement have been delineated by the *Filartiga* court and by Judge Edwards in *Tel-Oren.* Plaintiffs must plead a violation of the law of nations as it has evolved and exists in its contemporary form. Filartiga, 630 F.2d at 881; Tel–Oren, 726 F.2d at 777 (Edwards, J., concurring); Amerada Hess Shipping Corp. v. Argentine Republic, 830 F.2d 421, [425] (2d Cir.1987).... This "international tort" must be one which is definable, obligatory (rather than hortatory), and universally condemned. Filartiga, 630 F.2d at 881; *Tel-Oren,* 726 F.2d at 781 (Edwards, J., concurring); Guinto, *supra,* 654 F. Supp. at 279–80; *see also* Blum & Steinhardt, *Federal Jurisdiction over International Human Rights Claims: The Alien Tort Claims Act after* Filartiga v. Pena–Irala, 22

Harv. Int'l L.J. 53, 87–90 (1981) ["Blum & Steinhardt"]; Schneebaum, *The Enforceability of Customary Norms of Public International Law*, 8 Brooklyn J. Int'l L. 189, 301–02 (1982). The requirement of international consensus is of paramount importance, for it is that consensus which evinces the willingness of nations to be bound by the particular legal principle, and so can justify the court's exercise of jurisdiction over the international tort claim.

It is appropriate here to dispose of two arguments advanced by defendant. First, defendant's contention that the law of nations extends only to relations between sovereign states is unsupported. Defendant relies on the Second Circuit's statement in Dreyfus v. Von Finck, 534 F.2d 24, 30–31 (2d Cir.), *cert. denied*, 429 U.S. 835 ... (1976), that the law of nations deals "with the relationship among nations rather than individuals." The Second Circuit has expressly disavowed this dictum, at least insofar as it concerns individual injuries under the international law of human rights. Filartiga, 630 F.2d at 884; *see also* de Sanchez v. Banco Central de Nicaragua, 770 F.2d 1385, 1396 & n. 15 (5th Cir.1985). Second, it is evident that plaintiffs need not establish that every tort claim alleged constitutes an international tort within the meaning of § 1350....

The Court thus interprets 28 U.S.C. § 1350 to provide not merely jurisdiction but a cause of action, with the federal cause of action arising by recognition of certain "international torts" through the vehicle of § 1350. These international torts, violations of current customary international law, are characterized by universal consensus in the international community as to their binding status and their content. That is, they are universal, definable, and obligatory international norms. The Court now examines the allegations of the Complaint to determine whether plaintiffs have stated cognizable international torts for purposes of jurisdiction under § 1350.

B. Analysis Under 28 U.S.C. § 1350

In determining whether plaintiffs have stated cognizable claims under Section 1350, the Court has recourse to "the works of jurists, writing professedly on public law; ... the general usage and practice of nations; [and] judicial decisions recognizing and enforcing that law." United States v. Smith, 18 U.S. (5 Wheat.) 153, 160–61 ... (1820). For purposes of defendant's motion to dismiss, the Court must accept as true all of plaintiffs' allegations, construing them in the light most favorable to plaintiffs.... The Court may grant dismissal only if it is clear that plaintiffs can prove no set of facts which would entitle them to relief....

1. Official Torture

In Count One, plaintiffs both allege torture conducted by military and police personnel under defendant's command. The Court has no doubt that official torture constitutes a cognizable violation of the law of nations under § 1350. This was the very question addressed by the Second Circuit in *Filartiga, supra*. There, after examining numerous sources of international law, see Filartiga, 630 F.2d at 880–84 & n.16, the court concluded that the law of nations contains a "clear and unambiguous" prohibition of official torture. This proscription is universal, obligatory, and definable. Of course, purely private torture will not normally implicate the law of nations, since there is currently no international consensus regarding torture practiced by non-state actors. See Tel–Oren, 726 F.2d at 791–95 (Edwards, J., concurring). Here, however, plaintiffs allege torture by military and police personnel under the supervision and control of defendant while he served as Commander of the First Army Corps. The claim would thus allege torture committed by state officials and so fall within the international tort first recognized in *Filartiga*....

2. Prolonged Arbitrary Detention

In Count Four plaintiffs both allege a claim for prolonged arbitrary detention, stating that defendant "arbitrarily and without justification, cause or privilege, forcibly confined both plaintiff Benchoam and Nelida Azucena Sosa de Forti for a prolonged period." … Elsewhere plaintiffs allege that Benchoam was imprisoned for more than four years without ever being charged, while Forti's mother was arrested in 1977 but was never charged or released.

There is case law finding sufficient consensus to evince a customary international human rights norm against arbitrary detention. Rodriguez Fernandez v. Wilkinson, 505 F. Supp. 787, 795–98 (D.Kan.1980) (citing international treaties, cases, and commentaries), aff'd, 654 F.2d 1382 (10th Cir.1981); see also De Sanchez, supra, 770 F.2d at 1397 (right "not to be arbitrarily detained" incorporated into law of nations); Nguyen Da Yen v. Kissinger, 528 F.2d 1194, 1201 n. 13 (9th Cir.1975) (illegal detention may constitute international tort); but see Jean v. Nelson, 727 F.2d 957, 964 & n. 4 (11th Cir.1984) (disagreed with Rodriguez Fernandez in holding that detention of uninvited aliens under national sovereign's exclusion power is no violation of customary international law), aff'd, 472 U.S. 846 … (1985). The consensus is even clearer in the case of a state's prolonged arbitrary detention of its own citizens. See, e.g., Restatement (Revised) of the Foreign Relations Law of the United States § 702 (Tent. Draft No. 6, 1985) (prolonged arbitrary detention by state constitutes international law violation). The norm is obligatory, and is readily definable in terms of the arbitrary character of the detention. The Court finds that plaintiffs have alleged international tort claims for prolonged arbitrary detention.

3. Summary Execution

The Second Count alleges plaintiff Benchoam's claim for "murder and summary execution." Benchoam alleges that "defendant's torture, murder, beating and cruel, inhuman and degrading treatment of Ruben Benchoam resulted in and proximately caused his death." … In support of this claim, plaintiff cites several international documents which proscribe summary execution. Universal Declaration of Human Rights, art. 3, G.A. Res. 217A, U.N. Doc. A/810 (1948); International Covenant on Civil and Political Rights, art. 6, G.A. Res. 2200, 21 U.N. GAOR Supp. (No. 16), U.N. Doc. A/6316 (1966); American Convention on Human Rights, art. 5, OAS Treaty Series No. 36, OAS Off. Rec. OEA/Ser. 4 v/II 23, Doc. 21, rev. 2 (English ed. 1975). Similarly, murder—where practiced, encouraged, or condoned by a state—is listed among the international law violations to which Judge Edwards looked for guidance in identifying possible violations of the law of nations. See Tel–Oren, 726 F.2d at 781 (quoting Restatement (Revised) of the Foreign Relations Law of the United States § 702 (Tent. Draft No. 3, 1982)); see also Guinto, supra, 654 F. Supp. at 280. Further, the Fifth Circuit has acknowledged the right not to be murdered [by the state] as among the "basic rights" which "have been generally accepted—and hence incorporated into the law of nations." De Sanchez, supra, 770 F.2d at 1397.

The proscription of summary execution or murder by the state appears to be universal, is readily definable, and is of course obligatory. The Court emphasizes that plaintiff's allegations raise no issue as to whether or not the execution was within the lawful exercise of state power; rather, she alleges murder by state officials with neither authorization nor recourse to any process of law. Under these circumstances, the Court finds that plaintiff Benchoam has stated a cognizable claim under § 1350 for the 1977 murder/summary execution of her brother by Argentine military personnel.

4. Causing Disappearance

In Count Three plaintiff Forti alleges a claim for "causing the disappearance" of his mother, in that defendant "arbitrarily and without justification, cause or privilege, abducted Nelida Azucena Sosa de Forti, held her in secret captivity and caused her 'disappearance' to this day."...

Sadly, the practice of "disappearing" individuals—*i.e.*, abduction, secret detention, and torture, followed generally by either secret execution or release—during Argentina's "dirty war" is now well documented in the official report of the Argentine National Commission on the Disappeared, *Nunca Mas*. Nor are such practices necessarily restricted to Argentina. With mounting publicity over the years, such conduct has begun to draw censure as a violation of the basic right to life. Plaintiff cites a 1978 United Nations resolution and a 1980 congressional resolution to this effect. U.N. G.A. Res. /173 (1978); H.R. Con. Res. 285, 96th Cong., 2d Sess. The Court notes, too, that the proposed Restatement of the Law of Foreign Relations lists "the murder or causing the disappearance of individuals," where practiced, encouraged, or condoned by the state, as a violation of international law. Restatement (Revised) of the Foreign Relations Law of the United States, § 702 (Tent. Draft No. 6, 1985). However, plaintiffs do not cite the Court to any case finding that causing the disappearance of an individual constitutes a violation of the law of nations.

Before this Court may adjudicate a tort claim under § 1350, it must be satisfied that the legal standard it is to apply is one with universal acceptance and definition; on no other basis may the Court exercise jurisdiction over a claimed violation of the law of nations. Unfortunately, the Court cannot say, on the basis of the evidence submitted, that there yet exists the requisite degree of international consensus which demonstrates a customary international norm. Even if there were greater evidence of universality, there remain definitional problems. It is not clear precisely what conduct falls within the proposed norm, or how this proscription would differ from that of summary execution. The other torts condemned by the international community and discussed above—official torture, prolonged arbitrary detention, and summary execution—involve two types of conduct by the official actor: (1) taking the individual into custody; and (2) committing a wrongful, tortious act in excess of his authority over that person. In the case of "causing disappearance," only the first of these two actions can be proven—the taking into custody. However, the sole act of taking an individual into custody does not suffice to prove conduct which the international community proscribes. The Court recognizes the very real problems of proof presented by the disappearance of an individual following such custody. Yet there is no apparent international consensus as to the additional elements needed to make out a claim for causing the disappearance of an individual. For instance, plaintiffs have not shown that customary international law creates a presumption of causing disappearance upon a showing of prolonged absence after initial custody.

For these reasons the Court must dismiss Count Four for failure to state a claim upon which relief may be grounded....

5. Cruel, Inhuman and Degrading Treatment

Finally, in Count Five plaintiffs both allege a claim for "cruel, inhuman and degrading treatment" based on the general allegations of the Complaint and consisting specifically of the alleged torture, murder, forcible disappearance and prolonged arbitrary detention....

This claim suffers the same defects as Count Four. Plaintiffs do not cite, and the Court is not aware of, such evidence of universal consensus regarding the right to be free from "cruel, inhuman and degrading treatment as exists, for example, with respect to official torture." Further, any such right poses problems of definability. The difficulties for a district court in adjudicating such a claim are manifest. Because this right lacks readily ascertainable parameters, it is unclear what behavior falls within the proscription—beyond such obvious torts as are already encompassed by the proscriptions of torture, summary execution and prolonged arbitrary detention. Lacking the requisite elements of universality and definability, this proposed tort cannot qualify as a violation of the law of nations. Accordingly, the Court dismisses Count Five of the Complaint for failure to state a claim upon which relief may be granted.

In sum, the Court finds that plaintiffs have stated claims for prolonged arbitrary detention and summary execution. On the other hand, the Court dismisses with prejudice Counts Three ("causing disappearance") and Five ("cruel, inhuman and degrading treatment") for failure to state a claim—*i.e.*, failure to allege a violation of the law of nations cognizable under the Alien Tort Statute. The Court orders plaintiffs to amend Count One; to make a more definite statement of the acts upon which they allege the claim for official torture. It follows from the above statements that this Court has federal subject matter jurisdiction, with respect to both plaintiffs, under 28 U.S.C. § 1350.

C. Federal Question Jurisdiction

Alternatively, plaintiffs predicate jurisdiction on 28 U.S.C. § 1331, the federal question statute. Section 1331 provides that "the district courts shall have jurisdiction of all civil actions arising under the Constitution, laws, or treaties of the United States." This statute provides jurisdiction over claims founded on federal common law....

It has long been settled that federal common law incorporates international law. The Nereide, 13 U.S. (9 Cranch) 388, 423 ... (1815); The Paquete Habana, 175 U.S. 677, 700 ... (1900). More recently, the Supreme Court has held that the interpretation of international law is a federal question. *Sabbatino, supra*, 376 U.S. at 415. Thus, a case presenting claims arising under customary international law arises under the laws of the United States for purposes of federal question jurisdiction. See 13B C. Wright, A. Miller & E. Cooper, Federal Practice and Procedure § 3563, at 60–63 (2d ed. 1984)....

Defendant next argues that the act of state doctrine bars adjudication of plaintiffs' claims....

Here, ... plaintiffs allege acts by a subordinate government official in violation not of economic rights, but of fundamental human rights lying at the very heart of the individual's existence. These are not the public official acts of a head of government, nor is it clear at this stage of the proceedings to what extent defendant's acts were "ratified" by the *de facto* military government. Further, plaintiffs have submitted evidence that the acts, if committed, were illegal even under Argentine law at all relevant times....

Congress did not provide a statute of limitations for claims brought pursuant to 28 U.S.C. § 1350. When a federal statute provides a civil cause of action but includes no express limitations period, courts must generally borrow the most analogous state statute.... However, state statutes of limitations are not to be borrowed blindly....

... Since the Alien Tort Statute is a highly remedial statute, the limitations rule adopted should promote the policy of providing a forum for claims of violations of internationally recognized human rights....

Plaintiffs rely upon principles of equitable tolling of the statute of limitations to raise an issue of fact as to timeliness. Although the limitations period of a claim under the

Alien Tort Statute is governed by state law, because the claim itself is a federal claim, federal equitable tolling doctrines apply....

Forti v. Suarez–Mason, 694 F. Supp. 707 (N.D. Cal. 1988)

Jensen, J.

Plaintiffs subsequently filed this Motion, supported by numerous international legal authorities, as well as affidavits from eight renowned international law scholars. The Court has reviewed these materials and concludes that plaintiffs have met their burden of showing an international consensus as to the status and content of the international tort of "causing disappearance." Accordingly, the motion to reconsider is in this regard and the claim is reinstated. The Court also concludes that plaintiffs have again failed to establish that there is any international consensus as to what conduct falls within the category of "cruel, inhuman or degrading treatment." Absent such consensus as to the content of this alleged tort, it is not cognizable under the Alien Tort Statute. Therefore, the Motion to Reconsider dismissal of this claim is denied.

... The plaintiff's burden in stating a claim is to establish the existence of a "universal, definable, and obligatory international norm[]." ... To meet this burden plaintiffs need not establish unanimity among nations. Rather, they must show a general recognition among states that a specific practice is prohibited. It is with this standard in mind that the Court examines the evidence presented by plaintiffs....

The legal scholars whose declarations have been submitted in connection with this Motion are in agreement that there is universal consensus as to the two essential elements of a claim for "disappearance." In Professor Franck's words:

> The international community has also reached a consensus on the definition of a "disappearance." It has two essential elements: (a) abduction by a state official or by persons acting under state approval or authority; and (b) refusal by the state to acknowledge the abduction and detention.

Franck Declaration, para. 7. See also Falk Declaration, at 3; Henkin Declaration, para. 9; Steiner Declaration, para. 3, 5; Weissbrodt Declaration, para. 8(b); Weston Declaration, para. 5.

Plaintiffs cite numerous international legal authorities which support the assertion that "disappearance" is a universally recognized wrong under the law of nations. For example, United Nations General Assembly Resolution 33/173 recognizes "disappearance" as violative of many of the rights recognized in the Universal Declaration of Human Rights, G.A. Res. 217 A (III), adopted by the United Nations General Assembly, Dec. 10, 1948, U.N. Doc. A/810 (1948) [hereinafter Universal Declaration of Human Rights]. These rights include: (1) the right to life; (2) the right to liberty and security of the person; (3) the right to freedom from torture; (4) the right to freedom from arbitrary arrest and detention; and (5) the right to a fair and public trial. *Id.*, articles 3, 5, 9, 10, 11. See also International Covenant on Political and Civil Rights, G.A. Res. 2200 (XXI), adopted by the United Nations General Assembly, December 16, 1966, U.N. Doc. A/6316 (1966), articles 6, 7, 9, 10, 14, 15, 17.

Other documents support this characterization of "disappearance" as violative of universally recognized human rights. The United States Congress has denounced "prolonged detention without charges and trial" along with other "flagrant denial[s] of the right to life, liberty, or the security of person." 22 U.S.C. § 2304(d)(1). The recently published RESTATEMENT (THIRD) OF THE FOREIGN RELATIONS LAW OF THE UNITED STATES

§ 702 includes "disappearance" as a violation of the international law of human rights. The Organization of American States has also denounced "disappearance" as "an affront to the conscience of the hemisphere and … a crime against humanity." Organization of American States, Inter–American Commission on Human Rights, General Assembly Resolution 666 (November 18, 1983).

Of equal importance, plaintiffs' submissions support their assertion that there is a universally recognized legal definition of what constitutes the tort of "causing disappearance." The Court's earlier order expressed concern that "the sole act of taking an individual into custody does not suffice to prove conduct which the international community proscribes." 672 F. Supp. at 1543. Plaintiffs' submissions on this Motion, however, establish recognition of a second essential element — official refusal to acknowledge that the individual has been taken into custody. For example, the United Nations General Assembly has expressed concern at the:

> difficulties in obtaining reliable information from competent authorities as to the circumstances of such persons, including reports of the persistent refusal of such authorities or organizations to acknowledge that they hold such persons in custody or otherwise to account for them.

U.N. General Assembly Resolution 33/173 (December 20, 1978).

Likewise, the Organization of American States has recognized the importance of this element, commenting on the:

> numerous cases wherein the government systematically denies the detention of individuals, despite the convincing evidence that the claimants provide to verify their allegations that such persons have been detained by police or military authorities and, in some cases, that those persons are, or have been, confined in specified detention centers.

Organization of American States, Inter–American Commission on Human Rights, 1977 Annual Report, at 26. See also M. Berman & R. Clark, *State Terrorism: Disappearances*, 13 Rutgers L.J. 531, 533 (1982) ("The denial of accountability is the factor which makes disappearance unique among human rights violations.").

In the Court's view, the submitted materials are sufficient to establish the existence of a universal and obligatory international proscription of the tort of "causing disappearance." This tort is characterized by the following two essential elements: (1) abduction by state officials or their agents; followed by (2) official refusals to acknowledge the abduction or to disclose the detainee's fate....

In dismissing plaintiffs' earlier "cruel, inhuman or degrading treatment" claim this Court found that the proposed tort lacked "the requisite elements of universality and definability." 672 F. Supp. at 1543. Plaintiffs now submit the aforementioned declarations … and several international legal authorities in support of their argument that "the definition of cruel, inhuman or degrading treatment or punishment is inextricably related to that for torture." … Specifically, plaintiffs argue that the two are properly viewed on a continuum, and that "torture and cruel, inhuman or degrading treatment differ essentially in the degree of ill treatment suffered." *Id.* Thus while the latter treatment is not torture it is an analytically distinct tort which, in plaintiffs' view, is actionable under the Alien Tort Statute.

Plaintiffs emphasize that virtually all international legal authorities which prohibit torture also prohibit cruel, inhuman or degrading treatment. For example, § 702 of the Restatement (Third) of the Foreign Relations Law of the United States: "A state violates international law if, as a matter of state policy, it practices, encourages, or condones ... torture or other cruel, inhuman or degrading treatment or punishment." Likewise, 22 U.S.C. §2304(d)(1) lists "torture or cruel, inhuman or degrading treatment or punishment," among "gross violations of internationally recognized human rights." Article 5 of the Universal Declaration of Human Rights, *supra*, states that "no one shall be subjected to torture or to cruel, inhuman or degrading treatment." See also de Sanchez v. Banco Central De Nicaragua, 770 F.2d 1385, 1397 (5th Cir.1985) (recognizing "right not to be ... tortured, or otherwise subjected to cruel, inhuman or degrading treatment").

While these and other materials establish a recognized proscription of "cruel, inhuman or degrading treatment," they offer no guidance as to what constitutes such treatment. The RESTATEMENT does not define the term. The cited statute (22 U.S.C. §2304) and the Universal Declaration of Human Rights also both fail to offer a definition. The scholars whose declarations have been submitted likewise decline to offer any definition of the proposed tort. In fact, one of the declarations appears to concede the lack of a universally recognized definition. See Lillich Declaration, at 8 ("only the contours of the prohibition, not its existence as a norm of customary international law, are the subject of legitimate debate.").

... Absent some definition of what constitutes "cruel, inhuman or degrading treatment" this Court has no way of determining what alleged treatment is actionable, and what is not.

Plaintiffs cite The Greek Case, 12 T.B. Eur. Conv. on Human Rights 186 (1969), for a definition of "degrading treatment" as that which "grossly humiliates [the victim] before others or drives him to act against his will or conscience." ... But this definitional gloss is of no help. From our necessarily global perspective, conduct, particularly verbal conduct, which is humiliating or even grossly humiliating in one cultural context is of no moment in another. An international tort which appears and disappears as one travels around the world is clearly lacking in that level of common understanding necessary to create universal consensus. Likewise, the term "against his will or conscience" is too abstract to be of help. For example, a pacifist who is conscripted to serve in his country's military has arguably been forced to act "against his will or conscience." Would he thus have a claim for degrading treatment?

To be actionable under the Alien Tort Statute the proposed tort must be characterized by universal consensus in the international community as to its binding status *and its content*. In short, it must be a "universal, *definable*, and obligatory international norm[]." Forti, 672 F. Supp. at 1541 (emphasis added)....

Notes and Questions

1. Concerning lists of *jus cogens* norms, *see, e.g.*, Chapter 1, Section 1 F 3. *Compare*, for example, Section 702 of the U.S. RESTATEMENT and the Human Rights Committee's General Comment No. 24 *with* the opinions in *Forti I* and *Forti II*. Why was the RESTATEMENT not persuasive to the district judge? What was quite persuasive with respect to a definition of "disappearance"?

In its Memorial before the International Court of Justice in Case Concerning United States Diplomatic and Consular Staff in Tehran (United States v. Iran), 1980 I.C.J. Pleadings, the Executive Branch recognized that the following articles, among others, in the Universal Declaration of Human Rights reflect human rights guaranteed under customary international law: Articles 3, 5, 7, 9, 12, 13. Should these human rights be considered to provide needed specificity for judicial protection? What other rights recognized in the Universal Declaration provide sufficient normative content? Congress has also recognized that gross violations of human rights include: "torture or cruel, inhumane, or degrading treatment or punishment, prolonged arbitrary detention without charges, or other flagrant denial to life, liberty, and the security of person" as well as disappearances or secret detention. See 22 U.S.C. § 262 d(a).

2. Violations of international law actionable under the ATCA have not been limited to norms *jus cogens* and such a limit would be contrary to the clear language of the ATCA. For cases and Executive opinions addressing non-*jus cogens* violations, *see, e.g., Alvarez–Machain v. United States*, 331 F.3d 604 (9th Cir. 2003) (not limited to *jus cogens*, "guided by the language of the statute, not an imported restriction"); *id.*, 266 F.3d 1045 (9th Cir. 2001) ("never held that a *jus cogens* violation is required"); *Wiwa v. Royal Dutch Petroleum Co.*, 226 F.3d 88 (2d Cir. 2000), *cert. denied*, 532 U.S. 941 (2001) (imprisonment, among other violations); *Weisshaus v. Swiss Bankers Ass'n*, 225 F.3d 191 (2d Cir. 2000) (re: war crimes, among other violations); *Kadic v. Karadzic*, 70 F.3d at 242–43 (war crimes); *Nguyen da Yen v. Kissinger*, 528 F.2d 1194, 1201–02 n.13 (9th Cir. 1975); *Doe v. Islamic Salvation Front*, 993 F. Supp. 3, 5, 7–8 (D.D.C. 1998) (claims re: war crimes, hijacking, mutilation, among others); *Adra v. Clift*, 195 F. Supp. 857 (D. Md. 1961); *Bolchos v. Darrel*, 3 F. Cas. 810 (D.S.C. 1795); 26 Op. Att'y Gen. 250 (1907); 1 Op. Att'y Gen. 57 (1795); *see also M'Grath v. Candalero*, 16 F. Cas. at 128; *but see Doe v. Unocal*, 110 F. Supp.2d 1294, 1304 (C.D. Cal. 2000), settled (2005). The ATCA contains no list or limitations of applicable customary international law or treaties of the U.S. and expressly applies to "any" civil action for a tort in violation of such international law. For the judiciary to add limits that Congress has not chosen would be to rewrite the clear language of a long-standing federal statute and to violate the separation of powers. Further, at the time of formation of the ATCA the notion of a complete enumeration or short list of human rights would have been anathema to the Founders. *See, e.g.*, PAUST, *supra* at 174–75, 221 n.90, 330–32, 349–50 ns.45, 50. The same would have been true more generally with respect to the law of nations. *See, e.g., id.* at 8, 48–50 ns.60–88; Resolution of the Continental Congress (1781), *supra*. Still today, the general statute incorporating the laws of war by reference as offenses against the law of the United States does not attempt to list the numerous war crimes proscribed by international law. See 10 U.S.C. §§ 818, 821. These points are of importance after the Court's 2004 decision in *Sosa v. Alvarez–Machain*, addressed *infra*, since the majority opinion is clearly interested in what actionable violations of international law would have been evident to the Founders and early judiciary and the Court will also allow certain more modern claims.

3. Concerning recognized crimes against humanity, see also those listed in various instruments in the Documents Section (*e.g.*, The Charters of the I.M.T. at Nuremberg and the I.M.T. for the Far East) and the 1919 Report of the Responsibilities Commission (regarding offenses against the laws of humanity). Are "inhumane acts" covered? Are "persecution," torture, and rape covered? The crimes against humanity within the jurisdiction of the International Criminal Court (ICC) are quite limited, especially by phrases such as "widespread or systematic," "with knowledge of the attack," and "persecution against any identifiable group or collectivity." *See* Statute of the ICC, art. 7, in the Documents Section. Concerning secret detentions or disappearances as a crime against humanity, see also the International Convention for the Protection of All Persons From Enforced Disappearance, preamble; Inter–American Convention on the Forced Disappearance of Persons, preamble; Jordan J. Paust, *Post–9/11 Overreaction and Fallacies Regarding War and Defense, Guantanamo, the Status of Persons, Treatment, Judicial Review of Detention, and Due Process in Military Commissions*, 79 NOTRE DAME L. REV. 1335, 1352–56 (2004).

4. Is "universal consensus" required with respect to the content of customary international law? or treaty-based international law? See Chapter 1.

5. As stated in *Forti I*, is it true that "the law of nations clearly does not create or define civil actions"? *See, e.g.*, the Universal Declaration of Human Rights, art. 8; International Covenant on Civil and Political Rights, arts. 2, 14, and H.R. Comm., General Comments Nos. 7, 13, 15, 20, 24; Convention Against Torture, art. 14; Torture and Other Cruel, Inhuman or Degrading Treatment or Punishment, U.N. G.A. Res. 62/148, para. 13 (18 Dec. 2007); Basic Principles and Guidelines on the Right to a Remedy and Reparations for Victims of Gross Violations of International Human Rights and Serious Violations of International Humanitarian Law (2005); Paust, International Law as Law of the United States 224–29 (2 ed 2003).

Paul v. Avril, 812 F. Supp. 207 (S.D. Fla. 1993)

Palermo, Magistrate J.

This case involves an action by six (6) Haitians, Evans Paul, Jean–Auguste Mesyeux, Marino Etienne, Gerald Emile "Aby" Brun, Serge Gilles and Fernand Gerard Laforest. All six (6) Plaintiffs were citizens and residents of Haiti when this action was filed. The Plaintiffs seek compensatory and punitive damages against Defendant, Lieutenant General Prosper Avril (Avril), the former head of the Haitian military, for alleged "torture[,] cruel, inhuman or degrading treatment; arbitrary arrest and detention without trial; and other violations of customary international law." ... Since March 12, 1990, and at the time the Complaint was filed, Avril resided within the jurisdiction of the United States District Court for the Southern District of Florida. These acts allegedly all took place in Haiti.

The Complaint spans some twenty (20) pages delineating the acts committed upon Plaintiffs by soldiers and individuals allegedly acting under and with the "order, approval, instigation, and knowledge of Defendant Avril." ... These include acts such as severe beatings, being dragged up flights of stairs, having lit cigarettes inserted in the nostrils, being put in contortionistic positions while beaten with particular attention being paid to the skull and groin, refusal to administer medical treatment, being paraded on national television and falsely accused of being involved in an assassination plot, deliberate starvation and other equally indescribable acts of unmerciful treatment.... None of the acts enunciated are alleged to have been committed by Avril himself. The brutality of the acts committed is uncontroverted and undisputed.

The Complaint contains six (6) claims for relief: Torture; Arbitrary Detention; Cruel, Inhuman and Degrading Treatment; False Imprisonment; Assault and Battery; and Intentional Infliction of Emotional Distress. The Complaint prays for damages in excess of three million (3,000,000) dollars for each Plaintiff individually, and at least ten million (10,000,000) in punitive damages collectively....

The Defendant now moves to dismiss the complaint primarily relying on five (5) theories. First, that the Foreign Sovereign Immunities Act, 28 U.S.C. § 1602 *et seq.*, prohibits judicial consideration of the suit against Avril. Second, that Avril is immune from the jurisdiction of this court under the doctrine of Head of State Immunity. Third, Defendant argues there is no subject matter jurisdiction under 28 U.S.C. § 1350 as predicated by Plaintiffs. Fourth, Plaintiffs have not stated a justiciable cause of action under 28 U.S.C. §§ 1350–1351, and fifth, under the Act of State and Political Question doctrine this suit is nonjusticiable....

As stated, Defendant first contends that Avril is covered by the Foreign Sovereign Immunities Act ... and therefore this suit cannot be maintained. This argument is unconvincing for several reasons....

Plaintiffs do not argue the application of the FSIA exceptions, instead they argue the FSIA itself does not apply in three ways. First, they argue the FSIA offers no protection to individuals. Second, they claim that even if it does, Avril is not provided with immunity under the Act for acts that are outside of the scope of his authority. Last, Plaintiffs argue that any possible immunity has bean waived by the Haitian government.

The Government of Haiti, on April 9, 1991, waived any and all immunity enjoyed by Prosper Avril....

Defendant next argues that he is immune from the jurisdictional arm of this court under the Head of State doctrine. This argument must also fail....

... The waiver of immunity by the Haitian government is complete and also affects his residual head of state immunity. See *In Re* Doe, 860 F.2d at 46.

Defendant's third argument asserts there is no subject matter jurisdiction under the Alien Tort Statute, 28 U.S.C. § 1350, the statute Plaintiffs bring this action under. Defendant reasons that § 1350 is not applicable "to suits between aliens for actions arising outside the United States." ... The undersigned finds that contrary to Defendant's conclusions, there is subject matter under the statute.

Specifically, 28 U.S.C. § 1350 ... requires that jurisdiction be limited to cases: 1) involving aliens; 2) with a tort only; and 3) committed in violation of the law of nations or a treaty of the United States.... [the court addressed several cases] Additionally, these cases all involved torts, in violation of the laws of nations which occurred outside of the U.S.

Defendant's fourth argument centers around the theory that 28 U.S.C. § 1350 does not provide a cause of action, but merely provides a jurisdictional gateway to the court. The plain language of the statute and the use of the words "committed in violation" strongly implies that a well pled tort if committed in violation of the law of nations, would be sufficient. There are cases that hold 28 U.S.C. § 1350 as providing both a jurisdictional basis and a right of action. See Forti, 672 F. Supp. at 1540; Filartiga, 630 F. Supp. at 887; Handel v. Artukovic, 601 F. Supp. 1421, 1426–27 (C.D.Cal.1985) ("thus, while the 'violation' language of section 1350 may be interpreted as explicitly granting a cause of action, the 'arising under' language of section 1351 cannot be so interpreted"); Tel–Oren v. Libyan Arab Republic, 233 U.S. App. D.C. 384, 726 F.2d 774, 777–780 (D.C.Cir.1984) (Edwards, J., concurring) (plaintiffs, mostly Israeli citizens brought action against defendants, various Arab organizations under the law of nations and treaties of the United States for deaths occurring in a bus in Israel), *cert. denied*, 470 U.S. 1003 ... (1985).

Moreover, even if this were not the case, it is clear 28 U.S.C. § 1350 authorizes remedies for aliens suing for torts committed in violation of the law of nations. See Filartiga, 630 F.2d at 888; Jaffe v. Boyles, 616 F. Supp. 1371, 1379 (W.D.N.Y.1985) (recognized premise of Filartiga); Jones v. Petty Ray Geophysical Geosource, Inc., 722 F. Supp. 343, 348 (S.D.Tex.1989) (dismissed where plaintiff did not allege either alien status or tort committed in violation of the law of nations).

Last in this regard, Plaintiffs' causes of action sounding in False Imprisonment, Assault and Battery and Intentional Infliction of Emotional Distress under Florida law are cognizable at this stage of the proceedings under principles of pendant and ancillary jurisdiction. See Forti, 672 F. Supp. at 1540.

Defendant's fifth and final argument, that this suit is foreclosed because of the act of state and political question doctrines is completely devoid of merit. The acts as alleged in the complaint, if true would hardly qualify as official public acts. W.S. Kirkpatrick &

Co. v. Environmental Tectonics Corp., 493 U.S. 400, 403 ... (1990); Banco Nacional de Cuba v. Sabbatino, 376 U.S. 398, 428 ... (1964). Further, if the argument asserted by Defendant were true, and the federal courts would refuse to handle cases such as this one because the standards would be difficult to discern, discovery would be arduous to acquire, and the witnesses would have to travel substantial distances, cases such as *Forti, Siderman, Filartiga,* and Jimenez v. Aristeguieta, 311 F.2d 547, 557 (5th Cir.1962) (act of state doctrine applicable only where acts involved are official acts of state), would never have been adjudicated. Defendant has not distinguished this case from those precedents. The same is true with regard to Defendants' assertion of the political question doctrine. This case presents clearly justiciable legal issues as illustrated herein.

Question

1. Was the district court opinion in *Paul v. Avril* correct concerning the nature of defendants that are suable under the ATCA?

Xuncax v. Gramajo, 886 F. Supp. 162 (D. Mass. 1995)

Woodlock, J.

The plaintiffs allege that the defendant Gramajo, as Vice Chief of Staff and director of the Army General Staff [of Guatamala] from March of 1982 through 1983, as commander from July through December of 1982 of the military zone in which the plaintiffs resided, and as Minister of Defense from 1987 through 1990, was personally responsible for ordering and directing the implementation of the program of persecution and oppression that resulted in the terrors visited upon the plaintiffs and their families.... I find their allegations supported by the record. I also find that Gramajo may be held liable for the acts of members of the military forces under his command.

In Application of Yamashita, 327 U.S. 1 ... (1946), the commander of Japanese armed forces in the Philippine Islands during World War II was held responsible for numerous acts of atrocity committed by servicemembers under his command. The allegations contained in the prosecution's Bill of Particulars against Yamashita are eerily parallel to those made here:

> "a deliberate plan and purpose to massacre and exterminate a large part of the civilian population of Batangas Province, and to devastate and destroy public, private and religious property therein, as a result of which more than 25,000 men, women and children, all unarmed noncombatant civilians, were brutally mistreated and killed, without cause or trial, and entire settlements were devastated and destroyed wantonly and without military necessity."

372 U.S. at 14. The Court upheld Yamashita's conviction by a United States military tribunal, explaining:

> It is not denied that such acts directed against the civilian population of an occupied country and against prisoners of war are recognized in international law as violations of the law of war. But it is argued that the charge does not allege that petitioner has either committed or directed the commission of such acts, and consequently that no violation is charged as against him. But this overlooks the fact that the gist of the charge is an unlawful breach of duty by petitioner as an army commander to control the operations of the members of his command by "permitting them to commit" the extensive and widespread atrocities specified....

It is evident that the conduct of military operations by troops whose excesses are unrestrained by the orders or efforts of their commander would almost certainly result in violations which it is the purpose of the law of war to prevent.... Hence the law of war presupposes that its violation is to be avoided through the control of the operations of war by commanders who are to some extent responsible for their subordinates.

327 U.S. at 14–15 (citation to [1907] Hague Convention omitted).

In Forti v. Suarez–Mason, 672 F. Supp. 1531 (N.D. Cal.1987), the court held an Argentine General responsible for acts of brutality committed by military personnel in the defense zone under his command. The court explained:

Although the individual acts are alleged to have been committed by military and police officials, plaintiffs allege that these actors were all agents, employees, or representatives of defendant acting pursuant to a "policy, pattern and practice" of the First Army Corps under defendant's command. Plaintiffs assert that the defendant "held the highest position of authority" in Buenos Aires Province; that defendant was responsible for maintaining the prisons and detention centers there, as well as the conduct of Army officers and agents; and that he "authorized, approved, directed and ratified" the acts complained of.

672 F. Supp. at 1537–38 (citation omitted).

In enacting the Torture Victim Protection Act of 1991, Congress apparently endorsed this approach. As the Senate Committee Report explained:

The legislation is limited to lawsuits against persons who ordered, abetted, or assisted in the torture. It will not permit a lawsuit against a former leader of a country merely because an isolated act of torture occurred somewhere in that country. However, a higher official need not have personally performed or ordered the abuses in order to be held liable. Under international law, responsibility for torture, summary execution, or disappearances extends beyond the person or persons who actually committed those acts—anyone with higher authority who authorized, tolerated or knowingly ignored those acts is liable for them.

S. Rep. No. 249, 102d Cong., 1st Sess. 9 (1991) (footnote omitted). The Senate Committee Report used *Yamashita* and *Forti I* to illustrate this principal of "command responsibility:"

... although Suarez Mason was not accused of directly torturing or murdering anyone, he was found civilly liable for those acts which were committed by officers under his command about which he was aware and which he did nothing to prevent.

Similarly, in *In re Yamashita*, the Supreme Court held a general of the Imperial Japanese Army responsible for a pervasive pattern of war crimes committed by his officers when he knew or should have known that they were going on but failed to prevent or punish them. Such "command responsibility" is shown by evidence of a pervasive pattern and practice of torture, summary execution or disappearances. n3.

Id. (citation and one footnote omitted) (footnote in original).

In this case, plaintiffs have convincingly demonstrated that, at a minimum, Gramajo was aware of and supported widespread acts of brutality committed by personnel under his command resulting in thousands of civilian deaths.... Gramajo refused to act to prevent such atrocities. When publicly confronted with the murder of innocent civilians by soldiers under his command, Gramajo "did not deny the stated facts. He instead replied that he saw his actions as appropriate and involving the use of 'flexible' and 'humanitarian' tactics." ... In the face of public outcry, "the massacres continued and indeed got worse." ...

Indeed, the evidence suggests that Gramajo devised and directed the implementation of an indiscriminate campaign of terror against civilians such as plaintiffs and their relatives....

Upon review of the evidence adduced in support of default judgment, I find that the acts which form the basis of these actions exceed anything that might be considered to have been lawfully within the scope of Gramajo's official authority. Accordingly, I conclude that the defendant is not entitled to immunity under the FSIA, even if that statute were construed to apply to individuals acting in their official capacity. *Cf.* Letelier v. Republic of Chile, 488 F. Supp. 665, 673 (D.D.C.1980) (assassination is "clearly contrary to the precepts of humanity as recognized in both national and international law" and so cannot be part of official's "discretionary" authority), *cert. denied*, 471 U.S. 1125 ... (1985)....

... I conclude that retroactive application of the TVPA as the law in effect at the time of decision is entirely proper in this case.

Given retroactive application of the TVPA, federal statutory law clearly creates the cause of action upon which plaintiff Ortiz's lawsuit is founded. The case thus "arises under" the laws of the United States for purposes of federal question jurisdiction under 28 U.S.C. § 1331. *See, e.g.*, Merrell Dow Pharmaceuticals Inc. v. Thompson, 478 U.S. 804, 808 ... (1986) (*quoting* Franchise Tax Board v. Construction Laborers Vacation Trust, 463 U.S. 1, 8–9 ... (1983)). This Court therefore has subject matter jurisdiction to hear plaintiff Ortiz's TVPA claims....

Judicial opinions that have had occasion to impart meaning to § 1350 have not reached a consensus regarding the statute's import. A majority of courts, interpreting the statute broadly, have held that if an alien plaintiff can establish that the abuses allegedly inflicted upon her constitute violations of international law, § 1350 grants both a federal private cause of action as well as a federal forum in which to assert the claim. *See, e.g.*, Marcos Estate II, 25 F.3d at 1475 (9th Cir. 1994) (§ 1350 "creates a cause of action for violations of specific, universal and obligatory human rights standards,"); Amerada Hess Shipping Corp. v. Argentine Republic, 830 F.2d 421, 424–25 (2d Cir.1987), *rev'd on other grounds*, 488 U.S. 428 ... (1989); Filartiga v. Pena–Irala, 630 F.2d 876, 887 (2d Cir.1980); Paul v. Avril, 812 F. Supp. 207, 212 (S.D. Fla.1993); Forti v. Suarez–Mason, 672 F. Supp. 1531, 1539 (N.D.Cal.1987), on reconsideration on other grounds, 694 F. Supp. 707 (N.D. Cal.1988). The Ninth Circuit has concluded that § 1350 plaintiffs may look to municipal law as a source of substantive law. See Marcos Estate I, 978 F.2d at 503 (9th Cir. 1992), *cert. denied*, 113 S.Ct. 2960 (1993). See also Marcos Estate II, 25 F.3d at 1476 n.10. Judges of the District of Columbia Circuit, meanwhile, via separate concurrences, have at length and in a considered fashion propounded alternative views. See Tel–Oren v. Libyan Arab Republic, ... 726 F.2d 774 (D.C. Cir.1984); *id.* at 798 *et seq.* (Bork, J., concurring) (independent cause of action must be created by federal statute or international law itself, § 1350 inadequate to do so), *cert. denied*, 470 U.S. 1003 ... (1985), *id.* at 775, *et seq.* (Edwards, J., concurring) (suggesting domestic tort law may provide substantive cause of action under § 1350). After extended reflection, I find that § 1350 yields both a jurisdictional grant and a private right to sue for tortious violations of international law (or a treaty of the United States), without recourse to other law as a source of the cause of action.

a. The *Filartiga* Approach

In *Filartiga*, the wellspring of modern § 1350 case law, the Second Circuit first determined that the acts of torture there at issue violated international law. *Id.* at 882–84 n.18. The court then concluded that international law forms an integral part of the common law of the United States and that, accordingly, "federal jurisdiction over cases involving international law is clear." *Id.* at 887. In reaching this point, the Filartiga court flatly rejected the argument that, under the Constitution's grant of power to Congress to "define and punish ... offenses against the law of nations," Art. I, sec. 8, cl. 10, international law fell within federal common law "only to the extent that Congress has acted to define it," citing "numerous decisions applying rules of international law uncodified in any act of Congress." *Id.* at 886 (citations omitted). The court similarly rejected the notion that § 1350 itself was but a grant by Congress to the federal judiciary to define what constitutes a violation of international law....

2. *Xuncax Plaintiffs' Claims of Violations of International Law*

a. Peremptory Norms of International Law

As the Ninth Circuit has noted, "for a court to determine whether a plaintiff has a claim for a tort committed in violation of international law, it must [first] decide whether there is an applicable norm of international law ... and [then] whether it was violated in the particular case." Marcos Estate I, 978 F.2d at 502. In reaching such a decision, courts are guided by "the usage of nations, judicial opinions and the works of jurists" as "the sources from which customary international law is derived." Filartiga, 630 F.2d at 884. For further guidance regarding the "norms" of international law, courts and international law scholars look to whether the standard can be said to be "universal, definable and obligatory." Forti I, 672 F. Supp. at 1540. These qualifications essentially require that 1) no state condone the act in question and there is a recognizable "universal" consensus of prohibition against it; 2) there are sufficient criteria to determine whether a given action amounts to the prohibited act and thus violates the norm; 3) the prohibition against it is non-derogable and therefore binding at all times upon all actors. *See generally* Forti I, 672 F. Supp. at 1539–40; Aff. of Int'l Law Scholars, Ortiz Ex. M; Restatement (Third) of Foreign Relations Law §§ 701–02.

The Xuncax plaintiffs allege five violations of international law:

(1) Summary execution: Xuncax, for her husband's death, Doe, for his father's death, and Pedro–Pascual, for her sister's death;

(2) Disappearance: Callejas, based on his father's disappearance;

(3) Torture: Xuncax, for her husband, Doe, for his father, and Diego–Francisco, for himself and his wife;

(4) Arbitrary detention: Xuncax, for her husband, Doe, for his father, and Diego–Francisco, for himself and his wife;

(5) Cruel, inhuman and degrading treatment: Xuncax, Diego–Francisco, Doe, Pedro–Pascual, Francisco–Marcos, Manuel–Mendez, the Ruiz–Gomez brothers, and Callejas.

I am satisfied that four of these claims—torture, summary execution, disappearance, and arbitrary detention—constitute fully recognized violations of international law....

It is not necessary that every aspect of what might comprise a standard such as "cruel, inhuman or degrading treatment" be fully defined and universally agreed upon before a given action meriting the label is clearly proscribed under international law, any more than it is necessary to define all acts that may constitute "torture" or "arbitrary detention" in order to recognize certain conduct as actionable misconduct under that rubric. Accordingly, any act by the defendant which is proscribed by the Constitution of the United States and by a cognizable principle of international law plainly falls within the rubric of "cruel, inhuman or degrading treatment" and is actionable before this Court under § 1350.

Plaintiffs' contend that defendant is responsible for "cruel, inhuman or degrading treatment" because the actions taken at his direction "had the intent and the effect of grossly humiliating and debasing the plaintiffs, forcing them to act against their will and conscience, inciting fear and anguish, breaking physical or moral resistance, and/or forcing them to leave their homes and country and flee into exile[.]" (Xuncax Complaint p. 76.) This general allegation may be divided into two categories.

The first category includes acts by soldiers under defendant's command that caused a plaintiff to: (1) witness the torture (Xuncax and Doe) or severe mistreatment (Diego–Francisco) of an immediate relative; (2) watch soldiers ransack their home and threaten their family (Xuncax and Francisco–Marcos); (3) be bombed from the air (the Ruiz–Gomez brothers); or (4) have a grenade thrown at them (Callejas). I have no difficulty concluding that acts in this category constitute "cruel, inhuman or degrading treatment" in violation of international law. *See generally* The Greek Case, Y.B. Eur. Conv. on H.R. 186, 461–65 (1969) (describing cases where political detainees were subjected to acts of intimidation, humiliation, threats of reprisal against relatives, presence at torture of another, and interference with family life in violation of Article 3 of the European Convention on the Protection of Human Rights and Fundamental Freedom).

The second category consists of the claim that, as a consequence of Gramajo's acts, plaintiffs "were placed in great fear for their lives ... and were forced to leave their homes and country and flee into exile." Although I find that all plaintiffs have made such a showing, I do not agree that this showing independently constitutes "cruel, inhuman and degrading treatment" in violation of the law of nations and actionable under § 1350....

[the court awarded significant compensatory and punitive damages]

Notes and Questions

1. There were several errors in the full opinion in *Xuncax*. Can you spot any in the extract above? For a norm to be established under customary international law, is it necessary that "no state condone the act in question and there is a recognizable 'universal' consensus of prohibition against it"? Further, must every violation of customary international law, or treaty-based international law, implicate a "non-derogable" prohibition "binding at all times upon all actors"? Does even the Restatement require this?

2. Should U.S. standards as to what is "cruel" determine the content of applicable international law incorporated by reference in the ATCA? What exactly did the district court state in *Xuncax*?

Kadic v. Karadzic, 70 F.3d 232 (2d Cir. 1995), *cert. denied*, 518 U.S. 1005 (1996)

Newman, J.

Background

The plaintiffs-appellants are Croat and Muslim citizens of the internationally recognized nation of Bosnia-Herzegovina, formerly a republic of Yugoslavia. Their complaints, which we accept as true for purposes of this appeal, allege that they are victims, and representatives of victims, of various atrocities, including brutal acts of rape, forced prostitution, forced impregnation, torture, and summary execution, carried out by Bosnian-Serb military forces as part of a genocidal campaign conducted in the course of the Bosnian civil war. Karadzic, formerly a citizen of Yugoslavia and now a citizen of Bosnia-Herzegovina, is the President of a three-man presidency of the self-proclaimed Bosnian-Serb republic within Bosnia-Herzegovina, sometimes referred to as "Srpska," which claims to exercise lawful authority, and does in fact exercise actual control, over large parts of the territory of Bosnia-Herzegovina. In his capacity as President, Karadzic possesses ultimate command authority over the Bosnian-Serb military forces, and the injuries perpetrated upon plaintiffs were committed as part of a pattern of systematic human rights violations that was directed by Karadzic and carried out by the military forces under his command. The complaints allege that Karadzic acted in an official capacity either as the titular head of Srpska or in collaboration with the government of the recognized nation of the former Yugoslavia and its dominant constituent republic, Serbia.

The two groups of plaintiffs asserted causes of action for genocide, rape, forced prostitution and impregnation, torture and other cruel, inhuman, and degrading treatment, assault and battery, sex and ethnic inequality, summary execution, and wrongful death. They sought compensatory and punitive damages, attorney's fees, and, in one of the cases, injunctive relief. Plaintiffs grounded subject-matter jurisdiction in the Alien Tort Act, the Torture Victim Protection Act of 1991 ("Torture Victim Act"), Pub. L. No. 102-256, 106 Stat. 73 (1992), codified at 28 U.S.C. § 1350 note (Supp. V 1993), the general federal-question jurisdictional statute, 28 U.S.C. § 1331 (1988), and principles of supplemental jurisdiction, 28 U.S.C. § 1367 (Supp. V 1993)....

Karadzic contends that appellants have not alleged violations of the norms of international law because such norms bind only states and persons acting under color of a state's law, not private individuals. In making this contention, Karadzic advances the contradictory positions that he is not a state actor..., even as he asserts that he is the President of the self-proclaimed Republic of Srpska.... For their part, the Kadic appellants also take somewhat inconsistent positions in pleading defendant's role as President of Srpska..., and also contending that "Karadzic is not an official of any government."...

Judge Leisure accepted Karadzic's contention that "acts committed by non-state actors do not violate the law of nations," Doe, 866 F. Supp. at 739, and considered him to be a non-state actor. The Judge appears to have deemed state action required primarily on the basis of cases determining the need for state action as to claims of official torture, *see, e.g.,* Carmichael v. United Technologies Corp., 835 F.2d 109 (5th Cir. 1988), without consideration of the substantial body of law, discussed below, that renders private individuals liable for some international law violations.

We do not agree that the law of nations, as understood in the modern era, confines its reach to state action. Instead, we hold that certain forms of conduct violate the law of nations whether undertaken by those acting under the auspices of a state or only as private individuals. An early example of the application of the law of nations to the acts of private individuals is the prohibition against piracy. See United States v. Smith, 18 U.S. (5 Wheat.) 153, 161 ... (1820); United States v. Furlong, 18 U.S. (5 Wheat.) 184, 196-97 ... (1820). In The Brig Malek Adhel, 43 U.S. (2 How.) 210, 232 ... (1844), the

Supreme Court observed that pirates were "hostis humani generis" (an enemy of all mankind) in part because they acted "without … any pretense of public authority." *See generally* 4 WILLIAM BLACKSTONE, COMMENTARIES ON THE LAWS OF ENGLAND 68 (facsimile of 1st ed. 1765-1769, Univ. of Chi. ed., 1979). Later examples are prohibitions against the slave trade and certain war crimes. See M. CHERIF BASSIOUNI, CRIMES AGAINST HUMANITY IN INTERNATIONAL CRIMINAL LAW 193 (1992); Jordan Paust, *The Other Side of Right: Private Duties Under Human Rights Law*, 5 HARV. HUM. RTS. J. 51 (1992).

The liability of private persons for certain violations of customary international law and the availability of the Alien Tort Act to remedy such violations was early recognized by the Executive Branch in an opinion of Attorney General Bradford in reference to acts of American citizens aiding the French fleet to plunder British property off the coast of Sierra Leone in 1795. See Breach of Neutrality, 1 Op. Att'y Gen. 57, 59 (1795). The Executive Branch has emphatically restated in this litigation its position that private persons may be found liable under the Alien Tort Act for acts of genocide, war crimes, and other violations of international humanitarian law. See Statement of Interest of the United States at 5-13.

The RESTATEMENT (THIRD) OF THE FOREIGN RELATIONS LAW OF THE UNITED STATES (1986) ("Restatement (Third)") proclaims: "Individuals may be held liable for offenses against international law, such as piracy, war crimes, and genocide." Restatement (Third) pt. II, introductory note. The Restatement is careful to identify those violations that are actionable when committed by a state, Restatement (Third) §702, and a more limited category of violations of "universal concern," *id.* §404, partially overlapping with those listed in Section 702. Though the immediate focus of Section 404 is to identify those offenses for which a state has jurisdiction to punish without regard to territoriality or the nationality of the offenders, *cf. id.* §402(1)(a), (2), the inclusion of piracy and slave trade from an earlier era and aircraft hijacking from the modern era demonstrates that the offenses of "universal concern" include those capable of being committed by non-state actors. Although the jurisdiction authorized by Section 404 is usually exercised by application of criminal law, international law also permits states to establish appropriate civil remedies, *id.* §404, Comment [hereinafter cmt.] b, such as the tort actions authorized by the Alien Tort Act. Indeed, the two cases invoking the Alien Tort Act prior to *Filartiga* both applied the civil remedy to private action. See Adra v. Clift, 195 F. Supp. 857 (D. Md. 1961); Bolchos v. Darrel, 3 F. Cas. 810, 1 Bee 74 (D.S.C. 1795)(No. 1,607)….

2. Specific Application of Alien Tort Act to Appellants' Claims

In order to determine whether the offenses alleged by the appellants in this litigation are violations of the law of nations that may be the subject of Alien Tort Act claims against a private individual, we must make a particularized examination of these offenses, mindful of the important precept that "evolving standards of international law govern who is within the [Alien Tort Act's] jurisdictional grant." Amerada Hess, 830 F.2d at 425. In making that inquiry, it will be helpful to group the appellants' claims into three categories: (a) genocide, (b) war crimes, and (c) other instances of inflicting death, torture, and degrading treatment.

(a) Genocide. In the aftermath of the atrocities committed during the Second World War, the condemnation of genocide as contrary to international law quickly achieved broad acceptance by the community of nations. In 1946, the General Assembly of the United Nations declared that genocide is a crime under international law that is condemned by the civilized world, whether the perpetrators are "private individuals, public officials or statesmen." G.A. Res. 96 (I), 1 U.N. GAOR, U.N. Doc. A/64/Add.1, at 188-89 (1946). The General Assembly also affirmed the principles of Article 6 of the Agreement and Charter Establishing the Nuremberg War Crimes Tribunal for punishing "'persecutions on political, racial, or religious grounds,'" regardless of whether the offenders acted "'as individuals or as members of organizations,'" *In re* Extradition of Demjanjuk, 612 F. Supp. 544, 555 n.11 (N.D. Ohio 1985) (quoting Article 6). See G.A. Res. 95 (I), 1 U.N. GAOR, U.N. Doc. A/64/Add.1, at 188 (1946).

The Convention on the Prevention and Punishment of the Crime of Genocide, 78 U.N.T.S. 277, entered into force Jan. 12, 1951, for the United States Feb. 23, 1989 (hereinafter "Convention on Genocide"), provides a more specific articulation of the prohibition of genocide in international law. The Convention, which has been ratified by more than 120 nations, including the United States, see U.S. Dept. of State, Treaties in Force 345 (1994), defines "genocide" to mean any of the following acts committed with intent to destroy, in whole or in part, a national, ethnical, racial or religious group, as such:

(a) Killing members of the group;

(b) Causing serious bodily or mental harm to members of the group;

(c) Deliberately inflicting on the group conditions of life calculated to bring

about its physical destruction in whole or in part;

(d) Imposing measures intended to prevent births with the group;

(e) Forcibly transferring children of the group to another group.

Convention on Genocide art. II. Especially pertinent to the pending appeal, the Convention makes clear that "persons committing genocide ... shall be punished, whether they are constitutionally responsible rulers, public officials or private individuals." *Id.* art. IV (emphasis added). These authorities unambiguously reflect that, from its incorporation into international law, the proscription of genocide has applied equally to state and non-state actors.

The applicability of this norm to private individuals is also confirmed by the Genocide Convention Implementation Act of 1987, 18 U.S.C. § 1091 (1988), which criminalizes acts of genocide without regard to whether the offender is acting under color of law, see *id.* § 1091(a) ("whoever" commits genocide shall be punished), if the crime is committed within the United States or by a U.S. national, *id.* § 1091(d). Though Congress provided that the Genocide Convention Implementation Act shall not "be construed as creating any substantive or procedural right enforceable by law by any party in any proceeding," *id.* § 1092, the legislative decision not to create a new private remedy does not imply that a private remedy is not already available under the Alien Tort Act. Nothing in the Genocide Convention Implementation Act or its legislative history reveals an intent by Congress to repeal the Alien Tort Act insofar as it applies to genocide, and the two statutes are surely not repugnant to each other. Under these circumstances, it would be improper to construe the Genocide Convention Implementation Act as repealing the Alien Tort Act by implication. See Rodriguez v. United States, 480 U.S. 522, 524 ... (1987) ("Repeals by implication are not favored and will not be found unless an intent to repeal is clear and manifest.") (citations and internal quotation marks omitted); United States v. Cook, 922 F.2d 1026, 1034 (2d Cir.) ("mutual exclusivity" of statutes is required to demonstrate Congress's "clear, affirmative intent to repeal"), *cert. denied*, 500 U.S. 941 (1991).

Appellants' allegations that Karadzic personally planned and ordered a campaign of murder, rape, forced impregnation, and other forms of torture designed to destroy the religious and ethnic groups of Bosnian Muslims and Bosnian Croats clearly state a violation of the international law norm proscribing genocide, regardless of whether Karadzic acted under color of law or as a private individual. The District Court has subject-matter jurisdiction over these claims pursuant to the Alien Tort Act.

(b) War crimes. Plaintiffs also contend that the acts of murder, rape, torture, and arbitrary detention of civilians, committed in the course of hostilities, violate the law of war. Atrocities of the types alleged here have long been recognized in international law as violations of the law of war. See *In re* Yamashita, 327 U.S. 1, 14 ... (1946). Moreover, international law imposes an affirmative duty on military commanders to take appropriate measures within their power to control troops under their command for the prevention of such atrocities. *Id.* at 15-16.

After the Second World War, the law of war was codified in the four Geneva Conventions, which have been ratified by more than 180 nations, including the United States, see Treaties in Force, *supra*, at 398-99. Common article 3, which is substantially identical in each of the four Conventions, applies to "armed conflicts not of an international character" and binds "each Party to the conflict ... to apply, as a minimum, the following provisions":

> Persons taking no active part in the hostilities ... shall in all circumstances be treated humanely, without any adverse distinction founded on race, colour, religion or faith, sex, birth or wealth, or any other similar criteria.

To this end, the following acts are and shall remain prohibited at any time and in any place whatsoever with respect to the above-mentioned persons:

> (a) violence to life and person, in particular murder of all kinds, mutilation, cruel treatment and torture;
>
> (b) taking of hostages;
>
> (c) outrages upon personal dignity, in particular humiliating and degrading treatment;
>
> (d) the passing of sentences and carrying out of executions without previous judgment pronounced by a regularly constituted court....

Geneva Convention I art. 3 (1). Thus, under the law of war as codified in the Geneva Conventions, all "parties" to a conflict—which includes insurgent military groups—are obliged to adhere to these most fundamental requirements of the law of war.

The offenses alleged by the appellants, if proved, would violate the most fundamental norms of the law of war embodied in common article 3, which binds parties to internal conflicts regardless of whether they are recognized nations or roving hordes of insurgents. The liability of private individuals for committing war crimes has been recognized since World War I and was confirmed at Nuremberg after World War II, see Telford Taylor, *Nuremberg Trials: War Crimes and International Law*, 450 Int'l Conciliation 304 (April 1949) (collecting cases), and remains today an important aspect of international law, see Jordan Paust, *After My Lai: The Case for War Crimes Jurisdiction Over Civilians in Federal District Courts*, in 4 The Vietnam War and International Law 447 (R. Falk ed., 1976). The District Court has jurisdiction pursuant to the Alien Tort Act over appellants' claims of war crimes and other violations of international humanitarian law.

(c) Torture and summary execution. In *Filartiga*, we held that official torture is prohibited by universally accepted norms of international law, see 630 F.2d at 885, and the Torture Victim Act confirms this holding and extends it to cover summary execution. Torture Victim Act Secs. 2 (a), 3 (a). However, torture and summary execution—when not perpetrated in the course of genocide or war crimes—are proscribed by international law only when committed by state officials or under color of law. See Declaration on Torture art. 1 (defining torture as being "inflicted by or at the instigation of a public official"); Convention Against Torture and Other Cruel, Inhuman, or Degrading Treatment or Punishment pt. I, art. 1, 23 I.L.M. 1027 (1984), as modified, 24 I.L.M. 535 (1985), entered into force June 26, 1987, ratified by United States Oct. 21, 1994, 34 I.L.M. 590, 591 (1995) (defining torture as "inflicted by or at the instigation of or with the consent or acquiescence of a public official or other person acting in an official capacity"); Torture Victim Act § 2(a) (imposing liability on individuals acting "under actual or apparent authority, or color of law, of any foreign nation").

In the present case, appellants allege that acts of rape, torture, and summary execution were committed during hostilities by troops under Karadzic's command and with the specific intent of destroying appellants' ethnic-religious groups. Thus, many of the alleged atrocities are already encompassed within the appellants' claims of genocide and war crimes. Of course, at this threshold stage in the proceedings it cannot be known whether appellants will be able to prove the specific intent that is an element of genocide, or prove that each of the alleged torts were committed in the course of an armed conflict, as required to establish war crimes. It suffices to hold at this stage that the alleged atrocities are actionable under the Alien Tort Act, without regard to state action, to the extent that they were committed in pursuit of genocide or war crimes, and otherwise may be pursued against Karadzic to the extent that he is shown to be a state actor....

3. The State Action Requirement for International Law Violations

... Appellants' allegations entitle them to prove that Karadzic's regime satisfies the criteria for a state, for purposes of those international law violations requiring state action. Srpska is alleged to control defined territory, control populations within its power, and to have entered into agreements with other governments. It has a president, a legislature, and its own currency. These circumstances readily appear to satisfy the criteria for a state in all aspects of international law. Moreover, it is likely that the state action concept, where applicable for some violations like "official" torture, requires merely the semblance of official authority. The inquiry, after all, is whether a person purporting to wield official power has exceeded internationally recognized standards of civilized conduct, not whether statehood in all its formal aspects exists.

(b) Acting in concert with a foreign state. Appellants also sufficiently alleged that Karadzic acted under color of law insofar as they claimed that he acted in concert with the former Yugoslavia, the statehood of which is not disputed. The "color of law" jurisprudence of 42 U.S.C. § 1983 is a relevant guide to whether a defendant has engaged in official action for purposes of jurisdiction under the Alien Tort Act. See Forti v. Suarez-Mason, 672 F. Supp. 1531, 1546 (N.D. Cal. 1987), reconsideration granted in part on other grounds, 694 F. Supp. 707 (N.D. Cal. 1988). A private individual acts under color of law within the meaning of section 1983 when he acts together with state officials or with significant state aid. See Lugar v. Edmondson Oil Co., 457 U.S. 922, 937 ... (1982). The appellants are entitled to prove their allegations that Karadzic acted under color of law of Yugoslavia by acting in concert with Yugoslav officials or with significant Yugoslavian aid.

B. The Torture Victim Protection Act.... The Torture Victim Act, enacted in 1992, provides a cause of action for official torture and extrajudicial killing....

By its plain language, the Torture Victim Act renders liable only those individuals who have committed torture or extrajudicial killing "under actual or apparent authority, or color of law, of any foreign nation." Legislative history confirms that this language was intended to "make[] clear that the plaintiff must establish some governmental involvement in the torture or killing to prove a claim," and that the statute "does not attempt to deal with torture or killing by purely private groups." H.R. Rep. No. 367, 102d Cong., 2d Sess., at 5 (1991).... In construing the terms "actual or apparent authority" and "color of law," courts are instructed to look to principles of agency law and to jurisprudence under 42 U.S.C. § 1983, respectively. *Id*.

Though the Torture Victim Act creates a cause of action for official torture, this statute, unlike the Alien Tort Act, is not itself a jurisdictional statute. The Torture Victim Act permits the appellants to pursue their claims of official torture under the jurisdiction conferred by the Alien Tort Act and also under the general federal question jurisdiction of section 1331, see Xuncax v. Gramajo, 886 F. Supp. 162, 178 (D. Mass. 1995), to which we now turn.

C. Section 1331. The appellants contend that section 1331 provides an independent basis for subject-matter jurisdiction over all claims alleging violations of international law. Relying on the settled proposition that federal common law incorporates international law, see The Paquete Habana, 175 U.S. 677, 700 ... (1900); *In re* Estate of Ferdinand E. Marcos Human Rights Litigation (Marcos I), 978 F.2d 493, 502 (9th Cir. 1992), *cert. denied*, 125 L. Ed. 2d 661 ... (1993); Filartiga, 630 F.2d at 886, they reason that causes of action for violations of international law "arise under" the laws of the United States for purposes of jurisdiction under section 1331. Whether that is so is an issue of some uncertainty that need not be decided in this case.

In *Tel-Oren* Judge Edwards expressed the view that section 1331 did not supply jurisdiction for claimed violations of international law unless the plaintiffs could point to a remedy granted by the law of nations or argue successfully that such a remedy is implied. Tel-Oren, 726 F.2d at 779-80 n.4. The law of nations generally does not create private causes of action to remedy its violations, but leaves to each nation the task of defining the remedies that are available for international law violations. *Id*. at 778 (Edwards, J., concurring). Some district courts, however, have upheld section 1331 jurisdiction for international law violations. See Abebe-Jiri v. Negewo, No. 90-2010 (N.D. Ga. Aug. 20, 1993), appeal argued, No. 93-9133 (11th Cir. Jan. 10, 1995); Martinez-Baca v. Suarez-Mason, No. 87-2057, slip op. at 4-5 (N.D. Cal. Apr. 22, 1988); Forti v. Suarez-Mason, 672 F. Supp. 1531, 1544 (N.D. Cal. 1987).

We recognized the possibility of section 1331 jurisdiction in Filartiga, 630 F.2d at 887 n.22, but rested jurisdiction solely on the applicable Alien Tort Act. Since that Act appears to provide a remedy for the appellants' allegations of violations related to genocide, war crimes, and official torture, and the Torture Victim Act also appears to provide a remedy for their allegations of official torture, their causes of action are statutorily authorized, and, as in *Filartiga*, we need not rule definitively on whether any causes of action not specifically authorized by statute may be implied by international law standards as incorporated into United States law and grounded on section 1331 jurisdiction....

Two nonjurisdictional, prudential doctrines reflect the judiciary's concerns regarding separation of powers: the political question doctrine and the act of state doctrine. It is the "'constitutional' underpinnings" of these doctrines that influenced the concurring opinions of Judge Robb and Judge Bork in *Tel-Oren*. Although we too recognize the potentially detrimental effects of judicial action in cases of this nature, we do not embrace the rather categorical views as to the inappropriateness of judicial action urged by Judges Robb and Bork. Not every case "touching foreign relations" is nonjusticiable, see Baker v. Carr, 369 U.S. 186, 211 … (1962); Lamont v. Woods, 948 F.2d 825, 831-32 (2d Cir. 1991), and judges should not reflexively invoke these doctrines to avoid difficult and somewhat sensitive decisions in the context of human rights. We believe a preferable approach is to weigh carefully the relevant considerations on a case-by-case basis. This will permit the judiciary to act where appropriate in light of the express legislative mandate of the Congress in section 1350, without compromising the primacy of the political branches in foreign affairs.

Karadzic maintains that these suits were properly dismissed because they present nonjusticiable political questions. We disagree. Although these cases present issues that arise in a politically charged context, that does not transform them into cases involving nonjusticiable political questions. "The doctrine 'is one of "political questions," not one of "political cases.""" Klinghoffer, 937 F.2d at 49 (*quoting Baker*, 369 U.S. at 217).

… With respect to the first three factors, we have noted in a similar context involving a tort suit against the PLO that "the department to whom this issue has been 'constitutionally committed' is none other than our own—the Judiciary." Klinghoffer, 937 F.2d at 49. Although the present actions are not based on the common law of torts, as was *Klinghoffer*, our decision in *Filartiga* established that universally recognized norms of international law provide judicially discoverable and manageable standards for adjudicating suits brought under the Alien Tort Act, which obviates any need to make initial policy decisions of the kind normally reserved for nonjudicial discretion. Moreover, the existence of judicially discoverable and manageable standards further undermines the claim that such suits relate to matters that are constitutionally committed to another branch. See Nixon v. United States, 506 U.S. 224 … (1993)….

The act of state doctrine, under which courts generally refrain from judging the acts of a foreign state within its territory, see Banco Nacional de Cuba v. Sabbatino, 376 U.S. at 428 … ; Underhill v. Hernandez, 168 U.S. 250, 252 … (1897), might be implicated in some cases arising under section 1350. However, as in Filartiga, 630 F.2d at 889, we doubt that the acts of even a state official, taken in violation of a nation's fundamental law and wholly unratified by that nation's government, could properly be characterized as an act of state.

In the pending appeal, we need have no concern that interference with important governmental interests warrants rejection of appellants' claims. After commencing their action against Karadzic, attorneys for the plaintiffs in Doe wrote to the Secretary of State to oppose reported attempts by Karadzic to be granted immunity from suit in the United States; a copy of plaintiffs' complaint was attached to the letter. Far from intervening in the case to urge rejection of the suit on the ground that it presented political questions, the Department responded with a letter indicating that Karadzic was not immune from suit as an invitee of the United Nations. See Habib Letter, *supra*. After oral argument in the pending appeals, this Court wrote to the Attorney General to inquire whether the United States wished to offer any further views concerning any of the issues raised. In a "Statement of Interest," signed by the Solicitor General and the State Department's Legal Adviser, the United States has expressly disclaimed any concern that the political question doctrine should be invoked to prevent the litigation of these lawsuits: "Although there might be instances in which federal courts are asked to issue rulings under the Alien Tort Statute or the Torture Victim Protection Act that might raise a political question, this is not one of them." Statement of Interest of the United States at 3. Though even an assertion of the political question doctrine by the Executive Branch, entitled to respectful consideration, would not necessarily preclude adjudication, the Government's reply to our inquiry reinforces our view that adjudication may properly proceed.

As to the act of state doctrine, the doctrine was not asserted in the District Court and is not before us on this appeal. See Filartiga, 630 F.2d at 889. Moreover, the appellee has not had the temerity to assert in this Court that the acts he allegedly committed are the officially approved policy of a state. Finally, as noted, we think it would be a rare case in which the act of state doctrine precluded suit under section 1350. *Banco Nacional* was careful to recognize the doctrine "in the absence of . . . unambiguous agreement regarding controlling legal principles," 376 U.S. at 428, such as exist in the pending litigation, and applied the doctrine only in a context—expropriation of an alien's property—in which world opinion was sharply divided, see *id*. at 428-30. . . .

Notes and Questions

1. Is there a "state action" requirement with respect to human rights violations? Recall Chapter One, Section Three.

2. Despite dictum in *Kadic*, should the judiciary ever rightly conclude that if lawsuits are brought pursuant to a legislatively approved scheme (*e.g.*, under the ATCA or the TVPA), claims made pursuant to such a scheme raise nonjusticiable "political questions"?

3. Is nonimmunity with respect to officials and other state actors built into Section 2(a) of the TVPA? Is it also built into Article 2(3)(a) of the International Covenant on Civil and Political Rights?

4. With respect to nonimmunity for violations of international criminal law, the I.M.T. at Nuremberg affirmed: "The principle of international law, which under certain circumstances protects the representatives of a state, cannot be applied to acts which are condemned as criminal by international law. The authors of these acts cannot shelter themselves behind their official position," and one "cannot claim immunity while acting in pursuance of the authority of the State if the State in authorizing action moves outside its competence under international law."

More generally, acts in violation of international law are beyond the lawful authority of any state and are *ultra vires*. *See, e.g.*, PAUST, INTERNATIONAL LAW AS LAW OF THE UNITED STATES 422, 435-39 nn.69-72, 443-45 (2 ed. 2003); PAUST, VAN DYKE, MALONE, INTERNATIONAL LAW AND LITIGATION IN THE U.S. 24, 28, 347, 351, 514, 563, 573, 680-82, 694-95, 748, 754, 756, 769, 773-76, 779, 815, 987, 1030 (2 ed. 2005); *In re Estate of Ferdinand Marcos, Human Rights Litigation*, 25 F.3d 1467, 1470-71 (9th Cir. 1994); *Republic of the Philippines v. Marcos*, 806 F.2d 344 (2d Cir. 1986); *Doe v. Unocal Corp.*, 963 F. Supp. 880, 898-99 (C.D. Cal. 1997); *Xuncax v. Gramajo*, 886 F. Supp. 162, 175-76 (D. Mass. 1995); *Letelier v. Republic of Chile*, 488 F. Supp. 665, 673 (D.D.C. 1980); *see also Johnson v. Eisentrager*, 339 U.S. 763, 765, 789 (1950) (no public official immunity for war crimes); The *Santissima Trinidad*, 20 U.S. (7 Wheat.) 283, 350-55 (1822); *Hudson v. Guestier*, 8 U.S.(4 Cranch) 293, 294 (1808)(public acts violative of the law of nations are not entitled to recognition); *Rose v. Himely*, 8 U.S. (4 Cranch) 241, 276-77 (1808) (same); *Paul v. Avril*, 812 F. Supp. 207, 212 (S.D. Fla. 1993); *United States v. Noriega*, 746

F. Supp. 1506 (S.D. Fla. 1990) (violation of narcotics trafficking treaty); *Kalmich v. Bruno*, 450 F. Supp. 227, 229 n.2 (N.D. Ill. 1978); 9 Op. Att'y Gen. 356, 357 (1859).

5. Domestic amnesties, pardons, immunities, statutes of limitation, and limiting laws or orders are not valid internationally or binding in other states. *See, e.g.*, Principles of the Nuremberg Charter and Judgment, Principles II and IV, in the Documents Section; Charters of the I.M.T.s at Nuremberg and for the Far East; Statute of the ICC, arts. 27(2), 29, 33; Statute of the ICTY, art. 7(4); Statute of the ICTR, art. 6(4); U.N. S.C. Res. 1261, para. 3 (25 Aug. 1999); U.N. S.C. Res. 1315, preamble (14 Aug. 2000); U.N. G.A. Res. 47/133 (8 Dec. 1992); U.N. G.A. Res. 3074, para. 7 (1973).

6. With respect to the judicially-created act of state doctrine, only "public" acts are relevant and "the greater the degree of codification or consensus concerning a particular area of international law, the more appropriate it is for the judiciary to render decisions regarding it." *Banco Nacional de Cuba v. Sabbatino*, 376 U.S. 398, 428 (1964). *See also Sabbatino*, 376 U.S. at 430 n.34 ("There are, of course, areas of international law in which consensus as to standards is greater and which do not represent a battleground for conflicting ideologies. This decision in no way intimates that the courts of this country are broadly foreclosed from considering questions of international law"); Alfred *Dunhill of London, Inc. v. Republic of Cuba*, 425 U.S. 682, 707-11 (1976).

The trend among lower federal courts is to reject application of the act of state doctrine in cases involving violations of internationally protected human rights, especially since relevant conduct was *ultra vires* or beyond the lawful authority of any state. *See, e.g., Sarei v. Rio Tinto, PLC*, 487 F.3d 1193, 1209-10 (9th Cir. 2007) (race discrimination in violation of international law cannot be an "official" act within the act of state doctrine), citing *Siderman de Blake*, 965 F.2d at 717-18; *Doe I v. Unocal Corp.*, 395 F.3d 932, 958-59 (9th Cir. 2002); *In re Estate of Ferdinand Marcos, Human Rights Litigation Hilao v. Estate of Ferdinand Marcos*, 25 F.3d 1467, 1471 (9th Cir. 1994) (human rights violations, including torture, are not lawful public acts of state); *Liu v. Republic of China*, 892 F.2d 1419, 1432-33 (9th Cir. 1989) (act of state doctrine not applied to assassination, which is not in the "public interest," and a strong international consensus exists that it is illegal); *Presbyterian Church of Sudan v. Talisman Energy, Inc.*, 244 F. Supp.2d 289, 344-35 (S.D.N.Y. 2003) (adjudication of genocide, war crimes, enslavement, and torture is not barred by the act of state doctrine); *Xuncax v. Gramajo*, 886 F. Supp. 162, 176 (D. Mass. 1995) ("these actions exceed anything that might be considered to have been lawfully within the scope of Gramajo's official authority," and quoting *Letelier v. Republic of Chile*, 488 F. Supp. 665, 673 (D.D.C. 1980) (assassination is "clearly contrary to precepts of humanity as recognized in both national and international law" and so cannot be part of official discretionary authority), *cert. denied*, 471 U.S. 1125 (1985)); *Paul v. Avril*, 812 F. Supp. 207, 212 (S.D. Fla. 1993) (defendant's argument regarding "the act of state and political question doctrines is completely devoid of merit. The acts ... [of torture, cruel, inhuman and degrading treatment, and arbitrary detention in violation of customary international law] hardly qualify as official public acts" and regarding the political question doctrine, the claims present "clearly justiciable legal issues"); *Forti v. Suarez-Mason*, 672 F. Supp. 1531, 1546 (N.D. Cal. 1987) (torture, arbitrary detention, and summary execution "are not public official acts"); *see also Enahoro v. Abubakar*, 408 F.3d 877, 893 (7th Cir. 2005) (Cudahy, J., dissenting) ("officials receive no immunity for acts that violate international *jus cogens* human rights norms (which by definition are not legally authorized acts.)"); *Abebe-Jira v. Negewo*, 72 F.3d 844, 848 (11th Cir. 1996) (regarding the political question doctrine, "[i]n *Linder v. Portocarrero*, 963 F.2d 332, 337 (11th Cir. 1992), we held that the political question doctrine did not bar a tort action instituted against Nicaraguan Contra leaders [for war crimes in violation of common Article 3 of the Geneva Conventions]. Consequently, we reject Negewo's contention in light of *Linder*."); *Doe v. Unocal Corp.*, 963 F. Supp. 880, 892-95 (C.D. Cal. 1997) ("Because nations do not, and cannot under international law, claim a right to torture…, a finding that a nation committed such acts … should have no detrimental effect on the policies underlying the act of state doctrine. Accordingly, the Court need not apply the act of state doctrine in this case"). *See also* Senate Report, S.Rep. No. 249, 102nd Cong., 1st Sess. 8 (1991) (the act of state doctrine "applies only to 'public' acts, and no state commits torture as a matter of public policy," adding: "[a] state that practices torture and summary execution is not one that adheres to the rule of law. Consequently, the [TVPA] is designed to respond to this situation by providing a civil cause of action in US courts," and that the Senate Judiciary "Committee does not intend the 'act of state' doctrine to provide a shield from lawsuit….").

Evocative of the trend toward rejection of the act of state doctrine for acts beyond the scope of proper governmental authority was the Second Circuit's opinion in *Republic of Philippines v. Marcos,* 806 F.2d 344 (2d Cir.1986), *cert. denied sub nom.,* *New York Land Co. v. Republic of the Philippines,* 481 U.S. 1048 (1987) (Marcos I), and the Ninth Circuit's *en banc* decision in *Republic of the Philippines v. Marcos,* 862 F.2d 1355 (9th Cir.1988) (*en banc*), *cert. denied,* 490 U.S. 1035 (1989) (Marcos II). Although these cases involved claims that former President Marcos had looted the Philippine treasury, rather than his commission of human rights violations, they are significant in their rejection of a broad application of the act of state doctrine.

Almog v. Arab Bank, PLC 471 F. Supp.2d 257 (E.D.N.Y. 2007)

[Westlaw's note: "Multiple plaintiffs, United States and foreign nationals allegedly injured, or the survivors of those injured or killed, in terrorist attack in Israel, brought actions under, respectively, the Anti-Terrorism Act (ATA) and the Alien Tort Claims Act (ATS) [ATCA] against Jordanian bank alleged to have knowingly provided banking and other services that facilitated the actions of terrorist organizations."]

Ill. Alien Tort Claims Act Claims

… Neither the Almog nor the Afriat-Kurtzer plaintiffs assert that the torts they allege are in violation of a treaty of the United States; rather, they assert a violation of the law of nations. The essential issues in contention are therefore whether plaintiffs have pled a violation of the law of nations that should be recognized by this court under the ATS, and whether Arab Bank can be liable for aiding and abetting those violations….

The Supreme Court, in *Sosa* [v. Alvarez-Machain], stated that, "although the ATS is a jurisdictional statute creating no new causes of action…. [t]he jurisdictional grant is best read as having been enacted on the understanding that the common law would provide a cause of action for the modest number of international law violations with a potential for personal liability at the time" the ATS was enacted. Thus, under the ATS, courts can hear a limited category of claims "defined by the law of nations and recognized at common law." Sosa, 542 U.S. at 712….

Sosa instructs that courts consider the *current* state of the law of nations in deciding whether to recognize a claim under the ATS. *Id.* at 733. As the *Filartiga* Court stated, "courts must interpret international law not as it was in 1789, but as it has evolved and exists among the nations of the world today." 630 F.2d at 881. That rules of international law evolve and ripen over time was acknowledged by the Supreme Court as early as

1900 in *The Paquete Habana*, 175 U.S. 677, 694.... [Further,] that a norm of international law is honored in the breach does not diminish its binding effect as a norm of international law. *Filartiga*, 630 F.2d at 884 n.15; *cf Sosa*, 542 U.S. at 738 n.29....

A. Violation of the Law of Nations

I. Genocide and Crimes Against Humanity

Acts of genocide and crimes against humanity violate the law of nations and these norms are of sufficient specificity and definiteness to be recognized under the ATS. See *Flores*, 414 F.3d at 244 n.18 ("Customary international law rules proscribing crimes against humanity, including genocide, and war crimes, have been enforceable against individuals since World War II."); Kadic v. Karadzic, 70 F.3d 232, 241-42 (2d Cir. 1995) ("In 1946, the General Assembly of the United Nations declared that genocide is a crime under international law that is condemned by the civilized world, whether the perpetrators are private individuals, public officials or statesmen." (internal quotation marks omitted)); In re Agent Orange Prod Liab. Litig., 373 F. Supp.2d 7, 136 (E.D.N.Y. 2005) ("[C]rimes against humanity are also deemed to be part of jus cogens—the highest standing in international legal norms. Thus, they constitute a non-derogable rule of international law."); Wiwa v. Royal Dutch Petroleum Co., No. 96 Civ. 8386. 2002 WL 319887, at *9 (S.D.N.Y. Feb. 28, 2002) (stating that crimes against humanity violate "a norm that is customary, obligatory, and well-defined in international jurisprudence").

Defendant does not contest the availability of genocide or crimes against humanity claims under the ATS but argues that plaintiffs have not sufficiently pled a claim for genocide and crimes against humanity....

To be a crime against humanity, the emphasis must not be on the individual but rather on the collective—the individual is victimized not because of his or her individual attributes but because of membership in a targeted civilian population. *Id.* [*Wiwa* at *10] (citing Prosecutor v. Tadic, Case No. IT-94- I -T, Opinion and Jud., 644 (May 7, 1997)). Although the requirement of widespread or systematic action ensures that a plaintiff must allege not just one act but instead, a course of conduct, "a single act by a perpetrator, taken within the context of a widespread or systematic attack against a civilian population entails individual criminal responsibility and an individual perpetrator need not commit numerous offences to be held liable." *Id.*

Applying the standards provided in the Genocide Convention and the Rome Statute [of the ICC] to the facts alleged here, plaintiffs have successfully stated claims for genocide and crimes against humanity. The amended complaints allege that HAMAS, the PIJ, the AAMB, and the PFLP act with the united purpose and shared mission to eradicate the State of Israel, murder or throw out the Jews, and liberate the area by replacing it with an Islamic or Palestinian State through the use of suicide bombings and other shockingly egregious violent acts. These goals reflect an intent to target people based on criteria prohibited by both Genocide Convention and the Rome Statute.

Plaintiffs allege that the terrorist organizations seek to accomplish their shared goal by cooperating in the planning and commission of suicide bombings and other murderous attacks using explosives, incendiary weapons, and lethal devices in public places, which has resulted in the systematic and continuous killing and injury of thousands of unarmed innocent civilians in Israel, the West Bank, and the Gaza Strip....

2. Suicide Bombings and Other Murderous Attacks on Innocent Civilians Intended to Intimidate or Coerce a Civilian Population.

The third international norm which plaintiffs allege Arab Bank has violated is the financing of suicide bombings and other murderous attacks on innocent civilians which are intended to intimidate or coerce a civilian population. The underlying norm thus differs from the genocide norm with respect to the purpose of the perpetrators, and it differs from the more general crimes against humanity norm in that it specifically condemns bombings and other attacks intended to coerce or intimidate a civilian population. This particular claim for liability under the ATS is similar to the U.S. nationals' claims under the ATA, but the alien plaintiffs do not rely on domestic law; rather, they rely on the body of international law described above under the discussion of genocide and crimes against humanity, plus the additional sources of international law in the ensuing discussion.

In 1997, the United Nations General Assembly adopted the International Convention for the Suppression of Terrorist Bombings ("Bombing Convention"). G.A. Res, 52/164, 1, U.N. Doc. A/ RES/52/l 64 (Dec. 15, 1997)....

Two years after the Bombing Convention was adopted by the General Assembly, the International Convention for the Suppression of the Financing of Terrorism ("Financing Convention") was also adopted by the General Assembly of the United Nations. GA. Res. 54/109, 1, U.N. Doc. A/ RES/54/l09 (Dec. 9. 1999). It has been ratified by over 130 countries, including the United States (June 26. 2002). The United States implemented the Financing Convention via the Suppression of the Financing of Terrorism Convention Implementation Act of 2002. See 18 U.S.C. § 2339C....

The prohibition against attacks on innocent civilians that is reflected in both of these Conventions is not a new one. The three-century-old "principle of distinction," which requires parties to a conflict to at all times distinguish between civilians and combatants, forbids the deliberate attacking of civilians.... This principle is also reflected in Common Article 3 of the Geneva Conventions of 1949....

Under the customary law of armed conflict, as reflected in the Geneva Conventions, all "parties" to a conflict, including insurgent military groups, must adhere to these most fundamental requirements. *Kadic,* 70 F.3d at 243. While the principle of distinction and the Geneva Conventions apply expressly only in situations of armed conflict, their long-standing existence supports the conclusion, made explicit in the Bombing and Financing Conventions, that attacks against innocent civilians of the type alleged here are condemned by international law.

United Nations Security Council Resolution 1566 also supports this conclusion....

Resolution 1566 specifically condemns attacks against civilians intended to intimidate a civilian population, regardless of who commits the attacks or what the motivation behind such attacks may be. While such resolutions cannot be relied on as a sole source of international law, they are informative as to what the current state of international law is. See *Filartiga,* 630 F.2d at 882 n.9; *Presbyterian Church of Sudan,* 374 F. Supp.2d at 338: Bodner v. Banque Paribas, 114 F. Supp.2d 117, 128 (E.D.N.Y. 2000)....

In sum, in light of the universal condemnation of organized and systematic suicide bombings and other murderous acts intended to intimidate or coerce a civilian population, this court finds that such conduct violates an established norm of international law. The court further finds that the conduct alleged by plaintiffs is sufficiently specific and well-defined to be recognized as a claim under the ATS.

This court's consideration of whether to exercise its discretion to recognize a claim under the ATS is informed by the legislative guidance provided by Congress. See *Sosa,*

542 U.S. at 726-27 (expressing concern about the importance of legislative guidance and judgment in creating new common law claims). Although Congress has not created a cause of action under the ATS, it has created criminal penalties and, with respect to U.S. nationals, civil liability for the acts alleged by plaintiffs....

B. Arab Bank's Liability

Whether Arab Bank is liable for its alleged conduct under the ATS, like the question of whether the suicide bombings and attacks alleged by plaintiffs violate the law of nations, is a question of international law. *Sosa,* 542 U.S. at 732 n.20;:*Talisman Energy Inc.,* 374 F. Supp.2d at 333 (*Talisman II*). In a variety of ATS cases, courts have concluded that international law provides for the imposition of liability on a party that does not directly perform the underlying act. There is nothing novel or unusual under international law about imposing such liability. And the Genocide, Bombing, and Financing Conventions explicitly condemn acts of complicity or aiding and abetting by non-primary actors. Indeed, under the Financing Convention, the acts of Arab Bank alleged by plaintiff's amount to primary violations, as the entire focus of that Convention is on stopping the financing of terrorists and terrorist organizations which support offenses against civilians as defined in the Convention....

Standards for imposing liability where a non-primary actor is alleged to be liable for a violation of the law of nations emerge from the case law and Conventions. *Talisman I* sets forth the international law applicable in assessing aider and abettor liability under the ATS. In that case, the court relied on Article 7(l) of the Statute of the International Criminal Tribunal for the former Yugoslavia ("ICTY") and Article 6(l) of the Statute of the International Criminal Tribunal for Rwanda ("ICTR"), both of which provide for liability for planning, instigating, ordering, committing, or otherwise aiding and abetting in the planning, preparation or execution of acts of genocide or crimes against humanity. *Talisman I,* 244 F. Supp.2d at 322. The court stated that "the *actus reus* of aiding and abetting in international criminal law requires practical assistance, encouragement, or moral support which has a substantial effect on the perpetration of the crime." *Talisman I,* 244 F. Supp.2d at 323 (quoting Prosecutor v. Furundzija, Case No. IT-95- I 7/I -T. Judgment. 235 (Dec. 10. 1998). "While the assistance must be substantial, it 'need not constitute an indispensable element, that is, a *condition sine qua non* for the acts of the principal.'" *Id.* at 324 (quoting *Furundzija* para. 209). Participation in a crime is substantial if "the criminal act most probably would not have occurred in the same way had not someone acted in the role that the accused in fact assumed." *Id.* (quoting *Tadic* para. 688). The court also made clear that "some knowledge that the assistance will facilitate the crime is necessary." *Id.*

Talisman II, decided after the Supreme Court's decision in *Sosa,* reassessed the issue in light of *Sosa,* and fully endorsed the analysis in *Talisman I,* 374 F. Supp.2d at 337-41. The court explained that ICTY and ICTR decisions are appropriate sources for clarifying the content of aider and abettor liability in international law because the entire purpose of the ICTY and ICTR is to adjudicate violations of customary international law; although the tribunals do not create new rules of customary international law, they occupy a special role in enunciating the current content of customary international law norms. *Id.* at 338. The court noted that "ICTY and ICTR opinions typically engage in nuanced and exhaustive surveys of international legal sources, and as such, they are exceedingly useful as persuasive evidence of the content of customary international law norms." Id. at 338. The court also held that the international standards of liability with respect to the conduct of non-primary actors were defined with the specificity required to meet the requirements of *Sosa. Id.* at 340-41.

Note

1. The ICTY requirements of a "substantial effect" on perpetration of the crime by a principal is actually too limiting with respect to complicity or aiding and abetting. *See, e.g.*, JORDAN J. PAUST, M. CHERIF BASSIOUNI, *ET AL.*, INTERNATIONAL CRIMINAL LAW 69-74 (4 ed. 2013), also addressing *The Prosecutor v. Blaskic*, ICTY-95-14-T-A (Appeals Chamber, 29 Jul. 2004), para. 50 ("If he is aware that one of a number of crimes will probably be committed, and one of those crimes is in fact committed, he has intended to facilitate … that crime … and is guilty as an aider and abettor").

Sosa v. Alvarez Machain, 542 U.S. 692 (2004)

Souter, J.

The two issues are whether respondent Alvarez-Machain's allegation that the Drug Enforcement Administration instigated his abduction from Mexico for criminal trial in the United States supports a claim against the Government under the Federal Tort Claims Act (FTCA or Act), 28 U.S.C. § 1346(b)(1), §§ 2671-2680, and whether he may recover under the Alien Tort Statute (ATS) [ATCA], 28 U.S.C. § 1350. We hold that he is not entitled to a remedy under either statute. [Editors' note: the Court ruled that an exception to the FTCA's waiver of immunity for claims "arising in a foreign country" applied. 28 U.S.C. § 2680(k)]

We have considered the underlying facts before, United States v. Alvarez-Machain, 504 U.S. 655 … (1992) [That case was decided on the narrow ground that the abduction was not expressly a violation of a bilateral extradition treaty between the U.S. and Mexico]. In 1985, an agent of the Drug Enforcement Administration (DEA), Enrique Camarena-Salazar, was captured on assignment in Mexico and taken to a house in Guadalajara, where he was tortured over the course of a 2-day interrogation, then murdered. Based in part on eyewitness testimony, DEA officials in the United States came to believe that respondent Humberto Alvarez-Machain (Alvarez), a Mexican physician, was present at the house and acted to prolong the agent's life in order to extend the interrogation and torture. *Id.* at 657.

In 1990, a federal grand jury indicted Alvarez for the torture and murder of Camarena-Salazar, and the United States District Court for the Central District of California issued a warrant for his arrest. 331 F.3d 604, 609 (C.A.9 2003) (en banc). The DEA asked the Mexican Government for help in getting Alvarez into the United States, but when the requests and negotiations proved fruitless, the DEA approved a plan to hire Mexican nationals to seize Alvarez and bring him to the United States for trial. As so planned, a group of Mexicans, including petitioner Jose Francisco Sosa, abducted Alvarez from his house, held him overnight in a motel, and brought him by private plane to El Paso, Texas, where he was arrested by federal officers. *Ibid.*

Once in American custody, Alvarez moved to dismiss the indictment on the ground that his seizure was "outrageous governmental conduct," *Alvarez-Machain*, 504 U.S. at 568, and violated the extradition treaty between the United States and Mexico. The District Court agreed, the Ninth Circuit affirmed, and we reversed, *id.* at 670, holding that the fact of Alvarez's forcible seizure did not affect the jurisdiction of a federal court. The case was tried in 1992, and ended at the close of the Government's case, when the District Court granted Alvarez's motion for a judgment of acquittal.

In 1993, after returning to Mexico, Alvarez began the civil action before us here. He sued Sosa, Mexican citizen and DEA operative Antonio Garate-Bustamante, five unnamed Mexican civilians, the United States, and four DEA agents. 331 F.3d at 610. So far as it matters here, Alvarez sought damages from the United States under the FTCA, alleging false arrest, and from Sosa under the ATS, for a violation of the law of nations. The former statute authorizes suit "for ... personal injury ... caused by the negligent or wrongful act or omission of any employee of the Government while acting within the scope of his office or employment." 28 U.S.C. § 1346(b)(1). The latter provides in its entirety that "[t]he district courts shall have original jurisdiction of any civil action by an alien for a tort only, committed in violation of the law of nations or a treaty of the United States." § 1350....

Alvarez has also brought an action under the ATS against petitioner, Sosa, who argues (as does the United States supporting him) that there is no relief under the ATS because the statute does no more than vest federal courts with jurisdiction, neither creating nor authorizing the courts to recognize any particular right of action without further congressional action. Although we agree the statute is in terms only jurisdictional, we think that at the time of enactment the jurisdiction enabled federal courts to hear claims in a very limited category defined by the law of nations and recognized at common law. We do not believe, however, that the limited, implicit sanction to entertain the handful of international law *cum* common law claims understood in 1789 should be taken as authority to recognize the right of action asserted by Alvarez here....

The parties and *amici* here advance radically different historical interpretations of this terse provision. Alvarez says that the ATS was intended not simply as a jurisdictional grant, but as authority for the creation of a new cause of action for torts in violation of international law. We think that reading is implausible. As enacted in 1789, the ATS gave the district courts "cognizance" of certain causes of action, and the term bespoke a grant of jurisdiction, not power to mold substantive law. *See, e.g.,* THE FEDERALIST No. 81, pp. 447, 451 (J. Cooke ed. 1961) (A. Hamilton) (using "jurisdiction" interchangeably with "cognizance"). The fact that the ATS was placed in § 9 of the Judiciary Act, a statute otherwise exclusively concerned with federal-court jurisdiction, is itself support for its strictly jurisdictional nature. Nor would the distinction between jurisdiction and cause of action have been elided by the drafters of the Act or those who voted on it. As Fisher Ames put it, "there is a substantial difference between the jurisdiction of courts and rules of decision." 1 ANNALS OF CONG. 807 (Gales ed. 1834). It is unsurprising, then, that an authority on the historical origins of the ATS has written that "section 1350 clearly does not create a statutory cause of action," and that the contrary suggestion is "simply frivolous." Casto, *The Federal Courts' Protective Jurisdiction Over Torts Committed in Violation of the Law of Nations*, 18 CONN. L. REV. 467, 479, 480 (1986) (hereinafter Casto, *Law of Nations*); Cf. Dodge, *The Constitutionality of the Alien Tort Statute: Some Observations on Text and Context*, 42 VA. J. INT'L L. 687, 689 (2002). In sum, we think the statute was intended as jurisdictional in the sense of addressing the power of the courts to entertain cases concerned with a certain subject.

But holding the ATS jurisdictional raises a new question, this one about the interaction between the ATS at the time of its enactment and the ambient law of the era. Sosa would have it that the ATS was stillborn because there could be no claim for relief without a further statute expressly authorizing adoption of causes of action. *Amici* professors of federal jurisdiction and legal history take a different tack, that federal courts could entertain claims once the jurisdictional grant was on the books, because torts in violation of the law of nations would have been recognized within the common law of the time. Brief for Vikram Amar *et al.* as *Amici Curiae.* We think history and practice give the edge to this latter position.

"When the *United States* declared their independence, they were bound to receive the law of nations, in its modern state of purity and refinement." Ware v. Hylton, 3 Dall. 199, 281 ... (1796) (Wilson, J.). In the years of the early Republic, this law of nations comprised two principal elements, the first covering the general norms governing the behavior of national states with each other:"*the science which teaches the rights subsisting between nations or states, and the obligations correspondent to those rights,*" E. DE VATTEL, THE LAW OF NATIONS, PRELIMINARIES § 3 (J. Chitty *et al.* transl. and ed. 1883) (hereinafter Vattel) (footnote omitted), or "that code of public instruction which defines the rights and prescribes the duties of nations, in their intercourse with each other," 1 JAMES KENT COMMENTARIES *1. This aspect of the law of nations thus occupied the executive and legislative domains, not the judicial. See 4 W. BLACK- STONE, COMMENTARIES ON THE LAWS OF ENGLAND 68 (1769) (hereinafter Commen- taries) ("[O]ffenses against" the law of nations are "principally incident to whole states or nations").

The law of nations included a second, more pedestrian element, however, that did fall within the judicial sphere, as a body of judge-made law regulating the conduct of in- dividuals situated outside domestic boundaries and consequently carrying an interna- tional savor. To Blackstone, the law of nations in this sense was implicated "in mercan- tile questions, such as bills of exchange and the like; in all marine causes, relating to freight, average, demurrage, insurances, bottomry ... ; [and] in all disputes relating to prizes, to shipwrecks, to hostages, and ransom bills." *Id.,* at 67. The law merchant emerged from the customary practices of international traders and admiralty required its own transnational regulation. And it was the law of nations in this sense that our precursors spoke about when the Court explained the status of coast fishing vessels in wartime grew from "ancient usage among civilized nations, beginning centuries ago, and gradually ripening into a rule of international law...." The Paquete Habana, 175 U.S. 677, 686 ... (1900).

There was, finally, a sphere in which these rules binding individuals for the benefit of other individuals overlapped with the norms of state relationships. Blackstone referred to it when he mentioned three specific offenses against the law of nations addressed by the criminal law of England: violation of safe conducts, infringement of the rights of ambassadors, and piracy. 4 COMMENTARIES 68. An assault against an ambassador, for example, impinged upon the sovereignty of the foreign nation and if not adequately re- dressed could rise to an issue of war. See VATTEL 463-464. It was this narrow set of vio- lations of the law of nations, admitting of a judicial remedy and at the same time threat- ening serious consequences in international affairs, that was probably on minds of the men who drafted the ATS with its reference to tort.

Before there was any ATS, a distinctly American preoccupation with these hybrid in- ternational norms had taken shape owing to the distribution of political power from in- dependence through the period of confederation. The Continental Congress was ham- strung by its inability to "cause infractions of treaties, or of the law of nations to be punished," J. MADISON, JOURNAL OF THE CONSTITUTIONAL CONVENTION 60 (E. Scott ed. 1893), and in 1781 the Congress implored the States to vindicate rights under the law of nations. In words that echo Blackstone, the congressional resolution called upon state legislatures to "provide expeditious, exemplary, and adequate punishment" for "the violation of safe conducts or passports, ... of hostility against such as are in amity, ... with the United States, ... infractions of the immunities of ambassadors and other public ministers ... [and] "infractions of treaties and conventions to which the United States are a party." 21 Journals of the Continental Congress 1136-1137 (G. Hunt ed.1912) (hereinafter Journals of the Continental Congress). The resolution recommended that the States "authorise suits ... for damages by the party injured, and for compensation to the United States for damage sustained by them from an injury done to a foreign power by a citizen." *Id.*, at 1137; *cf.* Vattel 463-464 ("Whoever offends ... a public minister ... should be punished..., and ... the state should, at the expense of the delinquent, give full satisfaction to the sovereign who has been offended in the person of his minister"). Apparently only one State acted upon the recommendation, *see* First Laws of the State of Connecticut 82, 83 (J. Cushing ed. 1982) (1784 compilation; exact date of Act unknown), but Congress had done what it could to signal a commitment to enforce the law of nations.

Appreciation of the Continental Congress's incapacity to deal with this class of cases was intensified by the so-called Marbois incident of May 1784, in which a French adventurer, Longchamps, verbally and physically assaulted the Secretary of the French Legion in Philadelphia. See Respublica v. De Longchamps, 1 Dall. 111 ... (O.T. Phila. 1784). Congress called again for state legislation addressing such matters, and concern over the inadequate vindication of the law of nations persisted through the time of the constitutional convention. See 1 Records of the Federal Convention of 1787, p. 25 (M. Farrand ed. 1911) (speech of J. Randolph). During the Convention itself, in fact, a New York City constable produced a reprise of the Marbois affair and Secretary Jay reported to Congress on the Dutch Ambassador's protest, with the explanation that "the federal government does not appear ... to be vested with any judicial Powers competent to the Cognizance and Judgment of such Cases." Casto, *Law of Nations* 494, and n.152.

The Framers responded by vesting the Supreme Court with original jurisdiction over "all Cases affecting Ambassadors, other public ministers and Consuls." U.S. Const., Art. III, §2, and the First Congress followed through. The Judiciary Act reinforced this Court's original jurisdiction over suits brought by diplomats, see 1 Stat. 80, ch. 20, §13, created alienage jurisdiction, §11 and, of course, included the ATS, §9....

Although Congress modified the draft of what became the Judiciary Act, *see generally* Warren, *New Light on the History of the Federal Judiciary Act of 1789*, 37 Harv. L. Rev. 49 (1923), it made hardly any changes to the provisions on aliens, including what became the ATS, see Casto, *Law of Nations* 498. There is no record of congressional discussion about private actions that might be subject to the jurisdictional provision, or about any need for further legislation to create private remedies; there is no record even of debate on the section....

Still, the history does tend to support two propositions. First, there is every reason to suppose that the First Congress did not pass the ATS as a jurisdictional convenience to be placed on the shelf for use by a future Congress or state legislature that might, some day, authorize the creation of causes of action or itself decide to make some element of the law of nations actionable for the benefit of foreigners. The anxieties of the preconstitutional period cannot be ignored easily enough to think that the statute was not meant to have a practical effect. Consider that the principal draftsman of the ATS was apparently Oliver Ellsworth,previously a member of the Continental Congress that had passed the 1781 resolution and a member of the Connecticut Legislature that made good on that congressional request. *See generally* W. Brown, The Life of Oliver Ellsworth (1905). Consider, too, that the First Congress was attentive enough to the law of nations to recognize certain offenses expressly as criminal, including the three mentioned by Blackstone. See An Act for the Punishment of Certain Crimes Against the United States, §8, 1 Stat. 113-114 (murder or robbery, or other capital crimes, punishable as piracy if committed on the high seas), and §28, *id.*, at 118 (violation of safe conducts and assaults against ambassadors punished by imprisonment and fines described as "infract[ions of] the law of nations"). It would have been passing strange for Ellsworth and this very Congress to vest federal courts expressly with jurisdiction to entertain civil causes brought by aliens alleging violations of the law of nations, but to no effect whatever until the Congress should take further action. There is too much in the historical record to believe that Congress would have enacted the ATS only to leave it lying fallow indefinitely.

The second inference to be drawn from the history is that Congress intended the ATS to furnish jurisdiction for a relatively modest set of actions alleging violations of the law of nations. Uppermost in the legislative mind appears to have been offenses against ambassadors, see *id.*, at 118; violations of safe conduct were probably understood to be actionable, *ibid.*, and individual actions arising out of prize captures and piracy may well have also been contemplated. *Id.*, at 113-114. But the common law appears to have understood only those three of the hybrid variety as definite and actionable, or at any rate, to have assumed only a very limited set of claims. As Blackstone had put it, "offences against this law [of nations] are principally incident to whole states or nations," and not individuals seeking relief in court. 4 COMMENTARIES 68.

The sparse contemporaneous cases and legal materials referring to the ATS tend to confirm both inferences, that some, but few, torts in violation of the law of nations were understood to be within the common law. In Bolchos v. Darrel, 3 F. Cas. 810 (No. 1,607) (D.S.C. 1795), the District Court's doubt about admiralty jurisdiction over a suit for damages brought by a French privateer against the mortgagee of a British slave ship was assuaged by assuming that the ATS was a jurisdictional basis for the court's action. Nor is Moxon v. The Fanny, 17 F. Cas. 942 (No. 9,895) (D. Pa. 1793), to the contrary, a case in which the owners of a British ship sought damages for its seizure in United States waters by a French privateer. The District Court said in dictum that the ATS was not the proper vehicle for suit because "[i]t cannot be called a suit for a tort only, when the property, as well as damages for the supposed trespass, are sought for." *Id.* at 948. But the judge gave no intimation that further legislation would have been needed to give the District Court jurisdiction over a suit limited to damages.

Then there was the 1795 opinion of Attorney General William Bradford, who was asked whether criminal prosecution was available against Americans who had taken part in the French plunder of a British slave colony in Sierra Leone. 1 Op. Atty. Gen. 57. Bradford was uncertain, but he made it clear that a federal court was open for the prosecution of a tort action growing out of the episode:

> "But there can be no doubt that the company or individuals who have been injured by these acts of hostility have a remedy by a *civil* suit in the courts of the United States; jurisdiction being expressly given to these courts in all cases where an alien sues for a tort only, in violation of the laws of nations, or a treaty of the United States...." *Id.*, at 59.

Although it is conceivable that Bradford (who had prosecuted in the Marbois incident, see Casto, *Law of Nations* 503, n.201) assumed that there had been a violation of a treaty, 1 Op. Atty. Gen., at 58, that is certainly not obvious, and it appears likely that

Bradford understood the ATS to provide jurisdiction over what must have amounted to common law causes of action....

In sum, although the ATS is a jurisdictional statute creating no new causes of action, the reasonable inference from the historical materials is that the statute was intended to have practical effect the moment it became law. The jurisdictional grant is best read as having been enacted on the understanding that the common law would provide a cause of action for the modest number of international law violations with a potential for personal liability at the time.

We think it is correct, then, to assume that the First Congress understood that the district courts would recognize private causes of action for certain torts in violation of the law of nations, though we have found no basis to suspect Congress had any examples in mind beyond those torts corresponding to Blackstone's three primary offenses: violation of safe conducts, infringement of the rights of ambassadors, and piracy. We assume, too, that no development in the two centuries from the enactment of § 1350 to the birth of the modern line of cases beginning with Filartiga v. Pena-Irala, 630 F.2d 876 (C.A.2 1980), has categorically precluded federal courts from recognizing a claim under the law of nations as an element of common law; Congress has not in any relevant way amended § 1350 or limited civil common law power by another statute. Still, there are good reasons for a restrained conception of the discretion a federal court should exercise in considering a new cause of action of this kind. Accordingly, we think courts should require any claim based on the present-day law of nations to rest on a norm of international character accepted by the civilized world and defined with a specificity comparable to the features of the 18th-century paradigms we have recognized. This requirement is fatal to Alvarez's claim.

A series of reasons argue for judicial caution when considering the kinds of individual claims that might implement the jurisdiction conferred by the early statute. First, the prevailing conception of the common law has changed since 1789 in a way that counsels restraint in judicially applying internationally generated norms. When § 1350 was enacted, the accepted conception was of the common law as "a transcendental body of law outside of any particular State but obligatory within it unless and until changed by statute." Black and White Taxicab & Transfer Co. v. Brown and Yellow Taxicab & Transfer Co., 276 U.S. 518, 533 ... (1928) (Holmes, J., dissenting). Now, however, in most cases where a court is asked to state or formulate a common law principle in a new context, there is a general understanding that the law is not so much found or discovered as it is either made or created....

... [A] judge deciding in reliance on an international norm will find a substantial element of discretionary judgment in the decision.

Second, along with, and in part driven by, that conceptual development in understanding common law has come an equally significant rethinking of the role of the federal courts in making it. Erie R. Co. v. Tompkins, 304 U.S. 64 ... (1938), was the watershed in which we denied the existence of any federal "general" common law, *id.*, at 78, which largely withdrew to havens of specialty, some of them defined by express congressional authorization to devise a body of law directly, *e.g.*, Textile Workers v. Lincoln Mills of Ala., 353 U.S. 448 ... (1957) (interpretation of collective-bargaining agreements); Fed. Rule Evid. 501 (evidentiary privileges in federal-question cases). Elsewhere, this Court has thought it was in order to create federal common law rules in interstitial areas of particular federal interest. *E.g.,* United States v. Kimbell Foods, Inc., 440 U.S. 715, 726-727 ... (1979).And although we have even assumed competence to make judicial rules of decision of particular importance to foreign relations, such as the act of state doctrine, see Banco Nacional de Cuba v. Sabbatino, 376 U.S. 398, 427 ... (1964), the general practice has been to look for legislative guidance before exercising innovative authority over substantive law. It would be remarkable to take a more aggressive role in exercising a jurisdiction that remained largely in shadow for much of the prior two centuries.

Third, this Court has recently and repeatedly said that a decision to create a private right of action is one better left to legislative judgment in the great majority of cases.... [E]ven when Congress has made it clear by statute that a rule applies to purely domestic conduct, we are reluctant to infer intent to provide a private cause of action where the statute does not supply one expressly. While the absence of congressional action addressing private rights of action under an international norm is more equivocal than its failure to provide such a right when it creates a statute, the possible collateral consequences of making international rules privately actionable argue for judicial caution.

Fourth, the subject of those collateral consequences is itself a reason for a high bar to new private causes of action for violating international law, for the potential implications for the foreign relations of the United States of recognizing such causes should make courts particularly wary of impinging on the discretion of the Legislative and Executive Branches in managing foreign affairs. It is one thing for American courts to enforce constitutional limits on our own State and Federal Governments' power, but quite another to consider suits under rules that would go so far as to claim a limit on the power of foreign governments over their own citizens, and to hold that a foreign government or its agent has transgressed those limits. *Cf. Sabbatino, supra,* at 431-432. Yet modern international law is very much concerned with just such questions, and apt to stimulate calls for vindicating private interests in § 1350 cases. Since many attempts by federalcourts to craft remedies for the violation of new norms of international law would raise risks of adverse foreign policy consequences, they should be undertaken, if at all, with great caution. *Cf.* Tel-Oren v. Libyan Arab Republic, 726 F.2d 774, 813 (C.A.D.C. 1984) (Bork, J., concurring) (expressing doubt that § 1350 should be read to require "our courts [to] sit in judgment of the conduct of foreign officials in their own countries with respect to their own citizens").

The fifth reason is particularly important in light of the first four. We have no congressional mandate to seek out and define new and debatable violations of the law of nations, and modern indications of congressional understanding of the judicial role in the field have not affirmatively encouraged greater judicial creativity....

These reasons argue for great caution in adapting the law of nations to private rights. Justice Scalia (opinion concurring in part and concurring in judgment) concludes that caution is too hospitable, and a word is in order to summarize where we have come so far and to focus our difference with him on whether some norms of today's law of nations may ever be recognized legitimately by federal courts in the absence of congressional action beyond § 1350. is only jurisdictional. We also agree, or at least Justice Scalia does not dispute, that the jurisdiction was originally understood to be available to enforce a small number of international norms that a federal court could properly recognize as within the common law enforceable without further statutory authority. Justice Scalia concludes, however, that two subsequent developments should be understood to preclude federal courts from recognizing any further international norms as judicially enforceable today, absent further congressional action. As described before, we now tend to understand common law not as a discoverable reflection of universal reason but, in a positivistic way, as a product of human choice. And we now adhere to a conception of limited judicial power first expressed in reorienting federal diversity jurisdiction, see Erie v. Tompkins, 304 U.S. 64 … (1938), that federal courts have no authority to derive "general" common law.

Whereas Justice Scalia sees these developments as sufficient to close the door to further independent judicial recognition of actionable international norms, other considerations persuade us that the judicial power should be exercised on the understanding that the door is still ajar subject to vigilant doorkeeping, and thus open to a narrow class of international norms today. *Erie* did not in terms bar any judicial recognition of new substantive rules, no matter what the circumstances, and post-*Eire* understanding has identified limited enclaves in which federal courts may derive some substantive law in a common law way. For two centuries we have affirmed that the domestic law of the United States recognizes the law of nations. *See, e.g., Sabbatino*, 376 U.S. at 423 ("[I]t is, of course, true that United States courts apply international law as a part of our own in appropriate circumstances"); *The Paquete Habana,* 175 U.S. at 700 ("International law is part of our law, and must be ascertained and administered by the courts of justice of appropriate jurisdiction, as often as questions of right depending upon it are duly presented for their determination"); The Nereide, 9 Cranch 388, 423 … (18) (Marshall, C.J.) ("[T]he Court is bound by the law of nations which is a part of the law of the land"); see also Texas Industries, Inc. v. Radcliff Materials, Inc., 451 U.S. 630, 641 … (1981) (recognizing that "international disputes implicating … our relations with foreign nations" are one of the "narrow areas" in which "federal common law" continues to exist). It would take some explaining to say now that federal courts must avert their gaze entirely from any international norm intended to protect individuals.

We think an attempt to justify such a position would be particularly unconvincing in light of what we know about congressional understanding bearing on this issue lying at the intersection of the judicial and legislative powers. The First Congress, which reflected the understanding of the framing generation and included some of the Framers, assumed that federal courts could properly identify some international norms as enforceable in the exercise of § 1350 jurisdiction. We think it would be unreasonable to assume that the First Congress would have expected federal courts to lose all capacity to recognize enforceable international norms simply because the common law might lose some metaphysical cachet on the road to modern realism. Later Congresses seem to have shared our view. The position we take today has been assumed by some federal courts for 24 years, ever since the Second Circuit decided Filartiga v. Pena-Irala, 630 F.2d 876 (C.A.2 1980), and for practical purposes the point of today's disagreement has been focused since the exchange between Judge Edwards and Judge Bork in Tel-Oren v. Libyan Arab Republic, 726 F.2d 774 (C.A.D.C. 1984). Congress, however, has not only expressed no disagreement with our view of the proper exercise of the judicial power, but has responded to its most notable instance by enacting legislation supplementing the judicial determination in some detail.…

We must still, however, derive a standard or set of standards for assessing the particular claim Alvarez raises, and for this case it suffices to look to the historical antecedents. Whatever the ultimate criteria for accepting a cause of action subject to jurisdiction under § 1350, we are persuaded that federal courts should not recognize private claims under federal common law for violations of any international law norm with less definite content and acceptance among civilized nations than the historical paradigms familiar when § 1350 was enacted. *See, e.g.,* United States v. Smith, 5 Wheat. 153, 163-180 n.a … (1820) (illustrating the specificity with which the law of nations defined piracy). This limit upon judicial recognition is generally consistent with the reasoning of many of the courts and judges who faced the issue before it reached this Court. See

Filartiga, supra, at 890 ("[F]or purposes of civil liability, the torturer has become—like the pirate and slave trader before him—*hostis humani generis,* an enemy of all mankind"); *Tel-Oren, supra,* at 781 (Edwards, J., concurring) (suggesting that the "limits of section 1350' s reach" be defined by "a handful of heinous actions—each of which violates definable, universal and obligatory norms"); see also In re Estate of Marcos Human Rights Litigation, 25 F.3d 1467, 1475 (C.A.9 1994) ("Actionable violations of international law must be of a norm that is specific, universal, and obligatory"). And the determination whether a norm is sufficiently definite to support a cause of action should (and, indeed, inevitably must) involve an element of judgment about the practical consequences of making that cause available to litigants in the federal courts. [Court's note 21, in part: This requirement of clear definition is not meant to be the only principle limiting the availability of relief in the federal courts for violations of customary international law, though it disposes of this case....]

Thus, Alvarez's detention claim must be gauged against the current state of international law, looking to those sources we have long, albeit cautiously, recognized.... [the Court quoted *The Paquete Habana,* 175 U.S. at 700.]

To begin with, Alvarez cites two well-known international agreements that, despite their moral authority, have little utility under the standard set out in this opinion. He says that his abduction by Sosa was an "arbitrary arrest" within the meaning of the Universal Declaration of Human Rights (Declaration), G.A. Res. 217A (III), U.N. Doc. A/810 (1948). And he traces the rule against arbitrary arrest not only to the Declaration, but also to article nine of the International Covenant on Civil and Political Rights (Covenant), Dec. 19, 1996, 999 U.N.T.S. 171, to which the United States is a party, and to various other conventions to which it is not. But the Declaration does not of its own force impose obligations as a matter of international law. See Humphrey, *The UN Charter and the Universal Declaration of Human Rights,* in The International Protection of Human Rights 39, 50 (E. Luard ed.1967) (quoting Eleanor Roosevelt calling the Declaration "'a statement of principles ... setting up a common standard of achievement for all peoples and all nations'" and "'not a treaty or international agreement ... impos[ing] legal obligations'"). [Court's note 23, in part: It has nevertheless had substantial indirect effect on international law....] And, although the Covenant does bind the United States as a matter of international law, the United States ratified the Covenant on the express understanding that it was not self-executing and so did not itself create obligations enforceable in the federal courts. Accordingly, Alvarez cannot say that the Declaration and Covenant themselves establish the relevant and applicable rule of international law. He instead attempts to show that prohibition of arbitrary arrest has attained the status of binding customary international law.

Here, it is useful to examine Alvarez's complaint in greater detail. As he presently argues it, the claim does not rest on the cross-border feature of his abduction. [Court's note 24: Alvarez's brief contains one footnote seeking to incorporate by reference his arguments on cross-border abductions before the Court of Appeals. Brief for Respondent Alvarez-Machain 47, n.46. That is not enough to raise the question fairly, and we do not consider it.] Although the District Court granted relief in part on finding a violation of international law in taking Alvarez across the border from Mexico to the United States, the Court of Appeals rejected that ground of liability for failure to identify a norm of requisite force prohibiting a forcible abduction across a border. Instead, it relied on the conclusion that the law of the United States did not authorize Alvarez's arrest, because the DEA lacked extraterritorial authority under 21 U.S.C. §878, and because Federal Rule of Criminal Procedure 4(d)(2) limited the warrant for Alvarez's arrest to "the jurisdiction of the United States." It is this position that Alvarez takes now: that his arrest was arbitrary and as such forbidden by international law not because it infringed the prerogatives of Mexico, but because no applicable law authorized it.

Alvarez thus invokes a general prohibition of "arbitrary" detention defined as officially sanctioned action exceeding positive authorization to detain under the domestic law of some government, regardless of the circumstances. Whether or not this is an accurate reading of the Covenant, Alvarez cites little authority that a rule so broad has the status of a binding customary norm today. He certainly cites nothing to justify the federal courts in taking his broad rule as the predicate for a federal lawsuit, for its implications would be breathtaking. His rule would support a cause of action in federal court for any arrest, anywhere in the world, unauthorized by the law of the jurisdiction in which it took place, and would create a cause of action for any seizure of an alien in violation of the Fourth Amendment, supplanting the actions under Rev. Stat. § 1979, 42 U.S.C. § 1983 and Bivens. v. Six Unknown Fed. Narcotics Agents, 403 U.S. 388 ... (1971), that now provide damages remedies for such violations. It would create an action in federal court for arrests by state officers who simply exceed their authority; and for the violation of any limit that the law of any country might place on the authority of its own officers to arrest. And all of this assumes that Alvarez could establish that Sosa was acting on behalf of a government when he made the arrest, for otherwise he would need a rule broader still.

Alvarez's failure to marshal support for his proposed rule is underscored by the RESTATEMENT (THIRD) OF FOREIGN RELATIONS LAW OF THE UNITED STATES (1987), which says in its discussion of customary international human rights law that a "state violates international law if, as a matter of state policy, it practices, encourages, or condones ... prolonged arbitrary detention." *Id.* Although the Restatement does not explain its requirements of a "state policy" and of "prolonged" detention, the implication is clear. Any credible invocation of a principle against arbitrary detention that the civilized world accepts as binding customary international law requires a factual basis beyond relatively brief detention in excess of positive authority....

Whatever may be said for the broad principle Alvarez advances, in the present, imperfect world, it expresses an aspiration that exceeds any binding customary rule having the specificity we require. Creating a private cause of action to further that aspiration would go beyond any residual common law discretion we think it appropriate to exercise. It is enough to hold that a single illegal detention of less than a day, followed by the transfer of custody to lawful authorities and a prompt arraignment, violates no norm of customary international law so well defined as to support the creation of a federal remedy.

Breyer, J., concurring in part and concurring in the judgment

I join Justice Ginsburg's concurrence and join the Court's opinion in respect to the Alien Tort Statute (ATS) claim. The Court says that to qualify for recognition under the ATS a norm of international law must have a content as definite as, and an acceptance as widespread as, those that characterized 18th-century international norms prohibiting piracy.... The norm must extend liability to the type of perpetrator (*e.g.,* a private actor) the plaintiff seeks to sue.... And Congress can make clear that courts should not recognize any such norm, through a direct or indirect command or by occupying the field.... The Court also suggests that principles of exhaustion might apply, and that courts should give "serious weight" to the Executive Branch's view of the impact on foreign policy that permitting an ATS suit will likely have in a given case or type of case.... I believe all of these conditions are important.

I would add one further consideration. Since enforcement of an international norm by one nation's courts implies that other nations' courts may do the same, I would ask whether the exercise of jurisdiction under the ATS is consistent with those notions of comity that lead each nation to respect the sovereign rights of other nations by limiting the reach of its laws and their enforcement. In applying those principles, courts help assure that "the potentially conflicting laws of different nations" will "work together in harmony," a matter of increasing importance in an ever more interdependent world. F. Hoffman-La Roche Ltd. v. Empagram S.A., 542 U.S. 155 (2004); *cf.* Murray v. Schooner Charming Betsy, 2 Cranch 64, 118 … (1804). Such consideration is necessary to ensure that ATS litigation does not undermine the very harmony that it was intended to promote.…

These comity concerns normally do not arise (or at least are mitigated) if the conduct in question takes place in the country that provides the cause of action or if that conduct involves that country's own national—where, say, an American assaults a foreign diplomat and the diplomat brings suit in an American court. See RESTATEMENT (THIRD) OF FOREIGN RELATIONS LAW OF THE UNITED STATES §§ 402(1), (2) (1987) (hereinafter Restatement) (describing traditional bases of territorial and nationality jurisdiction). They do arise, however, when foreign persons injured abroad bring suit in the United States under the ATS, asking the courts to recognize a claim that a certain kind of foreign conduct violates an international norm.

Since different courts in different nations will not necessarily apply even similar substantive laws similarly, workable harmony, in practice, depends upon more than substantive uniformity among the laws of those nations. That is to say, substantive uniformity does not *automatically* mean that universal jurisdiction is appropriate. Thus, in the 18th century, nations reached consensus not only on the substantive principle that acts of piracy were universally wrong but also on the jurisdictional principle that any nation that found a pirate could prosecute him. *See, e.g.*, United States v. Smith, 5 Wheat. 153, 162 … (1820) (referring to "the general practice of all nations in punishing all persons, whether natives or foreigners, who have committed [piracy] against any persons whatsoever, with whom they are in amity").

Today international law will sometimes similarly reflect not only substantive agreement as to certain universally condemned behavior but also procedural agreement that universal jurisdiction exists to prosecute a subset of that behavior. See RESTATEMENT § 404, and Comment *a*; International Law Association, Final Report on the Exercise of Universal Jurisdiction in Respect of Gross Human Rights Offences 2 (2000). That subset includes torture, genocide, crimes against humanity, and war crimes. See *id.* at 5-8; see also, *e.g.*, Prosecutor v. Furundzija, Case No. IT-95-17/1-T, paras. 155-156 (International Tribunal for Prosecution of Persons Responsible for Serious Violations of International Humanitarian Law Committed in Territory of Former Yugoslavia since 1991 [ICTY], Dec. 10, 1998); Attorney Gen. of Israel v. Eichmann, 36 I.L.R. 277 (Sup.Ct. Israel 1962).

The fact that this procedural consensus exists suggests that recognition of universal jurisdiction in respect to a limited set of norms is consistent with principles of international comity. That is, allowing every nation's courts to adjudicate foreign conduct involving foreign parties in such cases will not significantly threaten the practical harmony that comity principles seek to protect. That consensus concerns criminal jurisdiction, but consensus as to universal criminal jurisdiction itself suggests that universal tort jurisdiction would be no more threatening. *Cf.* RESTATEMENT § 404, Comment *b*. That is because the criminal courts of many nations combine civil and criminal proceedings, allowing those injured by criminal conduct to be represented, and to recover damages, in the criminal proceeding itself. Brief for European Commission as

Amicus Curiae 21, n.48 (citing 3 Y. Donzallaz, La Convention de Lugano du 16 septembre 1998 concernant la competence judiciaire et l'execution des decisions en matiere civile et commerciale, paras. 5203-5272 (1998); EC Council Regulation Art. 5, §4, 44/2001, 2001 O.J. (L 12/1) (Jan. 16, 2001)). Thus, universal criminal jurisdiction necessarily contemplates a significant degree of civil tort recovery as well.

Taking these matters into account, as I believe courts should, I can find no similar procedural consensus supporting the exercise of jurisdiction in this case. That lack of consensus provides additional support for the Court's conclusion that the ATS does not recognize the claim at issue here—where the underlying substantive claim concerns arbitrary arrest, outside the United States, of a citizen of one foreign country by another.

Notes and Questions

1. The majority opinion in *Sosa* concluded that the ATCA (ATS) does not create a cause of action. It is unlikely that the Court will revisit its conclusion any time soon. Nevertheless, if it ever entertains the issue in the future it is of interest that no other judicial opinion had concluded that the ATCA does not create a cause of action other than the highly criticized concurring opinion of former Judge Bork in *Tel-Oren*. Early cases and opinions of the Attorneys General pointed the other way. *See, e.g.*, 1 Op. Att'y Gen. 57, 58 (1795) ("the company or individuals who have been injured by these acts of hostility have a remedy by a civil suit in the courts of the United States."); see also *United States v. Greene*, 26 F. Cas. 33, 33 (C.C.D. Maine 1827) (No. 15,258) (Story, J: "gives … right … to sue"); *M'Grath v. Candalero*, 16 F. Cas. 128 (D.S.C. 1794) (No. 6,810) ("sue here for a tort … the suit will be sustained"); *Jansen v. The Vrow Christina Magdalena*, 13 F. Cas. 356, 358 (D.S.C. 1794) (No. 7,216) ("the powers of the district courts are expressed … as to civil causes … where an alien sues for a tort only"); *Bolchos v. Darrel*, 3 F. Cas. 810, 810 (D.S.C. 1795) (No. 1,607) ("the original cause arose at sea … [and ATCA allows the court] to take cognizance of the cause"); 26 Op. Att'y Gen. 250, 252-53 (1907) (ATCA provides "a forum and a right of action"); Jordan J. Paust, *The History, Nature, and Reach of the Alien Tort Claims Act*, 16 FLA. J. INT'L L. 249, 250-52 n.3, 254 & n.11 (2004). Why did the Supreme Court ignore these early recognitions? Was there also a failure of counsel to raise them? See the Briefs filed in *Sosa*.

2. What is important after *Sosa* is the question concerning what types of violations of customary international law that the majority on the Court will recognize as actionable under the ATCA. The Court in *Sosa* was not fully briefed on the types of infractions of both treaties and the customary law of nations known to the Founders, Framers, and early judiciary and, in view of the majority opinion in *Sosa*, such a history should be revisited. In particular, Justice Souter cited portions of the 1781 Resolution of the Continental Congress, but he did not mention the point expressed in the Resolution that some of the listed infractions of the customary law of nations were only those that were most obvious. Additionally, it is curious why Justice Souter stated that "[i]t was … [a] narrow set of" three violations of the law of nations mentioned by Blackstone "that was probably on minds of the men who drafted the ATS" when Justice Souter had also recognized that the 1781 Resolution addressed two others: (1) acts of hostility against such as are in amity with the U.S. (also addressed in the 1795 Opinion of the Attorney General), and (2) all "infractions of treaties and conventions to which the United States are a party"—and having neglected a third: other less obvious customary "offences against the law of nations." These should also be considered if what was "on the minds of the men who drafted the" statute is important.

Importantly, Justice Breyer recognized that torture, war crimes, genocide, and crimes against humanity are actionable under the ATCA (124 S.Ct. at 2783 (Breyer, J., concurring)). It is also worth emphasizing that the Supreme Court recognized early in our history in *Talbot v. Janson*, 3 U.S. (3 Dall.) 133, 159-61 (1795) (Iredell, J.) that "all ... trespasses committed against the general law of nations, are enquirable, and may be proceeded against"). In *Fletcher v. Peck*, 10 U.S. (6 Cranch) 87, 133 (1810), Chief Justice Marshall also affirmed that our judicial tribunals "are established ... to decide on human rights." *See also The Julia*, 12 U.S. (8 Cranch) 181, 193 (1814) (Story, J., dissenting) ("rights of humanity" in time of war); *Chisholm v. Georgia*, 2 U.S. (2 Dall.) 419, 421 (counsel referring to "human rights"), 478 ("rights of men") (1793) (Jay, C.J.); *Vanhorne's Lessee v. Dorrance*, 2 U.S. (2 Dall.) 304, 310 (1795) (Paterson, J.) ("rights of man"); *Henfield's Case*, 11 F. Cas. 1099, 1120 (C.C.D. Pa. 1793) (No. 6,360) (Wilson, J., with Iredell, J., on circuit, and Judge Peters) ("rights of man"). Concerning later attention to human rights precepts in thousands of federal and state cases, *see, e.g.*, JORDAN J. PAUST, INTERNATIONAL LAW AS LAW OF THE UNITED STATES 210-23 (2 ed. 2003), and cases cited. Concerning other types of infractions known early in our history, *see, e.g.*, *id*. at 11-12.

3. How might other actionable modern violations of customary international law be discovered? Recall the majority opinion's recognition that "courts should require any claim based on the present day law of nations to rest on a norm of international character accepted by the civilized world and defined with a specificity comparable to the features of the 18th-century paradigms" recognized by the Court, which included piracy, acts of hostility or breaches of neutrality, infringements of rights of ambassadors, violations of safe conduct, and war crimes [and how were these defined?]. The majority opinion also addressed *United States v. Smith* as a case "illustrating the specificity with which the law of nations defined piracy" and *In re Estate of Marcos*, and stated that the issue is "whether a norm is sufficiently definite to support a cause of action."

4. Despite the statement about *The Paquete Habana* in the majority opinion, students should note that *The Paquete Habana* did not rest on the "law merchant" or "admiralty" law as such. The Court in *Paquete* expressly referred to "international law," the "law of war," and the "law of nations" as the bases for its decision that the Executive seizures abroad of enemy alien vessels and enemy aliens in time of war were illegal. The law merchant and admiralty law as such had long been separated from the law of nations by 1900. In *Paquete Habana*, what the Court had considered with respect to the proof of the content of international law were various forms of state practice and patterns of *opinio juris*. *See, e.g.*, PAUST, INTERNATIONAL LAW AS LAW OF THE UNITED STATES 172, 174-77 (2 ed. 2003).

5. The majority of the Court clearly rejected a radical ahistorical claim of a few textwriters that customary international law was mere common law, that such was law of the United States only insofar as Congress incorporated it, and that *Erie* had obviated its use in federal courts. Justice Scalia made that argument in dissent when claiming that the law of nations was mere "general common law" and that *Erie* (which did not address international law) precludes its use. 124 S.Ct. at 2770, also citing Young, *Sorting out the Debate Over Customary International Law*, 42 Va. J. Int'l L. 365, 374 (2002); Bradley & Goldsmith, *Customary International Law as Federal Common Law: A Critique of the Modern Position*, 110 Harv. L. Rev. 815, 824 (1997); Brief for Vikram Amar, *et al.*, as *Amici Curiae* 12-13. *But see* PAUST, *supra* at 7-9 & 39-43 n.50; Jordan J. Paust, *International Law Before the Supreme Court: A Mixed Record of Recognition*, 45 SANTA CLARA L. REV. & n.118 (2005); *Customary International Law and Human Rights Treaties* Are *Law of the United States*, 20 Mich. J. Int'l L. 301, 301-21 (1999); Jon Van Dyke, *The Role of*

Customary International Law in Federal and State Court Litigation, 26 U. Hawaii L. Rev. 361 (2004).

6. Article 9(1) of the International Covenant on Civil and Political Rights (ICCPR) prohibits "arbitrary" detention. Is arbitrary detention of less than a day covered by the prohibition? Under the circumstances, was the detention of Alvarez-Machain "arbitrary"? Was this the issue actually addressed by the *Sosa* majority? See the next note.

7. The Human Rights Committee created pursuant to and operating under the ICCPR and the European Court of Human Rights, among other international institutions, have concluded that abductions from other countries violate the human rights to liberty and personal security that are directly related to the prohibition of arbitrary detention. Moreover, the U.N. Security Council has previously affirmed that "abductions are offenses of grave concern to the international community, having severe adverse consequences for the rights of the victims" and it has condemned "unequivocally all acts of ... abduction." U.N. S.C. Res. 579 (1985). Was this the issue addressed in *Sosa*?

Footnote 24 and the accompanying and nearby text of the majority opinion in *Sosa* noted that Alvarez's attorney did not adequately raise the issue of "cross-border abductions," that the Court did "not consider it," and "[a]s he presently argues it, the claim does not rest on the cross-border feature of his abduction" but only on a claim that "his arrest was arbitrary ... because no applicable [federal] law authorized it" and because it was "officially sanctioned action exceeding positive authorization to detain under the domestic law of some government, regardless of the circumstances." If so, was this the best argument for his counsel to make? Furthermore, what exactly was the ruling in *Sosa* with respect to detentions? Was it that detention must be "beyond relatively brief detention in excess of positive authority," that "a single illegal detention [under domestic law] of less than a day" is not proscribed under customary international law or merely that such was not proven adequately by counsel? Would this be consistent with recognitions in cases such as *Rodriguez-Fernandez v. Wilkinson*, 505 F. Supp. 787 (D. Kan. 1980), *aff'd on other gds.*, 654 F.2d 1382 (10th Cir. 1981); *Forti v. Suarez-Mason*; and *Xuncax v. Gramajo*? *See also Kim Ho Ma v. Ashcroft*, 257 F3d 1095, 1114 (9th Cir. 2001); *Ma v. Reno*, 208 F.3d 815, 830 (9th Cir. 2000); *Martinez v. City of Los Angeles*, 141 F.3d 1373, 1384 (9th Cir. 1998); *De Sanchez v. Banco Central de Nicaragua*, 770 F.2d 1385, 1397 (5th Cir. 1985); *Chiminya Tachiona v. Mugabe*, 216 F. Supp.2d 262, 279-80 (S.D.N.Y. 2002); *Mehinovic v. Vuckovic*, 198 F. Supp.2d 1322, 1328-29, 1344, 1349-50, 1352, 1357-58, 1360 (N.D. Ga. 2002); *Wiwa v. Royal Dutch Petroleum Co.*, No. 96 CIV. 8386, 2002 WL 319887, at *6 (S.D.N.Y. Feb. 28, 2002)? Might the majority have assumed that if "detention of less than a day" occurred in Mexico, "the transfer of custody to lawful authorities ... [coupled with] a prompt arraignment" in the U.S. was not a continuation of a "detention" that started in Mexico? Would this be a proper characterization of an unlawful and continued "detention" or "abduction"?

8. The Court in *Sosa* was also not adequately briefed on the fact that the International Covenant on Civil and Political Rights (ICCPR) is at the very least partly self-executing. The U.S. declaration of partial non-self-execution is expressly inapplicable to Article 50 of the ICCPR, which mandates in clear, unavoidable, and self-executing terms that all of "[t]he provisions of the ... Covenant shall extend to all parts of federal States without any limitations or exceptions" whatsoever. Moreover, the U.S. understanding upon ratification and the Executive Explanation concerning Article 50 demonstrate the clear intent that the U.S. Executive and judiciary, among others, will comply with Article 50's mandate. *See, e.g.*, Paust, *supra* at 361-62, and references cited.

9. For cases finding that forced disappearance, a crime against humanity, is criminal and/or actionable, *see, e.g.*, *The Prosecutor v. Kupreskic*, IT-95-16-T (ICTY Trial Chamber, Judgment, 14 Jan. 2000); *In re Marcos, Human Rights Litigation*, 25 F.3d 1467, 1475 (9th Cir. 1994); *Bowoto v. Chevron Corp.*, WL 2349336 at *29 (N.D. Cal. 2007) ("there is sufficient circumstantial evidence of … forced disappearance [in Nigeria] to support tort claims"); *Tachiona v. Mugabe*, 234 F. Supp.2d 401, 416, 426 (S.D.N.Y. 2002); *Xuncax v. Gramajo*, 886 F. Supp. 162, 184-85 (D. Mass. 1995); *Forti v. Suarez-Mason*, 694 F. Supp. 707, 710-12 (N.D. Cal. 1988); 22 U.S.C. § 2151n(a) (2000); 22 U.S.C. § 2304(d) ("causing the disappearance of persons" is among "flagrant" and "gross violations of internationally recognized human rights"); S. Rep. No. 102-249, at 9 (1991), quoted in *Xuncax*, 886 F. Supp. at 172.

10. For cases other than *Sosa* finding genocide to be actionable, *see, e.g.*, *Khulumani v. Barclay Nat. Bank, Ltd.*, 504 F3d 254, 270 n.5, 273, 283 (2d Cir. 2007) (Katzmann, J., concurring); *Kadic v. Karadzic*, 70 F.3d 232, 241-42 (2d Cir. 1995), *cert. denied*, 518 U.S. 1005 (1996); *Almog v. Arab Bank*, PLC, 471 F. Supp.2d 257, 271, 274-78, 289, 293 (E.D.N.Y. 2007); *Presbyterian Church of Sudan v. Talisman Energy, Inc.*, 244 F. Supp.2d 289, 305-06, 327 (S.D.N.Y. 2003); *Mehinovic v. Vuckovic*, 198 F. Supp.2d 1322, 1354-55 (N.D. Ga. 2002); *Bodner v. Banque Paribas*, 114 F. Supp.2d 117, 128 (E.D.N.Y. 2000).

11. For cases addressing war crime liability under the Geneva Conventions and other laws of war, *see, e.g.*, *Weisshaus v. Swiss Bankers Ass'n*, 225 F.3d 191 (2d Cir. 2000); *Hilao v. Estate of Marcos*, 103 F.3d 767, 777 (9th Cir. 1996) (re: leader responsibility); *Kadic v. Karadzic*, 70 F.3d 232, 242–43 (2d Cir. 1995), *cert. denied*, 518 U.S. 1005 (1996); *Linder v. Portocarrero*, 963 F.2d 332, 336–37 (11th Cir. 1992); *Almog v. Arab Bank, PLC*, 471 F. Supp.2d 257, 279-80 (E.D.N.Y. 2007); *Estate of Rodriquez v. Drummond Co., Inc.*, 256 F. Supp.2d 1250 (N.D. Ala. 2003); *Presbyterian Church of Sudan v. Talisman Energy, Inc.*, 244 F. Supp.2d at 310–11; *Barrueto v. Larios*, 205 F. Supp.2d 1325, 1333 (S.D. Fla. 2002) (re: individual responsibility); *Mehinovic v. Vuckovic*, 198 F. Supp.2d 1322, 1350–54, 1358 (N.D. Ga. 2002); *In re World War II Era Japanese Forced Labor Litigation*, 114 F. Supp.2d 939 (N.D. Cal. 2000) (private claims were settled by international agreement); *Doe v. Islamic Salvation Front*, 993 F. Supp. 3, 8 (D.D.C. 1998); *Xuncax v. Gramajo*, 886 F. Supp. 162, 171–72 (D. Mass. 1995) (re: leader liability).

Since the beginning of the United States, private remedies have been available in courts for violations of the laws of war. *See, e.g.*, *Ex parte Quirin*, 317 U.S. 1, 27 (1942) ("From the very beginning of its history this Court has recognized and applied the law of war as including that part of the law of nations which prescribes … the status, right and duties of enemy … individuals"); *The Paquete Habana*, 175 U.S. 677, 698 ("law of war"), 714 (1900); *Freeland v. Williams*, 131 U.S. 405, 416–17 (1889) ("no civil liability attached" when no war crime occurred); *Ford v. Surget*, 97 U.S. 594, 605–06 (1878) (individuals "relieved from civil liability" where no war crime occurred); *Mitchell v. Harmony*, 54 U.S. (13 How.) 115, 137 (1851) (suit could be brought in "any district in which the defendant might be found"); *Bas v. Tingy*, 4 U.S. (4 Dall.) 37, 43 (1800) (Chase, J.); *Ware v. Hylton*, 3 U.S. (3 Dall.) 199, 279 (1796) (Iredell, J.) "rights … derived from the laws of war … and in that case the individual might have been entitled to compensation"); Paust, *supra*, at 64 n.130, 226–27, 291–92 nn.489–95.

12. For cases addressing water-boarding or the "water cure" (an interrogation tactic approved by President Bush and other members of his Administration during the so-called "war" on terror), *see, e.g.*, *Hudson v. McMillian*, 503 U.S. 1, 26 (1992) (Thomas, J., dissenting) ("water torture" violates 8th Amendment), quoting *Williams v. Boles*, 841 F.2d 181, 183 (7th Cir. 1988); *Robinson v. California*, 370 U.S. 660, 669 (1962) (Douglas,

J., concurring) ("water cures" are "terror"); *Abdel-Rahman v. Gonzales*, 493 F.3d 444, 448 (4th Cir. 2007) ("various types of torture, including simulated drownings" claimed); *Hernandez-Barrera v. Ashcroft*, 373 F.3d 9, 15 (1st Cir. 2004) ("water torture" claimed); *United States v. Yousef*, 327 F.3d 56, 127 (2d Cir. 2003) ("torture" would include "simulated drowning" if proved); *Hilao v. Estate of Marcos*, 103 F.3d 789, 790 (9th Cir. 1996) ("water torture" occurred through use of a towel over the nose and mouth and water poured down the nostrils to induce the fear of drowning); *United States v. Lee*, 744 F.2d 1124, 1125 (5th Cir. 1984) (civil rights of prisoners violated when they were subjected to "water torture"); *Iva Ikuko Toguri D'Aquino v. United States*, 192 F.2d 338, 361 (9th Cir. 1951) ("water torture" used by Japanese during WWII); *Struble v. Fountain*, 2008 WL 2074151 (S.D. Miss. 2008) ("simulated drowning" is "egregious" and can warrant punitive damages); *Yousuf v. Samantar*, 2007 WL 2220579, at *3 n.7 (E.D. Va. 2007) ("Waterboarding is a form of torture"); *Kaweesa v. Ashcroft*, 345 F. Supp.2d 79, 86 (D. Mass. 2004) ("water torture" during Idi Amin's regime in Uganda); *In re Estate of Ferdinand E. Marcos Human Rights Litigation*, 910 F. Supp. 1460, 1463 (D. Haw. 1995) ("forms of torture" include "[t]he 'water cure,' where a cloth was placed over the detainee's mouth and nose, and water poured over it producing a drowning sensation"); *Benjamin v. Jacobson*, 935 F. Supp. 332, 339 (S.D.N.Y. 1996) (addressing "water torture" in prisons); *Fisher v. State*, 145 Miss. 116, 110 So. 361, 363 (1926) ("water cure, a species of torture well known to the bench and bar of the country"); *White v. State*, 129 Miss. 182, 91 So. 903 (1922) ("water cure" causes "pain and horror" and is "barbarous"); *Commonwealth v. Chaitt*, 380 Pa. 532, 555, 112 A.2d 379 (1955) ("[t]here was a time when the rack, the dungeon, the water-cure and the thumbscrew were used"); *Cavazos v. State*, 143 Tex. Crim. 564, 566, 160 S.W.2d 260 (1942); Jordan J. Paust, Beyond the Law: The Bush Administration's Unlawful Responses in the "War" on Terror 13, 16, 28, 43, 150, 152, 161, 173, 178-79 (2007).

13. For cases addressing the prohibitions of torture or cruel, inhuman, or degrading treatment, *see. e.g.*, *Hilao v. Estate of Ferdinand Marcos*, 103 F.3d 767 (9th Cir. 1996); *Abebe-Jira v. Negewo*, 72 F.3d 844 (11th Cir. 1996); *Kadic v. Karadzic*, 70 F.3d 232, 242-43, 245 (2d Cir. 1995), *cert. denied*, 518 U.S. 1005 (1996); *Siderman de Blake v. Republic of Argentina*, 965 F.2d 699, 717 (9th Cir. 1992), *cert. denied*, 507 U.S. 1017 (1993); *Filartiga v. Pena-Irala*, 630 F.2d 876 (2d Cir. 1980); *Presbyterian Church of Sudan v. Talisman Energy, Inc.*, 244 F. Supp.2d 289, 305-06 (S.D.N.Y. 2003); *Mehinovic v. Vuckovic*, 198 F. Supp.2d 1322, 1344-49 (N.D. Ga. 2002); *Estate of Cabello v. Fernandez-Larios*, 157 F. Supp.2d 1345, 1360-61 (S.D. Fla. 2001); *Jama v. I.N.S.*, 22 F. Supp.2d 353, 363 (D. N.J. 1998); *Doe v. Islamic Salvation Front*, 993 F. Supp. 3, 8 (D.D.C. 1998) (including that covered under common Article 3 of the Geneva Conventions); *In re Estate of Ferdinand E. Marcos Human Rights Litigation*, 910 F. Supp. 1460, 1462-63 (D. Haw. 1995); *Xuncax v. Gramajo*, 886 F. Supp. 162, 187 (D. Mass. 1995); *Paul v. Avril*, 812 F. Supp. 207 (S.D. Fla. 1993).

Kiobel, *et al.* v. Royal Dutch Petroleum Co., *et al.*, __ U.S. __ (2013)

Roberts, C.J.

Petitioners, a group of Nigerian nationals residing in the United States, filed suit in federal court against certain Dutch, British, and Nigerian corporations. Petitioners sued under the Alien Tort Statute, 28 U.S.C. § 1350, alleging that the corporations aided and abetted the Nigerian Government in committing violations of the law of nations in Nigeria. The question presented is whether and under what circumstances courts may recognize a cause of action under the Alien Tort Statute, for violations of the law of nations occurring within the territory of a sovereign other than the United States.

I

Petitioners were residents of Ogoniland, an area of 250 square miles located in the Niger delta area of Nigeria and populated by roughly half a million people. When the complaint was filed, respondents Royal Dutch Petroleum Company and Shell Transport and Trading Company, p.l.c., were holding companies incorporated in the Netherlands and England, respectively. Their joint subsidiary, respondent Shell Petroleum Development Company of Nigeria, Ltd. (SPDC), was incorporated in Nigeria, and engaged in oil exploration and production in Ogoniland. According to the complaint, after concerned residents of Ogoniland began protesting the environmental effects of SPDC's practices, respondents enlisted the Nigerian Government to violently suppress the burgeoning demonstrations. Throughout the early 1990's, the complaint alleges, Nigerian military and police forces attacked Ogoni villages, beating, raping, killing, and arresting residents and destroying or looting property. Petitioners further allege that respondents aided and abetted these atrocities by, among other things, providing the Nigerian forces with food, transportation, and compensation, as well as by allowing the Nigerian military to use respondents' property as a staging ground for attacks.

Following the alleged atrocities, petitioners moved to the United States where they have been granted political asylum and now reside as legal residents. See Supp. Brief for Petitioners 3, and n.2. They filed suit in the United States District Court for the Southern District of New York, alleging jurisdiction under the Alien Tort Statute and requesting relief under customary international law. The ATS provides, in full, that "[t]he district courts shall have original jurisdiction of any civil action by an alien for a tort only, committed in violation of the law of nations or a treaty of the United States."

28 U.S.C. § 1350. According to petitioners, respondents violated the law of nations by aiding and abetting the Nigerian Government in committing (1) extrajudicial killings; (2) crimes against humanity; (3) torture and cruel treatment; (4) arbitrary arrest and detention; (5) violations of the rights to life, liberty, security, and association; (6) forced exile; and (7) property destruction. The District Court dismissed the first, fifth, sixth, and seventh claims, reasoning that the facts alleged to support those claims did not give rise to a violation of the law of nations. The court denied respondents' motion to dismiss with respect to the remaining claims, but certified its order for interlocutory appeal pursuant to § 1292(b).

The Second Circuit dismissed the entire complaint, reasoning that the law of nations does not recognize corporate liability. 621 F.3d 111 (2010). We granted certiorari to consider that question. 565 U.S. _ (2011). After oral argument, we directed the parties to file supplemental briefs addressing an additional question: "Whether and under what circumstances the [ATS] allows courts to recognize a cause of action for violations of the law of nations occurring within the territory of a sovereign other than the United States." 565 U.S. _ (2012). We heard oral argument again and now affirm the judgment below, based on our answer to the second question.

II

Passed as part of the Judiciary Act of 1789, the ATS was invoked twice in the late 18th century, but then only once more over the next 167 years. Act of Sept. 24, 1789, § 9, 1Stat. 77; see *Moxon* v. *The Fanny*, 17 F. Cas. 942 (No. 9,895) (DC Pa. 1793); *Bolchos* v. *Darrel*, 3 F. Cas. 810 (No.1,607) (DC SC 1795); *O'Reilly de Camara v. Brooke, 209* U.S. 45 (1908);

Khedivial Line, S.A.E. v. Seafarers' Int'l Union, 278 F.2d 49, 51-52 (CA2 1960) (*per curiam*). The statute provides district courts with jurisdiction to hear certain claims, but does not expressly provide any causes of action. We held in *Sosa v. Alvarez-Machain*, 542 U.S. 692, 714 (2004), however, that the First Congress did not intend the provision to be "stillborn." The grant of jurisdiction is instead "best read as having been enacted on the understanding that the common law would provide a cause of action for [a] modest number of international law violations." *Id.*, at 724. We thus held that federal courts may "recognize private claims [for such violations] under federal common law." *Id.*, at 732. The Court in *Sosa* rejected the plaintiff's claim in that case for "arbitrary arrest and detention," on the ground that it failed to state a violation of the law of nations with the requisite "definite content and acceptance among civilized nations." *Id.*, at 699, 732.

The question here is not whether petitioners have stated a proper claim under the ATS, but whether a claim may reach conduct occurring in the territory of a foreign sovereign. Respondents contend that claims under the ATS do not, relying primarily on a canon of statutory interpretation known as the presumption against extraterritorial application. That canon provides that "[w]hen a statute gives no clear indication of an extraterritorial application, it has none," *Morrison* v. *National Australia Bank Ltd.*, 561 U.S. (2010) (slip op., at 6), and reflects the "presumption that United States law governs domestically but does not rule the world," *Microsoft Corp.* v. *AT&T Corp.*, 550 U.S. 437, 454 (2007).

This presumption "serves to protect against unintended clashes between our laws and those of other nations which could result in international discord." *EEOC* v. *Arabian American Oil Co.*, 499 U.S. 244, 248 (1991) (*Aramco*). As this Court has explained:

> "For us to run interference in … a delicate field of international relations there must be present the affirmative intention of the Congress clearly expressed. It alone has the facilities necessary to make fairly such an important policy decision where the possibilities of international discord are so evident and retaliative action so certain." *Benz* v. *Campania Naviera Hidalgo, S.A.*, 353 U.S. 138, 147 (1957). The presumption against extraterritorial application helps ensure that the Judiciary does not erroneously adopt an interpretation of U.S. law that carries foreign policy consequences not clearly intended by the political branches.

We typically apply the presumption to discern whether an Act of Congress regulating conduct applies abroad. *See, e.g., Aramco, supra,* at 246 ("These cases present the issue whether Title VII applies extraterritorially to regulate the employment practices of United States employers who employ United States citizens abroad"); *Morrison, supra,* at (slip op., at 4) (noting that the question of extraterritorial application was a "merits question," not a question of jurisdiction). The ATS, on the other hand, is "strictly jurisdictional." *Sosa*n , 542 U.S., at 713. It does not directly regulate conduct or afford relief. It instead allows federal courts to recognize certain causes of action based on sufficiently definite norms of international law. But we think the principles underlying the canon of interpretation similarly constrain courts considering causes of action that may be brought under the ATS.

Indeed, the danger of unwarranted judicial interference in the conduct of foreign policy is magnified in the context of the ATS, because the question is not what Congress has done but instead what courts may do. This Court in *Sosa* repeatedly stressed the need for judicial caution in considering which claims could be brought under the ATS, in light of foreign policy concerns. As the Court explained, "the potential [foreign policy] implications ... of recognizing ... causes [under the ATS] should make courts particularly wary of impinging on the discretion of the Legislative and Executive Branches in managing foreign affairs." *Id.*, at 727; see also *id.*, at 727-728 ("Since many attempts by federal courts to craft remedies for the violation of new norms of international law would raise risks of adverse foreign policy consequences, they should be undertaken, if at all, with great caution"); *id.*, at 727 ("[T]he possible collateral consequences of making international rules privately actionable argue for judicial caution"). These concerns, which are implicated in any case arising under the ATS, are all the more pressing when the question is whether a cause of action under the ATS reaches conduct within the territory of another sovereign.

These concerns are not diminished by the fact that *Sosa* limited federal courts to recognizing causes of action only for alleged violations of international law norms that are "'specific, universal, and obligatory.'" *Id.*, at 732 (quoting *In re Estate of Marcos, Human Rights Litigation*, 25 F.3d 1467, 1475 (CA9 1994)). As demonstrated by Congress's enactment of the Torture Victim Protection Act of 1991, 106 Stat. 73, note following 28 U.S.C. §1350, identifying such a norm is only the beginning of defining a cause of action. See *id.*, §3 (providing detailed definitions for extrajudicial killing and torture); *id.*, §2 (specifying who may be liable, creating a rule of exhaustion, and establishing a statute of limitations). Each of these decisions carries with it significant foreign policy implications.

The principles underlying the presumption against extraterritoriality thus constrain courts exercising their power under the ATS.

III

Petitioners contend that even if the presumption applies, the text, history, and purposes of the ATS rebut it for causes of action brought under that statute. It is true that Congress, even in a jurisdictional provision, can indicate that it intends federal law to apply to conduct occurring abroad. *See, e.g.*, 18 U.S.C. §1091(e) (2006 ed., Supp. V) (providing jurisdiction over the offense of genocide "regardless of where the offense is committed" if the alleged offender is, among other things, "present in the United States"). But to rebut the presumption, the ATS would need to evince a "clear indication of extraterritoriality. *Morrison*, 561 U.S. at _ (slip op., at 16). It does not.

To begin, nothing in the text of the statute suggests that Congress intended causes of action recognized under it to have extraterritorial reach. The ATS covers actions by aliens for violations of the law of nations, but that does not imply extraterritorial reach—such violations affecting aliens can occur either within or outside the United States. Nor does the fact that the text reaches *any* civil action" suggest application to torts committed abroad; it is well established that generic terms like "any" or "every" do not rebut the presumption against extraterritoriality. *See, e.g., id.*, at (slip op., at 13-14); *Small v. United States*, 544 U.S. 385, 388 (2005); *Aramco*, 499 U.S., at 248-250;

Foley Bros., Inc. v. *Filardo*, 336 U.S. 281, 287 (1949).

Petitioners make much of the fact that the ATS provides jurisdiction over civil actions for "torts" in violation of the law of nations. They claim that in using that word, the First Congress "necessarily meant to provide for jurisdiction over extraterritorial transitory torts that could arise on foreign soil." Supp. Brief for Petitioners 18. For support, they cite the common-law doctrine that allowed courts to assume jurisdiction over such "transitory torts," including actions for personal injury, arising abroad. See *Mostyn v. Fabrigas*, 1 Cowp. 161, 177, 98 Eng. Rep. 1021, 1030 (1774) (Mansfield, L.) ("[A]ll actions of a transitory nature that arise abroad may be laid as happening in an English county"); *Dennick*

v. *Railroad Co.*, 103 U.S. 11, 18 (1881) ("Wherever, by either the common law or the statute law of a State, a right of action has become fixed and a legal liability incurred, that liability may be enforced and the right of action pursued in any court which has jurisdiction of such matters and can obtain jurisdiction of the parties").

Under the transitory torts doctrine, however, "the only justification for allowing a party to recover when the cause of action arose in another civilized jurisdiction is a well-founded belief that it was a cause of action in that place." *Cuba R. Co.* v. *Crosby*, 222 U.S. 473, 479 (1912) (majority opinion of Holmes, J.). The question under *Sosa* is not whether a federal court has jurisdiction to entertain a cause of action provided by foreign or even international law. The question is instead whether the court has authority to recognize a cause of action under U.S. law to enforce a norm of international law. The reference to "tort" does not demonstrate that the First Congress "necessarily meant" for those causes of action to reach conduct in the territory of a foreign sovereign. In the end, nothing in the text of the ATS evinces the requisite clear indication of extraterritoriality.

Nor does the historical background against which the ATS was enacted overcome the presumption against application to conduct in the territory of another sovereign. See *Morrison, supra*, at _ (slip op., at 16) (noting that "assuredly context can be consulted" in determining whether a cause of action applies abroad). We explained in *Sosa* that when Congress passed the ATS, "three principal offenses against the law of nations" had been identified by Blackstone: violation of safe conducts, infringement of the rights of ambassadors, and piracy. 542 U.S., at 723, 724; see 4 W. Blackstone, Commentaries on the Laws of England 68 (1769). The first two offenses have no necessary extraterritorial application. Indeed, Blackstone in describing them-did so in terms of conduct occur ring within the forum nation. See *ibid.* (describing the right of safe conducts for those "who are here"); 1 *id.*, at 251 (1765) (explaining that safe conducts grant a member of one society "a right to intrude into another"); *id.*, at 245-248 (recognizing the king's power to "receive ambassadors at home" and detailing their rights in the state "wherein they are appointed to reside"); see also E. De Vattel, Law of Nations 465 (J. Chitty et al. translated 1883) ("[O]n his entering the country to which he is sent, and making himself known, [the ambassador] is under the protection of the law of nations....").

Two notorious episodes involving violations of the law of nations occurred in the United States shortly before passage of the ATS. Each concerned the rights of ambassadors, and each involved conduct within the Union. In 1784, a French adventurer verbally and physically assaulted Francis Barbe Marbois—the Secretary of the French Legion—in Philadelphia. The assault led the French Minister Plenipotentiary to lodge a formal protest with the Continental Congress and threaten to leave the country unless an adequate remedy were provided. *Republica* v. *De Longchamps*, 1 Dall. 111 (O.T. Phila.

1784); *Sosa, supra*, at 716-717, and n.11. And in 1787, a New York constable entered the Dutch Ambassador's house and arrested one of his domestic servants. See Casto, The Federal Courts' Protective Jurisdiction over Torts Committed in Violation of the Law of Nations, 18 Conn. L. Rev. 467, 494 (1986). At the request of Secretary of Foreign Affairs John Jay, the Mayor of New York City arrested the constable in turn, but cautioned that because "'neither Congress nor our [State] Legislature have yet passed any act respecting a breach of the privileges of Ambassadors,'" the extent of any available relief would depend on the common law. See Bradley, The Alien Tort Statute and Article III, 42 Va. J. Int'l L. 587, 641-642 (2002) (quoting 3 Dept. of State, The Diplomatic Correspondence of the United States of America 447 (1837)). The two cases in which the ATS was invoked shortly after its passage also concerned conduct within the territory of the United States. See *Bolchos*, 3 F. Cas. 810 (wrongful seizure of slaves from a vessel while in port in the United States); *Moxon*, 17 F. Cas. 942 (wrongful seizure in United States territorial waters).

These prominent contemporary examples—immediately before and after passage of the ATS—provide no support for the proposition that Congress expected causes of action to be brought under the statute for violations of the law of nations occurring abroad.

The third example of a violation of the law of nations familiar to the Congress that enacted the ATS was piracy. Piracy typically occurs on the high seas, beyond the territorial jurisdiction of the United States or any other country. See 4 Blackstone, *supra*, at 72 ("The offence of piracy, by common law, consists of committing those acts of robbery and depredation upon the high seas, which, if committed upon land, would have amounted to felony there"). This Court has generally treated the high seas the same as foreign soil for purposes of the presumption against extraterritorial application. *See, e.g., Sale v. Haitian Centers Council, Inc.*, 509 U.S. 155, 173-174 (1993) (declining to apply a provision of the Immigration and Nationality Act to conduct occurring on the high seas); *Argentine Republic* v. *Amerada Hess Shipping Corp.*, 488 U.S. 428, 440 (1989) (declining to apply a provision of the Foreign Sovereign Immunities Act of 1976 to the high seas). Petitioners contend that because Congress surely intended the ATS to provide jurisdiction for actions against pirates, it necessarily anticipated the statute would apply to conduct occurring abroad.

Applying U.S. law to pirates, however, does not typically impose the sovereign will of the United States onto conduct occurring within the territorial jurisdiction of another sovereign, and therefore carries less direct foreign policy consequences. Pirates were fair game wherever found, by any nation, because they generally did not operate within any jurisdiction. See 4 Blackstone, *supra*, at 71. We do not think that the existence of a cause of action against them is a sufficient basis for concluding that other causes of action under the ATS reach conduct that does occur within the territory of another sovereign; pirates may well be a category unto themselves. See *Morrison*, 561 U.S., at _ (slip op., at 16) ("[W]hen a statute provides for some extraterritorial application, the presumption against extraterritoriality operates to limit that provision to its terms"); see also *Microsoft Corp.*, 550 U.S., at 455-456. Petitioners also point to a 1795 opinion authored by Attorney General William Bradford. See Breach of Neutrality, 1 Op. Atty. Gen. 57. In 1794, in the midst of war between France and Great Britain, and notwithstanding the American official policy of neutrality, several U.S. citizens joined a French privateer fleet and attacked and plundered the British colony of Sierra Leone. In response to a protest from the British Ambassador, Attorney General Bradford responded as follows:

> So far … as the transactions complained of originated or took place in a foreign country, they are not within the cognizance of our courts; nor can the actors be legally prosecuted or punished for them by the United States. But crimes committed on the high seas *are* within the jurisdiction of the … courts of the United States; and, so far as the offence was committed thereon, I am inclined to think that it may be legally prosecuted in … those courts.… But some doubt rests on this point, in consequence of the terms in which the [applicable criminal law] is expressed. But there can be no doubt that the company or individuals who have been injured by these acts of hostility have a remedy by a *civil* suit in the courts of the United States; jurisdiction being expressly given to these courts in all cases where an alien sues for a tort only, in violation of the laws of nations, or a treaty of the United States.…" *Id.*, at 58-59.

Petitioners read the last sentence as confirming that "The Founding generation understood the ATS to apply to law of nations violations committed on the territory of a foreign sovereign." Supp. Brief for Petitioners 33. Respondents counter that when Attorney General Bradford referred to "these acts of hostility," he meant the acts only insofar as they took place on the high seas, and even if his conclusion were broader, it was only because the applicable treaty had extraterritorial reach. See Supp. Brief for Respondents 28-30. The Solicitor General, having once read the opinion to stand for the proposition that an "ATS suit could be brought against American citizens for breaching neutrality with Britain only if acts did not take place in a foreign country," Supp. Brief for United States as *Amicus Curiae* 8, n.1 (internal quotation marks and brackets omitted), now suggests the opinion "could have been meant to encompass ... conduct [occurring within the foreign territory]," *id.*, at 8.

Attorney General Bradford's opinion defies a definitive reading and we need not adopt one here. Whatever its precise meaning, it deals with U.S. citizens who, by participating in an attack taking place both on the high seas and on a foreign shore, violated a treaty between the United States and Great Britain. The opinion hardly suffices to counter the weighty concerns underlying the presumption against extraterritoriality.

Finally, there is no indication that the ATS was passed to make the United States a uniquely hospitable forum for the enforcement of international norms. As Justice Story put it, "No nation has ever yet pretended to be the custos morum of the whole world...." *United States v. The La Jeune Eugenie*, 26 F. Cas. 832, 847 (No. 15,551) (CC. Mass. 1822). It is implausible to suppose that the First Congress wanted their fledgling Republic — struggling to receive international recognition — to be the first. Indeed, the parties offer no evidence that any nation, meek or mighty, presumed to do such a thing.

The United States was, however, embarrassed by its potential inability to provide judicial relief to foreign officials injured in the United States. Bradley, 42 Va. J. Int'l L., at 641. Such offenses against ambassadors violated the law of nations, "and if not adequately redressed could rise to an issue of war." *Sosa*, 542 U.S., at 715; cf. The Federalist No. 80, p. 536 (J. Cooke ed. 1961) (A. Hamilton) ("As the denial or perversion of justice ... is with reason classed among the just causes of war, it will follow that the federal judiciary ought to have cognizance of all causes in which the citizens of other countries are concerned"). The ATS ensured that the United States could provide a forum for adjudicating such incidents. See *Sosa*, *supra*, at 715-718, and n.11. Nothing about this historical context suggests that Congress also intended federal common law under the ATS to provide a cause of action for conduct occurring in the territory of another sovereign.

Indeed, far from avoiding diplomatic strife, providing such a cause of action could have generated it. Recent experience bears this out. See *Doe v. Exxon Mobil Corp.*, 654 F.3d 11, 77-78 (CADC 2011) (Kavanaugh, J., dissenting in part) (listing recent objections to extraterritorial applications of the ATS by Canada, Germany, Indonesia, Papua New Guinea, South Africa, Switzerland, and the United Kingdom). Moreover, accepting petitioners' view would imply that other nations, also applying the law of nations, could hale our citizens into their courts for alleged violations of the law of nations occurring in the United States, or anywhere else in the world. The presumption against extraterritoriality guards against our courts triggering such serious foreign policy consequences, and instead defers such decisions, quite appropriately, to the political branches.

We therefore conclude that the presumption against extraterritoriality applies to claims under the ATS, and that nothing in the statute rebuts that presumption. "There is no clear indication of extraterritoriality here," *Morrison*, 561 U.S., at _ (slip op., at 16), and petitioners' case seeking relief for violations of the law of nations occurring outside the United States is barred.

IV

On these facts, all the relevant conduct took place out side the United States. And even where the claims touch and concern the territory of the United States, they must do so with sufficient force to displace the presumption against extraterritorial application. See *Morrison*, 561 U.S. _ (slip op., at 17-24). Corporations are often present in many countries, and it would reach too far to say that mere corporate presence suffices. If Congress were to determine otherwise, a statute more specific than the ATS would be required. The judgment of the Court of Appeals is affirmed.

It is so ordered.

Kennedy, J., concurring

The opinion for the Court is careful to leave open a number of significant questions regarding the reach and interpretation of the Alien Tort Statute. In my view that is a proper disposition. Many serious concerns with respect to human rights abuses committed abroad have been addressed by Congress in statutes such as the Torture Victim Protection Act of 1991 (TVPA), 106 Stat. 73, note following 28 U.S.C. § 1350, and that class of cases will be determined in the future according to the detailed statutory scheme Congress has enacted. Other cases may arise with allegations of serious violations of international law principles protecting persons, cases covered neither by the TVPA nor by the reasoning and holding of today's case; and in those disputes the proper implementation of the presumption against extraterritorial application may require some further elaboration and explanation.

Alito, J., with Thomas, J, concurring

I concur in the judgment and join the opinion of the Court as far as it goes. Specifically, I agree that when Alien Tort Statute (ATS) "claims touch and concern the territory of the United States, they must do so with sufficient force to displace the presumption against extraterritorial application." *Ante*, at 14. This formulation obviously leaves much unanswered, and perhaps there is wisdom in the Court's preference for this narrow approach. I write separately to set out the broader standard that leads me to the conclusion that this case falls within the scope of the presumption.

In *Morrison* v. *National Australia Bank Ltd*., 561 U.S. (2010), we explained that "the presumption against extraterritorial application would be a craven watchdog indeed if it retreated to its kennel whenever *some* domestic activity is involved in the case." *Id*., at (slip op., at 17). We also reiterated that a cause of action falls outside the scope of the presumption — and thus is not barred by the presumption — only if the event or relationship that was "the 'focus' of congressional concern" under the relevant statute takes place within the United States. *Ibid*. (quoting *EEOC v. Arabian American Oil Co*., 499 U.S. Alito, J., concurring 244, 255 (1991)). For example, because "the focus of the [Securities] Exchange Act [of 1934] is not upon the place where the deception originated, but upon purchases and sales of securities in the United States," we held in *Morrison* that § 10(b) of the Exchange Act applies "only" to "transactions in securities listed on domestic exchanges, and domestic transactions in other securities." 561 U.S. at _ (slip op., at 17-18). The Court's decision in *Sosa v. Alvarez-Machain*, 542 U.S. 692 (2004), makes clear that when the ATS was enacted, "congressional concern" was "'focus[ed],'" *Morrison, supra*, at _ (slip op., at 17), on the "three principal offenses against the law of nations" that had been identified by Blackstone: violation of safe conducts, infringement of the rights of ambassadors, and piracy, *Sosa*, 542 U.S., at 723-724. The Court therefore held that "federal courts should not recognize private claims under federal common law for violations of any international law norm with less definite content and acceptance among civilized nations than the historical paradigms· familiar when [the ATS] was enacted." *Id.*, at 732. In other words, only conduct that satisfies *Sosa's* requirements of definiteness and acceptance among civilized nations can be said to have been "the 'focus' of congressional concern," *Morrison, supra* (slip op., at 17), when Congress enacted the ATS. As a result, a putative ATS cause of action will fall within the scope of the presumption against extraterritoriality—and will therefore be barred—unless the domestic conduct is sufficient to violate an international law norm that satisfies *Sosa's* requirements of definiteness and acceptance among civilized nations.

Breyer, J., with whom Ginsburg, J., Sotomayor, J., and Kagan, J., join, concurs in the judgment.

I agree with the Court's conclusion but not with its reasoning. The Court sets forth four key propositions of law: First, the "presumption against extraterritoriality applies to claims under" the Alien Tort Statute. *Ante*, at 13. Second, "nothing in the statute rebuts that presumption." *Ibid.* Third, there "is no clear indication of extraterritorial [application] here," where "all the relevant conduct took place outside the United States" and "where the claims" do not "touch and concern the territory of the United States ... with sufficient force to displace the presumption." *Ante*, at 13-14 (internal quotation marks omitted). Fourth, that is in part because "[c]orporations are often present in many countries, and it would reach too far to say that mere corporate presence suffices." *Ante*, at 14.

Unlike the Court, I would not invoke the presumption against extraterritoriality. Rather, guided in part by principles and practices of foreign relations law, I would find jurisdiction under this statute where (1) the alleged tort occurs on American soil, (2) the defendant is an American national, or (3) the defendant's conduct substantially and adversely affects an important American national interest, and that includes a distinct interest in preventing the United States from becoming a safe harbor (free of civil as well as criminal liability) for a torturer or other common enemy of mankind. See *Sosa* v. *Alvarez-Machain*, 542 U.S. 692, 732 (2004) ("'[F]or purposes of civil liability, the torturer has become—like the pirate and slave trader before him—*hostis humani generis*, an enemy of all mankind.'" (Quoting *Filartiga* v. *Pena-Irala*, 630 F.2d 876, 890 (CA2 1980) (alteration in original))). See also 1 Restatement (Third) of Foreign Relations Law of the United States §§ 402, 403, 404 (1986). In this case, however, the parties and relevant conduct lack sufficient ties to the United States for the ATS to provide jurisdiction.

I A

Our decision in *Sosa* frames the question. In *Sosa* the Court specified that the Alien Tort Statute (ATS), when enacted in 1789, "was intended as jurisdictional." 542 U.S. at 714. We added that the statute gives today's courts the power to apply certain "judge-made" damages law to victims of certain foreign affairs-related misconduct, including "three specific offenses" to which "Blackstone referred," namely "violation of safe conducts, infringement of the rights of ambassadors, and piracy." *Id.*, at 715. We held that the statute provides today's federal judges with the power to fashion "a cause of action" for a "modest number" of claims, "based on the present-day law of nations," and which "rest on a norm of international character accepted by the civilized world and defined with a specificity comparable to the features" of those three "18th-century paradigms." *Id.*, at 724-725. We further said that, in doing so, a requirement of "exhaust [ion]" of "remedies" might apply. *Id.*, at 733, n.21. We noted "a strong argument that federal court should give serious weight to the Executive Branch's view of the case's impact on foreign policy." *Ibid.* Adjudicating any such claim must, in my view, also be consistent with those notions of comity that lead each nation to respect the sovereign rights of other nations by limiting the reach of its own laws and their enforcement. *Id.*, at 761 (Breyer, J., concurring in part and concurring in judgment). See also *F. Hoffmann-La Roche Ltd v. Empagran S.A.*, 542 U.S. 155, 165-169 (2004).

Recognizing that Congress enacted the ATS to permit recovery of damages from pirates and others who violated basic international law norms as understood in 1789, *Sosa* essentially leads today's judges to ask: Who are today's pirates? See 542 U.S., at 724-725 (majority opinion). We provided a framework for answering that question by setting down principles drawn from international norms and designed to limit ATS claims to those that are similar in character and specificity to piracy. *Id.*, at 725. In this case we must decide the extent to which this jurisdictional statute opens a federal court's doors to those harmed by activities belonging to the limited class that *Sosa* set forth *when those activities take place abroad.* To help answer this question here, I would refer both to *Sosa* and, as in *Sosa,* to norms of international law. See Part II, *infra.*

B

In my view the majority's effort to answer the question by referring to the "presumption against extraterritoriality" does not work well. That presumption "rests on the perception that Congress ordinarily legislates with respect to domestic, not foreign matters." *Morrison v. National Australia Bank Ltd.*, 561 U.S. _ (2010) (slip op., at 5-6). See *ante*, at 4. The ATS, however, was enacted with "foreign matters" in mind. The statute's text refers explicitly to "alien[s]," "treat[ies]," and "the law of nations." 28 U.S.C. § 1350. The statute's purpose was to address "violations of the law of nations, admitting of a judicial remedy and at the same time threatening serious consequences in international affairs." *Sosa*, 542 U.S., at 715. And at least one of the three kinds of activities that we found to fall within the statute's scope, namely piracy, *ibid.*, normally takes place abroad. See 4 W. Blackstone, Commentaries on the Law of England 72 (1769). The majority cannot wish this piracy example away by emphasizing that piracy takes place on the high seas. See *ante*, at 10. That is because the robbery and murder that make up piracy do not normally take place in the water; they take place on a ship. And a ship is like land, in that it falls within the jurisdiction of the nation whose flag it flies. See *Mc-Culloch v. Sociedad Nacional de Marineros de Honduras*, 372 U.S. 10, 20-21 (1963); 2 Restatement § 502, Comment *d* ("[F]lag state has jurisdiction to prescribe with respect to any activity aboard the ship"). Indeed, in the early 19th century Chief Justice Marshall described piracy as an "offenc[e] against the nation under whose flag the vessel sails, and within whose particular jurisdiction all on board the vessel are." *United States v. Palmer*, 3 Wheat. 610, 632 (1818). See *United States v. Furlong*, 5 Wheat. 184, 197 (1820) (a crime committed "within the jurisdiction" of a foreign state and a crime committed "in the vessel of another nation" are "the same thing").

The majority nonetheless tries to find a distinction between piracy at sea and similar cases on land. It writes, "Applying U.S. law to pirates … does not typically impose the sovereign will of the United States onto conduct occurring within the *territorial* jurisdiction of another sovereign and therefore carries less direct foreign policy consequences." *Ante*, at 10 (emphasis added). But, as I have just pointed out, "[a]pplying U.S. law to pirates" *does* typically involve applying our law to acts taking place within the jurisdiction of another sovereign. Nor can the majority's words "territorial jurisdiction" sensibly distinguish land from sea for purposes of isolating adverse foreign policy risks, as the Barbary Pirates, the War of 1812, the sinking of the *Lusitania,* and the Lockerbie bombing make all too clear.

The majority also writes, "Pirates were fair game wherever found, by any nation, because they generally did not operate within any jurisdiction." *Ibid.* I very much agree that pirates were fair game "wherever found." Indeed, that is the point. That is why we asked, in *Sosa*, who are today's pirates? Certainly today's pirates include torturers and perpetrators of genocide. And today, like the pirates of old, they are "fair game" where they are found. Like those pirates, they are "common enemies of all mankind and all nations have an equal interest in their apprehension and punishment." 1 Restatement § 404 Reporters' Note 1, p. 256 (quoting *In re Demjanjuk*, 612 F. Supp. 544, 556 (N.D. Ohio 1985) (internal quotation marks omitted)). See *Sosa, supra,* at 732. And just as a nation that harbored pirates provoked the concern of other nations in past centuries, see *infra,* at 8, so harboring "common enemies of all mankind" provokes similar concerns today.

Thus the Court's reasoning, as applied to the narrow class of cases that *Sosa* described, fails to provide significant support for the use of any presumption against extraterritoriality; rather, it suggests the contrary. See also *ante,* at 10 (conceding and citing cases showing that this Court has "generally treated the high seas the same as foreign soil for purposes of the presumption against extraterritorial application").

In any event, as the Court uses its "presumption against extraterritorial application," it offers only limited help in deciding the question presented, namely "'under what circumstances the Alien Tort Statute ... allows courts to recognize a cause of action for violations of the law of nations occurring within the territory of a sovereign other than the United States.'" 565 U.S. _(2012). The majority echoes in this jurisdictional context *Sosa's* warning to use "caution" in shaping federal common-law causes of action. *Ante,* at 5. But it also makes clear that a statutory claim might sometimes "touch and concern the territory of the United States ... with sufficient force to displace the presumption." *Ante,* at 14. It leaves for another day the determination of just when the presumption against extraterritoriality might be "overcome." *Ante,* at 8.

II

In applying the ATS to acts "occurring within the territory of a[nother] sovereign," I would assume that Congress intended the statute's jurisdictional reach to match the statute's underlying substantive grasp. That grasp, defined by the statute's purposes set forth in *Sosa* includes compensation for those injured by piracy and its modern-day equivalents, at least where allowing such compensation avoids "serious" negative international "consequences" for the United States. 542 U.S., at 715. And just as we have looked to established international substantive norms to help determine the statute's substantive reach, *id.,* at 729, so we should look to international jurisdictional norms to help determine the statute's jurisdictional scope.

The Restatement (Third) of Foreign Relations Law is helpful. Section 402 recognizes that, subject to § 403's "reasonableness" requirement, a nation may apply its law (for example, federal common law, see 542 U.S., at 729-730) not only (1) to "conduct" that "takes place [or to persons or things] within its territory" but also (2) to the "activities, interests, status, or relations of its nationals outside as well as within its territory," (3) to "conduct outside its territory that has or is intended to have substantial effect within its territory," and (4) to certain foreign "conduct outside its territory ... that is directed against the security of the state or against a limited class of other state interests." In addition, § 404 of the Restatement explains that a "state has jurisdiction to define and prescribe punishment for certain offenses recognized by the community of nations as of universal concern, such as piracy, slave trade," and analogous behavior.

Considering these jurisdictional norms in light of both the ATS's basic purpose (to provide compensation for those injured by today's pirates) and *Sosa's* basic caution (to avoid international friction), I believe that the statute provides jurisdiction where (1) the alleged tort occurs on American soil, (2) the defendant is an American national, or (3) the defendant's conduct substantially and adversely affects an important American national interest, and that includes a distinct interest in preventing the United States from becoming a safe harbor (free of civil as well as criminal liability) for a torturer or other common enemy of mankind.

I would interpret the statute as providing jurisdiction only where distinct American interests are at issue. Doing so reflects the fact that Congress adopted the present statute at a time when, as Justice Story put it, "No nation ha[d] ever yet pretended to be the custos morum of the whole world." *United States* v. *La Jeune Eugenie*, 26 F. Cas. 832, 847 (No. 15,551) (C.C. Mass. 1822). That restriction also should help to minimize international friction. Further limiting principles such as exhaustion, *forum non conveniens*, and comity would do the same. So would a practice of courts giving weight to the views of the Executive Branch. See *Sosa*, 542 U.S., at 733, n. 21; *id.*, at 761 (opinion of Breyer, J.).

As I have indicated, we should treat this Nation's interest in not becoming a safe harbor for violators of the most fundamental international norms as an important jurisdiction-related interest justifying application of the ATS in light of

the statute's basic purposes—in particular that of compensating those who have suffered harm at the hands of, *e.g.*, torturers or other modern pirates. Nothing in the statute or its history suggests that our courts should turn a blind eye to the plight of victims in that "handful of heinous actions." *Tel-Oren* v. *Libyan Arab Republic*, 726 F.2d 774, 781 (C.A.D.C. 1984) (Edwards, J., concurring). See generally Leval, The Long Arm of International Law: Giving Victims of Human Rights Abuses Their Day in Court, 92 Foreign Affairs 16 (Mar.-Apr. 2013). To the contrary, the statute's language, history, and purposes suggest that the statute was to be a weapon in the "war" against those modern pirates who, by their conduct, have "declar[ed] war against all mankind." 4 Blackstone 71.

International norms have long included a duty not to permit a nation to become a safe harbor for pirates (or their equivalent). See generally A. Bradford, Flying the Black Flag: A Brief History of Piracy 19 (2007) ("Every polis by the sea ... which was suspected of sponsoring piracy or harboring pirates could be attacked and destroyed by the Athenians"); F. Sanborn, Origins of the Early English Maritime and Commercial Law 313 (1930) ("In 1490 Henry VII made a proclamation against harboring pirates or purchasing goods from them"); N. Risjord, Representative Americans: The Colonists 146 (1981) ("William Markham, Penn's lieutenant governor in the 1690s, was accused of harboring pirates in Philadelphia Governor Benjamin Fletcher of New York became the target of a royal inquiry after he issued privateering commissions to a band of notorious pirates"); 3 C. Yonge, A Pictorial History of the World's Great Nations 954 (1882) ("[In .the early 18th century, t]he government of Connecticut was accused of harboring pirates"); S. Menefee, Piracy, Terrorism, and the Insurgent Passenger: A Historical and Legal Perspective, in Maritime Terrorism and International Law 51 (N. Ronzitti ed. 1990) (quoting the judge who handled the seizure of the *Chesapeake* during the Civil War as stating that "'piracy *jure gentium* was justiciable by the court of New Brunswick, wherever committed'"); D. Field, Outlines of an International Code 33, Art. 84 (2d ed. 1876) (citing the 1794 treaty between the United States and Great Britain ("*Harboring pirates forbidden*. No nation can receive pirates into its territory, or permit any person within the same to receive, protect, conceal or assist them in any manner; but must punish all persons guilty of such acts")).

More recently two lower American courts have, in effect, rested jurisdiction primarily upon that kind of concern. In *Filartiga*, 630 F.2d 876, an alien plaintiff brought a lawsuit against an alien defendant for damages suffered through acts of torture that the defendant allegedly inflicted in a foreign nation, Paraguay. Neither plaintiff nor defendant was an American national and the actions underlying the lawsuit took place abroad. The defendant, however, "had ... resided in the United States for more than ninth months" before being sued, having overstayed his visitor's visa. *Id.*, at 878-879. Jurisdiction was deemed proper because the defendant's alleged conduct violated a well-established international law norm, and the suit vindicated our Nation's interest in not providing a safe harbor, free of damages claims, for those defendants who commit such conduct. In *Marcos*, the plaintiffs were nationals of the Philippines, the defendant was a Philippine national, and the alleged wrongful act, death by torture, took place abroad. *In re Estate of Marcos, Human Rights Litigation*, 25 F.3d 1467, 1469, 1475 (CA9 1994); *In re Estate of Marcos Human Rights Litigation*, 978 F.2d 493, 495-496, 500 (CA9 1992). A month before being sued, the defendant, "his family, and others loyal to [him] fled to Hawaii," where the ATS case was heard. *Marcos*, 25 F.3d, at 1469. As in *Filartiga*, the court found ATS jurisdiction. And in *Sosa* we referred to both cases with approval, suggesting that the ATS allowed a claim for relief in such circumstances. 542 U.S., at 732. See also *Flomo v. Firestone Natural Rubber Co.*, 643 F.3d 1013, 1025 (CA7 2011) (Posner, J.) ("*Sosa* was a case of nonmaritime extraterritorial conduct yet no Justice suggested that therefore it couldn't be maintained"). Not surprisingly, both before and after *Sosa*, courts have consistently rejected the notion that the ATS is categorically barred from extraterritorial application. See, *e.g.*, 643 F.3d, at 1025 ("[N]o court to our knowledge has ever held that it doesn't apply extraterritorially"); *Sarei v. Rio Tinto, PLC*, 671 F.3d 736, 747 (CA9 2011) (*en banc*) ("We therefore conclude that the ATS is not limited to conduct occurring within the United States"); *Doe v. Exxon Mobil Corp.*, 654 F.3d 11, 20 (CADC 2011) ("[W]e hold that there is no extraterritoriality bar").

Application of the statute in the way I have suggested is consistent with international law and foreign practice. Nations have long been obliged not to provide safe harbors for their own nationals who commit such serious crimes abroad. See E. de Vattel, Law of Nations, Book II, p. 163 (§ 76) ("pretty generally observed" practice in "respect to great crimes, which are equally contrary to the laws and safety of all nations," that a sovereign should not "suffer his subjects to molest the subjects of other states, or to do them an injury," but should "compel the transgressor to make reparation for the damage or injury," or be "deliver[ed] ... up to the offended state, to be there brought to justice").

Many countries permit foreign plaintiffs to bring suits against their own nationals based on unlawful conduct that took place abroad. See, e.g., Brief for Government of the Kingdom of the Netherlands et al. as *Amici Curiae* 19-23 (hereinafter Netherlands Brief) (citing *inter alia Guerrero v. Monterrico Metals PLC* [2009] EWHC (QB) 2475 (Eng.) (attacking conduct of U.K. companies in Peru); *Lubbe and Others v. Cape PLC* [2000] UKHL 41 (attacking conduct of U.K. companies in South Africa); *Rb. Gravenhage* [Court of the Hague], 30 December 2009, JOR 2010, 41 m.nt. Mr. RGJ de Haan (Oguro/Royal Dutch Shell PLC) (Neth.) (attacking conduct of Dutch respondent in Nigeria)). See also Brief for European Commission as *Amicus Curiae* 11 (It is "uncontroversial" that the "United States may ... exercise jurisdiction over ATS claims involving conduct committed by its own nationals within the territory of another sovereign, consistent with international law").

Other countries permit some form of lawsuit brought by a foreign national against a foreign national, based upon conduct taking place abroad and seeking damages. Certain countries, which find "universal" criminal "jurisdiction" to try perpetrators of particularly heinous crimes such as piracy and genocide, see Restatement §404, also permit private persons injured by that conduct to pursue "*actions civiles*" seeking civil damages in the criminal proceeding. Thompson, Ramasastry, & Taylor, Translating *Unocal:* The Expanding Web of Liability for Business Entities Implicated in International Crimes, 40 Geo. Wash. Int'l L. Rev. 841, 886 (2009). *See, e.g., Ely Ould Dah* v. *France,* App. No. 13113/03 (Eur. Ct. H.R.; Mar 30, 2009), 48 Int'l Legal Materials 884; Metcalf, Reparations for Displaced Torture Victims, 19 Cardozo J. Int'l & Comp. L. 451, 468-470 (2011). Moreover, the United Kingdom and the Netherlands, while not authorizing such damages actions themselves, tell us that they would have no objection to the exercise of American jurisdiction in cases such as *Filartiga* and *Marcos.* Netherlands Brief 15-16 and n.23.

At the same time Congress has ratified treaties obliging the United States to find and punish foreign perpetrators of serious crimes committed against foreign persons abroad. See Convention on the Prevention and Punishment of Crimes Against Internationally Protected Persons, Including Diplomatic Agents, Dec. 28, 1973, 28 U.S.T. 1975, T.I.A.S. No. 8532; Convention for the Suppression of Unlawful Acts Against the Safety of Civil Aviation, Sept. 23, 1971, 24 U.S.T. 565, T.I.A.S. No. 7570; Convention for the Suppression of Unlawful Seizure of Aircraft, Dec. 16, 1970, 22 U.S.T. 1641, T.I.A.S. No. 7192; Restatement §404 Reporters' Note 1, at 257 ("These agreements include an obligation on the parties to punish or extradite offenders, even when the offense was not committed within their territory or by a national"). See also International Convention for the Protection of All Persons from Enforced Disappearance, Art. 9(2) (2006) (state parties must take measures to establish jurisdiction "when the alleged offender is present in any territory under its jurisdiction, unless it extradites or surrenders him or her"); http://www.unhcr.org/refworld/docid/47fdfaebO.pdf (as visited Apr.1, 2013, and available in Clerk of Court's case file); Convention Against Torture and Other Cruel, Inhuman or Degrading Treatment of Punishment, Dec. 10, 1984, 1465 U.N.T.S. 85, Arts. 5(2), 7(1) (similar); Geneva Convention (III) Relative to the Treatment of Prisoners of War, Art. 129, Aug. 12, 1949, [1955] 6 U.S.T. 3316, T.I.A.S. No. 3364 (signatories must "search for persons alleged to have committed, or to have ordered to be committed, such grave breaches, and shall bring such persons, regardless of their nationality, before its own courts" or "hand such persons over for trial"). And Congress has sometimes authorized civil damages in such cases. See generally note following 28 U.S.C. §1350 (Torture Victim Protection Act of 1991 (TVPA) (private damages action for torture or extrajudicial killing committed under authority of a foreign nation)); S. Rep. No. 102-249, p. 4 (1991) (ATS "should not be replaced" by TVPA); H.R. Rep. No. 102-367, pt. 1, p. 4 (TVPA intended to "enhance the remedy already available under" the ATS). But cf. *Mohamad* v. *Palestinian Authority,* 566 U.S. _ (2012) (TVPA allows suits against only natural persons).

Congress, while aware of the award of civil damages under the ATS—including cases such as *Filartiga* with foreign plaintiffs, defendants, and conduct—has not sought to limit the statute's jurisdictional or substantive reach. Rather, Congress has enacted other statutes, and not only criminal statutes, that allow the United States to prosecute (or allow victims to obtain damages from) foreign persons who injure foreign victims by committing abroad torture, genocide, and other heinous acts. *See, e.g.,* 18 U.S.C. § 2340A(b)(2) (authorizing prosecution of torturers if "the alleged offender is present in the United States, irrespective of the nationality of the victim or alleged offender"); § 1091(e)(2)(D) (2006 ed., Supp. V) (genocide prosecution authorized when, "regardless of where the offense is committed, the alleged offender is ... present in the United States"); note following 28 U.S.C. § 1350, § 2(a) (private right of action on behalf of individuals harmed by an act of torture or extrajudicial killing committed "under actual or apparent authority, or color of law, of any foreign nation"). See also S. Rep. No. 102-249, *supra,* at 3-4 (purpose to "mak[e] sure that torturers and death squads will no longer have a safe haven in the United States," by "providing a civil cause of action in U.S. courts for torture committed abroad"). Thus, the jurisdictional approach that I would use is analogous to, and consistent with, the approaches of a number of other nations. It is consistent with the approaches set forth in the Restatement. Its insistence upon the presence of some distinct American interest, its reliance upon courts also invoking other related doctrines such as comity, exhaustion, and *forum non conveniens,* along with its dependence (for its workability) upon courts obtaining, and paying particular attention to, the view the Executive Branch, all should obviate the majority's concern that our jurisdictional example would lead "other nations, also applying the law of nations," to "hale our citizens into their courts for alleged violations of the law of nations occurring in the United States, or anywhere else in the world." *Ante,* at 13.

Most importantly, this jurisdictional view is consistent with the substantive view of the statute that we took in *Sosa.* This approach would avoid placing the statute's jurisdictional scope at odds with its substantive objectives, holding out "the word of promise" of compensation for victims of the torturer, while "break[ing] it to the hope."

III

Applying these jurisdictional principles to this case, however, I agree with the Court that jurisdiction does not lie. The defendants are two foreign corporations. Their shares, like those of many foreign corporations, are traded on the New York Stock Exchange. Their only presence in the United States consists of an office in New York City (actually owned by a separate but affiliated company) that helps to explain their business to potential investors. See Supp. Brief for Petitioners 4, n.3 (citing *Wiwa v. Royal Dutch Petroleum Co.,* 226 F.3d 88, 94 (CA2 2000)); App.55. The plaintiffs are not United States nationals but nationals of other nations. The conduct at issue took place abroad. And the plaintiffs allege, not that the defendants directly engaged in acts of torture, genocide, or the equivalent, but that they helped others (who are not American nationals) to do so. Under these circumstances, even if the New York office were a sufficient basis for asserting general jurisdiction, but see *Goodyear Dunlop Tires Operations, S.A. v. Brown,* 564 U.S. (2011), it would be farfetched to believe, based solely upon the defendants' minimal and indirect American presence, that this legal action helps to vindicate a distinct American interest, such as in not providing a safe harbor for an "enemy of all mankind." Thus I agree with the Court that here it would "reach too far to say" that such "mere corporate presence suffices." *Ante,* at 14.

I consequently join the Court's judgment but not its opinion.

Notes and Questions

1. If the main issue was that set forth in the first paragraph of the opinion of Chief Justice Roberts regarding violations of international law occurring within the territory

of a foreign state, in view of the extraterritorial aspects of conduct in violation of international law addressed in early cases such as *Bolchos, Moxon,* and those not addressed in his opinion should the answer have been yes? *Compare* Chief Justice Roberts ("The two cases in which the ATS was invoked shortly after its passage also concerned conduct within the territory of the United States. See *Bolchos,* 3 F. Cas. 810 (wrongful seizure of slaves from a vessel while in port in the United States); *Moxon,* 17 F. Cas. 942 (wrongful seizure in United States territorial tw9 waters)") *with* Jordan J. Paust, Kiobel, *10 Corporate Liability, and the Extraterritorial Reach of the ATS,* 53 Va. J. Int'l L. Digest 18, 27-28 (2012) [hereinafter Paust, *Kiobel*], available at http://ssrn.com/abstract=2173474 ("In *Moxon,* there were acts engaged in by French persons that originated from a French vessel onto an English vessel during its capture in U.S. waters and, as noted below [see Note 6 below], acts on a foreign flag vessel are acts within foreign state territory. In *Bolchos v. Darrel,* "the original cause arose at sea" on a Spanish vessel and the ATS allowed the court "to take cognizance of the cause" between two aliens, a Spanish claimant and an agent on behalf of a British national. Interesting dictum also appeared in some early extraterritorial cases [*See, e.g., Jansen v. The Vrow Christina Magdalena,* 13 F. Cas. 356, 358 (D.S.C. 1794) (No. 7,216) (dictum: "the powers of the district courts are expressed ... as to civil causes ... where an alien sues for a tort only," a case involving seizure of a Dutch vessel abroad); *M'Grath v. Candalero,* 16 F. Cas. 128 (D.S.C. 1794) (No.6,810) (dictum: where a vessel was seized abroad by a foreign vessel, "[i]f an alien sue here for a tort under the law of nations or a treaty ... the suit will be sustained"); Jordan J. Paust, *The History, Nature, and Reach of the Alien Tort Claims Act,* 16 Fla. J. Int'l L. 249, 250-51 n.3 (2004)]. A pre-*Filartiga* case in 1961 was also extraterritorial, involving recognized violations of international law within Lebanon and alien disputants [*Adra v. Clift,* 195 F. Supp. 857 (D. Md. 1961)]."). *Filartiga,* approved in *Sosa,* had also involved violations of international law occurring in a foreign territory. Why did Chief Justice Roberts mention only four cases that were decided prior to *Filartiga* in Part II of his opinion?

Was the answer to the question "yes" in part, since a majority of the Justices will allow at least partial extraterritorial application of the ATS? *See also* Breyer, J., opinion (2nd para. in Part I and lst para. in Part II).

2. Since, after *Sosa,* a right to a remedy or cause of action can arise under international law (as well as under an act of Congress or "common law") and the ATS is "jurisdictional," does enforcement of international law (1) as the substantive law incorporated by reference in the ATS, and/or (2) as the law that provides a right to an effective remedy pose a clash between "our laws and those of other nations" within the meaning of *Aramco*? Where, for example, human rights law provides a right to an effective remedy, it is international law as the substantive law as well as the law that provides a right to a remedy that is being enforced and not domestic law. *See also* Paust, *Kiobel, supra* at 20-21, 23. Further, it is international law over which there is a universal jurisdictional competence of the U.S. and other countries.

3. Indeed, if *Sosa* ruled that the ATS does not create a cause of action but the right to an effective remedy can arise under international law, was Chief Justice Roberts correct when stating "[t]he question under *Sosa* is not whether a federal court has jurisdiction to entertain a cause of action provided by foreign or even international law. The question is instead whether the court has authority to recognize a cause of action under U.S. law to enforce a norm of international law"?

4. If, given the language used in the ATS, violations of international law "can occur whether within or outside the United States" (Roberts, C.J.), which is true, doesn't this confirm the fact, from the face of the statute, that violations addressed in the ATS *can*

occur in a foreign state? Does the language necessarily "evince a 'clear indication of ex-traterritoriality'"? *See also* Breyer, J., concurring (in Part I B). Must the drafters have known this? Did the drafters or Congress at any subsequent time set a limit to its fa-cially possible extension to conduct abroad?

5. Under the transitory tort doctrine (whereby civil claims follow the person), isn't a cause of action under international law over which there is universal jurisdiction a cause of action "in that place" where the violation occurred as well as anywhere else?

6. Regarding piracy, Justice Breyer was correct to emphasize, contrary to Chief Justice Roberts, that piracy unavoidably involves the boarding of some other vessel flying the flag of some state and that, therefore, the piratical acts in violation of international law must necessarily occur in the equivalent of foreign state territory when the victim vessel is not a U.S. flag vessel. Concerning the fact that a foreign flag vessel or aircraft is the equivalent of foreign state territory, *see, e.g., Kiobel*, at _ (Breyer, J., concurring); Jordan J. Paust, M. Cherif Bassiouni, et al., International Criminal Law 196-97 (4 ed. 2013); Paust, *Kiobel*, *supra* at 28 & nn.46-47.

7. If international law over which there is universal jurisdiction is the substantive law that is being enforced, does the dictum from *La Jeune Eugenie* about no nation being the "custos morum of the whole world" have any direct relevance? especially when, under international law, there is a duty to provide a right to a remedy? Also note what Justice Story emphasized in that case: "in an American court of judicature, I am bound to con-sider the [slave] trade an offence against the universal law of society and in all cases, where it is not protected by a foreign government, to deal with it as an offence carrying with it the penalty of confiscation" and, "if the African slave trade is repugnant to the law of nations, no nation can rightly permit its subjects to carry it on, or exempt them ... [and] no nation can privilege itself to commit a crime against the law of na-tions," but no nation can sit in judgment of another nation as opposed to sitting in judgment against private perpetrators [see Note 8 below]. "It would be inconsistent with the equality and sovereignty of nations, which admit of no common superior. No nation has ever yet pretended to be the custos morum of the whole world." 26 F. Cas. at 847-51. Why did Chief Justice Roberts ignore this part of the opinion? *See also Talbot v. Janson*, 3 U.S. (3 Dall.) 133, 159-61 (1795) (Iredell, J., concurring) ("all ... trespasses committed against the general law of nations, are enquirable, and may be proceeded against, in any nation where no special exemption can be maintained, either by the gen-eral law of nations, or by some treaty which forbids or restrains it").

8. With respect to "foreign policy," compare *The Peterhoff*, 72 U.S. (5 Wall.) 28, 57 (1866) ("we administer the public law of nations, and are not at liberty to inquire what is for the particular ... disadvantage of our own or another country"); and *La Jeune Eu-genie*, 26 F. Cas. at 851 (where property is claimed by private violators of international law and would not go to their sovereign, "this court must follow the duty prescribed to it by law, independently of any wishes of our own government or of France"). *See also* Paust, *Kiobel*, *supra* at 23-25 n.27. Should "foreign policy" interests be identified and weighed by Congress and the Executive and not by unelected judges? See also Note 9 below.

9. Justice Breyer mentions § 403 of the Restatement. Despite the claim made in the Restatement, the comity-factors limitation of jurisdiction preferred in § 403 is not part of international law and expressly does not apply when § 404 is applicable (*i.e.*, when universal jurisdiction pertains even if, as recognized in § 404, there are no links

with the forum state). *See, e.g.*, Paust, Bassiouni, *et al.*, *supra* at 241-44; Paust, *Kiobel*, *supra* at 23.

10. Why was there a seeming focus on three violations of international law that happened to be addressed by Blackstone when the Framers and early judiciary had paid attention to several others, including breaches of neutrality addressed in 1 Op. Att'y Gen. 57 (1795) (Bradford, Att'y Gen.)? *Compare* the opinions of Chief Justice Roberts; Justice Alito (last para.); Justice Breyer (first para. in Section I A, but rightly using the word "including" and thereafter addressing other violations of customary international law and treaties of the United States) *with* Paust, Bassiouni, *et al.*, *supra* at 181-83; Paust, *Kiobel*, *supra* at 22-23 & nn.19-22; Chapter One.

11. Did Justice Breyer pay sufficient attention to the fact that complicitors of international crimes are also *hostis humani generis* when they aid or abet crimes under customary international law implicating universal jurisdiction when he stated that "plaintiffs allege, not that the defendants directly engaged in acts ... but that they helped others"? Concerning responsibility for complicitors under international law, *see, e.g.*, Paust, Bassiouni, *et al.*, *supra* at 69-74; Paust, *Kiobel*, *supra* at 27; 1 Op. Att'y Gen. 57, 58-59 (1795) ("and abetted").

12. Despite the fact that a majority of the Justices would allow at least partial extraterritorial application of the ATS, is there a majority view of what the criteria should be? What limits to extraterritoriality would Justice Alito prefer? What limits would Justice Breyer prefer? Does Justice Kennedy offer any guidance concerning "proper implementation" and the "open ... reach" of the ATS? What approach would you prefer?

13. Given the fact (1) that federal statutes should "never ... be construed to violate the law of nations if any other possible construction remains, and, consequently, can never be construed to violate ... rights ... further than is warranted by the law of nations," *Murray v. Schooner Charming Betsy*, 6 U.S. (2 Cranch) 64, 117-18 (1804) (Marshall, C.J.), and (2) that some forms of international law require that victims of violations have a right to an effective remedy, is it evident that "the *Charming Betsy* rule requires that the ATS not be interpreted restrictively to deny universal jurisdiction and rights under the law of nations" regarding the customary prohibition of "denial of justice" to aliens and custom ary and treaty-based human rights law? See Paust, *Kiobel*, *supra* at 29-31.

Does the focus in Justice Breyer's opinion on customary and treaty-based international legal duties not to provide a "safe haven" for those who commit international crimes partly support an interpretation of the ATS that, as he states, will serve "its substantive objectives, holding out 'the word of promise' of compensation for victims"? But has he paid sufficient attention to the nature of those duties (which apply, for example, "when the alleged offender is present") as if a "minimal ... presence" could not trigger a duty of the United States to comply with such obligations?

For further attention to the nature of the law that is expressly incorporated by reference in the ATS and its jurisdictional character and substantive grasp, the full set of early cases and opinions of the Attorneys General, congressional endorsement of the *Filartiga* line of cases, how the *Charming Betsy* rule supplements the need to interpret the statute consistently with universal jurisdiction and responsibility, and related matters, *see, e.g.*, Jordan J. Paust, Human Rights Through the ATS After *Kiobel*: Partial Extraterritoriality, Misconceptions, and Elusive and Problematic Judicially-Created Criteria, forthcoming, 6 Duke Forum for L. & Social Change (2014).

PART TWO

DOCUMENTS SECTION

United States Constitution

(extracts)

Article I.

Section 1. All legislative Powers herein granted shall be vested in a Congress of the United States, which shall consist of a Senate and House of Representatives.

Section 8. [1] The Congress shall have Power To lay and collect Taxes, Duties, Imposts and Excises, to pay the Debts and provide for the common Defence and general Welfare of the United States; but all Duties, Imposts and Excises shall be uniform throughout the United States;

[2] To borrow money on the credit of the United States;

[3] To regulate Commerce with foreign Nations, and among the several States, and with the Indian Tribes;

[4] To establish an uniform Rule of Naturalization, and uniform Laws on the subject of Bankruptcies throughout the United States;

[5] To coin Money, regulate the Value thereof, and of foreign Coin, and fix the Standard of Weights and Measures;

[6] To provide for the Punishment of counterfeiting the Securities and current Coin of the United States;

[7] To Establish Post Offices and Post Roads;

[8] To promote the Progress of Science and useful Arts, by securing for limited Times to Authors and Inventors the exclusive Right to their respective Writings and Discoveries;

[9] To constitute Tribunals inferior to the supreme Court;

[10] To define and punish Piracies and Felonies committed on the high Seas, and Offences against the Law of Nations;

[11] To declare War, grant Letters of Marque and Reprisal, and make Rules concerning Captures on Land and Water;

[12] To raise and support Armies, but no Appropriation of Money to that Use shall be for a longer Term than two Years;

[13] To provide and maintain a Navy;

[14] To make Rules for the Government and Regulation of the land and naval Forces;

[15] To provide for calling forth the Militia to execute the Laws of the Union, suppress Insurrections and repel Invasions;

[16] To provide for organizing, arming, and disciplining, the Militia, and for governing such Part of them as may be employed in the Service of the United States, reserving to the States respectively, the Appointment of the Officers, and the Authority of training the Militia according to the discipline prescribed by Congress; ...

[18] To make all Laws which shall be necessary and proper for carrying into Execution the foregoing Powers, and all other Powers vested by this Constitution in the Government of the United States, or in any Department or Officer thereof.

Section 9.

[2] The privilege of the Writ of Habeas Corpus shall not be suspended, unless when in Case of Rebellion or Invasion the public Safety may require it.

[3] No Bill of Attainder or ex post facto Law shall be passed.

Section 10.

[1] No State shall enter into any Treaty, Alliance, or Confederation; grant Letters of Marque and Reprisal....

[3] No State shall, without the Consent of Congress, ... enter into any Agreement or Compact with another State, or with a foreign Power or engage in War, unless actually invaded, or in such imminent Danger as will not admit of delay.

Article II.

Section 1. [1] The executive Power shall be vested in a President of the United States of America.

[8] Before he enter on the Execution of his Office, he shall take the following Oath or Affirmation:—"I do solemnly swear (or affirm) that I will faithfully execute the Office of President of the United States, and will to the best of my Ability, preserve, protect and defend the Constitution of the United States."

Section 2. [1] The President shall be Commander in Chief of the Army and Navy of the United States, and of the militia of the several States, when called into the actual Service of the United States; he may require the Opinion, in writing, of the principal Officer in each of the Executive Departments, upon any Subject relating to the Duties of their respective Offices, and he shall have Power to grant Reprieves and Pardons for Offenses against the United States, except in Cases of Impeachment.

[2] He shall have Power, by and with the Advice and Consent of the Senate to make Treaties, provided two thirds of the Senators present concur; and he shall nominate, and by and with the Advice and Consent of the Senate, shall appoint Ambassadors, other public Ministers and Consuls, Judges of the supreme Court, and all other Officers of the United States, whose Appointments are not herein otherwise provided for, and which shall be established by Law; but the Congress may by Law vest the Appointment of such inferior Officers, as they think proper, in the President alone, in the Courts of Law, or in the Heads of Departments....

Section 3.... [H]e shall receive Ambassadors and other public Ministers; he shall take Care that the Laws be faithfully executed, and shall Commission all the Officers of the United States.

Article III.

Section 1. The judicial Power of the United States, shall be vested in one supreme Court, and in such inferior Courts as the Congress may from time to time ordain and establish....

Section 2. [1] The judicial Power shall extend to all Cases, in Law and Equity, arising under this Constitution, the Laws of the United States, and Treaties made, or which shall be made, under their Authority;—to all Cases affecting Ambassadors, other public Ministers and Consuls;—to all Cases of admiralty and maritime Jurisdiction;—to Controversies to which the United States shall be a Party;—to Controversies between two or more States;—between a State and Citizens of another State;—between Citizens of different States;—between Citizens of the same State claiming Lands under the Grants of different States, and between a State, or the Citizens thereof, and foreign States, Citizens or Subjects.

[2] In all Cases affecting Ambassadors, other public Ministers and Consuls, and those in which a State shall be a Party, the supreme Court shall have original Jurisdiction. In all the other Cases before mentioned, the supreme Court shall have appellate Jurisdiction, both as to Law and Fact, with such Exceptions, and under such Regulations as the Congress shall make.

Article VI.

[2] This Constitution, and the Laws of the United States which shall be made in Pursuance thereof; and all Treaties made, or which shall be made, under the Authority of the United States, shall be the supreme Law of the Land; and the Judges in every State shall be bound thereby, any Thing in the Constitution or Laws of any State to the Contrary notwithstanding.

Amendment X.

The powers not delegated to the United States by the Constitution, nor prohibited by it to the States, are reserved to the States respectively, or to the people.

Charter of the United Nations, T.S. 993, 59 Stat. 1031, 1976 Y.B.U.N. 1043 (June 26, 1945)

WE THE PEOPLES OF THE UNITED NATIONS DETERMINED to save succeeding generations from the scourge of war, which twice in our lifetime has brought untold sorrow to mankind, and to reaffirm faith in fundamental human rights, in the dignity and worth of the human person, in the equal rights of men and women and of nations large and small, and to establish conditions under which justice and respect for the obligations arising from treaties and other sources of international law can be maintained, and to promote social progress and better standards of life in larger freedom,

AND FOR THESE ENDS to practice tolerance and live together in peace with one another as good neighbours, and to unite our strength to maintain international peace and security, and to ensure by the acceptance of principles and the institution of methods, that armed force shall not be used, save in the common interest, and to employ international machinery for the promotion of the economic and social advancement of all peoples,

HAVE RESOLVED TO COMBINE OUR EFFORTS TO ACCOMPLISH THESE AIMS Accordingly, our respective Governments, through representatives assembled in the city of San Francisco, who have exhibited their full powers found to be in good and due form, have agreed to the present Charter of the United Nations and do hereby establish an international organization to be known as the United Nations.

Chapter I. Purposes and Principles

Article 1

The Purposes of the United Nations are:

1. To maintain international peace and security, and to that end: to take effective collective measures for the prevention and removal of threats to the peace, and for the suppression of acts of aggression or other breaches of the peace, and to bring about by peaceful means, and in conformity with the principles of justice and international law, adjustment or settlement of international disputes or situations which might lead to a breach of the peace;

2. To develop friendly relations among nations based on respect for the principle of equal rights and self-determination of peoples, and to take other appropriate measures to strengthen universal peace;

3. To achieve international co-operation in solving international problems of an economic, social, cultural, or humanitarian character, and in promoting and encouraging respect for human rights and for fundamental freedoms for all without distinction as to race, sex, language, or religion; and

4. To be a centre for harmonizing the actions of nations in the attainment of these common ends.

Article 2

The Organization and its Members, in pursuit of the Purposes stated in Article 1, shall act in accordance with the following Principles.

1. The Organization is based on the principle of the sovereign equality of all its Members.

2. All Members, in order to ensure to all of them the rights and benefits resulting from membership, shall fulfil in good faith the obligations assumed by them in accordance with the present Charter.

3. All Members shall settle their international disputes by peaceful means in such a manner that international peace and security, and justice, are not endangered.

4. All Members shall refrain in their international relations from the threat or use of force against the territorial integrity or political independence of any state, or in any other manner inconsistent with the Purposes of the United Nations.

5. All Members shall give the United Nations every assistance in any action it takes in accordance with the present Charter, and shall refrain from giving assistance to any state against which the United Nations is taking preventive or enforcement action.

6. The Organization shall ensure that states which are not Members of the United Nations act in accordance with these Principles so far as may be necessary for the maintenance of international peace and security.

7. Nothing contained in the present Charter shall authorize the United Nations to intervene in matters which are essentially within the domestic jurisdiction of any state or shall require the Members to submit such matters to settlement under the present Charter; but this principle shall not prejudice the application of enforcement measures under Chapter VII....

Chapter III. Organs

Article 7

1. There are established as the principal organs of the United Nations: a General Assembly, a Security Council, an Economic and Social Council, a Trusteeship Council, an International Court of Justice, and a Secretariat.

2. Such subsidiary organs as may be found necessary may be established in accordance with the present Charter....

Chapter IV. The General Assembly

Composition

Article 9

1. The General Assembly shall consist of all the Members of the United Nations.

2. Each Member shall have not more than five representatives in the General Assembly.

Functions and Powers

Article 10

The General Assembly may discuss any questions or any matters within the scope of the present Charter or relating to the powers and functions of any organs provided for in the present Charter, and, except as provided in Article 12, may make recommendations to the Members of the United Nations or to the Security Council or to both on any such questions or matters.

Article 12

1. While the Security Council is exercising in respect of any dispute or situation the functions assigned to it in the present Charter, the General Assembly shall not make any recommendations with regard to that dispute or situation unless the Security Council so requests....

Article 13

1. The General Assembly shall initiate studies and make recommendations for the purpose of:

   a. promoting international cooperation in the political field and encouraging the progressive development of international law and its codification;

   b. promoting international cooperation in the economic, social, cultural, educational, and health fields, and assisting in the realization of human rights and fundamental freedoms for all without distinction as to race, sex, language, or religion.

2. The further responsibilities, functions, and powers of the General Assembly with respect to matters mentioned in paragraph 1 (b) above are set forth in Chapters IX and X.

Article 14

Subject to the provisions of Article 12, the General Assembly may recommend measures for the peaceful adjustment of any situation, regardless of origin, which it deems likely to impair the general welfare or friendly relations among nations, including situations resulting from a violation of the provisions of the present Charter setting forth the Purposes and Principles of the United Nations.

Article 22

The General Assembly may establish such subsidiary organs as it deems necessary for the performance of its functions....

Article 24

1. In order to ensure prompt and effective action by the United Nations, its Members confer on the Security Council primary responsibility for the maintenance of international peace and security, and agree that in carrying out its duties under this responsibility the Security Council acts on their behalf.

2. In discharging these duties the Security Council shall act in accordance with the Purposes and Principles of the United Nations. The specific powers granted to the Security Council for the discharge of these duties are laid down in Chapters VI, VII, VIII, and XII.

3. The Security Council shall submit annual and, when necessary, special reports to the General Assembly for its consideration.

Article 25

The Members of the United Nations agree to accept and carry out the decisions of the Security Council in accordance with the present Charter.

Chapter VI. Pacific Settlement of Disputes

Article 33

1. The parties to any dispute, the continuance of which is likely to endanger the maintenance of international peace and security, shall, first of all, seek a solution by negotiation, enquiry, mediation, conciliation, arbitration, judicial settlement, resort to regional agencies or arrangements, or other peaceful means of their own choice.

2. The Security Council shall, when it deems necessary, call upon the parties to settle their dispute by such means.

Article 34

The Security Council may investigate any dispute, or any situation which might lead to international friction or give rise to a dispute, in order to determine whether the continuance of the dispute or situation is likely to endanger the maintenance of international peace and security.

Chapter VII. Action with Respect to Threats to the Peace, Breaches of the Peace, or Acts of Aggression

Article 39

The Security Council shall determine the existence of any threat to the peace, breach of the peace, or act of aggression and shall make recommendations, or decide what measures shall be taken in accordance with Articles 41 and 42, to maintain or restore international peace and security.

Article 40

In order to prevent an aggravation of the situation, the Security Council may, before making the recommendations or deciding upon the measures provided for in Article 39, call upon the parties concerned to comply with such provisional measures as it deems necessary or desirable. Such provisional measures shall be without prejudice to the rights, claims, or position of the parties concerned. The Security Council shall duly take account of failure to comply with such provisional measures.

Article 41

The Security Council may decide what measures not involving the use of armed force are to be employed to give effect to its decisions, and it may call upon the Members of the United Nations to apply such measures. These may include complete or partial interruption of economic relations and of rail, sea, air, postal, telegraphic, radio, and other means of communication, and the severance of diplomatic relations.

Article 42

Should the Security Council consider that measures provided for in Article 41 would be inadequate or have proved inadequate, it may take such action by air, sea, or land forces as may be necessary to maintain or restore international peace and security. Such action may include demonstrations, blockade, and other operations by air, sea, or land forces of Members of the United Nations.

Article 43

1. All Members of the United Nations, in order to contribute to the maintenance of international peace and security, undertake to make available to the Security Council, on its call and in accordance with a special agreement or agreements, armed forces, assistance, and facilities, including rights of passage, necessary for the purpose of maintaining international peace and security.

2. Such agreement or agreements shall govern the numbers and types of forces, their degree of readiness and general location, and the nature of the facilities and assistance to be provided.

3. The agreement or agreements shall be negotiated as soon as possible on the initiative of the Security Council. They shall be concluded between the Security Council and Members or between the Security Council and groups of Members and shall be subject to ratification by the signatory states in accordance with their respective constitutional processes....

Article 45

In order to enable the United Nations to take urgent military measures, Members shall hold immediately available national air-force contingents for combined international enforcement action. The strength and degree of readiness of these contingents and plans for their combined action shall be determined, within the limits laid down in the special agreement or agreements referred to in Article 43, by the Security Council with the assistance of the Military Staff Committee.

Article 48

1. The action required to carry out the decisions of the Security Council for the maintenance of international peace and security shall be taken by all the Members of the United Nations or by some of them, as the Security Council may determine.

2. Such decisions shall be carried out by the members of the United Nations directly and through their action in the appropriate international agencies of which they are members.

Article 49

The Members of the United Nations shall join in affording mutual assistance in carrying out the measures decided upon by the Security Council.

Article 50

If preventive or enforcement measures against any state are taken by the Security Council, any other state, whether a Member of the United Nations or not, which finds itself confronted with special economic problems arising from the carrying out of those measures shall have the right to consult with the Security Council with regard to a solution of those problems.

Article 51

Nothing in the present Charter shall impair the inherent right of individual or collective self-defence if an armed attack occurs against a Member of the United Nations, until the Security Council has taken measures necessary to maintain international peace and security. Measures taken by Members in the exercise of this right of self-defence shall be immediately reported to the Security Council and shall not in any way affect the authority and responsibility of the Security Council under the present Charter to take at any time such action as it deems necessary in order to maintain or restore international peace and security.

Chapter VIII. Regional Arrangements

Article 52

1. Nothing in the present Charter precludes the existence of regional arrangements or agencies for dealing with such matters relating to the maintenance of international peace and security as are appropriate for regional action, provided that such arrangements or agencies and their activities are consistent with the Purposes and Principles of the United Nations.

2. The Members of the United Nations entering into such arrangements or constituting such agencies shall make every effort to achieve pacific settlement of local disputes through such regional arrangements or by such regional agencies before referring them to the Security Council.

3. The Security Council shall encourage the development of pacific settlement of local disputes through such regional arrangements or by such regional agencies either on the initiative of the states concerned or by reference from the Security Council.

4. This article in no way impairs the application of Articles 34 and 35.

Article 53

1. The Security Council shall, where appropriate, utilize such regional arrangements or agencies for enforcement action under its authority. But no enforcement action shall be taken under regional arrangements or by regional agencies without the authorization of the Security Council, with the exception of measures against any enemy state, as defined in paragraph 2 of this Article, provided for pursuant to Article 107 or in regional arrangements directed against renewal of aggressive policy on the part of any such state, until such time as the Organization may, on request of the Governments concerned, be charged with the responsibility for preventing further aggression by such a state.

2. The term enemy state as used in paragraph 1 of this article applies to any state which during the Second World War has been an enemy of any signatory of the present Charter.

Article 54

The Security Council shall at all times be kept fully informed of activities undertaken or in contemplation under regional arrangements or by regional agencies for the maintenance of international peace and security.

Chapter IX. International Economic and Social Cooperation

Article 55

With a view to the creation of conditions of stability and well-being which are necessary for peaceful and friendly relations among nations based on respect for the principle of equal rights and self-determination of peoples, the United Nations shall promote:

> a. higher standards of living, full employment, and conditions of economic and social progress and development;

> b. solutions of international economic, social, health, and related problems; and international cultural and educational cooperation; and

> c. universal respect for, and observance of, human rights and fundamental freedoms for all without distinction as to race, sex, language, or religion.

Article 56

All Members pledge themselves to take joint and separate action in cooperation with the Organization for the achievement of the purposes set forth in Article 55....

Article 103

In the event of a conflict between the obligations of the Members of the United Nations under the present Charter and their obligations under any other international agreement, their obligations under the present Charter shall prevail....

Declaration on Principles of International Law Concerning Friendly Relations and Co-operation Among States in Accordance with the Charter of the United Nations, October 24, 1970, U.N. G.A. Res. 2625, 25 U.N. GAOR, Supp. No. 28, at 121, U.N. Doc. A/8028 (1971)

PREAMBLE

The General Assembly,

Reaffirming in the terms of the Charter of the United Nations that the maintenance of international peace and security and the development of friendly relations and co-operation between nations are among the fundamental purposes of the United Nations,

Recalling that the peoples of the United Nations are determined to practice tolerance and live together in peace with one another as good neighbours,

Bearing in mind the importance of maintaining and strengthening international peace founded upon freedom, equality, justice and respect for fundamental human rights and of developing friendly relations among nations irrespective of their political, economic and social systems or the levels of their development,

Bearing in mind also the paramount importance of the Charter of the United Nations in the promotion of the rule of law among nations,

Considering that the faithful observance of the principles of international law concerning friendly relations and co-operation among States and the fulfillment in good faith of the obligations assumed by States, in accordance with the Charter, is of the greatest importance for the maintenance of international peace and security and for the implementation of the other purposes of the United Nations,

Convinced that the strict observance by States of the obligation not to intervene in the affairs of any other State is an essential condition to ensure that nations live together in peace with one another, since the practice of any form of intervention not only violates the spirit and letter of the Charter, but also leads to the creation of situations which threaten international peace and security,

Recalling the duty of States to refrain in their international relations from military, political, economic or any other form of coercion aimed against the political independence or territorial integrity of any State,

Considering it essential that all States shall refrain in their international relations from the threat or use of force against the territorial integrity or political independence of any State, or in any other manner inconsistent with the purposes of the United Nations,

Considering it equally essential that all States shall settle their international disputes by peaceful means in accordance with the Charter,

Reaffirming, in accordance with the Charter, the basic importance of sovereign equality and stressing that the purposes of the United Nations can be implemented only if States enjoy sovereign equality and comply fully with the requirements of this principle in their international relations,

Convinced that the subjection of peoples to alien subjugation, domination and exploitation constitutes a major obstacle to the promotion of international peace and security,

Convinced that the principle of equal rights and self-determination of peoples constitutes a significant contribution to contemporary international law, and that its effective application is of paramount importance for the promotion of friendly relations among States, based on respect for the principle of sovereign equality,

Convinced in consequence that any attempt aimed at the partial or total disruption of the national unity and territorial integrity of a State or country or at its political independence is incompatible with the purposes and principles of the Charter,

Considering the provisions of the Charter as a whole and taking into account the role of relevant resolutions adopted by the competent organs of the United Nations relating to the content of the principles,

Considering the progressive development and codification of the following principles:

(a) The principle that States shall refrain in their international relations from the threat or use of force against the territorial integrity or political independence of any State, or in any other manner inconsistent with the purposes of the United Nations,

(b) The principle that States shall settle their international disputes by peaceful means in such a manner that international peace and security and justice are not endangered,

(c) The duty not to intervene in matters within the domestic jurisdiction of any state, in accordance with the Charter,

(d) The duty of States to co-operate with one another in accordance with the Charter,

(e) The principle of equal rights and self-determination of peoples,

(f) The principle of sovereign equality of States,

(g) The principle that States shall fulfill in good faith the obligations assumed by them in accordance with the Charter, so as to secure their more effective application within the international community, would promote the realization of the purposes of the United Nations.

Having considered the principles of international law relating to friendly relations and co-operation among States,

1. *Solemnly proclaims* the following principles: ...

The duty of States to co-operate with one another in accordance with the Charter

States have the duty to co-operate with one another, irrespective of the differences of their political, economic and social systems, in the various spheres of international relations, in order to maintain international peace and security and to promote international economic stability and progress, the general welfare of nations and international cooperation free from discrimination based on such differences.

To this end:

(a) States shall co-operate with other States in the maintenance of international peace and security;

(b) States shall co-operate in the promotion of universal respect for, and observance of, human rights and fundamental freedoms for all, and in the elimination of all forms of racial discrimination and all forms of religious intolerance;

(c) States shall conduct their international relations in the economic, social, cultural technical and trade fields in accordance with the principles of sovereign equality and non-intervention,

(d) States Members of the United Nations have the duty to take joint and separate action in co-operation with the United Nations in accordance with the relevant provisions of the Charter.

States should co-operate in the economic, social and cultural fields as well as in the field of science and technology and for the promotion of international cultural and educational progress. States should cooperate in the promotion of economic growth throughout the world, especially that of the developing countries.

The principle of equal rights and self-determination of peoples

By virtue of the principle of equal rights and self-determination of peoples enshrined in the Charter of the United Nations, all peoples have the right freely to determine, without external interference their political status and to pursue their economic, social and cultural development, and every State has the duty to respect this right in accordance with the provisions of the Charter.

Every State has the duty to promote, through joint and separate action, realization of the principle of equal rights and self-determination of peoples, in accordance with the provisions of the Charter, and to render assistance to the United Nations in carrying out the responsibilities entrusted to it by the Charter regarding the implementation of the principle, in order:

(a) To promote friendly relations and co-operation among States, and

(b) To bring a speedy end of colonialism, having due regard to the freely expressed will of the peoples concerned;

and bearing in mind that subjection of peoples to alien subjugation, domination and exploitation constitutes a violation of the principle, as well as a denial of fundamental human rights, and is contrary to the Charter.

Every State has the duty to promote through joint and separate action universal respect for and observance of human rights and fundamental freedoms in accordance with the Charter.

The establishment of a sovereign and independent State, the free association or integration with an independent State or the emergence into any other political status freely determined by a people constitute modes of implementing the right of self-determination by that people.

Every State has the duty to refrain from any forcible action which deprives peoples referred to above in the elaboration of the present principle of their right to self-determination and freedom and independence. In their actions against, and resistance to, such forcible action in pursuit of the exercise of their right to self-determination, such peoples are entitled to seek and to receive support in accordance with the purposes and principles of the Charter.

The territory of a colony of other Non-Self-Governing Territory has, under the Charter, a status separate and distinct from the territory of the State administering it; and such separate and distinct status under the Charter shall exist until the people of the colony or Non-Self-Governing Territory have exercised their right of self-determination in accordance with the Charter, and particularly its purposes and principles.

Nothing in the foregoing paragraphs shall be construed as authorizing or encouraging any action which would dismember or impair, totally or in part, the territorial integrity or political unity of sovereign and independent States conducting themselves in compliance with the principle of equal rights and self-determination of peoples as described above and thus possessed of a government representing the whole people belonging to the territory without distinction as to race, creed or colour.

Every State shall refrain from any action aimed at the partial or total disruption of the national unity and territorial integrity of any other State or country....

Universal Declaration of Human Rights, U.N. G.A. Res. 217A, 3 U.N. GAOR, U.N. Doc. A/810, at 71 (1948)

Preamble

Whereas recognition of the inherent dignity and of the equal and inalienable rights of all members of the human family is the foundation of freedom, justice and peace in the world,

Whereas disregard and contempt for human rights have resulted in barbarous acts which have outraged the conscience of mankind, and the advent of a world in which human beings shall enjoy freedom of speech and belief and freedom from fear and want has been proclaimed as the highest aspiration of the common people,

Whereas it is essential, if man is not to be compelled to have recourse, as a last resort, to rebellion against tyranny and oppression, that human rights should be protected by the rule of law,

Whereas it is essential to promote the development of friendly relations between nations,

Whereas the peoples of the United Nations have in the Charter reaffirmed their faith in fundamental human rights, in the dignity and worth of the human person and in the equal rights of men and women and have determined to promote social progress and better standards of life in larger freedom,

Whereas Member States have pledged themselves to achieve, in cooperation with the United Nations, the promotion of universal respect for and observance of human rights and fundamental freedoms,

Whereas a common understanding of these rights and freedoms is of the greatest importance for the full realization of this pledge.

Now Therefore, The General Assembly *proclaims this universal declaration of human rights* as a common standard of achievement for all peoples and all nations, to the end that every individual and every organ of society, keeping this Declaration constantly in mind, shall strive by teaching and education to promote respect for these rights and freedoms and by progressive measures, national and international, to secure their universal and effective recognition and observance, both among the peoples of Member States themselves and among the peoples of territories under their jurisdiction.

Article 1

All human beings are born free and equal in dignity and rights. They are endowed with reason and conscience and should act towards one another in a spirit of brotherhood.

Article 2

Everyone is entitled to all the rights and freedoms set forth in this declaration, without discrimination of any kind, such as race, colour, sex, language, religion, political or other opinion, national or social origin, property, birth or other status.

Furthermore, no distinction shall be made on the basis of the political, jurisdictional or international status of the country or territory to which a person belongs, whether it be independent, trust, non-self-governing or under any other limitation of sovereignty.

Article 3

Everyone has the right to life, liberty and the security of person.

Article 4

No one shall be held in slavery or servitude; slavery and the slave trade shall be prohibited in all their forms.

Article 5

No one shall be subjected to torture or to cruel, inhuman or degrading treatment or punishment.

Article 6

Everyone has the right to recognition everywhere as a person before the law.

Article 7

All are equal before the law and are entitled without any discrimination to equal protection of the law. All are entitled to equal protection against any discrimination in violation of this Declaration and against any incitement to such discrimination.

Article 8

Everyone has the right to an effective remedy by the competent national tribunals for acts violating the fundamental rights granted him by the constitution or by law.

Article 9

No one shall be subjected to arbitrary arrest, detention or exile.

Article 10

Everyone is entitled in full equality to a fair and public hearing by an independent and impartial tribunal, in the determination of his rights and obligations and of any criminal charge against him.

Article 11

1. Everyone charged with a penal offence has the right to be presumed innocent until proved guilty according to law in a public trial at which he has had all the guarantees necessary for his defense.

2. No one shall be held guilty of any penal offence on account of any act or omission which did not constitute a penal offence, under national or international law, at the time when it was committed. Nor shall a heavier penalty be imposed than the one that was applicable at the time the penal offence was committed.

Article 12

No one shall be subjected to arbitrary interference with his privacy, family, home or correspondence, nor to attacks upon his honour and reputation. Everyone has the right to the protection of the law against such interference or attacks.

Article 13

1. Everyone has the right to freedom of movement and residence within the borders of each State.

2. Everyone has the right to leave any country, including his own, and to return to his country.

Article 14

1. Everyone has the right to seek and to enjoy in other countries asylum from persecution.

2. This right may not be invoked in the case of prosecutions genuinely arising from non-political crimes or from acts contrary to the purposes and principles of the United Nations.

Article 15

1. Everyone has the right to a nationality.

2. No one shall be arbitrarily deprived of his nationality nor denied the right to change his nationality.

Article 16

1. Men and women of full age, without any limitation due to race, nationality or religion, have the right to marry and to found a family. They are entitled to equal rights as to marriage, during marriage and at its dissolution.

2. Marriage shall be entered into only with the free and full consent of the intending spouses.

3. The family is the natural and fundamental group unit of society and is entitled to protection by society and the State.

Article 17

1. Everyone has the right to own property alone as well as in association with others.

2. No one shall be arbitrarily deprived of his property.

Article 18

Everyone has the right to freedom of thought, conscience and religion; this right includes freedom to change his religion or belief, and freedom, either alone or in community with others and in public or private, to manifest his religion or belief in teaching, practice, worship and observance.

Article 19

Everyone has the right to freedom of opinion and expression; this right includes freedom to hold opinions without interference and to seek, receive and impart information and ideas through any media and regardless of frontiers.

Article 20

1. Everyone has the right to freedom of peaceful assembly and association.

2. No one may be compelled to belong to an association.

Article 21

1. Everyone has the right to take part in the government of his country, directly or through freely chosen representatives.

2. Everyone has the right official access to public service in his country.

3. The will of the people shall be the basis of the authority of government; this will shall be expressed in periodic and genuine elections which shall be by universal and equal suffrage and shall be held by secret vote or by equivalent free voting procedures.

Article 22

Everyone, as a member of society, has the right to social security and is entitled to realization, through national effort and international cooperation and in accordance with the organization and resources of each State, of the economic, social and cultural rights indispensable for his dignity and the free development of his personality.

Article 23

1. Everyone has the right to work, to free choice of employment, to just and favorable conditions of work and to protection against unemployment.

2. Everyone, without any discrimination, has the right to equal pay for equal work.

3. Everyone who works has the right to just and favourable remuneration ensuring for himself and his family and existence worthy of human dignity, and supplemented, if necessary, by other means of social protection.

4. Everyone has the right to form and to join trade unions for the protection of his interests.

Article 24

Everyone has the right to rest and leisure, including reasonable limitation of working hours and periodic holidays with pay.

Article 25

1. Everyone has the right to a standard of living adequate for the health and well-being of himself and of his family, including food, clothing, housing and medical care and necessary social services, and the right to security in the event of unemployment, sickness, disability, widowhood, old age or other lack of livelihood in circumstances beyond his control.

2. Motherhood and childhood are entitled to special care and assistance. All children, whether born in or out of wedlock, shall enjoy the same social protection.

Article 26

1. Everyone has the right to education. Education shall be free, at least in the elementary and fundamental stages. Elementary education shall be compulsory. Technical and professional education shall be made generally available and higher education shall be equally accessible to all on the basis of merit.

2. Education shall be directed to the full development of the human personality and to the strengthening of respect for human rights and fundamental freedoms. It shall promote understanding, tolerance and friendship among all nations, racial or religious groups, and shall further the activities of the United Nations for the maintenance of peace.

3. Parents have a right to choose the kind of education that shall be given to their children.

Article 27

1. Everyone has the right freely to participate in the cultural life of the community, to enjoy the arts and to share in scientific advancement and its benefits.

2. Everyone has the right to the protection of the moral and material interests resulting from any scientific, literary or artistic production of which he is the author.

Article 28

Everyone is entitled to a social and international order in which the rights and freedoms set forth in this Declaration can be fully realized.

Article 29

1. Everyone has duties to the community in which alone the free and full development of his personality is possible.

2. In the exercise of his rights and freedoms, everyone shall be subject only to such limitations as are determined by law solely for the purpose of securing due recognition

and respect for the rights and freedoms of others and of meeting the just requirements of morality, public order and the general welfare in a democratic society.

3. These rights and freedoms may in no case be exercised contrary to the purposes and principles of the United Nations.

Article 30

Nothing in this Declaration may be interpreted as implying for any States, group or person any right to engage in any activity or to perform any act aimed at the destruction of any of the rights and freedoms set forth herein.

International Covenant on Civil and Political Rights, (ICCPR) 999 U.N.T.S. 171 (Dec. 9, 1966)

Preamble

The States Parties to the present Covenant,

Considering that, in accordance with the principles proclaimed in the Charter of the United Nations, recognition of the inherent dignity and of the equal and inalienable rights of all members of the human family is the foundation of freedom, justice and peace in the world,

Recognizing that these rights derive from the inherent dignity of the human person,

Recognizing that, in accordance with the Universal Declaration of Human Rights, the ideal of free human beings enjoying civil and political freedom and freedom from fear and want can only be achieved if conditions are created whereby everyone may enjoy his civil and political rights, as well as his economic, social and cultural rights,

Considering the obligation of States under the Charter of the United Nations to promote universal respect for, and observance of, human rights and freedoms,

Realizing that the individual, having duties to other individuals and to the community to which he belongs, is under a responsibility to strive for the promotion and observance of the rights recognized in the present Covenant,

Agree upon the following articles:

Part I

Article 1

1. All peoples have the right of self-determination. By virtue of that right they freely determine their political status and freely pursue their economic, social and cultural development.

2. All peoples may, for their own ends, freely dispose of their natural wealth and resources without prejudice to any obligations arising out of international economic co-

operation, based upon the principle of mutual benefit, and international law. In no case may a people be deprived of its own means of subsistence.

3. The States Parties to the present Covenant, including those having responsibility for the administration of Non-Self-Governing and Trust Territories, shall promote the realization of the right of self-determination, and shall respect that right, in conformity with the provisions of the Charter of the United Nations.

Part II

Article 2

1. Each State Party to the present Covenant undertakes to respect and to ensure to all individuals within its territory and subject to its jurisdiction the rights recognized in the present Covenant, without distinction of any kind, such as race, colour, sex, language, religion, political or other opinion, national or social origin, property, birth or other status.

2. Where not already provided for by existing legislative or other measures, each State Party to the present Covenant undertakes to take the necessary steps, in accordance with its constitutional processes and with the provisions of the present Covenant, to adopt such legislative or other measures as may be necessary to give effect to the rights recognized in the present Covenant.

3. Each State Party to the present Covenant undertakes:

(a) To ensure that any person whose rights or freedoms as herein recognized are violated shall have an effective remedy, notwithstanding that the violation has been committed by persons acting in an official capacity;

(b) To ensure that any person claiming such a remedy shall have his right thereto determined by competent judicial, administrative or legislative authorities, or by any other competent authority provided for by the legal system of the State, and to develop the possibilities of judicial remedy;

(c) To ensure that the competent authorities shall enforce such remedies when granted.

Article 3

The States Parties to the present Covenant undertake to ensure the equal right of men and women to the enjoyment of all civil and political rights set forth in the present Covenant.

Article 4

1. In time of public emergency which threatens the life of the nation and the existence of which is officially proclaimed, the States Parties to the present Covenant may take measures derogating from their obligations under the present Covenant to the extent strictly required by the exigencies of the situation, provided that such measures are not inconsistent with their other obligations under international law and do not involve discrimination solely on the ground of race, colour, sex, language, religion or social origin.

2. No derogation from Articles 6, 7, 8 (paragraphs 1 and 2), 11, 15, 16 and 18 may be made under this provision.

3. Any State Party to the present Covenant availing itself of the right of derogation shall immediately inform the other States Parties to the present Covenant, through the intermediary of the Secretary-General of the United Nations, of the provisions from which it has derogated and of the reasons by which it was actuated. A further communication shall be made, through the same intermediary, on the date on which it terminates such derogation.

Article 5

1. Nothing in the present Covenant may be interpreted as implying for any State, group or person any right to engage in any activity or perform any act aimed at the destruction of any of the rights and freedoms recognized herein or at their limitation to a greater extent than is provided for in the present Covenant.

2. There shall be no restriction upon or derogation from any of the fundamental human rights recognized or existing in any State Party to the present Covenant pursuant to law, conventions, regulations or custom on the pretext that the present Covenant does not recognize such rights or that it recognizes them to a lesser extent.

Part III

Article 6

1. Every human being has the inherent right to life. This right shall be protected by law. No one shall be arbitrarily deprived of his life.

2. In countries which have not abolished the death penalty, sentence of death may be imposed only for the most serious crimes in accordance with the law in force at the time of the commission of the crime and not contrary to the provisions of the present Covenant and to the Convention on the Prevention and Punishment of the Crime of Genocide. This penalty can only be carried out pursuant to a final judgment rendered by a competent court.

3. When deprivation of life constitutes the crime of genocide, it is understood that nothing in this article shall authorize any State Party to the present Covenant to derogate in any way from any obligation assumed under the provisions of the Convention on the Prevention and Punishment of the Crime of Genocide.

4. Anyone sentenced to death shall have the right to seek pardon or commutation of the sentence. Amnesty, pardon or commutation of the sentence of death may be granted in all cases.

5. Sentence of death shall not be imposed for crimes committed by persons below eighteen years of age and shall not be carried out on pregnant women.

6. Nothing in this article shall be invoked to delay or to prevent the abolition of capital punishment by any State Party to the present Covenant.

Article 7

No one shall be subjected to torture or to cruel, inhuman or degrading treatment or punishment. In particular, no one shall be subjected without his free consent to medical or scientific experimentation.

Article 8

1. No one shall be held in slavery; slavery and the slave trade in all their forms shall be prohibited.

2. No one shall be held in servitude.

3. (a) No one shall be required to perform forced or compulsory labour;

(b) Paragraph 3(a) shall not be held to preclude, in countries where imprisonment with hard labour may be imposed as a punishment for a crime, the performance of hard labour in pursuance of a sentence to such punishment by a competent court;

(c) For the purpose of this paragraph the term "forced or compulsory labour" shall not include:

(i) Any work or service, not referred to in sub-paragraph (b), normally required of a person who is under detention in consequence of a lawful order of a court, or of a person during conditional release from such detention;

(ii) Any service of a military character and, in countries where

conscientious objection is recognized, any national service required by law of conscientious objectors;

(iii) Any service exacted in cases of emergency or calamity threatening the life or well-being of the community;

(iv) Any work or service which forms part of normal civil obligations.

Article 9

1. Everyone has the right to liberty and security of person. No one shall be subjected to arbitrary arrest or detention. No one shall be deprived of his liberty except on such grounds and in accordance with such procedure as are established by law.

2. Anyone who is arrested shall be informed, at the time of arrest, of the reasons for his arrest and shall be promptly informed of any charges against him.

3. Anyone arrested or detained on a criminal charge shall be brought promptly before a judge or other officer authorized by law to exercise judicial power and shall be entitled to trial within a reasonable time or to release. It shall not be the general rule that persons awaiting trial shall be detained in custody, but release may be subject to guarantees to appear for trial, at any other stage of the judicial proceedings, and, should occasion arise, for execution of the judgment.

4. Anyone who is deprived of his liberty by arrest or detention shall be entitled to take proceedings before a court, in order that court may decide without delay on the lawfulness of his detention and order his release if the detention is not lawful.

5. Anyone who has been the victim of unlawful arrest or detention shall have an enforceable right to compensation.

Article 10

1. All persons deprived of their liberty shall be treated with humanity and with respect for the inherent dignity of the human person.

2. (a) Accused persons shall, save in exceptional circumstances, be segregated from convicted persons and shall be subject to separate treatment appropriate to their status as unconvicted persons;

(b) Accused juvenile persons shall be separated from adults and brought as speedily as possible for adjudication.

3. The penitentiary system shall comprise treatment of prisoners the essential aim of which shall be their reformation and social rehabilitation. Juvenile offenders shall be segregated from adults and be accorded treatment appropriate to their age and legal status.

Article 11

No one shall be imprisoned merely on the ground of inability to fulfil a contractual obligation.

Article 12

1. Everyone lawfully within the territory of a State shall, within that territory, have the right to liberty of movement and freedom to choose his residence.

2. Everyone shall be free to leave any country, including his own.

3. The above-mentioned rights shall not be subject to any restrictions except those which are provided by law, are necessary to protect national security, public order (*ordre public*), public health or morals or the rights and freedoms of others, and are consistent with the other rights recognized in the present Covenant.

4. No one shall be arbitrarily deprived of the right to enter his own country.

Article 13

An alien lawfully in the territory of a State Party to the present Covenant may be expelled therefrom only in pursuance of a decision reached in accordance with law and shall, except where compelling reasons of national security otherwise require, be allowed to submit the reasons against his expulsion and to have his case reviewed by, and be represented for the purpose before, the competent authority or a person or persons especially designated by the competent authority.

Article 14

1. All persons shall be equal before the courts and tribunals. In the determination of any criminal charge against him, or of his rights and obligations in a suit at law, everyone shall be entitled to a fair and public hearing by a competent, independent and impartial tribunal established by law. The Press and the public may be excluded from all or part of a trial for reasons of morals, public order (*ordre public*) or national security in a democratic society, or when the interest of the private lives of the parties so requires, or to the extent strictly necessary in the opinion of the court in special circumstances where publicity would prejudice the interests of justice; but any judgment rendered in a criminal case or in a suit at law shall be made public except where the interest of juve-

nile persons otherwise requires or the proceedings concern matrimonial disputes or the guardianship of children.

2. Everyone charged with a criminal offence shall have the right to be presumed innocent until proved guilty according to law.

3. In the determination of any criminal charge against him, everyone shall be entitled to the following minimum guarantees, in full equality:

(a) To be informed promptly and in detail in a language which he understands of the nature and cause of the charge against him;

(b) To have adequate time and facilities for the preparation of his defence and to communicate with counsel of his own choosing;

(c) To be tried without undue delay;

(d) To be tried in his presence, and to defend himself in person or through legal assistance of his own choosing; to be informed, if he does not have legal assistance, of this right; and to have legal assistance assigned to him, in any case where the interests of justice so require, and without payment by him in any such case if he does not have sufficient means to pay for it;

(e) To examine, or have examined, the witnesses against him and to obtain the attendance and examination of witnesses on his behalf under the same conditions as witnesses against him;

(f) To have the free assistance of an interpreter if he cannot understand or speak the language used in court;

(g) Not to be compelled to testify against himself or to confess guilt.

4. In the case of juvenile persons, the procedure shall be such as will take account of their age and the desirability of promoting their rehabilitation.

5. Everyone convicted of a crime shall have the right to his conviction and sentence being reviewed by a higher tribunal according to law.

6. When a person has by a final decision been convicted of a criminal offence and when subsequently his conviction has been reversed or he has been pardoned on the ground that a new or newly discovered fact shows conclusively that there has been a miscarriage of justice, the person who has suffered punishment as a result of such conviction shall be compensated according to law, unless it is proved that the non-disclosure of the unknown fact in time is wholly or partly attributable to him.

7. No one shall be liable to be tried or punished again for an offence for which he has already been finally convicted or acquitted in accordance with the law and penal procedure of each country.

Article 15

1. No one shall be held guilty of any criminal offence on account of any act or omission which did not constitute a criminal offence, under national or international law, at the time when it was committed. Nor shall a heavier penalty be imposed than the one that was applicable at the time when the criminal offence was committed. If, subsequent to the commission of the offence, provision is made by law for the imposition of a lighter penalty, the offender shall benefit thereby.

2. Nothing in this article shall prejudice the trial and punishment of any person for any act or omission which, at the time when it was committed, was criminal according to the general principles of law recognized by the community of nations.

Article 16

Everyone shall have the right to recognition everywhere as a person before the law.

Article 17

1. No one shall be subjected to arbitrary or unlawful interference with his privacy, family, home or correspondence, nor to unlawful attacks on his honour and reputation.

2. Everyone has the right to the protection of the law against such interference or attacks.

Article 18

1. Everyone shall have the right to freedom of thought, conscience and religion. This right shall include freedom to have or to adopt a religion or belief of his choice, and freedom, either individually or in community with others and in public or private, to manifest his religion or belief in worship, observance, practice and teaching.

2. No one shall be subject to coercion which would impair his freedom to have or to adopt a religion or belief of his choice.

3. Freedom to manifest one's religion or beliefs may be subject only to such limitations as are prescribed by law and are necessary to protect public safety, order, health, or morals or the fundamental rights and freedoms of others.

4. The States Parties to the present Covenant undertake to have respect for the liberty of parents and, when applicable, legal guardians to ensure the religious and moral education of their children in conformity with their own convictions.

Article 19

1. Everyone shall have the right to hold opinions without interference.

2. Everyone shall have the right to freedom of expression; this right shall include freedom to seek, receive and impart information and ideas of all kinds, regardless of frontiers, either orally, in writing or in print, in the form of art, or through any other media of his choice.

3. The exercise of the rights provided for in paragraph 2 of this article carries with it special duties and responsibilities. It may therefore be subject to certain restrictions, but these shall only be such as are provided by law and are necessary:

(a) For respect of the rights or reputations of others;

(b) For the protection of national security or of public order (*ordre public*), or of public health or morals.

Article 20

1. Any propaganda for war shall be prohibited by law.

2. Any advocacy of national, racial or religious hatred that constitutes incitement to discrimination, hostility or violence shall be prohibited by law.

Article 21

The right of peaceful assembly shall be recognized. No restrictions may be placed on the exercise of this right other than those imposed in conformity with the law and which are necessary in a democratic society in the interests of national security or public safety, public order (*ordre public*), the protection of public health or morals or the protection of the rights and freedoms of others.

Article 22

1. Everyone shall have the right to freedom of association with others, including the right to form and join trade unions for the protection of his interests.

2. No restrictions may be placed on the exercise of this right other than those which are prescribed by law and which are necessary in a democratic society in the interests of national security or public safety, public order (*ordre public*), the protection of public health or morals or the protection of the rights and freedoms of others. This article shall not prevent the imposition of lawful restrictions on members of the armed forces and of the police in their exercise of this right.

3. Nothing in this article shall authorize States Parties to the International Labour Organization Convention of 1948 concerning Freedom of Association and Protection of the Right to Organize to take legislative measures which would prejudice, or to apply the law in such a manner as to prejudice, the guarantees provided for in that Convention.

Article 23

1. The family is the natural and fundamental group unit of society and is entitled to protection by society and the State.

2. The right of men and women of marriageable age to marry and to found a family shall be recognized.

3. No marriage shall be entered into without the free and full consent of the intending spouses.

4. States Parties to the present Covenant shall take appropriate steps to ensure equality of rights and responsibilities of spouses as to marriage, during marriage and at its dissolution. In the case of dissolution, provision shall be made for the necessary protection of any children.

Article 24

1. Every child shall have, without any discrimination as to race, colour, sex, language, religion, national or social origin, property or birth, the right to such measures of protection as are required by his status as a minor, on the part of his family, society and the State.

2. Every child shall be registered immediately after birth and shall have a name.

3. Every child has the right to acquire a nationality.

Article 25

Every citizen shall have the right and the opportunity, without any of the distinctions mentioned in Article 2 and without unreasonable restrictions:

(a) To take part in the conduct of public affairs, directly or through freely chosen representatives;

(b) To vote and to be elected at genuine periodic elections which shall be by universal and equal suffrage and shall be held by secret ballot, guaranteeing the free expression of the will of the electors;

(c) To have access, on general terms of equality, to public service in his country.

Article 26

All persons are equal before the law and are entitled without any discrimination to the equal protection of the law. In this respect, the law shall prohibit any discrimination and guarantee to all persons equal and effective protection against discrimination on any ground such as race, colour, sex, language, religion, political or other opinion, national or social origin, property, birth or other status.

Article 27

In those States in which ethnic, religious or linguistic minorities exist, persons belonging to such minorities shall not be denied the right, in community with the other members of their group, to enjoy their own culture, to profess and practice their own religion, or to use their own language.

Part IV

Article 28

1. There shall be established a Human Rights Committee (hereafter referred to in the present Covenant as the Committee). It shall consist of eighteen members and shall carry out the functions hereinafter provided.

2. The Committee shall be composed of nationals of the States Parties to the present Covenant who shall be persons of high moral character and recognized competence in the field of human rights, consideration being given to the usefulness of the participation of some persons having legal experience.

3. The members of the Committee shall be elected and shall serve in their personal capacity.

Article 29

1. The members of the Committee shall be elected by secret ballot from a list of persons possessing the qualifications prescribed in Article 28 and nominated for the purpose by the State Parties to the present Covenant.

2. Each State Party to the present Covenant may nominate not more than two persons. These persons shall be nationals of the nominating State.

3. A person shall be eligible for renomination.

Article 30

1. The initial election shall be held no later than six months after the date of the entry into force of the present Covenant.

2. At least four months before the date of each election to the Committee, other than an election to fill a vacancy declared in accordance with Article 34, the Secretary-General of the United Nations shall address a written invitation to the States Parties to the present Covenant to submit their nominations for membership of the Committee within three months.

3. The Secretary-General of the United Nations shall prepare a list in alphabetical order of all the persons thus nominated, with an indication of the States Parties which have nominated them, and shall submit it to the States Parties to the present Covenant no later than one month before the date of each election.

4. Elections of the members of the Committee shall be held at a meeting of the States Parties to the present Covenant convened by the Secretary-General of the United Nations at the Headquarters of the United Nations. At that meeting, for which two thirds of the States Parties to the present Covenant shall constitute a quorum, the persons elected to the Committee shall be those nominees who obtain the largest number of votes and an absolute majority of the votes of the representatives of States Parties present and voting.

Article 31

1. The Committee may not include more than one national of the same State.

2. In the election of the Committee, consideration shall be given to equitable geographical distribution of membership and to the representation of the different forms of civilization and of the principal legal systems.

Article 32

1. The members of the Committee shall be elected for a term of four years. They shall be eligible for re-election if renominated. However, the terms of nine of the members elected at the first election shall expire at the end of two years; immediately after the first election, the names of these nine members shall be chosen by lot by the Chairman of the meeting referred to in Article 30, paragraph 4.

2. Elections at the expiry of office shall be held in accordance with the preceding articles of this part of the present Covenant.

Article 33

1. If, in the unanimous opinion of the other members, a member of the Committee has ceased to carry out his functions for any cause other than absence of a temporary character, the Chairman of the Committee shall notify the Secretary-General of the United Nations, who shall then declare the seat of that member to be vacant.

2. In the event of the death or the resignation of a member of the Committee, the Chairman shall immediately notify the Secretary-General of the United Nations, who shall declare the seat vacant from the date of death or the date on which the resignation takes effect.

Article 34

1. When a vacancy is declared in accordance with Article 33 and if the term of office of the member to be replaced does not expire within six months of the declaration of the vacancy, the Secretary-General of the United Nations shall notify each of the States Parties to the present Covenant, which may within two months submit nominations m accordance with Article 29 for the purpose of filling the vacancy.

2. The Secretary-General of the United Nations shall prepare a list in alphabetical order of the persons thus nominated and shall submit it to the States Parties to the present Covenant. The election to fill the vacancy shall then take place in accordance with the relevant provisions of this part of the present Covenant.

3. A member of the Committee elected to fill a vacancy declared in accordance with Article 33 shall hold office for the remainder of the term of the member who vacated the seat on the Committee under the provisions of that article.

Article 35

The members of the Committee shall, with the approval of the General Assembly of the United Nations, receive emoluments from United Nations resources on such terms and conditions as the General Assembly may decide, having regard to the importance of the Committee's responsibilities.

Article 36

The Secretary-General of the United Nations shall provide the necessary staff and facilities for the effective performance of the functions of the Committee under the present Covenant.

Article 37

1. The Secretary-General of the United Nations shall convene the initial meeting of the Committee at the Headquarters of the United Nations.

2. After its initial meeting, the Committee shall meet at such times as shall be provided in its rules of procedure.

3. The Committee shall normally meet at the Headquarters of the United Nations or at the United Nations Office at Geneva.

Article 38

Every member of the Committee shall, before taking up his duties, make a solemn declaration in open committee that he will perform his functions impartially and conscientiously.

Article 39

1. The Committee shall elect its officers for a term of two years. They may be re-elected.

2. The Committee shall establish its own rules of procedure, but these rules shall provide, *inter alia*, that:

(a) Twelve members shall constitute a quorum;

(b) Decisions of the Committee shall be made by a majority vote of the members present.

Article 40

1. The States Parties to the present Covenant undertake to submit reports on the measures they have adopted which give effect to the rights recognized herein and on the progress made in the enjoyment of those rights:

(a) Within one year of the entry into force of the present Covenant for the States Parties concerned;

(b) Thereafter whenever the Committee so requests.

2. All reports shall be submitted to the Secretary-General of the United Nations, who shall transmit them to the Committee for consideration. Reports shall indicate the factors and difficulties, if any, affecting the implementation of the present Covenant.

3. The Secretary-General of the United Nations may, after consultation with the Committee, transmit to the specialized agencies concerned copies of such parts of the reports as may fall within their field of competence.

4. The Committee shall study the reports submitted by the States Parties to the present

Covenant. It shall transmit its reports, and such general comments as it may consider appropriate, to the States Parties. The Committee may also transmit to the Economic and Social Council these comments along with the copies of the reports it has received from States Parties to the present Covenant.

5. The States Parties to the present Covenant may submit to the Committee observations on any comments that may be made in accordance with paragraph 4 of this article.

Article 41

1. A State Party to the present Covenant may at any time declare under this article that it recognizes the competence of the Committee to receive and consider communications to the effect that a State Party claims that another State Party is not fulfilling its obligations under the present Covenant. Communications under this article may be received and considered only if submitted by a State Party which has made a declaration recognizing in regard to itself the competence of the Committee. No communication shall be received by the Committee if it concerns a State Party which has not made such a declaration. Communications received under this article shall be dealt with in accordance with the following procedure:

(a) If a State Party to the present Covenant considers that another State Party is not giving effect to the provisions of the present Covenant, it may, by written communication, bring the matter to the attention of that State Party. Within three months after the receipt of the communication, the receiving State shall afford the State which sent the communication an explanation or any other statement m writing clarifying the matter, which should include, to the extent possible and pertinent, reference to domestic procedures and remedies taken, pending, or available in the matter.

(b) If the matter is not adjusted to the satisfaction of both States Parties concerned within six months after the receipt by the receiving State of the initial communication, either State shall have the right to refer the matter to the Committee, by notice given to the Committee and to the other State.

(c) The Committee shall deal with a matter referred to it only after it has ascertained that all available domestic remedies have been invoked and exhausted in the matter, in conformity with the generally recognized principles of international law. This shall not be the rule where the application of the remedies is unreasonably prolonged.

(d) The Committee shall hold closed meetings when examining communications under this article.

(e) Subject to the provisions of sub-paragraph (c), the Committee shall make available its good offices to the States Parties concerned with a view to a friendly solution of the matter on the basis of respect for human rights and fundamental freedoms as recognized in the present Covenant.

(f) In any matter referred to it, the Committee may call upon the States Parties concerned, referred to in sub-paragraph (b), to supply any relevant information.

(g) The States Parties concerned, referred to in sub-paragraph (b), shall have the right to be represented when the matter is being considered in the Committee and to make submissions orally and/or in writing.

(h) The Committee shall, within twelve months after the date of receipt of notice under sub-paragraph (b), submit a report:

(i) If a solution within the terms of sub-paragraph (e) is reached, the Committee shall confine its report to a brief statement of the facts and of the solution reached;

(ii) If a solution within the terms of sub-paragraph (e) is not reached, the Committee shall confine its report to a brief statement of the facts; the written submissions and record of the oral submissions made by the States Parties concerned shall be attached to the report. In every matter, the report shall be communicated to the States Parties concerned.

2. The provisions of this article shall come into force when ten States Parties to the present Covenant have made declarations under paragraph 1 of this article. Such declarations shall be deposited by the States Parties with the Secretary-General of the United Nations, who shall transmit copies thereof to the other States Parties. A declaration may be withdrawn at any time by notification to the Secretary-General. Such a withdrawal shall not prejudice the consideration of any matter which is the subject of a communication already transmitted under this article; no further communication by any State Party shall be received after the notification of withdrawal of the declaration has been received by the Secretary-General, unless the State Party concerned has made a new declaration.

Article 42

1. (a) If a matter referred to the Committee in accordance with Article 41 is not resolved to the satisfaction of the States Parties concerned, the Committee may, with the prior consent of the States Parties concerned, appoint an ad hoc Conciliation Commis-

sion (hereinafter referred to as the Commission). The good offices of the Commission shall be made available to the States Parties concerned with a view to an amicable solution of the matter on the basis of respect for the present Covenant;

> (b) The Commission shall consist of five persons acceptable to the States Parties concerned. If the States Parties concerned fail to reach agreement within three months on all or part of the composition of the Commission, the members of the Commission concerning whom no agreement has been reached shall be elected by secret ballot by a two-thirds majority vote of the Committee from among its members.

2. The members of the Commission shall serve in their personal capacity. They shall not be nationals of the States Parties concerned, or of a State not party to the present Covenant, or of a State Party which has not made a declaration under Article 41.

3. The Commission shall elect its own Chairman and adopt its own rules of procedure.

4. The meetings of the Commission shall normally be held at the Headquarters of the United Nations or at the United Nations Office at Geneva. However, they may be held at such other convenient places as the Commission may determine in consultation with the Secretary-General of the United Nations and the States Parties concerned.

5. The secretariat provided in accordance with Article 36 shall also service the commissions appointed under this article.

6. The information received and collated by the Committee shall be made available to the Commission and the Commission may call upon the States Parties concerned to supply any other relevant information.

7. When the Commission has fully considered the matter, but in any event not later than twelve months after having been seized of the matter, it shall submit to the Chairman of the Committee a report for communication to the States Parties concerned:

> (a) if the Commission is unable to complete its consideration of the matter within twelve months, it shall confine its report to a brief statement or the status of its consideration of the matter;

(b) if an amicable solution to the matter on the basis of respect for human rights as recognized in the present Covenant is reached, the Commission shall confine its report to a brief statement of the facts and of the solution reached;

> (c) if a solution within the terms of sub-paragraph (b) is not reached, the Commission's report shall embody its findings on all questions of fact relevant to the issues between the States Parties concerned, and its views on the possibilities of an amicable solution of the matter. This report shall also contain the written submissions and a record of the oral submissions made by the States Parties concerned;

> (d) if the Commission's report is submitted under subparagraph (c), the States Parties concerned shall, within three months of the receipt of the report, notify the Chairman of the Committee whether or not they accept the contents of the report of the Commission.

8. The provisions of this article are without prejudice to the responsibilities of the Committee under Article 41

9. The States Parties concerned shall share equally all the expenses of the members of the Commission in accordance with estimates to be provided by the Secretary-General of the United Nations.

10. The Secretary-General of the United Nations shall be empowered to pay the expenses of the members of the Commission, if necessary, before reimbursement by the States Parties concerned, in accordance with paragraph 9 of this article.

Article 43

The members of the Committee, and of the ad hoc conciliation commissions which may be appointed under Article 42, shall be entitled to the facilities, privileges and immunities of experts on mission for the United Nations as laid down in the relevant sections of the Convention on the Privileges and Immunities of the United Nations.

Article 44

The provisions for the implementation of the present Covenant shall apply without prejudice to the procedures prescribed in the field of human rights by or under the constituent instruments and the conventions of the United Nations and of the specialized agencies and shall not prevent the States Parties to the present Covenant from having recourse to other procedures for settling a dispute in accordance with general or special international agreements in force between them.

Article 45

The Committee shall submit to the General Assembly of the United Nations, through the Economic and Social Council, an annual report on its activities.

Part V

Article 46

Nothing in the present Covenant shall be interpreted as impairing the provisions of the Charter of the United Nations and of the constitutions of the specialized agencies which define the respective responsibilities of the various organs of the United Nations and of the specialized agencies in regard to the matters dealt with in the present Covenant.

Article 47

Nothing in the present Covenant shall be interpreted as impairing the inherent right of all peoples to enjoy and utilize fully and freely their natural wealth and resources.

Part VI

Article 48

1. The present Covenant is open for signature by any State Member of the United Nations or member of any of its specialized agencies, by any State Party to the Statute of the International Court of Justice, and by any other State which has been invited by the General Assembly of the United Nations to become a party to the present Covenant.

2. The present Covenant is subject to ratification. Instruments of ratification shall be deposited with the Secretary-General of the United Nations.

3. The present Covenant shall be open to accession by any State referred to in paragraph 1 of this article.

4. Accession shall be effected by the deposit of an instrument of accession with the Secretary-General of the United Nations.

5. The Secretary-General of the United Nations shall inform all States which have signed this Covenant or acceded to it of the deposit of each instrument of ratification or accession.

Article 49

1. The present Covenant shall enter into force three months after the date of the deposit with the Secretary-General of the United Nations of the thirty-fifth instrument of ratification or instrument of accession.

2. For each State ratifying the present Covenant or acceding to it after the deposit of the thirty-fifth instrument of ratification or instrument of accession, the present Covenant shall enter into force three months after the date of the deposit of its own instrument of ratification or instrument of accession.

Article 50

The provisions of the present Covenant shall extend to all parts of federal States without any limitations or exceptions.

Article 51

1. Any State Party to the present Covenant may propose an amendment and file it with the Secretary-General of the United Nations. The Secretary-General of the United Nations shall thereupon communicate any proposed amendments to the States Parties to the present Covenant with a request that they notify him whether they favor a conference of States Parties for the purpose of considering and voting upon the proposals. In the event that at least one third of the States Parties favors such a conference, the Secretary-General shall convene the conference under the auspices of the United Nations. Any amendment adopted by a majority of the States Parties present and voting at the conference shall be submitted to the General Assembly of the United Nations for approval.

2. Amendments shall come into force when they have been approved by the General Assembly of the United Nations and accepted by a two-thirds majority of the States Parties to the present Covenant in accordance with their respective constitutional processes.

3. When amendments come into force, they shall be binding on those States Parties which have accepted them, other States Parties still being bound by the provisions of the present Covenant and any earlier amendment which they have accepted.

Article 52

Irrespective of the notifications made under Article 48, paragraph 5, the Secretary-General of the United Nations shall inform all States referred to in paragraph 1 of the following particulars:

(a) Signatures, ratifications and accessions under Article 48;

(b) The date of the entry into force of the present Covenant under Article 49 and the date of the entry into force of any amendments under Article 51.

Article 53

1. The present Covenant, of which the Chinese, English, French, Russian and Spanish texts are equally authentic, shall be deposited in the archives of the United Nations.

American Declaration of the Rights and Duties of Man, OAS Res. XXX (1948), OAS Off. Rec. SEA/Ser. L/V/I.4 Rev. (1965)

Preamble

All men are born free and equal, in dignity and in rights, and, being endowed by nature with reason and conscience, they should conduct themselves as brothers one to another.

The fulfillment of duty by each individual is a prerequisite to the rights of all. Rights and duties are interrelated in every social and political activity of man. While rights exalt individual liberty, duties express the dignity of that liberty.

Duties of a juridical nature presuppose others of a moral nature which support them in principle and constitute their basis.

Inasmuch as spiritual development is the supreme end of human existence and the highest expression thereof, it is the duty of man to serve that end with all his strength and resources.

Since culture is the highest social and historical expression of that spiritual development, it is the duty of man to preserve, practice and foster culture by every means within his power.

And, since moral conduct constitutes the noblest flowering of culture, it is the duty of every man always to hold it in high respect.

Chapter One. Rights

Article I. Every human being has the right to life, liberty and the security of his person.

Article II. All persons are equal before the law and have the rights and duties established in this Declaration, without distinction as to race, sex, language, creed or any other factor.

Article III. Every person has the right freely to profess a religious faith, and to manifest and practice it both in public and in private.

Article IV. Every person has the right to freedom of investigation, of opinion, and of the expression and dissemination of ideas, by any medium whatsoever.

Article V. Every person has the right to the protection of the law against abusive attacks upon his honor, his reputation, and his private and family life.

Article VI. Every person has the right to establish a family, the basic element of society, and to receive protection therefor.

Article VII. All women, during pregnancy and the nursing period, and all children have the right to special protection, care and aid.

Article VIII. Every person has the right to fix his residence within the territory of the state of which he is a national, to move about freely within such territory, and not to leave it except by his own will.

Article IX. Every person has the right to the inviolability of his home.

Article X. Every person has the right to the inviolability and transmission of his correspondence.

Article XI. Every person has the right to the preservation of his health through sanitary and social measures relating to food, clothing, housing and medical care, to the extent permitted by public and community resources.

Article XII. Every person has the right to an education, which should be based on the principles of liberty, morality and human solidarity.

Likewise every person has the right to an education that will prepare him to attain a decent life, to raise his standard of living, and to be a useful member of society.

The right to an education includes the right to equality of opportunity in every case in accordance with natural talents, merit and the desire to utilize the resources that the state or the community is in a position to provide.

Every person has the right to receive, free, at least a primary education.

Article XIII. Every person has the right to take part in the cultural life of the community, to enjoy the arts, and to participate in the benefits that result from intellectual progress, especially scientific discoveries.

He likewise has the right to the protection of his moral and material interests as regards his inventions or any literary, scientific or artistic works of which he is the author.

Article XIV. Every person has the right to work, under proper conditions, and to follow his vocation freely, in so far as existing conditions of employment permit.

Every person who works has the right to receive such remuneration as will, in proportion to his capacity and skill, assure him a standard of living suitable for himself and for his family.

Article XV. Every person has the right to leisure time, to wholesome recreation, and to the opportunity for advantageous use of his free time to his spiritual, cultural and physical benefit.

Article XVI. Every person has the right to social security which will protect him from the consequences of unemployment, old age, and any disability arising from causes beyond his control that make it physically or mentally impossible for him to earn a living.

Article XVII. Every person has the right to be recognized everywhere as a person having rights and obligations, and to enjoy the basic civil rights.

Article XVIII. Every person may resort to the courts to ensure respect for his legal rights. There should likewise be available to him a simple, brief procedure whereby the courts will protect him from acts of authority that, to his prejudice, violate any fundamental constitutional rights.

Article XIX. Every person has the right to the nationality to which he is entitled by law and to change it, if he so wishes, for the nationality of any other country that is willing to grant it to him.

Article XX. Every person having legal capacity is entitled to participate in the government of his country, directly or through his representatives, and to take part in popular elections, which shall be by secret ballot, and shall be honest, periodic and free.

Article XXI. Every person has the right to assemble peaceably with others in a formal public meeting or an informal gathering, in connection with matters of common interest of any nature.

Article XXII. Every person has the right to associate with others to promote, exercise and protect his legitimate interests of a political, economic, religious, social, cultural, professional, labor union or other nature.

Article XXIII. Every person has a right to own such private property as meets the essential needs of decent living and helps to maintain the dignity of the individual and of the home.

Article XXIV. Every person has the right to submit respectful petitions to any competent authority, for reasons of either general or private interest, and the right to obtain a prompt decision thereon.

Article XXV. No person may be deprived of his liberty except in the cases and according to the procedures established by pre-existing law.

No person may be deprived of liberty for nonfulfillment of obligations of a purely civil character.

Every individual who has been deprived of his liberty has the right to have the legality of his detention ascertained without delay by a court, and the right to be tried without undue delay, or otherwise, to be released. He also has the right to humane treatment during the time he is in custody.

Article XXVI. Every accused person is presumed to be innocent until proved guilty.

Every person accused of an offense has the right to be given an impartial and public hearing, and to be tried by courts previously established in accordance with pre-existing laws, and not to receive cruel, infamous or unusual punishment.

Article XXVII. Every person has the right, in case of pursuit not resulting from ordinary crimes, to seek and receive asylum in foreign territory, in accordance with the laws of each country and with international agreements.

Article XVIII. The rights of man are limited by the rights of others, by the security of all, and by the just demands of the general welfare and the advancement of democracy.

Chapter Two. Duties

Article XXIX. It is the duty of the individual so to conduct himself in relation to others that each and every one may fully form and develop his personality.

Article XXX. It is the duty of every person to aid, support, educate and protect his minor children, and it is the duty of children to honor their parents always and to aid, support and protect them when they need it.

Article XXXI. It is the duty of every person to acquire at least an elementary education.

Article XXXII. It is the duty of every person to vote in the popular elections of the country of which he is a national, when he is legally capable of doing so.

Article XXXIII. It is the duty of every person to obey the law and other legitimate commands of the authorities of his country and those of the country in which he may be.

Article XXXIV. It is the duty of every able-bodied person to render whatever civil and military service his country may require for its defense and preservation, and, in case of public disaster, to render such services as may be in his power.

It is likewise his duty to hold any public office to which he may be elected by popular vote in the state of which he is a national.

Article XXXV. It is the duty of every person to cooperate with the state with respect to social security and welfare, in accordance with existing circumstances.

Article XXXVI. It is the duty of every person to pay the taxes established by law for the support of public services.

Article XXXVII. It is the duty of every person to work, as far as his capacity and possibilities permit, in order to obtain the means of livelihood or to benefit his community.

Article XXXVIII. It is the duty of every person to refrain from taking part in political activities that, according to law, are reserved exclusively to the citizens of the state in which he is an alien.

American Convention on Human Rights, OAS Treaty Ser. No. 36 (1969), 144 U.N.T.S. 123

Preamble

The American states signatory to this present Convention,

Reaffirming their intention to consolidate in this hemisphere, within the framework of democratic institutions, a system of personal liberty and social justice based on respect for the essential rights of man;

Recognizing that the essential rights of man are not derived from one's being a national of a certain state, but are based upon attributes of the human personality, and that they therefore justify international protection in the form of a convention reinforcing or complementing the protection provided by the domestic law of the American states;

Considering that these principles have been set forth in the Charter of the Organization of American States, in the American Declaration of the Rights and Duties of Man, and in the Universal Declaration of Human Rights, and that they have been reaffirmed and refined in other international instruments, worldwide as well as regional in scope;

Reiterating that, in accordance with the Universal Declaration of Human Rights, the ideal of free men enjoying freedom from fear and want can be achieved only if conditions are created whereby everyone may enjoy his economic, social, and cultural rights, as well as his civil and political rights; and

Considering that the Third Special Inter-American Conference (Buenos Aires, 1967) approved the incorporation into the Charter of the Organization itself of broader standards with respect to economic, social, and educational rights and resolved that an inter-American convention on human rights should determine the structure, competence, and procedure of the organs responsible for these matters,

Have agreed upon the following:

Part I. State Obligations and Rights Protected

Chapter I. General Obligations

Article 1. Obligation to Respect Rights

1. The States Parties to this Convention undertake to respect the rights and freedoms recognized herein and to ensure to all persons subject to their jurisdiction the free and full exercise of those rights and freedoms, without any discrimination for reasons of race, color, sex, language, religion, political or other opinion, national or social origin, economic status, birth, or any other social condition.

2. For the purposes of this Convention, "person" means every human being.

Article 2. Domestic Legal Effects

Where the exercise of any of the rights or freedoms referred to in Article 1 is not already ensured by legislative or other provisions, the States Parties undertake to adopt, in accordance with their constitutional processes and the provisions of this Convention, such legislative or other measures as may be necessary to give effect to those rights or freedoms.

Chapter II. Civil and Political Rights

Article 3. Right to Juridical Personality

Every person has the right to recognition as a person before the law.

Article 4. Right to Life

1. Every person has the right to have his life respected. This right shall be protected by law, and, in general, from the moment of conception. No one shall be arbitrarily deprived of his life.

2. In countries that have not abolished the death penalty, it may be imposed only for the most serious crimes and pursuant to a final judgment rendered by a competent court and in accordance with a law establishing such punishment, enacted prior to the commission of the crime. The application of such punishment shall not be extended to crimes to which it does not presently apply.

3. The death penalty shall not be reestablished in states that have abolished it.

4. In no case shall capital punishment be inflicted for political offences or related common crimes.

5. Capital punishment shall not be imposed upon persons who, at the time the crime was committed, were under 18 years of age or over 70 years of age; nor shall it be applied to pregnant women.

6. Every person condemned to death shall have the right to apply for amnesty, pardon, or commutation of sentence, which may be granted in all cases. Capital punishment shall not be imposed while such a petition is pending decision by the competent authority.

Article 5. Right to Humane Treatment

1. Every person has the right to have his physical, mental, and moral integrity respected.

2. No one shall be subjected to torture or to cruel, inhuman, or degrading punishment or treatment. All persons deprived of their liberty shall be treated with respect for the inherent dignity of the human person.

3. Punishment shall not be extended to any person other than the criminal.

4. Accused persons shall, save in exceptional circumstances, be segregated from convicted persons, and shall be subject to separate treatment appropriate to their status as unconvicted persons.

5. Minors while subject to criminal proceedings shall be separated from adults and brought before specialized tribunals, as speedily as possible, so that they may be treated in accordance with their status as minors.

6. Punishments consisting of deprivation of liberty shall have as an essential aim the reform and social readaptation of the prisoners.

Article 6. Freedom from Slavery

1. No one shall be subject to slavery or to involuntary servitude, which are prohibited in all their forms, as are the slave trade and traffic in women.

2. No one shall be required to perform forced or compulsory labor. This provision shall not be interpreted to mean that, in those countries in which the penalty established for certain crimes is deprivation of liberty at forced labor, the carrying out of such a sentence imposed by a competent court is prohibited. Forced labor shall not adversely affect the dignity or the physical or intellectual capacity of the prisoner.

3. For the purposes of this article the following do not constitute forced or compulsory labor:

(a) work or service normally required of a person imprisoned in execution of a sentence or formal decision passed by the competent judicial authority. Such work or service shall be carried out under the supervision and control of public authorities, and any persons performing such work or service shall not be placed at the disposal of any private party, company, or juridical person;

(b) military service and, in countries in which conscientious objectors are recognized, national service that the law may provide for in lieu of military service;

(c) service exacted in time of danger or calamity that threatens the existence or the well-being of the community; or

(d) work or service that forms part of normal civil obligations.

Article 7. Right to Personal Liberty

1. Every person has the right to personal liberty and security.

2. No one shall be deprived of his physical liberty except for the reasons and under the conditions established beforehand by the constitution of the State Party concerned or by a law established pursuant thereto.

3. No one shall be subject to arbitrary arrest or imprisonment.

4. Anyone who is detained shall be informed of the reasons for his detention and shall be promptly notified of the charge or charges against him.

5. Any person detained shall be brought promptly before a judge or other officer authorized by law to exercise judicial power and shall be entitled to trial within a reasonable time or to be released without prejudice to the continuation of the proceedings. His release may be subject to guarantees to assure his appearance for trial.

6. Anyone who is deprived of his liberty shall be entitled to recourse to a competent court, in order that the court may decide without delay on the lawfulness of his arrest or detention and order his release if the arrest or detention is unlawful. In States Parties whose laws provide that anyone who believes himself to be threatened with deprivation of his liberty is entitled to recourse to a competent court in order that it may decide on the lawfulness of such threat, this remedy may not be restricted or abolished. The interested party or another person in his behalf is entitled to seek these remedies.

7. No one shall be detained for debt. This principle shall not limit the orders of a competent judicial authority issued for nonfulfillment of duties of support.

Article 8. Right to a Fair Trial

1. Every person has the right to a hearing, with due guarantees and within a reasonable time, by a competent, independent, and impartial tribunal, previously established by law, in the substantiation of any accusation of a criminal nature made against him or for the determination of his rights and obligations of a civil, labor, fiscal, or any other nature.

2. Every person accused of a criminal offense has the right to be presumed innocent so long as his guilt has not been proven according to law. During the proceedings, every person is entitled, with full equality, to the following minimum guarantees:

    (a) the right of the accused to be assisted without charge by a translator or interpreter, if he does not understand or does not speak the language of the tribunal or court;

    (b) prior notification in detail to the accused of the charges against him;

    (c) adequate time and means for the preparation of his defense;

    (d) the right of the accused to defend himself personally or to be assisted by legal counsel of his own choosing, and to communicate freely and privately with his counsel;

    (e) the inalienable right to be assisted by counsel provided by the state, paid or not as the domestic law provides, if the accused does not defend himself personally or engage his own counsel within the time period established by law;

(f) the right of the defense to examine witnesses present in the court and to obtain the appearance, as witnesses, of experts or other persons who may throw light on the facts;

(g) the right not to be compelled to be a witness against himself or to plead guilty; and

(h) the right to appeal the judgment to a higher court.

3. A confession of guilt by the accused shall be valid only if it is made without coercion of any kind.

4. An accused person acquitted by a nonappealable judgment shall not be subjected to a new trial for the same cause.

5. Criminal proceedings shall be public, except insofar as may be necessary to protect the interests of justice.

Article 9. Freedom from Ex Post Facto Laws

No one shall be convicted of any act or omission that did not constitute a criminal offense, under the applicable law, at the time it was committed. A heavier penalty shall not be imposed than the one that was applicable at the time the criminal offense was committed. If subsequent to the commission of the offense the law provides for the imposition of a lighter punishment, the guilty person shall benefit therefrom.

Article 10. Right to Compensation

Every person has the right to be compensated in accordance with the law in the event he has been sentenced by a final judgment through a miscarriage of justice.

Article 11. Right to Privacy

1. Everyone has the right to have his honor respected and his dignity recognized.

2. No one may be the object of arbitrary or abusive interference with his private life, his family, his home, or his correspondence, or of unlawful attacks on his honor or reputation.

3. Everyone has the right to the protection of the law against such interference or attacks.

Article 12. Freedom of Conscience and Religion

1. Everyone has the right to freedom of conscience and religion. this right includes freedom to maintain or to change one's religion or beliefs, and freedom to profess or disseminate one's religion or beliefs either individually or together with others, in public or in private.

2. No one shall be subject to restrictions that might impair his freedom to maintain or to change his religion or beliefs.

3. Freedom to manifest one's religion and beliefs may be subject only to the limitations prescribed by law that are necessary to protect public safety, order, health, or morals, or the rights or freedoms of others.

4. Parents or guardians, as the case may be, have the right to provide for the religious and moral education of their children or wards that is in accord with their own convictions.

Article 13. Freedom of Thought and Expression

1. Everyone shall have the right to freedom of thought and expression. This right shall include freedom to seek, receive, and impart information and ideas of all kinds, regardless of frontiers, either orally, in writing, in print, in the form of art, or through any other medium of his choice.

2. The exercise of the right provided for in the foregoing paragraph shall not be subject to prior censorship but shall be subject to subsequent imposition of liability, which shall be expressly established by law to the extent necessary in order to ensure:

(a) respect for the rights or reputations of others; or

(b) the protection of national security, public order, or public health or morals.

3. The right of expression may not be restricted by indirect methods or means, such as the abuse of government or private controls over newsprint, radio broadcasting frequencies, or equipment used in the dissemination of information, or by any other means tending to impede the communication and circulation of ideas and opinions.

4. Notwithstanding the provisions of paragraph 2 above, public entertainments may be subject by law to prior censorship for the sole purpose of regulating access to them for the moral protection of childhood and adolescence.

5. Any propaganda for war and any advocacy of national, racial, or religious hatred that constitute incitements to lawless violence or to any other similar illegal action against any person or group of persons on any grounds including those of race, color, religion, language, or national origin shall be considered as offenses punishable by law.

Article 14. Right of Reply

1. Anyone injured by inaccurate or offensive statements or ideas disseminated to the public in general by a legally regulated medium of communication has the right to reply or make a correction using the same communications outlet, under such conditions as the law may establish.

2. The correction or reply shall not in any case remit other legal liabilities that may have been incurred.

3. For the effective protection of honor and reputation, every publisher, and every newspaper, motion picture, radio, and television company, shall have a person responsible, who is not protected by immunities or special privileges.

Article 15. Right of Assembly

The right of peaceful assembly, without arms, is recognized. No restrictions may be placed on the exercise of this right other than those imposed in conformity with the law and necessary in a democratic society in the interest of national security, public safety, or public order, or to protect public health, or morals or the rights or freedoms of others.

Article 16. Freedom of Association

1. Everyone has the right to associate freely for ideological, religious, political, economic, labor, social, cultural, sports, or other purposes.

2. The exercise of this right shall be subject only to such restrictions established by law as may be necessary in a democratic society, in the interest of national security, public safety, or public order, or to protect public health or morals or the rights and freedoms of others.

3. The provisions of this article do not bar the imposition of legal restrictions, including even deprivation of the exercise of the right of association, on members of the armed forces and the police.

Article 17. Rights of the Family

1. The family is the natural and fundamental group unit of society and is entitled to protection by society and the state.

2. The right of men and women of marriageable age to marry and to raise a family shall be recognized, if they meet the conditions required by domestic laws, insofar as such conditions do not affect the principle of nondiscrimination established in this Convention.

3. No marriage shall be entered into without the free and full consent of the intending spouses.

4. The States Parties shall take appropriate steps to ensure the equality of rights and the adequate balancing of responsibilities of the spouses as to marriage, during marriage, and in the event of its dissolution. In case of dissolution, provision shall be made for the necessary protection of any children solely on the basis of their own best interests.

5. The law shall recognize equal rights for children born out of wedlock and those born in wedlock.

Article 18. Right to a Name

Every person has the right to a given name and to the surnames of his parents or that of one of them. The law shall regulate the manner in which this right shall be ensured for all, by the use of assumed names if necessary.

Article 19. Rights of the Child

Every minor child has the right to the measures of protection required by his condition as a minor on the part of his family, society, and the state.

Article 20. Right to Nationality

1. Every person has the right to a nationality.

2. Every person has the right to the nationality of the state in whose territory he was born if he does not have the right to any other nationality.

3. No one shall be arbitrarily deprived of his nationality or of the right to change it.

Article 21. Right to Property

1. Everyone has the right to the use and enjoyment of his property. The law may subordinate such use and enjoyment to the interest of society.

2. No one shall be deprived of his property except upon payment of just compensation, for reasons of public utility or social interest, and in the cases and according to the forms established by law.

3. Usury and any other form of exploitation of man by man shall be prohibited by law.

Article 22. Freedom of Movement and Residence

1. Every person lawfully in the territory of a State Party has the right to move about in it and to reside in it subject to the provisions of the law.

2. Every person has the right to leave any country freely, including his own.

3. The exercise of the foregoing rights may be restricted only pursuant to a law to the extent necessary in a democratic society to prevent crime or to protect national security, public safety, public order, public morals, public health, or the rights or freedoms of others.

4. The exercise of the rights recognized in paragraph 1 may also be restricted by law in designated zones for reasons of public interest.

5. No one can be expelled from the territory of the state of which he is a national or be deprived of the right to enter it.

6. An alien lawfully in the territory of a State Party to this Convention may be expelled from it only pursuant to a decision reached in accordance with law.

7. Every person has the right to seek and be granted asylum in a foreign territory, in accordance with the legislation of the state and international conventions, in the event he is being pursued for political offenses or related common crimes.

8. In no case may an alien be deported or returned to a country, regardless of whether or not it is his country of origin, if in that country his right to life or personal freedom is in danger of being violated because of his race, nationality, religion, social status, or political opinions.

9. The collective expulsion of aliens is prohibited.

Article 23. Right to Participate in Government

1. Every citizen shall enjoy the following rights and opportunities:

   (a) to take part in the conduct of public affairs, directly or through freely chosen representatives;

   (b) to vote and to be elected in genuine periodic elections, which shall be by universal and equal suffrage and by secret ballot that guarantees the free expression of the will of the voters; and

   (c) to have access, under general conditions of equality, to the public services of his country.

2. The law may regulate the exercise of the rights and opportunities referred to in the preceding paragraph only on the basis of age, nationality, residence, language, educa-

tion, civil and mental capacity, or sentencing by a competent court in criminal proceedings.

Article 24. Right to Equal Protection

All persons are equal before the law. Consequently, they are entitled, without discrimination, to equal protection of the law.

Article 25. Right to Judicial Protection

1. Everyone has the right to simple and prompt recourse, or any other effective recourse, to a competent court or tribunal for protection against acts that violate his fundamental rights recognized by the constitution or laws of the state concerned or by this Convention, even though such violation may have been committed by persons acting in the course of their official duties.

2. The States Parties undertake:

(a) to ensure that any person claiming such remedy shall have his rights determined by the competent authority provided for by the legal system of the state;

(b) to develop the possibilities of judicial remedy; and

(c) to ensure that the competent authorities shall enforce such remedies when granted.

Chapter III. Economic, Social, and Cultural Rights

Article 26. Progressive Development

The States Parties undertake to adopt measures, both internally and through international cooperation, especially those of an economic and technical nature, with a view to achieving progressively, by legislation or other appropriate means, the full realization of the rights implicit in the economic, social, educational, scientific, and cultural standards set forth in the Charter of the Organization of American States as amended by the Protocol of Buenos Aires.

Chapter IV. Suspension of Guarantees, Interpretation, and Application

Article 27. Suspension of Guarantees

1. In time of war, public danger, or other emergency that threatens the independence or security of a State Party, it may take measures derogating from its obligations under the present Convention to the extent and for the period of time strictly required by the exigencies of the situation, provided that such measures are not inconsistent with its other obligations under international law and do not involve discrimination on the ground of race, color, sex, language, religion, or social origin.

2. The foregoing provision does not authorize any suspension of the following articles: Article 3 (Right to Juridical Personality), Article 4 (Right to Life), Article 5 (Right to Humane Treatment), Article 6 (Freedom from Slavery), Article 9 (Freedom from Ex Post Facto Laws), Article 12 (Freedom of Conscience and Religion), Article 17 (Rights of the Family), Article 18 (Right to a Name), Article 19 (Rights of the Child), Article 20 (Right to Nationality), and Article 23 (Right to Participate in Government), or of the judicial guarantees essential for the protection of such rights.

3. Any State Party availing itself of the right of suspension shall immediately inform the other States Parties, through the Secretary General of the Organization of American States, of the provisions the application of which it has suspended, the reasons that gave rise to the suspension, and the date set for the termination of such suspension.

Article 28. Federal Clause

1. Where a State Party is constituted as a federal state, the national government of such State Party shall implement all the provisions of the Convention over whose subject matter it exercises legislative and judicial jurisdiction.

2. With respect to the provisions over whose subject matter the constituent units of the federal state have jurisdiction, the national government shall immediately take suitable measures, in accordance with its constitution and its laws, to the end that the competent authorities of the constituent units may adopt appropriate provisions for the fulfillment of this Convention.

3. Whenever two or more States Parties agree to form a federation or other type of association, they shall take care that the resulting federal or other compact contains the provisions necessary for continuing and rendering effective the standards of this Convention in the new state that is organized.

Article 29. Restrictions Regarding Interpretation

No provision of this Convention shall be interpreted as:

(a) permitting any State Party, group, or person to suppress the enjoyment or exercise of the rights and freedoms recognized in this Convention or to restrict them to a greater extent than is provided for herein;

(b) restricting the enjoyment or exercise of any right or freedom recognized by virtue of the laws of any State Party or by virtue of another convention to which one of the said states is a party;

(c) precluding other rights or guarantees that are inherent in the human personality or derived from representative democracy as a form of government; or

(d) excluding or limiting the effect that the American Declaration of the Rights and Duties of Man and other international acts of the same nature may have.

Article 30. Scope of Restrictions

The restrictions that, pursuant to this Convention, may be placed on the enjoyment or exercise of the rights or freedoms recognized herein may not be applied except in accordance with laws enacted for reasons of general interest and in accordance with the purpose for which such restrictions have been established.

Article 31. Recognition of Other Rights

Other rights and freedoms recognized in accordance with the procedures established in Articles 76 and 77 may be included in the system of protection of this Convention.

Chapter V. Personal Responsibilities

Article 32. Relationship Between Duties and Rights

1. Every person has responsibilities to his family, his community, and mankind.

2. The rights of each person are limited by the rights of others, by the security of all, and by the just demands of the general welfare, in a democratic society....

Convention Against Torture and Other Cruel, Inhuman or Degrading Treatment or Punishment, 1465 U.N.T.S. 85 (Dec. 10, 1984)

The States Parties to this Convention,

Considering that, in accordance with the principles proclaimed in the Charter of the United Nations, recognition of the equal and inalienable rights of all members of the human family is the foundation of freedom, justice and peace in the world,

Recognizing that those rights derive from the inherent dignity of the human person,

Considering the obligation of States under the Charter, in particular Article 55, to promote universal respect for, and observance of, human rights and fundamental freedoms,

Having regard to Article 5 of the Universal Declaration of Human Rights and Article 7 of the International Covenant on Civil and Political Rights, both of which provide that no one may be subjected to torture or to cruel, inhuman or degrading treatment or punishment,

Having regard also to the Declaration on the Protection of All Persons from Being Subjected to Torture and Other Cruel, Inhuman or Degrading Treatment or Punishment, adopted by the General Assembly on 9 December 1975 (resolution 3452 (XXX)),

Desiring to make more effective the struggle against torture and other cruel, inhuman or degrading treatment or punishment throughout the world,

Have agreed as follows:

Part I

Article 1

1. For the purposes of this Convention, torture means any act by which severe pain or suffering, whether physical or mental, is intentionally inflicted on a person for such purposes as obtaining from him or a third person information or a confession, punishing him for an act he or a third person has committed or is suspected of having committed, or intimidating or coercing him or a third person, or for any reason based on discrimination of any kind, when such pain or suffering is inflicted by or at the instigation of or with the consent or acquiescence of a public official or other person acting in an official capacity. It does not include pain or suffering arising only from, inherent in or incidental to lawful sanctions.

2. This article is without prejudice to any international instrument or national legislation which does or may contain provisions of wider application.

Article 2

1. Each State Party shall take effective legislative, administrative, judicial or other measures to prevent acts of torture in any territory under its jurisdiction.

2. No exceptional circumstances whatsoever, whether a state of war or a threat of war, internal political instability or any other public emergency, may be invoked as a justification of torture.

3. An order from a superior officer or a public authority may not be invoked as a justification of torture.

Article 3

1. No State Party shall expel, return ("*refouler*") or extradite a person to another State where there are substantial grounds for believing that he would be in danger of being subjected to torture.

2. For the purpose of determining whether there are such grounds, the competent authorities shall take into account all relevant considerations including, where applicable, the existence in the State concerned of a consistent pattern of gross, flagrant or mass violations of human rights.

Article 4

1. Each State Party shall ensure that all acts of torture are offences under its criminal law. The same shall apply to an attempt to commit torture and to an act by any person which constitutes complicity or participation in torture.

2. Each State Party shall make these offences punishable by appropriate penalties which take into account their grave nature.

Article 5

1. Each State Party shall take such measures as may be necessary to establish its jurisdiction over the offences referred to in Article 4 in the following cases:

(a) When the offences are committed in any territory under its jurisdiction or on board a ship or aircraft registered in that State;

(b) When the alleged offender is a national of that State;

(c) When the victim is a national of that State if that State considers it appropriate.

2. Each State Party shall likewise take such measures as may be necessary to establish its jurisdiction over such offences in cases where the alleged offender is present in any territory under its jurisdiction and it does not extradite him pursuant to Article 8 to any of the States mentioned in paragraph 1 of this article.

3. This Convention does not exclude any criminal jurisdiction exercised in accordance with internal law.

Article 6

1. Upon being satisfied, after an examination of information available to it, that the circumstances so warrant, any State Party in whose territory a person alleged to have committed any offence referred to in Article 4 is present, shall take him into custody or

take other legal measures to ensure his presence. The custody and other legal measures shall be as provided in the law of that State but may be continued only for such time as is necessary to enable any criminal or extradition proceedings to be instituted.

2. Such State shall immediately make a preliminary inquiry into the facts.

3. Any person in custody pursuant to paragraph 1 of this article shall be assisted in communicating immediately with the nearest appropriate representative of the State of which he is a national, or, if he is a stateless person, to the representative of the State where he usually resides.

4. When a State, pursuant to this article, has taken a person into custody, it shall immediately notify the States referred to in Article 5, paragraph 1, of the fact that such person in is custody and of the circumstances which warrant his detention. The State which makes the preliminary inquiry contemplated in paragraph 2 of this article shall promptly report its findings to the said States and shall indicate whether it intends to exercise jurisdiction.

Article 7

1. The State Party in territory under whose jurisdiction a person alleged to have committed any offence referred to in Article 4 is found, shall in the cases contemplated in Article 5, if it does not extradite him, submit the case to its competent authorities for the purpose of prosecution.

2. These authorities shall take their decision in the same manner as in the case of any ordinary offence of a serious nature under the law of that State. In the cases referred to in Article 5, paragraph 2, the standards of evidence required for prosecution and conviction shall in no way be less stringent than those which apply in the cases referred to in Article 5, paragraph 1.

3. Any person regarding whom proceedings are brought in connection with any of the offenses referred to in Article 4 shall be guaranteed fair treatment at all stages of the proceedings.

Article 8

1. The offenses referred to in Article 4 shall be deemed to be included as extraditable offenses in any extradition treaty existing between States Parties. States Parties undertake to include such offenses as extraditable offenses in every extradition treaty to be concluded between them.

2. If a State Party which makes extradition conditional on the existence of a treaty receives a request for extradition from another State Party with which it has no extradition treaty, it may consider this Convention as the legal basis for extradition in respect of such offenses. Extradition shall be subject to the other conditions provided by the law of the requested State.

3. States Parties which do not make extradition conditional on the existence of a treaty shall recognize such offenses as extraditable offenses between themselves subject to the conditions provided by the law of the requested State.

4. Such offenses shall be treated, for the purpose of extradition between States Parties, as if they had been committed not only in the place in which they occurred but also

in the territories of the States required to establish their jurisdiction in accordance with Article 5, paragraph 1.

Article 9

1. States Parties shall afford one another the greatest measure of assistance in connection with criminal proceedings brought in respect of any of the offenses referred to in Article 4, including the supply of all evidence at their disposal necessary for the proceedings.

2. States Parties shall carry out their obligations under paragraph 1 of this article in conformity with any treaties on mutual judicial assistance that may exist between them.

Article 10

1. Each State Party shall ensure that education and information regarding the prohibition against torture are fully included in the training of law enforcement personnel, civil or military, medical personnel, public officials and other persons who may be involved in the custody, interrogation or treatment of any individual subjected to any form of arrest, detention or imprisonment.

2. Each State Party shall include this prohibition in the rules or instructions issued in regard to the duties and functions of any such persons.

Article 11

Each State Party shall keep under systematic review interrogation rules, instructions, methods and practices as well as arrangements for the custody and treatment of persons subjected to any form of arrest, detention or imprisonment in any territory under its jurisdiction, with a view to preventing any cases of torture.

Article 12

Each State Party shall ensure that its competent authorities proceed to a prompt and impartial investigation, wherever there is reasonable ground to believe that an act of torture has been committed in any territory under its jurisdiction.

Article 13

Each State Party shall ensure that any individual who alleges he has been subjected to torture in any territory under its jurisdiction has the right to complain to and to have his case promptly and impartially examined by its competent authorities. Steps shall be taken to insure that the complainant and witnesses are protected against all ill-treatment or intimidation as a consequence of his complaint or any evidence given.

Article 14

1. Each State Party shall ensure in its legal system that the victim of an act of torture obtains redress and has an enforceable right to fair and adequate compensation including the means for as full rehabilitation as possible. In the event of the death of the victim as a result of an act of torture, his dependents shall be entitled to compensation.

2. Nothing in this article shall affect any right of the victim or other persons to compensation which may exist under national law.

Article 15

Each State Party shall ensure that any statement which is established to have been made as a result of torture shall not be invoked as evidence in any proceedings, except against a person accused of torture as evidence that the statement was made.

Article 16

1. Each State Party shall undertake to prevent in any territory under its jurisdiction other acts of cruel, inhuman or degrading treatment or punishment which do not amount to torture as defined in Article 1, when such acts are committed by or at the instigation of or with the consent or acquiescence of a public official or other person acting in an official capacity. In particular, the obligations contained in Articles 10, 11, 12 and 13 shall apply with the substitution for references to torture of references to other forms of cruel, inhuman or degrading treatment or punishment.

2. The provisions of this Convention are without prejudice to the provisions of any other international instrument or national law which prohibit cruel, inhuman or degrading treatment or punishment or which relate to extradition or expulsion....

Instructions for the Government of Armies of the United States in the Field, General Orders No. 100 (1863) (the 1863 Lieber Code)

Article 11

The law of war does not only disclaim all cruelty and bad faith concerning engagements concluded with the enemy during war, but also the breaking of stipulations solemnly contracted by the belligerents in time of peace, and avowedly intended to remain in force in case of war between the contracting powers.

It disclaims all extortions and other transactions for individual gain; all acts of private revenge, or connivance in such acts.

Offenses to the contrary shall be severely punished, and especially so if committed by officers....

Article 13

Military jurisdiction is of two kinds: First, that which is conferred and defined by statute; second, that which is derived from the common law of war.... The character of the courts which exercise these jurisdictions depends upon the local laws of each particular country....

Article 14

Military necessity, as understood by modern civilized nations, consists in the necessity of those measures which are indispensable for securing the ends of the war, and which are lawful according to the modern law and usages of war.

Article 15

Military necessity admits of all direct destruction of life and limb of armed enemies, and other persons whose destruction is incidentally unavoidable in the armed contests of the war; it allows the capturing of every armed enemy, and every enemy of importance to the hostile government, or of particular danger to the captor; it allows all destruction of property, and obstruction of the ways and channels of traffic, travel, or communication, and of all withholding of sustenance or means of life from the enemy; of the appropriation of whatever an enemy's country affords necessary for the subsistence and safety of the army, and of such deception as does not involve the breaking of good faith either positively pledged, regarding agreements entered into during the war, or supposed by the modern laws of war to exist. Men who take up arms against one another in public war do not cease on this account to be moral beings, responsible to one another and to God.

Article 16

Military necessity does not admit of cruelty—that is the infliction of suffering for the sake of suffering or for revenge, nor of maiming or wounding except in fight, nor of torture to extort confessions. It does not admit of the use of poison in any way, nor the wanton devastation of a district. It admits of deception, but disclaims acts of perfidy; and, in general, military necessity does not include any act of hostility which makes the return to peace unnecessarily difficult.

Article 17

War is not carried on by arms alone. It is lawful to starve the hostile belligerent, armed or unarmed, so that it leads to the speedier subjection of the enemy.

Article 18

When a commander of a besieged place expels the noncombatants, in order to lessen the number of those who consume his stock of provisions, it is lawful, though an extreme measure, to drive them back, so as to hasten on the surrender....

Article 21

The citizen or native of a hostile country is thus an enemy, as one of the constituents of the hostile state or nation, and as such is subjected to the hardships of war.

Article 22

Nevertheless, as civilization has advanced during the last centuries, so has likewise steadily advanced, especially in war on land, the distinction between the private individual belonging to a hostile country and the hostile country itself, with its men in arms. The principle has been more and more acknowledged that the unarmed citizen is to be spared in person, property, and honor as much as the exigencies of war will admit.

Article 23

Private citizens are no longer murdered, enslaved, or carried off to distant parts, and the inoffensive individual is as little disturbed in his private relations as the commander of the hostile troops can afford to grant in the overruling demands of a vigorous war....

Article 34

As a general rule, the property belonging to churches, to hospitals, or other establishments of an exclusively charitable character, to establishments of education, or foundations for the promotion of knowledge, whether public schools, universities, academies of learning or observatories, museums of the fine arts, or of a scientific character–such property is not to be considered public property ... [for seizure or appropriation]; but it may be taxed or used when the public service may require it.

Article 35

Classical works of art, libraries, scientific collections, or precious instruments, such as astronomical telescopes, as well as hospitals, must be secured against all avoidable injury, even when they are contained in fortified places whilst besieged or bombarded.

Article 36

If such works of art, libraries, collections, or instruments belonging to a hostile nation or government, can be removed without injury, the ruler of the conquering state or nation may order them to be seized and removed for the benefit of the said nation. The ultimate ownership is to be settled by the ensuing treaty of peace.

In no case shall they be sold or given away, if captured by the armies of the United States, nor shall they ever be privately appropriated, or wantonly destroyed or injured.

Article 37

The United States acknowledge and protect, in hostile countries occupied by them, religion and morality; strictly private property; the persons of the inhabitants, especially those of women; and the sacredness of domestic relations. Offenses to the contrary shall be rigorously punished....

Article 44

All wanton violence committed against persons in the invaded country, all destruction of property not commanded by the authorized officer, all robbery, all pillage or sacking, even after taking a place by main force, all rape, wounding, maiming, or killing of such inhabitants, are prohibited under the penalty of death, or such other severe punishment as may seem adequate for the gravity of the offense.

A soldier, officer or private, in the act of committing such violence, and disobeying a superior ordering him to abstain from it, may be lawfully killed on the spot by such superior.

Article 45

All captures and booty belong, according to the modern law of war, primarily to the government of the captor....

Article 47

Crimes punishable by all penal codes, such as arson, murder, maiming, assaults, highway robbery, theft, burglary, fraud, forgery, and rape, if committed by an American soldier in a hostile country against the inhabitants, are not only punishable as at home, but in all cases in which death is not inflicted, the severer punishment shall be preferred....

Article 49

... All soldiers, of whatever species of arms; all men who belong to the rising en masse of the hostile country; all those who are attached to the army for its efficiency and promote directly the object of war ... are prisoners of war, and as such exposed to the inconveniences as well as entitled to the privileges of a prisoner of war.

Article 56

A prisoner of war is subject to no punishment for being a public enemy, nor is any revenge wreaked upon him by the intentional infliction of any suffering, or disgrace, by cruel imprisonment, want of food, by mutilation, death, or other barbarity.

Article 57

So soon as a man is armed by a sovereign government and takes the soldier's oath of fidelity, he is a belligerent; his killing, wounding, or other warlike acts are not individual crimes or offenses. No belligerent has a right to declare that enemies of a certain class, color, or condition, when properly organized as soldiers, will not be treated by him as public enemies.

Article 58

The law of nations knows no distinction of color, and if an enemy of the United States should enslave and sell any captured persons of their army, it would be a case of the severest retaliation, if not redressed upon complaint.

The United States cannot retaliate by enslavement; therefore death must be the retaliation for this crime against the law of nations.

Article 59

A prisoner of war remains answerable for his crimes committed against the captor's army or people....

Article 62

All troops of the enemy known or discovered to give no quarter in general, or to any portion of the army, receive none.

Article 63

Troops who fight in the uniform of their enemies, without any plain, striking, and uniform mark of distinction of their own, can expect no quarter....

Article 65

The use of the enemy's national standard, flag, or other emblem of nationality, for the purpose of deceiving the enemy in battle, is an act of perfidy by which they lose all claim to the protection of the laws of war....

Article 68

… Unnecessary or revengeful destruction of life is not lawful.

Article 70

The use of poison in any manner, be it to poison wells, or food, or arms, is wholly excluded from modern warfare. He that uses it puts himself out of the pale of the law and usages of war.

Article 71

Whoever intentionally inflicts additional wounds on an enemy already wholly disabled, or kills such an enemy, or who orders or encourages soldiers to do so, shall suffer death, if duly convicted, whether he belongs to the Army of the United States, or is an enemy captured after having committed his misdeed....

Article 76

Prisoners of war shall be fed upon plain and wholesome food, whenever practicable, and treated with humanity.

They may be required to work for the benefit of the captor's government, according to their rank and condition.

Article 77

A prisoner of war who escapes may be shot or otherwise killed in his flight, but neither death nor any other punishment shall be inflicted upon him simply for his attempt to escape....

Article 79

Every captured wounded enemy shall be medically treated, according to the ability of the medical staff....

Article 82

Men, or squads of men, who commit hostilities, whether by fighting, or inroads for destruction or plunder, or by raids of any kind, without commission, without being part and portion of the organized hostile army, and without sharing continuously in the war, but do so with intermitting returns to their homes and avocations, or with the occasional assumption of the semblance of peaceful pursuits, divesting themselves of the character or appearance of soldiers—such men, or squads of men, are public enemies, and therefore, if captured, are not entitled to the privileges of prisoners of war, but shall be treated summarily as highway robbers or pirates.

Article 83

Scouts, or single soldiers, if disguised in the dress of the country or in the uniform of the army hostile to their own, employed in obtaining information, if found within or lurking about the lines of the captor, are treated as spies, and suffer death....

Article 101

While deception in war is admitted as a just and necessary means of hostility, and is consistent with honorable warfare, the common law of war allows even capital punishment for clandestine or treacherous attempts to injure an enemy, because they are so dangerous, and it is so difficult to guard against them....

Article 148

The law of war does not allow proclaiming either an individual belonging to the hostile army, or a citizen, or a subject of the hostile government, an outlaw, who may be slain without trial by any captor, any more than the modern law of peace allows such intentional outlawry; on the contrary, it abhors such outrage.... Civilized nations look with horror upon offers of rewards for the assassination of enemies as relapses into barbarism.

Hague Convention (No. IV) Respecting the Laws and Customs of War on Land, and Annex, done at The Hague, Oct. 18, 1907, 36 Stat. 2277, T.S. No. 539, 1 Bevans 631

Preamble

... Considering that, while seeking means to preserve peace and prevent armed conflicts between nations, it is likewise necessary to bear in mind the case where an appeal to arms may be brought about by events which their solicitude could not avert;

Animated by the desire to serve, even in this extreme case, the interests of humanity and the ever progressive needs of civilization;

Thinking it important, with this object, to revise the general laws and customs of war, either with a view to defining them with greater precision or to confining them within such limits as would mitigate their severity as far as possible;

Have deemed in necessary to complete and render more precise in certain particulars the work of the First Peace Conference, which, following on the Brussels Conference of 1874, and inspired by the ideas dictated by a wise and generous forethought, adopted provisions intended to define and govern the usages of war on land.

According to the views of the High Contacting Parties, these provisions, the wording of which has been inspired by the desire to diminish the evils of war, so far as military requirements permit, are intended to serve as a general rule of conduct for the belligerents in their mutual relations and in their relations with the inhabitants.

It has not, however, been found possible at present to concert Regulations covering all the circumstances which arise in practice;

On the other hand, the High Contracting Parties clearly do not intend that unforeseen cases should, in the absence of a written undertaking, be let to the arbitrary judgment of military commanders.

Until a more complete code of the laws of war has been issued, the High Contracting Parties deem it expedient to declare that, in cases not included in the Regulations adopted by them, the inhabitants and the belligerents remain under the protection and the rule of the principles of the law of nations, as they result from the usages established among civilized peoples, from the laws of humanity, and from the dictates of the public conscience.

They declare that it is in this sense especially that Articles 1 and 2 of the Regulations adopted must be understood....

Who, after having deposited their full powers, found in good and due form, have agreed upon the following:

Article 1

The Contracting Parties shall issue instructions to their armed land forces which shall be in conformity with the Regulations respecting the Laws and Customs of War on Land, annexed to the present Convention.

Article 2

The provisions contained in the Regulations referred to in Article 1, as well as in the present Convention, do not apply except between Contracting Powers, and then only if all the belligerents are parties to the Convention.

Article 3

A belligerent party which violates the provisions of the said Regulations shall, if the case demands, be liable to pay compensation. It shall be responsible for all acts committed by persons forming part of its armed forces....

Annex to the Convention.

Regulations Respecting the Laws and Customs of War on Land

Section I. On Belligerents.

Chapter I. The Qualifications of Belligerents.

Article 1

The laws, rights, and duties of war apply not only to armies, but also to militia and volunteer corps fulfilling the following conditions:

1. To be commanded by a person responsible for his subordinates;

2. To have a fixed distinctive emblem recognizable at a distance;

3. To carry arms openly; and

4. To conduct their operations in accordance with the laws and customs of war.

In countries where militia or volunteer corps constitute the army, or form part of it, they are included under the denomination "army."

Article 2

The inhabitants of a territory which has not been occupied, who, on the approach of the enemy, spontaneously take up arms to resist the invading troops without having had time to organize themselves in accordance with Article 1, shall be regarded as belligerents if they carry arms openly and if they respect the laws and customs of war.

Article 3

The armed forces of the belligerent parties may consist of combatants and noncombatants. In the case of capture by the enemy, both have a right to be treated as prisoners of war.

Chapter II. Prisoners of War.

Article 4

Prisoners of war are in the power of the hostile Government, but not of the individuals or crops who capture them.

They must be humanely treated.

All their personal belongings, except arms, horses, and military papers, remain their property.

Article 5

Prisoners of war may be interned in a town, fortress, camp, or other place, under obligation not to go beyond certain fixed limits; but they can only be placed in confinement as an indispensable measure of safety and only while the circumstances which necessitate the measure continue to exist....

Article 20

After the conclusion of peace, the repatriation of prisoners of war shall be carried out as quickly as possible.

Chapter III. The Sick and Wounded.

Article 21

The obligations of belligerents with regard to the sick and wounded are governed by the Geneva Convention [of 1906].

Section II. Hostilities.

Chapter I. Means of Injuring the Enemy, Sieges, and Bombardments.

Article 22

The right of belligerents to adopt means of injuring the enemy is not unlimited.

Article 23

In addition to the prohibitions provided by special Conventions, it is especially forbidden:

(a) To employ poison or poisoned weapons;

(b) To kill or wound treacherously individuals belonging to the hostile nation or army;

(c) To kill or wound an enemy who, having laid down his arms, or having no longer means of defence, has surrendered at discretion;

(d) To declare that no quarter will be given;

(e) To employ arms, projectiles, or material of such as nature as to cause unnecessary suffering;

(f) To make improper use of a flag of truce, of the national flag, or of the military insignia and uniform of the enemy, as well as the distinctive badges of the Geneva Convention;

(g) To destroy or seize the enemy's property, unless such destruction or seizure be imperatively demanded by the necessities of war;

(h) To declare abolished, suspended, or inadmissible in a court of law the rights and actions of the nationals of the hostile party.

A belligerent is likewise forbidden to compel the nationals of the hostile party to take part in the operations of war directed against their own country, even if they were in the belligerent's service before the commencement of the war.

Article 24

Ruses of war and the employment of measures necessary for obtaining information about the enemy and the country are considered permissible.

Article 25

The attack or bombardment, by whatever means, of towns, villages, dwellings, or buildings which are undefended is prohibited.

Article 26

The officer in command of an attacking force must, before commencing bombardment, except in cases of assault, do all in his power to warn the authorities.

Article 27

In sieges and bombardments all necessary steps must be taken to spare, as far as possible, buildings dedicated to religion, art, science, or charitable purposes, historic monuments, hospitals, and places where the sick and wounded are collected, provided they are not being used at the time for military purposes.

It is the duty of the besieged to indicate the presence of such buildings or places by distinctive and visible signs, which shall be notified to the enemy beforehand.

Article 28

The pillage of a town or place, even when taken by assault, is prohibited.

Section III. Military Authority Over the Territory of the Hostile State.

Article 42

Territory is considered occupied when it is actually placed under the authority of the hostile army.

The occupation extends only to the territory where such authority has been established and can be exercised.

Article 43

The authority of the legitimate power having in fact passed into the hands of the occupant, the latter shall take all the measures in his power to restore, and ensure, as far as possible, public order and safety, while respecting, unless absolutely prevented, the laws in force in the country.

Article 44

A belligerent is forbidden to force the inhabitants of occupied territory to furnish information about the army of the other belligerent, or about its means of defence.

Article 45

It is forbidden to compel the inhabitants of occupied territory to swear allegiance to the hostile Power.

Article 46

Family honour and rights, the lives of persons, and private property, as well as religious convictions and practice, must be respected.

Private property cannot be confiscated.

Article 47

Pillage is formally forbidden.

Article 48

If, in the territory occupied, the occupant collects the taxes, dues, and tolls imposed for the benefit of the State, he shall do so, as far as is possible in accordance with the rules of assessment and incidence in force, and shall in consequence be bound to defray the expenses of the administration of the occupied territory to the same extent as the legitimate Government was so bound.

Article 49

If, in addition to the taxes mentioned in the above article, the occupant levies other money contributions in the occupied territory, this shall only be for the needs of the army or of the administration of the territory in question.

Article 50

No general penalty, pecuniary or otherwise, shall be inflicted upon the population on account of the acts of individuals for which they cannot be regarded as jointly and severally responsible.

Article 51

No contribution shall be collected except under a written order, and on the responsibility of a Commander-in-chief.

The collection of the said contribution shall only be effected as far as possible in accordance with the rules of assessment and incidence of the taxes in force.

For every contribution a receipt shall be given to the contributors....

Article 53

An army of occupation can only take possession of cash, funds, and realizable securities which are strictly the property of the State, depots of arms, means of transport, stores and supplies, and, generally, all movable property belonging to the State, which may be used for operations of the war.

All appliances, whether on land, at sea, or in the air, adapted for the transmission of news, or for the transport of persons or things, exclusive of cases governed by naval law, depots of arms, and, generally, all kinds of ammunition of war, may be seized, even if they belong to private individuals, but must be restored and compensation fixed when peace is made.

Article 54

Submarine cables connecting an occupied territory with a neutral territory shall not be seized or destroyed except in the case of absolute necessity. They must likewise be restored and compensation fixed when peace is made.

Article 55

The occupying State shall be regarded only as administrator and usufructuary of public buildings, real estate, forests, and agricultural estates belonging to the hostile State, and situated in the occupied country. It must safeguard the capital of these properties, and administer them in accordance with the rules of usufruct.

Article 56

The property of municipalities, that of institutions dedicated to religion, charity and education, the arts and sciences, even when State property, shall be treated as private property.

All seizure of, destruction or wilful damage done to institutions of this character, historic monuments, works of art and science, is forbidden, and should be made the subject of legal proceedings.

List of War Crimes Prepared by the Commission on the Responsibility of the Authors of the War and on Enforcement of Penalties, Presented to the Preliminary Peace Conference, Paris, 29 March 1919 (members: Belgium, British Empire, France, Greece, Italy, Japan, Poland, Roumania, Serbia, United States)

1. Murder and massacres—systematic terrorism.

2. Putting hostages to death.

3. Torture of civilians.

4. Deliberate starvation of civilians.

5. Rape.

6. Abduction of girls and women for the purpose of enforced prostitution.

7. Deportation of civilians.

8. Internment of civilians under inhuman conditions.

9. Forced labour of civilians in connection with the military operations of the enemy.

10. Usurpation of sovereignty during military occupation.

11. Compulsory enlistment of soldiers among the inhabitants of occupied territory.

12. Attempts to denationalize the inhabitants of occupied territory.

13. Pillage.

14. Confiscation of property.

15. Exaction of illegitimate or of exorbitant contributions and requisitions.

16. Debasement of the currency and issue of spurious currency.

17. Imposition of collective penalties.

18. Wanton devastation and destruction of property.

19. Deliberate bombardment of undefended places.

20. Wanton destruction of religious, charitable, educational and historic buildings and monuments.

21. Destruction of merchant ships and passenger vessels without warning and without provision for the safety of passengers and crew.

22. Destruction of fishing boats and relief ships.

23. Deliberate bombardment of hospitals.

24. Attack and destruction of hospital ships.

25. Breach of other rules relating to the Red Cross.

26. Use of deleterious and asphyxiating gases.

27. Use of explosive or expanding bullets and other inhuman appliances.

28. Directions to give no quarter.

29. Ill-treatment of wounded and prisoners of war.

30. Employment of prisoners of war on unauthorized works.

31. Misuse of flags of truce.

32. Poisoning of wells.

[Item added by the War Crimes Commission]

33. Indiscriminate mass arrests.

Geneva Convention Relative to the Treatment of Prisoners of War of 12 August 1949, 75 U.N.T.S. 135, 6 U.S.T. 3316, T.I.A.S. No. 3364

Part I. General Provisions

Article 1

The High Contracting Parties undertake to respect and to ensure respect for the present Convention in all circumstances.

Article 2

In addition to the provisions which shall be implemented in peacetime, the present Convention shall apply to all cases of declared war or of any other armed conflict which may arise between two or more of the High Contracting Parties, even if the state of war is not recognized by one of them.

The Convention shall also apply to all cases of partial or total occupation of the territory of a High Contracting Party, even if the said occupation meets with no armed resistance.

Although one of the Powers in conflict may not be a party to the present Convention, the Powers who are parties thereto shall remain bound by it in their mutual relations. They shall furthermore be bound by the Convention in relation to the said Power, if the latter accepts and applies the provisions thereof.

Article 3

In the case of armed conflict not of an international character occurring in the territory of one of the High Contracting Parties, each party to the conflict shall be bound to apply, as a minimum, the following provisions:

(1) Persons taking no active part in the hostilities, including members of armed forces who have laid down their arms and those placed *hors de combat* by sickness, wounds, detention, or any other cause, shall in all circumstances be treated humanely, without any adverse distinction founded on race, colour, religion or faith, sex, birth or wealth, or any other similar criteria.

To this end, the following acts are and shall remain prohibited at any time and in any place whatsoever with respect to the above-mentioned persons:

(a) violence to life and person, in particular murder of all kinds, mutilation, cruel treatment and torture;

(b) taking of hostages;

(c) outrages upon personal dignity, in particular, humiliating and degrading treatment;

(d) the passing of sentences and the carrying out of executions without previous judgment pronounced by a regularly constituted court, affording all the judicial guarantees which are recognized as indispensable by civilized peoples.

(2) The wounded and sick shall be collected and cared for.

An impartial humanitarian body, such as the International Committee of the Red Cross, may offer its services to the Parties to the conflict.

The Parties to the conflict should further endeavor to bring into force, by means of special agreements, all or part of the other provisions of the present Convention.

The application of the preceding provisions shall not affect the legal status of the Parties to the conflict.

Article 4

A. Prisoners of war, in the sense of the present Convention, are persons belonging to one of the following categories, who have fallen into the power of the enemy:

1. Members of the armed forces of a Party to the conflict, as well as members of militias or volunteer corps forming part of such forces.

2. Members of other militias and members of other volunteer corps, including those of organized resistance movements, belonging to a Party to the conflict and operating in or outside their own territory, even if this territory is occupied, provided that such militias or volunteer corps, including such organized resistance movements, fulfil the following conditions:

a. that of being commanded by a person responsible for his subordinates;

b. that of having a fixed distinctive sign recognizable at a distance;

c. that of carrying arms openly;

d. that of conducting their operations in accordance with the laws and customs of war.

3. Members of regular armed forces who profess allegiance to a government or an authority not recognized by the Detaining Power....

6. Inhabitants of a non-occupied territory, who on the approach of the enemy spontaneously take up arms to resist the invading forces, without having had time to form themselves into regular armed units provided they carry arms openly and respect the laws and customs of war....

C. This article shall in no way affect the status of medical personnel and chaplains as provided for in Article 33 of the present Convention.

Article 5

The present Convention shall apply to the persons referred to in Article 4 from the time they fall into the power of the enemy and until their final release and repatriation.

Should any doubt arise as to whether persons, having committed a belligerent act and having fallen into the hands of the enemy, belong to any of the categories enumerated in Article 4, such persons shall enjoy the protection of the present Convention until such time as their status has been determined by a competent tribunal.

Article 6

In addition to the agreements expressly provided for in Articles 10, 23, 28, 33, 60, 65, 66, 67, 72, 73, 109, 110, 118, 119, 122 and 132, the High Contracting Parties may conclude other special agreements for all matters concerning which they may deem it suitable to make separate provision. No special agreement shall adversely affect the situation of prisoners of war, as defined by the present Convention, nor restrict the rights which it confers upon them....

Article 7

Prisoners of war may in no circumstances renounce in part or in entirety the rights secured to them by the present Convention, and by the special agreements referred to in the foregoing article, if such there be ...

Part II. General Protection of Prisoners of War

Article 12

Prisoners of war are in the hands of the enemy Power, but not of the individuals or military units who have captured them. Irrespective of the individual responsibilities that may exist, the Detaining Power is responsible for the treatment given them.

Prisoners of war may only be transferred by the Detaining Power to a Power which is a party to the Convention and after the Detaining Power has satisfied itself of the willingness and ability of such transferee Power to apply the Convention. When prisoners of war are transferred under such circumstances, responsibility for the application of the Convention rests on the Power accepting them while they are in its custody.

Nevertheless, if that Power fails to carry out the provisions of the Convention in any important respect, the Power by whom the prisoners of war were transferred shall, upon being notified by the Protecting Power, take effective measures to correct the situation or shall request the return of the prisoners of war. Such requests must be complied with.

Article 13

Prisoners of war must at all times be humanely treated. Any unlawful act or omission by the Detaining Power causing death or seriously endangering the health of a prisoner of war in its custody is prohibited, and will be regarded as a serious breach of the present Convention. In particular, no prisoner of war may be subjected to physical mutilation or to medical or scientific experiments of any kind which are not justified by the medical, dental or hospital treatment of the prisoner concerned and carried out in his interest.

Likewise, prisoners of war must at all times be protected, particularly against acts of violence or intimidation and against insults and public curiosity.

Measures of reprisal against prisoners of war are prohibited.

Article 14

Prisoners of war are entitled in all circumstances to respect for their persons and their honour.

Women shall be treated with all the regard due to their sex and shall in all cases benefit by treatment as favourable as that granted to men.

Prisoners of war shall retain the full civil capacity which they enjoyed at the time of their capture. The Detaining Power may not restrict the exercise, either within or without its own territory, of the rights such capacity confers except in so far as the capacity requires.

Article 15

The Power detaining prisoners of war shall be bound to provide free of charge for their maintenance and for the medical attention required by their state of health.

Article 16

Taking into consideration the provisions of the present Convention relating to rank and sex, and subject to any privileged treatment which may be accorded to them by reason of their state of health, age or professional qualifications, all prisoners of war shall be treated alike by the Detaining Power, without any adverse distinction based on race, nationality, religious belief or political opinions, or any other distinction founded on similar criteria.

Part III. Captivity

Section I. Beginning of Captivity

Article 18

All effects and articles of personal use, except arms, horses, military equipment and military documents, shall remain in the possession of prisoners of war, likewise their metal helmets and gas masks and like articles issued for personal protection. Effects and articles used for their clothing or feeding shall likewise remain in their possession, even if such effects and articles belong to their regulation military equipment.

At no time should prisoners of war be without identity documents. The Detaining Power shall supply such documents to prisoners of war who possess none.

Badges of rank and nationality, decorations and articles having above all a personal or sentimental value may not be taken from prisoners of war.

Sums of money carried by prisoners of war may not be taken away from them except by order of an officer, and after the amount and particulars of the owner have been recorded in a special register and an itemized receipt has been given, legibly inscribed with the name, rank and unit of the person issuing the said receipt. Sums in the currency of the Detaining Power, or which are changed into such currency at the prisoner"s request, shall be placed to the credit of the prisoner"s account as provided in Article 64.

The Detaining Power may withdraw articles of value from prisoners of war only for reasons of security; when such articles are withdrawn, the procedure laid down for sums of money impounded shall apply.

Such objects, likewise sums taken away in any currency other than that of the Detaining Power and the conversion of which has not been asked for by the owners, shall be kept in the custody of the Detaining Power and shall be returned in their initial shape to prisoners of war at the end of their captivity.

Article 19

Prisoners of war shall be evacuated, as soon as possible after their capture, to camps situated in an area far enough from the combat zone for them to be out of danger.

Only those prisoners of war who, owing to wounds or sickness, would run greater risks by being evacuated than by remaining where they are, may be temporarily kept back in a danger zone.

Prisoners of war shall not be unnecessarily exposed to danger while awaiting evacuation from a fighting zone.

Article 20

The evacuation of prisoners of war shall always be effected humanely and in conditions similar to those for the forces of the Detaining Power in their changes of station.

The Detaining Power shall supply prisoners of war who are being evacuated with sufficient food and potable water, and with the necessary clothing and medical attention. The Detaining Power shall take all suitable precautions to ensure their safety during evacuation, and shall establish as soon as possible a list of the prisoners of war who are evacuated.

If prisoners of war must, during evacuation, pass through transit camps, their stay in such camps shall be as brief as possible....

Section II. Internment of Prisoners of War

Chapter I. General Observations.

Article 22

Prisoners of war may be interned only in premises located on land and affording every guarantee of hygiene and healthfulness. Except in particular cases which are justified by the interest of the prisoners themselves, they shall not be interned in penitentiaries.

Prisoners of war interned in unhealthy areas, or where the climate is injurious for them, shall be removed as soon as possible to a more favourable climate.

The Detaining Power shall assemble prisoners of war in camps or camp compounds according to their nationality, language and customs, provided that such prisoners shall not be separated from prisoners of war belonging to the armed forces with which they were serving at the time of their capture, except with their consent.

Article 23

No prisoner of war may at any time be sent to, or detained in areas where he may be exposed to the fire of the combat zone, nor may his presence be used to render certain points or areas immune from military operations.

Prisoners of war shall have shelters against air bombardment and other hazards of war, to the same extent as the local civilian population. With the exception of those engaged in the protection of their quarters against the aforesaid hazards, they may enter such shelters as soon as possible after the giving of the alarm. Any other protective measure taken in favour of the population shall also apply to them.

Detaining Powers shall give the Powers concerned, through the intermediary of the Protecting Powers, all useful information regarding the geographical location of prisoner of war camps.

Whenever military considerations permit, prisoner of war camps shall be indicated in the day-time by the letters PW or PG, placed so as to be clearly visible from the air. The Powers concerned may, however, agree upon any other system or marking. Only prisoner of war camps shall be marked as such.

Article 24

Transit or screening camps of a permanent kind shall be fitted out under conditions similar to those described in the present Section, and the prisoners therein shall have the same treatment as in other camps.

Chapter II. Quarters, Food and Clothing of Prisoners of War.

Chapter III. Hygiene and Medical Attention.

Chapter IV. Medical Personnel and Chaplains Retained to Assist Prisoners of War.

Article 33

Members of the medical personnel and chaplains while retained by the Detaining Power with a view to assisting prisoners of war, shall not be considered as prisoners of war. They shall, however, receive as a minimum the benefits and protection of the present Convention, and shall be granted all facilities necessary to provide for the medical care of, and religious ministration to prisoners of war....

Chapter V. Religious, Intellectual and Physical Activities.

Chapter VI. Discipline.

Chapter VII. Transfer of Prisoners of War After Their Arrival in Camp.

Section III. Labour of Prisoners of War

Section IV. Financial Resources of Prisoners of War

Section V. Relations of Prisoners of War with the Exterior

Section VI. Relations Between Prisoners of War and the Authorities

Chapter I. Complaints of Prisoners of War Respecting the Conditions of Captivity.

Chapter II. Prisoner of War Representatives.

Chapter III. Penal and Disciplinary Sanctions.

I. General Provisions

Article 82

A prisoner of war shall be subject to the laws, regulations and orders in force in the armed forces of the Detaining Power; the Detaining Power shall be justified in taking judicial or disciplinary measures in respect of any offence committed by a prisoner of war against such laws, regulations or orders. However, no proceedings or punishments contrary to the provisions of this Chapter shall be allowed.

Article 83

In deciding whether proceedings in respect of an offence alleged to have been committed by a prisoner of war shall be judicial or disciplinary, the Detaining Power shall ensure that the competent authorities exercise the greatest leniency and adopt, wherever possible, disciplinary rather than judicial measures.

Article 84

A prisoner of war shall be tried only by a military court, unless the existing laws of the Detaining Power expressly permit the civil courts to try a member of the armed forces of the Detaining Power in respect of the particular offence alleged to have been committed by the prisoner of war.

In no circumstances whatever shall a prisoner of war be tried by a court of any kind which does not offer the essential guarantees of independence and impartiality as generally recognized, and, in particular, the procedure of which does not afford the accused the rights and means of defence provided for in Article 105.

Article 85

Prisoners of war prosecuted under the laws of the Detaining Power for acts committed prior to capture shall retain, even if convicted, the benefits of the present Convention.

Article 86

No prisoner of war may be punished more than once for the same act or on the same charge.

Article 87

Prisoners of war may not be sentenced by the military authorities and courts of the Detaining Power to any penalties except those provided for in respect of members of the armed forces of said Power who have committed the same acts....

Collective punishment for individual acts, corporal punishment, imprisonment in premises without daylight and, in general, any form of torture or cruelty, are forbidden.

No prisoner of war may be deprived of his rank by the Detaining Power, or prevented from wearing his badges.

II. Disciplinary Sanctions

III. Judicial Proceedings

Article 99

No prisoner shall be tried or sentenced for an act which is not forbidden by the law of the Detaining Power or by international law, in force at the time the said act was committed.

No moral or physical coercion may be exerted on a prisoner of war in order to induce him to admit himself guilty of the act which he is accused.

No prisoner of war may be convicted without having had an opportunity to present his defence and the assistance of a qualified advocate or counsel.

Article 102

A prisoner of war can be validly sentenced only if the sentence has been pronounced by the same courts according to the same procedure as in the case of members of the armed forces of the Detaining Power, and if, furthermore, the provisions of the present Chapter have been observed.

Article 104

In any case in which the Detaining Power has decided to institute judicial proceedings against a prisoner of war, it shall notify the Protecting Power as soon as possible and at least three weeks before the opening of the trial....

Article 105

The prisoner of war shall be entitled to assistance by one of his prisoner comrades, to defence by a qualified advocate or counsel of his own choice, to the calling of witnesses and, if he deems it necessary, to the services of a competent interpreter. He shall be advised of these rights by the Detaining Power in due time before the trial.

Failing a choice by the prisoner of war, the Protecting Power shall find him an advocate or counsel, and shall have at least one week at its disposal for the purposes....

The advocate or counsel conducting the defence on behalf of the prisoner of war shall have at his disposal a period of two weeks at least before the opening of the trial, as well as the necessary facilities to prepare the defence of the accused. He may, in particular, freely visit the accused and interview him in private. He may also confer with any witnesses for the defence, including prisoners of war. He shall have the benefit of these facilities until the term of appeal or petition has expired.

Particulars of the charge or charges on which the prisoner of war is to be arraigned, as well as the documents which are generally communicated to the accused by virtue of the laws in force in the armed forces of the Detaining Power, shall be communicated to the accused prisoner of war in a language which he understands, and in good time before the opening of the trial. The same communication in the same circumstances shall be made to the advocate or counsel conducting the defence on behalf of the prisoner of war.

The representatives of the Protecting Power shall be entitled to attend the trial of the case, unless, exceptionally, this is held *in camera* in the interest of State security. In such a case the Detaining Power shall advise the Protecting Power accordingly.

Article 106

Every prisoner of war shall have, in the same manner as the members of the armed forces of the Detaining Power, the right of appeal or petition from any sentence pronounced upon him, with a view to the quashing or revising of the sentence or the reopening of the trial. He shall be fully informed of his right to appeal or petition and of the time limit within which he may do so.

Article 108

Sentences pronounced on prisoners of war after a conviction has become duly enforceable, shall be served in the same establishments and under the same conditions as in the case of members of the armed forces of the Detaining Power. These conditions shall in all cases conform to the requirements of health and humanity.

A woman prisoner of war on whom such a sentence has been pronounced shall be confined in separate quarters and shall be under the supervision of women....

Part IV. Termination of Captivity

Section I. Direct Repatriation and Accommodation in Neutral Countries

Section II. Release and Repatriation of Prisoners of War at the Close of Hostilities

Article 118

Prisoners of war shall be released and repatriated without delay after the cessation of active hostilities....

Article 119

Prisoners of war against whom criminal proceedings for an indictable offence are pending may be detained until the end of such proceedings, and, if necessary, until completion of the punishment. The same shall apply to prisoners of war already convicted for an indictable offence....

Part VI. Execution of the Convention

Section I. General Provisions

Article 126

Representatives or delegates of the Protecting Powers shall have permission to go to all places where prisoners of war may be, particularly to places of internment, imprisonment and labour, and shall have access to all premises occupied by prisoners of war; they shall also be allowed to go to the places of departure, passage and arrival of prisoners who are being transferred. They shall be able to interview the prisoners, and in particular the prisoners' representatives, without witnesses, either personally or through an interpreter....

Article 127

The High Contracting Parties undertake, in time of peace as in time of war, to disseminate the text of the present Convention as widely as possible in their respective countries, and, in particular, to include the study thereof in their programmes of military and, if possible, civil instruction, so that the principles thereof may become known to all their armed forces and to the entire population.

Any military or other authorities, who in time of war assume responsibilities in respect of prisoners of war, must possess the text of the Convention and be specially instructed as to its provisions.

Article 128

The High Contracting Parties shall communicate to one another through the Swiss Federal Council and, during hostilities, through the Protecting Powers, the official translations of the present Convention, as well as the laws and regulations which they may adopt to ensure the application thereof.

Article 129

The High Contracting Parties undertake to enact any legislation necessary to provide effective penal sanctions for persons committing, or ordering to be committed, any of the grave breaches of the present Convention defined in the following article.

Each High Contracting Party shall be under an obligation to search for persons alleged to have committed, or to have ordered to be committed, such grave breaches, and shall bring such persons, regardless of their nationality, before its own courts. It may also, if it prefers, and in accordance with the provisions of its own legislation, hand such persons over for trial to another High Contracting Party concerned, provided such High Contacting Party has made out a *prima facie* case.

Each High Contracting Party shall take measures necessary for the suppression of all acts contrary to the provisions of the present Convention other than grave breaches defined in the following article.

In all circumstances, the accused persons shall benefit by safeguards of proper trial and defence, which shall not be less favourable than those provided by Article 105 and those following of the present Convention.

Article 130

Grave breaches to which the preceding article relates shall be those involving any of the following acts, if committed against persons or property protected by the Convention: wilful killing, torture or inhuman treatment, including biological experiments, wilfully causing great suffering or serious injury to body or health, compelling a prisoner of war to serve in the forces of the hostile Power, or wilfully depriving a prisoner of war of the rights to fair and regular trial prescribed in this Convention.

Article 131

No High Contracting Part shall be allowed to absolve itself or any other High Contracting Party of any liability incurred by itself or by another High Contracting Party in respect of breaches referred to in the preceding article.

Article 132

At the request of a Party to the conflict, an enquiry shall be instituted, in a manner to be decided between the interested Parties, concerning any alleged violation of the Convention.

If agreement has not been reached concerning the procedure for the enquiry, the Parties should agree on the choice of an umpire who will decide upon the procedure to be followed.

Once the violation has been established, the Parties to the conflict shall put an end to it and shall repress it with the least possible delay....

Geneva Convention Relative to the Protection of Civilian Persons in Time of War of August 12, 1949 (GC)

75 U.N.T.S. 287, 6 U.S.T. 3516, T.I.A.S. No. 3365

Article 1

The High Contracting Parties undertake to respect and to ensure respect for the present Convention in all circumstances.

Article 2

In addition to the provisions which shall be implemented in peacetime, the present Convention shall apply to all cases of declared war or of any other armed conflict which may arise between two or more of the High Contracting Parties, even if the state of war is not recognized by one of them.

The Convention shall also apply to all cases of partial or total occupation of the territory of a High Contracting Party, even if the said occupation meets with no armed resistance.

Although one of the Powers in conflict may not be a party to the present Convention, the Powers who are parties thereto shall remain bound by it in their mutual relations. They shall furthermore be bound by the Convention in relation to the said Power, if the latter accepts and applies the provisions thereof.

Article 3

In the case of armed conflict not of an international character occurring in the territory of one of the High Contracting Parties, each party to the conflict shall be bound to apply, as a minimum, the following provisions:

(1) Persons taking no active part in the hostilities, including members of armed forces who have laid down their arms and those placed *hors de combat* by sickness, wounds, detention, or any other cause, shall in all circumstances be treated humanely, without any adverse distinction founded on race, colour, religion or faith, sex, birth or wealth, or any other similar criteria.

To this end, the following acts are and shall remain prohibited at any time and in any place whatsoever with respect to the above-mentioned persons:

> (a) violence to life and person, in particular murder of all kinds, mutilation, cruel treatment and torture;

> (b) taking of hostages;

> (c) outrages upon personal dignity, in particular, humiliating and degrading treatment;

> (d) the passing of sentences and the carrying out of executions without previous judgment pronounced by a regularly constituted court, affording all the judicial guarantees which are recognized as indispensable by civilized peoples.

(2) The wounded and sick shall be collected and cared for.

An impartial humanitarian body, such as the International Committee of the Red Cross, may offer its services to the Parties to the conflict.

The Parties to the conflict should further endeavor to bring into force, by means of special agreements, all or part of the other provisions of the present Convention.

The application of the preceding provisions shall not affect the legal status of the Parties to the conflict.

Article 4

Persons protected by the Convention are those who, at a given moment and in any manner whatsoever, find themselves, in case of a conflict or occupation, in the hands of a Party to the conflict or Occupying Power of which they are not nationals.

Nationals of a State which is not bound by the Convention are not protected by it. Nationals of a neutral State who find themselves in the territory of a belligerent State, and nationals of a co-belligerent State, shall not be regarded as protected persons while the State of which they are nationals has normal diplomatic representation in the State in whose hands they are.

The provisions of Part II are, however, wider in application, as defined in Article 13.

Persons protected by the Geneva Convention for the Amelioration of the Condition of the Wounded and Sick in Armed Forces in the Field of August 12, 1949, or by the Geneva Convention for the Amelioration of the Condition of Wounded, Sick and Shipwrecked Members of Armed Forces at Sea of August 12, 1949, or by the Geneva Convention Relative to the Treatment of Prisoners of War of August 12, 1949, shall not be considered as protected persons within the meaning of the present Convention.

Article 5

Where, in the territory of a Party to the conflict, the latter is satisfied that an individual protected person is definitely suspected of or engaged in activities hostile to the security of the State, such individual person shall not be entitled to claim such rights and privileges under the present Convention as would, if exercised in the favor of such individual person, be prejudicial to the security of such State.

Where in occupied territory an individual protected person is detained as a spy or saboteur, or as a person under definite suspicion of activity hostile to the security of the Occupying Power, such person shall, in those cases where absolute military security so requires, be regarded as having forfeited rights of communication under the present Convention.

In each case, such persons shall nevertheless be treated with humanity, and in case of trial, shall not be deprived of the rights of fair and regular trial prescribed by the present Convention. They shall also be granted the full rights and privileges of a protected person under the present Convention at the earliest date consistent with the security of the State or Occupying Power, as the case may be.

Article 6

The present Convention shall apply from the outset of any conflict or occupation mentioned in Article 2.

In the territory of Parties to the conflict, the application of the present Convention shall cease on the general close of military operations.

In the case of occupied territory, the application of the present Convention shall cease one year after the general close of military operations; however, the Occupying Power shall be bound, for the duration of the occupation, to the extent that such Power exercises the functions of government in such territory, by the provisions of the following articles of the present Convention: 1 to 12, 27, 29 to 34, 47, 49, 51, 52, 53, 59, 61 to 77, 143.

Protected persons whose release, repatriation or re-establishment may take place after such dates shall meanwhile continue to benefit by the present Convention.

Article 7

In addition to the agreements expressly provided for in Articles 11, 14, 15, 17, 36, 108, 109, 132, 133 and 149, the High Contracting Parties may conclude other special agreements for all matters concerning which they may deem it suitable to make separate provision. No special agreement shall adversely affect the situation of protected persons, as defined by the present Convention, nor restrict the rights which it confers upon them.

Protected persons shall continue to have the benefit of such agreements as long as the Convention is applicable to them, except where express provisions to the contrary are contained in the aforesaid or in subsequent agreements, or where more favourable measures have been taken with regard to them by one or other of the Parties to the conflict.

Article 8

Protected persons may in no circumstances renounce in part or in entirety the rights secured to them by the present Convention, and by the special agreements referred to in the foregoing article, if such there be....

Article 10

The provisions of the present Convention constitute no obstacle to the humanitarian activities which the International Committee of the Red Cross or any other impartial humanitarian organization may, subject to the consent of the Parties to the conflict concerned, undertake for the protection of civilian persons and for their relief....

Part II. General Protection of Populations Against Certain Consequences of War

Article 13

The provisions of Part II cover the whole of the populations of the countries in conflict, without any adverse distinction based, in particular, on race, nationality, religion or political opinion, and are intended to alleviate the sufferings caused by war.

Article 16

The wounded and sick, as well as the infirm, and expectant mothers, shall be the object of particular protection and respect.

As far as military considerations allow, each Party to the conflict shall facilitate the steps taken to search for the killed and wounded, to assist the shipwrecked and other persons exposed to grave danger, and to protect them against pillage and ill-treatment.

Article 17

The Parties to the conflict shall endeavour to conclude local agreements for the removal from besieged or encircled areas, of wounded, sick, infirm, and aged persons, children and maternity cases, and for the passage of ministers of all religions, medical personnel and medical equipment on their way to such areas.

Article 18

Civilian hospitals organized to give care to the wounded and sick, the infirm and maternity cases, may in no circumstances be the object of attack, but shall at all times be respected and protected by the Parties to the conflict....

Article 23

Each High Contracting Party shall allow the free passage of all consignments of medical and hospital stores and objects necessary for religious worship intended only for civilians of another High Contracting Party, even if the latter is its adversary. It shall likewise permit the free passage of all consignments of essential foodstuffs, clothing and tonics intended for children under fifteen, expectant mothers and maternity cases.

The obligation of a High Contracting Party to allow the free passage of consignments indicated in the preceding paragraph is subject to the condition that this Party is satisfied that there are no serious reasons for fearing:

   a. that the consignments may be diverted from their destination,

   b. that the control may not be effective, or

c. that a definite advantage may accrue to the military efforts or economy of the enemy through the substitution of the above-mentioned consignments for goods which would otherwise be provided or produced by the enemy or through the release of such material, services or facilities as would otherwise be required for the production of such goods....

Article 24

The Parties to the conflict shall take the necessary measures to ensure that children under fifteen, who are orphaned or are separated from their families as a result of the war, are not left to their own resources, and that their maintenance ... [is] facilitated in all circumstances....

Article 25

All persons in the territory of a Party to the conflict, or in a territory occupied by it, shall be enabled to give news of a strictly personal nature to members of their families, wherever they may be, and to receive news from them. This correspondence shall be forwarded speedily and without undue delay....

Article 26

Each Party to the conflict shall facilitate enquiries made by members of families dispersed owing to the war, with the object of renewing contact with one another and of meeting, if possible. It shall encourage, in particular, the work of organizations engaged on this task provided they are acceptable to it and conform to its security regulations.

Part III. Status and Treatment of Protected Persons

Section I. Provisions Common to the Territories of the Parties to the Conflict and to Occupied Territories

Article 27

Protected persons are entitled, in all circumstances, to respect for their persons, their honour, their family rights, their religious convictions and practices, and their manners and customs. They shall at all times be humanely treated, and shall be protected especially against all acts of violence or threats thereof and against insults and public curiosity.

Women shall be especially protected against any attack on their honour, in particular against rape, enforced prostitution, or any form of indecent assault.

Without prejudice to the provisions relating to their state of health, age and sex, all protected persons shall be treated with the same consideration by the Party to the conflict in whose power they are, without any adverse distinction based, in particular, on race, religion or political opinion.

However, the Parties to the conflict may take such measures of control and security in regard to protected persons as may be necessary as a result of the war.

Article 28

The presence of a protected person may not be used to render certain points or areas immune from military operations.

Article 29

The Party to the conflict in whose hands protected persons may be, is responsible for the treatment accorded to them by its agents, irrespective of any individual responsibility which may be incurred.

Article 30

Protected persons shall have every facility for making application to the Protecting Powers, the International Committee of the Red Cross, the National Red Cross (Red Crescent, Red Lion and Sun) Society of the country where they may be, as well as to any organization that might assist them.

These several organizations shall be granted all facilities for that purpose by the authorities, within the bounds set by military or security considerations.

Apart from the visits of the delegates of the Protecting Powers and of the International Committee of the Red Cross, provided for by Article 143, the Detaining or Occupying Powers shall facilitate as much as possible visits to protected persons by the representatives of other organizations whose object is to give spiritual aid or material relief to such persons.

Article 31

No physical or moral coercion shall be exercised against protected persons, in particular to obtain information from them or from third parties.

Article 32

The High Contracting Parties specifically agree that each of them is prohibited from taking any measure of such a character as to cause the physical suffering or extermination of protected persons in their hands. This prohibition applies not only to murder, torture, corporal punishment, mutilation and medical or scientific experiments not necessitated by the medical treatment of a protected person, but also to any other measures of brutality whether applied by civilian or military agents.

Article 33

No protected person may be punished for an offence he or she has not personally committed. Collective penalties and likewise all measures of intimidation or of terrorism are prohibited.

Pillage is prohibited.

Reprisals against protected persons and their property are prohibited.

Article 34

The taking of hostages is prohibited.

Section II. Aliens in the Territory of a Party to the Conflict

Article 35

All protected persons who may desire to leave the territory at the outset of, or during a conflict, shall be entitled to do so, unless their departure is contrary to the national interests of the State....

Article 42

The internment or placing in assigned residence of protected persons may be ordered only if the security of the Detaining Power makes it absolutely necessary....

Article 43

Any protected person who has been interned or placed in assigned residence shall be entitled to have such action reconsidered as soon as possible by an appropriate court or administrative board designated by the Detaining Power for that purpose. If the internment or placing in assigned residence is maintained, the court or administrative board shall periodically, at least twice yearly, give consideration to his or her case with a view to the favourable amendment of the initial decision, if circumstances permit.

Unless the persons concerned object, the Detaining Power shall, as rapidly as possible, give the Protecting Power the names of any protected persons who have been interned or subjected to assigned residence, or who have been released from internment or assigned residence. The decisions of the courts or boards mentioned in the first paragraph of the present Article shall also, subject to the same conditions, be notified as rapidly as possible to the Protecting Power.

Article 44

In applying the measures of control mentioned in the present Convention, the Detaining Power shall not treat as enemy aliens exclusively on the basis of their nationality *de jure* of an enemy State, refugees who do not, in fact, enjoy the protection of any government.

Article 45

Protected persons shall not be transferred to a Power which is not a party to the Convention.

This provision shall in no way constitute an obstacle to the repatriation of protected persons, or to their return to their country of residence after the cessation of hostilities.

Protected persons may be transferred by the Detaining Power only to a Power which is a party to the present Convention and after the Detaining Power has satisfied itself of the willingness and ability of such transferee Power to apply the present Convention. If protected persons are transferred under such circumstances, responsibility for the application of the present Convention rests on the Power accepting them, while they are in its custody. Nevertheless, if that Power fails to carry out the provisions of the present Convention in any important respect, the Power by which the protected persons were transferred shall, upon being so notified by the Protecting Power, take effective measures to correct the situation or shall request the return of the protected persons. Such request must be complied with.

In no circumstances shall a protected person be transferred to a country where he or she may have reason to fear persecution for his or her political opinions or religious beliefs.

The provisions of this Article do not constitute an obstacle to the extradition, in pursuance of extradition treaties concluded before the outbreak of hostilities, of protected persons accused of offences against ordinary criminal law.

Section III. Occupied Territories

Article 47

Protected persons who are in occupied territory shall not be deprived, in any case or in any manner whatsoever, of the benefits of the present Convention by any change introduced, as the result of the occupation of a territory, into the institutions or government of the said territory, nor by any agreement concluded between the authorities of the occupied territories and the Occupying Power, nor by any annexation by the latter of the whole or part of the occupied territory.

Article 48

Protected persons who are not nationals of the Power whose territory is occupied may avail themselves of the right to leave the territory subject to the provisions of Article 35, and decisions thereon shall be taken according to the procedure which the Occupying Power shall establish in accordance with the said article.

Article 49

Individual or mass forcible transfers, as well as deportations of protected persons from occupied territory to the territory of the Occupying Power or to that of any other country, occupied or not, are prohibited, regardless of their motive.

Nevertheless, the Occupying Power may undertake total or partial evacuation of a given area if the security of the population or imperative military reasons so demand. Such evacuations may not involve the displacement of protected persons outside the bounds of the occupied territory except when for material reasons it is impossible to avoid such displacement. Persons thus evacuated shall be transferred back to their homes as soon as hostilities in the area in question have ceased.

The Occupying Power undertaking such transfers of evacuations shall ensure, to the greatest practicable extent, that proper accommodation is provided to receive the protected persons, that the removals are effected in satisfactory conditions of hygiene, health, safety and nutrition, and that members of the same family are not separated.

The Protecting Power shall be informed of any transfers and evacuations as soon as they have taken place.

The Occupying Power shall not detain protected persons in an area particularly exposed to the dangers of war unless the security of the population or imperative military reasons so demand.

The Occupying Power shall not deport or transfer parts of its own civilian population into the territory it occupies.

Article 50

The Occupying Power shall, with the cooperation of the national and local authorities, facilitate the proper working of all institutions devoted to the care and education of children.

The Occupying Power shall take all necessary steps to facilitate the identification of children and the registration of their parentage. It may not, in any case, change their personal status, nor enlist them in formations or organizations subordinate to it....

Article 53

Any destruction by the Occupying Power of real or personal property ... is prohibited, except where such destruction is rendered absolutely necessary by military operations.

Article 54

The Occupying Power may not alter the status of public officials or judges in the occupied territories, or in any way apply sanctions to or take any measures of coercion or discrimination against them, should they abstain from fulfilling their functions for reasons of conscience.

This prohibition does not prejudice the application of the second paragraph of Article 51. It does not affect the right of the Occupying Power to remove public officials from their posts.

Article 55

To the fullest extent of the means available to it, the Occupying Power has the duty of ensuring the food and medical supplies of the population; it should, in particular, bring in the necessary foodstuffs, medical stores and other articles if the resources of the occupied territory are inadequate ... [and may] requisition ... [such for its forces and administrative personnel] only if the requirements of the civilian population have been taken into account....

Article 56

To the fullest extent of the means available to it, the Occupying Power has the duty of ensuring and maintaining, with the cooperation of national and local authorities, the medical and hospital establishments and services, public health and hygiene in the occupied territory, with particular reference to the adoption and application of the prophylactic and preventive measures necessary to combat the spread of contagious diseases and epidemics. Medical personnel of all categories shall be allowed to carry out their duties....

Article 58

The Occupying Power shall permit ministers of religion to give spiritual assistance to the members of their religious communities.

The Occupying Power shall also accept consignments of books and articles required for religious needs and shall facilitate their distribution in occupied territory.

Article 59

If the whole or part of the population of an occupied territory is inadequately supplied, the Occupying Power shall agree to relief schemes on behalf of the said population, and shall facilitate them by all the means at its disposal.

Such schemes, which may be undertaken either by States or by impartial humanitarian organizations such as the International Committee of the Red Cross, shall consist, in particular, of the provision of consignments of foodstuffs, medical supplies and clothing.

All Contracting Parties shall permit the free passage of these consignments and shall guarantee their protection.

A Power granting free passage ... shall, however, have the right to search the consignments, to regulate their passage according to prescribed times and routes, and to be reasonably satisfied ... that these consignments are to be used for the relief of the needy population and are not to be used for the benefit of the Occupying Power.

Article 60

Relief consignments shall in no way relieve the Occupying Power of any of its responsibilities under Articles 55, 56 and 59. The Occupying Power shall in no way whatsoever divert relief consignments from the purpose for which they are intended, except in cases of urgent necessity, in the interests of the population....

Article 64

The penal laws of the occupied territory shall remain in force, with the exception that they may be repealed or suspended by the Occupying Power in cases where they constitute a threat to its security or an obstacle to the application of the present Convention. Subject to the latter consideration and to the necessity for ensuring the effective administration of justice, the tribunals of the occupied territory shall continue to function in respect of all offences covered by the said laws.

The Occupying Power may, however, subject the population of the occupied territory to provisions which are essential to enable the Occupying power to fulfil its obligations under the present Convention, to maintain the orderly government of the territory, and to ensure the security of the Occupying Power, of the members and property of the occupying forces or administration, and likewise of the establishments and lines of communication used by them.

Article 65

The penal provisions enacted by the Occupying Power shall not come into force before they have been published and brought to the knowledge of the inhabitants in their own language. The effect of these penal provisions shall not be retroactive.

Article 66

In case of a breach of the penal provisions promulgated by it by virtue of the second paragraph of Article 64, the Occupying Power may hand over the accused to its properly constituted, non-political military courts, on condition that the said courts sit in the occupied country. Courts of appeal shall preferably sit in the occupied country.

Article 67

The courts shall apply only those provisions of law which were applicable prior to the offence, and which are in accordance with general principles of law, in particular the principle that the penalty shall be proportionate to the offence. They shall take into consideration the fact that the accused is not a national of the Occupying Power.

Article 68

Protected persons who commit an offence which is solely intended to harm the Occupying Power, but which does not constitute an attempt on the life or limb of members of the occupying forces or administration, nor a grave collective danger, nor seriously damage the property of the occupying forces or administration or the installations used by them, shall be liable to internment or simple imprisonment, provided the duration of such internment or imprisonment is proportionate to the offence committed. Furthermore, internment or imprisonment shall, for such offences, be the only measure adopted for depriving protected persons of liberty. The courts provided for under Article 66 of the present Convention may at their discretion convert a sentence of imprisonment to one of internment for the same period.

The penal provisions promulgated by the Occupying Power in accordance with Articles 64 and 65 may impose the death penalty on a protected person only in cases where the person is guilty of espionage, of serious acts of sabotage against the military installations of the Occupying Power or of intentional offences which have caused the death of one or more persons, provided that such offences were punishable by death under the law of the occupied territory in force before the occupation began.

The death penalty may not be pronounced against a protected person unless the attention of the court has been particularly called to the fact that since the accused is not a national of the Occupying Power, he is not bound to it by any duty of allegiance.

In any case, the death penalty may not be pronounced against a protected person who was under eighteen years of age at the time of the offence.

Article 69

In all cases, the duration of the period during which a protected person accused of an offence is under arrest awaiting trial or punishment shall be deducted from any period of imprisonment awarded.

Article 70

Protected persons shall not be arrested, prosecuted or convicted by the Occupying Power for acts committed or for opinions expressed before the occupation, or during a temporary interruption thereof, with the exception of breaches of the laws and customs of war.

Nationals of the Occupying Power who, before the outbreak of hostilities, have sought refuge in the territory of the occupied State, shall not be arrested, prosecuted, convicted or deported from the occupied territory, except for offences committed after the outbreak of hostilities, or for offence under common law committed before the outbreak of hostilities which, according to the law of the occupied State, would have justified extradition in time of peace.

Article 71

No sentence shall be pronounced by the competent courts of the Occupying Power except after a regular trial.

Accused persons who are prosecuted by the Occupying Power shall be promptly informed, in writing, in a language which they understand, of the particulars of the charges preferred against them, and shall be brought to trial as rapidly as possible. The Protecting Power shall be informed of all proceedings instituted by the Occupying Power against protected persons in respect of charges involving the death penalty or imprisonment for two years or more; it shall be enabled, at any time, to obtain information regarding the state of such proceedings. Furthermore, the Protecting Power shall be entitled, on request, to be furnished with all particulars of these and of any other proceedings instituted by the Occupying Power against protected persons.

The notification to the Protecting Power, as provided for in the second paragraph above, shall be sent immediately, and shall in any case reach the Protecting Power three weeks before the date of the first hearing. Unless, at the opening of the trial, evidence is submitted that the provisions of the article are fully complied with, the trial shall not proceed. The notification shall include the following particulars:

(a) description of the accused;

(b) place of residence or detention;

(c) specification of the charge or charges (with mention of the penal provisions under which it is brought);

(d) designation of the court which will hear the case;

(e) place and date of the first hearing.

Article 72

Accused persons shall have the right to present evidence necessary to their defence and may, in particular, call witnesses. They shall have the right to be assisted by a qualified advocate or counsel of their own choice, who shall be able to visit them freely and shall enjoy the necessary facilities for preparing the defence.

Failing a choice by the accused, the Protecting Power may provide him with an advocate or counsel. When an accused person has to meet a serious charge and the Protecting Power is not functioning, the Occupying Power, subject to the consent of the accused, shall provide an advocate or counsel.

Accused persons shall, unless they freely waive such assistance, be aided by an interpreter, both during preliminary investigation and during the hearing in court. They shall have the right at any time to object to the interpreter and to ask for his replacement.

Article 73

A convicted person shall have the right of appeal provided for by the laws applied by the court. He shall be fully informed of his right to appeal or petition and of the time limit within which he may do so.

The penal procedure provided in the present Section shall apply, as far as it is applicable, to appeals. Where the laws applied by the Court make no provision for appeals, the convicted person shall have the right to petition against the finding and sentence to the competent authority of the Occupying Power.

Article 74

Representatives of the Protecting Power shall have the right to attend the trial of any protected person, unless the hearing has, as an exceptional measure, to be held *in camera* in the interests of the security of the Occupying Power, which shall then notify the Protecting Power. A notification in respect of the date and place of trial shall be sent to the Protecting Power.

Any judgment involving a sentence of death, or imprisonment for two years or more, shall be communicated, with the relevant grounds, as rapidly as possible to the Protecting Power. The notification shall contain a reference to the notification made under Article 71, and, in the case of sentences of imprisonment, the name of the place where the sentence is to be served. A record of judgments other than those referred to above shall be kept by the court and shall be open to inspection by representatives of Protecting Power. Any period allowed for appeal in the case of sentences involving the death penalty, or imprisonment of two years or more, shall not run until notification of judgment has been received by the Protecting Power.

Article 75

In no case shall persons condemned to death be deprived of the right of petition for pardon or reprieve.

No death sentence shall be carried out before the expiration of a period of at least six months from the date of receipt by the Protecting Power of the notification of the final judgment confirming such death sentence, or of an order denying pardon or reprieve.

The six months period of suspension of the death sentence herein prescribed may be reduced in individual cases in circumstances of grave emergency involving an organized threat to the security of the Occupying Power or its forces, provided always that the Protecting Power is notified of such reduction and is given reasonable time and opportunity to make representations to the competent occupying authorities in respect of such death sentences.

Article 76

Protected persons accused of offences shall be detained in the occupied country, and if convicted they shall serve their sentences therein. They shall, if possible, be separated from other detainees and shall enjoy conditions of food and hygiene which will be sufficient to keep them in good health, and which will be at least equal to those obtaining in prisons in the occupied country.

They shall receive the medical attention required by their state of health.

They shall also have the right to receive any spiritual assistance which they may require.

Women shall be confined in separate quarters and shall be under the direct supervision of women.

Proper regard shall be paid to the special treatment due to minors.

Protected persons who are detained shall have the right to be visited by delegates of the Protecting Power and of the International Committee of the Red Cross, in accordance with the provisions of Article 143.

Such persons shall have the right to receive at least one relief parcel monthly.

Article 77

Protected persons who have been accused of offences or convicted by the courts in occupied territory, shall be handed over at the close of occupation, with the relevant records, to the authorities of the liberated territory.

Article 78

If the Occupying Power considers it necessary, for imperative reasons of security, to take safety measures concerning protected persons, it may, at the most, subject them to assigned residence or to internment.

Decisions regarding such assigned residence or internment shall be made according to a regular procedure to be prescribed by the Occupying Power in accordance with the provisions of the present Convention. This procedure shall include the right of appeal for the parties concerned. Appeals shall be decided with the least possible delay....

Section IV. Regulations for the Treatment of Internees

Chapter I. General Provisions.

Article 79

The Parties to the conflict shall not intern protected persons, except in accordance with the provisions of Articles 41, 42, 43, 68 and 78.

Article 80

Internees shall retain their full civil capacity and shall exercise such attendant rights as may be compatible with their status....

Chapter VIII. Relations with the Exterior ...

Article 106

As soon as he is interned, or at the least not more than one week after his arrival in a place of internment, and likewise in cases of sickness or transfer to another place of internment or to a hospital, every internee shall be enabled to send direct to his family, on the one hand, and to the Central Agency, provided for by Article 140, on the other, an internment card similar, if possible, to the model annexed to the present Convention, informing his relatives of his detention, address and state of health. The said cards shall be forwarded as rapidly as possible and may not be delayed in any way.

Article 107

Internees shall be allowed to send and receive letters and cards....

Chapter XII. Release, Repatriation, and Accommodation in Neutral Countries.

Article132

Each interned person shall be released by the Detaining Power as soon as the reasons which necessitated his internment no longer exist ...

Article 133

Internment shall cease as soon as possible after the close of hostilities ...

Article 134

The High Contracting Parties shall endeavour, upon the close of hostilities or occupation, to ensure the return of all internees to their last place of residence, or to facilitate their repatriation ...

Part IV. Execution of the Convention.

Section I. General Provisions ...

Article 143

Representatives or delegates of the Protecting Powers shall have permission to go to all places where protected persons are, particularly to places of internment, detention and work.

They shall have access to all premises occupied by protected persons and shall be able to interview the latter without witnesses, personally or through an interpreter.

Such visits may not be prohibited except for reasons of imperative military necessity, and then only as an exceptional and temporary measure. Their duration and frequency shall not be restricted....

The delegates of the International Committee of the Red Cross shall also enjoy the above prerogatives....

Article 144

The High Contracting Parties undertake, in time of peace as in time or war, to disseminate the text of the present Convention as widely as possible in their respective countries, and in particular, to include the study thereof in their programmes of military and, if possible, civil instruction, so that the principles thereof may become known to the entire population.

Any civilian, military, police or other authorities, who in time of war assume responsibilities in respect of protected persons, must possess the text of the Conventions and be specially instructed as to its provisions.

Article 145

The High Contracting Parties shall communicate to one another through the Swiss Federal Council and, during hostilities, through the Protecting Powers, the official translations of the present Convention, as well as the laws and regulations which they may adopt to ensure the application thereof.

Article 146

The High Contracting Parties undertake to enact any legislation necessary to provide effective penal sanctions for persons committing, or ordering to be committed, any of the grave breaches of the present Convention defined in the following article.

Each High Contracting Party shall be under the obligation to search for persons alleged to have committed, or to have ordered to be committed, such grave breaches, and shall bring such persons, regardless of their nationality, before its own courts. It may also, if it prefers, and in accordance with the provisions of its own legislation, hand such persons over for trial to another High Contracting Party concerned, provided such High Contracting Party has made out a *prima facie* case.

Each High Contracting Party shall take measures necessary for the suppression of all acts contrary to the provisions of the present Convention other than the grave breaches defined in the following article.

In all circumstances, the accused persons shall benefit by safeguards of proper trial and defence, which shall not be less favourable than those provided by Article 105 and those following of the Geneva Convention relative to the Treatment of Prisoners of War of August 12, 1949.

Article 147

Grave breaches to which the preceding article relates shall be those involving any of the following acts, if committed against persons or property protected by the present Convention: wilful killing, torture or inhuman treatment, including biological experiments, wilfully causing great suffering or serious injury to body or health, unlawful deportation or transfer or unlawful confinement of a protected person, compelling a protected person to serve in the forces of a hostile Power or wilfully depriving a protected person of the rights of fair and regular trial prescribed in the present Convention, taking of hostages and extensive destruction and appropriation of property, not justified by military necessity and carried out unlawfully and wantonly.

Article 148

No High Contracting Party shall be allowed to absolve itself or any other High Contracting Party of any liability incurred by itself or by another High Contracting Party in respect of breaches referred to in the preceding article.

Article 149

At the request of a Party to the conflict, an enquiry shall be instituted, in a manner to be decided between the interested Parties, concerning any alleged violation of the Convention.

If agreement has not been reached concerning the procedure for the enquiry, the Parties should agree on the choice of an umpire who will decide upon the procedure to be followed.

Once the violation has been established, the Parties to the conflict shall put an end to it and shall repress it with the least possible delay....

Protocol Additional to the Geneva Conventions of 12 August 1949, and relating to the protection of victims of international armed conflicts (Protocol I), 8 June 1977

Preamble

The High Contracting Parties, Proclaiming their earnest wish to see peace prevail among peoples,

Recalling that every State has the duty, in conformity with the Charter of the United Nations, to refrain in its international relations from the threat or use of force against the sovereignty, territorial integrity or political independence of any State, or in any other manner inconsistent with the purposes of the United Nations,

Believing it necessary nevertheless to reaffirm and develop the provisions protecting the victims of armed conflicts and to supplement measures intended to reinforce their application,

Expressing their conviction that nothing in this Protocol or in the Geneva Conventions of 12 August 1949 can be construed as legitimizing or authorizing any act of aggression or any other use of force inconsistent with the Charter of the United Nations,

Reaffirming further that the provisions of the Geneva Conventions of 12 August 1949 and of this Protocol must be fully applied in all circumstances to all persons who are protected by those instruments, without any adverse distinction based on the nature or origin of the armed conflict or on the causes espoused by or attributed to the Parties to the conflict,

Have agreed on the following:

PART I. GENERAL PROVISIONS

Article 1

General principles and scope of application

1. The High Contracting Parties undertake to respect and to ensure respect for this Protocol in all circumstances.

2. In cases not covered by this Protocol or by other international agreements, civilians and combatants remain under the protection and authority of the principles of international law derived from established custom, from the principles of humanity and from the dictates of public conscience.

3. This Protocol, which supplements the Geneva Conventions of 12 August 1949 for the protection of war victims, shall apply in the situations referred to in Article 2 common to those Conventions.

4. The situations referred to in the preceding paragraph include armed conflicts in which peoples are fighting against colonial domination and alien occupation and against racist regimes in the exercise of their right of self-determination, as enshrined in the Charter of the United Nations and the Declaration on Principles of International Law concerning Friendly Relations and Co-operation among States in accordance with the Charter of the United Nations....

Article 3

Beginning and end of application

Without prejudice to the provisions which are applicable at all times:

(a) the Conventions and this Protocol shall apply from the beginning of any situation referred to in Article 1 of this Protocol;

(b) the application of the Conventions and of this Protocol shall cease, in the territory of Parties to the conflict, on the general close of military operations and, in the case of occupied territories, on the termination of the occupation, except, in either circumstance, for those persons whose final release, repatriation or re-establishment takes place thereafter. These persons shall continue to benefit from the relevant provisions of the Conventions and of this Protocol until their final release, repatriation or re-establishment.

Article 4

Legal status of the Parties to the conflict

The application of the Conventions and of this Protocol, as well as the conclusion of the agreements provided for therein, shall not affect the legal status of the Parties to the conflict. Neither the occupation of a territory nor the application of the Conventions and this Protocol shall affect the legal status of the territory in question.

Part II. Wounded, Sick and Shipwrecked

Section I. General Protection

Article 10

Protection and care

1. All the wounded, sick and shipwrecked, to whichever Party they belong, shall be respected and protected.

2. In all circumstances they shall be treated humanely and shall receive, to the fullest extent practicable and with the least possible delay, the medical care and attention required by their condition. There shall be no distinction among them founded on any grounds other than medical ones.

Article 11

Protection of persons

1. The physical or mental health and integrity of persons who are in the power of the adverse Party or who are interned, detained or otherwise deprived of liberty as a result of a situation referred to in Article 1 shall not be endangered by any unjustified act or omission. Accordingly, it is prohibited to subject the persons described in this article to any medical procedure which is not indicated by the state of health of the person concerned and which is not consistent with generally accepted medical standards which would be applied under similar medical circumstances to persons who are nationals of the Party conducting the procedure and who are in no way deprived of their liberty.

2. It is, in particular, prohibited to carry out on such persons, even with their consent:

    (a) physical mutilations;

(b) medical or scientific experiments;

    (c) removal of tissue or organs for transplantation, except where these acts are justified in conformity with the conditions provided for in paragraph 1....

4. Any wilful act or omission which seriously endangers the physical or mental health or integrity of any person who is in the power of a Party other than the one on which he depends and which either violates any of the prohibitions in paragraphs 1 and 2 or fails to comply with the requirements of paragraph 3 shall be a grave breach of this Protocol....

Part III. Methods and Means of Warfare, Combatant and Prisoner-of-War Status

Section I. Methods and Means of Warfare

Article 35

Basic rules

1. In any armed conflict, the right of the Parties to the conflict to choose methods and means of warfare is not unlimited.

2. It is prohibited to employ weapons, projectiles and material and methods or warfare of a nature to cause superfluous injury or unnecessary suffering.

3. It is prohibited to employ methods or means of warfare which are intended, or may be expected, to cause widespread, long-term and severe damage to the natural environment.

Article 36

New weapons

In the study, development, acquisition or adoption of a new weapon, means or method of warfare, a High Contracting Party is under an obligation to determine whether its employment would, in some or all circumstances, be prohibited by this Protocol or by any other rule of international law applicable to the High Contracting Party.

Article 37

Prohibition of perfidy

1. It is prohibited to kill, injure or capture an adversary by resort to perfidy. Acts inviting the confidence of an adversary to lead him to believe that he is entitled to, or is obligated to accord, protection under the rules of international law applicable in armed conflict, with intent to betray that confidence, shall constitute perfidy. The following acts are examples of perfidy:

(a) the feigning of an intent to negotiate under a flag of truce or of a surrender;

(b) the feigning of an incapacitation by wounds or sickness;

(c) the feigning of civilian, non-combatant status; and

(d) the feigning of protected status by the use of signs, emblems or uniforms of the United Nations or of neutral or other States not Parties to the conflict.

2. Ruses of war are not prohibited. Such ruses are acts which are intended to mislead an adversary or to induce him to act recklessly but which infringe no rule of international law applicable in armed conflict and which are not perfidious because they do not invite the confidence of an adversary with respect to protection under that law. The following are examples of such ruses: the use of camouflage, decoys, mock operations and misinformation.

Article 40

Quarter

It is prohibited to order that there shall be no survivors, to threaten an adversary therewith or to conduct hostilities on this bases.

Part IV. Civilian Population

Section I. General Protection Against Effects of Hostilities

Chapter I. Basic Rule and Field of Application

Article 48

Basic rule

In order to ensure respect for and protection of the civilian population and civilian objects, the Parties to the conflict shall at all times distinguish between the civilian population and combatants and between civilian objects and military objectives and accordingly shall direct their operations only against military objectives.

Article 49

Definition of attacks and scope of application

1. "Attacks" means acts of violence against the adversary, whether in offence or in defence.

2. The provisions of this Protocol with respect to attacks apply to all attacks in whatever territory conducted, including the national territory belonging to a Party to the conflict but under the control of an adverse Party.

3. The provisions of this section apply to any land, air or sea warfare which may affect the civilian population, individual civilians or civilian objects on land. They further apply to all attacks from the sea or from the air against objectives on land but do not otherwise affect the ruled of international law applicable in armed conflict at sea or in the air.

4. The provisions of this section are additional to the rules concerning humanitarian protection contained in the Fourth Convention, particularly in part II thereof, and in other international agreements binding upon the High Contracting Parties, as well as to other rules of international law relating to the protection of civilians and civilian objects on land, at sea or in the air against the effects of hostilities.

Chapter II. Civilians and Civilian Population

Article 50

Definition of civilians and civilian population

1. A civilian is any person who does not belong to one of the categories of persons referred to in Article 4 (A) (1), (2), (3) and (6) of the Third Convention [GPW] and in

Article 43 of this Protocol. In case of doubt whether a person is a civilian, that person shall be considered to be a civilian.

2. The civilian population comprises all persons who are civilians.

3. The presence within the civilian population of individuals who do not come within the definition of civilians does not deprive the population of its civilian character.

Article 51

Protection of the civilian population

1. The civilian population and individual civilians shall enjoy general protection against dangers arising from military operations. To give effect to this protection, the following rules, which are additional to other applicable rules of international law, shall be observed in all circumstances.

2. The civilian population as such, as well as individual civilians, shall not be the object of attack. Acts or threats of violence the primary purpose of which is to spread terror among the civilian population are prohibited.

3. Civilians shall enjoy the protection afforded by this section, unless and for such time as they take a direct part in hostilities.

4. Indiscriminate attacks are prohibited. Indiscriminate attacks are:

(a) those which are not directed at a specific military objective;

(b) those which employ a method or means of combat which cannot be directed at a specific military objective; or

(c) those which employ a method or means of combat the effects of which cannot be limited as required by this Protocol;

and consequently, in each such case, are of a nature to strike military objectives and civilians or civilian objects without distinction.

5. Among others, the following types of attacks are to be considered as indiscriminate:

(a) an attack by bombardment by any methods or means which treats as a single military objective a number of clearly separated and distinct military objectives located in a city, town, village or other area containing a similar concentration of civilians or civilian objects; and

(b) an attack which may be expected to cause incidental loss of civilian life, injury to civilians, damage to civilian objects, or a combination thereof, which would be excessive in relation to the concrete and direct military advantage anticipated.

6. Attacks against the civilian population or civilians by way of reprisals are prohibited.

7. The presence or movements of the civilian population or individual civilians shall not be used to render certain points or areas immune from military operations, in particular in attempts to shield military objectives from attacks or to shield, favour or impede military operations. The Parties to the conflict shall not direct the movement of the civilian population or individual civilians in order to attempt to shield military objectives from attacks or to shield military operations.

8. Any violation of these prohibitions shall not release the Parties to the conflict from their legal obligations with respect to the civilian population and civilians, including the obligation to take the precautionary measures provided for in Article 57.

Chapter III. Civilian Objects

Article 52

General protection of civilian objects

1. Civilian objects shall not be the object of attack or of reprisal. Civilian objects are all objects which are not military objectives as defined in paragraph 2.

2. Attacks shall be limited strictly to military objectives. In so far as objets are concerned, military objectives are limited to those objects which by their nature, location, purpose or use make an effective contribution to military action and whose total or partial destruction, capture or neutralization, in the circumstances ruling at the time, offers a definite military advantage.

3. In case of doubt whether an object which is normally dedicated to civilian purposes, such as a place of worship, a house or other dwelling or a school, is being used to make an effective contribution to military action, it shall be presumed not to be so used.

Article 53

Protection of cultural objects and of places of worship

Without prejudice to the provisions of the Hague Convention for the Protection of Cultural Property in the Event of Armed Conflict of 14 May 1954, and of other relevant international instruments, it is prohibited:

(a) to commit any acts of hostility directed against the historic monuments, works of art or places of worship which constitute the cultural or spiritual heritage of peoples;

(b) to use such objects in support of the military effort;

(c) to make such objects the object of reprisals.

Article 54

Protection of objects indispensable to the survival of the civilian population

1. Starvation of civilians as a method of warfare is prohibited.

2. It is prohibited to attack, destroy, remove or render useless objects indispensable to the survival of the civilian population, such as food-stuffs, agricultural areas for the production of food-stuffs, crops, livestock, drinking water installations and supplies and irrigation works, for the specific purpose of denying them for their sustenance value to the civilian population or to the adverse Party, whatever the motive, whether in order to starve out civilians, to cause them to move away, or for any other motive.

3. The prohibitions in paragraph 2 shall not apply to such of the objects covered by it as are used by an adverse Party:

(a) as sustenance solely for the members of its armed forces; or

(b) if not as sustenance, then in direct support of military action, provided, however, that in no event shall actions against these objects be taken which may be expected to leave the civilian population with such inadequate food or water as to cause its starvation or force its movement.

4. These objects shall not be made the object of reprisals.

5. In recognition of the vital requirements of any Party to the conflict in the defence of its national territory against invasion, derogation from the prohibitions contained in paragraph 2 may be made by a Party to the conflict within such territory under its own control where required by imperative military necessity.

Article 55

Protection of the natural environment

1. Care shall be taken in warfare to protect the natural environment against widespread, long-term and severe damage. This prohibition includes a prohibition of the use of methods or means of warfare which are intended or may be expected to cause such damage to the natural environment and thereby to prejudice the health or survival of the population.

2. Attacks against the natural environment by way of reprisals are prohibited.

Article 56

Protection of works and installations containing dangerous forces

1. Works or installations containing dangerous forces, namely dams, dykes and nuclear electrical generating stations, shall not be made the object of attack, even where these objects are military objectives, if such attack may cause the release of dangerous forces and consequent severe losses among the civilian population. Other military objectives located at or in the vicinity of these works or installations shall not be made the object of attack if such attack may cause the release of dangerous forces from the works or installations and consequent severe losses among the civilian population.

2. The special protection against attack provided in paragraph 1 shall cease:

(a) for a dam or a dyke if it is used for other than its normal function and in regular, significant and direct support of military operations and if such attack is the only feasible way to terminate such support;

(b) for a nuclear electrical generating station only if it provides electric power in regular, significant and direct support of military operations and if such attack is the only feasible way to terminate such support;

(c) for other military objectives located at or in the vicinity of these works or installations only if they are used in regular, significant and direct support of military operations and if such attack is the only feasible way to terminate such support....

Chapter IV. Precautionary Measures

Article 57

Precautions in attack

1. In the conduct of military operations, constant care shall be taken to spare the civilian population, civilians and civilian objects.

2. With respect to attacks, the following shall be taken:

(a) those who plan or decide upon an attack shall:

(i) do everything feasible to verify that the objectives to be attacked are neither civilians nor civilian objects and are not subject to special protection but are military objectives within the meaning of paragraph 2 of Article 52 and that it is not prohibited by the provisions of this Protocol to attack them;

(ii) take all feasible precautions in the choice of means and methods of attack with a view to avoiding, and in any event to minimizing, incidental loss of civilian life, injury to civilians and damage to civilian objects;

(iii) refrain from deciding to launch an attack which may be expected to cause incidental loss of civilian life, injury to civilians, damage to civilian objects, or a combination thereof, which would be excessive in relation to the concrete and direct military advantage anticipated....

Section III. Treatment of Persons in the Power of a Party to the Conflict

Chapter I. Field of Application and Protection of Persons and Objects

Article 72

Field of application

The provisions of this Section are additional to the rules concerning humanitarian protection of civilians and civilian objects in the power of a Party to the conflict contained in the Fourth Convention [GC], particularly Parts I and III thereof, as well as to other applicable rules of international law relating to protection of fundamental human rights during international armed conflict.

Article 73

Refugees and stateless persons

Persons who, before the beginning of hostilities, were considered as stateless persons or refugees under the relevant international instruments accepted by the Parties concerned or under the national legislation of the State of refuge or State of residence shall be protected persons within the meaning of Parts I and III of the Fourth Convention, in all circumstances and without any adverse distinction.

Article 74

Reunion of dispersed families

The High Contracting Parties and the Parties to the conflict shall facilitate in every possible way the reunion of families dispersed as a result of armed conflicts and shall encourage in particular the work of the humanitarian organizations engaged in this task in accordance with the provisions of the Conventions and of this Protocol and in conformity with their respective security regulations.

Article 75

Fundamental guarantees

1. In so far as they are affected by a situation referred to in Article 1 of this Protocol, persons who are in the power of a Party to the conflict and who do not benefit from more favourable treatment under the Conventions or under this Protocol shall be treated humanely in all circumstances and shall enjoy, as a minimum, the protection provided by this article without any adverse distinction based upon race, colour, sex, language, religion or belief, political or other opinion, national or social origin, wealth, birth or other status, or on any other similar criteria. Each Party shall respect the person, honour, convictions and religious practices of all such persons.

2. The following acts are and shall remain prohibited at any time and in any place whatsoever, whether committed by civilian or by military agents:

(a) violence to the life, health, or physical or mental well-being of persons, in particular:

(i) murder;

(ii) torture of all kinds, whether physical or mental;

(iii) corporal punishment; and

(iv) mutilation;

(b) outrages upon personal dignity, in particular humiliating and degrading treatment, enforced prostitution and any form of indecent assault;

(c) the taking of hostages;

(d) collective punishments; and

(e) threats to commit any of the foregoing acts.

3. Any person arrested, detained or interned for actions related to the armed conflict shall be informed promptly, in a language he understands, of the reasons why these measures have been taken. Except in cases of arrest or detention for penal offences, such persons shall be released with the minimum delay possible and in any event as soon as the circumstances justifying the arrest, detention or internment have ceased to exist.

4. No sentence may be passed and no penalty may be executed on a person found guilty of a penal offence related to the armed conflict except pursuant to a conviction pronounced by an impartial and regularly constituted court respecting the generally recognized principles of regular judicial procedure, which include the following:

(a) the procedure shall provide for an accused to be informed without delay of the particulars of the offence alleged against him and shall afford the accused before and during his trial all necessary rights and means of defence;

(b) no one shall be convicted of an offence except on the basis of individual penal responsibility;

(c) no one shall be accused or convicted of a criminal offence on account of any act or omission which did not constitute a criminal offence under the national or international law to which he was subject at the time when it was committed; nor shall any heavier penalty be imposed than that which was applicable at the time when the criminal offence was committed; if, after the commission of the offence, provision is made by law for the imposition of a lighter penalty, the offender shall benefit thereby;

(d) anyone charged with an offence is presumed innocent until proved guilty according to law;

(e) anyone charged with an offence shall have the right to be tried in his presence;

(f) no one shall be compelled to testify against himself or to confess guilt;

(g) anyone charged with an offence shall have the right to examine, or have examined, the witnesses against him and to obtain the attendance and examination of witnesses on his behalf under the same conditions as witnesses against him;

(h) no one shall be prosecuted or punished by the same Party for an offence in respect of which a final judgment acquitting or convicting that person has been previously pronounced under the same law and judicial procedure;

(i) anyone prosecuted for an offence shall have the right to have the judgment pronounced publicly; and

(j) a convicted person shall be advised on conviction of his judicial and other remedies and of the time-limits within which they may be exercised.

5. Women whose liberty has been restricted for reasons related to the armed conflict shall be held in quarters separated from men's quarters. They shall be under the immediate supervision of women. Nevertheless, in cases where families are detained or interned, they shall, whenever possible, be held in the same place and accommodated as family units.

6. Persons arrested, detained or interned for reasons related to the armed conflict shall enjoy the protection provided by this article until their final release, repatriation or re-establishment, even after the end of the armed conflict.

7. In order to avoid any doubt concerning the prosecution and trial of persons accused of war crimes or crimes against humanity, the following principles shall apply:

(a) persons who are accused of such crimes should be submitted for the purpose of prosecution and trial in accordance with the applicable rules of international law; and

(b) any such persons who do not benefit from more favourable treatment under the Conventions or this Protocol shall be accorded the treatment provided by this article, whether or not the crimes of which they are accused constitute grave breaches of the Conventions or of this Protocol.

8. No provision of this article may be construed as limiting or infringing any other more favourable provision granting greater protection, under any applicable rules of international law, to persons covered by paragraph 1.

Chapter II. Measures in Favour of Women and Children

Article 76

Protection of Women

1. Women shall be the object of special respect and shall be protected in particular against rape, forced prostitution and any other form of indecent assault.

2. Pregnant women and mothers having dependent infants who are arrested, detained or interned for reasons related to the armed conflict, shall have their cases considered with the utmost priority.

3. To the maximum extent feasible, the Parties to the conflict shall endeavour to avoid the pronouncement of the death penalty on pregnant women or mothers having dependent infants, for an offence related to the armed conflict. The death penalty for such offences shall not be executed on such women.

Article 77

Protection of Children

1. Children shall be the object of special respect and shall be protected against any form of indecent assault. The Parties to the conflict shall provide them with the care and aid they require, whether because of their age or for any other reason.

2. The Parties to the conflict shall take all feasible measures in order that children who have not attained the age of fifteen years do not take a direct part in hostilities and, in particular, they shall refrain from recruiting them into their armed forces....

Part V. Execution of the Conventions and of this Protocol

Section I. General Provisions

Article 82

Legal advisers in armed forces

The High Contracting Parties at all times, and the Parties to the conflict in time of armed conflict, shall ensure that legal advisers are available, when necessary, to advise military commanders at the appropriate level on the application of the Conventions and this Protocol and on the appropriate instruction to be given to the armed forces on this subject.

Section II. Repression of Breaches of the Conventions and of this Protocol

Article 85

Repression of breaches of this Protocol

1. The provisions of the Conventions relating to the repression of breaches and grave breaches, supplemented by this Section, shall apply to the repression of breaches and grave breaches of this Protocol.

2. Acts described as grave breaches in the Conventions are grave breaches of this Protocol if committed against persons in the power of an adverse Party protected by Articles 44, 45 and 73 of this Protocol, or against the wounded, sick and shipwrecked of the adverse Party who are protected by this Protocol, or against those medical or religious personnel, medical units or medical transports which are under the control of the adverse Party and are protected by this Protocol.

3. In addition to the grave breaches defined in article 11, the following acts shall be regarded as grave breaches of this Protocol, when committed wilfully, in violation of the relevant provisions of this Protocol, and causing death or serious injury to body or health:

(a) making the civilian population or individual civilians the object of attack;

(b) launching an indiscriminate attack affecting the civilian population or civilian objects in the knowledge that such attack will cause excessive loss of life, injury to civilians or damage to civilian objects, as defined in Article 57, paragraph 2(a)(iii);

(c) launching an attack against works or installations containing dangerous forces in the knowledge that such attack will cause excessive loss of life, injury to civilians or damage to civilian objects, as defined in Article 57, paragraph 2(a)(iii);

(d) making non-defended localities and demilitarized zones the object of attack;

(e) making a person the object of attack in the knowledge that he is *hors de combat*;

(f) the perfidious use, in violation of Article 37, of the distinctive emblem of the red cross, red crescent or red lion and sun or of other protective signs recognized by the Convention or this Protocol.

4. In addition to the grave breaches defined in the preceding paragraphs and in the Conventions, the following shall be regarded as grave breaches of this Protocol, when committed wilfully and in violation of the Conventions or the Protocol:

(a) the transfer by the occupying Power of parts of its own civilian population into the territory it occupies, or the deportation or transfer of all or parts of the population of the occupied territory within or outside this territory, in violation of Article 49 of the Fourth Convention;

(b) unjustifiable delay in the repatriation of prisoners of war or civilians;

(c) practices of apartheid and other inhuman and degrading practices involving outrages upon personal dignity, based on racial discrimination;

(d) making the clearly-recognized historic monuments, works of art or places of worship which constitute the cultural or spiritual heritage of peoples and to which special protection has been given by special arrangement, for example, within the framework of a competent international organization, the object of attack, causing as a result extensive destruction thereof, where there is no evidence of the violation by the adverse Party of Article 53, subparagraph (b), and when such historic monuments, works of art and places of worship are not located in the immediate proximity of military objectives;

(e) depriving a person protected by the Conventions or referred to in paragraph 2 of this article of the rights of fair and regular trial.

5. Without prejudice to the application of the Conventions and of this Protocol, grave breaches of these instruments shall be regarded as war crimes.

Article 86

Failure to act

1. The High Contracting Parties and the Parties to the conflict shall repress grave breaches, and take measures necessary to suppress all other breaches, of the Conventions or of this Protocol which result from a failure to act when under a duty to do so.

2. The fact that a breach of the Conventions or of this Protocol was committed by a subordinate does not absolve his superiors from penal disciplinary responsibility, as the case may be, if they knew, or had information which should have enabled them to conclude in the circumstances at the time, that he was committing or was going to commit such a breach and if they did not take all feasible measures within their power to prevent or repress the breach.

Article 87

Duty of commanders

1. The High Contracting Parties and the Parties to the conflict shall require military commanders, with respect to members of the armed forces under their command and other persons under their control, to prevent and, where necessary, to suppress and to report to competent authorities breaches of the Conventions and of this Protocol.

2. In order to prevent and suppress breaches, High Contracting Parties and Parties to the conflict shall require that, commensurate with their level of responsibility, commanders ensure that members of the armed forces under their command are aware of their obligations under the Conventions and this Protocol.

3. The High Contracting Parties and Parties to the conflict shall require any commander who is aware that subordinates or other persons under his control are going to commit or have committed a breach of the Conventions or of this Protocol, to initiate such steps as are necessary to prevent such violations of the Conventions or this Protocol, and, where appropriate, to initiate disciplinary or penal action against violators thereof.

Article 88

Mutual assistance in criminal matters

1. The High Contracting Parties shall afford one another the greatest measure of assistance in connection with criminal proceedings brought in respect of grave breaches of the Convention or of this Protocol.

2. Subject to the rights and obligations established in the Conventions and in Article 85, paragraph 1 of this Protocol, and when circumstances permit, the High Contracting Parties shall co-operate in the matter of extradition. They shall give due consideration to the request of the State in whose territory the alleged offence has occurred.

3. The law of the High Contracting Party requested shall apply in all cases. the provisions of the preceding paragraphs shall not, however, affect the obligations arising from the provisions of any other treaty of a bilateral or multilateral nature which governs or will govern the whole or part of the subject of mutual assistance in criminal matters.

Article 89

Co-operation

In situations of serious violation of the Conventions or of this Protocol, the High Contracting Parties undertake to act jointly or individually, in co-operation with the United Nations and in conformity with the United Nations Charter.

Article 90

International Fact-Finding Commission

1. (a) An International Fact-Finding Commission ... consisting of 15 members of high moral standing and acknowledged impartiality shall be established;

(b) When not less than 20 High Contracting Parties have agreed to accept the competence of the Commission....

Article 91

Responsibility

A Party to the conflict which violates the provisions of the Conventions or this Protocol shall, if the case demands, be liable to pay compensation. It shall be responsible for all acts committed by persons forming part of its armed forces.

Protocol Additional to the Geneva Conventions of 12 August 1949, and relating to the protection of victims of non-international armed conflicts (Protocol II), 8 June 1977

PREAMBLE

The High Contracting Parties,

Recalling that the humanitarian principles enshrined in Article 3 common to the Geneva Conventions of 12 August 1949, constitute the foundation of respect for the human person in cases of armed conflict not of an international character,

Recalling furthermore that international instruments relating to human rights offer a basic protection to the human person,

Emphasizing the need to ensure a better protection for the victims of those armed conflicts,

Recalling that, in cases not covered by the law in force, the human person remains under the protection of the principles of humanity and the dictates of the public conscience,

Have agreed on the following:

Part I. Scope of this Protocol

Article 1—Material field of application

1. This Protocol, which develops and supplements Article 3 common to the Geneva Conventions of 12 August 1949 without modifying its existing conditions of application, shall apply to all armed conflicts which are not covered by Article 1 of ... Protocol I and which take place in the territory of a High Contracting Party between its armed forces and dissident armed forces or other organized armed groups which, under responsible command, exercise such control over a part of its territory as to enable them to carry out sustained and concerted military operations and to implement this Protocol.

2. This Protocol shall not apply to situations of internal disturbances and tensions, such as riots, isolated and sporadic acts of violence and other acts of a similar nature, as not being armed conflicts.

Article 2—Personal field of application

1. This Protocol shall be applied without any adverse distinction founded on race, colour, sex, language, religion or belief, political or other opinion, national or social origin, wealth, birth or other status, or on any other similar criteria (hereinafter referred to as "adverse distinction") to all persons affected by an armed conflict as defined in Article 1.

2. At the end of the armed conflict, all the persons who have been deprived of their liberty or whose liberty has been restricted for reasons related to such conflict, as well as those deprived of their liberty or whose liberty is restricted after the conflict for the same reasons, shall enjoy the protection of Articles 5 and 6 until the end of such deprivation or restriction of liberty.

Article 3—Non-intervention

1. Nothing in this Protocol shall be invoked for the purpose of affecting the sovereignty of a State or the responsibility of the government, by all legitimate means, to maintain or re-establish law and order in the State or to defend the national unity and territorial integrity of the State.

2. Nothing in this Protocol shall be invoked as a justification for intervening, directly or indirectly, for any reason whatever, in the armed conflict or in the internal or external affairs of the High Contracting Party in the territory of which that conflict occurs.

Part II. Human Treatment

Article 4—Fundamental guarantees

1. All persons who do not take a direct part or who have ceased to take part in hostilities, whether or not their liberty has been restricted, are entitled to respect for their person, honour and convictions and religious practices. They shall in all circumstances be treated humanely, without any adverse distinction. It is prohibited to order that there shall be no survivors.

2. Without prejudice to the generality of the foregoing, the following acts against the persons referred to in paragraph 1 are and shall remain prohibited at any time and in any place whatsoever:

(a) violence to the life, health and physical or mental well-being of persons, in particular murder as well as cruel treatment such as torture, mutilation or any form of corporal punishment;

(b) collective punishments;

(c) taking of hostages;

(d) acts of terrorism;

(e) outrages upon personal dignity, in particular humiliating and degrading treatment, rape, enforced prostitution and any form of indecent assault;

(f) slavery and the slave trade in all their forms;

(g) pillage;

(h) threats to commit any of the foregoing acts.

3. Children shall be provided with the care and aid they require, and in particular:

(a) they shall receive an education, including religious and moral education, in keeping with the wishes of their parents, or in the absence of parents, of those responsible for their care;

(b) all appropriate steps shall be taken to facilitate the reunion of families temporarily separated;

(c) children who have not attained the age of fifteen years shall neither be recruited in the armed forces or groups nor allowed to take part in hostilities;

(d) the special protection provided by this article to children who have not attained the age of fifteen years shall remain applicable to them if they take a direct part in hostilities despite the provisions of subparagraph (c) and are captured;

(e) measures shall be taken, if necessary, and whenever possible with the consent of their parents or persons who by law or custom are primarily responsible for their care, to remove children temporarily from the area in which hostilities are taking place to a safer area within the country and ensure that they are accompanied by persons responsible for their safety and well-being.

Article 5—Persons whose liberty has been restricted

1. In addition to the provisions of Article 4 the following provisions shall be respected as a minimum with regard to persons deprived of their liberty for reasons related to the armed conflict, whether they are interned or detained:

(a) the wounded and the sick shall be treated in accordance with Article 7;

(b) the persons referred to in this paragraph shall, to the same extent as the local civilian population, be provided with food and drinking water and be afforded safeguards as regards health and hygiene and protection against the rigours of the climate and the dangers of the armed conflict;

(c) they shall be allowed to receive individual or collective relief;

(d) they shall be allowed to practise their religion and, if requested and appropriate, to receive spiritual assistance from persons, such as chaplains, performing religious functions;

(e) they shall, if made to work, have the benefit of working conditions and safeguards similar to those enjoyed by the local civilian population.

2. Those who are responsible for the internment or detention of the persons referred to in paragraph 1 shall also, within the limits of their capabilities, respect the following provisions relating to such persons:

(a) except when men and women of a family are accommodated together, women shall be held in quarters separated from those of men and shall be under the immediate supervision of women;

(b) they shall be allowed to send and receive letters and cards, the number of which may be limited by competent authority if it deems necessary;

(c) places of internment and detention shall not be located close to the combat zone. The persons referred to in paragraph 1 shall be evacuated when the places where they are interned or detained become particularly exposed to danger arising out of the armed conflict, if their evacuation can be carried out under adequate conditions of safety;

(d) they shall have the benefit of medical examinations;

(e) their physical or mental health and integrity shall not be endangered by any unjustified act or omission. Accordingly, it is prohibited to subject the persons described in this article to any medical procedure which is not indicated by the state of health of the person concerned, and which is not consistent with the generally accepted medical standards applied to free persons under similar medical circumstances.

3. Persons who are not covered by paragraph 1 but whose liberty has been restricted in any way whatsoever for reasons related to the armed conflict shall be treated humanely in accordance with Article 4 and with paragraph 1 (a), (c) and (d), and 2 (b) of this article.

4. If it is decided to release persons deprived of their liberty, necessary measures to ensure their safety shall be taken by those so deciding.

Article 6—Penal prosecutions

1. This article applies to the prosecution and punishment of criminal offences related to the armed conflict.

2. No sentence shall be passed and no penalty executed on a person found guilty of an offence except pursuant to a conviction pronounced by a court offering the essential guarantees of independence and impartiality. In particular:

> (a) the procedure shall provide for an accused to be informed without delay of the particulars of the offence alleged against him and shall afford the accused before and during his trial all necessary rights and means of defence;

> (b) no one shall be convicted of an offence except on the basis of individual penal responsibility;

> (c) no one shall be held guilty of any criminal offence on account of any act or omission which did not constitute a criminal offence, under the law, at the time when it was committed; nor shall a heavier penalty be imposed than that which was applicable at the time when the criminal offence was committed; if, after the commission of the offence, provision is made by law for the imposition of a lighter penalty, the offender shall benefit thereby;

(d) anyone charged with an offence is presumed innocent until proved guilty according to law;

> (e) anyone charged with an offence shall have the right to be tried in his presence;

> (f) no one shall be compelled to testify against himself or confess guilt.

3. A convicted person shall be advised on conviction of his judicial and other remedies and of the time-limits within which they maybe exercised.

4. The death penalty shall not be pronounced on persons who were under the age of eighteen years at the time of the offence and shall not be carried out on pregnant women or mothers of young children.

5. At the end of hostilities, the authorities in power shall endeavour to grant the broadest possible amnesty to persons who have participated in the armed conflict, or those deprived of their liberty for reasons related to the armed conflict, weather they are interned or detained.

Part III. Wounded, Sick and Shipwrecked

Article 7—Protection and care

1. All the wounded, sick and shipwrecked, whether or not they have taken part in the armed conflict, shall be respected and protected.

2. In all circumstances they shall be treated humanely and shall receive to the fullest extent practicable and with the least possible delay, the medical care and attention required by their condition. There shall be no distinction among them founded on any grounds other than medical ones.

Article 8—Search

Whenever circumstances permit and particularly after an engagement, all possible measures shall be taken, without delay, to search for and collect the wounded, sick and shipwrecked, to protect them against pillage and ill-treatment, to ensure their adequate care, and to search for the dead, prevent their being despoiled, and decently dispose of them.

Article 9—Protection of medical and religious personnel

1. Medical and religious personnel shall be respected and protected and shall be granted all available help for the performance of their duties. They shall not be compelled to carry out tasks which are not compatible with their humanitarian mission.

2. In the performance of their duties medical personnel may not be required to give priority to any person except on medical grounds.

Article 10—General protection of medical duties

1. Under no circumstances shall any person be punished for having carried out medical activities compatible with medical ethics, regardless of the person benefitting therefrom.

2. Persons engaged in medical activities shall neither be compelled to perform acts or to carry out work contrary to, nor be compelled to refrain from acts required by, the rules of medical ethics or other rules designed for the benefit of the wounded and sick, or this Protocol.

3. The professional obligations of persons engaged in medical activities regarding information which they may acquire concerning the wounded and sick under their care shall, subject to national law, be respected.

4. Subject to national law, no person engaged in medical activities may be penalized in any way for refusing or failing to give information concerning the wounded and sick who are, or who have been, under his care.

Article 11—Protection of medical units and transports

1. Medical unites and transports shall be respected and protected at all times and shall not be the object of attack.

2. The protection to which medical units and transport are entitled shall not cease unless they are used to commit hostile acts, outside their humanitarian function. Protection may, however, cease only after a warning has been given setting, whenever appropriate, a reasonable time-limit, and after such warning has remained unheeded.

Article 12—The distinctive emblem

Under the direction of the competent authority concerned, the distinctive emblem of the red cross, red crescent or red lion and sun on a white ground shall be displayed by medical and religious personnel and medical units, and on medical transports. It shall be respected in all circumstances. It shall not be used improperly.

Part IV. Civilian Population

Article 13—Protection of the civilian population

1. The civilian population and individual civilians shall enjoy general protection against the dangers arising from military operations. To give effect to this protection, the following rules shall be observed in all circumstances.

2. The civilian population as such, as well as individual civilians, shall not be the object of attack. Acts or threats of violence the primary purpose of which is to spread terror among the civilian population are prohibited.

3. Civilians shall enjoy the protection afforded by this part, unless and for such time as they take a direct part in hostilities.

Article 14—Protection of objects indispensable to the survival of the civilian population

Starvation of civilians as a method of combat is prohibited. It is therefore prohibited to attack, destroy, remove or render useless, for that purpose, objects indispensable to the survival of the civilian population such as food-stuffs, agricultural areas for the production of food-stuffs, crops, livestock, drinking water installations and supplies and irrigation works.

Article 15—Protection of works and installations containing dangerous forces

Works or installations containing dangerous forces, namely dams, dykes and nuclear electrical generating stations, shall not be made the object of attack, even where these objects are military objectives, if such attack may cause the release of dangerous forces and consequent severe losses among the civilian population.

Article 16—Protection of cultural objects

Without prejudice to the provisions of the Hague Convention for the Protection of Cultural Property in the Event of Armed Conflict of 14 May 1954, it is prohibited to commit any acts of hostility directed against historic monuments, works of art or places of worship which constitute the cultural or spiritual heritage of peoples, and to use them in support of the military effort.

Article 17—Prohibition of forced movement of civilians

1. The displacement of the civilian population shall not be ordered for reasons related to the conflict unless the security of the civilians involved or imperative military reasons so demand. Should such displacements have to be carried out, all possible measures shall be taken in order that the civilian population may be received under satisfactory conditions of shelter, hygiene, health, safety and nutrition.

2. Civilians shall not be compelled to leave their own territory for reasons connected with the conflict.

Article 18—Relief societies and relief actions

1. Relief societies located in the territory of the High Contracting Party such as Red Cross (Red Crescent, Red Lion and Sun) organizations may offer their services for the

performance of their traditional functions in relation to the victims of the armed conflict. The civilian population may, even on its own initiative, offer to collect and care for the wounded, sick and shipwrecked.

2. If the civilian population is suffering undue hardship owing to a lack of the supplies essential for its survival, such as food-stuffs and medical supplies, relief actions for the civilian population which are of an exclusively humanitarian and impartial nature and which are conducted without any adverse distinction shall be undertaken subject to the consent of the High Contracting Party concerned.

Part V. Final Provisions

Article 19—Dissemination

This Protocol shall be disseminated as widely as possible.

Article 20—Signature

This Protocol shall be open for signature by the Parties to the Conventions six months after the signing of the Final Act and will remain open for a period of twelve months.

Article 21—Ratification

This Protocol shall be ratified as soon as possible. The instruments of ratification shall be deposited with the Swiss Federal Council, depository of the Conventions.

Article 22—Accession

This Protocol shall be open for accession by any Party to the Conventions which has not signed it. The instruments of accession shall be deposited with the depositary.

Article 28—Authentic texts

The original of this Protocol, of which the Arabic, Chinese, English, French, Russian and Spanish texts are equally authentic shall be deposited with the depository, which shall transmit certified true copies thereof to all the Parties to the Conventions.

Charter of the International Military Tribunal at Nuremberg, Annex to the London Agreement (8 Aug. 1945), 82 U.N.T.S. 279

I. Constitution of the International Military Tribunal

Article 1

In pursuance of the Agreement signed on the 8th day of August 1945 by the Government of the United States of America, the Provisional Government of the French Republic, the Government of the United Kingdom of Great Britain and Northern Ireland and the Government of the Union of Soviet Socialist Republics, there shall be established an International Military Tribunal (hereinafter called "the Tribunal") for the just and prompt trial and punishment of the major war criminals of the European Axis.

Article 2

The Tribunal shall consist of four members, each with an alternate. One member and one alternate shall be appointed by each of the Signatories. The alternates shall, so far as they are able, be present at all sessions of the Tribunal. In case of illness of any member of the Tribunal or his incapacity for some other reason to fulfill his functions, his alternate shall take his place.

Article 3

Neither the Tribunal, its members nor their alternates can be challenged by the prosecution, or by the Defendants or their Counsel. Each Signatory may replace its member of the Tribunal or his alternate for reasons of health or for other good reasons, except that no replacement may take place during a Trial, other than by an alternate.

Article 4

(a) The presence of all four members of the Tribunal or the alternate for any absent member shall be necessary to constitute the quorum.

(b) The members of the Tribunal shall, before any trial begins, agree among themselves upon the selection from their number of a President, and the President shall hold office during that trial, or as may otherwise be agreed by a vote of not less than three members. The principle of rotation or presidency for successive trials is agreed. If, however, a session of the Tribunal takes place on the territory of one of the four Signatories, the representative of that Signatory on the Tribunal shall preside.

(c) Save as aforesaid the Tribunal shall take decisions by a majority vote and in case the votes are evenly divided, the vote of the President shall be decisive: provided always that convictions and sentences shall only be imposed by affirmative votes of at least three members of the Tribunal.

Article 5

In case of need and depending on the number of the matters to be tried, other Tribunals may be set up; and the establishment, functions, and procedure of each Tribunal shall be identical, and shall be governed by this Charter.

II. Jurisdiction and General Principles

Article 6

The Tribunal established by the Agreement referred to in Article 1 hereof for the trial and punishment of the major war criminals of the European Axis countries shall have the power to try and punish persons who, acting in the interests of the European Axis countries, whether as individuals or as members of organizations, committed any of the following crimes.

The following acts, or any of them, are crimes coming within the jurisdiction of the Tribunal for which there shall be individual responsibility:

(a) *Crimes against peace*: namely, planning, preparation, initiation or waging of a war of aggression, or a war in violation of international treaties, agreements or assurances, or participation in a common plan or conspiracy for the accomplishment of any of the foregoing;

(b) *War crimes*: namely, violations of the laws or customs of war. Such violations shall include, but not be limited to, murder, ill-treatment or deportation to slave labour or for any other purpose of civilian population of or in occupied territory, murder or ill-treatment of prisoners of war or persons on the seas, killing of hostages, plunder of public or private property, wanton destruction of cities, towns or villages, or devastation not justified by military necessity;

(c) *Crimes against humanity*: namely, murder, extermination, enslavement, deportation, and other inhuman acts committed against any civilian population, before or during the war; or persecutions on political, racial or religious grounds in execution of or in connection with any crime within the jurisdiction of the Tribunal, whether or not in violation of the domestic law of the country where perpetrated.

Leaders, organizers, instigators and accomplices participating in the formulation or execution of a common plan or conspiracy to commit any of the foregoing crimes are responsible for all acts performed by any persons in execution of such plan.

Article 7

The official position of defendants, whether as Heads of State or responsible officials in Government Departments, shall not be considered as freeing them from responsibility or mitigating punishment.

Article 8

The fact that the Defendant acted pursuant to order of his Government or of a superior shall not free him from responsibility, but may be considered in mitigation of punishment if the Tribunal determines that justice so requires.

Article 9

At the trial of any individual member of any group or organization the Tribunal may declare (in connection with any act of which the individual may be convicted) that the group or organization of which the individual was a member was a criminal organization.

After receipt of the Indictment the Tribunal shall give notice as it thinks fit that the prosecution intends to ask the Tribunal to make such declaration and any member of the organization will be entitled to apply to the Tribunal for leave to be heard by the Tribunal upon the question of the criminal character of the organization. The Tribunal shall have the power to allow or reject the application. If the application is allowed, the Tribunal may direct in what manner the applicants shall be represented and heard.

Article 10

In cases where a group or organization is declared criminal by the Tribunal, the competent national authority of any Signatory shall have the right to bring individuals to trial for membership therein before national, military or occupation courts. In any such case the criminal nature of the group or organization is considered proved and shall not be questioned.

Article 11

Any person convicted by the Tribunal may be charged before a national, military or occupation court, referred to in Article 10 of this Charter, with a crime other than of membership in a criminal group or organization and such court may, after convicting him, impose upon him punishment independent of and additional to the punishment imposed by the Tribunal for participation in the criminal activities of such group or organization.

Article 12

The Tribunal shall have the right to take proceedings against a person charged with crimes set out in Article 6 of this Charter in his absence, if he has not been found or if the Tribunal, for any reason, finds it necessary, in the interests of justice, to conduct the hearing in his absence.

Article 13

The Tribunal shall draw up rules for its procedure. These rules shall not be inconsistent with the provisions of this Charter.

Article 14

Each Signatory shall appoint a Chief Prosecutor for the investigation of charges against and the prosecution of major war criminals.

The Chief Prosecutors shall act as a committee for the following purposes:

(a) to agree upon a plan of the individual work of each of the Chief Prosecutors and his staff,

(b) to settle the final designation of major war criminals to be tried by the Tribunal,

(c) to approve the Indictment and the documents to be submitted therewith,

(d) to lodge the Indictment and the accompanying documents with the Tribunal,

(e) to draw up and recommend to the Tribunal for its approval draft rules of procedure, contemplated by Article 13 of this Charter. The Tribunal shall have the power to accept, with or without amendments, or to reject, the rules so recommended.

The Committee shall act in all the above matters by a majority vote and shall appoint a Chairman as may be convenient and in accordance with the principle of rotation: provided that if there is an equal division of vote concerning the designation of a Defendant to be tried by the Tribunal, or the crimes with which he shall be charged, that proposal will be adopted which was made by the party which proposed that the particular Defendant be tried, or the particular charges be preferred against him.

Article 15

The Chief Prosecutors shall, individually, and acting in collaboration with one another, also undertake the following duties:

(a) investigation, collection and production before or at the Trial of all necessary evidence,

(b) the preparation of the Indictment for approval by the Committee in accordance with paragraph (c) of Article 14 hereof,

(c) the preliminary examination of all necessary witnesses and of the Defendants,

(d) to act as prosecutor at the Trial,

(e) to appoint representatives to carry out such duties as may be assigned to them,

(f) to undertake such other matters as may appear necessary to them for the purposes of the preparation for and conduct of the Trial.

It is understood that no witness or Defendant detained in any Signatory shall be taken out of the possession of that Signatory without its assent.

IV. Fair Trial for Defendants

Article 16

In order to ensure fair trial for the Defendants, the following procedures shall be followed:

(a) The Indictment shall include full particulars specifying in detail the charges against the Defendants. A copy of the Indictment and of all the documents lodged with the Indictment, translated into a language which he understands, shall be furnished to the Defendant as a reasonable time before the Trial.

(b) During any preliminary examination or trial of a Defendant he shall have the right to give any explanation relevant to the charges made against him.

(c) A preliminary examination of a Defendant and his Trial shall be conducted in, or translated into, a language which the Defendant understands.

(d) A defendant shall have the right to conduct his own defense before the Tribunal or to have the assistance of Counsel.

(e) A defendant shall have the right through himself or through his Counsel to present evidence at the Trial in support of his defense, and to cross-examine any witness called by the Prosecution.

V. Powers of the Tribunal and Conduct of the Trial

Article 17

The Tribunal shall have the power:

(a) to summon witnesses to the Trial and to require their attendance and testimony and to put questions to them,

(b) to interrogate any Defendant,

(c) to require the production of documents and other evidentiary material,

(d) to administer oaths to witnesses,

(e) to appoint officers for the carrying out of any task designated by the Tribunal including the power to have evidence taken on commission.

Article 18

The Tribunal shall:

(a) confine Trial strictly to an expeditious hearing of the issues raised by the charges,

(b) take strict measures to prevent any action which will cause unreasonable delay, and rule out irrelevant issues and statements of any kind whatsoever,

(c) deal summarily with any contumacy, imposing appropriate punishment, including exclusion of any Defendant or his Counsel from some or all further proceedings, but without prejudice to the determination of the charges.

Article 19

The Tribunal shall not be bound by technical rules of evidence. It shall adopt and apply to the greatest possible extent expeditious and non-technical procedure, and shall admit any evidence which it deems to have probative value.

Article 20

The Tribunal may require to be informed of the nature of any evidence before it is offered so that it may rule upon the relevance thereof.

Article 21

The Tribunal shall not require proof of facts of common knowledge but shall take judicial notice thereof. It shall also take judicial notice of official governmental documents and reports of the United Nations, including the acts and documents of the committees set up in the various Allied countries for the investigation of war crimes, and the records and findings of military or other Tribunals of any of the United Nations.

Article 22

The permanent seat of the Tribunal shall be in Berlin. The first meetings of the members of the Tribunal and of the Chief Prosecutors shall be held at Berlin in a place to be designated by the Control Council for Germany. The first trial shall be held at Nuremberg, and any subsequent trials shall be held at such places as the Tribunal may decide.

Article 23

One or more of the Chief Prosecutors may take part in the prosecution at each Trial. The function of any Chief Prosecutor may be discharged by him personally, or by any person or persons authorised by him.

The function of ... [Counsel] for a Defendant may be discharged at the Defendant's request by any Counsel professionally qualified to conduct cases before the Courts of his own country, or by any other person who may be specially authorised thereto by the Tribunal.

Article 24

The proceedings at the Trial shall take the following course:

(a) The Indictment shall be read in court.

(b) The Tribunal shall ask each Defendant whether he pleads "guilty" or "not guilty".

(c) The Prosecution shall make an opening statement.

(d) The Tribunal shall ask the Prosecution and the Defence what evidence (if any) they wish to submit to the Tribunal, and the Tribunal shall rule upon the admissibility of any such evidence.

(e) The witnesses for the Prosecution shall be examined and after that the witnesses for the Defence. Thereafter such rebutting evidence as may be held by the Tribunal to be admissible shall be called by either the Prosecution or the Defence.

(f) The Tribunal may put any question to any witness and to any Defendant, at any time.

(g) The Prosecution and the Defence shall interrogate and may cross-examine any witness and any Defendant who gives testimony.

(h) Defence shall address the court.

(i) The Prosecution shall address the court.

(j) Each Defendant may make a statement to the Tribunal.

(k) The Tribunal shall deliver judgment and pronounce sentence.

Article 25

All official documents shall be produced, and all court proceedings conducted, in English, French and Russian, and in the language of the Defendant. So much of the record and of the proceedings may also be translated into the language of any country in which the Tribunal is sitting, as the Tribunal considers desirable in the interests of justice and public opinion.

VI. Judgment and Sentence

Article 26

The judgment of the Tribunal as to the guilt or the innocence of any Defendant shall give the reasons on which it is based, and shall be final and not subject to review.

Article 27

The Tribunal shall have the right to impose upon a Defendant, on conviction, death or such other punishment as shall be determined by it to be just.

Article 28

In addition to any punishment imposed by it, the Tribunal shall have the right to deprive the convicted person of any stolen property and order its delivery to the Control Council for Germany.

Article 29

In case of guilt, sentences shall be carried out in accordance with the orders of the Control Council for Germany, which may at any time reduce or otherwise alter the sentences, but may not increase the severity thereof. If the Control Council for Germany, after any defendant has been convicted and sentenced, discovers fresh evidence which, in its opinion, would found a fresh charge against him, the Council shall report accordingly to the Committee established under Article 14 hereof for such action as they may consider proper, having regard to the interests of justice.

VII. Expenses

Article 30

The expenses of the Tribunal and of the Trials shall be charged by the Signatories against the funds allotted for maintenance of the Control Council for Germany.

Tokyo Charter for the International Military Tribunal for the Far East (1946), as amended by General Orders No. 20 (26 April 1946), T.I.A.S. No. 1589

Section I. Constitution of Tribunal

Article 1

Tribunal Established. The International Tribunal for the Far East is hereby established for the just and prompt trial and punishment of the major war criminals in the Far East. The permanent seat of the Tribunal is in Tokyo.

Article 2

Members. The Tribunal shall consist of not less than five nor more than nine Members, appointed by the Supreme Commander for the Allied Powers from the names submitted by the Signatories to the Instrument of Surrender, India, and the Commonwealth of the Philippines.

Article 3

Offices and Secretariat.

a. *President*. The Supreme Commander for the Allied Powers shall appoint a Member to be President of the Tribunal.

b. *Secretariat*.

(1) The Secretariat of the Tribunal shall be composed of a General Secretary to be appointed by the Supreme Commander for the Allied Powers and such assistant secretaries, clerks, interpreters, and other personnel as may be necessary.

(2) The General Secretary shall organize and direct the work of the Secretariat.

(3) The Secretariat shall receive all documents addressed to the Tribunal, maintain the records of the Tribunal, provide necessary clerical services to the Tribunal and its members, and perform such other duties as may be designated by the Tribunal.

Article 4

Convening and Quorum, Voting, and Absence.

a. *Convening and Quorum.* When as many as six members of the Tribunal are present, they may convene the Tribunal in formal session. The presence of a majority of all members shall be necessary to constitute a quorum.

b. *Voting.* All decisions and judgments of this Tribunal, including convictions and sentences, shall be by a majority vote of those members of the Tribunal present. In case the votes are evenly divided, the vote of the President shall be decisive.

c. *Absence.* If a member at any time is absent and afterwards is able to be present, he shall take part in all subsequent proceedings; unless he declares in open court that he is disqualified by reason of insufficient familiarity with the proceedings which took place in his absence.

Section II. Jurisdiction and General Provisions

Article 5

Jurisdiction Over Persons and Offenses. The Tribunal shall have the power to try and punish Far Eastern war criminals who as individuals or as members of organizations are charged with offenses which include Crimes against Peace. The following acts, or any of them, are crimes coming within the jurisdiction of the Tribunal for which there shall be individual responsibility:

a. *Crimes against Peace*: Namely, the planning, preparation, initiation or waging of a declared or undeclared war of aggression, or a war in violation of international law, treaties, agreements or assurances, or participation in a common plan or conspiracy for the accomplishment of any of the foregoing;

b. *Conventional War Crimes*: Namely, violations of the laws or customs of war;

c. *Crimes against Humanity*: Namely, murder, extermination, enslavement, deportation, and other inhumane acts committed before or during the war, or persecutions on political or racial grounds in execution of or in connection with any crime within the jurisdiction of the Tribunal, whether or not in violation of the domestic law of the country where perpetrated.

Leaders, organizers, instigators and accomplices participating in the formulation or execution of a common plan or conspiracy to commit any of the foregoing crimes are responsible for all acts performed by any person in execution of such plan.

Article 6

Responsibility of Accused. Neither the official position, at any time, of an accused, nor the fact that an accused acted pursuant to order of his government or of a superior shall, of itself, be sufficient to free such accused from responsibility for any crime with which he is charged, but such circumstances may be considered in mitigation of punishment if the Tribunal determines that justice so requires.

Article 7

Rules of Procedure. The Tribunal may draft and amend rules of procedure consistent with the fundamental provisions of this Charter.

Article 8

Counsel.

a. *Chief Counsel.* The Chief of Counsel designated by the Supreme Commander for the Allied Powers is responsible for the investigation and prosecution of charges against war criminals within the jurisdiction of this Tribunal and will render such legal assistance to the Supreme Commander as is appropriate.

b. *Associate Counsel.* Any United Nation with which Japan has been at war may appoint an Associate Counsel to assist the Chief of Counsel.

Section III. Fair Trial for Accused

Article 9

Procedure for Fair Trial. In order to insure fair trial for the accused, the following procedure shall be followed:

a. *Indictment.* The indictment shall consist of a plain, concise and adequate statement of each offense charged. Each accused shall be furnished in adequate time for defense a copy of the indictment, including any amendment, and of this Charter, in a language understood by the accused.

b. *Language.* The trial and related proceedings shall be conducted in English and in the language of the accused. Translations of documents and other papers shall be provided as needed and requested.

c. *Counsel for Accused.* Each accused shall have the right to be represented by counsel of his own selection, subject to the disapproval of such counsel at any time by the Tribunal. The accused shall file with the General Secretary of the Tribunal the name of his counsel. If an accused is not represented by counsel and in open court requests the appointment of counsel, the Tribunal shall designate counsel for him. In the absence of such request the Tribunal may appoint counsel for an accused if in its judgment such appointment is necessary to provide a fair trial.

d. *Evidence for Defense.* An accused shall have the right, through himself or through his counsel (but not through both), to conduct his defense, including the right to examine any witness, subject to reasonable restrictions as the Tribunal may determine.

e. *Production of Evidence for the Defense.* An accused may apply in writing to the Tribunal for the production of witnesses or of documents. The application shall state where the witness or document is thought to be located. It shall also state the facts proposed to be proved by the witness or the document and the relevancy of such facts to the defense. If the Tribunal grants the application the Tribunal shall be given such aid in obtaining production of the evidence as the circumstances require.

Article 10

Applications and Motions before Trial. All motions, applications, or other requests addressed to the Tribunal prior to the commencement of trial shall be made in writing and filed with the General Secretary of the Tribunal for action by the Tribunal.

Section IV. Powers of Tribunal and Conduct of Trial

Article 11

Powers. The Tribunal shall have the power:

a. To summon witnesses to the trial, to require them to attend and testify, and to question them.

b. To interrogate each accused and to permit comment on his refusal to answer any question.

c. To require the production of documents and other evidentiary material.

d. To require of each witness an oath, affirmation, or such declaration as is customary in the country of the witness, and to administer oaths.

e. To appoint officers for the carrying out of any task designated by the Tribunal, including the power to have evidence taken on commission.

Article 12

Conduct of Trial. The Tribunal shall:

a. Confine the trial strictly to an expeditious hearing of the issues raised by the charges.

b. Take strict measures to prevent any action which would cause any unreasonable delay and rule out irrelevant issues and statements of any kind whatsoever.

c. Provide for the maintenance of order at the trial and deal summarily with any contumacy, imposing appropriate punishment, including exclusion of any accused or his counsel from some or all further proceedings, but without prejudice to the determination of the charges.

d. Determine the mental and physical capacity of any accused to proceed to trial.

Article 13

Evidence.

a. *Admissibility.* The Tribunal shall not be bound by technical rules of evidence. It shall adopt and apply to the greatest possible extent expeditious and non-technical procedure, and shall admit any evidence which it deems to have probative value. All purported admissions or statements of the accused are admissible.

b. *Relevance.* The Tribunal may require to be informed of the nature of any evidence before it is offered in order to rule upon the relevance.

c. *Specific evidence admissible.* In particular, and without limiting in any way the scope of the foregoing general rules, the following evidence may be admitted:

(1) A document, regardless of its security classification and without proof of its issuance or signature, which appears to the Tribunal to have been signed or issued by any officer, department, agency or member of the armed forces of any government.

(2) A report which appears to the Tribunal to have been signed or issued by the International Red Cross or a member thereof, or by a doctor of medicine or any medical service personnel, or by an investigator or intelligence officer, of by

any other person who appears to the Tribunal to have personal knowledge of the matters contained in the report.

(3) An affidavit, deposition or other signed statement.

(4) A diary, letter or other document, including sworn or unsworn statements, which appear to the Tribunal to contain information relating to the charge.

(5) A copy of a document or other secondary evidence of its contents, if the original is not immediately available.

d. *Judicial Notice.* The Tribunal shall neither require proof of facts of common knowledge, nor of the authenticity of official government documents and reports of any nation or of the proceedings, records, and findings of military or other agencies of any of the United Nations.

e. *Records, Exhibits, and Documents.* The transcript of the proceedings, and exhibits and documents submitted to the Tribunal, will be filed with the General Secretary of the Tribunal and will constitute part of the Record.

Article 14

Place of Trial. The first trial will be held in Tokyo, and any subsequent trials will be held at such places as the Tribunal decides.

Article 15

Course of Trial Proceedings. The proceedings of the Trial will take the following course:

a. The indictment will be read in court unless reading is waived by all accused.

b. The Tribunal will ask each accused whether he pleads "guilty" or "not guilty."

c. The prosecution and each accused (by counsel only, if represented) may make a concise opening statement.

d. The prosecution and defense may offer evidence, and the admissibility of the same shall be determined by the Tribunal.

e. The prosecution and each accused (by counsel only, if represented) may examine each witness and each accused who gives testimony.

f. Accused (by counsel only, if represented) may address the Tribunal.

g. The prosecution may address the Tribunal.

h. The Tribunal will deliver judgment and pronounce sentence.

Section V. Judgment and Sentence

Article 16

Penalty. The Tribunal shall have the power to impose upon an accused, on conviction, death, or such other punishment as shall be determined by it to be just.

Article 17

Judgment and Review. The judgment will be announced in open court and will give the reasons on which it is based. The record of the trial will be transmitted directly to the Supreme Commander for the Allied Powers for his action. Sentence will be carried out in accordance with the Order of the Supreme Commander for the Allied Powers, who may at any time reduce or otherwise alter the sentence, except to increase its severity.

Allied Control Council Law No. 10 (20 Dec. 1945), Control Council for Germany, Official Gazette 50 (Jan. 31, 1946)

Punishment of Persons Guilty of War Crimes, Crimes Against Peace, and Crimes Against Humanity

In order to give effect to the terms of the Moscow Declaration of 30 October 1943 and the London Agreement of 8 August 1945, and the Charter issued pursuant thereto and in order to establish a uniform legal basis in Germany for the prosecution of war criminals and other similar offenders, other than those dealt with by the International Military Tribunal, the Control Council enacts as follows:

Article I

The Moscow Declaration of 30 October 1943 "Concerning Responsibility of Hitlerites for Committed Atrocities" and the London Agreement of 8 August 1945 "Concerning Prosecution and Punishment of Major War Criminals of the European Axis" are made integral parts of this Law. Adherence to the provisions of the London Agreement by any of the United Nations, as provided for in Article V of that Agreement, shall not entitle such Nation to participate or interfere in the operation of this Law within the Control Council area of authority in Germany.

Article II

1. Each of the following acts is recognized as a crime:

a) *Crimes against Peace.* Initiation of invasions of other countries and wars of aggression in violation of international laws and treaties, including but not limited to planning, preparation, initiation or waging a war of aggression, or a war ... [in] violation of international treaties, agreements or assurances, or participation in a common plan or conspiracy for the accomplishment of any of the foregoing

(b) *War Crimes.* Atrocities or offenses against persons or property constituting violations of the laws or customs of war, including, but not limited to, murder, ill treatment or deportation to slave labour or for any other purpose, of civilian population from occupied territory, murder or ill treatment of prisoners of war or persons on the seas, killing of hostages, plunder of public or private property, wanton destruction of cities, towns or villages, or devastation not justified by military necessity.

(c) *Crimes against Humanity.* Atrocities and offenses, including but not limited to murder, extermination, enslavement, deportation, imprisonment, torture, rape, or other inhumane acts committed against any civilian population, or persecutions on political, racial or religious grounds whether or not in violation of the domestic laws of the country where perpetrated.

(d) Membership in categories of a criminal group or organization declared criminal by the International Military Tribunal.

2. Any person without regard to nationality or the capacity in which he acted, is deemed to have committed a crime as defined in paragraph 1 of this article, if he was (a) a principal or (b) was an accessory to the commission of any such crime or ordered or abetted the same or (c) took a consenting part therein or (d) was connected with plans or enterprises involving its commission or (e) was a member of any organization or group connected with the commission of any such crime or (f) with reference to paragraph 1 (a) if he held a high political, civil or military (including General Staff) position in Germany or in one of its Allies, co-belligerents or satellites or held high position in financial, industrial or economic life of any such country.

3. Any person found guilty of any of the crimes above mentioned may upon conviction be punished as shall be determined by the tribunal to be just. Such punishment may consist of one or more of the following:

(a) Death.

(b) Imprisonment for life or a term of years, with or without hard labour.

(c) Fine, and imprisonment with or without hard labour, in lieu thereof.

(d) Forfeiture of property.

(e) Restitution of property wrongfully acquired.

(f) Deprivation of some or all civil rights.

Any property declared to be forfeited or the restitution of which is ordered by the Tribunal shall be delivered to the Control Council for Germany, which shall decide on its disposal.

4. (a) The official position of any person, whether as Head of State or as a responsible official in a Government Department, does not free him from responsibility for a crime or entitle him to mitigation of punishment.

(b) The fact that any person acted pursuant to the order of his Government or of a superior does not relieve him from responsibility for a crime, but may be considered in mitigation.

5. In any trial or prosecution for a crime herein referred to, the accused shall not be entitled to the benefits of any statute of limitation in respect of the period from 30 January 1933 to 1 July 1945, nor shall any immunity, pardon or amnesty granted under the Nazi regime be admitted as a bar to trial or punishment.

Article III

1. Each occupying authority, within its Zone of occupation,

(a) shall have the right to cause persons within such Zone suspected of having committed a crime, including those charged with crime by one of the United Nations, to be arrested and shall take under control the property, real and personal, owned or controlled by the said persons, pending decisions as to its eventual disposition.

(b) shall report to the Legal Directorate the names of all suspected criminals, the reasons for and the places of their detention, if they are detained, and the names and location of witnesses.

(c) shall take appropriate measures to see that witnesses and evidence will be available when required.

(d) shall have the right to cause all persons so arrested and charged, and not delivered to another authority as herein provided, or released, to be brought to trial before an appropriate tribunal. Such tribunal may, in the case of crimes committed by persons of German citizenship or nationality against other persons of German citizenship or nationality, or stateless persons, be a German Court, if authorized by the occupying authorities.

2. The tribunal by which persons charged with offenses hereunder shall be tried and the rules and procedure thereof shall be determined or designated by each Zone Commander for his respective Zone. Nothing herein is intended to, or shall impair or limit the jurisdiction or power of any court or tribunal now or hereafter established in any Zone by the Commander thereof, or of the International Military Tribunal established by the London Agreement of 8 August 1945.

3. Persons wanted for trial by an International Military Tribunal will not be tried without the consent of the Committee of Chief Prosecutors. Each Zone Commander will deliver such persons who are within his Zone to that committee upon request and will make witnesses and evidence available to it.

4. Persons known to be wanted for trial in another Zone or outside Germany will not be tried prior to decision under Article IV unless the fact of their apprehension has been reported in accordance with Section 1(b) of this Article, three months have elapsed thereafter, and no request for delivery of the type contemplated by Article IV has been received by the Zone Commander concerned.

5. The execution of death sentences may be deferred by not to exceed one month after the sentence has become final when the Zone Commander concerned has reason to believe that the testimony of those under sentence would be of value in the investigation and trial of crimes within or without his Zone.

6. Each Zone Commander will cause such effect to be given to the judgments of courts of competent jurisdiction, with respect to the property taken under his control pursuant thereto, as he may deem proper in the interest of justice.

Article IV

1. When any person in a Zone in Germany is alleged to have committed a crime, as defined in Article II, in a country other than Germany or in another Zone, the government of that nation or the Commander of the latter Zone, as the case may be, may request the Commander of the Zone in which the person is located for his arrest and delivery for trial to the country or Zone in which the crime was committed. Such request for delivery shall be granted by the Commander receiving it unless he believes such person is wanted for trial or as a witness by an International Military Tribunal, or in Germany, or in a nation other than the one making the request, or the Commander is not satisfied that delivery should be made, in any of which cases he shall have the right to forward the said request to the Legal Directorate of the Allied Control Authority. A similar procedure shall apply to witnesses, material exhibits and other forms of evidence.

2. The Legal Directorate shall consider all requests referred to it, and shall determine the same in accordance with the following principles, its determination to be communicated to the Zone Commander.

(a) A person wanted for trial or as witness by an International Military Tribunal shall not be delivered for trial or required to give evidence outside Germany, as the case may be, except upon approval by the Committee of Chief Prosecutors acting under the London Agreement of 8 August 1945.

(b) A person wanted for trial by several authorities (other than an International Military Tribunal) shall be disposed of in accordance with the following priorities:

(1) If wanted for trial in the Zone in which he is, he should not be delivered unless arrangements are made for his return after trial elsewhere;

(2) If wanted for trial in a Zone other than that in which he is, he should be delivered to that Zone in preference to delivery outside Germany unless arrangements are made for his return to that Zone after trial elsewhere;

(3) If wanted for trial outside Germany by two or more of the United Nations, of one of which he is a citizen, that one should have priority;

(4) If wanted for trial outside Germany by several countries, not all of which are United Nations, United Nations should have priority;

(5) If wanted for trial outside Germany by two or more of the United Nations, then, subject to Article IV 2 (b) (3) above, that which has the most serious charges against him, which are moreover supported by evidence, should have priority.

Article V

The delivery, under Article IV of this Law, of persons for trial shall be made on demands of the Governments or Zone Commanders in such a manner that the delivery of criminals to one jurisdiction will not become the means of defeating or unnecessarily delaying the carrying out of justice in another place. If within six months the delivered person has not been convicted by the Court of the zone or country to which he has been delivered, then such person shall be returned upon demand of the Commander of the Zone where the person was located prior to delivery.

Done at Berlin, 20 December 1945.

Principles of the Nuremberg Charter and Judgment, Formulated by the International Law Commission, 5 U.N. GAOR, Supp. No. 12, at 11–14, para. 99, U.N. Doc. A/1316 (1950)

I. Any person who commits an act which constitutes a crime under international law is responsible therefor and liable to punishment.

II. The fact that internal law does not impose a penalty for an act which constitutes a crime under international law does not relieve the person who committed the act from responsibility under international law.

III. The fact that a person who committed an act which constitutes a crime under international law acted as Head of State or responsible Government official does not relieve him from responsibility under international law.

IV. The fact that a person acted pursuant to order of his Government or of a superior does not relieve him from responsibility under international law, provided a moral choice was in fact possible to him..

V. Any person charge with a crime under international law has the right to a fair trial on the facts and law.

VI. The crimes hereinafter set out are punishable as crimes under international law:

a. Crimes against peace:

(i) Planning, preparation, initiation or waging of a war of aggression, or a war in violation of international treaties, agreements or assurances;

(ii) Participation in a common plan or conspiracy for the accomplishment of any of the acts mentioned under (i).

b. War crimes: Violation of the laws and customs of war which include, but are not limited to, murder, ill-treatment of prisoners of war or of persons on the seas, killing of hostages, plunder of public or private property, wanton destruction of cities, towns, or villages, or devastation not justified by military necessity.

c. Crimes against humanity: Murder, extermination, enslavement, deportation and other inhuman acts done against any civilian population, or persecution on political, racial or religious grounds, when such acts are done or such persecutions are carried on in execution of or in connection with any crime against peace or any war crime.

VII. Complicity in the commission of a crime against peace, a war crime, or a crime against humanity as set forth in Principle VI is a crime under international law.

Statute of the International Criminal Tribunal for Former Yugoslavia, U.N. S.C. Res. 827 (1993)

Article 1

Competence of the International Tribunal

The International Tribunal shall have the power to prosecute persons responsible for serious violations of international humanitarian law committed in the territory of the former Yugoslavia since 1991 in accordance with the provisions of the present Statute.

Article 2

Grave breaches of the Geneva Conventions of 1949

The International Tribunal shall have the power to prosecute persons committing or ordering to be committed grave breaches of the Geneva Conventions of 12 August 1949, namely the following acts against persons or property protected under the provisions of the relevant Geneva Convention:

(a)   wilful killing;

(b)   torture or inhuman treatment, including biological experiments;

(c)   wilfully causing great suffering or serious injury to body or health;

(d)   extensive destruction and appropriation of property, not justified by military necessity and carried out unlawfully and wantonly;

(e)   compelling a prisoner of war or a civilian to serve in the forces of a hostile power;

(f)   wilfully depriving a prisoner of war or a civilian of the rights of fair and regular trial;

(g)   unlawful deportation or transfer or unlawful confinement of a civilian;

(h)   taking civilians as hostages.

Article 3

Violations of the laws or customs of war

The International Tribunal shall have the power to prosecute persons violating the laws or customs of war. Such violations shall include, but not be limited to:

(a)   employment of poisonous weapons or other weapons calculated to cause unnecessary suffering;

(b)   wanton destruction of cities, towns or villages, or devastation not justified by military necessity;

(c)   attack, or bombardment, by whatever means, of undefended towns, villages, dwellings, or buildings;

(d)   seizure of, destruction or wilful damage done to institutions dedicated to religion, charity and education, the arts and sciences, historic monuments and works of art and science;

(e)   plunder of public or private property.

Article 4

Genocide

1. The International Tribunal shall have the power to prosecute persons committing genocide as defined in paragraph 2 of this article or of committing any of the other acts enumerated in paragraph 3 of this article.

2. Genocide means any of the following acts committed with intent to destroy, in whole or in part, a national, ethnical, racial or religious group, as such:

(a)   killing members of the group;

(b)   causing serious bodily or mental harm to members of the group

(c)   deliberately inflicting on the group conditions of life calculated to bring about its physical destruction in whole or in part;

(d)   imposing measures intended to prevent births within the group;

(e)forcibly transferring children of the group to another group.

3. The following acts shall be punishable:

(a)   genocide;

(b)   conspiracy to commit genocide;

(c)   direct and public incitement to commit genocide;

(d)   attempt to commit genocide;

(e)   complicity in genocide.

Article 5

Crimes against humanity

The International Tribunal shall have the power to prosecute persons responsible for the following crimes when committed in armed conflict, whether international or internal in character, and directed against any civilian population:

(a)   murder;

(b)   extermination;

(c)   enslavement;

(d)   deportation;

(e)   imprisonment;

(f)   torture;

(g)   rape;

(h)   persecutions on political, racial and religious grounds

(i)   other inhumane acts.

Article 6

Personal jurisdiction

The International Tribunal shall have jurisdiction over natural persons pursuant to the provisions of the present Statute.

Article 7

Individual criminal responsibility

1. A person who planned, instigated, ordered, committed or otherwise aided and abetted in the planning, preparation or execution of a crime referred to in articles 2 to 5 of the present Statute, shall be individually responsible for the crime.

2. The official position of any accused person, whether as Head of State or Government or as a responsible Government official, shall not relieve such person of criminal responsibility nor mitigate punishment.

3. The fact that any of the acts referred to in articles 2 to 5 of the present Statute was committed by a subordinate does not relieve his superior of criminal responsibility if he knew or had reason to know that the subordinate was about to commit such acts or had done so and the superior failed to take the necessary and reasonable measures to prevent such acts or to punish the perpetrators thereof.

4. The fact that an accused person acted pursuant to an order of a Government or of a superior shall not relieve him of criminal responsibility, but may be considered in mitigation of punishment if the International Tribunal determines that justice so requires.

Article 8

Territorial and temporal jurisdiction

The territorial jurisdiction of the International Tribunal shall extend to the territory of the former Socialist Federal Republic of Yugoslavia, including its land surface, airspace and territorial waters. The temporal jurisdiction of the International Tribunal shall extend to a period beginning on 1 January 1991.

Article 9

Concurrent jurisdiction

1. The International Tribunal and national courts shall have concurrent jurisdiction to prosecute persons for serious violations of international humanitarian law committed in the territory of the former Yugoslavia since 1 January 1991.

2. The International Tribunal shall have primacy over national courts. At any stage of the procedure, the International Tribunal may formally request national courts to defer to the competence of the International Tribunal in accordance with the present Statute and the Rules of Procedure and Evidence of the International Tribunal.

Article 10

Non-bis-in-idem

1. No person shall be tried before a national court for acts constituting serious violations of international humanitarian law under the present Statute, for which he or she has already been tried by the International Tribunal.

2. A person who has been tried by a national court for acts constituting serious violations of international humanitarian law may be subsequently tried by the International Tribunal only if:

(a)   the act for which he or she was tried was characterized as an ordinary crime; or

(b)   the national court proceedings were not impartial or independent, were designed to shield the accused from international criminal responsibility, or the case was not diligently prosecuted.

3. In considering the penalty to be imposed on a person convicted of a crime under the present Statute, the International Tribunal shall take into account the extent to which any penalty imposed by a national court on the same person for the same act has already been served.

Article 11

Organization of the International Tribunal

The International Tribunal shall consist of the following organs:

(a)   The Chambers, comprising two Trial Chambers and an Appeals Chamber;

(b)   The Prosecutor, and

(c)   A Registry, servicing both the Chambers and the Prosecutor.

Article 12

Composition of the Chambers

The Chambers shall be composed of eleven independent judges, no two of whom may be nationals of the same State, who shall serve as follows:

(a)   Three judges shall serve in each of the Trial Chambers;

(b)   Five judges shall serve in the Appeals Chamber.

Article 13

Qualifications and election of judges

1. The judges shall be persons of high moral character, impartiality and integrity who possess the qualifications required in their respective countries for appointment to the highest judicial offices. In the overall composition of the Chambers due account shall be

taken of the experience of the judges in criminal law, international law, including international humanitarian law and human rights law.

2. The judges of the International Tribunal shall be elected by the General Assembly from a list submitted by the Security Council, in the following manner:

(a)   The Secretary-General shall invite nominations for judges of the International Tribunal from States Members of the United Nations and non-member States maintaining permanent observer missions at United Nations Headquarters;

(b)   Within sixty days of the date of the invitation of the Secretary-General, each State may nominate up to two candidates meeting the qualifications set out in paragraph 1 above, no two of whom shall be of the same nationality;

(c)   The Secretary-General shall forward the nominations received to the Security Council. From the nominations received the Security Council shall establish a list of not less than twenty-two and not more than thirty-three candidates, taking due account of the adequate representation of the principal legal systems of the world;

(d)   The President of the Security Council shall transmit the list of candidates to the President of the General Assembly. From that list the General Assembly shall elect the eleven judges of the International Tribunal. The candidates who receive an absolute majority of the votes of the States Members of the United Nations and of the non-Member States maintaining permanent observer missions at United Nations Headquarters, shall be declared elected. Should two candidates of the same nationality obtain the required majority vote, the one who received the higher number of votes shall be considered elected.

3. In the event of a vacancy in the Chambers, after consultation with the Presidents of the Security Council and of the General Assembly, the Secretary-General shall appoint a person meeting the qualifications of paragraph 1 above, for the remainder of the term of office concerned.

4. The judges shall be elected for a term of four years. The terms and conditions of service shall be those of the judges of the International Court of Justice. They shall be eligible for re-election.

Article 14

Officers and members of the Chambers

1. The judges of the International Tribunal shall elect a President.

2. The President of the International Tribunal shall be a member of the Appeals Chamber and shall preside over its proceedings.

3. After consultation with the judges of the International Tribunal, the President shall assign the judges to the Appeals Chamber and to the Trial Chambers. A judge shall serve only in the Chamber to which he or she was assigned.

4. The judges of each Trial Chamber shall elect a Presiding Judge, who shall conduct all of the proceedings of the Trial Chamber as a whole.

Article 15

Rules of procedure and evidence

The judges of the International Tribunal shall adopt rules of procedure and evidence for the conduct of the pre-trial phase of the proceedings, trials and appeals, the admission of evidence, the protection of victims and witnesses and other appropriate matters.

Article 16

The Prosecutor

1. The Prosecutor shall be responsible for the investigation and prosecution of persons responsible for serious violations of international humanitarian law committed in the territory of the former Yugoslavia since 1 January 1991.

2. The Prosecutor shall act independently as a separate organ of the International Tribunal. He or she shall not seek or receive instructions from any Government or from any other source.

3. The Office of the Prosecutor shall be composed of a Prosecutor and such other qualified staff as may be required.

4. The Prosecutor shall be appointed by the Security Council on nomination by the Secretary-General. He or she shall be of high moral character and possess the highest level of competence and experience in the conduct of investigations and prosecutions of criminal cases. The Prosecutor shall serve for a four-year term and be eligible for reappointment. The terms and conditions of service of the Prosecutor shall be those of an Under-Secretary-General of the United Nations.

5. The staff of the Office of the Prosecutor shall be appointed by the Secretary-General on the recommendation of the Prosecutor.

Article 17

The Registry

1. The Registry shall be responsible for the administration and servicing of the International Tribunal.

2. The Registry shall consist of a Registrar and such other staff as may be required.

3. The Registrar shall be appointed by the Secretary-General after consultation with the President of the International Tribunal. He or she shall serve for a four-year term and be eligible for reappointment. The terms and conditions of service of the Registrar shall be those of an Assistant Secretary-General of the United Nations.

4. The staff of the Registry shall be appointed by the Secretary-General on the recommendation of the Registrar.

Article 18

Investigation and preparation of indictment

1. The Prosecutor shall initiate investigations ex-officio or on the basis of information obtained from any source, particularly from Governments, United Nations organs, intergovernmental and non-governmental organizations. The Prosecutor shall assess the information received or obtained and decide whether there is sufficient basis to proceed.

2. The Prosecutor shall have the power to question suspects, victims and witnesses, to collect evidence and to conduct on-site investigations. In carrying out these tasks, the Prosecutor may, as appropriate, seek the assistance of the State authorities concerned.

3. If questioned, the suspect shall be entitled to be assisted by counsel of his own choice, including the right to have legal assistance assigned to him without payment by him in any such case if he does not have sufficient means to pay for it, as well as to necessary translation into and from a language he speaks and understands.

4. Upon a determination that a prima facie case exists, the Prosecutor shall prepare an indictment containing a concise statement of the facts and the crime or crimes with which the accused is charged under the Statute. The indictment shall be transmitted to a judge of the Trial Chamber.

Article 19

Review of the indictment

1. The judge of the Trial Chamber to whom the indictment has been transmitted shall review it. If satisfied that a prima facie case has been established by the Prosecutor, he shall confirm the indictment. If not so satisfied, the indictment shall be dismissed.

2. Upon confirmation of an indictment, the judge may, at the request of the Prosecutor, issue such orders and warrants for the arrest, detention, surrender or transfer of persons, and any other orders as may be required for the conduct of the trial.

Article 20

Commencement and conduct of trial proceedings

1. The Trial Chambers shall ensure that a trial is fair and expeditious and that proceedings are conducted in accordance with the rules of procedure and evidence, with full respect for the rights of the accused and due regard for the protection of victims and witnesses.

2. A person against whom an indictment has been confirmed shall, pursuant to an order or an arrest warrant of the International Tribunal, be taken into custody, immediately informed of the charges against him and transferred to the International Tribunal.

3. The Trial Chamber shall read the indictment, satisfy itself that the rights of the accused are respected, confirm that the accused understands the indictment, and instruct the accused to enter a plea. The Trial Chamber shall then set the date for trial.

4. The hearings shall be public unless the Trial Chamber decides to close the proceedings in accordance with its rules of procedure and evidence.

Article 21

Rights of the accused

1. All persons shall be equal before the International Tribunal.

2. In the determination of charges against him, the accused shall be entitled to a fair and public hearing, subject to article 22 of the Statute.

3. The accused shall be presumed innocent until proved guilty according to the provisions of the present Statute.

4. In the determination of any charge against the accused pursuant to the present Statute, the accused shall be entitled to the following minimum guarantees, in full equality:

(a)   to be informed promptly and in detail in a language which he understands of the nature and cause of the charge against him;

(b)   to have adequate time and facilities for the preparation of his defence and to communicate with counsel of his own choosing;

(c)   to be tried without undue delay;

(d)   to be tried in his presence, and to defend himself in person or through legal assistance of his own choosing; to be informed, if he does not have legal assistance, of this right; and to have legal assistance assigned to him, in any case where the interests of justice so require, and without payment by him in any such case if he does not have sufficient means to pay for it;

(e)   to examine, or have examined, the witnesses against him and to obtain the attendance and examination of witnesses on his behalf under the same conditions as witnesses against him;

(f)   to have the free assistance of an interpreter if he cannot understand or speak the language used in the International Tribunal;

(g)   not to be compelled to testify against himself or to confess guilt.

Article 22

Protection of victims and witnesses

The International Tribunal shall provide in its rules of procedure and evidence for the protection of victims and witnesses. Such protection measures shall include, but shall not be limited to, the conduct of in camera proceedings and the protection of the victim's identity.

Article 23

Judgement

1. The Trial Chambers shall pronounce judgements and impose sentences and penalties on persons convicted of serious violations of international humanitarian law.

2. The judgement shall be rendered by a majority of the judges of the Trial Chamber, and shall be delivered by the Trial Chamber in public. It shall be accompanied by a reasoned opinion in writing, to which separate or dissenting opinions may be appended.

Article 24

Penalties

1. The penalty imposed by the Trial Chamber shall be limited to imprisonment. In determining the terms of imprisonment, the Trial Chambers shall have recourse to the general practice regarding prison sentences in the courts of the former Yugoslavia.

2. In imposing the sentences, the Trial Chambers should take into account such factors as the gravity of the offence and the individual circumstances of the convicted person.

3. In addition to imprisonment, the Trial Chambers may order the return of any property and proceeds acquired by criminal conduct, including by means of duress, to their rightful owners.

Article 25

Appellate proceedings

1. The Appeals Chamber shall hear appeals from persons convicted by the Trial Chambers or from the Prosecutor on the following grounds:

(a)   an error on a question of law invalidating the decision; or

(b)   an error of fact which has occasioned a miscarriage of justice.

2. The Appeals Chamber may affirm, reverse or revise the decisions taken by the Trial Chambers.

Article 26

Review proceedings

Where a new fact has been discovered which was not known at the time of the proceedings before the Trial Chambers or the Appeals Chamber and which could have been a decisive factor in reaching the decision, the convicted person or the Prosecutor may submit to the International Tribunal an application for review of the judgement.

Article 27

Enforcement of sentences

Imprisonment shall be served in a State designated by the International Tribunal from a list of States which have indicated to the Security Council their willingness to accept convicted persons. Such imprisonment shall be in accordance with the applicable law of the State concerned, subject to the supervision of the International Tribunal.

Article 28

Pardon or commutation of sentences

If, pursuant to the applicable law of the State in which the convicted person is imprisoned, he or she is eligible for pardon or commutation of sentence, the State concerned shall notify the International Tribunal accordingly. The President of the International Tribunal, in consultation with the judges, shall decide the matter on the basis of the interests of justice and the general principles of law.

Article 29

Cooperation and judicial assistance

1. States shall cooperate with the International Tribunal in the investigation and prosecution of persons accused of committing serious violations of international humanitarian law.

2. States shall comply without undue delay with any request for assistance or an order issued by a Trial Chamber, including, but not limited to:

(a) the identification and location of persons;

(b) the taking of testimony and the production of evidence;

(c) the service of documents;

(d) the arrest or detention of persons;

(e) the surrender or the transfer of the accused to the International Tribunal.

Article 30

The status, privileges and immunities of the International Tribunal

1. The Convention on the Privileges and Immunities of the United Nations of 13 February 1946 shall apply to the International Tribunal, the judges, the Prosecutor and his staff, and the Registrar and his staff.

2. The judges, the Prosecutor and the Registrar shall enjoy the privileges and immunities, exemptions and facilities accorded to diplomatic envoys, in accordance with international law.

3. The staff of the Prosecutor and of the Registrar shall enjoy the privileges and immunities accorded to officials of the United Nations under articles V and VII of the Convention referred to in paragraph 1 of this article.

4. Other persons, including the accused, required at the seat of the International Tribunal shall be accorded such treatment as is necessary for the proper functioning of the International Tribunal.

Article 31

Seat of the International Tribunal

The International Tribunal shall have its seat at The Hague.

Article 32

Expenses of the International Tribunal

The expenses of the International Tribunal shall be borne by the regular budget of the United Nations in accordance with Article 17 of the Charter of the United Nations.

Article 33

Working languages

The working languages of the International Tribunal shall be English and French.

Article 34

Annual report

The President of the International Tribunal shall submit an annual report of the International Tribunal to the Security Council and to the General Assembly.

Statute of the International Criminal Tribunal for Rwanda, U.N. S.C. Res. 955 (8 Nov. 1994)

The Security Council,

Reaffirming all its previous resolutions on the situation in Rwanda,

Having considered the reports of the Secretary-General pursuant to paragraph 3 of resolution 935 (1994) 1 July 1994 (S/1994/879 and S/1994/906), and having taken note of the reports of the Special Rapporteur for Rwanda of the United Nations Commission on Human Rights (S/1994/1157, annex I and annex II),

Expressing appreciation for the work of the Commission of Experts established pursuant to resolution 935 (1994), in particular its preliminary report on violations of international humanitarian law in Rwanda transmitted by the Secretary-General's letter of 1 October 1994 (S/1994/1125),

Expressing once again its grave concern at the reports indicating that genocide and other systematic, widespread and flagrant violations of international humanitarian law have been committed in Rwanda,

Determining that this situation continues to constitute a threat to international peace and security,

Determined to put an end to such crimes and to take effective measures to bring to justice the persons who are responsible for them,

Convinced that in the particular circumstances of Rwanda, the prosecution of persons responsible for serious violations of international humanitarian law would enable this aim to be achieved and would contribute to the process of national reconciliation and to the restoration and maintenance of peace,

Believing that the establishment of an international tribunal for the prosecution of persons responsible for genocide and the other above-mentioned violations of international humanitarian law will contribute to ensuring that such violations are halted and effectively redressed,

Stressing also the need for international cooperation to strengthen the courts and judicial system of Rwanda, having regard in particular to the necessity for those courts to deal with large numbers of suspects,

Considering that the Commission of Experts established pursuant to resolution 935 (1994) should continue on an urgent basis the collection of information relating to evidence of grave violations of international humanitarian law committed in the territory of Rwanda and should submit its final report to the Secretary-General by 30 November 1994,

Acting under Chapter VII of the Charter of the United Nations,

1. *Decides* hereby, having received the request of the Government of Rwanda (S/1994/1115), to establish an international tribunal for the sole purpose of prosecuting persons responsible for genocide and other serious violations of international humanitarian law committed in the territory of Rwanda and Rwandan citizens responsible for genocide and other such violations committed in the territory of neighbouring states, between 1 January 1994 and 31 December 1994 and to this end to adopt the Statute of the International Criminal Tribunal for Rwanda annexed hereto;

2. *Decides* that all States shall cooperate fully with the International Tribunal and its organs in accordance with the present resolution and the Statute of the International Tribunal and that consequently all States shall take any measures necessary under their domestic law to implement the provisions of the present resolution and the Statute, including the obligation of States to comply with requests for assistance or orders issued by a Trial Chamber under Article 28 of the Statute, and requests States to keep the Secretary-General informed of such measures;

3. *Considers* that the Government of Rwanda should be notified prior to the taking of decisions under articles 26 and 27 of the Statute;

4. *Urges* States and intergovernmental and non-governmental organisations to contribute funds, equipment and services to the International Tribunal, including the offer of expert personnel;

5. *Requests* the Secretary-General to implement this resolution urgently and in particular to make practical arrangements for the effective functioning of the International Tribunal, including recommendations to the Council as to possible locations for the seat of the International Tribunal at the earliest time to report periodically to the Council;

6. *Decides* that the seat of the International Tribunal shall be determined by the Council having regard to considerations of justice and fairness as well as administrative

efficiency, including access to witnesses, and economy, and subject to the conclusion of appropriate arrangements between the United Nations and the State of the seat, acceptable to the Council, having regard to the fact that the International Tribunal may meet away from its seat when it considers necessary for the efficient exercise of its functions; and decides that an office will be established and proceedings will be conducted in Rwanda, where feasible and appropriate, subject to the conclusion of similar appropriate arrangements;

7. *Decides* to consider increasing the number of judges and Trial Chambers of the International Tribunal if it becomes necessary;

8. *Decides* to remain actively seized of the matter.

Annex

Statute of the International Tribunal for Rwanda

Having been established by the Security Council acting under Chapter VII of the Charter of the United Nations, the International Criminal Tribunal for the Prosecution of Persons Responsible for Genocide and Other Serious Violations of International Humanitarian Law Committed in the Territory of Rwanda and Rwandan Citizens responsible for genocide and other such violations committed in the territory of neighbouring States, between 1 January 1994 and 31 December 1994 (hereinafter referred to as "The International Tribunal for Rwanda") shall function in accordance with the provisions of the present Statute.

Article 1. Competence of the International Tribunal for Rwanda

The International Tribunal for Rwanda shall have the power to prosecute persons responsible for serious violations of international humanitarian law committed in the territory of Rwanda and Rwandan citizens responsible for such violations committed in the territory of neighbouring States between 1 January 1994 and 31 December 1994, in accordance with the provisions of the present Statute.

Article 2. Genocide

1. The International Tribunal for Rwanda shall have the power to prosecute persons committing genocide as defined in paragraph 2 of this article or of committing any of the other acts enumerated in paragraph 3 of this article.

2. Genocide means any of the following acts committed with intent to destroy, in whole or in part, a national, ethnical, racial or religious group, as such:

(a) Killing members of the group;

(b) Causing serious bodily or mental harm to members of the group;

(c) Deliberately inflicting on the group conditions of life calculated to bring about its physical destruction in whole or in part;

(d) Imposing measures intended to prevent births within the group;

(e) Forcibly transferring children of the group to another group.

3. The following acts shall be punishable:

(a) Genocide;

(b) Conspiracy to commit genocide;

(c) Direct and public incitement to commit genocide;

(d) Attempt to commit genocide;

(e) Complicity in genocide.

Article 3. Crimes against Humanity

The International Tribunal for Rwanda shall have the power to prosecute persons responsible for the following crimes when committed as part of a widespread or systematic attack against any civilian population on national, political, ethnic, racial or religious grounds:

(a) Murder;

(b) Extermination;

(c) Enslavement;

(d) Deportation;

(e) Imprisonment;

(f) Torture;

(g) Rape;

(h) Persecutions on political, racial and religious grounds;

(i) Other inhumane acts.

Article 4. Violations of Article 3 common to the Geneva Conventions and of Additional Protocol II

The International Tribunal for Rwanda shall have the power to prosecute persons committing or ordering to be committed serious violations of Article 3 common to the Geneva Conventions of 12 August 1949 for the Protection of War Victims, and of Additional Protocol II thereto of 8 June 1977. These violations shall include, but shall not be limited to:

(a) Violence to life, health and physical or mental well-being of persons, in particular murder as well as cruel treatment such as torture, mutilation or any form of corporal punishment;

(b) Collective punishments;

(c) Taking of hostages;

(d) Acts of terrorism;

(e) Outrages upon personal dignity, in particular humiliating and degrading treatment, rape, enforced prostitution and any form of indecent assault;

(f) Pillage;

(g) The passing of sentences and the carrying out of executions without previous judgement pronounced by a regularly constituted court, affording all the judicial guarantees which are recognised as indispensable by civilised peoples;

(h) Threats to commit any of the foregoing acts.

Article 5. Personal jurisdiction

The International Tribunal for Rwanda shall have jurisdiction over natural persons pursuant to the provisions of the present Statute.

Article 6. Individual Criminal Responsibility

1. A person who planned, instigated, ordered, committed or otherwise aided and abetted in the planning, preparation or execution of a crime referred to in Articles 2 to 4 of the present Statute, shall be individually responsible for the crime.

2. The official position of any accused person, whether as Head of State or Government or as a responsible Government official, shall not relieve such person of criminal responsibility nor mitigate punishment.

3. The fact that any of the acts referred to in Articles 2 to 4 of the present Statute was committed by a subordinate does not relieve his or her superior of criminal responsibility if he or she knew or had reason to know that the subordinate was about to commit such acts or had done so and the superior failed to take the necessary and reasonable measures to prevent such acts or to punish the perpetrators thereof.

4. The fact that an accused person acted pursuant to an order of a Government or of a superior shall not relieve him or her of criminal responsibility, but may be considered in mitigation of punishment if the International Tribunal for Rwanda determines that justice so requires.

Article 7. Territorial and temporal jurisdiction

The territorial jurisdiction of the International Tribunal for Rwanda shall extend to the territory of Rwanda including its land surface and airspace as well as to the territory of neighbouring States in respect of serious violations of international humanitarian law committed by Rwandan citizens. The temporal jurisdiction of the International Tribunal for Rwanda shall extend to a period beginning on 1 January 1994 and ending on 31 December 1994.

Article 8. Concurrent jurisdiction

1. The International Tribunal for Rwanda and national courts shall have concurrent jurisdiction to prosecute persons for serious violations of international humanitarian law committed in the territory of Rwanda and Rwandan citizens for such violations committed in the territory of the neighbouring States, between 1 January 1994 and 31 December 1994.

2. The International Tribunal for Rwanda shall have the primacy over the national courts of all States. At any stage of the procedure, the International Tribunal for Rwanda may formally request national courts to defer to its competence in accordance with the present Statute and the Rules of Procedure and Evidence of the International Tribunal for Rwanda.

Article 9. *Non bis in idem*

1. No person shall be tried before a national court for acts constituting serious violations of international humanitarian law under the present Statute, for which he or she has already been tried by the International Tribunal for Rwanda.

2. A person who has been tried before a national court for acts constituting serious violations of international humanitarian law may be subsequently tried by the International Tribunal for Rwanda only if:

(a) The act for which he or she was tried was characterised as an ordinary crime; or

(b) The national court proceedings were not impartial or independent, were designed to shield the accused from international criminal responsibility, or the case was not diligently prosecuted.

3. In considering the penalty to be imposed on a person convicted of a crime under the present Statute, the International Tribunal for Rwanda shall take into account the extent to which any penalty imposed by a national court on the same person for the same act has already been served.

Article 10. Organisation of the International Tribunal for Rwanda

The International Tribunal for Rwanda shall consist of the following organs:

(a) The Chambers, comprising three Trial Chambers and an Appeals Chamber;

(b) The Prosecutor;

(c) A registry.

Article 11. Composition of the Chambers

The Chambers shall be composed of fourteen independent judges, no two of whom may be nationals of the same State, who shall serve as follows:

(a) Three judges shall serve in each of the Trial Chambers;

(b) Five judges shall serve in the Appeals Chamber.

Article 12. Qualification and election of judges

1. The judges shall be persons of high moral character, impartiality and integrity who possess the qualifications required in their respective countries for appointment to the highest judicial offices. In the overall composition of the Chambers due account shall be taken of the experience of the judges in criminal law, international law, including international humanitarian law and human rights law.

2. The members of the Appeals Chamber of the International Tribunal for the Prosecution of Persons Responsible for Serious Violations of International Humanitarian Law Committed in the Territory of the former Yugoslavia since 1991 (hereinafter referred to as "the International Tribunal for the former Yugoslavia") shall also serve as the members of the Appeals Chamber of the International Tribunal for Rwanda.

3. The judges of the Trial Chambers of the International Tribunal for Rwanda shall be elected by the General Assembly from a list submitted by the Security Council, in the following manner:

(a) The Secretary-General shall invite nominations for judges of the Trial Chambers from States Members of the United Nations and non-member States maintaining permanent observer missions at the United Nations Headquarters;

(b) Within thirty days of the date of the invitation of the Secretary-General, each State may nominate up to two candidates meeting the qualifications set out in paragraph 1 above, no two of whom shall be of the same nationality and neither of whom shall be one of the same nationality as any judge on the Appeals Chamber;

(c) The Secretary-General shall forward the nominations received to the Security Council. From the nominations received the Security Council shall establish a list of not less that eighteen and not more that twenty-seven candidates, taking due account of adequate representation on the International Tribunal for Rwanda of the principal legal systems of the world;

(d) The President of the Security Council shall transmit the list of candidates to the President of the General Assembly. From that list the General Assembly shall elect the nine judges of the Trial Chambers. The candidates who receive an absolute majority of the votes of the States Members of the United Nations and of the non-member States maintaining permanent observer missions at United Nations headquarters, shall be declared elected. Should two candidates of the same nationality obtain the required majority vote, the one who received the higher number of votes shall be considered elected.

4. In the event of a vacancy in the Trial Chambers, after consultation with the Presidents of the Security Council and of the General Assembly, the Secretary-General shall appoint a person meeting the qualifications of paragraph 1 above, for the remainder of the term of office concerned.

5. The judges of the Trial Chambers shall be elected for a term of four years. The terms and conditions of service shall be those of the judges of the International Tribunal for the former Yugoslavia. They shall be eligible for re-election.

Article 13. Officers and members of the Chambers

1. The judges of the International Tribunal for Rwanda shall elect a President.

2. After consultation with the judges of the International Tribunal for Rwanda, the President shall assign the judges to the Trial Chambers. A judge shall serve only in the Chamber to which he or she was assigned.

3. The judges of each Trial Chamber shall elect a Presiding Judge, who shall conduct all of the proceedings of that Trial Chamber as a whole.

Article 14. Rules of procedure and evidence

The judges of the International Tribunal for Rwanda shall adopt, for the purpose of proceedings before the International Tribunal for Rwanda, the rules of procedure and evidence for the conduct of the pre-trial phase of the proceedings, trials and appeals, the admission of evidence, the protection of victims and witnesses and other appropriate matters of the International Tribunal for the former Yugoslavia with such changes as they deem necessary.

Article 15. The Prosecutor

1. The Prosecutor shall be responsible for the investigation and prosecution of persons responsible for serious violations of international humanitarian law committed in the territory of Rwanda and Rwandan citizens responsible for such violations committed in the territory of neighbouring States, between 1 January 1994 and 31 December 1994.

2. The Prosecutor shall act independently as a separate organ of the International Tribunal for Rwanda. He or she shall not seek or receive instructions from any Government or from any other source.

3. The Prosecutor of the International Tribunal for the Former Yugoslavia shall also serve as the Prosecutor of the International Tribunal for Rwanda. He or she shall have additional staff, including an additional Deputy Prosecutor, to assist with prosecutions before the International Tribunal for Rwanda. Such staff shall be appointed by the Secretary-General on the recommendation of the Prosecutor.

Article 16. The Registry

1. The Registry shall be responsible for the administration and servicing of the International Tribunal for Rwanda.

2. The Registry shall consist of a Registrar and such other staff as may be required.

3. The Registrar shall be appointed by the Secretary-General after consultation with the President of the International Tribunal for Rwanda. He or she shall serve for a four-year term and be eligible for re-appointment. The terms and conditions of service of the Registrar shall be those of an Assistant Secretary-General of the United Nations.

4. The Staff of the Registry shall be appointed by the Secretary-General on the recommendation of the Registrar.

Article 17. Investigation and preparation of indictment

1. The Prosecutor shall initiate investigations ex-officio or on the basis of information obtained from any source, particularly from Governments, United Nations organs, intergovernmental and non-governmental organisations. The Prosecutor shall assess the information received or obtained and decide whether there is sufficient basis to proceed.

2. The Prosecutor shall have the power to question suspects, victims and witnesses, to collect evidence and to conduct on-site investigations. In carrying out these tasks, the Prosecutor may, as appropriate, seek the assistance of the State authorities concerned.

3. If questioned, the suspect shall be entitled to be assisted by counsel of his or her own choice, including the right to have legal assistance assigned to the suspect without payment by him or her in any such case if he or she does not have sufficient means to pay for it, as well as necessary translation into and from a language he or she speaks and understands.

4. Upon a determination that a *prima facie* case exists, the Prosecutor shall prepare an indictment containing a concise statement of the facts and the crime or crimes with which the accused is charged under the Statute. The indictment shall be transmitted to a judge of the Trial Chamber.

Article 18. Review of the Indictment

1. The judge of the Trial Chamber to whom the indictment has been transmitted shall review it. If satisfied that a *prima facie* case has been established by the Prosecutor, he or she shall confirm the indictment. If not so satisfied, the indictment shall be dismissed.

2. Upon confirmation of an indictment, the judge may, at the request of the Prosecutor, issue such orders and warrants for the arrest, detention, surrender or transfer of persons, and any other orders as may be required for the conduct of the trial.

Article 19. Commencement and conduct of trial proceedings

1. The Trial Chambers shall ensure that a trial is fair and expeditious and that proceedings are conducted in accordance with the rules of procedure and evidence, with full respect for the rights of the accused with due regard for the protection of victims and witnesses.

2. A person against whom an indictment has been confirmed shall, pursuant to an order or an arrest warrant of the International Tribunal for Rwanda, be taken into custody, immediately informed of the charges against him or her and transferred to the International Tribunal for Rwanda.

3. The Trial Chamber shall read the indictment, satisfy itself that the rights of the accused are respected, confirm that the accused understands the indictment, and instruct the accused to enter a plea. The Trial Chamber shall then set the date for trial.

4. The hearings shall be public unless the Trial Chamber decides to close the proceedings in accordance with its rules of procedure and evidence.

Article 20. Rights of the Accused

1. All persons shall be equal before the International Tribunal for Rwanda.

2. In the determination of charges against him or her, the accused shall be entitled to a fair and public hearing, subject to Article 21 of the Statute.

3. The accused shall be presumed innocent until proven guilty according to the provisions of the present Statute.

4. In determination of any charge against the accused pursuant to the present Statute, the accused shall be entitled to the following minimum guarantees, in full equality:

(a) To be informed promptly and in detail in a language which he or she understands of the nature and cause of the charge against him or her;

(b) To have adequate time and facilities for the preparation of his or her defence and to communicate with counsel of his or her own choosing;

(c) To be tried without undue delay;

(d) To be tried in his or her presence, and to defend himself or herself in person or through legal assistance of his or her own choosing; to be informed, if he or she does not have legal assistance, of this right; and to have legal assistance assigned to him or her, in any case where the interest of justice so require, and without payment by him or her in any such case if he or she does not have sufficient means to pay for it;

(e) To examine, or have examined, the witnesses against him or her and to obtain the attendance and examination of witnesses on his or her behalf under the same conditions as witnesses against him or her;

(f) To have the free assistance of an interpreter if her or she cannot understand or speak the language used in the International Tribunal for Rwanda;

(g) Not to be compelled to testify against himself or herself or to confess guilt.

Article 21. Protection of victims and witnesses

The International Tribunal for Rwanda shall provide in its rules of procedure and evidence for the protection of victims and witnesses. Such protection measures shall include, but shall not be limited to, the conduct of in camera proceedings and the protection of the victim's identity.

Article 22. Judgement

1. The Trial Chambers shall pronounce judgements and impose sentences and penalties on persons convicted of serious violations of international humanitarian law.

2. The judgement shall be rendered by a majority of the judges of the Trial Chamber, and shall be delivered by the Trial Chamber in public. It shall be accompanied by a reasoned opinion in writing, to which separate or dissenting opinions may be appended.

Article 23. Penalties

1. The penalty imposed by the Trial Chamber shall be limited to imprisonment. In determining the terms of imprisonment, the Trial Chambers shall have recourse to the general practice regarding prison sentences in the courts of Rwanda.

2. In imposing the sentences, the Trial Chambers should take into account such factors as the gravity of the offence and the individual circumstances of the convicted person.

3. In addition to imprisonment, the Trial Chambers may order the return of any property and proceeds acquired by criminal conduct, including by means of duress, to their rightful owners.

Article 24. Appellate Proceedings

1. The Appeals Chamber shall hear appeals from persons convicted by the Trial Chambers or from the Prosecutor on the following grounds:

(a) An error on a question of law invalidating the decision; or

(b) An error of fact which has occasioned a miscarriage of justice.

2. The Appeals Chamber may affirm, reverse or revise the decisions taken by the Trial Chambers.

Article 25. Review Proceedings

Where a new fact has been discovered which was not known at the time of the proceedings before the Trial Chambers or the Appeals Chamber and which could have been a decisive factor in reaching the decision, the convicted person or the Prosecutor may submit to the International Tribunal for Rwanda an application for review of the judgement.

Article 26. Enforcement of Sentences

Imprisonment shall be served in Rwanda or any of the States on a list of States which have indicated to the Security Council their willingness to accept convicted persons, as designated by the International Tribunal for Rwanda. Such imprisonment shall be in accordance with the applicable law of the State concerned, subject to the supervision of the International Tribunal for Rwanda.

Article 27. Pardon or commutation of sentences

If, pursuant to the applicable law of the State in which the convicted person is imprisoned, he or she is eligible for pardon or commutation of sentence, the State concerned shall notify the International Tribunal for Rwanda accordingly. There shall only be pardon or commutation of sentence if the President of the International Tribunal for Rwanda, in consultation with the judges, so decides on the basis of the interests of justice and the general principles of law.

Article 28. Cooperation and judicial assistance

1. States shall cooperate with the International Tribunal for Rwanda in the investigation and prosecution of persons accused of committing serious violations of international humanitarian law.

2. States shall comply without undue delay with any request for assistance or an order issued by a Trial Chamber, including but not limited to:

(a) The identification and location of persons;

(b) The taking of testimony and the production of evidence;

(c) The service of documents;

(d) The arrest or detention of persons;

(e) The surrender or the transfer of the accused to the International Tribunal for Rwanda.

Article 29. The status, privileges and immunities of the International Tribunal for Rwanda

1. The Convention on the Privileges and Immunities of the United Nations of 13 February 1946 shall apply to the Registrar and his or her staff.

2. The judges, the Prosecutor and the Registrar shall enjoy the privileges and immunities, exemptions and facilities accorded to diplomatic envoys, in accordance with international law.

3. The staff of the Prosecutor and of the Registrar shall enjoy the privileges and immunities accorded to officials of the United Nations under Articles V and VII of the Convention referred to in paragraph 1 of this article.

4. Other persons, including the accused, required at the seat or meeting place of the International Tribunal for Rwanda shall be accorded such treatment as is necessary for the proper functioning of the International Tribunal for Rwanda.

Article 30. Expenses of the International Tribunal for Rwanda

The expenses of the International Tribunal for Rwanda shall be expenses of the Organisation in accordance with Article 17 of the Charter of the United Nations.

Article 31. Working languages

The working languages of the International Tribunal for Rwanda shall be English and French.

Article 32. Annual Report

The President of the International Tribunal for Rwanda shall submit an annual report of the International Tribunal for Rwanda to the Security Council and to the General Assembly.

Rome Statute of the International Criminal Court, Adopted by the U.N. Diplomatic Conference, July 17, 1998

Preamble

Conscious that all peoples are united by common bonds, their cultures pieced together in a shared heritage, and concerned that this delicate mosaic may be shattered at any time,

Mindful that during this century millions of children, women and men have been victims of unimaginable atrocities that deeply shock the conscience of humanity,

Recognizing that such grave crimes threaten the peace, security and well-being of the world,

Affirming that the most serious crimes of concern to the international community as a whole must not go unpunished and that their effective prosecution must be ensured by taking measures at the national level and by enhancing international cooperation,

Determined to put an end to impunity for the perpetrators of these crimes and thus to contribute to the prevention of such crimes,

Recalling that it is the duty of every State to exercise its criminal jurisdiction over those responsible for international crimes,

Reaffirming the Purposes and Principles of the Charter of the United Nations, and in particular that all States shall refrain from the threat or use of force against the territorial integrity or political independence of any State, or in any other manner inconsistent with the Purposes of the United Nations,

Emphasizing in this connection that nothing in this Statute shall be taken as authorizing any State Party to intervene in an armed conflict in the internal affairs of any State,

Determined to these ends and for the sake of present and future generations, to establish an independent permanent International Criminal Court in relationship with the United Nations system, with jurisdiction over the most serious crimes of concern to the international community as a whole,

Emphasizing that the International Criminal Court established under this Statute shall be complementary to national criminal jurisdictions,

Resolved to guarantee lasting respect for the enforcement of international justice,

Have agreed as follows:

Part 1. Establishment of the Court

Article 1. The Court

An International Criminal Court ("the Court") is hereby established. It shall be a permanent institution and shall have the power to exercise its jurisdiction over persons for the most serious crimes of international concern, as referred to in this Statute, and shall be complementary to national criminal jurisdictions. The jurisdiction and functioning of the Court shall be governed by the provisions of this Statute.

Article 2. Relationship of the Court with the United Nations

The Court shall be brought into relationship with the United Nations through an agreement to be approved by the Assembly of States Parties to this Statute and thereafter concluded by the President of the Court on its behalf.

Article 3. Seat of the Court

1. The seat of the Court shall be established at The Hague in the Netherlands ("the host State").

2. The Court shall enter into a headquarters agreement with the host State, to be approved by the Assembly of States Parties and thereafter concluded by the President of the Court on its behalf.

3. The Court may sit elsewhere, whenever it considers it desirable, as provided in this Statute.

Article 4. Legal status and powers of the Court

1. The Court shall have international legal personality. It shall also have such legal capacity as may be necessary for the exercise of its functions and the fulfilment of its purposes.

2. The Court may exercise its functions and powers, as provided in this Statute, on the territory of any State Party and, by special agreement, on the territory of any other State.

Part 2. Jurisdiction, Admissibility and Applicable Law

Article 5. Crimes within the jurisdiction of the Court

1. The jurisdiction of the Court shall be limited to the most serious crimes of concern to the international community as a whole. The Court has jurisdiction in accordance with this Statute with respect to the following crimes:

    (a) The crime of genocide;

    (b) Crimes against humanity;

    (c) War crimes;

    (d) The crime of aggression.

2. The Court shall exercise jurisdiction over the crime of aggression once a provision is adopted in accordance with Articles 121 and 123 defining the crime and setting out the conditions under which the Court shall exercise jurisdiction with respect to this

crime. Such a provision shall be consistent with the relevant provisions of the Charter of the United Nations.

Article 6. Genocide

For the purpose of this Statute, "genocide" means any of the following acts committed with intent to destroy, in whole or in part, a national, ethnical, racial or religious group, as such:

(a) Killing members of the group;

(b) Causing serious bodily or mental harm to members of the group;

(c) Deliberately inflicting on the group conditions of life calculated to bring about its physical destruction in whole or in part;

(d) Imposing measures intended to prevent births within the group;

(e) Forcibly transferring children of the group to another group.

Article 7. Crimes against humanity

1. For the purpose of this Statute, "crime against humanity" means any of the following acts when committed as part of a widespread or systematic attack directed against any civilian population, with knowledge of the attack:

(a) Murder;

(b) Extermination;

(c) Enslavement;

(d) Deportation or forcible transfer of population;

(e) Imprisonment or other severe deprivation of physical liberty in violation of fundamental rules of international law;

(f) Torture;

(g) Rape, sexual slavery, enforced prostitution, forced pregnancy, enforced sterilization, or any other form of sexual violence of comparable gravity;

(h) Persecution against any identifiable group or collectivity on political, racial, national, ethnic, cultural, religious, gender as defined in paragraph 3, or other grounds that are universally recognised as impermissible under international law, in connection with any act referred to in this paragraph or any crime within the jurisdiction of the Court;

(i) Enforced disappearance of persons;

(j) The crime of apartheid;

(k) Other inhumane acts of a similar character intentionally causing great suffering, or serious injury to body or to mental or physical health.

2. For the purpose of paragraph 1:

(a) "Attack directed against any civilian population" means a course of conduct involving the multiple commission of acts referred to in paragraph 1 against any civilian population, pursuant to or in furtherance of a State or organizational policy to commit such attack;

(b) "Extermination" includes the intentional infliction of conditions of life, *inter alia* the deprivation of access to food and medicine, calculated to bring about the destruction of part of a population;

(c) "Enslavement" means the exercise of any or all of the powers attaching to the right of ownership over a person and includes the exercise of such power in the course of trafficking in persons, in particular women and children;

(d) "Deportation or forcible transfer of population" means forced displacement of the persons concerned by expulsion or other coercive acts from the area in which they are lawfully present, without grounds permitted under international law;

(e) "Torture" means the intentional infliction of severe pain or suffering, whether physical or mental, upon a person in the custody or under the control of the accused; except that torture shall not include pain or suffering arising only from, inherent in or incidental to, lawful sanctions;

(f) "Forced pregnancy" means the unlawful confinement, of a woman forcibly made pregnant, with the intent of affecting the ethnic composition of any population or carrying out other grave violations of international law. This definition shall not in any way be interpreted as affecting national laws relating to pregnancy;

(g) "Persecution" means the intentional and severe deprivation of fundamental rights contrary to international law by reason of the identity of the group or collectivity;

(h) "The crime of apartheid" means inhumane acts of a character similar to those referred to in paragraph 1, committed in the context of an institutionalized regime of systematic oppression and domination by one racial group over any other racial group or groups and committed with the intention of maintaining that regime;

(i) "Enforced disappearance of persons" means the arrest, detention or abduction of persons by, or with the authorization, support or acquiescence of, a State or a political organization, followed by a refusal to acknowledge that deprivation of freedom or to give information on the fate or whereabouts of those persons, with the intention of removing them from the protection of the law for a prolonged period of time.

3. For the purpose of this Statute, it is understood that the term "gender" refers to the two sexes, male and female, within the context of society. The term "gender" does not indicate any meaning different from the above.

Article 8

1. The Court shall have jurisdiction in respect of war crimes in particular when committed as a part of a plan or policy or as part of a large-scale commission of such crimes.

2. For the purpose of this Statute, "war crimes" means:

(a) Grave breaches of the Geneva Conventions of 12 August 1949, namely, any of the following acts against persons or property protected under the provisions of the relevant Geneva Convention:

(i) Wilful killing;

(ii) Torture or inhuman treatment, including biological experiments;

(iii) Wilfully causing great suffering, or serious injury to body or health;

(iv) Extensive destruction and appropriation of property, not justified by military necessity and carried out unlawfully and wantonly;

(v) Compelling a prisoner of war or other protected person to serve in the forces of a hostile Power;

(vi) Wilfully depriving a prisoner of war or other protected person of the rights of fair and regular trial;

(vii) Unlawful deportation or transfer or unlawful confinement;

(viii) Taking of hostages.

(b) Other serious violations of the laws and customs applicable in international armed conflict, within the established framework of international law, namely, any of the following acts:

(i) Intentionally directing attacks against the civilian population as such or against individual civilians not taking direct part in hostilities;

(ii) Intentionally directing attacks against civilian objects, that is, objects which are not military objectives;

(iii) Intentionally directing attacks against personnel, installations, material, units or vehicles involved in a humanitarian assistance or peacekeeping mission in accordance with the Charter of the United Nations, as long as they are entitled to the protection given to civilians or civilian objects under the international law of armed conflict;

(iv) Intentionally launching an attack in the knowledge that such attack will cause incidental loss of life or injury to civilians or damage to civilian objects or widespread, long-term and severe damage to the natural environment which would be clearly excessive in relation to the concrete and direct overall military advantage anticipated;

(v) Attacking or bombarding, by whatever means, towns, villages, dwellings or buildings which are undefended and which are not military objectives;

(vi) Killing or wounding a combatant who, having laid down his arms or having no longer means of defence, has surrendered at discretion;

(vii) Making improper use of a flag of truce, of the flag or of the military insignia and uniform of the enemy or of the United Nations, as well as of the distinctive emblems of the Geneva Conventions, resulting in death or serious personal injury;

(viii) The transfer, directly or indirectly, by the Occupying Power of parts of its own civilian population into the territory it occupies, or the deportation or transfer of all or parts of the population of the occupied territory within or outside this territory;

(ix) Intentionally directing attacks against buildings dedicated to religion, education, art, science or charitable purposes, historic monuments, hospitals and places where the sick and wounded are collected, provided they are not military objectives;

(x) Subjecting persons who are in the power of an adverse party to physical mutilation or to medical or scientific experiments of any kind which are neither justified by the medical, dental or hospital treatment of the person concerned nor carried out in his or her interest, and which cause death to or seriously endanger the health of such person or persons;

(xi) Killing or wounding treacherously individuals belonging to the hostile nation or army;

(xii) Declaring that no quarter will be given;

(xiii) Destroying or seizing the enemy's property unless such destruction or seizure be imperatively demanded by the necessities of war;

(xiv) Declaring abolished, suspended or inadmissible in a court of law the rights and actions of the nationals of the hostile party;

(xv) Compelling the nationals of the hostile party to take part in the operations of war directed against their own country, even if they were in the belligerent's service before the commencement of the war;

(xvi) Pillaging a town or place, even when taken by assault;

(xvii) Employing poison or poisoned weapons;

(xviii) Employing asphyxiating, poisonous or other gases, and all analogous liquids, materials or devices;

(xix) Employing bullets which expand or flatten easily in the human body, such as bullets with a hard envelope which does not entirely cover the core or is pierced with incisions;

(xx) Employing weapons, projectiles and material and methods of warfare which are of a nature to cause superfluous injury or unnecessary suffering or which are inherently indiscriminate in violation of the international law of armed conflict, provided that such weapons, projectiles and material and methods of warfare are the subject of a comprehensive prohibition and are included in an annex to this Statute, by an amendment in accordance with the relevant provisions set forth in Articles 121 and 123;

(xxi) Committing outrages upon personal dignity, in particular humiliating and degrading treatment;

(xxii) Committing rape, sexual slavery, enforced prostitution, forced pregnancy, as defined in Article 7, paragraph 2 (f), enforced sterilization, or any other form of sexual violence also constituting a grave breach of the Geneva Conventions;

(xxiii) Utilizing the presence of a civilian or other protected person to render certain points, areas or military forces immune from military operations;

(xxiv) Intentionally directing attacks against buildings, material, medical units and transport, and personnel using the distinctive emblems of the Geneva Conventions in conformity with international law;

(xxv) Intentionally using starvation of civilians as a method of warfare by depriving them of objects indispensable to their survival, including wilfully impeding relief supplies as provided for under the Geneva Conventions;

(xxvi) Conscripting or enlisting children under the age of fifteen years into the national armed forces or using them to participate actively in hostilities.

(c) In the case of an armed conflict not of an international character, serious violations of Article 3 common to the four Geneva Conventions of 12 August 1949, namely, any of the following acts committed against persons taking no active part in the hostilities, including members of armed forces who have laid down their arms and those placed *hors de combat* by sickness, wounds, detention or any other cause:

(i) Violence to life and person, in particular murder of all kinds, mutilation, cruel treatment and torture;

(ii) Committing outrages upon personal dignity, in particular humiliating and degrading treatment;

(iii) Taking of hostages;

(iv) The passing of sentences and the carrying out of executions without previous judgement pronounced by a regularly constituted court, affording all judicial guarantees which are generally recognized as indispensable.

(d) Paragraph 2 (c) applies to armed conflicts not of an international character and thus does not apply to situations of internal disturbances and tensions, such as riots, isolated and sporadic acts of violence or other acts of a similar nature.

(e) Other serious violations of the laws and customs applicable in armed conflicts not of an international character, within the established framework of international law, namely, any of the following acts:

(i) Intentionally directing attacks against the civilian population as such or against individual civilians not taking direct part in hostilities;

(ii) Intentionally directing attacks against buildings, material, medical units and transport, and personnel using the distinctive emblems of the Geneva Conventions in conformity with international law;

(iii) Intentionally directing attacks against personnel, installations, material, units or vehicles involved in a humanitarian assistance or peacekeeping mission in accordance with the Charter of the United Nations, as long as they are entitled to the protection given to civilians or civilian objects under the law of armed conflict;

(iv) Intentionally directing attacks against buildings dedicated to religion, education, art, science or charitable purposes, historic monuments, hospitals and places where the sick and wounded are collected, provided they are not military objectives;

(v) Pillaging a town or place, even when taken by assault;

(vi) Committing rape, sexual slavery, enforced prostitution, forced pregnancy, as defined in Article 7, paragraph 2 (f), enforced sterilization, and any other form of sexual violence also constituting a serious violation of Article 3 common to the four Geneva Conventions;

(vii) Conscripting or enlisting children under the age of fifteen years into armed forces or groups or using them to participate actively in hostilities;

(viii) Ordering the displacement of the civilian population for reasons related to the conflict, unless the security of the civilians involved or imperative military reasons so demand;

(ix) Killing or wounding treacherously a combatant adversary;

(x) Declaring that no quarter will be given;

(xi) Subjecting persons who are in the power of another party to the conflict to physical mutilation or to medical or scientific experiments of any kind which are neither justified by the medical, dental or hospital treatment of the person concerned nor carried out in his or her interest, and which cause death to or seriously endanger the health of such person or persons;

(xii) Destroying or seizing the property of an adversary unless such destruction or seizure be imperatively demanded by the necessities of the conflict;

(f) Paragraph 2 (e) applies to armed conflicts not of an international character and thus does not apply to situations of internal disturbances and tensions, such as riots, isolated and sporadic acts of violence or other acts of a similar nature. It applies to armed conflicts that take place in the territory of a State when there is protracted armed conflict between governmental authorities and organized armed groups or between such groups.

3. Nothing in paragraphs 2 (c) and (d) shall affect the responsibility of a Government to maintain or reestablish law and order in the State or to defend the unity and territorial integrity of the State, by all legitimate means.

Article 9

1. Elements of Crimes shall assist the Court in the interpretation and application of Articles 6, 7 and 8. They shall be adopted by a two-thirds majority of the members of the Assembly of States Parties.

2. Amendments to the Elements of Crimes may be proposed by:

(a) Any State Party;

(b) The judges acting by an absolute majority;

(c) The Prosecutor.

Such amendments shall be adopted by a two-thirds majority of the members of the Assembly of States Parties.

3. The Elements of Crimes and amendments thereto shall be consistent with this Statute.

Article 10

Nothing in this Part shall be interpreted as limiting or prejudicing in any way existing or developing rules of international law for purposes other than this Statute.

Article 11

1. The Court has jurisdiction only with respect to crimes committed after the entry into force of this Statute.

2. If a State becomes a Party to this Statute after its entry into force, the Court may exercise its jurisdiction only with respect to crimes committed after the entry into force of this Statute for that State, unless that State has made a declaration under Article 12, paragraph 3.

Article 12. Preconditions to the exercise of jurisdiction

1. A State which becomes a Party to this Statute thereby accepts the jurisdiction of the Court with respect to the crimes referred to in Article 5.

2. In the case of Article 13, paragraph (a) or (c), the Court may exercise its jurisdiction if one or more of the following States are Parties to this Statute or have accepted the jurisdiction of the Court in accordance with paragraph 3:

> (a) The State on the territory of which the conduct in question occurred or, if the crime was committed on board a vessel or aircraft, the State of registration of that vessel or aircraft;

> (b) The State of which the person accused of the crime is a national.

3. If the acceptance of a State which is not a Party to this Statute is required under paragraph 2, that State may, by declaration lodged with the Registrar, accept the exercise of jurisdiction by the Court with respect to the crime in question. The accepting State shall cooperate with the Court without any delay or exception in accordance with Part 9.

Article 13. Exercise of jurisdiction

The Court may exercise its jurisdiction with respect to a crime referred to in Article 5 in accordance with the provisions of this Statute if:

> (a) A situation in which one or more of such crimes appears to have been committed is referred to the Prosecutor by a State Party in accordance with Article 14;

> (b) A situation in which one or more of such crimes appears to have been committed is referred to the Prosecutor by the Security Council acting under Chapter VII of the United Nations; or

> (c) The Prosecutor has initiated an investigation in respect of such a crime in accordance with Article 15.

Article 14. Referral of a situation by a State Party

1. A State Party may refer to the Prosecutor a situation in which one or more crimes within the jurisdiction of the Court appear to have been committed requesting the Prosecutor to investigate the situation for the purpose of determining whether one or more specific persons should be charged with the commission of such crimes.

2. As far as possible, a referral shall specify the relevant circumstances and be accompanied by such supporting documentation as is available to the State referring the situation.

Article 15. Prosecutor

1. The Prosecutor may initiate investigations *proprio motu* on the basis of information on crimes within the jurisdiction of the Court.

2. The Prosecutor shall analyse the seriousness of the information received. For this purpose, he or she may seek additional information from States, organs of the United Nations, intergovernmental or non-governmental organizations, or other reliable sources that he or she deems appropriate, and may receive written or oral testimony at the seat of the Court.

3. If the Prosecutor concludes that there is a reasonable basis to proceed with an investigation, he or she shall submit to the Pre-Trial Chamber a request for authorization of an investigation, together with any supporting material collected. Victims may make representations to the Pre-Trial Chamber, in accordance with the Rules of Procedure and Evidence.

4. If the Pre-Trial Chamber, upon examination of the request and the supporting material, considers that there is a reasonable basis to proceed with an investigation, and that the case appears to fall within the jurisdiction of the Court, it shall authorize the commencement of the investigation, without prejudice to subsequent determinations by the Court with regard to the jurisdiction and admissibility of a case.

5. The refusal of the Pre-Trial Chamber to authorize the investigation shall not preclude the presentation of a subsequent request by the Prosecutor based on new facts or evidence regarding the same situation.

6. If, after the preliminary examination referred to in paragraphs 1 and 2, the Prosecutor concludes that the information provided does not constitute a reasonable basis for an investigation, he or she shall inform those who provided the information. This shall not preclude the Prosecutor from considering further information submitted to him or her regarding the same situation in the light of new facts or evidence.

Article 16. Deferral of investigation or prosecution

No investigation or prosecution may be commenced or proceeded with under this Statute for a period of 12 months after the Security Council, in a resolution adopted under Chapter VII of the Charter of the United Nations, has requested the Court to that effect; that request may be renewed by the Council under the same conditions.

Article 17. Issues of admissibility

1. Having regard to paragraph 10 of the Preamble and Article 1, the Court shall determine that a case is inadmissible where:

(a) The case is being investigated or prosecuted by a State which has jurisdiction over it, unless the State is unwilling or unable genuinely to carry out the investigation or prosecution;

(b) The case has been investigated by a State which has jurisdiction over it and the State has decided not to prosecute the person concerned, unless the decision resulted from the unwillingness or inability of the State genuinely to prosecute;

(c) The person concerned has already been tried for conduct which is the subject of the complaint, and a trial by the Court is not permitted under Article 20, paragraph 3;

(d) The case is not of sufficient gravity to justify further action by the Court.

2. In order to determine unwillingness in a particular case, the Court shall consider, having regard to the principles of due process recognized by international law, whether one or more of the following exist, as applicable:

(a) The proceedings were or are being undertaken or the national decision was made for the purpose of shielding the person concerned from criminal responsibility for crimes within the jurisdiction of the Court referred to in Article 5;

(b) There has been an unjustified delay in the proceedings which in the circumstances is inconsistent with an intent to bring the person concerned to justice;

(c) The proceedings were not or are not being conducted independently or impartially, and they were or are being conducted in a manner which, in the circumstances, is inconsistent with an intent to bring the person concerned to justice.

3. In order to determine inability in a particular case, the Court shall consider whether, due to a total or substantial collapse or unavailability of its national judicial system, the State is unable to obtain the accused or the necessary evidence and testimony or otherwise unable to carry out its proceedings.

Article 18. Preliminary rulings regarding admissibility

1. When a situation has been referred to the Court pursuant to Article 13 (a) and the Prosecutor has determined that there would be a reasonable basis to commence an investigation, or the Prosecutor initiates an investigation pursuant to Articles 13 (c) and 15, the Prosecutor shall notify all States Parties and those States which, taking into account the information available, would normally exercise jurisdiction over the crimes concerned. The Prosecutor may notify such States on a confidential basis and, where the Prosecutor believes it necessary to protect persons, prevent destruction of evidence or prevent the absconding of persons, may limit the scope of the information provided to States.

2. Within one month of receipt of that notice, a State may inform the Court that it is investigating or has investigated its nationals or others within its jurisdiction with respect to criminal acts which may constitute crimes referred to in Article 5 and which relate to the information provided in the notification to States. At the request of that State, the Prosecutor shall defer to the State's investigation of those persons unless the Pre-Trial Chamber, on the application of the Prosecutor, decides to authorize the investigation.

3. The Prosecutor's deferral to a State's investigation shall be open to review by the Prosecutor six months after the date of deferral or at any time when there has been a significant change of circumstances based on the State's unwillingness or inability genuinely to carry out the investigation.

4. The State concerned or the Prosecutor may appeal to the Appeals Chamber against a ruling of the Pre-Trial Chamber, in accordance with Article 82, paragraph 2. The appeal may be heard on an expedited basis.

5. When the Prosecutor has deferred an investigation in accordance with paragraph 2, the Prosecutor may request that the State concerned periodically inform the Prosecutor of the progress of its investigations and any subsequent prosecutions. States Parties shall respond to such requests without undue delay.

6. Pending a ruling by the Pre-Trial Chamber, or at any time when the Prosecutor has deferred an investigation under this article, the Prosecutor may, on an exceptional basis, seek authority from the Pre-Trial Chamber to pursue necessary investigative steps for the purpose of preserving evidence where there is a unique opportunity to obtain important evidence or there is a significant risk that such evidence may not be subsequently available.

7. A State which has challenged a ruling of the Pre-Trial Chamber under this article may challenge the admissibility of a case under Article 19 on the grounds of additional significant facts or significant change of circumstances.

Article 19. Challenges to the jurisdiction of the Court or the admissibility of a case

1. The Court shall satisfy itself that it has jurisdiction in any case brought before it. The Court may, on its own motion, determine the admissibility of a case in accordance with Article 17.

2. Challenges to the admissibility of a case on the grounds referred to in Article 17 or challenges to the jurisdiction of the Court may be made by:

(a) An accused or a person for whom a warrant of arrest or a summons to appear has been issued under Article 58;

(b) A State which has jurisdiction over a case, on the ground that it is investigating or prosecuting the case or has investigated or prosecuted; or

(c) A State from which acceptance of jurisdiction is required under Article 12.

3. The Prosecutor may seek a ruling from the Court regarding a question of jurisdiction or admissibility. In proceedings with respect to jurisdiction or admissibility, those who have referred the situation under Article 13, as well as victims, may also submit observations to the Court.

4. The admissibility of a case or the jurisdiction of the Court may be challenged only once by any person or State referred to in paragraph 2. The challenge shall take place prior to or at the commencement of the trial. In exceptional circumstances, the Court may grant leave for a challenge to be brought more than once or at a time later than the commencement of the trial. Challenges to the admissibility of a case, at the commencement of a trial, or subsequently with the leave of the Court, may be based only on Article 17, paragraph 1 (c).

5. A State referred to in paragraph 2 (b) and (c) shall make a challenge at the earliest opportunity.

6. Prior to the confirmation of the charges, challenges to the admissibility of a case or challenges to the jurisdiction of the Court shall be referred to the Pre-Trial Chamber. After confirmation of the charges, they shall be referred to the Trial Chamber. Decisions with respect to jurisdiction or admissibility may be appealed to the Appeals Chamber in accordance with Article 82.

7. If a challenge is made by a State referred to in paragraph 2 (b) or (c), the Prosecutor shall suspend the investigation until such time as the Court makes a determination in accordance with Article 17.

8. Pending a ruling by the Court, the Prosecutor may seek authority from the Court:

(a) To pursue necessary investigative steps of the kind referred to in Article 18, paragraph 6;

(b) To take a statement or testimony from a witness or complete the collection and examination of evidence which had begun prior to the making of the challenge; and

(c) In cooperation with the relevant States, to prevent the absconding of persons in respect of whom the Prosecutor has already requested a warrant of arrest under Article 58.

9. The making of challenge shall not affect the validity of any act performed by the Prosecutor or any order or warrant issued by the Court prior to the making of the challenge.

10. If the Court has decided that a case is inadmissible under Article 17, the Prosecutor may submit a request for a review of the decision when he or she is fully satisfied that new facts have arisen which negate the basis on which the case had previously been found inadmissible under Article 17.

11. If the Prosecutor, having regard to the matters referred to in Article 17, defers an investigation, the Prosecutor may request that the relevant State make available to the Prosecutor information on the proceedings. That information shall, at the request of the State concerned, be confidential. If the Prosecutor thereafter decides to proceed with an investigation, he or she shall notify the State in respect of the proceedings of which deferral has taken place.

Article 20. *Ne bis in idem*

1. Except as provided in this Statute, no person shall be tried before the Court with respect to conduct which formed the basis of crimes for which the person has been convicted or acquitted by the Court.

2. No person shall be tried before another court for a crime referred to in Article 5 for which that person has already been convicted or acquitted by the Court.

3. No person who has been tried by another court for conduct also proscribed under Articles 6, 7 or 8 shall be tried by the Court with respect to the same conduct unless the proceedings in the other court:

(a) Were for the purpose of shielding the person concerned from criminal responsibility for crimes within the jurisdiction of the Court; or

(b) Otherwise were not conducted independently or impartially in accordance with the norms of due process recognized by international law and were conducted in a manner which, in the circumstances, was inconsistent with an intent to bring the person concerned to justice.

Article 21. Applicable law

1. The Court shall apply:

(a) In the first place, this Statute, Elements of Crimes and its Rules of Procedure and Evidence;

(b) In the second place, where appropriate, applicable treaties and the principles and rules of international law, including the established principles of the international law of armed conflict;

(c) Failing that, general principles of law derived by the Court from national laws and legal systems of the world....

2. The Court may apply principles and rules of law as interpreted in its previous decisions.

3. The application and interpretation of law pursuant to this article must be consistent with internationally recognized human rights, and be without any adverse distinction founded on grounds such as gender, as defined in Article 7, paragraph 3, age, race, colour, language, religion or belief, political or other opinion, national, ethnic or social origin, wealth, birth or other status.

Part 3. General Principles of Criminal Law

Article 22. *Nullum crimen sine lege*

1. A person shall not be criminally responsible under this Statute unless the conduct in question constitutes, at the time it takes place, a crime within the jurisdiction of this Court.

2. The definition of a crime shall be strictly construed and shall not be extended by analogy. In case of ambiguity, the definition shall be interpreted in favour of the person being investigated, prosecuted or convicted.

3. This article shall not affect the characterization of any conduct as criminal under international law independently of this Statute.

Article 23. *Nulla poena sine lege*

A person convicted by the Court may be punished only in accordance with this Statute.

Article 24. Non-retroactivity *ratione personae*

1. No person shall be criminally responsible under this Statute for conduct prior to entry into force of the Statute.

2. In the event of a change in the law applicable to a given case prior to a final judgment, the law more favourable to the person being investigated, prosecuted or convicted shall apply.

Article 25. Individual criminal responsibility

1. The Court shall have jurisdiction over natural persons pursuant to this Statute.

2. A person who commits a crime within the jurisdiction of the Court shall be individually responsible and liable for punishment in accordance with this Statute.

3. In accordance with this Statute, a person shall be criminally responsible and liable for punishment for a crime within the jurisdiction of the Court if that person:

(a) Commits such a crime, whether as an individual, jointly with another or through another person, regardless of whether that other person is criminally responsible;

(b) Orders, solicits or induces the commission of such a crime which in fact occurs or is attempted;

(c) For the purpose of facilitating the commission of such a crime, aids, abets or otherwise assists in its commission or its attempted commission, including providing the means for its commission;

(d) In any other way contributes to the commission or attempted commission of such a crime by a group of persons acting with a common purpose. Such contribution shall be intentional and shall either:

(i) Be made with the aim of furthering the criminal activity or criminal purpose of the group, where such activity or purpose involves the commission of a crime within the jurisdiction of the Court; or

(ii) Be made in the knowledge of the intention of the group to commit the crime;

(e) In respect of the crime of genocide, directly and publicly incites others to commit genocide;

(f) Attempts to commit such a crime by taking action that commences its execution by means of a substantial step, but the crime does not occur because of circumstances independent of the person's intentions. However, a person who abandons the effort to commit the crime or otherwise prevents the completion of the crime shall not be liable for punishment under this Statute for the attempt to commit that crime if that person completely and voluntarily gave up the criminal purpose.

4. No provision in this Statute relating to individual criminal responsibility shall affect the responsibility of States under international law.

Article 26. Exclusion of jurisdiction over persons under eighteen

The Court shall have no jurisdiction over any person who was under the age of 18 at the time of the alleged commission of a crime.

Article 27. Irrelevance of official capacity

1. This Statute shall apply equally to all persons without any distinction based on official capacity. In particular, official capacity as a Head of State or Government, a member of a Government or parliament, an elected representative or a government official shall in no case exempt a person from criminal responsibility under this Statute, nor shall it, in and of itself, constitute a ground for reduction of sentence.

2. Immunities or special procedural rules which may attach to the official capacity of a person, whether under national or international law, shall not bar the Court from exercising its jurisdiction over such a person.

Article 28. Responsibility of commanders and other superiors

In addition to other grounds of criminal responsibility under this Statute for crimes within the jurisdiction of the Court:

1. A military commander or person effectively acting as a military commander shall be criminally responsible for crimes within the jurisdiction of the Court committed by forces under his or her effective command and control, or effective authority and control as the case may be, as a result of his or her failure to exercise control properly over such forces, where:

(a) That military commander or person either knew or, owing to the circumstances at the time, should have known that the forces were committing or about to commit such crimes; and

(b) That military commander or person failed to take all necessary and reasonable measures within his or her power to prevent or repress their commission or to submit the matter to the competent authorities for investigation and prosecution.

2. With respect to superior and subordinate relationships not described in paragraph 1, a superior shall be criminally responsible for crimes within the jurisdiction of the Court committed by subordinates under his or her effective authority and control, as a result of his or her failure to exercise control properly over such subordinates, where:

(a) The superior either knew, or consciously disregarded information which clearly indicated, that the subordinates were committing or about to commit such crimes;

(b) The crimes concerned activities that were within the effective responsibility and control of the superior; and

(c) The superior failed to take all necessary and reasonable measures within his or her power to prevent or repress their commission or to submit the matter to the competent authorities for investigation and prosecution.

Article 29. Non-applicability of statute of limitations

The crimes within the jurisdiction of the Court shall not be subject to any statute of limitations.

Article 30. Mental Element

1. Unless otherwise provided, a person shall be criminally responsible and liable for punishment for a crime within the jurisdiction of the Court only if the material elements are committed with intent and knowledge.

2. For the purposes of this article, a person has intent where:

(a) In relation to conduct, that person means to engage in the conduct;

(b) In relation to a consequence, that person means to cause that consequence or is aware that it will occur in the ordinary course of events.

3. For the purposes of this article, "knowledge" means awareness that a circumstance exists or a consequence will occur in the ordinary course of events. "Know" and "knowingly" shall be construed accordingly.

Article 31. Grounds for excluding criminal responsibility

1. In addition to other grounds for excluding criminal responsibility provided for in this Section, a person shall not be criminally responsible if, at the time of that person's conduct:

(a) The person suffers from a mental disease or defect that destroys that person's capacity to appreciate the unlawfulness or nature of his or her conduct, or capacity to control his or her conduct to conform to the requirements of law;

(b) The person is in a state of intoxication that destroys that person's capacity to appreciate the unlawfulness or nature of his or her conduct, or capacity to control his or her conduct to conform to the requirements of law, unless the person has become voluntarily intoxicated under such circumstances that the person knew, or disregarded the risk, that, as a result of the intoxication, he or she was likely to engage in conduct constituting a crime within the jurisdiction of the Court;

(c) The person acts reasonably to defend himself or herself or another person or, in the case of war crimes, property which is essential for the survival of the person or another person or property which is essential for accomplishing a military mission, against an imminent and unlawful use of force in a manner proportionate to the degree of danger to the person or the other person or property protected. The fact that the person was involved in a defensive operation conducted by forces shall not in itself constitute a ground for excluding criminal responsibility under this subparagraph;

(d) The conduct which is alleged to constitute a crime within the jurisdiction of the Court has been caused by duress resulting from a threat of imminent death or of continuing or imminent serious bodily harm against that person or another person, and the person acts necessarily and reasonably to avoid this threat, provided that the person does not intend to cause a greater harm than the one sought to be avoided. Such a threat may either be:

(i) Made by other persons; or

(ii) Constituted by other circumstances beyond that person's control.

2. The Court shall determine the applicability of the grounds for excluding criminal responsibility provided for in this Statute to the case before it.

3. At trial, the Court may consider a ground for excluding criminal responsibility other than those referred to in paragraph 1 where such a ground is derived from applicable law as set forth in Article 21. The procedure relating to the consideration of such a ground shall be provided for in the Rules of Procedure and Evidence.

Article 32. Mistake of fact or mistake of law

1. A mistake of fact shall be a ground for excluding criminal responsibility only if it negates the mental element required by the crime.

2. A mistake of law as to whether a particular type of conduct is a crime within the jurisdiction of the Court shall not be a ground for excluding criminal responsibility. A mistake of law may, however, be a ground for excluding criminal responsibility if it negates the mental element required by such a crime, or as provided for in Article 33.

Article 33. Superior orders and prescription of law

1. The fact that a crime within the jurisdiction of the Court has been committed by a person pursuant to an order of a Government or of a superior, whether military or civilian, shall not relieve that person of criminal responsibility unless:

(a) The person was under a legal obligation to obey orders of the Government or the superior in question;

(b) The person did not know that the order was unlawful; and

(c) The order was not manifestly unlawful.

2. For the purposes of this article, orders to commit genocide or crimes against humanity are manifestly unlawful.

Part 4. Composition and Administration of the Court

Article 34. Organs of the Court

The Court shall be composed of the following organs:

(a) The Presidency;

(b) An Appeals Division, a Trial Division and a Pre-Trial Division;

(c) The Office of the Prosecutor;

(d) The Registry.

Article 35. Service of judges

1. All judges shall be elected as full-time members of the Court and shall be available to serve on that basis from the commencement of their terms of office.

2. The judges composing the Presidency shall serve on a full-time basis as soon as they are elected.

3. The Presidency may, on the basis of the workload of the Court and in consultation with its members, decide from time to time to what extent the remaining judges shall be required to serve on a full-time basis. Any such arrangement shall be without prejudice to the provisions of Article 40.

4. The financial arrangements for judges not required to serve on a full-time basis shall be made in accordance with Article 49.

Article 36. Qualifications, nomination and election of judges

1. Subject to the provisions of paragraph 2, there shall be 18 judges of the Court.

2. (a) The Presidency, acting on behalf of the Court, may propose an increase in the number of judges specified in paragraph 1, indicating the reasons why this is considered necessary and appropriate. The Registrar shall promptly circulate any such proposal to all States Parties.

(b) Any such proposal shall then be considered at a meeting of the Assembly of States Parties to be convened in accordance with Article 112. The proposal shall be considered adopted if approved at the meeting by a vote of two-thirds of the members of the Assembly of States Parties and shall enter into force at such time as decided by the Assembly of States Parties.

(c) (i) Once a proposal for an increase in the number of judges has been adopted under subparagraph (b), the election of the additional judges shall take place at the next session of the Assembly of States Parties in accordance with paragraphs 3 to 8 inclusive, and Article 37, paragraph 2;

(ii) Once a proposal for an increase in the number of judges has been adopted and brought into effect under subparagraphs (b) and (c) (i), it shall be open to the Presidency at any time thereafter, if the workload of the Court justifies it, to propose a reduction in the number of judges, provided that the number of judges shall not be reduced below that specified in paragraph 1. The proposal shall be dealt with in accordance with the procedure laid down in subparagraphs (a) and (b). In the event that the proposal is adopted, the number of judges shall be progressively decreased as the terms of office of serving judges expire, until the necessary number has been reached.

3. (a) The judges shall be chosen from among persons of high moral character, impartiality and integrity who possess the qualifications required in their respective States for appointment to the highest judicial offices.

(b) Every candidate for election to the Court shall:

(i) Have established competence in criminal law and procedure, and the necessary relevant experience, whether as judge, prosecutor, advocate or in other similar capacity, in criminal proceedings; or

(ii) Have established competence in relevant areas of international law such as international humanitarian law and the law of human rights, and extensive experience in a professional legal capacity which is of relevance to the judicial work of the Court;

(c) Every candidate for election to the Court shall have an excellent knowledge of and be fluent in at least one of the working languages of the Court.

4. (a) Nominations of candidates for election to the Court may be made by any State Party to this Statute, and shall be made either:

(i) By the procedure for the nomination of candidates for appointment to the highest judicial offices in the State in question; or

(ii) By the procedure provided for the nomination of candidates for the International Court of Justice in the Statute of that Court. Nominations shall be accompanied by a statement in the necessary detail specifying how the candidate fulfils the requirements of paragraph 3.

(b) Each State Party may put forward one candidate for any given election who need not necessarily be a national of that State Party but shall in any case be a national of a State Party.

(c) The Assembly of States Parties may decide to establish, if appropriate, an Advisory Committee on nominations. In that event, the Committee's composition and mandate shall be established by the Assembly of States Parties.

5. For the purposes of the election, there shall be two lists of candidates:

List A containing the names of candidates with the qualifications specified in paragraph 3 (b) (i); and

List B containing the names of candidates with the qualifications specified in paragraph 3 (b) (ii).

A candidate with sufficient qualifications for both lists may choose on which list to appear. At the first election to the Court, at least nine judges shall be elected from list A and at least five judges from list B. Subsequent elections shall be so organized as to maintain the equivalent proportion on the Court of judges qualified on the two lists.

6. (a) The judges shall be elected by secret ballot at a meeting of the Assembly of States Parties convened for that purpose under Article 112. Subject to paragraph 7, the persons elected to the Court shall be the 18 candidates who obtain the highest number of votes and a two-thirds majority of the States Parties present and voting.

(b) In the event that a sufficient number of judges is not elected on the first ballot, successive ballots shall be held in accordance with the procedures laid down in subparagraph (a) until the remaining places have been filled.

7. No two judges may be nationals of the same State. A person who, for the purposes of membership in the Court, could be regarded as a national of more than one State shall be deemed to be a national of the State in which that person ordinarily exercises civil and political rights.

8. (a) The States Parties shall, in the selection of judges, take into account the need, within the membership of the Court, for:

(i) The representation of the principal legal systems of the world;

(ii) Equitable geographical representation; and

(iii) A fair representation of female and male judges.

(b) States Parties shall also take into account the need to include judges with legal expertise on specific issues, including, but not limited to, violence against women or children.

9. (a) Subject to subparagraph (b), judges shall hold office for a term of nine years and, subject to subparagraph (c) and to Article 37, paragraph 2, shall not be eligible for re-election.

(b) At the first election, one third of the judges elected shall be selected by lot to serve for a term of three years; one third of the judges elected shall be selected by lot to serve for a term of six years; and the remainder shall serve for a term of nine years.

(c) A judge who is selected to serve for a term of three years under subparagraph (b) shall be eligible for re-election for a full term.

10. Notwithstanding paragraph 9, a judge assigned to a Trial or Appeals Chamber in accordance with Article 39 shall continue in office to complete any trial or appeal the hearing of which has already commenced before that Chamber.

Article 37. Judicial Vacancies

1. In the event of a vacancy, an election shall be held in accordance with Article 36 to fill the vacancy.

2. A judge elected to fill a vacancy shall serve for the remainder of the predecessor's term and, if that period is three years or less, shall be eligible for re-election for a full term under Article 36.

Article 38. The Presidency

1. The President and the First and Second Vice-Presidents shall be elected by an absolute majority of the judges. They shall each serve for a term of three years or until the

end of their respective terms of office as judges, whichever expires earlier. They shall be eligible for re-election once.

2. The First Vice-President shall act in place of the President in the event that the President is unavailable or disqualified. The Second Vice-President shall act in place of the President in the event that both the President and the First Vice-President are unavailable or disqualified.

3. The President, together with the First and Second Vice-Presidents, shall constitute the Presidency, which shall be responsible for:

(a) The proper administration of the Court, with the exception of the Office of the Prosecutor; and

(b) The other functions conferred upon it in accordance with this Statute.

4. In discharging its responsibility under paragraph 3 (a), the Presidency shall coordinate with and seek the concurrence of the Prosecutor on all matters of mutual concern.

Article 39. Chambers

1. As soon as possible after the election of the judges, the Court shall organize itself into the divisions specified in Article 34, paragraph (b). The Appeals Division shall be composed of the President and four other judges, the Trial Division of not less than six judges and the Pre-Trial Division of not less than six judges. The assignment of judges to divisions shall be based on the nature of the functions to be performed by each division and the qualifications and experience of the judges elected to the Court, in such a way that each division shall contain an appropriate combination of expertise in criminal law and procedure and in international law. The Trial and Pre-Trial Divisions shall be composed predominantly of judges with criminal trial experience.

2. (a) The judicial functions of the Court shall be carried out in each division by Chambers.

(b) (i) The Appeals Chamber shall be composed of all the judges of the Appeals Division;

(ii) The functions of the Trial Chamber shall be carried out by three judges of the Trial Division;

(iii) The functions of the Pre-Trial Chamber shall be carried out either by three judges of the Pre-Trial Division or by a single judge of that division in accordance with this Statute and the Rules of Procedure and Evidence;

(c) Nothing in this paragraph shall preclude the simultaneous constitution of more than one Trial Chamber or Pre-Trial Chamber when the efficient management of the Court's workload so requires.

3. (a) Judges assigned to the Trial and Pre-Trial Divisions shall serve in those divisions for a period of three years, and thereafter until the completion of any case the hearing of which has already commenced in the division concerned.

(b) Judges assigned to the Appeals Division shall serve in that division for their entire term of office.

4. Judges assigned to the Appeals Division shall serve only in that division. Nothing in this article shall, however, preclude the temporary attachment of judges from the

Trial Division to the Pre-Trial Division or vice versa, if the Presidency considers that the efficient management of the Court's workload so requires, provided that under no circumstances shall a judge who has participated in the pre-trial phase of a case be eligible to sit on the Trial Chamber hearing that case.

Article 40. Independence of the judges

1. The judges shall be independent in the performance of their functions.

2. Judges shall not engage in any activity which is likely to interfere with their judicial functions or to affect confidence in their independence.

3. Judges required to serve on a full-time basis at the seat of the Court shall not engage in any other occupation of a professional nature.

4. Any question regarding the application of paragraphs 2 and 3 shall be decided by an absolute majority of the judges. Where any such question concerns an individual judge, that judge shall not take part in the decision.

Article 41. Excusing and disqualification of judges

1. The Presidency may, at the request of a judge, excuse that judge from the exercise of a function under this Statute, in accordance with the Rules of Procedure and Evidence.

2. (a) A judge shall not participate in any case in which his or her impartiality might reasonably be doubted on any ground. A judge shall be disqualified from a case in accordance with this paragraph if, *inter alia*, that judge has previously been involved in any capacity in that case before the Court or in a related criminal case at the national level involving the person being investigated or prosecuted. A judge shall also be disqualified on such other grounds as may be provided for in the Rules of Procedure and Evidence.

(b) The Prosecutor or the person being investigated or prosecuted may request the disqualification of a judge under this paragraph.

(c) Any question as to the disqualification of a judge shall be decided by an absolute majority of the judges. The challenged judge shall be entitled to present his or her comments on the matter, but shall not take part in the decision.

Article 42. The Office of the Prosecutor

1. The Office of the Prosecutor shall act independently as a separate organ of the Court. It shall be responsible for receiving referrals and any substantiated information on crimes within the jurisdiction of the Court, for examining them and for conducting investigations and prosecutions before the Court. A member of the Office shall not seek or act on instructions from any external source.

2. The Office shall be headed by the Prosecutor. The Prosecutor shall have full authority over the management and administration of the Office, including the staff, facilities and other resources thereof. The Prosecutor shall be assisted by one or more Deputy Prosecutors, who shall be entitled to carry out any of the acts required of the Prosecutor under this Statute. The Prosecutor and the Deputy Prosecutors shall be of different nationalities. They shall serve on a full-time basis.

3. The Prosecutor and the Deputy Prosecutors shall be persons of high moral character, be highly competent in and have extensive practical experience in the prosecution or trial of criminal cases. They shall have an excellent knowledge of and be fluent in at least one of the working languages of the Court.

4. The Prosecutor shall be elected by secret ballot by an absolute majority of the members of the Assembly of States Parties. The Deputy Prosecutors shall be elected in the same way from a list of candidates provided by the Prosecutor. The Prosecutor shall nominate three candidates for each position of Deputy Prosecutor to be filled. Unless a shorter term is decided upon at the time of their election, the Prosecutor and the Deputy Prosecutors shall hold office for a term of nine years and shall not be eligible for re-election.

5. Neither the Prosecutor nor a Deputy Prosecutor shall engage in any activity which is likely to interfere with his or her prosecutorial functions or to affect confidence in his or her independence. They shall not engage in any other occupation of a professional nature.

6. The Presidency may excuse the Prosecutor or a Deputy Prosecutor, at his or her request, from acting in a particular case.

7. Neither the Prosecutor nor a Deputy Prosecutor shall participate in any matter in which their impartiality might reasonably be doubted on any ground. They shall be disqualified from a case in accordance with this paragraph if, *inter alia*, they have previously been involved in any capacity in that case before the Court or in a related criminal case at the national level involving the person being investigated or prosecuted.

8. Any question as to the disqualification of the Prosecutor or a Deputy Prosecutor shall be decided by the Appeals Chamber.

(a) The person being investigated or prosecuted may at any time request the disqualification of the Prosecutor or a Deputy Prosecutor on the grounds set out in this article.

(b) The Prosecutor or the Deputy Prosecutor, as appropriate, shall be entitled to present his or her comments on the matter.

9. The Prosecutor shall appoint advisers with legal expertise on specific issues, including, but not limited to, sexual and gender violence and violence against children.

Article 43. The Registry

1. The Registry shall be responsible for the non-judicial aspects of the administration and servicing of the Court, without prejudice to the functions and powers of the Prosecutor in accordance with Article 42.

2. The Registry shall be headed by the Registrar, who shall be the principal administrative officer of the Court. The Registrar shall exercise his or her functions under the authority of the President of the Court.

3. The Registrar and the Deputy Registrar shall be persons of high moral character, be highly competent and have an excellent knowledge of and be fluent in at least one of the working languages of the Court.

4. The judges shall elect the Registrar by an absolute majority by secret ballot, taking into account any recommendation by the Assembly of States Parties. If the need arises

and upon the recommendation of the Registrar, the judges shall elect, in the same manner, a Deputy Registrar.

5. The Registrar shall hold office for a term of five years, shall be eligible for re-election once and shall serve on a full-time basis. The Deputy Registrar shall hold office for a term of five years or such shorter term as may be decided upon by an absolute majority of the judges, and may be elected on the basis that the Deputy Registrar shall be called upon to serve as required.

6. The Registrar shall set up a Victims and Witnesses Unit within the Registry. This Unit shall provide, in consultation with the Office of the Prosecutor, protective measures and security arrangements, counselling and other appropriate assistance for witnesses, victims who appear before the Court and others who are at risk on account of testimony given by such witnesses. The Unit shall include staff with expertise in trauma, including trauma related to crimes of sexual violence.

Article 44. Staff

1. The Prosecutor and the Registrar shall appoint such qualified staff as may be required to their respective offices. In the case of the Prosecutor, this shall include the appointment of investigators.

2. In the employment of staff, the Prosecutor and the Registrar shall ensure the highest standards of efficiency, competency and integrity, and shall have regard, mutatis mutandis, to the criteria set forth in Article 36, paragraph 8.

3. The Registrar, with the agreement of the Presidency and the Prosecutor, shall propose Staff Regulations which include the terms and conditions upon which the staff of the Court shall be appointed, remunerated and dismissed. The Staff Regulations shall be approved by the Assembly of States Parties.

4. The Court may, in exceptional circumstances, employ the expertise of gratis personnel offered by States Parties, intergovernmental organizations or non-governmental organizations to assist with the work of any of the organs of the Court. The Prosecutor may accept any such offer on behalf of the Office of the Prosecutor. Such gratis personnel shall be employed in accordance with guidelines to be established by the Assembly of States Parties.

Article 45. Solemn undertaking

Before taking up their respective duties under this Statute, the judges, the Prosecutor, the Deputy Prosecutors, the Registrar and the Deputy Registrar shall each make a solemn undertaking in open court to exercise his or her respective functions impartially and conscientiously.

Article 46. Removal from office

1. A judge, the Prosecutor, a Deputy Prosecutor, the Registrar or the Deputy Registrar shall be removed from office if a decision to this effect is made in accordance with paragraph 2, in cases where that person:

> (a) Is found to have committed serious misconduct or a serious breach of his or her duties under this Statute, as provided for in the Rules of Procedure and Evidence; or

(b) Is unable to exercise the functions required by this Statute.

2. A decision as to the removal from office of a judge, the Prosecutor or a Deputy Prosecutor under paragraph 1 shall be made by the Assembly of States Parties, by secret ballot:

(a) In the case of a judge, by a two-thirds majority of the States Parties upon a recommendation adopted by a two-thirds majority of the other judges;

(b) In the case of the Prosecutor, by an absolute majority of the States Parties;

(c) In the case of a Deputy Prosecutor, by an absolute majority of the States Parties upon the recommendation of the Prosecutor.

3. A decision as to the removal from office of the Registrar or Deputy Registrar shall be made by an absolute majority of the judges.

4. A judge, Prosecutor, Deputy Prosecutor, Registrar or Deputy Registrar whose conduct or ability to exercise the functions of the office as required by this Statute is challenged under this article shall have full opportunity to present and receive evidence and to make submissions in accordance with the Rules of Procedure and Evidence. The person in question shall not otherwise participate in the consideration of the matter.

Article 47. Disciplinary measures

A judge, Prosecutor, Deputy Prosecutor, Registrar or Deputy Registrar who has committed misconduct of a less serious nature than that set out in Article 46, paragraph 1, shall be subject to disciplinary measures, in accordance with the Rules of Procedure and Evidence.

Article 48. Privileges and immunities

1. The Court shall enjoy in the territory of each State Party such privileges and immunities as are necessary for the fulfilment of its purposes.

2. The judges, the Prosecutor, the Deputy Prosecutors and the Registrar shall, when engaged on or with respect to the business of the Court, enjoy the same privileges and immunities as are accorded to heads of diplomatic missions and shall, after the expiry of their terms of office, continue to be accorded immunity from legal process of every kind in respect of words spoken or written and acts performed by them in their official capacity.

3. The Deputy Registrar, the staff of the Office of the Prosecutor and the staff of the Registry shall enjoy the privileges and immunities and facilities necessary for the performance of their functions, in accordance with the agreement on the privileges and immunities of the Court.

4. Counsel, experts, witnesses or any other person required to be present at the seat of the Court shall be accorded such treatment as is necessary for the proper functioning of the Court, in accordance with the agreement on the privileges and immunities of the Court.

5. The privileges and immunities of:

(a) A judge or the Prosecutor may be waived by an absolute majority of the judges;

(b) The Registrar may be waived by the Presidency;

(c) The Deputy Prosecutors and staff of the Office of the Prosecutor may be waived by the Prosecutor;

(d) The Deputy Registrar and staff of the Registry may be waived by the Registrar.

Article 49. Salaries, allowances and expenses

The judges, the Prosecutor, the Deputy Prosecutors, the Registrar and the Deputy Registrar shall receive such salaries, allowances and expenses as may be decided upon by the Assembly of States Parties. These salaries and allowances shall not be reduced during their terms of office.

Article 50. Official and working languages

1. The official languages of the Court shall be Arabic, Chinese, English, French, Russian and Spanish. The judgements of the Court, as well as other decisions resolving fundamental issues before the Court, shall be published in the official languages. The Presidency shall, in accordance with the criteria established by the Rules of Procedure and Evidence, determine which decisions may be considered as resolving fundamental issues for the purposes of this paragraph.

2. The working languages of the Court shall be English and French. The Rules of Procedure and Evidence shall determine the cases in which other official languages may be used as working languages.

3. At the request of any party to a proceeding or a State allowed to intervene in a proceeding, the Court shall authorize a language other than English or French to be used by such a party or State, provided that the Court considers such authorization to be adequately justified.

Article 51. Rules of Procedure and Evidence

1. The Rules of Procedure and Evidence shall enter into force upon adoption by a two-thirds majority of the members of the Assembly of States Parties.

2. Amendments to the Rules of Procedure and Evidence may be proposed by:

(a) Any State Party;

(b) The judges acting by an absolute majority; or

(c) The Prosecutor.

Such amendments shall enter into force upon adoption by a two-thirds majority of the members of the Assembly of States Parties.

3. After the adoption of the Rules of Procedure and Evidence, in urgent cases where the Rules do not provide for a specific situation before the Court, the judges may, by a two-thirds majority, draw up provisional Rules to be applied until adopted, amended or rejected at the next ordinary or special session of the Assembly of States Parties.

4. The Rules of Procedure and Evidence, amendments thereto and any provisional Rule shall be consistent with this Statute. Amendments to the Rules of Procedure and Evidence as well as provisional Rules shall not be applied retroactively to the detriment of the person who is being investigated or prosecuted or who has been convicted.

5. In the event of conflict between the Statute and the Rules of Procedure and Evidence, the Statute shall prevail.

Article 52. Regulations of the Court

1. The judges shall, in accordance with this Statute and the Rules of Procedure and Evidence, adopt, by an absolute majority, the Regulations of the Court necessary for its routine functioning.

2. The Prosecutor and the Registrar shall be consulted in the elaboration of the Regulations and any amendments thereto.

3. The Regulations and any amendments thereto shall take effect upon adoption unless otherwise decided by the judges. Immediately upon adoption, they shall be circulated to States Parties for comments. If within six months there are no objections from a majority of States Parties, they shall remain in force.

PART 5. INVESTIGATION AND PROSECUTION

Article 53. Initiation of an investigation

1. The Prosecutor shall, having evaluated the information made available to him or her, initiate an investigation unless he or she determines that there is no reasonable basis to proceed under this Statute. In deciding whether to initiate an investigation, the Prosecutor shall consider whether:

(a) The information available to the Prosecutor provides a reasonable basis to believe that a crime within the jurisdiction of the Court has been or is being committed;

(b) The case is or would be admissible under Article 17; and

(c) Taking into account the gravity of the crime and the interests of victims, there are nonetheless substantial reasons to believe that an investigation would not serve the interests of justice.

If the Prosecutor determines that there is no reasonable basis to proceed and his or her determination is based solely on subparagraph (c) above, he or she shall inform the Pre-Trial Chamber.

2. If, upon investigation, the Prosecutor concludes that there is not a sufficient basis for a prosecution because:

(a) There is not a sufficient legal or factual basis to seek a warrant or summons under Article 58;

(b) The case is inadmissible under Article 17; or

(c) A prosecution is not in the interests of justice, taking into account all the circumstances, including the gravity of the crime, the interests of victims and the age or infirmity of the alleged perpetrator, and his or her role in the alleged crime;

The Prosecutor shall inform the Pre-Trial Chamber and the State making a referral under Article 14 or the Security Council in a case under Article 13, paragraph (b), of his or her conclusion and the reasons for the conclusion.

3. (a) At the request of the State making a referral under Article 14 or the Security Council under Article 13, paragraph (b), the Pre-Trial Chamber may review a decision of the Prosecutor under paragraph 1 or 2 not to proceed and may request the Prosecutor to reconsider that decision.

(b) In addition, the Pre-Trial Chamber may, on its own initiative, review a decision of the Prosecutor not to proceed if it is based solely on paragraph 1(c) or 2(c). In such a case, the decision of the Prosecutor shall be effective only if confirmed by the Pre-Trial Chamber.

4. The Prosecutor may, at any time, reconsider a decision whether to initiate an investigation prosecution based on new facts or information.

Article 54. Duties and powers of the Prosecutor with respect to investigations

1. The Prosecutor shall:

(a) In order to establish the truth, extend the investigation to cover all facts and evidence relevant to an assessment of whether there is criminal responsibility under this Statute, and, in doing so, investigate incriminating and exonerating circumstances equally;

(b) Take appropriate measures to ensure the effective investigation and prosecution of crimes within the jurisdiction of the Court, and in doing so, respect the interests and personal circumstances of victims and witnesses, including age, gender as defined in Article 7, paragraph 3, and health, and take into account the nature of the crime, in particular where it involves sexual violence, gender violence or violence against children; and

(c) Fully respect the rights of persons arising under this Statute.

2. The Prosecutor may conduct investigations on the territory of a State:

(a) In accordance with the provisions of Part 9; or

(b) As authorized by the Pre-Trial Chamber under Article 57, paragraph 3 (d).

3. The Prosecutor may:

(a) Collect and examine evidence;

(b) Request the presence of and question persons being investigated, victims and witnesses;

(c) Seek the cooperation of any State or intergovernmental organization or arrangement in accordance with its respective competence and/or mandate;

(d) Enter into such arrangements or agreements, not inconsistent with this Statute, as may be necessary to facilitate the cooperation of a State, intergovernmental organization or person;

(e) Agree not to disclose, at any stage of the proceedings, documents or information that the Prosecutor obtains on the condition of confidentiality and solely for the purpose of generating new evidence, unless the provider of the information consents; and

(f) Take necessary measures, or request that necessary measures be taken, to ensure the confidentiality of information, the protection of any person or the preservation of evidence.

Article 55. Rights of persons during an investigation

1. In respect of an investigation under this Statute, a person:

(a) Shall not be compelled to incriminate himself or herself or to confess guilt;

(b) Shall not be subjected to any form of coercion, duress or threat, to torture or to any other form of cruel, inhuman or degrading treatment or punishment; and

(c) Shall, if questioned in a language other than a language the person fully understands and speaks, have, free of any cost, the assistance of a competent interpreter and such translations as are necessary to meet the requirements of fairness;

(d) Shall not be subjected to arbitrary arrest or detention; and shall not be deprived of his or her liberty except on such grounds and in accordance with such procedures as are established in the Statute.

2. Where there are grounds to believe that a person has committed a crime within the jurisdiction of the Court and that person is about to be questioned either by the Prosecutor, or by national authorities pursuant to a request made under Part 9 of this Statute, that person shall also have the following rights of which he or she shall be informed prior to being questioned:

(a) To be informed, prior to being questioned, that there are grounds to believe that he or she has committed a crime within the jurisdiction of the Court;

(b) To remain silent, without such silence being a consideration in the determination of guilt or innocence;

(c) To have legal assistance of the person's choosing, or, if the person does not have legal assistance, to have legal assistance assigned to him or her, in any case where the interests of justice so require, and without payment by the person in any such case if the person does not have sufficient means to pay for it;

(d) To be questioned in the presence of counsel unless the person has voluntarily waived his or her right to counsel.

Article 56. Role of the Pre-Trial Chamber in relation to a unique investigative opportunity

1. (a) Where the Prosecutor considers an investigation to present a unique opportunity to take testimony or a statement from a witness or to examine, collect or test evidence, which may not be available subsequently for the purposes of a trial, the Prosecutor shall so inform the Pre-Trial Chamber.

(b) In that case, the Pre-Trial Chamber may, upon request of the Prosecutor, take such measures as may be necessary to ensure the efficiency and integrity of the proceedings and, in particular, to protect the rights of the defence.

(c) Unless the Pre-Trial Chamber orders otherwise, the Prosecutor shall provide the relevant information to the person who has been arrested or appeared in response to a summons in connection with the investigation referred to in subparagraph (a), in order that he or she may be heard on the matter.

2. The measures referred to in paragraph 1(b) may include:

(a) Making recommendations or orders regarding procedures to be followed;

(b) Directing that a record be made of the proceedings;

(c) Appointing an expert to assist;

(d) Authorizing counsel for a person who has been arrested, or appeared before the Court in response to a summons, to participate, or where there has not yet been such an arrest or appearance or counsel has not been designated, appointing another counsel to attend and represent the interests of the defence;

(e) Naming one of its members or, if necessary, another available judge of the Pre-Trial or Trial Division to observe and make recommendations or orders regarding the collection and preservation of evidence and the questioning of persons;

(f) Taking such other action as may be necessary to collect or preserve evidence.

3. (a) Where the Prosecutor has not sought measures pursuant to this article but the Pre-Trial Chamber considers that such measures are required to preserve evidence that it deems would be essential for the defence at trial, it shall consult with the Prosecutor as to whether there is good reason for the Prosecutor's failure to request the measures. If upon consultation, the Pre-Trial Chamber concludes that the Prosecutor's failure to request such measures is unjustified, the Pre-Trial Chamber may take such measures on its own initiative.

(b) A decision of the Pre-Trial Chamber to act on its own initiative under this paragraph may be appealed by the Prosecutor. The appeal shall be heard on an expedited basis.

4. The admissibility of evidence preserved or collected for trial pursuant to this article, or the record thereof, shall be governed at trial by Article 69, and given such weight as determined by the Trial Chamber.

Article 57. Functions and powers of the Pre-Trial Chamber

1. Unless otherwise provided for in this Statute, the Pre-Trial Chamber shall exercise its functions in accordance with the provisions of this article.

2. (a) Orders or rulings of the Pre-Trial Chamber issued under Articles 15, 18, 19, 54, paragraph 2, 61, paragraph 7, and 72 must be concurred in by a majority of its judges.

(b) In all other cases, a single judge of the Pre-Trial Chamber may exercise the functions provided for in this Statute, unless otherwise provided for in the Rules of Procedure and Evidence or by a majority of the Pre-Trial Chamber.

3. In addition to its other functions under this Statute, the Pre-Trial Chamber may:

(a) At the request of the Prosecutor, issue such orders and warrants as may be required for the purposes of an investigation;

(b) Upon the request of a person who has been arrested or has appeared pursuant to a summons under Article 58, issue such orders, including measures such as those described in Article 56, or seek such cooperation pursuant to Part 9 as may be necessary to assist the person in the preparation of his or her defence;

(c) Where necessary, provide for the protection and privacy of victims and witnesses, the preservation of evidence, the protection of persons who have been arrested or appeared in response to a summons, and the protection of national security information;

(d) Authorize the Prosecutor to take specific investigative steps within the territory of a State Party without having secured the cooperation of that State under Part 9 if, whenever possible having regard to the views of the State concerned, the Pre-Trial Chamber has determined in that case that the State is clearly unable to execute a request for cooperation due to the unavailability of any authority or any component of its judicial system competent to execute the request for cooperation under Part 9.

(e) Where a warrant of arrest or a summons has been issued under Article 58, and having due regard to the strength of the evidence and the rights of the parties concerned, as provided for in this Statute and the Rules of Procedure and Evidence, seek the cooperation of States pursuant to Article 93, paragraph 1(j), to take protective measures for the purpose of forfeiture in particular for the ultimate benefit of victims.

Article 58. Issuance by the Pre-Trial Chamber of a warrant of arrest or a summons to appear

1. At any time after the initiation of an investigation, the Pre-Trial Chamber shall, on the application of the Prosecutor, issue a warrant of arrest of a person if, having examined the application and the evidence or other information submitted by the Prosecutor, it is satisfied that:

(a) There are reasonable grounds to believe that the person has committed a crime within the jurisdiction of the Court; and

(b) The arrest of the person appears necessary:

(i) To ensure the person's appearance at trial.

(ii) To ensure that the person does not obstruct or endanger the investigation or the court proceedings, or

(iii) Where applicable, to prevent the person from continuing with the commission of that crime or a related crime which is within the jurisdiction of the Court and which arises out of the same circumstances.

2. The application of the Prosecutor shall contain:

(a) The name of the person and any other relevant identifying information;

(b) A specific reference to the crimes within the jurisdiction of the Court which the person is alleged to have committed;

(c) A concise statement of the facts which are alleged to constitute those crimes;

(d) A summary of the evidence and any other information which establish reasonable grounds to believe that the person committed those crimes; and

(e) The reason why the Prosecutor believes that the arrest of the person is necessary.

3. The warrant of arrest shall contain:

(a) The name of the person and any other relevant identifying information;

(b) A specific reference to the crimes within the jurisdiction of the Court for which the person's arrest is sought; and

(c) A concise statement of the facts which are alleged to constitute those crimes.

4. The warrant of arrest shall remain in effect until otherwise ordered by the Court.

5. On the basis of the warrant of arrest, the Court may request the provisional arrest or the arrest and surrender of the person under Part 9.

6. The Prosecutor may request the Pre-Trial Chamber to amend the warrant of arrest by modifying or adding to the crimes specified therein. The Pre-Trial Chamber shall so amend the warrant if it is satisfied that there are reasonable grounds to believe that the person committed the modified or additional crimes.

7. As an alternative to seeking a warrant of arrest, the Prosecutor may submit an application requesting that the Pre-Trial Chamber issue a summons for the person to appear. If the Pre-Trial Chamber is satisfied that there are reasonable grounds to believe that the person committed the crime alleged and that a summons is sufficient to ensure the person's appearance, it shall issue the summons, with or without conditions restricting liberty (other than detention) if provided for by national law, for the person to appear. The summons shall contain:

(a) The name of the person and any other relevant identifying information;

(b) The specified date on which the person is to appear;

(c) A specific reference to the crimes within the jurisdiction of the Court which the person is alleged to have committed; and

(d) A concise statement of the facts which are alleged to constitute the crime.

The summons shall be served on the person.

Article 59. Arrest proceedings in the custodial State

1. A State Party which has received a request for provisional arrest or for arrest and surrender shall immediately take steps to arrest the person in question in accordance with its laws and the provisions of Part 9.

2. A person arrested shall be brought promptly before the competent judicial authority in the custodial State which shall determine, in accordance with the law of that State, that:

(a) The warrant applies to that person;

(b) The person has been arrested in accordance with the proper process; and

(c) The person's rights have been respected.

3. The person arrested shall have the right to apply to the competent authority in the custodial State for interim release pending surrender.

4. In reaching a decision on any such application, the competent authority in the custodial State shall consider whether, given the gravity of the alleged crimes, there are urgent and exceptional circumstances to justify interim release and whether necessary safeguards exist to ensure that the custodial State can fulfil its duty to surrender the person to the Court. It shall not be open to the competent authority of the custodial State to consider whether the warrant of arrest was properly issued in accordance with Article 58, paragraph 1(a) and (b).

5. The Pre-Trial Chamber shall be notified of any request for interim release and shall make recommendations to the competent authority in the custodial State. The competent authority in the custodial State shall give full consideration to such recommendations, including any recommendations on measures to prevent the escape of the person, before rendering its decision.

6. If the person is granted interim release, the Pre-Trial Chamber may request periodic reports on the status of the interim release.

7. Once ordered to be surrendered by the custodial State, the person shall be delivered to the Court as soon as possible.

Article 60. Initial proceedings before the Court

1. Upon the surrender of the person to the Court, or the person's appearance before the Court voluntarily or pursuant to a summons, the Pre-Trial Chamber shall satisfy itself that the person has been informed of the crimes which he or she is alleged to have committed, and of his or her rights under this Statute, including the right to apply for interim release pending trial.

2. A person subject to a warrant of arrest may apply for interim release pending trial. If the Pre-Trial Chamber is satisfied that the conditions set forth in Article 58, paragraph 1, are met, the person shall continue to be detained. If it is not so satisfied, the Pre-Trial Chamber shall release the person, with or without conditions.

3. The Pre-Trial Chamber shall periodically review its ruling on the release or detention of the person, and may do so at any time on the request of the Prosecutor or the person. Upon such review, it may modify its ruling as to detention, release or conditions of release, if it is satisfied that changed circumstances so require.

4. The Pre-Trial Chamber shall ensure that a person is not detained for an unreasonable period prior to trial due to inexcusable delay by the Prosecutor. If such delay occurs, the Court shall consider releasing the person, with or without conditions.

5. If necessary, the Pre-Trial Chamber may issue a warrant of arrest to secure the presence of a person who has been released.

Article 61. Confirmation of the charges before trial

1. Subject to the provisions of paragraph 2, within a reasonable time after the person's surrender or voluntary appearance before the Court, the Pre-Trial Chamber shall hold a hearing to confirm the charges on which the Prosecutor intends to seek trial. The hearing shall be held in the presence of the Prosecutor and the person charged, as well as his or her counsel.

2. The Pre-Trial Chamber may, upon request of the Prosecutor or on its own motion, hold a hearing in the absence of the person charged to confirm the charges on which the Prosecutor intends to seek trial when the person has:

(a) Waived his or her right to be present; or

(b) Fled or cannot be found and all reasonable steps have been taken to secure his or her appearance before the Court and to inform the person of the charges and that a hearing to confirm those charges will be held.

In that case, the person shall be represented by counsel where the Pre-Trial Chamber determines that it is in the interests of justice.

3. Within a reasonable time before the hearing, the person shall:

(a) Be provided with a copy of the document containing the charges on which the Prosecutor intends to bring the person to trial; and

(b) Be informed of the evidence on which the Prosecutor intends to rely at the hearing.

The Pre-Trial Chamber may issue orders regarding the disclosure of information for the purposes of the hearing.

4. Before the hearing, the Prosecutor may continue the investigation and may amend or withdraw any charges. The person shall be given reasonable notice before the hearing of any amendment to or withdrawal of charges. In case of a withdrawal of charges, the Prosecutor shall notify the Pre-Trial Chamber of the reasons for the withdrawal.

5. At the hearing, the Prosecutor shall support each charge with sufficient evidence to establish substantial grounds to believe that the person committed the crime charged. The Prosecutor may rely on documentary or summary evidence and need not call the witnesses expected to testify at the trial.

6. At the hearing, the person may:

(a) Object to the charges;

(b) Challenge the evidence presented by the Prosecutor; and

(c) Present evidence.

7. The Pre-Trial Chamber shall, on the basis of the hearing, determine whether there is sufficient evidence to establish substantial grounds to believe that the person committed each of the crimes charged. Based on its determination, the Pre-Trial Chamber shall:

(a) Confirm those charges in relation to which it has determined that there is sufficient evidence; and commit the person to a Trial Chamber for trial on the charges as confirmed;

(b) Decline to confirm those charges in relation to which it has determined that there is insufficient evidence;

(c) Adjourn the hearing and request the Prosecutor to consider;

(i) Providing further evidence or conducting further investigation with respect to a particular charge; or

(ii) Amending a charge because the evidence submitted appears to establish a different crime within the jurisdiction of the Court.

8. Where the Pre-Trial Chamber declines to confirm a charge, the Prosecutor shall not be precluded from subsequently requesting its confirmation if the request is supported by additional evidence.

9. After the charges are confirmed and before the trial has begun, the Prosecutor may, with the permission of the Pre-Trial Chamber and after notice to the accused, amend the charges. If the Prosecutor seeks to add additional charges or to substitute more serious charges, a hearing under this article to confirm those charges must be held. After commencement of the trial, the Prosecutor may, with the permission of the Trial Chamber, withdraw the charges.

10. Any warrant previously issued shall cease to have effect with respect to any charges which have not been confirmed by the Pre-Trial Chamber or which have been withdrawn by the Prosecutor.

11. Once the charges have been confirmed in accordance with this article, the Presidency shall constitute a Trial Chamber which, subject to paragraph 8 and to Article 64, paragraph 4, shall be responsible for the conduct of subsequent proceedings and may

exercise any function of the Pre-Trial Chamber that is relevant and capable of application in those proceedings.

PART 6. THE TRIAL

Article 62. Place of trial

Unless otherwise decided, the place of the trial shall be the seat of the Court.

Article 63. Trial in the presence of the accused

1. The accused shall be present during the trial.

2. If the accused, being present before the Court, continues to disrupt the trial, the Trial Chamber may remove the accused and shall make provision for him or her to observe the trial and instruct counsel from outside the courtroom, through the use of communications technology, if required. Such measures shall be taken only in exceptional circumstances after other reasonable alternatives have proved inadequate, and only for such duration as is strictly required.

Article 64. Functions and powers of the Trial Chamber

1. The functions and powers of the Trial Chamber set out in this article shall be exercised in accordance with this Statute and the Rules of Procedure and Evidence.

2. The Trial Chamber shall ensure that a trial is fair and expeditious and is conducted with full respect for the rights of the accused and due regard for the protection of victims and witnesses.

3. Upon assignment of a case for trial in accordance with this Statute, the Trial Chamber assigned to deal with the case shall:

(a) Confer with the parties and adopt such procedures as are necessary to facilitate the fair and expeditious conduct of the proceedings;

(b) Determine the language or languages to be used at trial; and

(c) Subject to any other relevant provisions of this Statute, provide for disclosure of documents or information not previously disclosed, sufficiently in advance of the commencement of the trial to enable adequate preparation for trial.

4. The Trial Chamber may, if necessary for its effective and fair functioning, refer preliminary issues to the Pre-Trial Chamber or, if necessary, to another available judge of the Pre-Trial Division.

5. Upon notice to the parties, the Trial Chamber may, as appropriate, direct that there be joinder or severance in respect of charges against more than one accused.

6. In performing its functions prior to trial or during the course of a trial, the Trial Chamber may, as necessary:

(a) Exercise any functions of the Pre-Trial Chamber referred to in Article 61, paragraph 11;

(b) Require the attendance and testimony of witnesses and production of documents and other evidence by obtaining, if necessary, the assistance of States as provided in this Statute;

(c) Provide for the protection of confidential information;

(d) Order the production of evidence in addition to that already collected prior to the trial or presented during the trial by the parties;

(e) Provide for the protection of the accused, witnesses and victims; and

(f) Rule on any other relevant matters.

7. The trial shall be held in public. The Trial Chamber may, however, determine that special circumstances require that certain proceedings be in closed session for the purposes set forth in Article 68, or to protect confidential or sensitive information to be given in evidence.

8. (a) At the commencement of the trial, the Trial Chamber shall have read to the accused the charges previously confirmed by the Pre-Trial Chamber. The Trial Chamber shall satisfy itself that the accused understands the nature of the charges. It shall afford him or her the opportunity to make an admission of guilt in accordance with Article 65 or to plead not guilty.

(b) At the trial, the presiding judge may give directions for the conduct of proceedings, including to ensure that they are conducted in a fair and impartial manner. Subject to any directions of the presiding judge, the parties may submit evidence in accordance with the provisions of this Statute.

9. The Trial Chamber shall have, *inter alia*, the power on application of a party or on its own motion to:

(a) Rule on the admissibility or relevance of evidence; and

(b) Take all necessary steps to maintain order in the course of a hearing.

10. The Trial Chamber shall ensure that a complete record of the trial, which accurately reflects the proceedings, is made and that it is maintained and preserved by the Registrar.

Article 65. Proceedings on an admission of guilt

1. Where the accused makes an admission of guilt pursuant to Article 64, paragraph 8 (a), the Trial Chamber shall determine whether:

(a) The accused understands the nature and consequences of the admission of guilt;

(b) The admission is voluntarily made by the accused after sufficient consultation with defence counsel; and

(c) The admission of guilt is supported by the facts of the case that are contained in:

(i) The charges brought by the Prosecutor and admitted by the accused;

(ii) Any materials presented by the Prosecutor which supplement the charges and which the accused accepts; and

(iii) Any other evidence, such as the testimony of witnesses, presented by the Prosecutor or the accused.

2. Where the Trial Chamber is satisfied that the matters referred to in paragraph 1 are established, it shall consider the admission of guilt, together with any additional evidence presented, as establishing all the essential facts that are required to prove the

crime to which the admission of guilt relates, and may convict the accused of that crime.

3. Where the Trial Chamber is not satisfied that the matters referred to in paragraph 1 are established, it shall consider the admission of guilt as not having been made, in which case it shall order that the trial be continued under the ordinary trial procedures provided by this Statute and may remit the case to another Trial Chamber.

4. Where the Trial Chamber is of the opinion that a more complete presentation of the facts of the case is required in the interests of justice, in particular the interests of the victims, the Trial Chamber may:

> (a) Request the Prosecutor to present additional evidence, including the testimony of witnesses; or

> (b) Order that the trial be continued under the ordinary trial procedures provided by this Statute, in which case it shall consider the admission of guilt as not having been made and may remit the case to another Trial Chamber.

5. Any discussions between the Prosecutor and the defence regarding modification of the charges, the admission of guilt or the penalty to be imposed shall not be binding on the Court.

Article 66. Presumption of innocence

1. Everyone shall be presumed innocent until proved guilty before the Court in accordance with the applicable law.

2. The onus is on the Prosecutor to prove the guilt of the accused.

3. In order to convict the accused, the Court must be convinced of the guilt of the accused beyond reasonable doubt.

Article 67. Rights of the accused

1. In the determination of any charge, the accused shall be entitled to a public hearing, having regard to the provisions of this Statute, to a fair hearing conducted impartially, and to the following minimum guarantees, in full equality:

> (a) To be informed promptly and in detail of the nature, cause and content of the charge, in a language which the accused fully understands and speaks;

> (b) To have adequate time and facilities for the preparation of the defence and to communicate freely with counsel of the accused's choosing in confidence;

> (c) To be tried without undue delay;

> (d) Subject to Article 63, paragraph 2, to be present at the trial, to conduct the defence in person or through legal assistance of the accused's choosing, to be informed, if the accused does not have legal assistance, of this right and to have legal assistance assigned by the Court in any case where the interests of justice so require, and without payment if the accused lacks sufficient means to pay for it;

> (e) To examine, or have examined, the witnesses against him or her and to obtain the attendance and examination of witnesses on his or her behalf under the same conditions as witnesses against him or her. The accused shall also be entitled to raise defences and to present other evidence admissible under this Statute;

(f) To have, free of any cost, the assistance of a competent interpreter and such translations as are necessary to meet the requirements of fairness, if any of the proceedings of or documents presented to the Court are not in a language which the accused fully understands and speaks;

(g) Not to be compelled to testify or to confess guilt and to remain silent, without such silence being a consideration in the determination of guilt or innocence;

(h) To make an unsworn oral or written statement in his or her defence; and

(i) Not to have imposed on him or her any reversal of the burden of proof or any onus of rebuttal.

2. In addition to any other disclosure provided for in this Statute, the Prosecutor shall, as soon as practicable, disclose to the defence evidence in the Prosecutor's possession or control which he or she believes shows or tends to show the innocence of the accused, or to mitigate the guilt of the accused, or which may affect the credibility of prosecution evidence. In case of doubt as to the application of this paragraph, the Court shall decide.

Article 68. Protection of the victims and witnesses and their participation in the proceedings

1. The Court shall take appropriate measures to protect the safety, physical and psychological well-being, dignity and privacy of victims and witnesses. In so doing, the Court shall have regard to all relevant factors, including age, gender as defined in Article 2, paragraph 3, and health, and the nature of the crime, in particular, but not limited to, where the crime involves sexual or gender violence or violence against children. The Prosecutor shall take such measures particularly during the investigation and prosecution of such crimes. These measures shall not be prejudicial to or inconsistent with the rights of the accused and a fair and impartial trial.

2. As an exception to the principle of public hearings provided for in Article 67, the Chambers of the Court may, to protect victims and witnesses or an accused, conduct any part of the proceedings in camera or allow the presentation of evidence by electronic or other special means. In particular, such measures shall be implemented in the case of a victim of sexual violence or a child who is a victim or a witness, unless otherwise ordered by the Court, having regard to all the circumstances, particularly the views of the victim or witness.

3. Where the personal interests of the victims are affected, the Court shall permit their views and concerns to be presented and considered at stages of the proceedings determined to be appropriate by the Court and in a manner which is not prejudicial to or inconsistent with the rights of the accused and a fair and impartial trial. Such views and concerns may be presented by the legal representatives of the victims where the Court considers it appropriate, in accordance with the Rules of Procedure and Evidence.

4. The Victims and Witnesses Unit may advise the Prosecutor and the Court on appropriate protective measures, security arrangements, counselling and assistance as referred to in Article 43, paragraph 6.

5. Where the disclosure of evidence or information pursuant to this Statute may lead to the grave endangerment of the security of a witness or his or her family, the Prosecutor may, for the purposes of any proceedings conducted prior to the commencement of the trial, withhold such evidence or information and instead submit a summary thereof.

Such measures shall be exercised in a manner which is not prejudicial to or inconsistent with the rights of the accused and a fair and impartial trial.

6. A State may make an application for necessary measures to be taken in respect of the protection of its servants or agents and the protection of confidential or sensitive information.

Article 69. Evidence

1. Before testifying, each witness shall, in accordance with the Rules of Procedure and Evidence, give an undertaking as to the truthfulness of the evidence to be given by that witness.

2. The testimony of a witness at trial shall be given in person, except to the extent provided by the measures set forth in Article 68 or in the Rules of Procedure and Evidence. The Court may also permit the giving of *viva voce* (oral) or recorded testimony of a witness by means of video or audio technology, as well as the introduction of documents or written transcripts, subject to this Statute and in accordance with the Rules of Procedure and Evidence. These measures shall not be prejudicial to or inconsistent with the rights of the accused.

3. The parties may submit evidence relevant to the case, in accordance with Article 64. The Court shall have the authority to request the submission of all evidence that it considers necessary for the determination of the truth.

4. The Court may rule on the relevance or admissibility of any evidence, taking into account, *inter alia*, the probative value of the evidence and any prejudice that such evidence may cause to a fair trial or to a fair evaluation of the testimony of a witness, in accordance with the Rules of Procedure and Evidence.

5. The Court shall respect and observe privileges on confidentiality as provided for in the Rules of Procedure and Evidence.

6. The Court shall not require proof of facts of common knowledge but may take judicial notice of them.

7. Evidence obtained by means of a violation of this Statute or internationally recognized human rights shall not be admissible if:

(a) The violation casts substantial doubt on the reliability of the evidence; or

(b) The admission of the evidence would be antithetical to and would seriously damage the integrity of the proceedings.

8. When deciding on the relevance or admissibility of evidence collected by a State, the Court shall not rule on the application of the State's national law.

Article 70. Offences against the administration of justice

1. The Court shall have jurisdiction over the following offences against its administration of justice when committed intentionally:

(a) Giving false testimony when under an obligation pursuant to Article 69, paragraph 1, to tell the truth;

(b) Presenting evidence that the party knows is false or forged;

(c) Corruptly influencing a witness, obstructing or interfering with the attendance or testimony of a witness, retaliating against a witness for giving testimony or destroying, tampering with or interfering with the collection of evidence;

(d) Impeding, intimidating or corruptly influencing an official of the Court for the purpose of forging or persuading the official not to perform, or to perform improperly, his or her duties;

(e) Retaliating against an official of the Court on account of duties performed by that or another official;

(f) Soliciting or accepting a bribe as an official of the Court in conjunction with his or her official duties.

2. The principles and procedures governing the Court's exercise of jurisdiction over offences under this articles shall be those provided for in the Rules of Procedure and Evidence. The conditions for providing international cooperation to the Court with respect to its proceedings under this article shall be governed by the domestic laws of the requested State.

3. In the event of conviction, the Court may impose a term of imprisonment not exceeding five years, or a fine in accordance with the Rules of Procedure and Evidence, or both.

4. (a) Each State Party shall extend its criminal laws penalizing offences against the integrity of its own investigative or judicial process to offences against the administration of justice referred to in this article, committed on its territory, or by one of its nationals;

(b) Upon request by the Court, whenever it deems it proper, the State Party shall submit the case to its competent authorities for the purpose of prosecution. Those authorities shall treat such cases with diligence and devote sufficient resources to enable them to be conducted effectively.

Article 71. Sanctions for misconduct before the Court

1. The Court may sanction persons present before it who commit misconduct, including disruption of its proceedings or deliberate refusal to comply with its directions, by administrative measures other than imprisonment, such as temporary or permanent removal from the courtroom, a fine or other similar measures provided for in the Rules of Procedure and Evidence.

2. The procedures governing the imposition of the measures set forth in paragraph 1 shall be those provided for in the Rules of Procedure and Evidence.

Article 72. Protection of national security information

1. This article applies in any case where the disclosure of the information or documents of a State would, in the opinion of that State, prejudice its national security interests. Such cases include those falling within the scope of Article 56, paragraphs 2 and 3, Article 61, paragraph 3, Article 64, paragraph 3, Article 67, paragraph 2, Article 68, paragraph 6, Article 87, paragraph 6 and Article 93, as well as cases arising at any other stage of the proceedings where such disclosure may be at issue.

2. This article shall also apply when a person who has been requested to give information or evidence has refused to do so or has referred the matter to the State on the

ground that disclosure would prejudice the national security interests of a State and the State concerned confirms that it is of the opinion that disclosure would prejudice its national security interests.

3. Nothing in this article shall prejudice the requirements of confidentiality applicable under Article 54, paragraph 3(e) and (f), or the application of Article 73.

4. If a State learns that information or documents of the State are being, or are likely to be, disclosed at any stage of the proceedings, and it is of the opinion that disclosure would prejudice its national security interests, that State shall have the right to intervene in order to obtain resolution of the issue in accordance with this article.

5. If, in the opinion of a State, disclosure of information would prejudice its national security interests, all reasonable steps will be taken by the State, acting in conjunction with the Prosecutor, the Defence or the Pre-Trial Chamber or Trial Chamber, as the case may be, to seek to resolve the matter by cooperative means. Such steps may include:

(a) Modification or clarification of the request;

(b) A determination by the Court regarding the relevance of the information or evidence sought, or a determination as to whether the evidence, though relevant, could be or has been obtained from a source other than the requested State;

(c) Obtaining the information or evidence from a different source or in a different form; or

(d) Agreement on conditions under which the assistance could be provided including, among other things, providing summaries or redactions, limitations on disclosure, use of in camera or *ex parte* proceedings, or other protective measures permissible under the Statute and the Rules.

6. Once all reasonable steps have been taken to resolve the matter through cooperative means, and if the State considers that there are no means or conditions under which the information or documents could be provided or disclosed without prejudice to its national security interests, it shall so notify the Prosecutor or the Court of the specific reasons for its decision, unless a specific description of the reasons would itself necessarily result in such prejudice to the State's national security interests.

7. Thereafter, if the Court determines that the evidence is relevant and necessary for the establishment of the guilt or innocence of the accused, the Court may undertake the following actions:

(a) Where disclosure of the information or document is sought pursuant to a request for cooperation under Part 9 or the circumstances described in paragraph 2, and the State has invoked the ground for refusal referred to in Article 93, paragraph 4:

(i) The Court may, before making any conclusion referred to in subparagraph 7 (a)(ii), request further consultations for the purpose of considering the State's representations, which may include, as appropriate, hearings in camera and *ex parte*;

(ii) If the Court concludes that, by invoking the ground for refusal under Article 93, paragraph 4, in the circumstances of the case, the requested State is not acting in accordance with its obligations under the Statute, the Court may refer the matter in accordance with Article 87, paragraph 7, specifying the reasons for its conclusion; and

(iii) The Court may make such inference in the trial of the accused as to the existence or non-existence of a fact, as may be appropriate in the circumstances; or

(b) In all other circumstances:

(i) Order disclosure; or

(ii) To the extent it does not order disclosure, make such inference in the trial of the accused as to the existence or non-existence of a fact, as may be appropriate in the circumstances.

Article 73. Third-party information or documents

If a State Party is requested by the Court to provide a document or information in its custody, possession or control, which was disclosed to it in confidence by a State, intergovernmental organization or international organization, it shall seek the consent of the originator to disclose that document or information. If the originator is a State Party, it shall either consent to disclosure of the information or document or undertake to resolve the issue of disclosure with the Court, subject to the provisions of Article 72. If the originator is not a State Party and refuses consent to disclosure, the requested State shall inform the Court that it is unable to provide the document or information because of a pre-existing obligation of confidentiality to the originator.

Article 74. Requirements for the decision

1. All the judges of the Trial Chamber shall be present at each stage of the trial and throughout their deliberations. The Presidency may, on a case-by-case basis, designate, as available, one or more alternate judges to be present at each stage of the trial and to replace a member of the Trial Chamber if that member is unable to continue attending.

2. The Trial Chamber's decision shall be based on its evaluation of the evidence and the entire proceedings. The decision shall not exceed the facts and circumstances described in the charges and any amendments to the charges. The Court may base its decision only on evidence submitted and discussed before it at the trial.

3. The judges shall attempt to achieve unanimity in their decision, failing which the decision shall be taken by a majority of the judges.

4. The deliberations of the Trial Chamber shall remain secret.

5. The decision shall be in writing and shall contain a full and reasoned statement of the Trial Chamber's findings on the evidence and conclusions. The Trial Chamber shall issue one decision. When there is no unanimity, the Trial Chamber's decision shall contain the views of the majority and the minority. The decision or a summary thereof shall be delivered in open court.

Article 75. Reparations to victims

1. The Court shall establish principles relating to reparations to, or in respect of, victims, including restitution, compensation and rehabilitation. On this basis, in its decision the Court may, either upon request or on its own motion in exceptional circumstances, determine the scope and extent of any damage, loss and injury to, or in respect of, victims and will state the principles on which it is acting.

2. The Court may make an order directly against a convicted person specifying appropriate reparations to, or in respect of, victims, including restitution, compensation and rehabilitation. Where appropriate, the Court may order that the award for reparations be made through the Trust Fund provided for in Article 79.

3. Before making an order under this article, the Court may invite and shall take account of representations from or on behalf of the convicted person, victims, other interested persons or interested States.

4. In exercising its power under this article, the Court may, after a person is convicted of a crime within the jurisdiction of the Court, determine whether, in order to give effect to an order which it may make under this article, it is necessary to seek measures under Article 93, paragraph 1.

5. A State Party shall give effect to a decision under this article as if the provisions of Article 109 were applicable to this article.

6. Nothing in this article shall be interpreted as prejudicing the rights of victims under national or international law.

Article 76. Sentencing

1. In the event of a conviction, the Trial Chamber shall consider the appropriate sentence to be imposed and shall take into account the evidence presented and submissions made during the trial that are relevant to the sentence.

2. Except where Article 65 applies and before the completion of the trial, the Trial Chamber may on its own motion and shall, at the request of the Prosecutor or the accused, hold a further hearing to hear any additional evidence or submissions relevant to the sentence, in accordance with the Rules of Procedure and Evidence.

3. Where paragraph 2 applies, any representations under Article 75 shall be heard during the further hearing referred to in paragraph 2 and, if necessary, during any additional hearing.

4. The sentence shall be pronounced in public and, wherever possible, in the presence of the accused.

PART 7. PENALTIES

Article 77. Applicable penalties

1. Subject to Article 110, the Court may impose one of the following penalties on a person convicted of a crime under Article 5 of this Statute:

(a) Imprisonment for a specified number of years, which may not exceed a maximum of 30 years; or

(b) A term of life imprisonment when justified by the extreme gravity of the crime and the individual circumstances of the convicted person.

2. In addition to imprisonment, the Court may order:

(a) A fine under the criteria provided for in the Rules of Procedure and Evidence;

(b) A forfeiture of proceeds, property and assets derived directly or indirectly from that crime, without prejudice to the rights of bona fide third parties.

Article 78. Determination of the sentence

1. In determining the sentence, the Court shall, in accordance with the Rules of Procedure and Evidence, take into account such factors as the gravity of the crime and the individual circumstances of the convicted person.

2. In imposing a sentence of imprisonment, the Court shall deduct the time, if any, previously spent in detention in accordance with an order of the Court. The Court may deduct any time otherwise spent in detention in connection with conduct underlying the crime.

3. When a person has been convicted of more than one crime, the Court shall pronounce a sentence for each crime and a joint sentence specifying the total period of imprisonment. This period shall be no less than the highest individual sentence pronounced and shall not exceed 30 years imprisonment or a sentence of life imprisonment in conformity with Article 77, paragraph 1(b).

Article 79. Trust Fund

1. A Trust Fund shall be established by decision of the Assembly of States Parties for the benefit of victims of crimes within the jurisdiction of the Court, and of the families of such victims.

2. The Court may order money and other property collected through fines or forfeiture to be transferred, by order of the Court, to the Trust Fund.

3. The Trust Fund shall be managed according to criteria to be determined by the Assembly of States Parties.

Article 80. Non-prejudice to national application of penalties and national laws

Nothing in this Part of the Statute affects the application by States of penalties prescribed by their national law, nor the law of States which do not provide for penalties prescribed in this Part.

PART 8. APPEAL AND REVISION

Article 81. Appeal against decision of acquittal or conviction or against sentence

1. A decision under Article 74 may be appealed in accordance with the Rules of Procedure and Evidence as follows:

    (a) The Prosecutor may make an appeal on any of the following grounds:

        (i) Procedural error,

        (ii) Error of fact, or

        (iii) Error of law;

    (b) The convicted person or the Prosecutor on that person's behalf may make an appeal on any of the following grounds:

        (i) Procedural error,

        (ii) Error of fact,

        (iii) Error of law, or

(iv) Any other ground that affects the fairness or reliability of the proceedings or decision.

2. (a) A sentence may be appealed, in accordance with the Rules of Procedure and Evidence, by the Prosecutor or the convicted person on the ground of disproportion between the crime and the sentence;

(b) If on an appeal against sentence the Court considers that there are grounds on which the conviction might be set aside, wholly or in part, it may invite the Prosecutor and the convicted person to submit grounds under Article 81, paragraph 1(a) or (b), and may render a decision on conviction in accordance with Article 83;

(c) The same procedure applies when the Court, on an appeal against conviction only, considers that there are grounds to reduce the sentence under paragraph 2 (a).

3. (a) Unless the Trial Chamber orders otherwise, a convicted person shall remain in custody pending an appeal;

(b) When a convicted person's time in custody exceeds the sentence of imprisonment imposed, that person shall be released, except that if the Prosecutor is also appealing, the release may be subject to the conditions under subparagraph (c) below;

(c) In case of an acquittal, the accused shall be released immediately, subject to the following:

(i) Under exceptional circumstances, and having regard, *inter alia*, to the concrete risk of flight, the seriousness of the offence charged and the probability of success on appeal, the Trial Chamber, at the request of the Prosecutor, may maintain the detention of the person pending appeal;

(ii) A decision by the Trial Chamber under subparagraph (c)(i) may be appealed in accordance with the Rules of Procedure and Evidence.

4. Subject to the provisions of paragraph 3(a) and (b), execution of the decision or sentence shall be suspended during the period allowed for appeal and for the duration of the appeal proceedings.

Article 82. Appeal against other decisions

1. Either party may appeal any of the following decisions in accordance with the Rules of Procedure and Evidence:

(a) A decision with respect to jurisdiction or admissibility;

(b) A decision granting or denying release of the person being investigated or prosecuted;

(c) A decision of the Pre-Trial Chamber to act on its own initiative under Article 56, paragraph 3;

(d) A decision that involves an issue that would significantly affect the fair and expeditious conduct of the proceedings or the outcome of the trial, and for which, in the opinion of the Pre-Trial or Trial Chamber, an immediate resolution by the Appeals Chamber may materially advance the proceedings.

2. A decision of the Pre-Trial Chamber under Article 57, paragraph 3(d), may be appealed against by the State concerned or by the Prosecutor, with the leave of the Pre-Trial Chamber. The appeal shall be heard on an expedited basis.

3. An appeal shall not of itself have suspensive effect unless the Appeals Chamber so orders, upon request, in accordance with the Rules of Procedure and Evidence.

4. A legal representative of the victims, the convicted person or a bona fide owner of property adversely affected by an order under Article 73 may appeal against the order for reparations, as provided in the Rules of Procedure and Evidence.

Article 83. Proceedings on appeal

1. For the purposes of proceedings under Article 81 and this article, the Appeals Chamber shall have all the powers of the Trial Chamber.

2. If the Appeals Chamber finds that the proceedings appealed from were unfair in a way that affected the reliability of the decision or sentence, or that the decision or sentence appealed from was materially affected by error of fact or law or procedural error, it may:

(a) Reverse or amend the decision or sentence; or

(b) Order a new trial before a different Trial Chamber.

For these purposes, the Appeals Chamber may remand a factual issue to the original Trial Chamber for it to determine the issue and to report back accordingly, or may itself call evidence to determine the issue. When the decision or sentence has been appealed only by the person convicted, or the Prosecutor on that person's behalf, it cannot be amended to his or her detriment.

3. If in an appeal against sentence the Appeals Chamber finds that the sentence is disproportionate to the crime, it may vary the sentence in accordance with Part 7.

4. The judgement of the Appeals Chamber shall be taken by a majority of the judges and shall be delivered in open court. The judgement shall state the reasons on which it is based. When there is no unanimity, the judgement of the Appeals Chamber shall contain the views of the majority and the minority, but a judge may deliver a separate or dissenting opinion on a question of law.

5. The Appeals Chamber may deliver its judgement in the absence of the person acquitted or convicted.

Article 84. Revision of conviction or sentence

1. The convicted person or, after death, spouses, children, parents or one person alive at the time of the accused's death who has been given express written instructions from the accused to bring such a claim, or the Prosecutor on the person's behalf, may apply to the Appeals Chamber to revise the final judgement of conviction or sentence on the grounds that:

(a) New evidence has been discovered that:

(i) Was not available at the time of trial, and such unavailability was not wholly or partially attributable to the party making application; and

(ii) Is sufficiently important that had it been proved at trial it would have been likely to have resulted in a different verdict;

(b) It has been newly discovered that decisive evidence, taken into account at trial and upon which the conviction depends, was false, forged or falsified;

(c) One or more of the judges who participated in conviction or confirmation of the charges has committed, in that case, an act of serious misconduct or serious breach of duty of sufficient gravity to justify the removal of that judge or those judges from office under Article 46.

2. The Appeals Chamber shall reject the application if it considers it to be unfounded. If it determines that the application is meritorious, it may, as appropriate:

(a) Reconvene the original Trial Chamber;

(b) Constitute a new Trial Chamber; or

(c) Retain jurisdiction over the matter, with a view to, after hearing the parties in the manner set forth in the Rules of Procedure and Evidence, arriving at a determination on whether the judgement should be revised.

Article 85. Compensation to an arrested or convicted person

1. Anyone who has been the victim of unlawful arrest or detention shall have an enforceable right to compensation.

2. When a person has by a final decision been convicted of a criminal offence, and when subsequently his or her conviction has been reversed on the ground that a new or newly discovered fact shows conclusively that there has been a miscarriage of justice, the person who has suffered punishment as a result of such conviction shall be compensated according to law, unless it is proved that the non-disclosure of the unknown fact in time is wholly or partly attributable to him or her.

3. In exceptional circumstances, where the Court finds conclusive facts showing that there has been a grave and manifest miscarriage of justice, it may in its discretion award compensation, according to the criteria provided in the Rules of Procedure and Evidence, to a person who has been released from detention following a final decision of acquittal or a termination of the proceedings for that reason.

PART 9. INTERNATIONAL COOPERATION AND JUDICIAL ASSISTANCE

Article 86. General obligation to cooperate

States Parties shall, in accordance with the provisions of this Statute, cooperate fully with the Court in its investigation and prosecution of crimes within the jurisdiction of the Court.

Article 87. Requests for cooperation: general provisions

1. (a) The Court shall have the authority to make requests to States Parties for cooperation. The requests shall be transmitted through the diplomatic channel or any other appropriate channel as may be designated by each State Party upon ratification, acceptance, approval or accession. Subsequent changes to the designation shall be made by each State Party in accordance with the Rules of Procedure and Evidence.

(b) When appropriate, without prejudice to the provisions of subparagraph (a), requests may also be transmitted through the International Criminal Police Organization or any appropriate regional organization.

2. Requests for cooperation and any documents supporting the request shall either be in or be accompanied by a translation into an official language of the requested State or in one of the working languages of the Court, in accordance with the choice made by that State upon ratification, acceptance, approval or accession.

Subsequent changes to this choice shall be made in accordance with the Rules of Procedure and Evidence.

3. The requested State shall keep confidential a request for cooperation and any documents supporting the request, except to the extent that the disclosure is necessary for execution of the request.

4. In relation to any request for assistance presented under Part 9, the Court may take such measures, including measures related to the protection of information, as may be necessary to ensure the safety or physical or psychological well-being of any victims, potential witnesses and their families. The Court may request that any information that is made available under Part 9 shall be provided and handled in a manner that protects the safety and physical or psychological well-being of any victims, potential witnesses and their families.

5. The Court may invite any State not party to this Statute to provide assistance under this Part on the basis of an ad hoc arrangement, an agreement with such State or any other appropriate basis. Where a State not party to this Statute, which has entered into an ad hoc arrangement or an agreement with the Court, fails to cooperate with requests pursuant to any such arrangement or agreement, the Court may so inform the Assembly of States Parties or, where the Security Council referred the matter to the Court, the Security Council.

6. The Court may ask any intergovernmental organization to provide information or documents. The Court may also ask for other forms of cooperation and assistance which may be agreed upon with such an organization and which are in accordance with its competence or mandate.

7. Where a State Party fails to comply with a request to cooperate by the Court contrary to the provisions of this Statute, thereby preventing the Court from exercising its functions and powers under this Statute, the Court may make a finding to that effect and refer the matter to the Assembly of States Parties or, where the Security Council referred the matter to the Court, to the Security Council.

Article 88. Availability of procedures under national law

States Parties shall ensure that there are procedures available under their national law for all of the forms of cooperation which are specified under this Part.

Article 89. Surrender of persons to the Court

1. The Court may transmit a request for the arrest and surrender of a person, together with the material supporting the request outlined in Article 91, to any State on the territory of which that person may be found and shall request the cooperation of that State in the arrest and surrender of such a person. States Parties shall, in accordance with the provisions of this Part and the procedure under their national law, comply with requests for arrest and surrender.

2. Where the person sought for surrender brings a challenge before a national court on the basis of the principle of *ne bis in idem* as provided in Article 20, the requested

State shall immediately consult with the Court to determine if there has been a relevant ruling on admissibility. If the case is admissible, the requested State shall proceed with the execution of the request. If an admissibility ruling is pending, the requested State may postpone the execution of the request for surrender of the person until the Court makes a determination on admissibility.

3. (a) A State Party shall authorize, in accordance with its national procedural law, transportation through its territory of a person being surrendered to the Court by another State, except where transit through that State would impede or delay the surrender.

(b) A request by the Court for transit shall be transmitted in accordance with Article 87. The request for transit shall contain:

(i) A description of the person being transported;

(ii) A brief statement of the facts of the case and their legal characterization; and

(iii) The warrant for arrest and surrender;

(c) A person being transported shall be detained in custody during the period of transit;

(d) No authorization is required if the person is transported by air and no landing is scheduled on the territory of the transit State;

(e) If an unscheduled landing occurs on the territory of the transit State, that State may require a request for transit from the Court as provided for in subparagraph (b). The transit State shall detain the person being transported until the request for transit is received and the transit is effected; provided that detention for purposes of this subparagraph may not be extended beyond 96 hours from the unscheduled landing unless the request is received within that time.

4. If the person sought is being proceeded against or is serving a sentence in the requested State for a crime different from that for which surrender to the Court is sought, the requested State, after making its decision to grant the request, shall consult with the Court.

Article 90. Competing requests

1. A State Party which receives a request from the Court for the surrender of a person under Article 89 shall, if it also receives a request from any other State for the extradition of the same person for the same conduct which forms the basis of the crime for which the Court seeks the person's surrender, notify the Court and the requesting State of that fact.

2. Where the requesting State is a State Party, the requested State shall give priority to the request from the Court if:

(a) The Court has, pursuant to Articles 18 and 19, made a determination that the case in respect of which surrender is sought is admissible and that determination takes into account the investigation or prosecution conducted by the requesting State in respect of its request for extradition; or

(b) The Court makes the determination described in subparagraph (a) pursuant to the requested State's notification under paragraph 1.

3. Where a determination under paragraph 2 (a) has not been made, the requested State may, at its discretion, pending the determination of the Court under paragraph 2 (b), proceed to deal with the request for extradition from the requesting State but shall not extradite the person until the Court has determined that the case is inadmissible. The Court's determination shall be made on an expedited basis.

4. If the requesting State is a State not Party to this Statute the requested State, if it is not under an international obligation to extradite the person to the requesting State, shall give priority to the request for surrender from the Court, if the Court has determined that the case is admissible.

5. Where a case under paragraph 4 has not been determined to be admissible by the Court, the requested State may, at its discretion, proceed to deal with the request for extradition from the requesting State.

6. In cases where paragraph 4 applies except that the requested State is under an existing international obligation to extradite the person to the requesting State not Party to this Statute, the requested State shall determine whether to surrender the person to the Court or extradite the person to the requesting State. In making its decision, the requested State shall consider all the relevant factors, including but not limited to:

(a) The respective dates of the requests;

(b) The interests of the requesting State including, where relevant, whether the crime was committed in its territory and the nationality of the victims and of the person sought; and

(c) The possibility of subsequent surrender between the Court and the requesting State.

7. Where a State Party which receives a request from the Court for the surrender of a person also receives a request from any State for the extradition of the same person for conduct other than that which constitutes the crime for which the Court seeks the person's surrender:

(a) The requested State shall, if it is not under an existing international obligation to extradite the person to the requesting State, give priority to the request from the Court;

(b) The requested State shall, if it is under an existing international obligation to extradite the person to the requesting State, determine whether to surrender the person to the Court or extradite the person to the requesting State. In making its decision, the requested State shall consider all the relevant factors, including but not limited to those set out in paragraph 6, but shall give special consideration to the relative nature and gravity of the conduct in question.

8. Where pursuant to a notification under this article, the Court has determined a case to be inadmissible, and subsequently extradition to the requesting State is refused, the requested State shall notify the Court of this decision.

Article 91. Contents of request for arrest and surrender

1. A request for arrest and surrender shall be made in writing. In urgent cases, a request may be made by any medium capable of delivering a written record, provided that the request shall be confirmed through the channel provided for in Article 87, paragraph 1 (a).

2. In the case of a request for the arrest and surrender of a person for whom a warrant of arrest has been issued by the Pre-Trial Chamber under Article 58, the request shall contain or be supported by:

(a) Information describing the person sought, sufficient to identify the person, and information as to that person's probable location;

(b) A copy of the warrant of arrest; and

(c) Such documents, statements or information as may be necessary to meet the requirements for the surrender process in the requested State, except that those requirements should not be more burdensome than those applicable to requests for extradition pursuant to treaties or arrangements between the requested State and other States and should, if possible, be less burdensome, taking into account the distinct nature of the Court.

3. In the case of a request for the arrest and surrender of a person already convicted, the request shall contain or be supported by:

(a) A copy of any warrant of arrest for that person;

(b) A copy of the judgement of conviction;

(c) Information to demonstrate that the person sought is the one referred to in the judgement of conviction; and

(d) If the person sought has been sentenced, a copy of the sentence imposed and, in the case of a sentence for imprisonment, a statement of any time already served and the time remaining to be served.

4. Upon the request of the Court, a State Party shall consult with the Court, either generally or with respect to a specific matter, regarding any requirements under its national law that may apply under paragraph 2 (c). During the consultations, the State Party shall advise the Court of the specific requirements of its national law.

Article 92. Provisional arrest

1. In urgent cases, the Court may request the provisional arrest of the person sought, pending presentation of the request for surrender and the documents supporting the request as specified in Article 91.

2. The request for provisional arrest shall be made by any medium capable of delivering a written record and shall contain:

(a) Information describing the person sought, sufficient to identify the person, and information as to that person's probable location;

(b) A concise statement of the crimes for which the person's arrest is sought and of the facts which are alleged to constitute those crimes, including, where possible, the date and location of the crime;

(c) A statement of the existence of a warrant of arrest or a judgement of conviction against the person sought; and

(d) A statement that a request for surrender of the person sought will follow.

3. A person who is provisionally arrested may be released from custody if the requested State has not received the request for surrender and the documents supporting the request as specified in Article 91 within the time limits specified in the Rules of Pro-

cedure and Evidence. However, the person may consent to surrender before the expiration of this period if permitted by the law of the requested State. In such a case, the requested State shall proceed to surrender the person to the Court as soon as possible.

4. The fact that the person sought has been released from custody pursuant to paragraph 3 shall not prejudice the subsequent arrest and surrender of that person if the request for surrender and the documents supporting the request are delivered at a later date.

Article 93. Other forms of cooperation

1. States Parties shall, in accordance with the provisions of this Part and under procedures of national law, comply with requests by the Court to provide the following assistance in relation to investigations or prosecutions:

(a) The identification and whereabouts of persons or the location of items;

(b) The taking of evidence, including testimony under oath, and the production of evidence, including expert opinions and reports necessary to the Court;

(c) The questioning of any person being investigated or prosecuted;

(d) The service of documents, including judicial documents;

(e) Facilitating the voluntary appearance of persons as witnesses or experts before the Court;

(f) The temporary transfer of persons as provided in paragraph 7;

(g) The examination of places or sites, including the exhumation and examination of grave sites;

(h) The execution of searches and seizures;

(i) The provision of records and documents, including official records and documents;

(j) The protection of victims and witnesses and the preservation of evidence;

(k) The identification, tracing and freezing or seizure of proceeds, property and assets and instrumentalities of crimes for the purpose of eventual forfeiture, without prejudice to the rights of bona fide third parties; and

(l) Any other type of assistance which is not prohibited by the law of the requested State, with a view to facilitating the investigation and prosecution of crimes within the jurisdiction of the Court.

2. The Court shall have the authority to provide an assurance to a witness or an expert appearing before the Court that he or she will not be prosecuted, detained or subjected to any restriction of personal freedom by the Court in respect of any act or omission that preceded the departure of that person from the requested State.

3. Where execution of a particular measure of assistance detailed in a request presented under paragraph 1, is prohibited in the requested State on the basis of an existing fundamental legal principle of general application, the requested State shall promptly consult with the Court to try to resolve the matter. In the consultations, consideration should be given to whether the assistance can be rendered in another manner or subject to conditions. If after consultations the matter cannot be resolved, the Court shall modify the request as necessary.

4. In accordance with Article 72, a State Party may deny a request for assistance, in whole or in part, only if the request concerns the production of any documents or disclosure of evidence which relates to its national security.

5. Before denying a request for assistance under paragraph 1 (1), the requested State shall consider whether the assistance can be provided subject to specified conditions, or whether the assistance can be provided at a later date or in an alternative manner, provided that if the Court or the Prosecutor accepts the assistance subject to conditions, the Court of the Prosecutor shall abide by them.

6. If a request for assistance is denied, the requested State Party shall promptly inform the Court or the Prosecutor of the reasons for such denial.

7. (a) The Court may request the temporary transfer of a person in custody for purposes of identification or for obtaining testimony or other assistance. The person may be transferred if the following conditions are fulfilled:

> (i) The person freely gives his or her informed consent to the transfer; and

> (ii) The requested State agrees to the transfer, subject to such conditions as that State and the Court may agree.

(b) The person being transferred shall remain in custody. When the purposes of the transfer have been fulfilled, the Court shall return the person without delay to the requested State.

8. (a) The Court shall ensure the confidentiality of documents and information, except as required for the investigation and proceedings described in the request.

> (b) The requested State may, when necessary, transmit documents or information to the Prosecutor on a confidential basis. The Prosecutor may then use them solely for the purpose of generating new evidence;

> (c) The requested State may, on its own motion or at the request of the Prosecutor, subsequently consent to the disclosure of such documents or information. They may then be used as evidence pursuant to the provisions of Parts 5 and 6 and in accordance with the Rules of Procedure and Evidence.

9. (a) (i) In the event that a State Party receives competing requests, other than for surrender or extradition, from the Court and from another State pursuant to an international obligation, the State Party shall endeavour, in consultation with the Court and the other State, to meet both requests, if necessary by postponing or attaching conditions to one or the other request.

> (ii) Failing that, competing requests shall be resolved in accordance with the principles established in Article 90.

> (b) Where, however, the request from the Court concerns information, property or persons which are subject to the control of a third State or an international organization by virtue of an international agreement, the requested States shall so inform the Court and the Court shall direct its request to the third State or international organization.

10. (a) The Court may, upon request, cooperate with and provide assistance to a State Party conducting an investigation into or trial in respect of conduct which constitutes a crime within the jurisdiction of the Court or which constitutes a serious crime under the national law of the requesting State.

(b) (i) The assistance provided under subparagraph (a) shall include, *inter alia*:

(1) The transmission of statements, documents or other types of evidence obtained in the course of an investigation or a trial conducted by the Court; and

(2) The questioning of any person detained by order of the Court;

(ii) In the case of assistance under subparagraph (b)(i)(1):

(1) If the documents or other types of evidence have been obtained with the assistance of a State, such transmission shall require the consent of that State;

(2) If the statements, documents or other types of evidence have been provided by a witness or expert, such transmission shall be subject to the provisions of Article 68.

(c) The Court may, under the conditions set out in this paragraph, grant a request for assistance under this paragraph from a State which is not a Party to the Statute.

Article 94. Postponement of execution of a request in respect of ongoing investigation or prosecution

1. If the immediate execution of a request would interfere with an ongoing investigation or prosecution of a case different from that to which the request relates, the requested State may postpone the execution of the request for a period of time agreed upon with the Court. However, the postponement shall be no longer than is necessary to complete the relevant investigation or prosecution in the requested State. Before making a decision to postpone, the requested State should consider whether the assistance may be immediately provided subject to certain conditions.

2. If a decision to postpone is taken pursuant to paragraph 1, the Prosecutor may, however, seek measures to preserve evidence, pursuant to Article 93, paragraph 1(j).

Article 95. Postponement of execution of a request in respect of an admissibility challenge

Without prejudice to Article 53, paragraph 2, where there is an admissibility challenge under consideration by the Court pursuant to Articles 18 or 19, the requested State may postpone the execution of a request under this Part pending a determination by the Court, unless the Court has specifically ordered that the Prosecutor may pursue the collection of such evidence pursuant to Articles 18 or 19.

Article 96. Contents of request for other forms of assistance under Article 93

Upon the request for other forms of assistance referred to in Article 93 shall be made in writing. In urgent cases, a request may be made by any medium capable of delivering a written record, provided that the request shall be confirmed through the channel provided for in Article 87, paragraph 1 (a).

2. The request shall, as applicable, contain or be supported by the following:

(a) A concise statement of the purpose of the request and the assistance sought, including the legal basis and the grounds for the request;

(b) As much detailed information as possible about the location or identification of any person or place that must be found or identified in order for the assistance sought to be provided;

(c) A concise statement of the essential facts underlying the request;

(d) The reasons for and details of any procedure or requirement to be followed;

(e) Such information as may be required under the law of the requested State in order to execute the request; and

(f) Any other information relevant in order for the assistance sought to be provided.

3. Upon the request of the Court, a State Party shall consult with the Court, either generally or with respect to a specific matter, regarding any requirements under its national law that may apply under paragraph 2 (e). During the consultations, the State Party shall advise the Court of the specific requirements of its national law.

4. The provisions of this article shall, where applicable, also apply in respect of a request for assistance made to the Court.

Article 97. Consultations

Where a State Party receives a request under this Part in relation to which it identifies problems which may impede or prevent the execution of the request, that State shall consult with the Court without delay in order to resolve the matter. Such problems may include, *inter alia*:

(a) Insufficient information to execute the request;

(b) In the case of a request for surrender, the fact that despite best efforts, the person sought cannot be located or that the investigation conducted has determined that the person in the custodial State is clearly not the person named in the warrant; or

(c) The fact that execution of the request in its current form would require the requested State to breach a pre-existing treaty obligation undertaken with respect to another State.

Article 98. Cooperation with respect to waiver of immunity and consent to surrender

1. The Court may not proceed with a request for surrender or assistance which would require the requested State to act inconsistently with its obligations under international law with respect to the State or diplomatic immunity of a person or property of a third State, unless the Court can first obtain the cooperation of that third State for the waiver of the immunity.

2. The Court may not proceed with a request for surrender which would require the requested State to act inconsistently with its obligations under international agreements pursuant to which the consent of a sending State is required to surrender a person of that State to the Court, unless the Court can first obtain the cooperation of the sending State for the giving of consent for the surrender.

Article 99. Execution of requests under Articles 93 and 96

1. Requests for assistance shall be executed in accordance with the relevant procedure under the law of the requested State and, unless prohibited by such law, in the manner specified in the request, including following any procedure outlined therein or permitting persons specified in the request to be present at and assist in the execution process.

2. In the case of an urgent request, the documents or evidence produced in response shall, at the request of the Court, be sent urgently.

3. Replies from the requested State shall be transmitted in their original language and form.

4. Without prejudice to other articles in this Part, where it is necessary for the successful execution of a request which can be executed without any compulsory measures, including specifically the interview of or taking evidence from a person on a voluntary basis, including doing so without the presence of the authorities of the requested State Party if it is essential for the request to be executed, and the examination without modification of a public site or other public place, the Prosecutor may execute such request directly on the territory of a State as follows:

> (a) When the State Party requested is a State on the territory of which the crime is alleged to have been committed, and there has been a determination of admissibility pursuant to Articles 18 or 19, the Prosecutor may directly execute such request following all possible consultations with the requested State Party;

> (b) In other cases, the Prosecutor may execute such request following consultations with the requested State Party and subject to any reasonable conditions or concerns raised by that State Party. Where the requested State Party identifies problems with the execution of a request pursuant to this subparagraph it shall, without delay, consult with the Court to resolve the matter.

5. Provisions allowing a person heard or examined by the Court under Article 72 to invoke restrictions designed to prevent disclosure of confidential information connected with national defence or security shall also apply to the execution of requests for assistance under this article.

Article 100. Costs

1. The ordinary costs for execution of requests in the territory of the requested State shall be borne by that State, except for the following, which shall be borne by the Court:

> (a) Costs associated with the travel and security of witnesses and experts or the transfer under Article 93 of persons in custody;

> (b) Costs of translation, interpretation and transcription;

> (c) Travel and subsistence costs of the judges, the Prosecutor, the Deputy Prosecutors, the Registrar, the Deputy Registrar and staff of any organ of the Court;

> (d) Costs of any expert opinion or report requested by the Court;

> (e) Costs associated with the transport of a person being surrendered to the Court by a custodial State; and

> (f) Following consultations, any extraordinary costs that may result from the execution of a request.

2. The provisions of paragraph 1 shall, as appropriate, apply to requests from States Parties to the Court. In that case, the Court shall bear the ordinary costs of execution.

Article 101. Rule of speciality

1. A person surrendered to the Court under this Statute shall not be proceeded against, punished or detained for any conduct committed prior to surrender, other than the conduct or course of conduct which forms the basis of the crimes for which that person has been surrendered.

2. The Court may request a waiver of the requirements of paragraph 1 from the State which surrendered the person to the Court and, if necessary, the Court shall provide additional information in accordance with Article 91. States Parties shall have the authority to provide a waiver to the Court and should endeavour to do so.

Article 102. Use of terms

For the purposes of this Statute:

(a) "surrender" means the delivering up of a person by a State to the Court, pursuant to this Statute.

(b) "extradition" means the delivering up of a person by one State to another as provided by treaty, convention or national legislation.

PART 10. ENFORCEMENT

Article 103. Role of States in enforcement of sentences of imprisonment

1. (a) A sentence of imprisonment shall be served in a State designated by the Court from a list of States which have indicated to the Court their willingness to accept sentenced persons.

(b) At the time of declaring its willingness to accept sentenced persons, a State may attach conditions to its acceptance as agreed by the Court and in accordance with this Part.

(c) A State designated in a particular case shall promptly inform the Court whether it accepts the Court's designation.

2. (a) The State of enforcement shall notify the Court of any circumstances, including the exercise of any conditions agreed under paragraph 1, which could materially affect the terms or extent of the imprisonment. The Court shall be given at least 45 days' notice of any such known or foreseeable circumstances. During this period, the State of enforcement shall take no action that might prejudice its obligations under Article 110.

(b) Where the Court cannot agree to the circumstances referred to in subparagraph (a), it shall notify the State of enforcement and proceed in accordance with Article 104, paragraph 1.

3. In exercising its discretion to make a designation under paragraph 1, the Court shall take into account the following:

(a) The principle that States Parties should share the responsibility for enforcing sentences of imprisonment, in accordance with principles of equitable distribution, as provided in the Rules of Procedure and Evidence;

(b) The application of widely accepted international treaty standards governing the treatment of prisoners;

(c) The views of the sentenced person; and

(d) The nationality of the sentenced person;

(e) Such other factors regarding the circumstances of the crime or the person sentenced, or the effective enforcement of the sentence, as may be appropriate in designating the State of enforcement.

4. If no State is designated under paragraph 1, the sentence of imprisonment shall be served in a prison facility made available by the host State, in accordance with the conditions set out in the headquarters agreement referred to in Article 3, paragraph 2. In such a case, the costs arising out of the enforcement of a sentence of imprisonment shall be borne by the Court.

Article 104. Change in designation of State of enforcement

1. The Court may, at any time, decide to transfer a sentenced person to a prison of another State.

2. A sentenced person may, at any time, apply to the Court to be transferred from the State of enforcement.

Article 105. Enforcement of the sentence

1. Subject to conditions which a State may have specified in accordance with Article 103, paragraph 1 (b), the sentence of imprisonment shall be binding on the States Parties, which shall in no case modify it.

2. The Court alone shall have the right to decide any application for appeal and revision. The State of enforcement shall not impede the making of any such application by a sentenced person.

Article 106. Supervision of enforcement of sentences and conditions of imprisonment

1. The enforcement of a sentence of imprisonment shall be subject to the supervision of the Court and shall be consistent with widely accepted international treaty standards governing treatment of prisoners.

2. The conditions of imprisonment shall be governed by the law of the State of enforcement and shall be consistent with widely accepted international treaty standards governing treatment of prisoners; in no case shall such conditions be more or less favourable than those available to prisoners convicted of similar offences in the State of enforcement.

3. Communications between a sentenced person and the Court shall be unimpeded and confidential.

Article 107. Transfer of the person upon completion of sentence

1. Following completion of the sentence, a person who is not a national of the State of enforcement may, in accordance with the law of the State of enforcement, be transferred to a State which is obliged to receive him or her, or to another State which agrees to receive him or her, taking into account any wishes of the person to be transferred to

that State, unless the State of enforcement authorizes the person to remain in its territory.

2. If no State bears the costs arising out of transferring the person to another State pursuant to paragraph 1, such costs shall be borne by the Court.

3. Subject to the provisions of Article 108, the State of enforcement may also, in accordance with its national law, extradite or otherwise surrender the person to the State which has requested the extradition or surrender of the person for purposes of trial or enforcement of a sentence.

Article 108. Limitation on the prosecution or punishment of other offences

1. A sentenced person in the custody of the State of enforcement shall not be subject to prosecution or punishment or to extradition to a third State for any conduct engaged in prior to that person's delivery to the State of enforcement, unless such prosecution, punishment or extradition has been approved by the Court at the request of the State of enforcement.

2. The Court shall decide the matter after having heard the views of the sentenced person.

3. Paragraph 1 shall cease to apply if the sentenced person remains voluntarily for more than 30 days in the territory of the State of enforcement after having served the full sentence imposed by the Court, or returns to the territory of that State after having left it.

Article 109. Enforcement of fines and forfeiture measures

1. States Parties shall give effect to fines or forfeitures ordered by the Court under Part 7, without prejudice to the rights of bona fide third parties, and in accordance with the procedure of their national law.

2. If a State Party is unable to give effect to an order for forfeiture, it shall take measures to recover the value of the proceeds, property or assets ordered by the Court to be forfeited, without prejudice to the rights of bona fide third parties.

3. Property, or the proceeds of the sale of real property or, where appropriate, the sale of other property, which is obtained by a State Party as a result of its enforcement of a judgement of the Court shall be transferred to the Court.

Article 110. Review by the Court concerning reduction of sentence

1. The State of enforcement shall not release the person before expiry of the sentence pronounced by the Court.

2. The Court alone shall have the right to decide any reduction of sentence, and shall rule on the matter after having heard the person.

3. When the person has served two thirds of the sentence, or 25 years in the case of life imprisonment, the Court shall review the sentence to determine whether it should be reduced. Such a review shall not be conducted before that time.

4. In its review under paragraph 3, the Court may reduce the sentence if it finds that one or more of the following factors are present:

(a) The early and continuing willingness of the person to cooperate with the Court in its investigations and prosecutions;

(b) The voluntary assistance of the person in enabling the enforcement of the judgements and orders of the Court in other cases, and in particular providing assistance in locating assets subject to orders of fine, forfeiture or reparation which may be used for the benefit of victims; or

(c) Other factors establishing a clear and significant change of circumstances sufficient to justify the reduction of sentence, as provided in the Rules of Procedure and Evidence.

5. If the Court determines in its initial review under paragraph 3 that it is not appropriate to reduce the sentence, it shall thereafter review the question of reduction of sentence at such intervals and applying such criteria as provided for in the Rules of Procedure and Evidence.

Article 111. Escape

If a convicted person escapes from custody and flees the State of enforcement, that State may, after consultation with the Court, request the person's surrender from the State in which the person is located pursuant to existing bilateral or multilateral arrangements, or may request that the Court seek the person's surrender. It may direct that the person be delivered to the State in which he or she was serving the sentence or to another State designated by the Court.

PART 11. ASSEMBLY OF STATES PARTIES

Article 112. Assembly of States Parties

1. An Assembly of States Parties to this Statute is hereby established. Each State Party shall have one representative in the Assembly who may be accompanied by alternates and advisers. Other States which have signed the Statute or the Final Act may be observers in the Assembly.

2. The Assembly shall:

(a) Consider and adopt, as appropriate, recommendations of the Preparatory Commission;

(b) Provide management oversight to the Presidency, the Prosecutor and the Registrar regarding the administration of the Court;

(c) Consider the reports and activities of the Bureau established under paragraph 3 and take appropriate action in regard thereto;

(d) Consider and decide the budget for the Court;

(e) Decide whether to alter, in accordance with Article 36, the number of judges;

(f) Consider pursuant to Article 87, paragraphs 5 and 7, any question relating to non-cooperation;

(g) Perform any other function consistent with this Statute or the Rules of Procedure and Evidence.

3. (a) The Assembly shall have a Bureau consisting of a President, two Vice-Presidents and 18 members elected by the Assembly for three-year terms.

(b) The Bureau shall have a representative character, taking into account, in particular, equitable geographical distribution and the adequate representation of the principal legal systems of the world.

(c) The Bureau shall meet as often as necessary, but at least once a year. It shall assist the Assembly in the discharge of its responsibilities.

4. The Assembly may establish such subsidiary bodies as may be necessary, including an independent oversight mechanism for inspection, evaluation and investigation of the Court, in order to enhance its efficiency and economy.

5. The President of the Court, the Prosecutor and the Registrar or their representatives may participate, as appropriate, in meetings of the Assembly and of the Bureau.

6. The Assembly shall meet at the seat of the Court or at the Headquarters of the United Nations once a year and, when circumstances so require, hold special sessions. Except as otherwise specified in this Statute, special sessions shall be convened by the Bureau on its own initiative or at the request of one third of the States Parties.

7. Each State Party shall have one vote. Every effort shall be made to reach decisions by consensus in the Assembly and in the Bureau. If consensus cannot be reached, except as otherwise provided in the Statute:

(a) Decisions on matters of substance must be approved by a two-thirds majority of those present and voting provided that an absolute majority of States Parties constitutes the quorum for voting;

(b) Decisions on matters of procedure shall be taken by a simple majority of States Parties present and voting.

8. A State Party which is in arrears in the payment of its financial contributions towards the costs of the Court shall have no vote in the Assembly and in the Bureau if the amount of its arrears equals or exceeds the amount of the contributions due from it for the preceding two full years. The Assembly may, nevertheless, permit such a State Party to vote in the Assembly and in the Bureau if it is satisfied that the failure to pay is due to conditions beyond the control of the State Party.

9. The Assembly shall adopt its own rules of procedure.

10. The official and working languages of the Assembly shall be those of the General Assembly of the United Nations.

PART 12. FINANCING

Article 113. Financial Regulations

Except as otherwise specifically provided, all financial matters related to the Court and the meetings of the Assembly of States Parties, including its Bureau and subsidiary bodies, shall be governed by this Statute and the Financial Regulations and Rules adopted by the Assembly of States Parties.

Article 114. Payment of expenses

Expenses of the Court and the Assembly of States Parties, including its Bureau and subsidiary bodies, shall be paid from the funds of the Court.

Article 115. Funds of the Court and of the Assembly of States Parties

The expenses of the Court and the Assembly of States Parties, including its Bureau and subsidiary bodies, as provided for in the budget decided by the Assembly of States Parties, shall be provided by the following sources:

(a) Assessed contributions made by States Parties;

(b) Funds provided by the United Nations, subject to the approval of the General Assembly, in particular in relation to the expenses incurred due to referrals by the Security Council.

Article 116. Voluntary contributions

Without prejudice to Article 115, the Court may receive and utilize, as additional funds, voluntary contributions from Governments, international organizations, individuals, corporations and other entities, in accordance with relevant criteria adopted by the Assembly of States Parties.

Article 117. Assessment of contributions

The contributions of States Parties shall be assessed in accordance with an agreed scale of assessment, based on the scale adopted by the United Nations for its regular budget and adjusted in accordance with the principles on which that scale is based.

Article 118. Annual audit

The records, books and accounts of the Court, including its annual financial statements, shall be audited annually by an independent auditor.

PART 13. FINAL CLAUSES

Article 119. Settlement of disputes

1. Any dispute concerning the judicial functions of the Court shall be settled by the decision of the Court.

2. Any other dispute between two or more States Parties relating to the interpretation or application of this Statute which is not settled through negotiations within three months of their commencement shall be referred to the Assembly of States Parties. The Assembly may itself seek to settle the dispute or make recommendations on further means of settlement of the dispute, including referral to the International Court of Justice in conformity with the Statute of that Court.

Article 120. Reservations

No reservations may be made to this Statute.

Article 121. Amendments

1. After the expiry of seven years from the entry into force of this Statute, any State Party may propose amendments thereto. The text of any proposed amendment shall be submitted to the Secretary-General of the United Nations, who shall promptly circulate it to all States Parties.

2. No sooner than three months from the date of notification, the next Assembly of States Parties shall, by a majority of those present and voting, decide whether to take up the proposal. The Assembly may deal with the proposal directly or convene a Review Conference if the issue involved so warrants.

3. The adoption of an amendment at a meeting of the Assembly of States Parties or at a Review Conference on which consensus cannot be reached shall require a two-thirds majority of States Parties.

4. Except as provided in paragraph 5, an amendment shall enter into force for all States Parties one year after instruments of ratification or acceptance have been deposited with the Secretary-General of the United Nations by seven-eighths of them.

5. Any amendment to Article 5 of this Statute shall enter into force for those States Parties which have accepted the amendment one year after the deposit of their instruments of ratification or acceptance. In respect of a State Party which has not accepted the amendment, the Court shall not exercise its jurisdiction regarding a crime covered by the amendment when committed by that State Party's nationals or on its territory.

6. If an amendment has been accepted by seven-eighths of States Parties in accordance with paragraph 4, any State Party which has not accepted the amendment may withdraw from the Statute with immediate effect, notwithstanding paragraph 1 of Article 127, but subject to paragraph 2 of Article 127, by giving notice no later than one year after the entry into force of such amendment.

7. The Secretary-General of the United Nations shall circulate to all States Parties any amendment adopted at a meeting of the Assembly of States Parties or at a Review Conference.

Article 122. Amendments to provisions of an institutional nature

1. Amendments to provisions of the Statute which are of an exclusively institutional nature, namely, Article 35, Article 36, paragraphs 8 and 9 Article 37, Article 38, Article 39, paragraphs 1 (first two sentences), 2 and 4, Article 42, paragraphs 4 to 9, Article 43, paragraphs 2 and 3, and Articles 44, 46, 47 and 49, may be proposed at any time, notwithstanding Article 121, paragraph 1, by any State Party. The text of any proposed amendment shall be submitted to the Secretary-General of the United Nations or such other person designated by the Assembly of States Parties who shall promptly circulate it to all States Parties and to others participating in the Assembly.

2. Amendments under this article on which consensus cannot be reached shall be adopted by the Assembly of States Parties or by a Review Conference, by a two-thirds majority of States Parties. Such amendments shall enter into force for all States Parties six months after their adoption by the Assembly or, as the case may be, by the Conference.

Article 123. Review of the Statute

1. Seven years after the entry into force of this Statute the Secretary-General of the United Nations shall convene a Review Conference to consider any amendments to this Statute. Such review may include, but is not limited to, the list of crimes contained in Article 5. The Conference shall be open to those participating in the Assembly of States Parties and on the same conditions.

2. At any time thereafter, at the request of a State Party and for the purposes set out in paragraph 1, the Secretary-General of the United Nations shall, upon approval by a majority of States Parties, convene a Review Conference.

3. The provisions of Article 121, paragraphs 3 to 7, shall apply to the adoption and entry into force of any amendment to the Statute considered at a Review Conference.

Article 124. Transitional Provision

Notwithstanding Article 12, paragraph 1, a State, on becoming a party to this Statute, may declare that, for a period of seven years after the entry into force of this Statute for the State concerned, it does not accept the jurisdiction of the Court with respect to the category of crimes referred to in Article 8 when a crime is alleged to have been committed by its nationals or on its territory. A declaration under this article may be withdrawn at any time. The provisions of this article shall be reviewed at the Review Conference convened in accordance with Article 123, paragraph 1.

Article 125. Signature, ratification, acceptance, approval or accession

1. This Statute shall be open for signature by all States in Rome, at the headquarters of the Food and Agriculture Organization of the United Nations, on 17 July 1998. Thereafter, it shall remain open for signature in Rome at the Ministry of Foreign Affairs of Italy until 17 October 1998. After that date, the Statute shall remain open for signature in New York, at United Nations Headquarters, until 31 December 2000.

2. This Statute is subject to ratification, acceptance or approval by signatory States. Instruments of ratification, acceptance or approval shall be deposited with the Secretary-General of the United Nations.

3. This Statute shall be open to accession by all States. Instruments of accession shall be deposited with the Secretary-General of the United Nations.

Article 126. Entry into force

1. This Statute shall enter into force on the first day of the month after the 60th day following the date of the deposit of the 60th instrument of ratification, acceptance, approval or accession with the Secretary-General of the United Nations.

2. For each State ratifying, accepting, approving or acceding to the Statute after the deposit of the 60th instrument of ratification, acceptance, approval or accession, the Statute shall enter into force on the first day of the month after the 60th day following the deposit by such State of its instrument of ratification, acceptance, approval or accession.

Article 127. Withdrawal

1. A State Party may, by written notification addressed to the Secretary-General of the United Nations, withdraw from this Statute. The withdrawal shall take effect one year after the date of receipt of the notification, unless the notification specifies a later date.

2. A State shall not be discharged, by reason of its withdrawal, from the obligations arising from this Statute while it was a Party to the Statute, including any financial obligations which may have accrued. Its withdrawal shall not affect any cooperation with the Court in connection with criminal investigations and proceedings in relation

to which the withdrawing State had a duty to cooperate and which were commenced prior to the date on which the withdrawal became effective, nor shall it prejudice in any way the continued consideration of any matter which was already under consideration by the Court prior to the date on which the withdrawal became effective.

Article 128. Authentic texts

The original of this Statute, of which the Arabic, Chinese, English, French, Russian and Spanish texts are equally authentic, shall be deposited with the Secretary-General of the United Nations, who shall send certified copies thereof to all States.

IN WITNESS WHEREOF, the undersigned, being duly authorized thereto by their respective Governments, have signed this Statute.

DONE at Rome, this 17th day of July 1998.

Convention on the Prevention and Punishment of the Crime of Genocide, 78 U.N.T.S. 277 (1948)

The Contracting Parties,

Having considered the declaration made by the General Assembly of the United Nations in its resolution 96(I) dated 11 December 1946 that genocide is a crime under international law, contrary to the spirit and aims of the United Nations and condemned by the civilized world;

Recognizing that at all periods of history genocide has inflicted great losses on humanity; and

Being convinced that, in order to liberate mankind from such an odious scourge, international co-operation is required;

Hereby agree as hereinafter provided.

Article I

The Contracting Parties confirm that genocide, whether committed in time of peace or in time of war, is a crime under international law which they undertake to prevent and to punish.

Article II

In the present Convention, genocide means any of the following acts committed with intent to destroy, in whole or in part, a national, ethnical, racial or religious group as such:

(a) Killing members of the group;

(b) Causing serious bodily or mental harm to members of the group;

(c) Deliberately inflicting on the group conditions of life calculated to bring about its physical destruction in whole or in part;

(d) Imposing measures intended to prevent births within the group;

(e) Forcibly transferring children of the group to another group.

Article III

The following acts shall be punishable:

   (a) Genocide;

   (b) Conspiracy to commit genocide;

   (c) Direct and public incitement to commit genocide;

   (d) Attempt to commit genocide;

   (e) Complicity in genocide.

Article IV

Persons committing genocide or any of the other acts enumerated in Article III shall be punished, whether they are constitutionally responsible rulers, public officials or private individuals.

Article V

The Contracting Parties undertake to enact, in accordance with their respective Constitutions, the necessary legislation to give effect to the provisions of the present Convention and, in particular, to provide effective penalties for persons guilty of genocide or any of the other acts enumerated in Article III.

Article VI

Persons charged with genocide or any of the other acts enumerated in Article III shall be tried by a competent tribunal of the State in the territory of which the act was committed, or by such international penal tribunal as may have jurisdiction with respect to those Contracting Parties which shall have accepted its jurisdiction.

Article VII

Genocide and the other acts enumerated in Article III shall not be considered as political crimes for the purpose of extradition.

The Contracting Parties pledge themselves in such cases to grant extradition in accordance with their laws and treaties in force.

Article VIII

Any Contracting Party may call upon the competent organs of the United Nations to take such action under the Charter of the United Nations as they consider appropriate for the prevention and suppression of acts of genocide or any of the other acts enumerated in Article III.

Article IX

Disputes between the Contracting Parties relating to the interpretation, application or fulfilment of the present Convention, including those relating to the responsibility of a State for genocide or any of the other acts enumerated in Article II, shall be submitted to the International Court of Justice at the request of any of the parties to the dispute.

Article X

The present Convention, of which the Chinese, English, French, Russian and Spanish texts are equally authentic, shall bear the date of 9 December 1948....

International Convention on the Suppression and Punishment of the Crime of "Apartheid," done in New York, Nov. 30, 1973, 1015 U.N.T.S. 243 (1974)

Article I

(1) The States Parties to the present Convention declare that apartheid is a crime against humanity and that inhuman acts resulting from the policies and practices of apartheid and similar policies and practices of racial segregation and discrimination, as defined in Article II of the Convention, are crimes violating the principles of international law, in particular the purposes and principles of the Charter of the United Nations, and constituting a serious threat to international peace and security.

(2) States Parties to the present Convention declare criminal those organizations, institutions and individuals committing the crime of apartheid.

Article II

For the purpose of the present Convention, the term "the crime of apartheid " which shall include similar policies and practices of racial segregation and discrimination as practiced in southern Africa, shall apply to the following inhuman acts committed for the purpose of establishing and maintaining domination by one racial group of persons over any other racial group of persons and systematically oppressing them:

(a) Denial to a member or members of a racial group or groups of the right to life and liberty of person:

(i) By murder of members of a racial group or groups;

(ii) By the infliction upon the members of a racial group or groups of serious bodily or mental harm by the infringement of their freedom or dignity, or by subjecting them to torture or to cruel, inhuman or degrading treatment or punishment;

(iii) By arbitrary arrest and illegal imprisonment of the members of a racial group or groups;

(b) Deliberate imposition on a racial group or groups of living conditions calculated to cause its or their physical destruction in whole or in part;

(c) Any legislative measures and other measures calculated to prevent a racial group or groups from participation in the political, social, economic and cultural life of the country and the deliberate creation of conditions preventing the full development of such a group or groups, in particular by denying to members of a racial group or groups basic human rights and freedoms, including the right to work, the right to form recognized trade unions, the right to education, the right to leave and to return to their country, the right to freedom of opinion and expression, and the right to freedom of peaceful assembly and association;

(d) Any measures, including legislative measures, designed to divide the population along racial lines by the creation of separate reserves and ghettos for the members of a racial group or groups, the prohibition of mixed marriages among members of various racial groups, the expropriation of landed property belonging to a racial group or groups or to members thereof;

(e) Exploitation of the labour of the members of a racial group or groups, in particular by submitting them to forced labour;

(f) Persecution of organizations and persons, by depriving them of fundamental rights and freedoms, because they oppose apartheid.

Article III

International criminal responsibility shall apply, irrespective of the motive involved, to individuals, members of organizations and institutions and representatives of the State, whether residing in the territory of the State in which the acts are perpetrated or in some other State, whenever they:

(a) Commit, participate in, directly incite or conspire in the commission of the acts mentioned in Article II of the present Convention;

(b) Directly abet, encourage or co-operate in the commission of the crime of *apartheid.*

Article IV

The States Parties to the present Convention undertake:

(a) To adopt any legislative or other measure necessary to suppress as well as to prevent any encouragement of the crime of apartheid and similar segregationist policies or their manifestations and to punish persons guilty of that crime;

(b) To adopt legislative, judicial and administrative measures to prosecute, bring to trial and punish in accordance with their jurisdiction persons responsible for, or accused of, the acts defined in Article II of the present Convention, whether or not such persons reside in the territory of the State in which the acts are committed or are nationals of that State or of some other State or are stateless persons.

Article V

Persons charged with the acts enumerated in Article II of the present Convention may be tried by a competent tribunal of any State Party to the Convention which may acquire jurisdiction with respect to those State Parties which shall have accepted its jurisdiction.

Article VI

The States Parties to the present Convention undertake to accept and carry out in accordance with the Charter of the United Nations the decisions taken by the Security Council aimed at the prevention, suppression and punishment of the crime of apartheid, and to co-operate in the implementation of decisions adopted by other competent organs of the United Nations with a view to achieving the purposes of the Convention.

Article XI

(1) Acts enumerated in Article II of the present Convention shall not be considered political crimes for the purpose of extradition.

(2) The States Parties to the present Convention undertake in such cases to grant extradition with their legislation and with the treaties in force.

International Convention on the Elimination of All Forms of Racial Discrimination, 660 U.N.T.S. 195 (1966)

Part I

Article 1

1. In this Convention, the term "racial discrimination" shall mean any distinction, exclusion, restriction or preference based on race, colour, descent, or national or ethnic origin which has the purpose or effect of nullifying or impairing the recognition, enjoyment or exercise, on an equal footing, of human rights and fundamental freedoms in the political, economic, social, cultural or any other field of public life.

2. This Convention shall not apply to distinctions, exclusions, restrictions or preferences made by a State Party to this Convention between citizens and non-citizens.

3. Nothing in this Convention may be interpreted as affecting in any way the legal provisions of States Parties concerning nationality, citizenship or naturalization, provided that such provisions do not discriminate against any particular nationality.

4. Special measures taken for the sole purpose of securing adequate advancement of certain racial or ethnic groups or individuals requiring such protection as may be necessary in order to ensure such groups or individuals equal enjoyment or exercise of human rights and fundamental freedoms shall not be deemed racial discrimination, provided, however, that such measures do not, as a consequence, lead to the maintenance of separate rights for different racial groups and that they shall not be continued after the objectives for which they were taken have been achieved.

Article 2

1. States Parties condemn racial discrimination and undertake to pursue by all appropriate means and without delay a policy of eliminating racial discrimination in all its forms and promoting understanding among all races, and, to this end:

  (a) Each State Party undertakes to engage in no act or practice of racial discrimination against persons, groups of persons or institutions and to ensure that all public authorities and public institutions, national and local, shall act in conformity with this obligation;

  (b) Each State Party undertakes not to sponsor, defend or support racial discrimination by any persons or organizations;

  (c) Each State Party shall take effective measures to review governmental, national and local policies, and to amend, rescind or nullify any laws and regulations which have the effect of creating or perpetuating racial discrimination wherever it exists;

(d) Each State Party shall prohibit and bring to an end, by all appropriate means, including legislation as required by circumstances, racial discrimination by any persons, group or organization;

(e) Each State Party undertakes to encourage, where appropriate, integrationist multi-racial organizations and movements and other means of eliminating barriers between races, and to discourage anything which tends to strengthen racial division.

2. States Parties shall, when the circumstances so warrant, take, in the social, economic, cultural and other fields, special and concrete measures to ensure the adequate development and protection of certain racial groups or individuals belonging to them, for the purpose of guaranteeing them the full and equal enjoyment of human rights and fundamental freedoms. These measures shall in no case entail as a consequence the maintenance or unequal or separate rights for different racial groups after the objectives for which they were taken have been achieved.

Article 3

States Parties particularly condemn racial segregation and apartheid and undertake to prevent, prohibit and eradicate all practices of this nature in territories under their jurisdiction.

Article 4

States Parties condemn all propaganda and all organizations which are based on ideas or theories of superiority of one race or group of persons of one colour or ethnic origin, or which attempt to justify or promote racial hatred and discrimination in any form, and undertake to adopt immediate and positive measures designed to eradicate all incitement to, or acts of, such discrimination and, to this end, with due regard to the principles embodied in the Universal Declaration of Human Rights and the rights expressly set forth in Article 5 of this Convention, inter alia:

(a) Shall declare an offence punishable by law all dissemination of ideas based on racial superiority or hatred, incitement to racial discrimination, as well as all acts of violence or incitement to such acts against any race or group of persons of another colour or ethnic origin, and also the provision of any assistance to racist activities, including the financing thereof;

(b) Shall declare illegal and prohibit organizations, and also organized and all other propaganda activities, which promote and incite racial discrimination, and shall recognize participation in such organizations or activities as an offence punishable by law;

(c) Shall not permit public authorities or public institutions, national or local, to promote or incite racial discrimination.

Article 5

In compliance with the fundamental obligations laid down in Article 2 of this Convention, States Parties undertake to prohibit and to eliminate racial discrimination in all its forms and to guarantee the right of everyone, without distinction as to race, colour, or national or ethnic origin, to equality before the law, notably in the enjoyment of the following rights:

(a) The right to equal treatment before the tribunals and all other organs administering justice;

(b) The right to security of person and protection by the State against violence or bodily harm, whether inflicted by government officials or by any individual, group or institution;

(c) Political rights, in particular the rights to participate in elections—to vote and to stand for election—on the basis of universal and equal suffrage, to take part in the Government as well as in the conduct of public affairs at any level and to have equal access to public service;

(d) Other civil rights, in particular:

   (i) The right to freedom of movement and residence within the border of the State;

   (ii) The right to leave any country, including one's own, and to return to one's country;

   (iii) The right to nationality;

   (iv) The right to marriage and choice of spouse;

   (v) The right to own property alone as well as in association with others;

   (vi) The right to inherit;

   (vii) The right to freedom of thought, conscience and religion;

   (viii) The right to freedom of opinion and expression;

   (ix) The right to freedom of peaceful assembly and association;

(e) Economic, social and cultural rights, in particular:

   (i) The rights to work, to free choice of employment, to just and favourable conditions of work, to protection against unemployment, to equal pay for equal work, to just and favourable remuneration;

   (ii) The right to form and join trade unions;

   (iii) The right to housing;

   (iv) The right to public health, medical care, social security and social services;

   (v) The right to education and training;

   (vi) The right to equal participation in cultural activities;

(f) The right of access to any place or service intended for use by the general public, such as transport, hotels, restaurants, cafes, theatres and parks.

Article 6

States Parties shall assure to everyone within their jurisdiction effective protection and remedies, through the competent national tribunals and other State institutions, against any acts of racial discrimination which violate his human rights and fundamental freedoms contrary to this Convention, as well as the right to seek from such tribunals just and adequate reparation or satisfaction for any damage suffered as a result of such discrimination.

Article 7

States Parties undertake to adopt immediate and effective measures, particularly in the fields of teaching, education, culture and information, with a view to combating prejudices which lead to racial discrimination and to promoting understanding, tolerance and friendship among nations and racial or ethnical groups, as well as to propagating the purposes and principles of the Charter of the United Nations, the Universal Declaration of Human Rights, the United Nations Declaration on the Elimination of All Forms of Racial Discrimination, and this Convention.

Part II

Article 8

1. There shall be established a Committee on the Elimination of Racial Discrimination (hereinafter referred to as the Committee) consisting of eighteen experts of high moral standing and acknowledged impartiality elected by States Parties from among their nationals, who shall serve in their personal capacity, consideration being given to equitable geographical distribution and to the representation of the different forms of civilization as well as of the principal legal systems.

2. The members of the Committee shall be elected by secret ballot from a list of persons nominated by the States Parties. Each State Party may nominate one person from among its own nationals.

3. The initial election shall be held six months after the date of the entry into force of this Convention. At least three months before the date of each election the Secretary-General of the United Nations shall address a letter to the States Parties inviting them to submit their nominations within two months. The Secretary-General shall prepare a list in alphabetical order of all persons thus nominated, indicating the States Parties which have nominated them, and shall submit it to the States Parties.

4. Elections of the members of the Committee shall be held at a meeting of States Parties convened by the Secretary-General at United Nations Headquarters. At that meeting, for which two-thirds of the States Parties shall constitute a quorum, the persons elected to the Committee shall be those nominees who obtain the largest number of votes and an absolute majority of the votes of the representatives of States Parties present and voting.

5. (a) The members of the Committee shall be elected for a term of four years. However, the terms of nine of the members elected at the first election shall expire at the end of two years; immediately after the first election the names of these nine members shall be chosen by lot by the Chairman of the Committee.

(b) For the filling of casual vacancies, the State Party whose expert has ceased to function as a member of the Committee shall appoint another expert from among its nationals, subject to the approval of the Committee.

6. States Parties shall be responsible for the expenses of the members of the Committee while they are in performance of Committee duties.

Article 9

1. States Parties undertake to submit to the Secretary-General of the United Nations, for consideration by the Committee, a report on the legislative, judicial, administrative or other measures which they have adopted and which give effect to the provisions of this Convention:

(a) within one year after the entry into force of the Convention for the State concerned; and

(b) thereafter every two years and whenever the Committee so requests. The Committee may request further information from the States Parties.

2. The Committee shall report annually, through the Secretary-General, to the General Assembly of the United Nations on its activities and may make suggestions and general recommendations based on the examination of the reports and information received from the States Parties. Such suggestions and general recommendations shall be reported to the General Assembly together with comments, if any, from States Parties.

Article 10

1. The Committee shall adopt its own rules of procedure.

2. The Committee shall elect its officers for a term of two years.

3. The secretariat of the Committee shall be provided by the Secretary-General of the United Nations.

4. The meetings of the Committee shall normally be held at United Nations Headquarters.

Article 11

1. If a State Party considers that another State Party is not giving effect to the provisions of this Convention, it may bring the matter to the attention of the Committee. The Committee shall then transmit the communication to the State Party concerned. Within three months, the receiving State shall submit to the Committee written explanations or statements clarifying the matter and the remedy, if any, that may have been taken by that State.

2. If the matter is not adjusted to the satisfaction of both parties, either by bilateral negotiations or by any other procedure open to them, within six months after the receipt by the receiving State of the initial communication, either State shall have the right to refer the matter again to the Committee by notifying the Committee and also the other State.

3. The Committee shall deal with a matter referred to it in accordance with paragraph 2 of this article after it has ascertained that all available domestic remedies have been invoked and exhausted in the case, in conformity with the generally recognized principles of international law. This shall not be the rule where the application of the remedies is unreasonably prolonged.

4. In any matter referred to it, the Committee may call upon the States Parties concerned to supply any other relevant information.

5. When any matter arising out of this article is being considered by the Committee, the States Parties concerned shall be entitled to send a representative to take part in the

proceedings of the Committee, without voting rights, while the matter is under consideration.

Article 12

1. (a) After the Committee has obtained and collated all the information it deems necessary, the Chairman shall appoint an ad hoc Conciliation Commission (hereinafter referred to as the Commission) comprising five persons who may or may not be members of the Committee. The members of the Commission shall be appointed with the unanimous consent of the parties to the dispute, and its good offices shall be made available to the States concerned with a view to an amicable solution of the matter on the basis or respect for this Convention.

(b) If the States Parties to the dispute fail to reach agreement within three months on all or part of the composition of the Commission, the members of the Commission not agreed upon by the States parties to the dispute shall be elected by secret ballot by a two-thirds majority vote of the Committee from among its own members.

2. The members of the Commission shall serve in their personal capacity. They shall not be nationals of the States parties to the dispute or of a State not Party to this Convention.

3. The Commission shall elect its own Chairman and adopt its own rules of procedure.

4. The meetings of the Commission shall normally be held at United Nations Headquarters or at any other convenient place as determined by the Commission.

5. The secretariat provided in accordance with Article 10, paragraph 3, of this Convention shall also service the Commission whenever a dispute among States Parties brings the Commission into being.

6. The States parties to the dispute shall share equally all the expenses of the members of the Commission in accordance with estimates to be provided by the Secretary-General of the United Nations.

7. The Secretary-General shall be empowered to pay the expenses of the members of the Commission, if necessary, before reimbursement by the States parties to the dispute in accordance with paragraph 6 of this article.

8. The information obtained and collated by the Committee shall be made available to the Commission, and the Commission may call upon the States concerned to supply any other relevant information.

Article 13

1. When the Commission has fully considered the matter, it shall prepare and submit to the Chairman of the Committee a report embodying its findings on all questions of fact relevant to the issue between the parties and containing such recommendations as it may think proper for the amicable solution of the dispute.

2. The Chairman of the Committee shall communicate the report of the Commission to each of the States Parties to the dispute. These States shall, within three months, inform the Chairman of the Committee whether or not they accept the recommendations contained in the report of the Commission.

3. After the period provided for in paragraph 2 of Chairman of the Committee shall communicate the report of the Commission and the declarations of the States Parties concerned to the other States Parties to this Convention.

Article 14

1. A State Party may at any time declare that it recognizes the competence of the Committee to receive and consider communications from individuals or groups of individuals within its jurisdiction claiming to be victims of a violation by that State Party of any of the rights set forth in this Convention. No communication shall be received by the Committee if it concerns a State Party which has not made such a declaration.

2. Any State Party which makes a declaration as provided for in paragraph 1 of this article may establish or indicate a body within its national legal order which shall be competent to receive and consider petitions from individuals and groups of individuals within its jurisdiction who claim to be victims of a violation of any of the rights set forth in this Convention and who have exhausted other available local remedies.

3. A declaration made in accordance with paragraph 1 of this article and the name of any body established or indicated in accordance with paragraph 2 of this article shall be deposited by the State Party concerned with the Secretary-General of the United Nations, who shall transmit copies thereof to the other States Parties. A declaration may be withdrawn at any time by notification to the Secretary-General, but such a withdrawal shall not affect communications pending before the Committee.

4. A register of petitions shall be kept by the body established or indicated in accordance with paragraph 2 of this article, and certified copies of the register shall be filed annually through appropriate channels with the Secretary-General on the understanding that the contents shall not be publicly disclosed.

5. In the event of failure to obtain satisfaction from the body established or indicated in accordance with paragraph 2 of this article, the petitioner shall have the right to communicate the matter to the Committee within six months.

6. (a) The Committee shall confidentially bring any communication referred to it to the attention of the State Party alleged to be violating any provision of this Convention, but the identity of the individual or groups of individuals concerned shall not be revealed without his or their express consent. The Committee shall not receive anonymous communications.

   (b) Within three months, the receiving State shall submit to the Committee written explanations or statements clarifying the matter and the remedy, if any, that may have been taken by that State.

7. (a) The Committee shall consider communications in the light of all information made available to it by the State Party concerned and by the petitioner. The Committee shall not consider any communication from a petitioner unless it has ascertained that the petitioner has exhausted all available domestic remedies. However, this shall not be the rule where the application of the remedies is unreasonably prolonged.

   (b) The Committee shall forward its suggestions and recommendations, if any, to the State Party concerned and to the petitioner.

8. The Committee shall include in its annual report a summary of such communications and, where appropriate, a summary of the explanations and statements of the States Parties concerned and of its own suggestions and recommendations.

9. The Committee shall be competent to exercise the functions provided for in this article only when at least ten States Parties to this Convention are bound by declarations in accordance with paragraph 1 of this article.

Article 20

1. The Secretary-General of the United Nations shall receive and circulate to all States which are or may become Parties to this Convention reservations made by States at the time of ratification or accession. Any State which objects to the reservation shall, within a period of ninety days from the date of the said communication, notify the Secretary-General that it does not accept it.

2. A reservation incompatible with the object and purpose of this Convention shall not be permitted, nor shall a reservation the effect of which would inhibit the operation of any of the bodies established by this Convention be allowed. A reservation shall be considered incompatible or inhibitive if at least two-thirds of the States Parties to this Convention object to it.

3. Reservations may be withdrawn at any time by notification to this effect addressed to the Secretary-General. Such notification shall take effect on the date on which it is received.

Article 22

Any dispute between two or more States Parties with respect to the interpretation or application of this Convention, which is not settled by negotiation or by the procedures expressly provided for in this Convention, shall, at the request of any of the parties to the dispute, be referred to the International Court of Justice for decision, unless the disputants agree to another mode of settlement.

International Convention Against the Taking of Hostages, 1316 U.N.T.S. 205 (1979)

The States Parties to this Convention,

Having in mind the purposes and principles of the Charter of the United Nations concerning the maintenance of international peace and security and the promotion of friendly relations and co-operation among States,

Recognizing in particular that everyone has the right to life, liberty and security of person, as set out in the Universal Declaration of Human Rights and the International Covenant on Civil and Political Rights,

Reaffirming the principle of equal rights and self-determination of peoples as enshrined in the Charter of the United Nations and the Declaration on Principles of International Law concerning Friendly Relations and Co-operation among States in accordance with the Charter of the United Nations, as well as in other relevant resolutions of the General Assembly,

Considering that the taking of hostages is an offence of grave concern to the international community and that, in accordance with the provisions of this Convention, any person committing an act of hostage taking shall either be prosecuted or extradited,

Being convinced that it is urgently necessary to develop international co-operation between States in devising and adopting effective measures for the prevention, prosecution and punishment of all acts of taking of hostages as manifestations of international terrorism,

Have agreed as follows:

Article 1

1. Any person who seizes or detains and threatens to kill, to injure or to continue to detain another person (hereinafter referred to as the "hostage") in order to compel a third party, namely, a State, an international intergovernmental organization, a natural or juridical person, or a group of persons, to do or abstain from doing any act as an explicit or implicit condition for the release of the hostage commits the offence of taking of hostages ("hostage-taking") within the meaning of this Convention.

2. Any person who:

(a) attempts to commit an act of hostage-taking, or

(b) participates as an accomplice of anyone who commits or attempts to commit an act of hostage-taking likewise commits an offence for the purposes of this Convention.

Article 2

Each State Party shall make the offences set forth in Article 1 punishable by appropriate penalties which take into account the grave nature of those offences.

Article 3

1. The State Party in the territory of which the hostage is held by the offender shall take all measures it considers appropriate to ease the situation of the hostage, in particular, to secure his release and, after his release, to facilitate, when relevant, his departure.

2. If any object which the offender has obtained as a result of the taking of hostages comes into the custody of a State Party, that State Party shall return it as soon as possible to the hostage or the third party referred to in Article 1, as the case may be, or to the appropriate authorities thereof.

Article 4

States Parties shall co-operate in the prevention of the offences set forth in Article 1, particularly by:

(a) taking all practicable measures to prevent preparations in their respective territories for the commission of those offences within or outside their territories, including measures to prohibit in their territories illegal activities of persons, groups and organizations that encourage, instigate, organize or engage in the perpetration of acts of taking of hostages;

(b) exchanging information and co-ordinating the taking of administrative and other measures as appropriate to prevent the commission of those offences.

Article 5

1. Each State Party shall take such measures as may be necessary to establish its jurisdiction over any of the offences set forth in Article 1 which are committed:

(a) in its territory or on board a ship or aircraft registered in that State;

(b) by any of its nationals or, if that State considers it appropriate, by those stateless persons who have their habitual residence in its territory;

(c) in order to compel that State to do or abstain from doing any act; or

(d) with respect to a hostage who is a national of that State, if that State considers it appropriate.

2. Each State Party shall likewise take such measures as may be necessary to establish its jurisdiction over the offences set forth in Article 1 in cases where the alleged offender is present in its territory and it does not extradite him to any of the States mentioned in paragraph 1 of this article.

3. This Convention does not exclude any criminal jurisdiction exercised in accordance with internal law.

Article 6

1. Upon being satisfied that the circumstances so warrant, any State Party in the territory of which the alleged offender is present shall, in accordance with its laws, take him into custody or take other measures to ensure his presence for such time as is necessary to enable any criminal or extradition proceedings to be instituted. That State Party shall immediately make a preliminary inquiry into the facts.

2. The custody or other measures referred to in paragraph 1 of this article shall be notified without delay directly or through the Secretary-General of the United Nations to:

(a) the State where the offence was committed;

(b) the State against which compulsion has been directed or attempted;

(c) the State of which the natural or juridical person against whom compulsion has been directed or attempted is a national;

(d) the State of which the hostage is a national or in the territory of which he has his habitual residence;

(e) the State of which the alleged offender is a national or, if he is a stateless person, in the territory of which he has his habitual residence;

(f) the international intergovernmental organization against which compulsion has been directed or attempted;

(g) all other States concerned.

3. Any person regarding whom the measures referred to in paragraph 1 of this article are being taken shall be entitled:

(a) to communicate without delay with the nearest appropriate representative of the State of which he is a national or which is otherwise entitled to establish such communication or, if he is a stateless person, the State in the territory of which he has his habitual residence;

(b) to be visited by a representative of that State.

4. The rights referred to in paragraph 3 of this article shall be exercised in conformity with the laws and regulations of the State in the territory of which the alleged offender is present subject to the proviso, however, that the said laws and regulations must enable full effect to be given to the purposes for which the rights accorded under paragraph 3 of this article are intended.

5. The provisions of paragraphs 3 and 4 of this article shall be without prejudice to the right of any State Party having a claim to jurisdiction in accordance with paragraph 1(b) of Article 5 to invite the International Committee of the Red Cross to communicate with and visit the alleged offender.

6. The State which makes the preliminary inquiry contemplated in paragraph 1 of this article shall promptly report its findings to the States or organization referred to in paragraph 2 of this article and indicate whether it intends to exercise jurisdiction.

Article 7

The State Party where the alleged offender is prosecuted shall in accordance with its laws communicate the final outcome of the proceedings to the Secretary-General of the United Nations, who shall transmit the information to the other States concerned and the international intergovernmental organizations concerned.

Article 8

1. The State Party in the territory of which the alleged offender is found shall, if it does not extradite him, be obliged, without exception whatsoever and whether or not the offence was committed in its territory, to submit the case to its competent authorities for the purpose of prosecution, through proceedings in accordance with the laws of that State. Those authorities shall take their decision in the same manner as in the case of any ordinary offence of a grave nature under the law of that State.

2. Any person regarding whom proceedings are being carried out in connection with any of the offences set forth in Article 1 shall be guaranteed fair treatment at all stages of the proceedings, including enjoyment of all the rights and guarantees provided by the law of the State in the territory of which he is present.

Article 9

1. A request for the extradition of an alleged offender, pursuant to this Convention, shall not be granted if the requested State Party has substantial grounds for believing:

(a) that the request for extradition for an offence set forth in Article 1 has been made for the purpose of prosecuting or punishing a person on account of his race, religion, nationality, ethnic origin or political opinion; or

(b) that the person's position may be prejudiced:

(i) for any of the reasons mentioned in subparagraph (a) of this paragraph; or

(ii) for the reason that communication with him by the appropriate authorities of the State entitled to exercise rights of protection cannot be effected.

2. With respect to the offences as defined in this Convention the provisions of all extradition treaties and arrangements applicable between States Parties are modified as between States Parties to the extent that they are incompatible with this Convention.

Article 10

1. The offences set forth in Article 1 shall be deemed to be included as extraditable offences in any extradition treaty existing between States Parties. States Parties undertake to include such offences as extraditable offences in every extradition treaty to be concluded between them.

2. If a State Party which makes extradition conditional on the existence of a treaty receives a request for extradition from another State Party with which it has no extradition treaty, the requested State may at its option consider this Convention as the legal basis for extradition in respect of the offences set forth in Article 1. Extradition shall be subject to the other conditions provided by the law of the requested State.

3. States Parties which do not make extradition conditional on the existence of a treaty shall recognize the offences set forth in Article 1 as extraditable offences between themselves subject to the conditions provided by the law of the requested State.

4. The offences set forth in Article 1 shall be treated, for the purpose of extradition between States Parties, as if they had been committed not only in the place in which they occurred but also in the territories of the States required to establish their jurisdiction in accordance with paragraph 1 of Article 5.

Article 11

1. States Parties shall afford one another the greatest measure of assistance in connection with criminal proceedings brought in respect of the offences set forth in Article 1, including the supply of all evidence at their disposal necessary for the proceedings.

2. The provisions of paragraph 1 of this article shall not affect obligations concerning mutual judicial assistance embodied in any other treaty.

Article 12

In so far as the Geneva Conventions of 1949 for the protection of war victims or the Additional Protocols to those Conventions are applicable to a particular act of hostage-taking, and in so far as States Parties to this Convention are bound under those conventions to prosecute or hand over the hostage-taker, the present Convention shall not apply to an act of hostage-taking committed in the course of armed conflicts as defined in the Geneva Conventions of 1949 and the Protocols thereto, including armed conflicts mentioned in Article 1, paragraph 4, of Additional Protocol I of 1977, in which peoples are fighting against colonial domination and alien occupation and against racist regimes in the exercise of their right of self-determination, as enshrined in the Charter of the United Nations and the Declaration on Principles of International Law concerning Friendly Relations and Co-operation among States in accordance with the Charter of the United Nations.

Article 13

This Convention shall not apply where the offence is committed within a single State, the hostage and the alleged offender are nationals of that State and the alleged offender is found in the territory of that State.

Article 14

Nothing in this Convention shall be construed as justifying the violation of the territorial integrity or political independence of a State in contravention of the Charter of the United Nations.

Article 15

The provisions of this Convention shall not affect the application of the Treaties on Asylum, in force at the date of the adoption of this Convention, as between the States which are parties to those Treaties; but a State Party to this Convention may not invoke those Treaties with respect to another State Party to this Convention which is not a party to those treaties....

International Convention for the Protection of All Persons From Enforced Disappearance, adopted by U.N. G.A. Res. 61/177 (20 Dec. 2006)

Preamble

The States Parties to this Convention,

Considering *the obligation of States under the Charter of the United Nations to promote universal respect for, and observance of, human rights and fundamental freedoms,*

Having regard to the Universal Declaration of Human Rights,

Recalling *the International Covenant on Economic, Social and Cultural Rights, the International Covenant on Civil and Political Rights and the other relevant international instruments in the fields of human rights, humanitarian law and international criminal law,*

Also recalling the Declaration on the Protection of All Persons from Enforced Disappearance adopted by the General Assembly of the United Nations in its resolution 47/ 133 of 18 December 1992,

Aware of the extreme seriousness of enforced disappearance, which constitutes a crime and, in certain circumstances defined in international law, a crime against humanity,

Determined to prevent enforced disappearances and to combat impunity for the crime of enforced disappearance,

Considering the right of any person not to be subjected to enforced disappearance, the right of victims to justice and to reparation,

Affirming the right of any victim to know the truth about the circumstances of an enforced disappearance and the fate of the disappeared person, and the right to freedom to seek, receive and impart information to this end,

Have agreed on the following articles:

Part I

Article 1

1. No one shall be subjected to enforced disappearance.

2. No exceptional circumstances whatsoever, whether a state of war or a threat of war, internal political instability or any other public emergency, may be invoked as a justification for enforced disappearance.

Article 2

For the purposes of this Convention, "enforced disappearance" is considered to be the arrest, detention, abduction or any other form of deprivation of liberty by agents of the State or by persons or groups of persons acting with the authorization, support or acquiescence of the State, followed by a refusal to acknowledge the deprivation of liberty or by concealment of the fate or whereabouts of the disappeared person, which place such a person outside the protection of the law.

Article 3

Each State Party shall take appropriate measures to investigate acts defined in article 2 committed by persons or groups of persons acting without the authorization, support or acquiescence of the State and to bring those responsible to justice.

Article 4

Each State Party shall take the necessary measures to ensure that enforced disappearance constitutes an offence under its criminal law.

Article 5

The widespread or systematic practice of enforced disappearance constitutes a crime against humanity as defined in applicable international law and shall attract the consequences provided for under such applicable international law.

Article 6

1. Each State Party shall take the necessary measures to hold criminally responsible at least:

   (a) Any person who commits, orders, solicits or induces the commission of, attempts to commit, is an accomplice to or participates in an enforced disappearance;

   (b) A superior who:

      (i) Knew, or consciously disregarded information which clearly indicated, that subordinates under his or her effective authority and control were committing or about to commit a crime of enforced disappearance;

      (ii) Exercised effective responsibility for and control over activities which were concerned with the crime of enforced disappearance; and

      (iii) Failed to take all necessary and reasonable measures within his or her power to prevent or repress the commission of an enforced disappearance or to submit the matter to the competent authorities for investigation and prosecution;

   (c) Subparagraph *(b)* above is without prejudice to the higher standards of responsibility applicable under relevant international law to a military commander or to a person effectively acting as a military commander.

2. No order or instruction from any public authority, civilian, military or other, may be invoked to justify an offence of enforced disappearance.

Article 7

1. Each State Party shall make the offence of enforced disappearance punishable by appropriate penalties which take into account its extreme seriousness.

2. Each State Party may establish:

(a) Mitigating circumstances, in particular for persons who, having been implicated in the commission of an enforced disappearance, effectively contribute to bringing the disappeared person forward alive or make it possible to clarify cases of enforced disappearance or to identify the perpetrators of an enforced disappearance;

(b) Without prejudice to other criminal procedures, aggravating circumstances, in particular in the event of the death of the disappeared person or the commission of an enforced disappearance in respect of pregnant women, minors, persons with disabilities or other particularly vulnerable persons.

Article 8

Without prejudice to article 5,

1. A State Party which applies a statute of limitations in respect of enforced disappearance shall take the necessary measures to ensure that the term of limitation for criminal proceedings:

(a) Is of long duration and is proportionate to the extreme seriousness of this offence;

(b) Commences from the moment when the offence of enforced disappearance ceases, taking into account its continuous nature.

2. Each State Party shall guarantee the right of victims of enforced disappearance to an effective remedy during the term of limitation.

Article 9

1. Each State Party shall take the necessary measures to establish its competence to exercise jurisdiction over the offence of enforced disappearance:

I>(a) *When the offence is committed in any territory under its jurisdiction or on board a ship or aircraft registered in that State;*

(b) When the alleged offender is one of its nationals;

(c) When the disappeared person is one of its nationals and the State Party considers it appropriate.

2. Each State Party shall likewise take such measures as may be necessary to establish its competence to exercise jurisdiction over the offence of enforced disappearance when the alleged offender is present in any territory under its jurisdiction, unless it extradites or surrenders him or her to another State in accordance with its international obligations or surrenders him or her to an international criminal tribunal whose jurisdiction it has recognized.

3. This Convention does not exclude any additional criminal jurisdiction exercised in accordance with national law.

Article 10

1. Upon being satisfied, after an examination of the information available to it, that the circumstances so warrant, any State Party in whose territory a person suspected of having committed an offence of enforced disappearance is present shall take him or her into custody or take such other legal measures as are necessary to ensure his or her presence. The custody and other legal measures shall be as provided for in the law of that State Party but may be maintained only for such time as is necessary to ensure the person's presence at criminal, surrender or extradition proceedings.

2. A State Party which has taken the measures referred to in paragraph 1 of this article shall immediately carry out a preliminary inquiry or investigations to establish the facts. It shall notify the States Parties referred to in article 9, paragraph 1, of the measures it has taken in pursuance of paragraph 1 of this article, including detention and the circumstances warranting detention, and of the findings of its preliminary inquiry or its investigations, indicating whether it intends to exercise its jurisdiction.

3. Any person in custody pursuant to paragraph 1 of this article may communicate immediately with the nearest appropriate representative of the State of which he or she is a national, or, if he or she is a stateless person, with the representative of the State where he or she usually resides.

Article 11

1. The State Party in the territory under whose jurisdiction a person alleged to have committed an offence of enforced disappearance is found shall, if it does not extradite that person or surrender him or her to another State in accordance with its international obligations or surrender him or her to an international criminal tribunal whose jurisdiction it has recognized, submit the case to its competent authorities for the purpose of prosecution.

2. These authorities shall take their decision in the same manner as in the case of any ordinary offence of a serious nature under the law of that State Party. In the cases referred to in article 9, paragraph 2, the standards of evidence required for prosecution and conviction shall in no way be less stringent than those which apply in the cases referred to in article 9, paragraph 1.

3. Any person against whom proceedings are brought in connection with an offence of enforced disappearance shall be guaranteed fair treatment at all stages of the proceedings. Any person tried for an offence of enforced disappearance shall benefit from a fair trial before a competent, independent and impartial court or tribunal established by law.

Article 12

1. Each State Party shall ensure that any individual who alleges that a person has been subjected to enforced disappearance has the right to report the facts to the competent authorities, which shall examine the allegation promptly and impartially and, where necessary, undertake without delay a thorough and impartial investigation. Appropriate steps shall be taken, where necessary, to ensure that the complainant, wit-

nesses, relatives of the disappeared person and their defence counsel, as well as persons participating in the investigation, are protected against all ill-treatment or intimidation as a consequence of the complaint or any evidence given.

2. Where there are reasonable grounds for believing that a person has been subjected to enforced disappearance, the authorities referred to in paragraph 1 of this article shall undertake an investigation, even if there has been no formal complaint.

3. Each State Party shall ensure that the authorities referred to in paragraph 1 of this article:

(*a*) Have the necessary powers and resources to conduct the investigation effectively, including access to the documentation and other information relevant to their investigation;

(*b*) Have access, if necessary with the prior authorization of a judicial authority, which shall rule promptly on the matter, to any place of detention or any other place where there are reasonable grounds to believe that the disappeared person may be present.

4. Each State Party shall take the necessary measures to prevent and sanction acts that hinder the conduct of an investigation. It shall ensure in particular that persons suspected of having committed an offence of enforced disappearance are not in a position to influence the progress of an investigation by means of pressure or acts of intimidation or reprisal aimed at the complainant, witnesses, relatives of the disappeared person or their defence counsel, or at persons participating in the investigation.

Article 13

1. For the purposes of extradition between States Parties, the offence of enforced disappearance shall not be regarded as a political offence or as an offence connected with a political offence or as an offence inspired by political motives. Accordingly, a request for extradition based on such an offence may not be refused on these grounds alone.

2. The offence of enforced disappearance shall be deemed to be included as an extraditable offence in any extradition treaty existing between States Parties before the entry into force of this Convention.

3. States Parties undertake to include the offence of enforced disappearance as an extraditable offence in any extradition treaty subsequently to be concluded between them.

4. If a State Party which makes extradition conditional on the existence of a treaty receives a request for extradition from another State Party with which it has no extradition treaty, it may consider this Convention as the necessary legal basis for extradition in respect of the offence of enforced disappearance.

5. States Parties which do not make extradition conditional on the existence of a treaty shall recognize the offence of enforced disappearance as an extraditable offence between themselves.

6. Extradition shall, in all cases, be subject to the conditions provided for by the law of the requested State Party or by applicable extradition treaties, including, in particular, conditions relating to the minimum penalty requirement for extradition and the grounds upon which the requested State Party may refuse extradition or make it subject to certain conditions.

7. Nothing in this Convention shall be interpreted as imposing an obligation to extradite if the requested State Party has substantial grounds for believing that the request has been made for the purpose of prosecuting or punishing a person on account of that person's sex, race, religion, nationality, ethnic origin, political opinions or membership of a particular social group, or that compliance with the request would cause harm to that person for any one of these reasons.

Article 14

1. States Parties shall afford one another the greatest measure of mutual legal assistance in connection with criminal proceedings brought in respect of an offence of enforced disappearance, including the supply of all evidence at their disposal that is necessary for the proceedings.

2. Such mutual legal assistance shall be subject to the conditions provided for by the domestic law of the requested State Party or by applicable treaties on mutual legal assistance, including, in particular, the conditions in relation to the grounds upon which the requested State Party may refuse to grant mutual legal assistance or may make it subject to conditions.

Article 15

States Parties shall cooperate with each other and shall afford one another the greatest measure of mutual assistance with a view to assisting victims of enforced disappearance, and in searching for, locating and releasing disappeared persons and, in the event of death, in exhuming and identifying them and returning their remains.

Article 16

1. No State Party shall expel, return ("refouler"), surrender or extradite a person to another State where there are substantial grounds for believing that he or she would be in danger of being subjected to enforced disappearance.

2. For the purpose of determining whether there are such grounds, the competent authorities shall take into account all relevant considerations, including, where applicable, the existence in the State concerned of a consistent pattern of gross, flagrant or mass violations of human rights or of serious violations of international humanitarian law.

Article 17

1. No one shall be held in secret detention.

2. Without prejudice to other international obligations of the State Party with regard to the deprivation of liberty, each State Party shall, in its legislation:

> (a) Establish the conditions under which orders of deprivation of liberty may be given;

> (b) Indicate those authorities authorized to order the deprivation of liberty;

> (c) Guarantee that any person deprived of liberty shall be held solely in officially recognized and supervised places of deprivation of liberty;

> (d) Guarantee that any person deprived of liberty shall be authorized to communicate with and be visited by his or her family, counsel or any other person of his

or her choice, subject only to the conditions established by law, or, if he or she is a foreigner, to communicate with his or her consular authorities, in accordance with applicable international law;

(e) Guarantee access by the competent and legally authorized authorities and in-stitutions to the places where persons are deprived of liberty, if necessary with prior authorization from a judicial authority;

(f) Guarantee that any person deprived of liberty or, in the case of a suspected en-forced disappearance, since the person deprived of liberty is not able to exercise this right, any persons with a legitimate interest, such as relatives of the person de-prived of liberty, their representatives or their counsel, shall, in all circumstances, be entitled to take proceedings before a court, in order that the court may decide without delay on the lawfulness of the deprivation of liberty and order the per-son's release if such deprivation of liberty is not lawful.

3. Each State Party shall assure the compilation and maintenance of one or more up-to-date official registers and/or records of persons deprived of liberty, which shall be made promptly available, upon request, to any judicial or other competent authority or institution authorized for that purpose by the law of the State Party concerned or any relevant international legal instrument to which the State concerned is a party. The in-formation contained therein shall include, as a minimum:

(a) The identity of the person deprived of liberty;

(b) The date, time and place where the person was deprived of liberty and the identity of the authority that deprived the person of liberty;

(c) The authority that ordered the deprivation of liberty and the grounds for the deprivation of liberty;

(d) The authority responsible for supervising the deprivation of liberty;

(e) The place of deprivation of liberty, the date and time of admission to the place of deprivation of liberty and the authority responsible for the place of deprivation of liberty;

(f) Elements relating to the state of health of the person deprived of liberty;

(g) In the event of death during the deprivation of liberty, the circumstances and cause of death and the destination of the remains;

(h) The date and time of release or transfer to another place of detention, the des-tination and the authority responsible for the transfer.

Article 18

1. Subject to articles 19 and 20, each State Party shall guarantee to any person with a legitimate interest in this information, such as relatives of the person deprived of liberty, their representatives or their counsel, access to at least the following information:

(a) The authority that ordered the deprivation of liberty;

(b) The date, time and place where the person was deprived of liberty and admit-ted to the place of deprivation of liberty;

(c) The authority responsible for supervising the deprivation of liberty;

(d) The whereabouts of the person deprived of liberty, including, in the event of a transfer to another place of deprivation of liberty, the destination and the authority responsible for the transfer;

(e) The date, time and place of release;

(f) Elements relating to the state of health of the person deprived of liberty;

(g) In the event of death during the deprivation of liberty, the circumstances and cause of death and the destination of the remains.

2. Appropriate measures shall be taken, where necessary, to protect the persons referred to in paragraph 1 of this article, as well as persons participating in the investigation, from any ill-treatment, intimidation or sanction as a result of the search for information concerning a person deprived of liberty.

Article 19

1. Personal information, including medical and genetic data, which is collected and/or transmitted within the framework of the search for a disappeared person shall not be used or made available for purposes other than the search for the disappeared person. This is without prejudice to the use of such information in criminal proceedings relating to an offence of enforced disappearance or the exercise of the right to obtain reparation.

2. The collection, processing, use and storage of personal information, including medical and genetic data, shall not infringe or have the effect of infringing the human rights, fundamental freedoms or human dignity of an individual.

Article 20

1. Only where a person is under the protection of the law and the deprivation of liberty is subject to judicial control may the right to information referred to in article 18 be restricted, on an exceptional basis, where strictly necessary and where provided for by law, and if the transmission of the information would adversely affect the privacy or safety of the person, hinder a criminal investigation, or for other equivalent reasons in accordance with the law, and in conformity with applicable international law and with the objectives of this Convention. In no case shall there be restrictions on the right to information referred to in article 18 that could constitute conduct defined in article 2 or be in violation of article 17, paragraph 1.

2. Without prejudice to consideration of the lawfulness of the deprivation of a person's liberty, States Parties shall guarantee to the persons referred to in article 18, paragraph 1, the right to a prompt and effective judicial remedy as a means of obtaining without delay the information referred to in article 18, paragraph 1. This right to a remedy may not be suspended or restricted in any circumstances.

Article 21

Each State Party shall take the necessary measures to ensure that persons deprived of liberty are released in a manner permitting reliable verification that they have actually been released. Each State Party shall also take the necessary measures to assure the physical integrity of such persons and their ability to exercise fully their rights at the time of release, without prejudice to any obligations to which such persons may be subject under national law.

Article 22

Without prejudice to article 6, each State Party shall take the necessary measures to prevent and impose sanctions for the following conduct:

(a) Delaying or obstructing the remedies referred to in article 17, paragraph 2 *(f)*, and article 20, paragraph 2;

(b) Failure to record the deprivation of liberty of any person, or the recording of any information which the official responsible for the official register knew or should have known to be inaccurate;

(c) Refusal to provide information on the deprivation of liberty of a person, or the provision of inaccurate information, even though the legal requirements for providing such information have been met.

Article 23

1. Each State Party shall ensure that the training of law enforcement personnel, civil or military, medical personnel, public officials and other persons who may be involved in the custody or treatment of any person deprived of liberty includes the necessary education and information regarding the relevant provisions of this Convention, in order to:

(a) Prevent the involvement of such officials in enforced disappearances;

(b) Emphasize the importance of prevention and investigations in relation to enforced disappearances;

(c) Ensure that the urgent need to resolve cases of enforced disappearance is recognized.

2. Each State Party shall ensure that orders or instructions prescribing, authorizing or encouraging enforced disappearance are prohibited. Each State Party shall guarantee that a person who refuses to obey such an order will not be punished.

3. Each State Party shall take the necessary measures to ensure that the persons referred to in paragraph 1 of this article who have reason to believe that an enforced disappearance has occurred or is planned report the matter to their superiors and, where necessary, to the appropriate authorities or bodies vested with powers of review or remedy.

Article 24

1. For the purposes of this Convention, "victim" means the disappeared person and any individual who has suffered harm as the direct result of an enforced disappearance.

2. Each victim has the right to know the truth regarding the circumstances of the enforced disappearance, the progress and results of the investigation and the fate of the disappeared person. Each State Party shall take appropriate measures in this regard.

3. Each State Party shall take all appropriate measures to search for, locate and release disappeared persons and, in the event of death, to locate, respect and return their remains.

4. Each State Party shall ensure in its legal system that the victims of enforced disappearance have the right to obtain reparation and prompt, fair and adequate compensation.

5. The right to obtain reparation referred to in paragraph 4 of this article covers material and moral damages and, where appropriate, other forms of reparation such as:

(a) Restitution;

(b) Rehabilitation;

(c) Satisfaction, including restoration of dignity and reputation;

(d) Guarantees of non-repetition.

6. Without prejudice to the obligation to continue the investigation until the fate of the disappeared person has been clarified, each State Party shall take the appropriate steps with regard to the legal situation of disappeared persons whose fate has not been clarified and that of their relatives, in fields such as social welfare, financial matters, family law and property rights.

7. Each State Party shall guarantee the right to form and participate freely in organizations and associations concerned with attempting to establish the circumstances of enforced disappearances and the fate of disappeared persons, and to assist victims of enforced disappearance.

Article 25

1. Each State Party shall take the necessary measures to prevent and punish under its criminal law:

(a) The wrongful removal of children who are subjected to enforced disappearance, children whose father, mother or legal guardian is subjected to enforced disappearance or children born during the captivity of a mother subjected to enforced disappearance;

(b) The falsification, concealment or destruction of documents attesting to the true identity of the children referred to in subparagraph (a) above.

2. Each State Party shall take the necessary measures to search for and identify the children referred to in paragraph 1 (a) of this article and to return them to their families of origin, in accordance with legal procedures and applicable international agreements.

3. States Parties shall assist one another in searching for, identifying and locating the children referred to in paragraph 1 (a) of this article.

4. Given the need to protect the best interests of the children referred to in paragraph 1 (a) of this article and their right to preserve, or to have re-established, their identity, including their nationality, name and family relations as recognized by law, States Parties which recognize a system of adoption or other form of placement of children shall have legal procedures in place to review the adoption or placement procedure, and, where appropriate, to annul any adoption or placement of children that originated in an enforced disappearance.

5. In all cases, and in particular in all matters relating to this article, the best interests of the child shall be a primary consideration, and a child who is capable of forming his or her own views shall have the right to express those views freely, the views of the child being given due weight in accordance with the age and maturity of the child.

Part II

Article 26

1. A Committee on Enforced Disappearances (hereinafter referred to as "the Committee") shall be established to carry out the functions provided for under this Convention. The Committee shall consist of ten experts of high moral character and recognized competence in the field of human rights, who shall serve in their personal capacity and be independent and impartial. The members of the Committee shall be elected by the States Parties according to equitable geographical distribution. Due account shall be taken of the usefulness of the participation in the work of the Committee of persons having relevant legal experience and of balanced gender representation.

2. The members of the Committee shall be elected by secret ballot from a list of persons nominated by States Parties from among their nationals, at biennial meetings of the States Parties convened by the Secretary-General of the United Nations for this purpose. At those meetings, for which two thirds of the States Parties shall constitute a quorum, the persons elected to the Committee shall be those who obtain the largest number of votes and an absolute majority of the votes of the representatives of States Parties present and voting.

3. The initial election shall be held no later than six months after the date of entry into force of this Convention. Four months before the date of each election, the Secretary-General of the United Nations shall address a letter to the States Parties inviting them to submit nominations within three months. The Secretary-General shall prepare a list in alphabetical order of all persons thus nominated, indicating the State Party which nominated each candidate, and shall submit this list to all States Parties.

4. The members of the Committee shall be elected for a term of four years. They shall be eligible for re-election once. However, the term of five of the members elected at the first election shall expire at the end of two years; immediately after the first election, the names of these five members shall be chosen by lot by the chairman of the meeting referred to in paragraph 2 of this article.

5. If a member of the Committee dies or resigns or for any other reason can no longer perform his or her Committee duties, the State Party which nominated him or her shall, in accordance with the criteria set out in paragraph 1 of this article, appoint another candidate from among its nationals to serve out his or her term, subject to the approval of the majority of the States Parties. Such approval shall be considered to have been obtained unless half or more of the States Parties respond negatively within six weeks of having been informed by the Secretary-General of the United Nations of the proposed appointment.

6. The Committee shall establish its own rules of procedure.

7. The Secretary-General of the United Nations shall provide the Committee with the necessary means, staff and facilities for the effective performance of its functions. The Secretary-General of the United Nations shall convene the initial meeting of the Committee.

8. The members of the Committee shall be entitled to the facilities, privileges and immunities of experts on mission for the United Nations, as laid down in the relevant sections of the Convention on the Privileges and Immunities of the United Nations.

9. Each State Party shall cooperate with the Committee and assist its members in the fulfilment of their mandate, to the extent of the Committee's functions that the State Party has accepted.

Article 27

A Conference of the States Parties will take place at the earliest four years and at the latest six years following the entry into force of this Convention to evaluate the functioning of the Committee and to decide, in accordance with the procedure described in article 44, paragraph 2, whether it is appropriate to transfer to another body—without excluding any possibility—the monitoring of this Convention, in accordance with the functions defined in articles 28 to 36.

Article 28

1. In the framework of the competencies granted by this Convention, the Committee shall cooperate with all relevant organs, offices and specialized agencies and funds of the United Nations, with the treaty bodies instituted by international instruments, with the special procedures of the United Nations and with the relevant regional intergovernmental organizations or bodies, as well as with all relevant State institutions, agencies or offices working towards the protection of all persons against enforced disappearances.

2. As it discharges its mandate, the Committee shall consult other treaty bodies instituted by relevant international human rights instruments, in particular the Human Rights Committee instituted by the International Covenant on Civil and Political Rights, with a view to ensuring the consistency of their respective observations and recommendations.

Article 29

1. Each State Party shall submit to the Committee, through the Secretary-General of the United Nations, a report on the measures taken to give effect to its obligations under this Convention, within two years after the entry into force of this Convention for the State Party concerned.

2. The Secretary-General of the United Nations shall make this report available to all States Parties.

3. Each report shall be considered by the Committee, which shall issue such comments, observations or recommendations as it may deem appropriate. The comments, observations or recommendations shall be communicated to the State Party concerned, which may respond to them, on its own initiative or at the request of the Committee.

4. The Committee may also request States Parties to provide additional information on the implementation of this Convention.

Article 30

1. A request that a disappeared person should be sought and found may be submitted to the Committee, as a matter of urgency, by relatives of the disappeared person or their legal representatives, their counsel or any person authorized by them, as well as by any other person having a legitimate interest.

2. If the Committee considers that a request for urgent action submitted in pursuance of paragraph 1 of this article:

(a) Is not manifestly unfounded;

(b) Does not constitute an abuse of the right of submission of such requests;

(c) Has already been duly presented to the competent bodies of the State Party concerned, such as those authorized to undertake investigations, where such a possibility exists;

(d) Is not incompatible with the provisions of this Convention; and

(e) The same matter is not being examined under another procedure of international investigation or settlement of the same nature;

it shall request the State Party concerned to provide it with information on the situation of the persons sought, within a time limit set by the Committee.

3. In the light of the information provided by the State Party concerned in accordance with paragraph 2 of this article, the Committee may transmit recommendations to the State Party, including a request that the State Party should take all the necessary measures, including interim measures, to locate and protect the person concerned in accordance with this Convention and to inform the Committee, within a specified period of time, of measures taken, taking into account the urgency of the situation. The Committee shall inform the person submitting the urgent action request of its recommendations and of the information provided to it by the State as it becomes available.

4. The Committee shall continue its efforts to work with the State Party concerned for as long as the fate of the person sought remains unresolved. The person presenting the request shall be kept informed.

Article 31

1. A State Party may at the time of ratification of this Convention or at any time afterwards declare that it recognizes the competence of the Committee to receive and consider communications from or on behalf of individuals subject to its jurisdiction claiming to be victims of a violation by this State Party of provisions of this Convention. The Committee shall not admit any communication concerning a State Party which has not made such a declaration.

2. The Committee shall consider a communication inadmissible where:

(a) The communication is anonymous;

(b) The communication constitutes an abuse of the right of submission of such communications or is incompatible with the provisions of this Convention;

(c) The same matter is being examined under another procedure of international investigation or settlement of the same nature; or where

(d) All effective available domestic remedies have not been exhausted. This rule shall not apply where the application of the remedies is unreasonably prolonged.

3. If the Committee considers that the communication meets the requirements set out in paragraph 2 of this article, it shall transmit the communication to the State Party concerned, requesting it to provide observations and comments within a time limit set by the Committee.

4. At any time after the receipt of a communication and before a determination on the merits has been reached, the Committee may transmit to the State Party concerned for its urgent consideration a request that the State Party will take such interim mea-

sures as may be necessary to avoid possible irreparable damage to the victims of the alleged violation. Where the Committee exercises its discretion, this does not imply a determination on admissibility or on the merits of the communication.

5. The Committee shall hold closed meetings when examining communications under the present article. It shall inform the author of a communication of the responses provided by the State Party concerned. When the Committee decides to finalize the procedure, it shall communicate its views to the State Party and to the author of the communication.

Article 32

A State Party to this Convention may at any time declare that it recognizes the competence of the Committee to receive and consider communications in which a State Party claims that another State Party is not fulfilling its obligations under this Convention. The Committee shall not receive communications concerning a State Party which has not made such a declaration, nor communications from a State Party which has not made such a declaration.

Article 33

1. If the Committee receives reliable information indicating that a State Party is seriously violating the provisions of this Convention, it may, after consultation with the State Party concerned, request one or more of its members to undertake a visit and report back to it without delay.

2. The Committee shall notify the State Party concerned, in writing, of its intention to organize a visit, indicating the composition of the delegation and the purpose of the visit. The State Party shall answer the Committee within a reasonable time.

3. Upon a substantiated request by the State Party, the Committee may decide to postpone or cancel its visit.

4. If the State Party agrees to the visit, the Committee and the State Party concerned shall work together to define the modalities of the visit and the State Party shall provide the Committee with all the facilities needed for the successful completion of the visit.

5. Following its visit, the Committee shall communicate to the State Party concerned its observations and recommendations.

Article 34

If the Committee receives information which appears to it to contain well-founded indications that enforced disappearance is being practiced on a widespread or systematic basis in the territory under the jurisdiction of a State Party, it may, after seeking from the State Party concerned all relevant information on the situation, urgently bring the matter to the attention of the General Assembly of the United Nations, through the Secretary-General of the United Nations.

Article 35

1. The Committee shall have competence solely in respect of enforced disappearances which commenced after the entry into force of this Convention.

2. If a State becomes a party to this Convention after its entry into force, the obligations of that State vis-à-vis the Committee shall relate only to enforced disappearances which commenced after the entry into force of this Convention for the State concerned....

Inter-American Convention on the Forced Disappearance of Persons, done in Belen, Brazil, June 9, 1994

The Member States of the Organization of American States,

Disturbed by the persistence of the forced disappearance of persons;

Reaffirming that the true meaning of American solidarity and good neighborliness can be none other than that of consolidating in this Hemisphere, in the framework of democratic institutions, a system of individual freedom and social justice based on respect for essential human rights;

Considering that the forced disappearance of persons is an affront to the conscience of the Hemisphere and a grave and abominable offense against the inherent dignity of the human being, and one that contradicts the principles and purposes enshrined in the Charter of the Organization of American States;

Considering that the forced disappearance of persons violates numerous non-derogable and essential human rights enshrined in the American Convention on Human Rights, in the American Declaration of the Rights and Duties of Man, and in the Universal Declaration of Human Rights;

Recalling that the international protection of human rights is in the form of a convention reinforcing or complementing the protection provided by domestic law and is based upon the attributes of the human personality;

Reaffirming that the systematic practice of the forced disappearance of persons constitutes a crime against humanity;

Hoping that this Convention may help to prevent, punish, and eliminate the forced disappearance of persons in the Hemisphere and make a decisive contribution to the protection of human rights and the rule of law,

Resolve to adopt the following Inter-American Convention on the Forced Disappearance of Persons:

Article I

The States Parties to this Convention undertake:

(a) Not to practice, permit, or tolerate the forced disappearance of persons, even in states of emergency or suspension of individual guarantees;

(b) To punish within their jurisdictions those persons who commit or attempt to commit the crime of forced disappearance of persons and their accomplices and accessories;

(c) To cooperate with one another in helping to prevent, punish and eliminate the forced disappearance of persons;

(d) To take legislative, administrative, judicial, and any other measures necessary to comply with the commitments undertaken in this Convention.

Article II

For the purposes of this Convention, forced disappearance is considered to be the act of depriving a person or persons of his or their freedom, in whatever way, perpetrated by agents of the state or by persons or groups of persons acting with the authorization, support, or acquiescence of the state, followed by an absence of information or a refusal to acknowledge that deprivation of freedom or to give information on the whereabouts of that person, thereby impeding his or her recourse to the applicable legal remedies and procedural guarantees.

Article III

The States Parties undertake to adopt, in accordance with their constitutional procedures, the legislative measures that may be needed to define the forced disappearance of persons as an offense and to impose an appropriate punishment commensurate with its extreme gravity. This offense shall be deemed continuous or permanent as long as the fate or whereabouts of the victim has not been determined.

The States Parties may establish mitigating circumstances for persons who have participated in acts constituting forced disappearance when they help to cause the victim to reappear alive or provide information that sheds light on the forced disappearance of a person.

Article IV

The acts constituting the forced disappearance of persons shall be considered offenses in every State Party. Consequently, each State Party shall take measures to establish its jurisdiction over such cases in the following instances:

(a) When the forced disappearance of persons or any act constituting such offense was committed within its jurisdiction;

(b) When the accused is a national of that state;

(c) When the victim is a national of that state and that state sees fit to do so.

Every State Party shall, moreover, take the necessary measures to establish its jurisdiction over the crime described in this Convention when the alleged criminal is within its territory and it does not proceed to extradite him.

This Convention does not authorize any State Party to undertake, in the territory of another State Party, the exercise of jurisdiction or the performance of functions that are placed within the exclusive purview of the authorities of that other Party by its domestic law.

Article V

The forced disappearance of persons shall not be considered a political offense for purposes of extradition.

The forced disappearance of persons shall be deemed to be included among the extraditable offenses in every extradition treaty entered into between State Parties.

The States Parties undertake to include the offense of forced disappearance as one which is extraditable in every extradition treaty to be concluded between them in the future.

Every State Party that makes extradition conditional on the existence of a treaty and receives a request for extradition from another State Party with which it has no extradition treaty may consider this Convention as the necessary legal basis for extradition with respect to the offense of forced disappearance.

State Parties which do not make extradition conditional on the existence of a treaty shall recognize such offense as extraditable, subject to the conditions imposed by the law of the requested state.

Extradition shall be subject to the provisions set forth in the constitution and other laws of the requested state.

Article VI

When a State Party does not grant the extradition, the case shall be submitted to its competent authorities as if the offense had been committed within its jurisdiction, for the purposes of investigation and when appropriate, for criminal action, in accordance with its national law. Any decision adopted by these authorities shall be communicated to the state that has requested the extradition.

Article VII

Criminal prosecution for the forced disappearance of persons and the penalty judicially imposed on its perpetrator shall not be subject to statutes of limitations.

However, if there should be a norm of a fundamental character preventing application of the stipulation contained in the previous paragraph, the period of limitation shall be equal to that which applies to the gravest crime in the domestic laws of the corresponding State Party.

Article VIII

The defense of due obedience to superior orders or instructions that stipulate, authorize, or encourage forced disappearance shall not be admitted.

All persons who receive such orders have the right and duty not to obey them.

The States Parties shall ensure that the training of public law-enforcement personnel or officials includes the necessary education on the offense of forced disappearance of persons.

Article IX

Persons alleged to be responsible for the acts constituting the offense of forced disappearance of persons may be tried only in the competent jurisdictions of ordinary law in each state, to the exclusion of all other special jurisdictions, particularly military jurisdictions.

The acts constituting forced disappearance shall not be deemed to have been committed in the course of military duties.

Privileges, immunities, or special dispensations shall not be admitted in such trials, without prejudice to the provisions set forth in the Vienna Convention on Diplomatic Relations.

Article X

In no case may exceptional circumstances such as a state of war, the threat of war, internal political instability, or any other public emergency be invoked to justify the forced disappearance of persons. In such cases, the right to expeditious and effective judicial procedures and recourse shall be retained as a means of determining the whereabouts or state of health of a person who has been deprived of freedom, or of identifying the official who ordered or carried out such deprivation of freedom.

In pursuing such procedures or recourse, and in keeping with applicable domestic law, the competent judicial authorities shall have free and immediate access to all detention centers and to each of their units, and to all places where there is reason to believe the disappeared person might be found, including places that are subject to military jurisdiction.

Article XI

Every person deprived of liberty shall be held in an officially recognized place of detention and be brought before a competent judicial authority without delay, in accordance with applicable domestic law.

The States Parties shall establish and maintain official up-to-date registries of their detainees and, in accordance with their domestic law, shall make them available to relatives, judges, attorneys, any other person having a legitimate interest, and other authorities.

Article XII

The States Parties shall give each other mutual assistance in the search for, identification, location, and return of minors who have been removed to another state or detained therein as a consequence of the forced disappearance of their parents or guardians.

Article XIII

For the purposes of this Convention, the processing of petitions or communications presented to the Inter-American Commission on Human Rights alleging the forced disappearance of persons shall be subject to the procedures established in the American Convention on Human Rights and to the Statute and Regulations of the Inter-American Commission on Human Rights and to the Statute and Rules of Procedure of the Inter-American Court of Human Rights, including the provisions on precautionary measures.

Article XIV

Without prejudice to the provisions of the preceding article, when the Inter-American Commission on Human Rights receives a petition or communication regarding an alleged forced disappearance, its Executive Secretariat shall urgently and confidentially address the respective government and shall request that government to provide as soon as possible information as to the whereabouts of the allegedly disappeared person together with any other information it considers pertinent, and such request shall be without prejudice as to the admissibility of the petition.

Article XV

None of the provisions of this Convention shall be interpreted as limiting other bilateral or multilateral treaties or other agreements signed by the Parties.

This Convention shall not apply to the international armed conflicts governed by the 1949 Geneva Convention and its Protocol concerning protection of wounded, sick, and shipwrecked members of the armed forces; and prisoners of war and civilians in time of war.

Article XVI

This Convention is open for signature by the member states of the Organization of American States.

Article XVII

This Convention is subject to ratification. The instruments of ratification shall be deposited with the General Secretariat of the Organization of American States.

Article XVIII

This Convention shall be open to accession by any other state. The instruments of accession shall be deposited with the General Secretariat of the Organization of American States.

Article XIX

The states may make reservations with respect to this Convention when signing, ratifying or acceding to it, unless such reservations are incompatible with the object and purpose of the Convention and as long as they refer to one or more specific provisions.

Article XX

This Convention shall enter into force for the ratifying states on the thirtieth day from the date of deposit of the second instrument of ratification.

For each state ratifying or acceding to the Convention after the second instrument of ratification has been deposited, the Convention shall enter into force on the thirtieth day from the date on which that state deposited its instrument of ratification or accession.

Article XXI

This Convention shall remain in force indefinitely, but may be denounced by any State Party. The instrument of denunciation shall be deposited with the General Secretariat of the Organization of American States. The Convention shall cease to be in effect for the denouncing state and shall remain in force for the other State Parties one year from the date of deposit of the instrument of denunciation.

Article XXII

The original instrument of this Convention, the Spanish, English, Portuguese and French texts of which are equally authentic, shall be deposited with the General Secretariat of the Organization of American States, which shall forward certified copies thereof to the United Nations Secretariat, for registration and publication, in accordance with Article 102 of the Charter of the United Nations. The General Secretariat of the Organization of American States shall notify member states of the Organization and states acceding to the Convention of the signatures and deposit of instruments of ratification, accession or denunciation, as well as of any reservations that may be expressed.

In Witness Whereof the undersigned Plenipotentiaries, being duly authorized thereto by their respective governments, have signed this Convention, which shall be called the "Inter-American Convention on the Forced Disappearance of Persons."

Protection of Human Rights and Fundamental Freedoms While Countering Terrorism, U.N. G.A. Res. 59/191 (20 Dec. 2004)

The General Assembly,

Reaffirming the purposes and principles of the Charter of the United Nations,

Reaffirming also the fundamental importance, including in response to terrorism and the fear of terrorism, of respecting all human rights and fundamental freedoms and the rule of law,

Recalling that States are under the obligation to protect all human rights and fundamental freedoms of all persons, and deploring violations of human rights and fundamental freedoms in the context of the fight against terrorism,

Recognizing that the respect for human rights, the respect for democracy and the respect for the rule of law are interrelated and mutually reinforcing,

Noting the declarations, statements and recommendations of a number of human rights treaty monitoring bodies and special procedures on the question of the compatibility of counter-terrorism measures with human rights obligations, …

Reaffirming that acts, methods and practices of terrorism in all its forms and manifestations are activities aimed at the destruction of human rights, fundamental freedoms and democracy, threatening the territorial integrity and the security of States and destabilizing legitimately constituted Governments, and that the international community should take the necessary steps to enhance cooperation to prevent and combat terrorism, …

Reaffirming its unequivocal condemnation of all acts, methods and practices of terrorism in all its forms and manifestations, wherever and by whomever committed, regardless of their motivation, as criminal and unjustifiable, and renewing its commitment to strengthen international cooperation to prevent and combat terrorism,

Deploring the suffering caused by terrorism to the victims and their families and expressing its profound solidarity with them,

Stressing that everyone is entitled to all the rights and freedoms recognized in the Universal Declaration of Human Rights without distinction of any kind, including on the grounds of race, colour, sex, language, religion, political or other opinion, national or social origin, property, birth or other status,

1. *Reaffirms* that States must ensure that any measure taken to combat terrorism complies with their obligations under international law, in particular international human rights, refugee and humanitarian law;

2. *Also reaffirms* the obligations of States, in accordance with article 4 of the International Covenant on Civil and Political Rights, to respect certain rights as non-derogable in any circumstances, recalls, in regard to all other Covenant rights, that any measures derogating from the provisions of the Covenant must be in accordance with that article in all cases, and underlines the exceptional and temporary nature of any such derogations;

3. *Calls upon* States to raise awareness about the importance of these obligations among national authorities involved in combating terrorism....

Human Rights and Terrorism, U.N. G.A. Res. 59/195 (20 Dec. 2004)

The General Assembly,

Guided by the Charter of the United Nations, the Universal Declaration of Human Rights, the Declaration on Principles of International Law concerning Friendly Relations and Cooperation among States in accordance with the Charter of the United Nations and the International Covenants on Human Rights, ...

Recalling previous resolutions of the Commission on Human Rights on the issue of human rights and terrorism, as well as on hostage-taking,

Bearing in mind all other relevant General Assembly resolutions,

Bearing in mind also relevant Security Council resolutions,

Aware that, at the dawn of the twenty-first century, the world is witness to historic and far-reaching transformations, in the course of which forces of aggressive nationalism and religious and ethnic extremism continue to produce fresh challenges,

Alarmed that acts of terrorism in all its forms and manifestations aimed at the destruction of human rights have continued despite national and international efforts,

Convinced that terrorism in all its forms and manifestations, wherever and by whomever committed, can never be justified in any instance, including as a means to promote and protect human rights, ...

Bearing in mind that the right to life is the basic human right, without which a human being can exercise no other right,

Bearing in mind also that terrorism creates an environment that destroys the right of people to live in freedom from fear,

Reiterating that all States have an obligation to promote and protect all human rights and fundamental freedoms and to ensure effective implementation of their obligations under international law,

Seriously concerned about the gross violations of human rights perpetuated by terrorist groups,

Expressing its deepest sympathy and condolences to all the victims of terrorism and their families,

Alarmed in particular at the possibility that terrorist groups may exploit new technologies to facilitate acts of terrorism, which may cause massive damage, including huge loss of life,

Emphasizing the need to intensify the fight against terrorism at the national level, to enhance effective international cooperation in combating terrorism in conformity with international law, including relevant State obligations under international human rights and international humanitarian law, and to strengthen the role of the United Nations in this respect,

Emphasizing also that States shall deny safe haven to those who finance, plan, support or commit terrorist acts or provide safe haven,

Reaffirming that all measures to counter terrorism must be in strict conformity with international law, including international human rights standards and obligations,

Mindful of the need to protect the human rights of and guarantees for the individual in accordance with the relevant human rights principles and instruments, in particular the right to life,

Noting the growing consciousness within the international community of the negative effects of terrorism in all its forms and manifestations on the full enjoyment of human rights and fundamental freedoms and on the establishment of the rule of law and democratic freedoms enshrined in the Charter of the United Nations and the International Covenants on Human Rights,

Concerned by the tendencies to link terrorism and violence with religion, …

1. *Reiterates* its unequivocal condemnation of the acts, methods and practices of terrorism in all its forms and manifestations as activities aimed at the destruction of human rights, fundamental freedoms and democracy, threatening the territorial integrity and the security of States, destabilizing legitimately constituted Governments, undermining pluralistic civil society and having adverse consequences for the economic and social development of States;

2. *Strongly condemns* the violations of the right to life, liberty and security;

3. *Rejects* the identification of terrorism with any religion, nationality or culture;

4. *Profoundly deplores* the increasing number of innocent persons, including women, children and the elderly, killed, massacred and maimed by terrorists in indiscriminate and random acts of violence and terror, which cannot be justified in any circumstances;

5. *Expresses its solidarity* with the victims of terrorism;

6. *Reaffirms* the decision of the Heads of State and Government, as contained in the United Nations Millennium Declaration [res. 55/2], to take concerted action against international terrorism and to accede as soon as possible to all the relevant regional and international conventions;

7. *Urges* the international community to enhance cooperation at the regional and international levels in the fight against terrorism in all its forms and manifestations, in accordance with relevant international instruments, including those relating to human rights, with the aim of its eradication;

8. *Calls upon* States to take all necessary and effective measures, in accordance with relevant provisions of international law, including international human rights standards, to prevent, combat and eliminate terrorism in all its forms and manifestations, wherever and by whomever it is committed, and also calls upon States to strengthen, where appropriate, their legislation to combat terrorism in all its forms and manifestations;

9. *Urges* all States to deny safe haven to terrorists;

10. *Calls upon* States to take appropriate measures, in conformity with relevant provisions of national and international law, including human rights standards, before granting refugee status, for the purpose of ensuring that an asylum-seeker has not planned, facilitated or participated in the commission of terrorist acts, including assassinations, and to ensure, in conformity with international law, that refugee status is not abused by the perpetrators, organizers or facilitators of terrorist acts and that claims of political motivation are not recognized as grounds for refusing requests for the extradition of alleged terrorists; …

12. *Condemns* the incitement to ethnic hatred, violence and terrorism;

13. *Stresses* that every person, regardless of nationality, race, sex, religion or any other distinction, has a right to protection from terrorism and terrorist acts;

14. *Expresses concern* that the growing connection between terrorist groups and other criminal organizations engaged in the illegal traffic in arms and drugs at the national and international levels, as well as the consequent commission of serious crimes such as murder, extortion, kidnapping, assault, the taking of hostages and robbery, and requests the relevant United Nations bodies to continue to give special attention to this question;....

Lawfulness of Detentions by the United States in Guantanamo Bay, Parliamentary Assembly, Council of Europe, Resolution 1433 (26 April 2005)

1. The Parliamentary Assembly recalls and restates its outrage and disgust at the terrorist attacks on the United States of America of 11 September 2001, the horror of which has not been dimmed by the passage of time. It shares the United States' determination to combat international terrorism and fully endorses the importance of detecting and preventing terrorist crimes, prosecuting and punishing terrorists and protecting human lives.

2. Whilst the Assembly therefore offers its full support to the United States in its efforts to fight terrorism, this must be on condition that all measures taken are fully respectful of human rights and the rule of law. Conformity with international human rights and humanitarian law is not a weakness in the fight against terrorism but a weapon, ensuring the widest international support for actions and avoiding situations which could provoke misplaced sympathy for terrorists or their causes.

3. The United States has long been a beacon of democracy and a champion of human rights throughout the world and its positive influence on European development in this respect since the Second World War is greatly appreciated. Nevertheless, the Assembly considers that the United States Government has betrayed its own highest principles in the zeal with which it has attempted to pursue the "war on terror". These errors have perhaps been most manifest in relation to Guantánamo Bay.

4. At no time have detentions at Guantánamo Bay been within a "legal black hole". International human rights law has at all times been fully applicable to all detainees. For those captured during the international armed conflict in Afghanistan, protection of certain rights may have been complemented by the provisions of international humanitarian law (IHL) for the duration of that conflict. Since that international armed con-

flict ceased, however, international human rights standards have applied in the normal fashion.

5. The Assembly applauds and supports the work of the International Committee of the Red Cross (ICRC) and the various United Nations human rights protection mechanisms, along with that of non-governmental organisations including Human Rights First, the Center for Constitutional Rights and Amnesty International, in striving to improve detention conditions at Guantánamo Bay and ensure that detainees' rights are respected. It also thanks the European Commission for Democracy through Law (Venice Commission) for its opinion on the possible need for further development of the Geneva Conventions, produced in response to a request from the Assembly's Committee on Legal Affairs and Human Rights.

6. The Assembly recalls the evidence provided by Mr. Jamal Al Harith, former detainee, along with lawyers representing current and former detainees and other international experts, at the hearing held by its Committee on Legal Affairs and Human Rights in Paris on 17 December 2004.

7. On the basis of an extensive review of legal and factual material from these and other reliable sources, the Assembly concludes that the circumstances surrounding detentions by the United States at Guantánamo Bay show unlawfulness and inconsistency with the rule of law, on the following grounds:

> i. many if not all detainees have been subjected to cruel, inhuman or degrading treatment occurring as a direct result of official policy, authorised at the very highest levels of government;

> ii. many detainees have been subjected to ill-treatment amounting to torture which has occurred systematically and with the knowledge and complicity of the United States Government;

> iii. the right of those detained in connection with the international armed conflict previously conducted by the United States in Afghanistan to be presumptively recognised as prisoners of war (POWs) and to have their status independently determined by a competent tribunal was not respected;

> iv. there have been numerous violations of various aspects of all detainees' rights to liberty and security of the person, making their detention arbitrary;

> v. there have been numerous violations of various aspects of all detainees' rights to fair trial, amounting to a flagrant denial of justice;

> vi. the United States has engaged in the unlawful practice of secret detention;

> vii. the United States has, by practising "rendition" (removal of persons to other countries, without judicial supervision, for purposes such as interrogation or detention), allowed detainees to be subjected to torture and to cruel, inhuman or degrading treatment, in violation of the prohibition on *non-refoulement*;

> viii. the United States' proposals to return or transfer detainees to other countries, even where reliant on "diplomatic assurances" concerning the detainees' subsequent treatment, risk violating the prohibition on *non-refoulement*.

8. The Assembly therefore calls on the United States Government to ensure respect for the rule of law and human rights by remedying these situations and in particular:

i. to cease immediately all ill-treatment of Guantánamo Bay detainees;

ii. to investigate, prosecute and punish all instances of unlawful mistreatment of detainees, no matter what the status or office of the person responsible;

iii. to allow all detainees to challenge the lawfulness of their detention before a regularly constituted court competent to order their release if detention is not lawful;

iv. to release immediately all those detainees against whom there is not sufficient evidence to justify laying criminal charges;

v. to charge those suspected of criminal offences and bring them for trial before a competent, independent and impartial tribunal guaranteeing all the procedural safeguards required by international law, without delay, whilst excluding imposition of the death penalty against them;

vi. to respect its obligations under international law and the Constitution of the United States to exclude any statement established to have been made as a result of torture or other cruel, inhuman or degrading treatment or punishment from any proceedings, except against a person accused of such ill-treatment as evidence that the statement was made;

vii. to cease immediately the practice of secret detentions and to ensure full respect for the rights of any detainees currently held in secret, in particular the prohibition on torture and cruel, inhuman or degrading treatment and the right to have relatives informed of the fact of detention, to recognition as a person before the law, to judicial review of the lawfulness of detention and to release or trial without delay;

viii. to allow access to all detainees by family members, legal representatives, consular representatives and officials of international humanitarian and human rights organisations;

ix. to cease the practice of "rendition" in violation of the prohibition on *non-refoulement*;

x. not to return or transfer detainees in reliance on "diplomatic assurances" from countries known to engage in the systematic practice of torture and in all cases unless the absence of a risk of ill-treatment is firmly established;

xi. to comply fully and promptly with the recommendations of the ICRC and to avoid any actions that might have the effect of undermining its activities, reputation or standing.

9. Furthermore, the Assembly also calls on the United States Government to ensure that the "war on terror" is conducted in all respects in accordance with international law, particularly international human rights and humanitarian law.

10. In addition, the Assembly calls on member states of the Council of Europe:

i. to enhance their diplomatic and consular efforts to protect the rights and ensure the release of any of their citizens, nationals or former residents currently detained at Guantánamo Bay, whether legally obliged to do so or not;

ii. with respect to any of their citizens, nationals or former residents who have been returned or transferred from detention at Guantánamo Bay:

a. to treat such persons according to the usual provisions of criminal law, respecting the presumption in favour of immediate liberty on arrival;

b. to provide such persons with all necessary support and assistance, in particular legal aid to bring cases relating to detention at Guantánamo Bay;

c. to protect such persons from prejudice or discrimination and to ensure their mental and physical well-being during the process of reintegration;

d. to ensure that such persons do not suffer detriment to their rights or interests as a result of being held in unlawful detention at Guantánamo Bay, especially in relation to immigration status;

iii. not to permit their authorities to participate or assist in the interrogation of Guantánamo Bay detainees;

iv. to respect their obligations under international law to exclude any statement established to have been made as a result of torture or other cruel, inhuman or degrading treatment or punishment from any proceedings, except against a person accused of such ill-treatment as evidence that the statement was made;

v. to refuse to comply with United States' requests for extradition of terrorist suspects liable to detention at Guantánamo Bay;

vi. to refuse to comply with United States' requests for mutual legal assistance in relation to Guantánamo Bay detainees, other than by providing exculpatory evidence, or unless in connection with legal proceedings before a regularly constituted court;

vii. to ensure that their territory and facilities are not used in connection with practices of secret detention or rendition in possible violation of international human rights law;

viii. to respect the *erga omnes* nature of human rights by taking all possible measures to persuade the United States authorities to respect fully the rights under international law of all Guantánamo Bay detainees.

11. Finally, the Assembly resolves to pursue this issue further through bilateral dialogue with the United States Congress.